Fundamentals of
Organizational
Communication

Fundamentals of Organizational Communication

Knowledge, Sensitivity, Skills, Values

Eighth Edition

PAMELA S. SHOCKLEY-ZALABAK

University of Colorado

Allyn & Bacon

Boston   Columbus   Indianapolis   New York   San Francisco   Upper Saddle River
Amsterdam   Cape Town   Dubai   London   Madrid   Milan   Munich   Paris   Montreal   Toronto
Delhi   Mexico City   Sao Paulo   Sydney   Hong Kong   Seoul   Singapore   Taipei   Tokyo

Editor-in-Chief, Communication: Karon Bowers
Senior Acquisitions Editor: Jeanne Zalesky
Editorial Assistant: Stephanie Chaisson
Associate Managing Editor: Bayani Mendoza de Leon
Production Project Manager: Clara Bartunek
Marketing Manager: Blair Tuckman
Art Director: Jayne Conte
Project Coordination, Text Design, and Electronic Page Makeup: Aptara®, Inc.
Cover Designer: Suzanne Duda

Library of Congress Cataloging-in-Publication Data

Shockley-Zalabak, Pamela.
  Fundamentals of organizational communication / Pamela S. Shockley-Zalabak.—8th ed.
    p. cm.
  ISBN-13: 978-0-205-78108-9
  ISBN-10: 0-205-78108-X
  1. Communication in organizations.   I. Title.
  HD30.3.S55 2012
  658.4'5—dc22

                                                    2010027103

1 2 3 4 5 6 7 8 9 10—CRW—13   12   11   10

Allyn & Bacon
is an imprint of

www.pearsonhighered.com   ISBN-10:   0-205-78108-X
                          ISBN-13: 978-0-205-78108- 9

To Charles Zalabak
and
Leatha and Jim Shockley

BRIEF CONTENTS

Chapter 1   Organizational Communication: A Competency-Based Approach   1

Chapter 2   Perspectives for Organizational Communication   27

Chapter 3   Communication Implications of Major Organizational Theories   69

Chapter 4   Organizational Communication: Values and Ethical Communication Behaviors   101

Chapter 5   Individuals in Organizations   136

Chapter 6   Groups in Organizations   181

Chapter 7   Leadership and Management Communication   210

Chapter 8   Participating in Organizations: Developing Critical Organizational Communication Competencies   250

Chapter 9   Organizational Conflict: Communicating for Effectiveness   283

Chapter 10   Strategic Organizational Communication: Professional Applications of Organizational Communication   323

Chapter 11   Organizational Change and Communication   355

Chapter 12   Career Options for Organizational Communication   384

CONTENTS

Preface   xiv

CHAPTER 1

Organizational Communication: A Competency-Based Approach   1

The Changing Nature of Organizations and Work   1

Challenges for Individuals and Organizations   2

The Communications Era   2

Communication: The Key to Organizational Excellence   4

Excellence in Communication: Communication Competency   5

Organizational Communication: A Competency-Based Approach   7
- The "What Business Is This of Ours?" Case   8

Basics of Human Communication   9
Defining Communication   10

The Human Communication Process   10
Source/Receiver   10
Encoding/Decoding   11
Message   11
Channel   11
Noise   12
Competence   12
Field of Experience   12
Communication Context   13
Effect   13

The Construction of Shared Realities   14

Concepts of Organizations   15

Definitions of Organizational Communication   16
Organizational Communication as Process   16
Organizational Communication as People   16
Organizational Communication as Messages   17
Organizational Communication as Meaning   17
Organizational Communication as Purpose   17

Self-Assessment of Personal Development Needs   18

Chapter Highlights   24

Workshop   24
- The Case Against Hiring Karen Groves   25
- The "What Do You Mean I'm Not Getting a Raise?" Case   25

Tips for Effective Communication   25

References and Suggested Readings   26

CHAPTER 2

Perspectives for Organizational Communication   27
- The Coronado Company's Quality Defects Case   27

Introduction   28

The Functional Tradition   30
Organizational Communication Systems: Component Parts   31
Communication Inputs   31
Communication Throughput   32
Communication Output   32
Open versus Closed Systems   32
Message Functions   33
Organizing Functions   34
Relationship Functions   34
Change Functions   35
Message Structure   35
Communication Networks   36
Communication Channels   37
Message Direction   38
Communication Load   39
Message Distortion   40
The Functional Tradition: Summary of Essential Characteristics   41

The Meaning-Centered Approach   41
    Communication as Organizing and Decision Making   41
    Communication as Influence   44
    Identification   44
    Socialization   45
    Communication Rules   46
    Power   48
    Communication as Culture   49
    Communication Climate   50
    The Meaning-Centered Approach: Summary of Essential
    Characteristics   51

Emerging Perspectives   51
    Communication as Constitutive Process   52
    Communication Constitutes Organization   52
    Postmodernism and Organizational Communication   54
    Critical Theory and Organizational Communication   55
    Feminist and Race Perspectives and Organizational
    Communication   56
    Institutions and Organizational Communication   58
    Global Cultures and Organizational Communication   60
    Technology and Organizational Communication   61
    Emerging Perspectives: Summary of Essential Issues   62
    Practical Theory and Organizational Communication   62

Chapter Highlights   63

Workshop   64
    ■ The United Concepts Advertising Agency
      Dilemma Case   64
    ■ The "Newcomers Aren't Welcome Here"
      Case   64

Tips for Effective Communication   65

References and Suggested Readings   65

CHAPTER 3

Communication Implications of Major Organizational Theories   69

    ■ The Davis Instrument Company's
      Manufacturing Crisis   69

Introduction   70

The Scientific Management School   72
    Principles and Basic Activities for Scientific
    Management   72
        Frederick Taylor
    Principles of Management   73
        Henri Fayol
    Principles of Bureaucracy   74
        Max Weber

    Communication Implications of Scientific Management
    Theories in Contemporary Organizations   75

The Human Behavior School   76
    Major Human Behavior Theories   77
        Mary Parker Follett • Elton Mayo •
        Douglas McGregor • Rensis Likert
    Communication Implications of Human Behavior
    Theories in Contemporary Organizations   81

Integrated Perspectives Viewpoints   82
    Process and Environmental Approaches   82
        Herbert Simon • Eric L. Trist and Kenneth
        W. Bamforth • Joan Woodward, Paul
        Lawrence, and Jay Lorsch • Daniel Katz
        and Robert Kahn • Gareth Morgan •
        Margaret Wheatley • Peter Senge
    Cultural Approaches   87
        Edgar Schein • Terrence Deal and Allen
        Kennedy • Thomas Peters and Robert
        Waterman • Joanne Martin and Peter
        Frost • Karl Weick
    Communication Implications of Integrated Perspectives
    in Contemporary Organizations   92

Postmodern, Critical, and Feminist
Perspectives   93
        Stewart Clegg • Jurgen Habermas • Marta
        Calás and Linda Smircich • Karen Ashcraft
    Communication Implications of Postmodern, Critical,
    and Feminist Perspectives in Contemporary
    Organizations   96

Chapter Highlights   97

Workshop   97
    ■ The "What Do You Mean I'm Not Going to
      Graduate?" Case   98
    ■ The "We Never Had to Advertise Before"
      Case   99

Tips for Effective Communication   99

References and Suggested Readings   99

CHAPTER 4

Organizational Communication: Values and Ethical Communication Behaviors   101

    ■ The Presidential Fact-Finding (Witch-
      Hunt?) Case   101

Introduction   102

Values in Organizational Communication   103
    Organizational Value Systems   104

Organizational Values, Globalization, and Diversity 105
Individual Values 107

Appraising Your Individual Value System 109

Ethics in Organizational Communication 112
The Abuse of Ethics 112
Defining Ethics 112
Making Ethical Decisions 113
Defining Ethical Communication 114
Influences for Ethical Organizational Communication 116
Evaluating Ethical Behavior 116

Organizational Conundrums 118

Ethical Dilemmas in Organizational Communication 120
Representing Skills and Abilities 120
Communication Behaviors Related to Money 121
Communication Behaviors Related to Information Collection, Dissemination, Problem Solving, and Decision Making 122
Personal Communication Behaviors 122
Communication Behaviors and Technology 123
Destructive Communication Behaviors 124
Planned Organizational Communication 125
Courage, Responsibility, Trust, and Ethics 126

Developing Ethical Standards in Organizational Communication 126
Ethical Dilemmas in Organizational Communication 126

Chapter Highlights 130

Workshop 130
People, Planet, and Profit: Sustainability and the Triple Bottom Line, *Laura Quinn* 130
GreenBean Coffee, Inc. — Is It Our Responsibility? *Laura Quinn* 132

Tips for Effective Communication 133

References and Suggested Readings 133

CHAPTER 5

Individuals in Organizations 136
■ Dave Green's First Real Job 136

Introduction 137

Individuals in Organizations 138

The Intrapersonal Experience 139

■ Dave Green: The Intrapersonal Experience 140
Motivation 140
Abraham Maslow • Frederick Herzberg • B. F. Skinner • Gerald Salancik and Jeffrey Pfeffer
Predispositions for Organizational Communication Behaviors 146
Leadership and Conflict Preferences 147
Communication Competency 148

Interpersonal Experiences 148
■ Dave Green: Interpersonal Experiences 148

Forming Interpersonal Relationships 149
Supervisors and Employees 150
Peers 154
Customers, Clients, and Vendors 157
Communication Networks and Interpersonal Relationships 157
Diversity and Interpersonal Relationships 161

Trust and Interpersonal Relationships 162

Workplace Emotion, Balance, and Interpersonal Relationships 163

Technology and Interpersonal Relationships 164

Increasing Interpersonal Effectiveness 166
Cultural Intelligence 166
Valuing Diversity 167
Active Listening 170
Guidelines for Good Listening 172
Descriptive Messages 172

Chapter Highlights 174

Workshop 175

Tips for Effective Communication 176

References and Suggested Readings 177

CHAPTER 6

Groups in Organizations 181
■ Dave Green's Small-Group Experiences 181

Introduction 182

Small-Group Experiences 182

Types of Groups 183
Primary Work Teams 184
Directional Groups 186

Quality Teams 187
Task Force Groups 188
Steering Committees 189
Focus Groups 189
Geographically Diverse Teams 190
Social Support Groups 190
Communities of Practice 190

The Team-Based Organization 191
High-Reliability Organizations 193

Group Processes 194
Workplace Democracy 194
Group Norms and Communication Roles 194

Working in Groups 196
Diverse Work Groups 197
Creativity and Collaboration 198
Virtual Groups 199
Groups and Technology Use 201

Increasing Group Participation
Effectiveness 202
Negative Participation Behaviors 202
Positive Participation Behaviors 203

Chapter Highlights 204

Workshop 205

Tips for Effective Communication 208

References and Suggested Readings 208

CHAPTER 7

Leadership and Management Communication 210

■ The Case of the Invisible Manager 210

Introduction 211

The Importance of Leadership and Management
Communication 212

Theories of Leadership and Management 213
Trait Approaches 215
Style Approaches 216
Situational Approaches 219
Transformational Approaches 222
Discursive Approaches 224

Distinctions between Leadership
and Management 225

Leadership and Management Challenges 227
Changing Organizational Forms 227
Global and Multicultural Changes 228
High-Speed Management 229
Inclusive-Participation Processes 229
Building Trust 229

Determinants of Leadership Effectiveness 230
Communication Competencies as Determinants of
Leadership Effectiveness 230
Predispositions for Leadership Communication 231
Strategic Communication Objectives for
Leadership 231
Communication Tactics for Leadership 234
Power Bases for Leaders 234
Situational Analysis for Leadership 239

Increasing Leadership Effectiveness 239
Principled, Excellent, and Ethical Leadership 240
Identifying Constructive Communication Behaviors for
Leadership 242

Chapter Highlights 243

Workshop 244
Leadership That Transforms, Michael Z.
Hackman and Craig Johnson 244

Tips for Effective Communication 247

References and Suggested Readings 248

CHAPTER 8

Participating in Organizations: Developing Critical Organizational Communication Competencies 250

■ The Decisions, Problems, More Decisions
Case 250

Introduction 251

Defining Decision Making and Problem
Solving 252

Influences for Decision Making and Problem
Solving 253
Culture 253
The Decision/Problem Issue 254
Communication Competency 254
Technical Competency 255

Methods for Decision Making and Problem
Solving 255

Individual Approaches 255
Leader Mandate 256
Majority Rule 256
Powerful Minority 256
Consensus 257

Barriers to Effective Decision Making and
Problem Solving 257
Organizational Barriers 257
Task and Procedural Barriers 258
Interpersonal Barriers 258

Problem-Solving Processes 259
The Standard Agenda: A Rational Model 259
Brainstorming 260
Experientially Based Processes 260

Increasing Decision-Making and Problem-Solving
Effectiveness 261
Interaction Process Skills 261
Fact-Finding and Evaluation Skills 262
Information Criteria 262
■ The Spending More to Save More
Presentation Case 263

Interviews in Organizations 264
The Informational Interview 264
The Employment Interview 266
The Performance Appraisal Interview 266
The Complaint Interview 267
The Counseling Interview 267
The Media Interview 268

Increasing Interview Effectiveness 268

Presentations in Organizations 269

Types of Organizational Presentations 271
Training/Educational Presentations 271
Informational Presentations 272
Persuasive Presentations 272

Increasing Presentation Effectiveness 273
Increasing Credibility 273
Audience and Context Analysis 274
Preparation of Material 274
Preparation for Presenting 275
Handling Participation 275

Communications Technology in Organizations 275
Preparation for Communications Technology 278

Chapter Highlights 278

Workshop 279
The Training Manager of Food Service
Industries E-Mail Exercise 280

Tips for Effective Communication 281

References and Suggested Readings 281

CHAPTER 9

Organizational Conflict: Communicating for Effectiveness 283

■ The Middlesex Insurance Company
Case 283

Introduction 284

Defining and Describing Conflict
Processes 285
Defining Conflict 285
Conflict Contexts 285
Conflict Causes 286
Conflict Episodes 289

The Individual in Organizational Conflict 292
Orientations/Predispositions/Styles 295
Strategic Objectives 298
Communication Tactics in Conflict 299
Emotion during Conflict 302

Groups in Organizational Conflict 303
Group Members in Conflict 304
Framing and Sensemaking 304
Procedural Conflict 305
Interpersonal Issues 305
Substantive Issues 306
Groupthink 306
Group Conflict Management Processes 306
Power and Organizational Conflict 307
Conflict with Customers and Vendors 308

Special Types of Organizational Conflict:
Sexual Harassment, Discrimination, Ethical
Abuses 309

Productively Engaging in Conflict 312
*Supportive Climates, Ethical Behaviors, Principled
Negotiation, and Co-Construction 313*

Guidelines for Productive Conflict 316
A Process for Productive Conflict 317
The Process 317

Chapter Highlights 319

Workshop 319

Tips for Effective Communication 321

References and Suggested Readings 321

CHAPTER 10

Strategic Organizational Communication: Professional Applications of Organizational Communication 323

- The Press and the Stockholders Want to Know Case 323

Introduction 324

Describing Strategic Organizational Communication 325
- Perspectives on Strategic Organizational Communication 326

The Organization and Its Environment 327
- Multiple Publics 328
- Environmental Scanning 329
- The Global Environment 330

Strategic Management 330

Strategic Organizational Communication 332
- Public Relations 332
- Managing an Organization's Image or Reputation 333
- Internal Communications 334
- Public Affairs and Issues Management 335
- Media Relations 335
- Risk and Crisis Communication 336
- Marketing 340
- Integrated Marketing Communications 341
- The Marketing Mix 341
- Advertising 342
- Branding 343
- Relationship Marketing and the Use of Marketing Databases 343
- Technology and Strategic Organizational Communication 344
- Evaluating Strategic Organizational Communication 345

Ethical Issues in Strategic Organizational Communication 345

Chapter Highlights 346

Workshop 346
- Communication about Risk and Crisis in the Twenty-first Century, Sherwyn P. Morreale 347

Southwest Airlines: Social Media in Action, Adam Saffer 348

Tips for Effective Communication 352

References and Suggested Readings 352

CHAPTER 11

Organizational Change and Communication 355

- The Techtron Computers "Want to Survive, Go Public, and Then What?" Case 355

Introduction 356

The Pace of Change 357

Developing and Sustaining Organizational Excellence 359

Barriers to Change 360
- Complacency 360
- Organizational Silence 360
- Knowledge or Information Deficits 361
- Risk Perception 361
- Uncertainty 361
- Contradictions and Misalignments 362
- Active and Passive Resistance 362
- Organizational Leaders 363
- Organizational Trust 363
- Organizational Decline 363

The Leadership of Development and Change 364

Models and Processes for Development and Change 365
- Organizational Transformation Process 365
- Diffusion of Innovation 365
- Stakeholder Theory 366
- The Purchase Model 367
- The Doctor–Patient Model 367
- The Process Model 367
- Appreciative Inquiry 368

Planned Development and Change 368
- Data Collection 368
- Data Evaluation 370
- Planning and Implementing Solutions 371
- Evaluating Results 373

Communicating about Change 374

Chapter Highlights 375

Workshop   376
- ■ Jane Edwards' Problem Employee   376
- ■ The Case of the Poorly Written Manual   376
- ■ The Transition of Stanley Manufacturing   376
- ■ The Crisis at Homes for the Homeless   376
- ■ Mason Financial Is Working at Capacity   377
- ■ Changes for Hewlett Designers   377
- ■ Into the Pit and Out Again: An Organizational Turnaround, *Nina Polok*   378

Tips for Effective Communication   382

References and Suggested Readings   382

CHAPTER 12

Career Options for Organizational Communication   384

- ■ The "Where Do We Go from Here?" Case   384

Introduction   385

Choosing a Communication Career   386
- *Knowledge for Employment Matching*   386
- *Sensitivity for Employment Matching*   387
- *Skills for Employment Matching*   388
- *Values for Employment Matching*   388

Career Choices in Organizational Communication   389
- *Internal Communication*   391
- *External Communications*   392
- *Sales*   393
- *Human Services*   393
- *Education*   393
- *Research: Information Management*   394
- *Management*   394
- *Consulting*   395
- *Additional Options for Organizational Communication*   395

Educational Preparation for Organizational Communication Careers   396

Careers in the Twenty-first Century   397
- *Old versus New Career Paradigms*   397
- *Protean Careers*   398
- *The Boundaryless Career*   399
- *Twenty-first-Century Organizational Forms and Career Skills*   399
- *Networked Organization*   400
- *Cellular Organization*   400
- *Team-Based Careers*   401

Chapter Highlights   401

Workshop   402

Tips for Effective Communication   408

References and Suggested Readings   408

APPENDIX

Putting it All Together   409

Cases   409
- *I Can't Believe Our Entire World Is Wired*   412
- *How Did This Harm Occur?*   413
- *Granite City's Homeless Shelter: Doing More with Less*   414
- *Dennison Computer Corporation—A Lesson in Organizational Culture*   415
- *China, India, and Oklahoma City: Working Together, but How?*   418
- *Don Augustine's Disappointed Staff*   418
- *Dora Cartwright's Leadership Dilemma*   420
- *Kathy's Stubborn, Smart Streak*   421
- *Brian James Doesn't Know What to Believe*   421
- *I Am Tired and Stressed*   422
- *I Thought I Gave Them Everything*   423
- *Ann Cartwright, Vice President of Drummond Industries*   423
- *The Rule Here Is to Do What Management Wants*   424
- *Two Men—Two Issues—Two Japanese Workers, Rieko McAdams*   425
- *I Thought We Were a Team*   426
- *The Internal Communications Dilemma*   426
- *The Reluctant Team Member*   427
- *What Happened to the Value of Networking?*   428
- *The "Walking the Talk" Manager*   428
- *Working Together at a Distance*   429
- *Career and Personal Needs Just Don't Mix*   430
- *The Competitive Leak Is More Than a Crisis*   430
- *The CEO Puts Her Foot in Her Mouth*   431
- *The Only U.S.A. Communicator on the Team*   431
- *Working across Time and Space*   432
- *Are We a High-Reliability Team or Not?*   433

Author Index   434

Subject Index   439

PREFACE

We are in transition from an information and knowledge age to a conceptual age with rapid change in the institutions and organizations with which we are most familiar. *Fundamentals of Organizational Communication: Knowledge, Sensitivity, Skills, Values* was written to help readers experience twenty-first-century organizational challenges within the context of learning about communication and organizations.

The eighth edition of this book presents the concepts of organizational communication within a unique competency-based approach that incorporates personal knowledge, interpersonal sensitivity, communication skills, and ethical values. It blends theory, practice, and analysis with an emphasis on knowledge, sensitivity, skills, and values.

Why a competency-based approach? The answer is simple: organizing material by competency components is academically relevant and important to contemporary organizations. Favorable responses to earlier editions from both students and faculty support the competency-based mix of theory and application. In addition, studies in the United States of America and internationally describe both human and technological communication as the keys to excellence in the twenty-first century. Numerous employer surveys have found that accurately processing large volumes of information within organizations, although necessary, is not sufficient for excellence; employers need individuals who take personal responsibility for building relationships that contribute to trust, quality communication, innovation, and change.

NEW TO THIS EDITION

We are in one of the most turbulent and exciting periods in human history. The twenty-first century presents unprecedented challenges and opportunities, particularly for the discipline of organizational communication. The changes in the eighth edition of *Fundamentals of Organizational Communication* directly address the rapid changes in the field and provide students with the most current information available from which to make both academic and professional choices. A brief overview of some of the most important changes to the eighth edition includes:

- Expanded discussions of globalization and communications technologies, including social media, throughout the text
- New discussions of practical theory and communication constitutes organizations (CCO) (Chapter 2)
- New discussions of race perspectives for organizational communication (Chapter 2)
- Expanded discussion of global values and ethical implications (Chapter 4)
- New discussions of the importance of trust throughout the text

- Expansion of discussions of emotion in organizations and discussions of bullying and mobbing (Chapter 5)
- Introduction of the concept of high-reliability organizations (Chapter 6)
- New discussions of discursive leadership and the importance of discourse for leadership (Chapter 7)
- New discussion of framing and sensemaking during conflict (Chapter 9)
- New discussion of strategic communication and social media (Chapter 10)
- New discussions of contradictions and misalignments during change (Chapter 11)
- New discussion of organizational decline (Chapter 11)
- New discussion of Stakeholder Theory (Chapter 11)
- An updated appendix with new cases not included in previous editions

THE COMPETENCY FRAMEWORK

Knowledge

Theoretical concepts important to the study of organizational communication are presented so that students can develop personal knowledge. Knowledge competencies are what we come to know about the theory and principles of a particular field of study, in this case organizational communication. Knowledge competencies support sensitivity in organizational life, guide our development of skills, and assist us in understanding the application of ethical standards and our personal values in organizational settings. To this end, this book examines various frameworks for understanding organizational communication, communication implications of major organizational theories, and communication processes in organizations.

Sensitivity

The sensitivity component in the competency framework refers to our ability to sense or become aware of a variety of organizational meanings and feelings. It is related to our ability and willingness to understand what others are feeling and doing. To help students develop the sensitivity competency, this book encourages them to study and analyze various roles and relationships within organizations. Individual sensitivity can be developed by analyzing the impact of personal behaviors in organizational settings, such as individuals in organizations, dyadic relationships (specifically supervisor–employee relationships), group processes, conflict, and leadership and management communication, each examined in the text. In addition, the text emphasizes the importance of the sensitivity component for our increasingly diverse, multicultural, and global organizational world.

Skills

The skills component of the framework focuses on developing important analytical capabilities as well as the ability to communicate effectively in a variety of settings. It is designed to help students develop both initiating and receiving communication skills. Key organizational communication skills (e.g., decision making, problem solving, fact-finding, interviewing, using communications technologies, and making presentations) are identified, and analysis and practice opportunities appropriate for each are provided. Also, analysis opportunities provided in case studies and research opportunities contribute to students' skill development.

Values

The values component in the competency framework is key to the integration of knowledge, sensitivity, and skills. To understand the realities of organizational life, we must first examine how individual and organizational values or ethics can shape organizational communication behavior. Students develop values and ethics through case studies that present ethical dilemmas and value issues in organizational settings. We adopt different value positions and ethical perspectives to analyze cases, recommend courses of action, and predict outcomes.

FEATURES OF *FUNDAMENTALS OF ORGANIZATIONAL COMMUNICATION*

Each chapter of *Fundamentals of Organizational Communication* attempts to contribute to competency development through the constant interaction of theory, practice, and analysis. Chapters begin with a statement of objectives and a short case study illustrating the concepts to be studied. Key terms and concepts are identified in margins, and chapters end with highlights, communication tips, and a workshop posing questions and issues in each of the competency areas: knowledge, sensitivity, skills, and values. The appendix provides additional practice and opportunities for analysis.

Chapters 1 through 3 develop students' knowledge through an understanding of what contributes to comprehensive communication competency and how we can understand this phenomenon called organizational communication. These chapters emphasize major organizational theories and their communication implications.

Chapter 4 focuses on the interaction of personal, organizational, and professional ethics and values. It presents the values component of communication competency, placing particular emphasis on how organizational values contribute to organizational culture and effectiveness.

Chapters 5 through 9 develop the sensitivity component of communication competency. These chapters describe individuals in organizations and their intrapersonal, interpersonal, and small-group experiences. In addition, they emphasize the increasing diversity and multiculturalism of organizations as well as the study of conflict and leadership. Research indicates that conflict and leadership may well be the focal processes for effective communication in organizations. Texts in organizational communication frequently treat these topics mechanically, without emphasizing underlying subtleties such as organizational climate or the complex interactions of individual predispositions, strategies, and tactics. This book supports understanding of individual preferences in these crucial areas of organizational behavior by using self-assessment instruments.

Chapter 10 through 12 develop competency in the skills component, identifying key applications and career options for organizational communication skills and making specific suggestions for skill development.

The appendix contributes to the comprehensive development of all four competency components through an interaction of theory, practice, and analysis. Materials in the appendix are to be used as supplements to the other chapters to apply the concepts learned through practical and realistic examples.

SUPPLEMENTAL RESOURCES FOR INSTRUCTORS

Instructor's Manual and Test Bank

For each chapter in the text, the *Instructor's Manual and Test Bank* provides a chapter focus, learning objectives, key terms, and discussion activities and exercises. The Test Bank portion offers hundreds of test questions in multiple-choice, true/false, short-answer, and essay formats. Available only online on our Instructor's Resource Center at www.ablongman.com/irc (please contact your Pearson representative for an access code).

Computerized Test Bank

The user-friendly interface enables instructors to view, edit, and add questions; transfer questions into tests; and print tests in a variety of fonts. Search and Sort features allow instructors to locate questions quickly and arrange them in a preferred order. Available only online on our Instructor's Resource Center at www.ablongman.com/irc (please contact your Pearson representative for an access code).

PowerPoint Presentation Package

A PowerPoint presentation provides lecture slides based on key concepts in the text. Available only online on our Instructor's Resource Center at www.ablongman.com/irc (please contact your Pearson representative for an access code).

ACKNOWLEDGMENTS

I wrote this book for four primary reasons: my experiences with students who appreciate the importance of the study of organizational communication, my research interests in organizational communication, my twenty-plus years of business experience in both the private and public sectors, and my fundamental belief that organizations and the discipline of organizational communication must undergo significant change as the world around us changes. When taken together, these experiences and beliefs have been invaluable to me in relating theory to practice and in projecting competency needs for the future.

I am grateful for the help and support of many individuals in the development of this manuscript. Sherry Morreale and Mike Hackman, along with my colleagues in the Department of Communication at the University of Colorado at Colorado

Springs, have stimulated my thinking. Adam Saffer, an outstanding graduate student, has made excellent contributions to research and the development of new cases. I also want to thank the many special students at the University of Colorado at Colorado Springs, who reviewed and critiqued most of the exercises and cases contained in the text.

I also am grateful to the following individuals who reviewed the manuscript and provided helpful suggestions: Sherwyn Morreale, University of Colorado, Colorado Springs, and Susan Dunlap, Argosy University.

On a personal note, I wrote this book with the continuing guidance, love, and support of my family. My father and mother, Jim and Leatha Shockley, provided the foundation for a special pursuit of learning. Without my husband, Charles, the professional years simply would not have occurred. His continuous love and encouragement made all dreams possible. Our daughter and granddaughter, Yvonne and Carissa, continue in his light.

This book was written for students who want to change and improve organizations and themselves, who are willing to risk excellence, and who love engaging in human communication. Therefore, to students (past, present, and future) and to my family (Charles, Yvonne, Carissa, Mom, and Dad), I dedicate this book.

Organizational Communication

A Competency-Based Approach

DEVELOPING COMPETENCIES THROUGH ...

KNOWLEDGE Describing communication in the information-rich world
Defining and describing communication competency
Defining and describing the human communication process
Identifying descriptions of organizations
Surveying definitions of organizational communication

SENSITIVITY Understanding communication as a key to organizational excellence
Developing awareness of our personal communication competencies
Understanding human communication as attempting to create shared realities, shared meanings
Distinguishing among interpersonal, small-group, and organizational communication

SKILLS Assessing personal development needs
Practicing analysis capabilities

VALUES Understanding communication competency as a personal and organizational need
Clarifying a contemporary "good communicator" theme
Understanding communication as fundamental to the process of organizing
Evaluating communication for ethics and effectiveness

THE CHANGING NATURE OF ORGANIZATIONS AND WORK

We are in one of the most turbulent periods in history. This statement is not profound but is real nevertheless. Our twenty-first-century world is more complex, and the knowledge we bring to bear on our problems often adds to confusion and disagreement. We have unprecedented opportunities and unprecedented problems. Most of us seek a firm direction that is outmoded. Uncertainty has become the norm. We need new thinking, new criticisms, new knowledge, new approaches, and new understandings. Creativity and innovation are more important than ever.

Nowhere is the current turbulence more evident than in contemporary organizations. Increased economic pressures, globalization, rapidly diversifying employee and customer bases, changing technology, an increasing awareness of organizational relationships to society in general, and a host of other factors contribute to new organization types, new relationships between organizations and employees, and a growing acknowledgment of the complexity of all organizational life. The virtual organization, e-commerce, high-performing teams, contract employment, increased contact with a culturally diverse world, and home-based work are but a few of the changes with impacts on interpersonal relationships, group interactions, management and leadership, personal and professional ethics, time management, and nonwork life.

What many have called the old social contract—mutual loyalty and support between employees and their employers—has been replaced by frequent shifts from one employer to another, increased global competition, downsizing in workforces, part-time employment, flatter organizations, and a generally changing relationship between management and workers. Critics of the changing nature of our work lives call for increased workplace democracy, whereas advocates defend the changes as necessary for survival.

CHALLENGES FOR INDIVIDUALS AND ORGANIZATIONS

The environments individuals and organizations encounter are complex, fragile, turbulent, and uncertain. The opportunities for innovation and change are enormous. J. F. Rischard (2002) describes the challenges individuals and organizations face as problems of sharing our planet, our humanity, and a global rule book. Rischard identifies global warming, biodiversity, deforestation, poverty, education, the digital divide, e-commerce rules, international labor and migration rules, the global financial architecture, and several other problems as issues so pressing they must be addressed in the next twenty years by individuals and organizations including for-profit, not-for-profit, governmental, and educational institutions. Individuals and organizations experience increasingly diverse environments characterized by age, gender, race, and cultural differences. Individuals and organizations are challenged to engage these differences to create opportunities, generate innovation, and contribute to productive change.

THE COMMUNICATIONS ERA

Regardless of the position taken about the changing nature of organizations and work, few disagree the communications era surrounds us. We live, work, and play in complex communications environments. Sophisticated communications technologies have changed the way we do everything. The rapid development and use of communications technologies has made the world more interconnected than at any previous point in human history.

All of us are experiencing a unique time in history with two unprecedented shifts—globalization and the nature of innovation—driving changes impacting all aspects of our lives. Innovation can occur anywhere, and participation in the creation of new products and processes is no longer limited to super-powers and highly developed countries. The United States of America, Japan, Germany, and the United Kingdom have all seen white-collar jobs move to countries such as India, China, and Russia. Millions of routine jobs have disappeared, while new and more stimulating jobs requiring communications expertise are being created. With more than half of America's workforce and gross national product in knowledge industries, virtually all agree we are in a postindustrial **information society** moving to a **conceptual age**. Daniel Pink (2005), who describes the shift from the information to the conceptual age, suggests, "The future belongs to a very different kind of person with a very different kind of mind—creators and empathizers, pattern recognizers, and meaning makers. These people—artists, inventors, designers, storytellers, caregivers, consolers, big picture thinkers—will now reap society's richest rewards and share its greatest joys" (p. 1). Thomas Friedman (2006) believes "we are now connecting all the knowledge centers on the planet together into a single global network, which—if politics and terrorism do not get in the way—could usher in an amazing era of prosperity, innovation, and collaboration, by companies, communities, and individuals" (p. 8).

Information society ■ Environment in which more jobs create, process, or distribute information than directly produce goods. The environment is characterized by mass production of information, which requires the constant learning of new activities and processes.

Conceptual age ■ Environment in which inventive, empathic, big-picture capabilities are required for the most fulfilling jobs. Written and oral communication, inquiry, critical and creative thinking, quantitative literacy, cultural knowledge, teamwork, synthesis of learning, and strong personal ethics are highly valued.

As an individual you are likely to spend most of your working life employed in a "knowledge/information" or "conceptual" job. You are more likely to create, process, or distribute information than you are to be directly involved in the production of goods. There is a greater need for salespeople, teachers, lawyers, financial analysts, media producers, bankers, consultants, scientists, engineers, doctors, architects, writers, information managers, editors, and social workers and a decreased need for manufacturing assembly workers, service support workers, miners, toolmakers, machinists, builders, and welders.

One of the most important characteristics of the "communications" era is the rapid change associated with mass production of information, change requiring us all to be constantly involved in the learning of new activities and processes. Most of us have already experienced rapid change brought about by new technologies. For example, although checks can still be written by hand, many of us pay our bills online or with plastic cards and use computer terminals to deposit money in or withdraw money from our bank accounts. We can still go to the movies, or we can bring movies to our homes through discs, satellites, and Internet connections. We can write letters and memos to send through "regular" mail, or we can use sophisticated electronic systems to send and receive all types of correspondence and files rapidly. We use our cellular phones for talking with others but also as our Web connections, cameras (both still and video), instant messaging devices, calculators, clocks, e-mail processors, televisions, and a host of other functions. Social networking of all types increasingly is prevalent in both our personal and organizational environments.

Fiber-optic connections, wireless networks, and global telecommunications and computer networks have literally changed the ways in which we do research, changed those with whom we can stay in constant contact, and altered notions of time and space. We are connected daily with both close friends and strangers. Most students reading this book are in traditional classrooms with "live" instructors. For some students now, and for more in the future, however, "live" means that the instructor is located at a remote site equipped with audio, video, and computer interconnects supported by e-books. *Convergence* is the term of the day, with computing, wireless technologies, and more traditional media such as television converging into integrated tools for work, school, family, and leisure environments.

We have so much information that, for individuals and organizations, the challenge is how to deal with our information alternatives. This daily increase in information (based on innovations in communications and computer technology) brings with it rapid change in activities, processes, and products.

Workers in the communications era of microelectronics, computers, and telecommunications have an abundance of information for decision making and a growing concern for information overload. Research suggests virtually all knowledge workers use e-mail and voicemail, with use of mobile phones, conference calls, corporate intranets, IM/text messaging, corporate Web sites, information portals, and corporate extranets on the rise. We can routinely communicate across both geography and organizational levels. It is not unusual, for example, for employees of an organization in Boston to interact with their counterparts in Los Angeles, whom they have never met, while both groups prepare a portion of a single report or recommendation. And for a growing number of individuals, this report can be generated without ever leaving their homes as they "telecommute" from automated home workstations to offices around the globe.

The complexity of all organizational life and the rapid increase in communications technologies place increasing demands on our individual communication abilities. These demands are best met with the perspective that becoming and staying competent is an ongoing process requiring lifelong learning.

COMMUNICATION: THE KEY TO ORGANIZATIONAL EXCELLENCE

Organizational excellence ■ Ability of people to work together and utilize technology for the creative solving of increasingly complex problems.

In this complex and information-rich conceptual society, the key to **organizational excellence** is effective communication. Communication systems within organizations—both human and technological—are responsible for solving increasingly complex problems creatively. People using the machines of the communications era must coordinate large volumes of information for the performance of new and dynamic tasks. There is widespread recognition, however, that excellence in organizational problem solving is more than the efficient management of large volumes of facts. Organizational excellence stems from the dedicated commitment of people, people who are motivated to work together and who share similar values and visions about the results of their efforts.

Viewing communications as the key to organizational excellence is not new. As early as 1938, Chester Barnard, in his now-famous work *The Functions of the Executive,* described as a primary responsibility of executives the development and maintenance of a system of communication. Research since then has linked organizational communication to managerial effectiveness, the integration of work units across organizational levels, characteristics of effective supervision, job and communication satisfaction, innovation, adaptability, creativity, and overall organizational effectiveness and performance. In fact, numerous scholars have gone as far as to suggest that organizations are essentially complex communication processes that create and change events. For both the industrial society of the past and the information and conceptual societies of today and tomorrow, there is broad agreement about the centrality of organizational communication and that organizational communication plays a significant part in contributing to or detracting from organizational excellence.

With this emphasis on the complex, fast-paced information conceptual society and the importance of human communication, questions arise concerning what skills and abilities organizations need from their future employees. How should individuals prepare themselves for the information responsibilities and opportunities that almost inevitably will be a part of the future? What does it take to contribute to organizational communication excellence?

Put simply, organizations of today and tomorrow need competent communicators at all organizational levels. With more complex decisions, rapid change, more information, and less certainty about what the decisions should be, excellence in a conceptual world depends on the abilities, commitment, and creativity of all organizational members. As a result, students, communication teachers and researchers, and active organizational members must work together to understand what contributes to organizational communication competency and how best to develop personal potential.

EXCELLENCE IN COMMUNICATION: COMMUNICATION COMPETENCY

Quintilian, an early Latin rhetorician, is credited with introducing the ideal of the "good man speaking well," an ideal that is not as far removed from contemporary concepts of organizational communication competency as history might suggest. In fact, Michael Hackman and Craig Johnson (2004) identified a contemporary "good communicator" theme when reviewing research from personnel administrators throughout the United States of America. Today's organizations need people who can speak well, listen, write, persuade others, demonstrate interpersonal skills, gather information, and exhibit small-group problem-solving expertise. In other words, organizations in our complex and turbulent world need flexible and creative people who have diverse and well-developed communication abilities. Yet how do we determine if we are competent organizational communicators? Who decides? On what do we base our conclusions?

Researchers differ in how they define **communication competency.** Some believe that a person is competent if he or she knows what is appropriate in a specific situation, whether or not that behavior actually occurs. A student, for example, who realizes that class participation is required for a high grade may choose not to participate, yet the student can be considered competent because of the knowledge or awareness of the appropriate behavior. Other researchers extend the competency concept beyond

Communication competency ■
Composed of knowledge, sensitivity, skills, and values. Competence arises from interaction of theory, practice, and analysis.

knowledge of appropriate behaviors to include actual language performance and the achievement of interpersonal goals. The student, from this perspective, must not only recognize appropriate participation behaviors but also participate so as to demonstrate communication competency.

Fred Jablin and Patricia Sias (2001), in their comprehensive discussion of communication competency, suggested that the concept of communication competency is best understood by an ecological model that revolves around four systems:

> (1) the microsystem, which contains the developing organizational member and other persons in the immediate work environment (e.g., supervisors, coworkers, and clients); (2) the mesosystem, which represents the interrelations among various microsystems (e.g., what individuals learn in their project teams may affect their competence in the functional work groups in which they are members); (3) the macrosystem, which does not represent the immediate context in which an individual works, but does impinge on him or her (i.e., major divisions of the organization and the organization itself as a whole); and (4) the exosystem, which represents the overarching cultural belief system, forms of knowledge, social, technological, and political ideologies. . . . In brief, an ecological perspective emphasizes system embeddedness. That is, the actions of one element of the system affect the other elements. (pp. 836–837)

Jablin and Sias specifically described how globalization and technology have changed forever notions of what is a competent communicator. It is fair to conclude they expand previous notions of communication competency to extend to groups and to the organization as a whole within its broad environment. In recent work, Sherry Morreale (2008) suggests linkage between communication competence and ethics. Specifically, Morreale identifies issues of competence related to pursuing self-interest versus the interest of others, to engaging in information sharing versus manipulation, and to recognizing the long-term effects of communication across time and diverse relationships.

Stephen Littlejohn and David Jabusch (1982) have proposed a particularly useful definition of communication competency for the organizational setting. They suggest that communication competency is "the ability and willingness of an individual to participate responsibly in a transaction in such a way as to maximize the outcomes of shared meanings." This definition requires not only knowledge of appropriate behaviors but also motivation to engage in communication that results in mutual understanding. In other words, communication competency involves our personal willingness and ability to communicate so that our meanings are understood and we understand the meanings of others. Finally, this definition can be applied to the group and macro-organizational levels so important in the ecological model proposed by Jablin and Sias. Regardless of differences in perspectives, organizational communication competency relates to message encoding and decoding abilities, the process of communication initiation and consumption.

When we begin to think about our personal communication competency, we quickly realize that we form impressions of our own competency while making evaluations about the competency of others. We try to decide what is appropriate for us as well as for others, and we determine whether that behavior is effective in a particular circumstance. In other words, my impression of my own competency and the competency of others is related to my evaluation of whether we exhibited the "right" behaviors and achieved "desirable" results in a particular situation. Determining what is "right" and "desirable" is not always easy, however. Think for a moment about your personal experiences. Have you ever been in a situation where others thought you did a good job although you were disappointed in yourself? Who was right? Were you competent or incompetent? Can both be correct?

Earlier we said that organizational excellence depends on the communication competencies of all organizational members. Specifically, we described the need for creative problem solving among diverse groups of people who often share little common information. With this emphasis on communication and technology, the real question becomes what individuals should do to prepare themselves to meet their future communication needs. In other words, how do we develop and evaluate our communication competencies?

Our answer begins by returning to the Littlejohn and Jabusch approach to communication competency. Littlejohn and Jabusch (1982) contend that competency arises out of four basic components: process understanding, interpersonal sensitivity, communication skills, and ethical responsibility. Process understanding refers to the cognitive ability to understand the dynamics of the communication event. Interpersonal sensitivity is the ability to perceive feelings and meanings. Communication skills are the ability to develop and interpret message strategies in specific situations. The ethical component of competency is the attitudinal set that governs concern for the well-being of all participants in taking responsibility for communication outcomes. Finally, Littlejohn and Jabusch believe that competence comes from the interaction of three primary elements: theory, practice, and analysis. When applied to the organizational setting, the Littlejohn and Jabusch approach can be modified and expanded to include the competency components this book seeks to develop: knowledge, sensitivity, skills, and values.

ORGANIZATIONAL COMMUNICATION: A COMPETENCY-BASED APPROACH

This book is designed to help you develop communication competencies for effective organizational communication. The goal of the book is to provide theory, practice, and analysis opportunities that contribute to knowledge, sensitivity, skills, and values important for organizational excellence.

Knowledge: the ability to understand the organizational communication environment. Knowledge competencies are what we come to know about a particular field. Knowledge is the learning of theory and principles. Knowledge competencies are fundamental to support our sensitivity to organizational life, to guide our skill development, and to assist us in understanding the application of ethical standards and our personal values in a variety of organizational settings. **Knowledge competency** develops through the exploration of the interactive process nature of human communication. We examine what organizational communication is and the major theoretical approaches for its

> **Knowledge competency** ■ Ability to understand the organizational communication environment.

study. We explore the roles of individuals in organizations and examine communication implications of major organizational theories. Finally, we discuss vital organizational subjects such as conflict, leadership, and strategic communication.

Sensitivity: the ability to sense accurately organizational meanings and feelings. It is related to our ability and willingness to understand what others feel and do. **Sensitivity competency** develops through the examination of our personal "theories-in-use" about communication and organizations. We assess individual preferences for leadership and conflict, as well as the impact of personal differences and similarities within organizational settings. We place emphasis on how we come to understand our complex organizational environments.

Sensitivity competency ■ Ability to sense organizational meanings and feelings accurately.

Skills: the ability to analyze organizational situations accurately and to initiate and consume organizational messages effectively. The skills competency focuses on developing important analytical capabilities as well as the ability to communicate effectively in a variety of settings. **Skills competency** develops through analysis and practice opportunities. Specifically, analytical skills develop by applying knowledge and sensitivity to case studies and individual experiences. We also present and practice problem-solving and conflict-management skills.

Skills competency ■ Ability to analyze organizational situations accurately and to initiate and consume organizational messages effectively.

Values: the importance of taking personal responsibility for effective communication, thereby contributing to organizational excellence. **Values competency** develops through discussion of personal responsibility for participation in organizational communication. We examine ethical dilemmas relating to organizational communication and the importance of values to organizational culture. Finally, we use case studies to illustrate ethical and value issues common in organizations.

Values competency ■ Importance of taking responsibility for effective communication, thereby contributing to organizational excellence.

THE "WHAT BUSINESS IS THIS OF OURS?" CASE

The following case describes a problem at Quality Engineering, a medium-sized company located in Denver, Colorado. The case is based on a real situation at Quality, although the name of the supplier in question has been changed. You will use this case to think about the human communication process and to begin to understand the concept of organizational communication.

John and Mary were the only two buyers in the purchasing department of Quality Engineering. Both had been with the company for several years and were experienced in handling purchases for the manufacturing, research, finance, and marketing areas of Quality. Mary typically handled purchases for the manufacturing and research areas, and John was the principal buyer for the rest of the organization. At times their individual workloads required that they cross departments and help each other. Their boss, Mike Anderson, the accountant for Quality, believed they were the best purchasing team with whom he had ever worked. He was proud of their efforts and willingness to cooperate with each other. He frequently commented to Quality management that John and Mary made money for the company by getting the best possible prices for goods and services.

Mike was surprised and concerned to overhear John and Mary in a heated discussion.

JOHN: I can't believe you are still using Anderson Printing as one of our suppliers. I told you last month that their last two orders for my groups were late and part of the printing had to be sent back because of errors. I told them then that I wouldn't accept any more of their bids on our jobs. It makes me look like a fool when I hear from them that you are still ordering their products for manufacturing and research. How can we enforce good quality from our suppliers if we don't present a united front?

MARY: Just a minute. Anderson Printing has been one of our good suppliers for over ten years. I know we have had some problems with them in the past year but I don't think we should drop them flat. They have pulled us out of a lot of jams when we needed printing in a big hurry. I never agreed to drop them from our supplier list. You just told them they were gone and expected me to support your decision. You should have talked to me about it first. I don't care if you think you looked like a fool. We are in this together and need to make those types of decisions as a team.

JOHN: I'll admit we should have talked about it, but Anderson made me so mad on that last deal that I just told them they were through. I expected you to support me. We both want what is best for Quality. Our reputations are good because we always get the company the best products for the lowest price. I would have supported you.

MARY: Yes, I suspect you would have, but John, you can't lose your temper like that. We need to work together on these decisions. You and I can usually work out a solution when we try hard enough. I don't want to drop any supplier on the spur of the moment, especially when we may have trouble replacing them. John, sometimes I think we have worked together for so long that we take each other for granted. We are friends and I want it to remain that way, but that shouldn't stop us from doing business with each other as true professionals.

JOHN: Wait a minute. Are you saying that I don't act like a professional—?

MARY: No, see what I mean? You get mad when I even suggest we might improve the way we do things.

JOHN: Well, I just think friends should support each other. I know I may not have handled the Anderson thing just right, but as my friend I expected more support from you.

MARY: Oh, John, there you go again! ■

BASICS OF HUMAN COMMUNICATION

Are John and Mary engaged in interpersonal or organizational communication, or both? Does the setting make the difference? Can we distinguish between interpersonal and organizational communication? When we talk about developing our personal communication competencies, is it different for our personal and organizational lives? The answers to these questions lie in understanding what human communication is, how it works, and how organizations and human communication relate. In other words, frameworks for understanding organizational communication can be found in descriptions of human communication and organizations.

Although the discussion between John and Mary is typical of human communication exchanges that occur daily in organizations, it also is typical of communication between two people regardless of the setting. In fact, the discussion between John and Mary illustrates some of the important basics necessary for understanding human communication.

Defining Communication

Analyzing the exchange between John and Mary will help us describe human communication. John and Mary transfer information, they elicit responses from each other, and they engage in social interaction. Further, it is possible to say that they use symbols (words) to attempt to create shared meaning (mutual understanding). Their disagreement about how to handle problems with Anderson Printing will influence not only what happens to Anderson as a supplier to Quality Engineering but their interpersonal relationship as well. Put another way, their exchange is an example of communication behaviors creating and shaping both relationships and events through a culturally dependent process of assigning meaning to symbols.

John wants Mary to share his reality that Anderson has made serious mistakes that disqualify it from providing goods and services to Quality. Furthermore, he expects Mary to accept another reality: that friends and coworkers should support each other's decisions, even if decisions are made on the spur of the moment and in anger. Mary has a different set of realities that she wants John to understand. Although she agrees about recent problems with Anderson, part of her reality includes Anderson's past service to Quality and the possible difficulty of replacing its goods and services with another supplier. She also believes that John should have included her in his decision. We do not know from this exchange how open or direct John and Mary intend to be with each other. We do not have enough information to determine if other agendas influence their exchange. We do know John and Mary make conscious choices about the realities they exchange. When John and Mary exchange their individual realities, their communication is an attempt to construct shared realities.

Although they may not agree, their communication enables each to share the realities of the other.

THE HUMAN COMMUNICATION PROCESS

When John and Mary construct their shared realities, they engage in what we call the **human communication process**. Both John and Mary serve as *sources* and *receivers* of messages. Both engage in message *encoding* and *decoding* and in selecting verbal and nonverbal *channels* for message transmission. Both are influenced by their individual *competence* and their perception of the competence of the other. Each brings to the exchange a different set of *experiences,* and each may view the context of their interaction differently. Thus, all their messages are subject to distortion or noise. The *effect,* or what happens between John and Mary, is a result of the complex interaction of all these elements.

Human communication process ■ Attempts to construct shared realities through social interaction.

Source/Receiver

Source/Receiver ■ Individuals send messages as sources and receive messages as receivers. The process is often so rapid as to appear simultaneous.

Each individual engaged in communication with others is both a message **source** and a message **receiver**. We talk (send messages) while closely monitoring the nonverbal reactions of others (receiving messages). We listen (receive messages) and determine how to respond (send messages). Often message-sending and message-receiving activities occur so rapidly that they seem to be happening simultaneously.

Encoding/Decoding

As a message source and receiver, each individual encodes and decodes messages. Message **encoding** is the process of formulating messages, choosing content and symbols to convey meaning. Message encoding is determining what we want to be understood (content) and how we believe that it can best be presented (choosing symbols). Message **decoding** is the process of assigning meaning in the role of receiver to message symbols generated by the message source. Decoding is taking what we see and hear from others and deciding how it should be interpreted or understood. Both encoding and decoding are influenced by our communicative competence (knowledge, sensitivity, skills, and values), our specific intentions (desire for clarity, openness, manipulation, deceit, control, and so forth), our past experiences, our perception of the competence of others, and the communication context.

> **Encoding/Decoding** ■ Message encoding is the process of formulating messages, choosing content and symbols to convey meaning. Message decoding is the process of assigning meaning in the role of receiver to message symbols generated by the message source.

Message

The **message** is the symbolic attempt to transfer meaning; it is the signal that serves as a stimulus for a receiver. Sources send messages consisting of auditory, visual, olfactory, gustatory, or tactile stimuli in any combination of these five senses. Sources of messages intend meaning, but messages in and of themselves do not carry meaning. Meanings, or interpretations of messages, are assigned when the receiver decodes the message. Messages serve as symbols for meaning and as such are subject to situational and cultural influences. In other words, to understand a message as a source intends requires an understanding of the source's symbol system (language and actions and intent of language and actions) in a particular situation.

> **Message** ■ Symbolic attempt to transfer meaning; the signal that serves as a stimulus for a receiver.

Channel

The **channel** is the medium through which the message is transmitted. It is the link or links between source and receiver. Channels include the five senses and any technological means used for message transmission. Channels are frequently used in combination (verbal and nonverbal, oral and written, face to face, and telemediated), with certain channels generally more credible than others. When verbal and nonverbal messages appear to contradict, for example, researchers tell us that most people will find the nonverbal channel more credible than the verbal one. In other words, most of us believe that it is more difficult to lie nonverbally than verbally. Channels can distort messages both technologically and in sensory reception. Indeed, the very selection of one channel over another may become a message in and of itself. Written channels, for example, are more often used than face-to-face channels for giving

> **Channel** ■ Medium through which the message is transmitted.

bad news. Evidence is growing suggesting e-mail and text messages are often more harsh than face-to-face communication. Receiving a memo or e-mail from your boss—the bad-news channel—may be cause for alarm even before the actual message has been read.

Noise

Noise ■ Distortion or interference that contributes to discrepancies between the meaning intended by the source of a message and the meaning assigned by the receiver.

Noise is the distortion or interference that contributes to discrepancies between the meaning intended by the source and the meaning assigned by the receiver. Noise can be anything: physical distractions, channel interference, communicative competence, communication context, or psychological predispositions. Noise is always present in one form or another, and the type or types of noise contribute to the meanings assigned to messages by receivers and to the encoding of new messages. Think for a moment about your reaction to receiving an important message from a person whose credibility you have reason to doubt. What meaning do you assign to the message based on your prior relationship with this individual? Assume next that you receive the same message from a trusted friend. Is your reaction different? What type of noise was generated by your past experiences with both individuals? How did that noise affect meaning?

Competence

Each individual brings knowledge, sensitivity, skills, and values to communication interactions. Our ability to understand appropriate behaviors, our specific intentions, our willingness to engage in communication, and our ability to interact with others to generate shared realities all contribute to our impression of our own *competence*. Also, we continually evaluate and form impressions about the competence of those with whom we communicate. Our impression of our own competence and the impression we have of the competence of others contribute to both the encoding and decoding of messages. Ultimately, competence contributes to communication effects and how we evaluate the effectiveness of our interactions.

Field of Experience

Field of experience ■ Set of specific experiences or background that all parties in communication bring to bear on the interaction.

All parties in a communication interaction bring a specific set of experiences or background to bear on the interaction. What we do in a particular situation is related to how much we know about the situation from past experiences and whether we share any common past experiences. We may behave very differently in situations in which we have considerable past experience than we would in situations that are new and unfamiliar. The **field of experience** is situation specific and may or may not relate to broader evaluations of self-competence. In other words, although we may feel less competent in situations in which we have little past experience, that impression does not automatically transfer to other circumstances in which we have more background.

Generally, it is believed that the more common the field of experience among those communicating, the easier it is to share similar meanings or to construct shared realities. Have you ever tried, for example, to explain an American sporting event to a visitor from another country where the sport is not played and has never been televised? Did you even know where to begin? Chances are that the lack of any prior experience on the part of your receiver (no common field of experience between you) required you to engage in considerable detail, making it difficult even to begin to describe the event. You can imagine that your approach would be entirely different if you described the same event to a longtime fan of the sport.

Communication Context

The **communication context** is the environment for the communication interaction. Context includes not only the specific time and place of the interaction but also the roles, relationships, and status of communication participants. As such, prior interactions among participants contribute to the construction of the current communication context. It is fair to say context contributes to our specific intentions in a given circumstance. Communication intentions, as most of us have experienced, can range from full disclosure, openness, and clarity seeking to deception, ambiguity, manipulation, and control. Most of us recognize we communicate differently depending on how well we know people, what their formal position is in relation to us, and how visible our communication is to others. The way we express ourselves in the privacy of our own homes may differ from what we will say and do in our work environments. Openly disagreeing with a friend or coworker is different from openly disagreeing with our boss. The way we express ourselves is related to whether we believe others to be more knowledgeable or competent than we are or whether we believe that we possess the best information in a specific setting. The way we express ourselves also reflects the expectations of the particular culture or environment in which we communicate. We can therefore say that context is both culturally and physically influenced, and as with other elements in the communication process, perception of context can differ from one communication participant to another.

Communication context ■ Environment for the communication interaction.

Effect

The communication **effect** is the result, consequence, or outcome of the communication exchange. Effects can be observed to be directly related to communication interactions. When people have an argument and terminate relationships at the end of the argument, we witness what we would call an obvious effect. At other times, the effect is not immediately observable or is, at best, delayed in time and context. A student does not contribute to a group project; the project is completed and all group members receive the same grade. Nothing appears to happen until the next class project begins and members of the group ask the instructor to reassign the student to another team. Although less direct, this effect nevertheless should be understood as an outcome of previous communication exchanges.

Effect ■ Result, consequence, or outcome of communication exchanges.

In addition to being viewed in terms of results, the effect of an interaction is evaluated by communication participants for effectiveness and ethics. Did the outcomes result from the free, informed choices of all parties? Did one or more parties feel manipulated? Were all parties empathically supported? Were the best alternatives considered as a result of the interaction? It is in this evaluative area—ethics and effectiveness—that future interactions are influenced. Perceptions of whether past interactions were ethical and effective influence perceptions of the desirability of future communication.

THE CONSTRUCTION OF SHARED REALITIES

Shared realities ■ Meanings resulting from the communication process; attempts to have others understand our world as we do or as we intend for it to be understood and our efforts to comprehend the world of those around us.

Human communication is the process of attempting to construct **shared realities,** to create shared meanings. It is our attempts to have others understand our world as we do or as we want them to understand it and our efforts to comprehend the world of those around us. As Robert Craig (2007) describes, "A first-order constitutive model of communication posits that communication, rather than merely a neutral conduit for transmitting independently existing information, is the primary social process through which our meaningful common world is constructed." As a process for the construction of shared realities, human communication is culturally and contextually influenced, dynamic, and ever-changing.

When this process occurs between two individuals with some type of ongoing relationship, we call the process *interpersonal communication*. When the process occurs among several individuals, we describe it as *group communication*. When large numbers of people are involved (either personally or through technological channels), we call the process *public* or *mass media communication*. Finally, we refer to the human communication process in organizations as *organizational communication*, the subject of our text. Whether in interpersonal, group, public, mass media/networked/telemediated, or organizational contexts, the human communication process involves attempts to construct shared realities among people to generate shared meaning. Think back to the "What Business Is This of Ours?" case. What were the shared realities at Quality Engineering? Describe the fields of experience and the context of the interaction between John and Mary. What were the noise factors? Can you predict the effect of their interaction? Will they be able to work together in the future?

A word of caution is appropriate at this point. Although we continue to describe human communication as the process of constructing shared realities and creating shared meanings, we must remember that shared meanings are always incomplete and characterized by ambiguity. The human communication process as an attempt to construct shared realities can represent openness and clarity but also be characterized by manipulation, control, or deceit. I can deliberately attempt to have you understand a situation as I understand it, hoping for a shared reality characterized by openness, but I can also deliberately attempt to have you understand a situation very differently from what I know the facts to be. Suppose that I want you to share with me a reality that I choose but not one based on my more complete knowledge, experience, or awareness. My messages then generate a shared reality between us that is characterized by deceit. The important concept here is that the construction of meaning is an intentional process between us related to our knowledge, sensitivity, skills, and values.

CONCEPTS OF ORGANIZATIONS

We have defined and described the human communication process in a variety of possible contexts. Our particular interests are, of course, communication and organizations and how communication influences organizational processes and events. We begin to explore the relationship between communication and organizations by first identifying what an organization is and what it does. The term **organization** is applied to the results of the process of organizing. Organizing is an attempt to bring order out of chaos or establish organizations, entities in which purposeful and ordered activity takes place. Organizing is accomplished through purposeful activities generated as a result of communication behaviors. In other words, the process we call organizing is accomplished through human communication as individuals seek to bring order out of chaos and establish entities for purposeful activities.

Organization ■ Result of the process of organizing; dynamic system in which individuals engage in collective efforts for goal accomplishment.

Amitai Etzioni (1964) described organizations as social units or groupings of people deliberately constructed and reconstructed to strive for specific goals. As such, organizations are characterized by divisions of labor for goal achievement. These efforts also are directed by relatively continuous patterns of authority and leadership. Interdependence exists among organizational components as well as with the external environment. This complex interdependence requires coordination achieved through communication.

Katherine Miller (2003) identified five features she believed are possessed by all organizations: two or more people (a social collectivity), goals, coordinating activity, structure, and environmental embeddedness. Gerald Pepper (1995) provided a communication-based definition when he described organizations as consisting of the organizing activities of their members. Pepper argued, "Though this definition may seem circular, it really is quite descriptive of a communication explanation of organizations. The definition accounts for traditional, pyramidal organizational form just as easily as it accounts for nontraditional democratic, 'feminist' organizational forms, because the key to the definition is the communicative relationships among the members, rather than arbitrary components assumed to define the organization" (pp. 17–18).

Taken as a whole, these definitions and issues help us understand organizations from their structure and from the ways they continually create and change what they do and how they do it. This process occurs through communication behaviors. Put another way, understanding what an organization is and how it works requires an understanding of the process of organizational communication.

Throughout the next several chapters, we explore many different types of organizations. We examine organizations with which you have personal contact and involvement. We discuss traditional hierarchical organizations, profit-making organizations, and nonprofit groups. We describe organizations in which hierarchy is replaced by flatter forms and the use of technology to create virtual groups or entire organizations. We explore partnerships, entrepreneurial opportunities, and home-based work as well as global ventures. For all these "types" of organization, you will come to understand human communication behaviors as creating and shaping both relationships and events.

DEFINITIONS OF ORGANIZATIONAL COMMUNICATION

Organizational communication ■
Process through which organizations are created and in turn create and shape events. The process can be understood as a combination of process, people, messages, meaning, and purpose.

Organizational communication is both similar to and distinct from other types of communication. Organizational communication has sources and receivers who engage in the encoding and decoding of messages. Messages are transmitted over channels distorted by noise. As with other forms of communication, organizational communication is related to the competencies of individuals, their fields of experience, the communicative context, and the effects or results of interactions. Yet organizational communication is more than the daily interactions of individuals within organizations. It is the process through which organizations create and shape events. Next, we describe organizational communication as a complex interaction of process, people, messages, meaning, and purpose.

Organizational Communication as Process

As with other forms of communication, organizational communication is best understood as an ongoing process without distinct beginnings and ends. The process includes patterns of interactions that develop among organizational members and those external to the organization and how these interactions shape organizations.

Because the process is ever-changing, it can be described as evolutionary and culturally dependent. In other words, the ongoing process of creating and transmitting organizational messages reflects the shared agreements and disagreements resulting from previous message exchanges and evolves to generate new realities that create and shape events.

The process occurs in developing strategy, planning, decision making, and executing the work of the organization. The process also occurs, however, during unexpected crises, changes in the external environment, encounters with competitors, and in a host of less visible ways. The process occurs between individuals whether performing daily work or socializing and includes messages to large numbers of employers, customers, and stakeholders. All these interactions taken together create and shape the ongoing organization.

Organizational Communication as People

Individuals bring to organizations sets of characteristics that influence how information is processed. Organizational communication contributes to creating relationships and assists both individuals and organizations in achieving diverse purposes. Organizational communication occurs between and among people who share both work and interpersonal relationships. Organizational communication also occurs between and among people who are geographically separated and who may speak different languages and have widely differing cultural perspectives. It is fair to say that organizational communication occurs across networks of people who seek to obtain a variety of objectives requiring communication interactions.

Organizational Communication as Messages

Organizational communication is the creation and exchange of messages. It is the movement or transmission of verbal and nonverbal behaviors and the sharing of information throughout the organization. Communicators are linked together by channels, and messages are described with such terms as *frequency, amount,* and *type*. Concern is expressed for message fidelity, or the extent to which messages are similar or accurate at all links through the channels. Organizational messages increasingly are telemediated (via the use of complex technologies to exchange messages), extending their geographic reach, changing notions of time and space, and altering who participates in communication processes.

Organizational Communication as Meaning

Organizational communication creates and shapes organizational events. Role taking occurs as individuals engage in social interaction within the ever-changing organizational context. Organizational communication is the symbolic behavior of individuals and organizations that, when interpreted, affects all organizational activities. Organizational communication does not create a singular set of meanings for organizational members and activities. The interactions of ever-changing behaviors often create multiple perceptions of events and multiple realities that become the process through which organizational meanings are generated.

Organizational Communication as Purpose

Organizational communication is organizing, decision making, planning, controlling, and coordinating. Organizational communication seeks to reduce environmental uncertainty. It is people, messages, and meaning. It is intentional and unintentional messages explaining the workings of the organization. It is the process through which individuals and organizations attempt goal-oriented behavior in dealing with their environments.

Stanley Deetz (1994) provided an important summary perspective to our discussion of definitions for organizational communication. Deetz suggested: "Communication, in the view I am suggesting, refers to the social processes by which meanings, identities, psychological states, social structures, and the various means of the contact of the organization with the environment are both produced, reproduced, or changed. In both its constitutive and reproductive modes, communication processes are central to how perceptions, meanings, and routines are held in common. In all interactions, including those in organizations, perception, meaning, and data transmission are all complex, multileveled phenomena produced out of and producing conflicting motives and structures" (p. 90).

Can you now answer the question about the differences between organizational and other types of communication? You should be able to do so. Whereas interpersonal and group communication occur in organizations, organizational communication is a more comprehensive process including, but not limited to, one-on-one and group exchanges. Competencies for organizational communication include interpersonal abilities, but organizational communication competencies also require effectiveness in complex and changing environments where diverse groups of people join in purposeful activity. The goal of this book is to help you identify and develop important competencies for organizational communication. The next several chapters concentrate on knowledge, sensitivity, skills, and values important in interpersonal, group, and organization-wide contexts.

Let us return to our case study. Describe the interaction between John and Mary from an organizational communication perspective. Can you identify organizational factors influencing their exchange? Do John and Mary have a work relationship, or are they communicating as friends? Can they be both? Is this an example of organizational goal-directed behavior? How might their exchange affect Quality Engineering?

It is difficult to be certain about our answers for this case. The chances are that most of us feel the need for additional information about John and Mary and Quality Engineering. Yet the lack of complete information is characteristic of many, if not most, of our organizational experiences. In fact, it is probable that even with more information we can never be certain of all the shared realities between John and Mary. Indeed, as we begin our study of organizational communication, a key to our personal development rests with our ability to analyze thoughtfully while recognizing the limits of our understanding.

SELF-ASSESSMENT OF PERSONAL DEVELOPMENT NEEDS

The material in the next eleven chapters is designed to help you develop important competencies for organizational communication. Before you begin to study that material, however, please complete Figure 1.1. The following chapters will be more meaningful if you approach theory, practice, and analysis opportunities with a personal assessment of your current strengths and weaknesses. You are about to complete the first of several self-assessments contained in your text. Before you proceed, it is important to understand both the strengths and weaknesses of self-assessment. Self-assessments are generated by you about you. They can be helpful guides to understanding behavior, perceptions, and attitudes important for your communication behaviors. Self-assessment, however, is not a complete or final analysis about you. The questions asked determine the profiles developed. Sometimes we tend to answer the way we think we should as opposed to what we really believe or do. Important questions or issues for you as an individual may not be considered in a particular assessment. Also, although assessments can guide development, they should not be used to develop profiles of "this is the way I am," or "this is the way I am not." In other words, the self-assessments in the text should be used to stimulate your thinking about you and your experiences, not to develop rigid categories or self-descriptive labels.

The following organizational communication competencies are presented for your self-evaluation. For each area, you are asked to determine whether your present competencies are highly developed, moderately developed, somewhat limited, or needing development.

As I begin this course, I would describe my KNOWLEDGE *in . . .*	*Highly Developed*	*Moderately Developed*	*Somewhat Limited*	*Needing Development*
1. defining and understanding organizational communication as . . .				
2. understanding major theories of how organizations work as . . .				
3. determining how an individual experiences organizational life as . . .				
4. describing what organizational conflict is and how it relates to productive organizations as . . .				
5. identifying characteristics of leadership and management communication as . . .				
6. understanding decision making and problem solving as . . .				

(*continued*)

FIGURE 1.1
Self-Assessment of Personal Development Needs

	Highly Developed	Moderately Developed	Somewhat Limited	Needing Development
7. understanding strategic organizational communication as . . .				
8. locating career opportunities in organizational communication as . . .				
9. distinguishing between values and ethics in organizational communication as . . .				

As I begin this course, I would describe my *SENSITIVITY* to . . .	Highly Developed	Moderately Developed	Somewhat Limited	Needing Development
10. my personal responsibilities for organizational communication as . . .				
11. how "shared realities" are generated through organizational communication as . . .				
12. why and how people work together as . . .				
13. what motivates me and what is likely to motivate others as . . .				
14. the importance of interpersonal relationships with supervisors, peers, and employees as . . .				

	Highly Developed	Moderately Developed	Somewhat Limited	Needing Development
15. personal preferences for a variety of approaches to conflict as . . .				
16. the influence of the environment of organizations as . . .				
17. personal preferences for leadership and management communication as . . .				
18. organizational influences for decision making and problem solving as . . .				
19. past achievements, values, and skills that can guide career choices as . . .				
20. how values and ethics contribute to organizational effectiveness as . . .				

As I begin this course, I would describe my SKILLS in . . .	*Highly Developed*	*Moderately Developed*	*Somewhat Limited*	*Needing Development*
21. analyzing a variety of organizational problems as . . .				
22. developing effective organizational messages as . . .				

(*continued*)

23. engaging in active listening as . . .				
24. contributing to supportive organizational environments as . . .				
25. participating in productive conflict management as . . .				
26. leadership communication as . . .				
27. leading and participating in effective group meetings as . . .				
28. fact-finding and evaluation as . . .				
29. gathering information for decision making and problem solving as . . .				
30. analyzing data for decision making and problem solving as . . .				
31. developing and making public presentations as . . .				
32. using a variety of communications technologies as . . .				

As I begin this course, I would describe my VALUE for . . .	Highly Developed	Moderately Developed	Somewhat Limited	Needing Development
33. accepting personal responsibility for communication as . . .				
34. relating individual communication behavior to organizational effectiveness as . . .				
35. using conflict for productive outcomes as . . .				
36. professional applications of organizational communication as . . .				
37. determining how leaders and managers should behave as . . .				
38. influencing my career choices as . . .				
39. understanding organizational values, ethics, and dilemmas as . . .				

After you have completed your self-evaluation, compile a complete list of items for which you rated your competencies as *Highly Developed*. Next compile lists for those competency items rated *Moderately Developed, Somewhat Limited,* and *Needing Development*. Use these lists to help establish personal objectives for the study of this text. All the competencies evaluated in your self-assessment are presented in the following chapters with theory, practice, and analysis opportunities.

CHAPTER HIGHLIGHTS

The information-rich conceptual world is a reality of our lives that places increasing importance on our individual communication competencies. Organizations of today and tomorrow must depend on people and the machines of the communications era to solve problems creatively and to adapt to rapid change. In this fast-paced environment, organizational excellence is directly related to effective communication from all members of the organization. To prepare for the communication responsibilities and opportunities of the future, individuals need to develop broad-based communication competency. **Communication competency** is best understood as a complex interaction of **knowledge, sensitivity, skills,** and **values.**

Human communication is the process through which we attempt to construct shared realities. The **human communication process** includes **sources and receivers, message encoding and decoding, channels, noise, communicative competence,** participants' **fields of experience, contexts,** and **effects.** The process is evaluated for effectiveness and ethical behaviors, with these evaluations influencing future interactions. Organizations are the products of organizing activities and can be described as deliberately constructed social units designed to strive for specific goals. As such, organizations are dynamic mergers of human behaviors and technological operations. Organizational communication includes all the descriptors in the human communication process. It is also the process through which organizations are created and in turn create and shape events. As such, **organizational communication** can be understood as a combination of process, people, messages, meaning, and purpose. ∎

WORKSHOP

1. Review online or in hard copy the Sunday edition of your city's largest newspaper. Identify all the stories that relate to an "information" or "conceptual" age and the technologies of the communications era. Bring copies of selected articles to class for group discussion.

2. Small groups should use The Case against Hiring Karen Groves, which follows, to determine how communication behaviors influenced Hockaday's management team to vote against hiring Karen Groves.

3. Visit one of the numerous job-search sites on the Internet. Identify at least fifty job titles that represent information jobs. Bring your list to class for discussion.

4. Identify all the organizations of which you are a member. Include the school you currently attend. Describe shared realities for each organization. Discuss as a class the shared realities of your school.

5. Shared meanings or shared realities are what organizational communication is all about. My Meaning, Your Meaning, Our Meanings, an exercise to illustrate the importance of meanings and shared realities, is found below. Divide the class into groups of six members each and complete the exercise. Discuss what you have learned about meanings and shared realities.

6. The following case, "What Do You Mean I'm Not Getting a Raise?" illustrates organizational messages with multiple meanings. Study the case and attempt to understand how people receiving the same message can arrive at very different meanings.

My Meaning, Your Meaning, Our Meanings

Read each of the following four statements and write your response. You may agree, disagree, or take no position on the statement. Your response should accurately reflect the statement's meaning to you.

1. Oral skills are more important than written communication skills for most jobs. I (agree with, disagree with, don't know about) this statement. It means to me. . . .

2. People who are the most intelligent make the best grades and are the most successful. I (agree with, disagree with, don't know about) this statement. It means to me. . . .

3. The successful organizational member must be competitive and persuasive. I (agree with, disagree

with, don't know about) this statement. It means to me. . . .

4. The successful organizational member is more analytical than others and believes technical skills are more important than communication abilities. I (agree with, disagree with, don't know about) this statement. It means to me. . . .

Discuss your responses and compare similarities and differences in groups of six. What influenced the similarities and differences in your answers? How do these influences contribute to the meanings we assign to messages?

Next, consider the following four professions: minister, salesperson, lawyer, television executive. As a group, attempt to determine how you think that most people in these professions would react to the four statements. Again, what does that tell us about how meanings are influenced? How accurate can you be about your perceptions of the meanings others might assign?

Finally, as a group, attempt to develop a response to each statement that all group members can support. (Total agreement is not necessary, only general support.) How do these group statements differ from your individual statements? Did your statements become a shared reality for your group? If so, why? If not, why not? (If time permits, compare your group's statements with those of other groups in your class. What are the similarities and differences? Are there any surprises?) ∎

THE CASE AGAINST HIRING KAREN GROVES

John Murphy, the head of personnel for Hockaday Corporation, was excited about the application of Karen Groves to become Hockaday's new training director. Karen's educational background in organizational communication and business, her work in the training department of a major competitor of Hockaday's, and her excellent letters of recommendation made her an appealing candidate. John's initial interview with Karen had gone well and he was anxious for her to meet Hockaday's management staff, who approved John's hiring decisions for major company positions.

John was surprised and dismayed when Hockaday's president reported to John that the staff did not favor hiring Karen.

According to the president, Karen surprised the group when she said _____ and _____. They did not believe that she would be good for Hockaday because of her _____.

In groups of four to six members, fill in the blanks to account for what might have happened to create the case against hiring Karen. Describe how the communication abilities of all involved may have contributed to the negative decision. Following individual group discussions, each group should present to the class as a whole its members' description of the situation and how they believe communication affected the outcome. ∎

THE "WHAT DO YOU MEAN I'M NOT GETTING A RAISE?" CASE

Jane Jackson, division manager of AMC, Inc., had spent the day in the cafeteria meeting with each of AMC's three manufacturing shifts. She had good news and had been eager to make the announcement that the company would not begin the layoffs rumored to occur at the end of the present round of contracts. Instead of layoffs, management had decided to freeze wages and evaluate in six months when cost-of-living and merit increases could resume. Jane had been careful with the announcement, reading the press release exactly as it was written from corporate headquarters.

Following her cafeteria meetings, Jane asked her section managers to meet with individual supervisors on each of the three shifts to determine how the news was being received. Jane had been concerned about the layoff rumors and expected a generally favorable response to the announcement. She was not prepared for her section managers' feedback. Several supervisors reported that although there was considerable relief that layoffs were not imminent, many workers did not understand that they would not receive their annual increases at performance appraisal time. Numerous workers believed management intended to consider layoffs again at the end of the six-month freeze period, and others thought that the wage freeze meant no new people were being hired. Jane could not understand how all this confusion was possible. After all, everyone got exactly the same message.

What would you tell Jane about messages and meanings? What are the probable reasons for this confusion? What would you do if you were Jane and her section managers? ∎

TIPS FOR EFFECTIVE COMMUNICATION

1. Ask for (and listen to) feedback on your communication strengths and weaknesses.

2. Identify which new communications technologies you should learn. Make a plan for skill development.

3. Identify three excellent communicators with whom you can talk. Ask them for personal advice about communication.

4. Give at least five speeches during the upcoming year.

5. Practice asking others to describe what they think you meant when having important conversations. Listen, and learn to clarify if descriptions do not match your intentions. ■

REFERENCES AND SUGGESTED READINGS

Barnard, C. 1938. *The functions of the executive.* Cambridge, MA: Harvard University Press.

Bronowski, J. 1958. The creative process. *Scientific American* 199(3): 59–64.

Craig, R. T. 2007. Pragmatism in the field of communication theory. *Communication Theory* 17(2): 125–145.

Deetz, S. A. 1992. *Democracy in an age of corporate colonization.* Albany: State University of New York Press.

Deetz, S. 1994. *Transforming communication, transforming business: Building responsive and responsible workplaces.* Cresskill, NJ: Hampton.

Etzioni, A. 1964. *Modern organizations.* Englewood Cliffs, NJ: Prentice Hall.

Friedman, T. 2006. *The world is flat.* New York: Farrar, Straus and Giroux.

Hackman, M., and C. Johnson. 2004. *Leadership: A communication perspective.* 4th ed. Prospect Heights, IL: Waveland.

Jablin, F., and P. Sias. 2001. Communication competence. In *The new handbook of organizational communication: Advances in theory, research, and methods,* eds. F. Jablin and L. Putnam, 819–864. Thousand Oaks, CA: Sage.

Kennedy, G. 1969. *Quintilian.* New York: Twayne.

Littlejohn, S. W., and D. M. Jabusch. 1982. Communication competence: Model and application. *Journal of Applied Communication Research* 10(1): 29–37.

Miller, K. 2003. *Organizational communication: Approaches and processes.* Belmont, CA: Wadsworth.

Morreale, S. 2008. Competent and incompetent communication. In *21st century communication: A reference handbook,* ed. W. Eadie, 444–453. Thousand Oaks, CA: Sage.

Pepper, G. 1995. *Communicating in organizations: A cultural approach.* New York: McGraw-Hill.

Pink, D. 2005. *A whole new mind: Moving from the information age to the conceptual age.* New York: Riverhead Books.

Rischard, J. F. 2002. *High noon: 20 global problems 20 years to solve them.* New York: Basic Books. ■

Perspectives for Organizational Communication

DEVELOPING COMPETENCIES THROUGH ...

KNOWLEDGE   Describing the Functional tradition to organizational communication
Describing the Meaning-Centered approach to organizational communication
Describing Emerging Perspectives for organizational communication
Distinguishing among the Functional tradition, the Meaning-Centered approach, and Emerging Perspectives

SENSITIVITY   Understanding the importance of meaning generation for organizational communication
Identifying how organizational communication creates and shapes organizational events

SKILLS   Developing analysis abilities using the Functional tradition, the Meaning-Centered approach, and Emerging Perspectives
Practicing analysis abilities

VALUES   Viewing communication as the fundamental organizational process
Relating organizational communication to a variety of value and ethical issues

THE CORONADO COMPANY'S QUALITY DEFECTS CASE

Coronado Manufacturing Company, located in Trenton, New Jersey, is a small-appliance manufacturer providing house brand products to a series of major chain stores. The situation you are about to examine was once a major issue for Coronado, threatening their long-term survival. We use their quality defects problem to assist in understanding major theoretical perspectives for organizational communication.

Bill Drake, president of Coronado Manufacturing Company, could hardly believe the conclusions in the consultant's report. Product quality had always been a strength of Coronado Manufacturing, and now defective products were being blamed for declining sales in the company's small appliances. The report went on to say that the sales department for Coronado was not passing along customer complaints to anyone in manufacturing. Furthermore, Drake was confused by his own lack of personal knowledge about customer dissatisfaction and about problems in manufacturing. After all, he met weekly with the management team responsible for spotting these problems, and they all knew that he felt that the customer was number one.

Drake thought about the history of Coronado Manufacturing. Coronado had been founded some fifty years ago by Drake's father and uncle. Both men had worked most of their lives for a major manufacturer of small appliances well known for its quality products and customer concern. In founding Coronado, both men had hired people who cared about quality and understood customers. In fact, stories were told about the founders personally emphasizing quality to newcomers on the manufacturing line and making "surprise" visits to customers to check on how "their" products were working. When Bill Drake's father retired, he had admonished Bill not to forget the basics that had made the business successful.

Bill Drake had assumed he was successfully carrying on Coronado's quality and customer traditions. Was the report accurate? Was his management team withholding information? How could he determine what to do?

Bill Drake is confronted with a management problem requiring immediate action. The decisions he makes, the action he takes, and what ultimately happens to Coronado Manufacturing provide examples of how organizational communication creates and shapes events. ■

INTRODUCTION

In Chapter 1 we defined organizational communication as the process through which organizations create and shape events. This chapter is designed to help us understand this process and to develop our competencies in determining how Bill Drake might approach his problem. Three different approaches—Functional, Meaning-Centered, and Emerging Perspectives—are presented as ways to understand the processes of organizational communication and are used as frameworks to help analyze specific organizational situations, experiences, and problems. The approaches in this chapter are communication approaches or theory perspectives focusing specifically on organizational communication. In Chapter 3 we will discuss theories and approaches from an organizational perspective. Chapter 3 helps us understand the communication implications of how organizations have been described over time. It is important to distinguish between communication perspectives and organizational perspectives to develop our abilities to understand the significance of organizational communication.

The Functional and Meaning-Centered approaches ask different questions about organizational communication. The Functional tradition asks how and why communication works, whereas the Meaning-Centered approach asks what communication is. The Functional tradition asks what purpose communication serves within organizations and how messages move. The Meaning-Centered approach asks if communication is the process through which organizing, decision making, influence, and culture occur. The Functional approach describes organizational reality in such terms as chains of command, positions, roles, and communications channels, whereas the Meaning-Centered approach defines as reality the symbolic significance of these terms. The Functional tradition subordinates the importance of the individual to his or her organizational position and function, whereas in the Meaning-Centered approach the significance of the individual is the key focus.

The Emerging Perspectives we discuss ask questions about communication as a constitutive or basic process of social construction. Emerging Perspectives focus attention on power and control and on the marginalization of voices other than those of the dominant control structure. They also begin our discussion of influences beyond a specific organization, namely, the concepts of institutions, globalization, and technology.

After studying this chapter, you will be able to answer several questions about the Functional tradition, the Meaning-Centered approach, and Emerging Perspectives. Specifically you will begin to utilize perspectives for organizational communication as **practical theory**. Based on the work of Robert Craig and Karen Tracy (1995), Vernon Cronen (2001), and Stephen Littlejohn and Karen Foss (2008), we describe how perspectives and theories can be utilized to understand and improve organizational life. Littlejohn and Foss suggest, "A practical theory does not prescribe the action you should take, but enables you to act in a coherent way that leads to understanding how you might improve the situation. A good practical theory enables you to (1) focus on a real situation you are facing; (2) explore what is unique about this situation; (3) consider both the powers and limits of each action you could take; (4) take actions that enhance your life and achieve positive outcomes as well; and (5) learn from experience in the actual situations you face and prepare you to manage new ones" (pp. 25–26).

> **Practical theory** ■ A set of principles enabling communicators to construct tentative models and approaches relevant to broad ranges of practical situations.

The Functional Tradition

1. What are different types of organizational messages?
2. How do organizing, relationship, and change messages differ?
3. How can communication networks be described?
4. How do different communications channels affect messages?
5. What is communication load?
6. What is distortion in organizational communication?

The Meaning-Centered Approach

1. How is "reality" generated through human interaction?
2. Why are communicating and organizing almost synonymous processes?
3. How does communication contribute to decision making?
4. What is meant by sensemaking?
5. What are influence processes in organizations?
6. What are communication rules?
7. What is the difference between treating culture as something an organization has versus something an organization is?
8. What is meant by communication climate?

Emerging Perspectives

1. What is meant by the constitutive role of communication?
2. What are the issues for organizational communication when adopting a postmodern viewpoint?
3. What is the emphasis of critical organizational communication theory?
4. What is feminist organizational communication theory?

5. How do the values evidenced in Emerging Perspectives differ from the Functional tradition and Meaning-Centered approaches?
6. How does practical theory relate to the Functional tradition, Meaning-Centered approaches, and other Emerging Perspectives?
7. What is the common ground among the three perspectives? What are the most important differences?
8. How does the concept of institutions influence individual organizations?
9. What is the relationship between global cultures and organizational communication?
10. What is the relationship of communications technologies to issues in the Functional, Meaning-Centered, and Emerging Perspectives approaches?

Think back to the Coronado Quality Defects case. Which of these questions should Bill Drake ask? As you study the material in this chapter, try to determine how the Functional tradition, the Meaning-Centered approach, and Emerging Perspectives can help Bill Drake solve his problem at Coronado Manufacturing.

This chapter contributes to *knowledge* competencies by describing and contrasting three approaches to organizational communication. It contributes to the development of individual *sensitivity* competencies by examining the development of meaning in organizations and individual communication behaviors that shape and change organizational events. It contributes to *skill* development by applying Functional, Meaning-Centered, and Emerging Perspectives approaches to cases and exercises. Finally, it encourages *value* competencies by examining organizational communication as the fundamental organizational process including multiple ethical issues and concerns.

THE FUNCTIONAL TRADITION

Functional tradition ■ Way of understanding organizational communication by describing what messages do and how they move through organizations.

The **Functional tradition** helps us understand organizational communication by describing what messages do and how they move through organizations. The Functional tradition describes how communication produces organizational outcomes. This perspective describes communication as a complex organizational process that serves organizing, relationship, and change functions: what messages do. The way messages move through organizations is described by examining communication networks, channels, message directions, communication load, and distortion. The Functional tradition suggests communication transmits rules, regulations, and information throughout the organization. Communication establishes and defines human relationships, helps individuals identify with goals and opportunities, and is the process by which the organization generates and manages change. These functions occur during the repetitive patterns of communication interactions in which organizational members engage.

In Chapter 1 we described organizations as dynamic systems in which individuals engage in collective efforts to accomplish goals. We found that organizations can be understood not only in terms of their structure but also by the way they continually create and change what they do and how they do it. We claimed that, as such, organizations emerge and evolve through communication behaviors. The Functional tradition describes organizations as dynamic communication systems with the various parts of the system working together to create and shape organizational events.

Organizational Communication Systems: Component Parts

Before we can examine what messages do and how they move in organizations, we need to understand the concept of an **organizational communication system** on which the Functional tradition is based. What are the main parts of the system? What parts work together to create and shape organizational events? How does communication contribute to keeping a system dynamic? What role did communication play in organizations that cease to exist?

> Organizational communication system ■ Number of related units and processes that operate together within the organization and with its environment to create and shape organizational events. Information processing is the primary function of the communication system.

In the Functional tradition, information processing is seen as the primary function of organizational communication systems. It takes place in a number of related units that when taken together are called organizations or suprasystems. The individual units, sometimes called subsystems, are related by some degree of structure and when described as a whole can be distinguished from other organizations in the environment by their boundaries. The individual units are interdependent and permeable to other units and the external environment.

The Coronado Manufacturing Company provides an example of an organizational communication system with its manufacturing and sales units; Bill Drake as president represents a management unit. These units relate to one another to produce a product that customers in the external environment, outside the Coronado boundary, will buy. Coronado Manufacturing Company is the suprasystem with management, manufacturing, and sales subsystems. The external environment, however, is important to Coronado. Sales are slipping. Bill Drake needs external information (from the consultant and customers) to make decisions about internal operations, decisions that in turn will influence future sales.

Communication Inputs

This relationship between external environment information and internal information processing is important for understanding organizational communication systems. Information in the external environment, commonly known as **communication inputs**, is any information that can potentially influence the decision making of the suprasystem (organization). It is crucial for an organization to have accurate and timely information inputs to adapt and change. Bill Drake realizes that the future

> Communication inputs ■ Information in the external environment that may influence the decision making of the organization.

of Coronado Manufacturing is related to the accuracy of the inputs about quality defects from his customers. Without this information his understanding of the sales problem is incomplete. Only with accurate information about quality problems can he make informed decisions.

Communication Throughput

When information enters the organization, the communication system begins a process known as **communication throughput,** or the transforming and changing of input information for internal organizational use. Bill Drake, in taking the consultant's report and evaluating what to do, is taking inputs and transforming them into organizational action. His decisions and the decisions of people in sales and manufacturing can be described as throughput communication. In other words, the internal subsystems (management, sales, manufacturing) of Coronado move messages through the organization that will influence the production of products and ultimately customer satisfaction. The quality of throughput communication will determine whether the defects problem is solved. Even with accurate and timely inputs, the subsystems of Coronado require effective internal communication to increase sales. Bill Drake questions the throughput communication of his organization when he realizes that despite weekly staff meetings, he was unaware of the quality problem.

Communication Output

Messages to the external environment from within the organization are known as **communication output.** Outputs can be thought of as the results of the input and throughput process and are both intentional and unintentional. Coronado Manufacturing, through its sales force and advertising, generates intentional output communication. The defects in its products, however, have become unintentional output messages with important consequences. The low-quality message from the defective products is a potentially more powerful message than positive messages from advertising and sales campaigns.

Open versus Closed Systems

The response of the environment (in Coronado's case, the customers) to organizational communication is feedback that in turn becomes new inputs to the system. The way the organization responds to these new inputs with throughput efforts and new outputs determines whether it has an open or closed system. **Open systems** continually take in new information, transform that information, and give information back to the environment. By contrast, **closed systems** are characterized by a lack of input communication, making it difficult to make good decisions and stay current with the needs of the environment. Open systems use a variety of problem-solving approaches. There is no one best way to do things. This ability to use a variety of approaches is called **equifinality,** meaning that there are many ways to reach system goals.

Bill Drake wants Coronado Manufacturing to operate as an open system. He listens to customer complaints to try to decide what to do. He can consider a new advertising campaign or new approaches from his sales staff. He knows, however, that he is unlikely to be successful until the defects problem is solved. In the long term, if Bill Drake pays no attention to

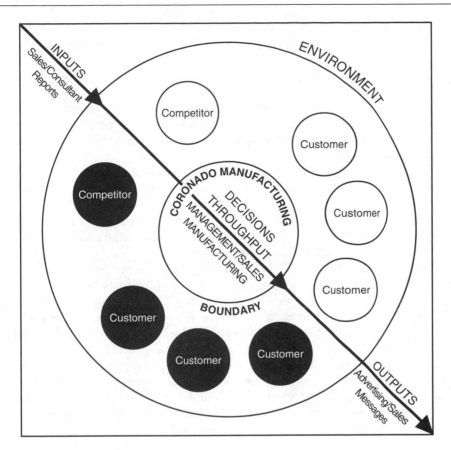

FIGURE 2.1
Coronado Manufacturing Communication System

sales or quality problems, he increases the likelihood that Coronado Manufacturing will go out of business. As we can see from studying the Coronado case, however, Bill Drake has more than one way to approach his problems. He can work with both manufacturing and sales, he can work only with manufacturing, he can assign responsibility to others, he can retain much of the responsibility himself, and he has other options. There are a number of ways (equifinality) to solve Coronado's problems. Figure 2.1 illustrates the Coronado Manufacturing communication system.

Message Functions

When we talk about **message functions** within organizations, we are talking about what communication does or how it contributes to the overall functioning of the organization. In our attempt to understand organizational communication from the Functional approach, we describe message functions in three broad categories—organizing functions, relationship functions, and change functions. Each function is seen as

Message functions ■ What communication does or how it contributes to the overall functioning of the organization.

necessary for an open communication system, although the exact balance among message functions will vary by organizational type and circumstance.

Organizing Functions

People who work together talk more about doing tasks than any other subject. This finding is not surprising. To engage in organized activity in pursuit of goals, people in organizations must develop and exchange messages about rules, regulations, policies, and tasks.

Organizing functions ■ Messages that establish the rules and regulations of a particular environment.

Organizing functions establish the rules and regulations of a particular environment. Policy manuals, employee handbooks, orientation training, newsletters, and a variety of other sources convey information about how the organization expects to work and what it requires of its members. These organizing messages define and clarify tasks, develop work instructions, and evaluate task accomplishment.

Organizing messages can be found in every aspect of our lives. The school you attend publishes standards for admissions and requirements for specific majors and degrees. Instructors establish requirements and define performance expectations. You converse with teachers and peers about assignments and responsibilities. All these messages and many more describe how your school is organized, how it is supposed to work, and how you fit into that process.

The adequacy and effectiveness of organizing messages can be evaluated by how well organizational members understand and perform tasks, how rules and regulations are understood and followed, and how adequately daily operations support organizational goals. In sum, the organizing function of communication guides, directs, and controls organizational activity.

Relationship Functions

Relationship functions ■ Communication that helps individuals define their roles and assess the compatibility of individual and organizational goals.

The **relationship function** of organizational communication helps individuals define their roles and assess the compatibility of individual and organizational goals. Relationship communication contributes to individuals' identification with an organization or sense of "belonging" in their work environment. Frequently referred to as integrative or maintenance messages, relationship communication contributes to employee morale and maintains or integrates individuals with their work environments.

Communication establishes relationships between supervisors and employees and within peer groups. Relationship messages range from informal conversations to visible symbols of status such as large offices and reserved parking spaces. Job titles, awards, and promotions are other examples of relationship communication that determine how individuals identify with or relate to the organization.

Whereas organizing messages communicate how the organization operates, relationship messages establish the human interactions that make such operation possible. Chances are, for example, that your sense of belonging with your school or lack of it closely relates to your interpersonal interactions with teachers and other students. In fact, your ability to meet performance expectations successfully may be influenced by your relationships with your instructors and how comfortable you are in exchanging ideas with them. The same may be true of your relationships with other students. The quality of your work on a team project is probably influenced by how much you feel a part of—or integrated with—your group. The effectiveness of relationship messages is reflected in individual satisfaction with work relationships, productivity, employee turnover, overall support for organizational practices, and a variety of other less obvious ways.

Change Functions

Change functions help organizations adapt what they do and how they do it and are essential to an open system. Change messages occur in organizational problem solving, individual decision making, feedback from the environment, and numerous other choice-making situations. Change communication is the processing of new ideas and information as well as the altering of existing procedures and processes. It is essential for continual adaptation to the environment and for meeting the complex needs of individuals working together.

Change functions ■ Messages that help organizations adapt what they do and how they do it; viewed as essential to an open system.

Experiences in decision-making groups help illustrate how change messages function. When working with a group of students to develop a class presentation, chances are you can recall messages speculating about the best approach and who should take what type of responsibility. Furthermore, you probably attempted to reduce the ambiguity of the assignment by determining what the instructor wanted and what would be appropriate for the time you had. Your group's ability to exchange innovative messages and adapt to the requirements of the assignment influenced your effectiveness and final grade. In the Coronado case, Bill Drake became aware of his quality problem through change messages, specifically through declining sales and a consultant's report. His attempt to correct the problem will require change messages with his sales and manufacturing staffs and new approaches to reverse the negative reactions of his customers.

The ultimate effectiveness of change communication is the survival of the organization. Without appropriate change, organizational systems stagnate and die. Change communication is necessary for innovation and adaptation and is the process through which the organization obtains new information, chooses among various alternatives, and weighs current practices against emerging needs. Timely and creative change communication is required for a dynamic and open system. The effectiveness of change messages can be determined by whether the organization gathers information from the best available sources and acts on that information with a timely, quality decision. Figure 2.2 illustrates organizing, relationship, and change functions.

Message Structure

The movement of organizing, relationship, and change messages throughout the organization and between the organization and its external environment is the **message structure** of organizational communication. The Functional tradition approach to structure asks questions about the repetitive patterns of interactions among

Message structure ■ Movement of organizing, relationship, and change messages throughout the organization and between the organization and its external environment.

Organizing Messages

Rules and regulations
Organizational policies
Task definition
Task instruction
Task evaluation

Relationship Messages

Individual role definition
Individual/organizational goals
Status symbols
Integration among supervisor/employees, peers

Change Messages

Decision making
Market analysis
New idea processing
Environmental inputs
Employee suggestions
Problem solving

FIGURE 2.2
The Functional Tradition

members of the organization (networks), the use of a variety of channels for communication, message directions, and the amount of messages and the types of distortions that can be expected to occur in organizational communication. In other words, the structure of organizational communication can be understood in terms of networks, channels, message directions, load, and distortion.

Communication Networks

Networks ■ Formal and informal patterns of communication that link organizational members together.

Communication **networks** are the formal and informal patterns of communication that link organizational members together. Networks can be described by how formally or informally they are organized, by the links between people, and by the roles people perform as they link.

Communication networks develop as a result of both formal organization and informal social contact. Organizations divide work by function and task. Organization charts that map out who reports to whom and in what area of responsibility can be described as blueprints for the way decisions are to be made, the way conflicts are to be resolved, and which groups are responsible for "networking" to reach organizational goals. The formal organization (as illustrated by the organization chart just mentioned) prescribes who has the right to tell others what to do, who is to work together as a unit or team, and who has the final authority in disagreements. In other words, the formal act of organizing creates organizational communication networks or the formal communication system.

As individuals work together, interpersonal relationships develop and extend beyond the specific requirements of the work group. Informal networks emerge, with individuals exchanging diverse types of information related both to the organization and to their social relationships. The organizational grapevine is perhaps the most frequently discussed example of an informal network.

Supervisors and employees, task forces, committees, quality circles, and other types of decision-making bodies are examples of formal communication networks. Formal networks also are established with various forms of technology such as computers and video systems. Generally speaking, these telemediated networks establish communication links that geographic separation would otherwise make difficult and costly. These new technologies change literally all aspects of formal and informal networks. Fluid and geographically diverse organizational structures link networks of individuals who may never meet in any face-to-face interaction. Supervisors manage workers with whom they communicate only through technology. The around-the-clock organization of work creates networks of people who regularly interact with each other across time zones and vast distances.

Informal networks emerge as a result of formal networks and are formed by individuals who have interpersonal relationships, who exchange valuable information across reporting chains, and who disregard formal status and timing. Typically, informal networks exclude numerous individuals who are designated for network inclusion by the formal chain of command.

Formal and informal networks exist side by side; individuals maintain membership in both. Formal and informal networks contribute to organizational reality, and both networks change and shape organizational events. Message structure within organizations cannot be understood without evaluating how both formal and informal patterns of interaction take place.

Think about your own personal networks. What formal networks exist in the organizations of which you are a member? What types of networks exist in your school? How do you establish your informal networks? Which type of network is more meaningful to you? We are all involved in both formal and informal networks. When we evaluate our personal experiences, we can better understand how organizational networks function and how they contribute to the movement of organizing, relationship, and change messages.

Communication Channels

Channels are the means for transmission of messages. Organizations typically have a wide variety of channels available for transmitting oral and written messages. Face-to-face interaction, group meetings, memos, letters, computer-mediated exchanges, Web sites, presentations, and teleconferencing are among the channels commonly used in contemporary organizations. Increasing emphasis is placed on developing new and improved technical channels that speed information transfer and shorten decision-making response time. Indeed, it is fair to say the choice and availability of communication channels influence the way the organization can and does operate.

Channels ■ Means for the transmission of messages. Common means are face-to-face interaction, group meetings, memos, letters, computer-mediated exchanges, Web sites, presentations, and teleconferencing.

Questions arise as to the effectiveness of various channels and what is communicated by channel selection. Although most of us take channel use for granted, selecting one channel over another can communicate subtle and important attitudes about both the message receiver and the message itself. For example, most of us like to communicate good news in face-to-face interaction. We enjoy the reactions of others and deliberately choose channels that permit close, immediate contact. If the news is not positive, we may prefer another channel. Negative messages, more than good news, are likely to be transmitted in a less immediate channel such as letters or memos, the telephone, e-mail, or a third-party announcement. In fact, research suggests that our attitude about the message and our willingness to have contact with the receiver significantly influence the channels we use for communication.

Attitudes about messages and receivers are not the only factors that influence channel selection. Power and status, work requirements, technical capability, and judgments about channel effectiveness all contribute to the mode or modes we use. High-status organizational members, for example, can determine what channels they personally want to use and what modes others must use in communicating with them. The president of the company can initiate face-to-face interaction with just about anyone in the organization. The chances are good, however, that not all organizational members can walk into the president's office for an unscheduled visit. In the Coronado case, Bill Drake can require the consultant to submit a report and recommendations in writing. Drake can require his sales and manufacturing people to meet with him and make detailed presentations of their ideas. It is unlikely that the consultant or the sales and manufacturing managers could make the same requirement of Bill Drake.

Bill Drake will be confronted with channel selection as he works on the defects problem. He will use internal channels, and once the problem is solved he must consider how to communicate to his customers. How would you advise Drake? Are particular channels more appropriate than others as he seeks to regain lost sales? Attempt to describe the criteria Drake should use for channel selection.

Message Direction

Direction ■ Description of the movement of messages in organizations based on authority or position levels of message senders and receivers; typically described as downward, upward, and horizontal communication.

As messages move through channels, we begin to think about that movement in terms of **direction**. Researchers typically describe three primary message directions in organizations: downward, upward, and horizontal. Downward communication describes message movement from a person in a position of authority to an employee or group with lesser authority. It is characterized by those with higher authority developing messages to transmit to those lower in authority, with authority being defined by the chain of command or the formal structure of the organization. We have downward communication, for example, when the board of regents for the university votes to raise tuition for the upcoming semester. The board formally informs the school's president, who in turn informs officials in admissions and records; finally, students, who will pay the new fees, are advised of the bad news.

Upward communication describes message movement that begins with lower organizational levels and is transmitted to higher levels of authority. As with downward communication, the formal organization defines authority levels.

Employees engage in upward communication when they complain about working conditions to a supervisor, who in turn reports their concerns to higher management.

Horizontal communication moves laterally across the organization among individuals of approximately the same level and without distinct reporting relationships to one another. In other words, horizontal flow occurs when various department heads come together to discuss common problems from their respective groups. This communication generally moves messages more quickly across the organization than if the messages were to follow the vertical chain of command.

Increasingly, information flow cannot be described in terms of specific direction. Informal network flow such as the grapevine and flow between organizational members and the organizational environment (i.e., customers, vendors, stockholders, regulators) may move both vertically and horizontally, all within the transmission of a single message. The call a salesperson makes to a customer does not specify a place in a single organizational hierarchy for either individual with regard to the other. Messages may move among people of different organizational authority levels and different organizations without the message having anything to do with authority or reporting relationships. When the research engineer speculates about the feasibility of a new product with the head of the marketing department, they represent different authority levels. One is a manager and one is not. We do not, however, label that flow as up or down the chain of command because the exchange is about a subject not related to the authority of the two individuals. The widespread use of communications technologies has altered whàt is possible in directional flow, increasing the likelihood of messages moving without regard to formal direction, structure, time, or geographic location.

Communication Load

The number of messages moving through the communication system is yet another important variable for describing the message structure of organizational communication. We commonly refer to the number of messages as communication **load**, or the volume, rate, and complexity of messages processed by an individual or the organization as a whole.

Load is a common term for most of us. In fact, it is a rare student who does not proclaim himself or herself to be in information overload during midterms or final examinations. The concept of load, however, is not limited to the overload state. Load, for example, can be defined as the optimum or ideal volume, rate, and complexity of messages for a particular individual or organization. Underload is present when the volume, rate, and complexity of messages to an individual or organization are lower than the capacity of the individual or system. Underload is frequently found when individuals engage in routine, repetitive tasks that have been thoroughly learned and no longer present challenges. This situation leads to boredom and the underutilization of human potential. Overload, on the other hand, occurs when the volume, rate, and complexity of messages exceed the system's capacity. It generates stress and strains the capacity of individuals to deal with information. In fact, one of the continuing

Load ■ Number of messages moving through the communication system; commonly referred to as load, overload, and underload.

concerns with the increasing use of communications technologies is the ease with which we can process large volumes of messages, generating a permanent overload in many jobs, a situation that actually impairs rather than strengthens the decision-making process.

Message Distortion

Distortion ■ Anything that contributes to alterations in meaning as messages move through the organization.

Closely related to the concept of load are the types of communication problems, or **distortions**, which occur as messages move throughout the organization. These distortions occur because of load, message direction, channel usage, and the very composition of the networks themselves. Put simply, distortions are those things that contribute to alterations in meaning as messages move through the organization. Distortions are noise in the organizational communication system.

Organizational communication is characterized by the serial transmission of messages. Messages pass first to individuals as receivers, who then become senders of information. Supervisors learn of changes in policies and have the responsibility to transmit those changes to an employee group. Messages are influenced by the numbers of people involved (the network), the channels for transmission (oral, written, or a variety of electronic combinations), the speed of message exchanges, and the direction of flow (vertical, horizontal, informal). Research consistently finds that original messages change or are distorted in the serial transmission process. Information is lost from or added to the message, the interpretation of facts changes, and new interpretations develop.

These distortions in serial transmission are brought about in part by perceptual differences among people, differences influenced by role and status. A manager may view a change in work hours as much less important than do the employees, who believe that no one was concerned about them when making the decision. The manager sees the change as necessary to accommodate a new schedule; whereas the workers are convinced the company never takes them into consideration. These perceptual differences affect the amount of attention given to the message and the interpretation of its meaning. They also influence the ability of the manager and members of the group to transmit the message to others. In addition to role, status, experience, values, and personal style, numerous other influences contribute to perception and how individuals knowingly or unknowingly distort organizational messages.

Finally, the very language of the message is subject to distortion. Definitions of terms and concepts vary throughout the organization. An excellent example of this phenomenon occurred in a small East Coast manufacturing company involved in introducing computer-assisted manufacturing processes. The president of the company announced the "entry of Cooper Manufacturing into the information age."

Training classes were scheduled for all personnel working in areas where the new systems were being installed. Instead of the expected positive response, management was amazed when the director of personnel reported employee concern that the training programs were designed for people to fail and were really a way to push them out of jobs.

The Functional Tradition: Summary of Essential Characteristics

The Functional tradition helps us understand organizational communication by describing **message function** and **structure**. Based on a view of organizations as complex communication systems, the Functional tradition identifies **organizing**, **relationship**, and **change functions** for messages and describes message structure as the movement of messages through formal and informal **networks**. Network members use diverse **channels** that transmit messages in lateral, vertical, and less structured **directions**. The **load** of these messages on the networks is the capacity measure of the organizational communication system. Finally, the Functional tradition suggests all messages are subject to numerous and predictable types of **distortions**, distortions that affect both message movement and meaning.

Can you now answer the questions asked at the beginning of the chapter? Could you use the Functional tradition as a practical theory to help advise Bill Drake about Coronado Manufacturing? More important, can you describe your school as an organizational communication system?

THE MEANING-CENTERED APPROACH

The second major approach for understanding organizational communication is the **Meaning-Centered approach**. This approach asks what communication is, not how and why it works. The Meaning-Centered perspective is concerned with how organizational reality is generated through human interaction. As such, message purposes (functions) and message movement (structure) are secondary to understanding communication as the construction of shared realities (human interaction). Specifically, the Meaning-Centered approach describes organizational communication as the process for generating shared realities that become organizing, decision making, sensemaking, influence, and culture. Figure 2.3 summarizes key assumptions of the Meaning-Centered perspective.

> **Meaning-Centered approach** ■ Way of understanding organizational communication by discovering how organizational reality is generated through human interaction. The approach describes organizational communication as the process for generating shared realities that become organizing, decision making, sensemaking, influence, and culture.

Think back to Coronado Manufacturing. Proponents of the Meaning-Centered approach would have Bill Drake ask questions about which human interactions contributed to the shift away from the company's quality culture. They would encourage him to discover why his perception of the values of the company seems not to be shared in either manufacturing or sales. They would advise him to understand his present problem by reviewing Coronado's organizing and decision-making activities.

Communication as Organizing and Decision Making

Organizing   In Chapter 1 we described **organizing** as bringing order out of chaos and organizations as the products of the organizing process. The Meaning-Centered approach to organizational communication describes communicating and organizing as almost synonymous processes. Decision making, or the process of choice from among uncertain alternatives, also is viewed as essentially a communication phenomenon and part of the organizing process.

> **Organizing** ■ Bringing order out of chaos with organizations as the products of the organizing process; described as almost synonymous with the communication process.

1. All ongoing human interaction is communication in one form or another.
2. Organizations exist through human interaction; structures and technologies result from the information to which individuals react.
3. Shared organizational realities reflect the collective interpretations by organizational members of all organizational activities.
4. Organizing and decision making are essentially communication phenomena.
5. Sensemaking combines action and interpretation.
6. Identification, socialization, communication rules, and power all are communication processes that reflect how organizational influence occurs.
7. Organizing, decision making, and influence processes describe the cultures of organizations by describing how organizations do things and how they talk about how they do things.
8. Organizational cultures and subcultures reflect the shared realities in the organization and how these realities create and shape organizational events.
9. Communication climate is the subjective, evaluative reaction of organization members to the organization's communication events, their reaction to organizational culture.

FIGURE 2.3
Key Assumptions of the Meaning-Centered Approach

What do we mean when we say that communicating, organizing, and decision making are essentially similar processes? Karl Weick, in his important book *The Social Psychology of Organizing* (1979), provided helpful insight for answering our questions. Weick proposed organizations as such do not exist but rather are in the process of existing through ongoing human interaction. In other words, there is no such thing as an organization; there is only the ongoing interaction among human activities, interaction that continually creates and shapes events. As previously discussed, all ongoing human interaction is communication in one form or another.

The Weick perspective suggested Coronado Manufacturing can be better understood as fifty years in the process of evolution rather than as an organization that was founded and structured fifty years ago. Bill Drake's father and uncle initiated the ongoing process, and Drake is part of the continuing stream of interactions. Put another way, the Weick model contended organizations do not exist apart from the human interactions of members. As Weick has described, communication is "the substance of organizing."

Weick focused on the organizational environment as the communication links and messages that are the basis of human interaction. He is not as concerned with the physical or technical structure of organizations as he is with the information to which individuals react. Weick contended that human reactions "enact" organizational environments through information exchanges and the active creation of meanings. This creation or enactment of organizational environments differs among individuals, resulting in multiple and diverse meanings and interpretations. Weick explained that organizational members use rules and communication cycles to continually process what he calls "equivocal" messages or messages susceptible to varying interpretations. Organizational rules are the relatively stable procedures or known processes that guide organizational behavior. In Coronado's case, the processing of a sales request has some fairly specific procedures for internal communication response. These rules (procedures) can be used as guidance for most inquiries. The defects problem is not as well defined. Communication cycles—conversations among those involved with the problem—become important to reduce the equivocality of the Coronado problem. Weick described the use of rules and communication cycles as "selection" processes or the use of selected information to reduce uncertainty. Selected rules and communication cycles, however, will vary in their effectiveness for actually reducing equivocality. When the selection process is effective, Weick proposed, individuals engage in "retention" to literally save rules and cycles for future guidance. Weick described this retained information as causal maps used to make sense of future equivocality. Weick concluded that the main goal of the process of organizing is an attempt to reduce equivocality—ambiguity—in order to predict future responses to organizational behaviors.

Supervisors reduce equivocality for their employees by the organizing of work assignments and the communication of task requirements. The supervisor gives an employee an assignment (desired action); the employee attempts the assignment (response); the supervisor evaluates the assignment (feedback). This interaction reduces equivocality for both the supervisor and the employee. The supervisor understands what the employee believed the assignment to be by evaluating what was accomplished. The feedback to the employee (often in the form of rewards or punishment) reduces uncertainty about the adequacy of the performance. This cycle—repeated at all organizational levels—is the organizing process.

Bill Drake is processing equivocal messages. He is attempting to determine if the consultant's report is accurate. He is more concerned with the effect of quality defects than specific technical problems. Even if assembly-line improvements are needed, it is through human communication that problems will be identified and solved. Drake does not understand how the company values of quality and customer service have changed. He is uncomfortable with the equivocality (ambiguity) of his interactions with sales and manufacturing management. He needs to figure out what his alternatives are and what to do next.

Decision Making   The process of choosing from among numerous alternatives—**decision making**—is the organizing process of directing behaviors and resources toward organizational goals. Decision making, as with other organizing efforts, is accomplished primarily through communication. Decision making is the process in which Bill Drake and his staff must engage.

> Decision making ■ Process of choosing from among numerous alternatives; the part of the organizing process necessary for directing behaviors and resources toward organizational goals.

A practical example helps to illustrate decision making as an organizing process. When you work with a group of students on a major class project, one of your goals may be a high grade from your instructor. There are numerous ways to approach this goal. Choosing from among these alternatives (decision making) is the first step toward assigning individual responsibilities within the project and deciding what resources the group will need (organizing). This choosing or decision making results from the communication interactions of the group. The quality of the group's decisions will influence the quality of the project and whether the group reaches its goals.

What influences the way this decision making occurs? Each member of the group brings different experiences, abilities, and expectations to the group. Each member operates with a set of premises or propositions about what he or she believes to be true. Decision making is the attempt to merge these individual premises into more general ones (shared realities) that most members of the group can accept.

Think for a moment about a group of students working on an assignment. One student may operate from the premise that group projects are not worth much time and effort. Others may believe that the project is important for the course grade and needs careful planning and attention. Another may believe that his or her idea for the topic is superior. These premises (propositions about what is true) influence individual behavior and the types of alternatives the group will consider. Also, some members may identify (experience a sense of "we") with the efforts of the group, whereas others may feel no sense of belonging or commitment. Those individuals who identify with one another are more likely to attempt a decision that most members of the group believe is appropriate than are those members who identify elsewhere.

Organizational decision making is the process that sets in motion much of the "doing" of the organization. Decision making reduces message equivocality by choosing from among numerous alternatives. These choosing activities occur through human communication.

Communication as Influence

Influence ■ Organizational and individual attempts to persuade; frequently seen in organizational identification, socialization, communication rules, and power.

The Meaning-Centered approach proposes that **influence** is a necessary process for creating and changing organizational events. In other words, who and what are viewed as influential, the way people seek to influence others, and how people respond to influence all contribute to organizing and decision making. Questions about the influence process in organizations focus on how individuals identify with their organizations, how organizations attempt to socialize members, how communication rules emerge to direct behavior, and how power is used. Identification, socialization, communication rules, and power all are essentially communication processes that help us understand how organizational influence occurs. From the Meaning-Centered perspective, the influence process is fundamental to the development of shared organizational realities and ultimately to creating and shaping organizational events. Indeed, it is fair to say that from a Meaning-Centered approach organizational communication is the process through which organizational influence takes place.

Identification

Identity ■ Relatively stable characteristics, including core beliefs, values, attitudes, preferences, decisional premises, and more that make up the self.

We all come to organizational experiences with a sense of self, or our personal **identity** or identities. Our identity can be described as relatively stable characteristics that include our core beliefs, values, attitudes, preferences, and decisional premises. We are more likely to be receptive to influence attempts in organizations with which we identify or have a sense of "we" or belonging. **Identification** or the lack of it results from the identity or identities we bring to our organizational experiences and from a variety of organizational relationships (supervisors, peers, employees). As such, identification can be understood as an active process to which both individuals and organizations contribute.

Most organizations encourage members to identify with the organization. Chances are that when you entered school you were encouraged to join various organizations, attend sporting functions, and oppose your school's most important rivals. Although most of these activities are enjoyable in and of themselves, they also develop a sense of "we" with the school. This sense of "we" means that our school's interests become our own and are influential in our choices.

It is likely that when people perceive the goals of an organization as compatible with their individual goals, they identify with the organization. The person who identifies is likely to accept the organization's decisional premises or reasoning. We can therefore say that the person who identifies is more likely to be positively influenced by the organization. An employee, for example, is more likely to be persuaded that a need for operating changes is favorable if the employee identifies with the organization and his or her supervisor. On the other hand, the employee who does not identify with the organization may view the same decision with resistance and suspicion. As organizations face increasing challenges to change, the issue of identification as influence takes on particular importance. Organizations need constructive work-related opinions, concerns, or ideas from employees in diverse organizational positions. Recent research suggests that identification moderates how employees will respond to speaking up when change may be needed. Employees with strong organizational identification who believe they have personal control in their work setting are likely to give voice to their opinions. Interestingly enough, employees who believe they have little personal control in their work setting are unlikely to speak up if they have high organizational identification. These findings support the perspective that all organizational members must be concerned not only with the positive aspects of identification but also with the potential limitations of identification. Identification contributes to problems if its influence contributes to silence or to a suspension of critical thinking. Practically speaking, we can all see how identification works by looking at our personal and organizational lives. The chances are that we are more likely to be influenced by individuals and groups with whom we feel a strong sense of "we" than by those with whom we feel no such relationship.

Identification ■ Dynamic social process by which identities are constructed; includes perceptions of a sense of belonging. Usually associated with the belief that individual and organizational goals are compatible.

Socialization

Closely associated with identification is the influence process of **socialization,** or active organizational attempts to help members learn appropriate behaviors, norms, and values. The socialization process attempts to help new members understand how their interests overlap with those of the organization.

Socialization ■ Active organizational attempts to help members learn appropriate behaviors, norms, and values.

Anticipatory socialization ■ Pre-entry information about the organization and the anticipated work role.

Encounter socialization ■ Early organizational experiences reducing uncertainty about all aspects of organizational life.

Metamorphosis socialization ■ Initial mastery of basic skills and information and adjustments to organizational life.

Socialization efforts frequently are categorized in phases or stages: **anticipatory socialization, encounter socialization,** and **metamorphosis socialization.** Anticipatory socialization begins before individuals enter organizations and results from past work experiences and interactions with family, friends, and institutions such as schools, churches, or social organizations. Anticipatory socialization is shaped by pre-entry information about the organization and the anticipated work role. Anticipatory socialization is the readiness an individual brings to the "reality shock" of organizational entry. Anticipatory socialization also includes what individuals learn about particular organizations prior to entry. The employment interview is an important example. Organizational representatives conducting interviews provide important socialization information while assessing the potential fit of the candidate to the organization. In addition, interviews are important opportunities for individuals to determine whether their expectations match their perceptions of the expectations of the organization.

The encounter stage for socialization involves new employee training, supervisor coaching, peer groups, and formal organizational documents. Newcomers learn tasks, develop relationships, and reduce uncertainty about most aspects of organizational life. The encounter phase includes social activities, messages about performance proficiency, and other experiences that contribute to learning about the organization.

Finally, the metamorphosis phase of socialization occurs when the newcomer begins to master basic organizational requirements and adjusts to the organization. The phases, however, should be considered only general descriptions of the socialization process with full realization that differences in individuals and influence attempts generate very different socialization experiences.

Generally speaking, during socialization processes individuals learn role-related information and organizational culture information. Presumably, as with the identification process, the greater the degree of socialization, the more likely individuals will be to respond favorably to organizational persuasion. In fact, little doubt remains that socialization relates to organizational commitment, decision making, perceptions of communications climate, and overall job satisfaction.

It is important to note socialization efforts are not solely the purview of the organization. New organizational members don't just wait for information from the organization but also seek information which contributes to socialization. Newcomers often want to find out for themselves how they can succeed in an organization, gain a variety of competencies, and, in general, reduce the uncertainty of new environments. Newcomers want to know how they are perceived by others and whether they are accepted in their new roles. Although information-seeking tactics vary among newcomers, it is fair to say information seeking by newcomers is a powerful part of the socialization process.

Communication rules ■ General prescriptions about appropriate communication behaviors in particular settings. Thematic rules are general prescriptions of behavior reflecting the values and beliefs of the organization, whereas tactical rules prescribe specific behaviors as related to more general themes.

Communication Rules

Communication rules are general prescriptions about appropriate communication behaviors in particular settings. Rules operate to influence behavior, are specific enough to be followed, and occur in particular contexts. In other words, communication rules are informal norms about what type of communication is desirable in a particular organization. Rules tell us, for example, whether disagreement is encouraged or discouraged, how we are expected to contribute our ideas, and whether we should ask for a raise or never mention the subject of salary in a particular situation. Rules aid in socialization and are therefore likely to be used by those high in organizational identification, those who want to exhibit a sense of "we" with the organization. Generally, rules are learned through informal communication such as organizational stories, rituals, and myths.

Communication rules are of two general types, thematic and tactical. Thematic rules are general prescriptions of behavior reflecting the values and beliefs of the organization. Tactical rules prescribe specific behaviors as related to more general themes. Several tactical rules may evolve from one general thematic rule. A major Midwest computer company has a strong thematic rule of "Communicate your commitment to the company." Several tactical rules have developed that relate to that theme, such as "Come in on Saturday to finish up, but make sure you tell someone," "Complain about how tough the challenge really is," and "Use the term *family* to refer to the company." These examples illustrate the contextual nature of thematic and tactical rules. Although the preceding statements are not only acceptable but also desirable in one particular company, they make little or no sense outside that context. Compliance with thematic and tactical rules indicates that an individual has received socializing information and identifies, at least to some extent, with the organization.

In an interesting expansion of our understanding of rules, Jennifer Ziegler (2007) describes the functions and problems with organizational lists. Lists can be described as organizationally developed statements designed to control a process or direct behavior. Ziegler's study of firefighters' 10 Standard Fire Orders illustrates a list which is intended to provide control in crisis situations but also is subject to cultural and individual differences in interpretations. She has demonstrated how these differences have contributed at times to significant problems. Ziegler goes on to identify numerous organizational lists, such as pilots' checklists, codes of conduct, recall lists, and others which, on the surface, are developed to provide rules to solve enduring organizational problems but may result in rules which create new problems.

Marshall Scott Poole and Robert McPhee (1983) and Poole, David Seibold, and McPhee (1985) added the dimension of **structuration** when they contended structurational rules theory provides a dynamic view of communication rules where diverse rule sets emerge through complex formal and informal interactions. As Stephen Littlejohn and Karen Foss (2008) describe, ". . . structuration is a process in which the unintended consequences of action create norms, rules, roles, and other social structures that constrain or affect future action. Structuration occurs constantly in all social systems." Structurational theory proposes that rules not only influence behavior but also are influenced by members' conceptions of appropriate behaviors. Poole and McPhee (1983) explained:

Structuration ■ Production and reproduction of social systems via the application of generative rules and resources in interaction.

> Structuration refers to the production and reproduction of social systems via the application of generative rules and resources in interaction. For example, the status hierarchy in a work group is an observable system. The structure underlying

this system consists of rules, such as norms about who takes problems to the boss, and resources, such as a special friendship with the boss or seniority. The status system exists because of the constant process of structuration in which rules and resources are both the medium and outcome of interaction. Members use rules and resources to maintain their places or to attempt to rise in the hierarchy; the structure of rules and resources thus produces the status system. (p. 210)

We expand our understanding of communication rules when we discuss communication as culture.

Power

Power ■ Attempts to influence another person's behavior to produce desired outcomes. The process occurs through communication and is related to resources, dependencies, and alternatives.

An additional communication dynamic that influences behavior is the use of power. In its most general sense, **power** has been defined as an attempt to influence another person's behavior to produce desired outcomes. As such, *power* is a neutral term subject to positive use as well as abuse. The power process occurs through communication and relates to resources, dependencies, and alternatives.

A resource is something owned or controlled by an individual, group, or entire organization. Resources are materials, information, knowledge, money, and a variety of other possible assets. Either owning or controlling resources allows individuals or organizations to influence interactions with others. A manager may control budget allocations within a department. Individual department members control important technical information not known to the manager. Both are resources influential in interactions between the manager and employees. Resources are closely linked to alternatives. A resource is more valuable if few alternatives to the use of the resource are available. Generally speaking, the individual controlling scarce resources is in a more influential (higher-power) position than the individual who controls resources with ample alternatives.

Although it is an outmoded notion, many believe power is a fixed commodity rather than a process of human interaction. In other words, many individuals behave as if the more power they have, the less is left for others. In reality, power is not a commodity but an influence process that permits all involved to gain more power, lose power, or share power. Therefore, when influence attempts result in abuse, evidence suggests we will seek other alternatives and lessen our dependency on the power abuser. Communication between supervisors and employees can illustrate this phenomenon. Supervisors and employees both have resources. The supervisor has the formal authority established by the chain of command. The supervisor controls information flow and performance evaluation. Employees control technical performance and have vital firsthand information about the progress of work. Both are dependent on each other; the supervisor directs, but without compliance and performance, no work is accomplished. If the supervisor becomes abusive in directing the work, an employee group may seek other alternatives by withdrawing from interaction with the supervisor or withholding information the supervisor needs to make good decisions. At an extreme the employee group may complain to others in management, transfer to other departments, or leave the organization. Power is one of the central issues we discuss in the Emerging Perspectives section of this chapter.

Communication as Culture

Organizing, decision making, and influence processes, when taken together, help us describe the **culture** of organizations by describing how organizations do things and how they talk about how they do things. Put another way, organizational culture is the unique sense of the place that organizations generate through ways of doing and ways of communicating about the organization. Organizational culture reflects the shared realities and shared practices in the organization and how these realities create and shape organizational events. Organizational culture is the unique symbolic common ground that becomes the self-definitions or self-images of the organization.

Culture ■ Unique sense of the place that organizations generate through ways of doing and ways of communicating about the organization; reflects the shared realities and shared practices in the organization and how they create and shape organizational events.

Metaphors help us understand the differences between the Functional tradition and Meaning-Centered approach to organizational cultures. Metaphors are ways of describing the likeness of one concept or person to another concept or person by speaking of the first as if it were the second. We say "She is the life of the party" or "He is the salt of the earth." Managers are referred to as quarterbacks, coaches, or lions in battle, with organizational decisions described as game or battle plans. These metaphors give us underlying assumptions for understanding behavior or concepts based on our knowledge of what we say something is like. We use our knowledge of what quarterbacks do, for example, to understand what managers do (a common metaphor supporting a bias toward male managers). We use the metaphor of a string quartet to explain excellence in teamwork based on the varying talents of individual contributors. Organization-wide metaphors used for the Functional tradition and Meaning-Centered approach work in much the same way.

When we described the Functional tradition to organizational communication, we talked about communication systems with inputs, throughput, and outputs. We described subsystems, suprasystems, and boundaries to external environments. We were using the organic metaphor of the dynamic system taken from the study of biology for conceptualizing or understanding organizational communication. The systems metaphor provided a distinct and descriptive set of assumptions about the way organizational communication works. Culture, in the systems metaphor, is one of many organizational variables.

In the Meaning-Centered approach the cultural metaphor replaces the systems metaphor of the Functional tradition. This culture metaphor describes communication as culture rather than describing culture and communication as separate processes. The culture metaphor promotes understanding communication as a process for generating shared realities and practices that in turn we call organizational culture.

When culture is used as a metaphor for organizational communication, we attempt to understand communication by understanding the uniqueness or shared realities in particular organizations. We explore how organizations use language, the symbols, jargon, and specialized vocabulary used by people working together. We examine behaviors exhibited in rituals and rites of organizational life and listen for the general standards or values of the organization as described in stories, legends, and reminiscences. We focus on how communication activities generate uniqueness or symbolic common ground. There is a danger, however, in oversimplifying culture as a single set of commonly held values, beliefs, actions, practices, rules, and dialogues mutually supported by all organizational members. In reality, organizations commonly reflect subcultural consensus and even lack of consensus about values, beliefs, actions, practices, rules, and dialogues. Embedded in this notion of culture as a metaphor for organizational communication is a view of organizations as dynamic, continually changing, and meaning producing.

Members of organizations working together communicate to create the activity and practice of the organization and to interpret the meaning of that activity and practice. Observing who is involved in important decisions, how influence takes place, and how people treat one another helps in understanding the "uniqueness" of an organization. Words, actions, artifacts, routine practices, and texts are the regular communication interactions among organizational members that generate uniqueness or culture(s). Differences in the cultural knowledge organizational members possess can lead to subcultures and use of cultural information for personal benefit. For example, longer-term organizational members may provide cultural information to newcomers, or they may choose to withhold that information, making organizational entry difficult. Communication provides organizational members with similar experiences and realities (if not similar levels of agreement and values about experiences and realities). In this dynamic view of culture as communication, these realities are constantly subject to change as organizational members react to new information and circumstances.

Whether personal, task, social, or organizational, rituals help define what is important or the values of the culture and provide a communication process to transmit those values. Awards ceremonies, Friday afternoon get-togethers, graduation, and numerous daily routines are all rituals that both provide regularity and signify importance in organizational life.

Organizational storytelling infuses passion or interest into everyday activities. Stories generate a sense of history about organizational existence and identify values through descriptions of success and failure. In the Coronado case, stories about the founders transmitted important information about the Coronado values of quality and customers. The Meaning-Centered approach suggests Coronado's manufacturing problem partly can be described in terms of a shift in culture or values.

Bill Drake must understand the communication interactions that have contributed to a change at Coronado in terms of what constitutes quality. Stories about his father and uncle have not been sufficient to maintain the earlier focus on customers. Can you suggest ways he might find out about the current focus on customers? How can his perception of the values of Coronado be different from that of others in the company? What should Drake do to determine what the culture of Coronado Manufacturing really is?

Communication Climate

Communication climate ■ Reaction to the organization's culture; determination or evaluation of the desirability of a culture.

The culture of an organization describes the unique sense of the place, its practices, and how that organization describes itself. The reaction to an organization's culture is the organization's **communication climate**.

We are used to thinking of climate in geographic terms. We think about temperature, humidity, winds, and rainfall and react somewhat subjectively to what we believe is a desirable climate. So it is with a climate for communication. The climate is a subjective reaction to organization members' perceptions of communication events. The subjective reaction is shared to a great extent by either individual groups or the entire organization.

Think for a moment about the culture of your school. By now you probably know how things are supposed to work. You know who holds power, what some of the rituals are, and how socializing generally takes place. You can describe the unique sense of the place to others, but your description does not necessarily tell whether you think it is a good place. Your positive or negative attitude—climate evaluation—is your reaction to the culture, not a description of the culture itself.

Identify the organizations of which you are a member. How would you describe their climate? How does a positive view of climate influence your behavior? What are the differences when your view is negative?

The Meaning-Centered Approach: Summary of Essential Characteristics

The **Meaning-Centered approach** to organizational communication understands communication as a complex process that creates and shapes organizational events. As such, communication is **organizing, decision making, influence,** and **culture.** Organizing is viewed as an ongoing process of human interactions attempting to reduce message equivocality. Decision making is part of organizing and is the process responsible for moving individuals and resources toward accomplishment of organizational goals. Influence is the process in which individuals and organizations engage to generate desired behaviors and is therefore closely related to organizing and decision making. Culture, as a metaphor for organizational communication, is the unique sense of a place that reflects the way things are done and how people talk about the way things are done. Finally, communication climate is the subjective reaction to the communication events that contribute to uniqueness or culture. The Meaning-Centered approach makes only limited distinctions among organizing, decision making, influence, and culture. All are seen as processes of communication, and all help us understand how organizations create and shape events through human interaction.

Now return to the beginning of the chapter. Can you answer each of the questions about the Meaning-Centered approach? How does it differ from the Functional tradition? What are the similarities? Earlier you described the communication system of your school. Now describe the culture of your school. Are there particular stories or rituals that come to mind? What are the communication rules?

EMERGING PERSPECTIVES

Emerging Perspectives for organizational communication expand, critique, and challenge many of the basic assumptions and interpretations found in the Functional and Meaning-Centered approaches and provide important value propositions for our consideration. In the next section of this chapter we introduce the concept of communication as a constitutive process and describe four approaches—communication constitutes organizations (CCO), postmodernism, critical theory, and feminist and race theory—as important perspectives for the study of organizational communication.

The rising interest in CCO, postmodernism, critical theory, and feminist and race theory can be understood when we consider the magnitude and rate of change in almost all aspects of our lives and the failure of more traditional approaches to guide our uncertainty. Organizations are increasing in size and complexity, with communications technologies changing even the most basic of organizational processes. Globalization both influences organizing processes and changes the very nature of work itself. Almost simultaneously we experience the influence of mass culture and the fact that fewer and fewer of us use similar information sources. In addition, our awareness of issues of diversity, difference, and marginalization grows. Put simply, this current time of turbulence and rapid change has given rise to a contemporary context in which new questions and new challenges are important for understanding our organizational lives.

Communication as Constitutive Process

Constitutive process ■
Communication seen as a process of meaning development and social production of perceptions, identities, social structures, and affective responses.

Stanley Deetz (1992) helped us understand the concept of communication as **constitutive process** when he suggested, "Communication cannot be reduced to an informational issue where meanings are assumed to be already existing, but must be seen as a process of meaning development and social production of perceptions, identities, social structures, and affective responses." Deetz suggested we move beyond Functional concerns for message production and transfer and the Meaning-Centered issues of "realities" and cultures to a fundamental view of communication that constitutes or brings about self and social environments. Communication is not synonymous with organizing, decision making, and influence but is better understood as the process that literally produces organizing, decision making, and influence.

This view of communication as a constitutive process, and the call for more participative communication processes can be seen in each of the four approaches to the study of organizational communication that follow. Additionally, we describe emerging discussions of institutions, global cultures, and technology as they relate to organizational communication. We begin with the communication constitutes organization (CCO) perspective.

Communication Constitutes Organization (CCO) ■
Communication processes or flows which generate and sustain organizations.

Communication Constitutes Organization (CCO)

Earlier in this chapter we described the work of Karl Weick with relationship to the ongoing processes of organizing and decision making. Influenced by the concepts of Weick and others, an important perspective for organizational communication known as communication constitutes organization (CCO) has emerged. Generally speaking, CCO rejects the notion portrayed in the Functional tradition that the organization contains a variety of discrete and independent communication interactions which are manifested in an identifiable structure with known boundaries. CCO expands what Weick and numerous others have described as the organization in the continual process of becoming through the numerous interactions of participants—essentially the Meaning-Centered approach described earlier. CCO extends the Meaning-Centered approach by discussing how organizations develop identities, exercise power and influence, and sustain themselves. This extended approach has been described by Gail Fairhurst and Linda Putnam (2004) as an action perspective anchoring the organization in the continuous flow of communication. In summarizing the Fairhurst and Putnam perspective as it relates to CCO, Putnam, Anne Nicotera, and Robert McPhee (2009) suggested, "This approach aims for a balance between structure and agency rather than privileging one or the other. Organizations never emerge as entities per se, but as systems, objects anchored in social practices, texts, or memory traces derived from the properties of language and action. Communication and organization are not equivalent concepts per se, but they are mutually constitutive" (p. 9). In other words, CCO attempts to understand the interactions and balances among agency (communicative actions) and broad structures. CCO addresses how agency and structures are mutually constitutive, that is, how they construct each other.

McPhee and Pamela Zaug (2000/2009) focus on the flows of communication which are present in ongoing organizing processes. The McPhee and Zaug framework describes four flows which work in complex ways to constitute and sustain organizations. The four flows are (1) relationships of members to the organization; (2) organizational self-structuring features for ongoing design and control; (3) activity coordination for work processes; and (4) institutional positioning with external stakeholders. Specifically, the first flow addresses how members address their roles, statuses, and overall relationships to the organization; the second flow describes how leaders design, implement, and deal with problems of control and decision; the third flow focuses on work design and implementation; and the fourth flow deals with complex relationships to stakeholders or other organizations.

Larry Browning, Ronald Greene, S. B. Sitkin, Kathleen Sutcliffe, and David Obstfeld (2009) add concepts of complexity to understanding the four flows and CCO in general. Browning and his colleagues contend, "Constitutive complexity allows us to search for multiple dimensions that explain a particular question, rather than accepting one and only one 'correct' answer. As dynamic relationships in organizations move from singular, to paired, to group processes, the concept of dynamic complexity emerges. . . . evolved complexity, accounts for units developing in different ways despite originating in quite similar circumstances" (p. 91). In other words, complexity helps us understand that the flows are not mutually exclusive and often overlap. While they can be described as separate processes, the overlap and the complexity generated are critical to understanding how organizations develop and sustain themselves. François Cooren and Gail Fairhurst (2009) caution us to not lose sight of the importance of human interactions and nonhuman signs and symbols when describing communication flows and complexity. They argue for what they call a "bottom-up perspective" which continues to focus on human interactions as creating what we refer to as structure. Cooren and Fairhurst contend, "There is no structure overarching human interactions to the extent that what makes human actors do things (which is usually what we have in mind when we use the term 'structure') is nothing but other human or non-human actors" (p. 137). They go on to explain,

> If the idea of the communicative constitution of organization makes any sense, it is for us on the sole condition that the concept of "communication" is extended to what non-humans do. For instance, this means that we need to acknowledge that the sign indeed *tells* visitors what behavior has to be adopted upon entering the building, that the security system *dissuades* visitors from squeezing in without checking in at the front desk, or that the procedure *leads* the concierge to ask visitors specific questions. Only if these contributions are acknowledged can we expect to find in communication and interaction the building blocks of organization. Going back to the four flows identified by McPhee and Zaug (2000), we can then adopt a bottom-up perspective and translate them to show that they are the product of these micro-associations between humans and non-humans. (p. 142)

James Taylor and his colleagues focus on language and foster the concept that organizing occurs when people interact around particular concerns. Taylor calls this process "co-orientation," which creates through conversation the construction of organizations. Taylor (2009) clarifies his position,

> I have argued that it will be taking account of the properties of language, and the practices of language-users, that we will advance. Language is both how people relate to each other, and how they express their understandings of such relating. Interaction mediated by language is thus reflexive, and retrospective, as both Giddens and Weick have pointed out, in that people monitor the interaction they are caught up in and make sense of it in retrospect. . . . It is, furthermore, in this recursive, retrospective dynamic that the identities of objects, individuals, technologies, communities, and finally, the organization itself are born. (p. 181)

Regardless of the specific positions regarding CCO, the perspective expands prior thinking about the complex relationships and structures which we call organizational communication.

Postmodernism and Organizational Communication

Postmodernism ■ Theoretical perspectives representing an alienation from the past, skepticism about authority structures, ambiguity of meanings, and mass culture.

The term **postmodernism** has been variously defined and hotly debated in fields as diverse as architecture, film, education, philosophy, sociology, and communication. Generally referring to perspectives that reject former notions of authority and power, stability of meanings, and concepts of effectiveness, postmodernism has become known as theoretical perspectives that represent an alienation from the past, skepticism about authority structures, ambiguity of meanings, and mass culture. Historical modernism is viewed as preceding postmodernity in time and experience, with postmodernism presenting challenges to the established traditions of modernism.

Postmodern theorists reject the claims of the Functional and Meaning-Centered perspectives as overly simplistic and lacking in understanding of a world characterized by rapid change, multiple meanings, and pervasive ambiguity. The notion of grand master narratives—stories with broad application and explanatory power (e.g., principles of scientific management or prescriptions for strong cultures) are replaced by the micronarratives of individual organization members. Postmodern theorists look at individual behaviors without implying relationships to underlying values, assumptions, and rationales. In particular, postmodern organizational communication seeks to understand how multiple meanings and multiple interpretations of organizational events influence multiple and diverse behaviors.

Deconstruction is the method of postmodern analysis. Put simply, deconstruction refers to the examination of taken-for-granted assumptions, the examination of the myths we use to explain how things are the way they are, and the uncovering of the interests involved in socially constructed meanings. The value base of postmodern organizational communication rests with shared power, concepts of empowerment and interdependence, and multiple interpretations of everyday events.

Deconstruction ■ The examination of taken-for-granted assumptions, the examination of the myths we use to explain how things are the way they are, and the uncovering of the interests involved in socially constructed meanings.

Postmodern analysis challenges traditional notions of rationality and, as such, rejects many of the tenets of the Functional tradition as well as the emphasis on shared realities in the Meaning-Centered perspective.

What can Bill Drake learn from the postmodern perspective? Are individual behaviors in his management team contributing to multiple meanings about what he should know or about what should be communicated between sales and manufacturing? Has he been taking for granted the assumption that his team agrees that the customer is number one? Does he need to deconstruct his own myths about how things are? Although admittedly complex in its propositions and concepts, postmodern organizational communication analysis provides additional useful ways for Bill Drake to ask questions about the communication in Coronado Manufacturing.

Critical Theory and Organizational Communication

Critical theory focuses our attention on studying privilege and power with specific attention to abuses of power through communication and organization. As Deetz (2001) explained, "The central goal of critical theory in organizational communication studies has been to create a society and workplaces that are free from domination and where all members can contribute equally to produce systems that meet human needs and lead to the progressive development of all" (p. 26). As Dennis Mumby (1993) claimed, "One of the principal tenets of the critical studies approach is that organizations are not simply neutral sites of meaning formation; rather, they are produced and reproduced in the context of struggles between competing interest groups and systems of representation" (p. 21).

Critical theory ■ Focuses attention on studies of power and abuses of power through communication and organization.

The critical theory approach depicts organizations where dominant groups control the development of ideologies or basic assumptions about how things should be. From these assumptions come legitimized controls (sometimes referred to as reified controls) in which power is hidden from ready observation and accepted as normal if not desirable. This notion of pervasive power that is not visible or overt and is generally accepted based on our myths of "how things came to be" is called **hegemony**. Hegemony is a process of control based on a dominant group leading others

Hegemony ■ Process of control based on a dominant group leading others to believe that their subordination is the norm.

to believe that their subordination is normal or the norm. Hegemony implies to some (but not all) critical theorists that certain people in organizations are oppressed even when they do not recognize their experience as such. This perspective is in direct contradiction to both the Functional and Meaning-Centered approaches, which rely heavily on overt communication actions and practices.

Critical theory seeks to understand power structures and identify interests served by various types and alignments of power. Critical theory also seeks to uncover power abuses in order to contribute to more fulfilling organizations and entire societies. Critical theory, more than our earlier perspectives, seeks to support both analysis and action, whether stimulating resistance, promoting change, or focusing on emancipating those abused by power structures.

For critical theorists, power and communication are closely intertwined. Power is exercised through communication, and power influences communication rules and structures. Dennis Mumby (1987) characterized organizational power controls as domination based on getting people to organize their behavior around particular rule systems. Legitimate control emerges through stories, myths, rituals, and a variety of other symbolic forms. These forms in turn become the rules that prescribe appropriate behavior. This "legitimate" yet hidden exercise of power can contribute to the suspension of critical thinking.

As Deetz (2001) described: "While organizations could be positive social institutions providing forums for the articulation and resolution of important group conflicts over the use of natural resources, distribution of income, production of desirable goods and services, the development of personal qualities, and the direction of society, various forms of power and domination have led to skewed decision making and fostered social harms and significant waste and inefficiency" (p. 26).

Critical theory helps us ask questions about how we can change and reform organizational practices to better represent a variety of stakeholders with competing interests.

Distinctions between postmodern and critical approaches generally focus on differences in approach to organizational understandings. Specifically, postmodern approaches emphasize deconstruction and the unmasking of myths and assumptions to open up the possibility of new understandings and new processes. Critical approaches, on the other hand, use value-laden ideological critiques to demonstrate domination and to produce opposition.

What questions should Bill Drake ask using critical theory? Are there hidden power struggles contributing to the defects problem? Is someone or a group of people attempting to silence others in order to keep problems from Drake? How can he know? Is there something wrong in the organization that is more important than the defects problem? Bill Drake would be well advised to think about potential power abuses as he evaluates the problems he faces.

Feminist and Race Perspectives and Organizational Communication

Feminist theory focuses on the marginalization and domination of women in the workplace and the devaluing of women's voices in all organizational processes. Although diverse in perspective and approaches, feminist theory generally attempts to move our society beyond patriarchal forms and social practices by critiquing power relationships that devalue women. **Race perspectives** and organizational communication currently are less developed, emerging, and of significant importance. Race perspectives focus on the domination of those not of a majority race and the uncovering of practices which both silence and devalue minority voices.

> **Feminist and race theory** ■ Focuses on the marginalization and domination of women and persons of color in the workplace and the valuing of diverse voices in all organizational processes.

Judi Marshall (1993) described male forms as the norms to which organizational members adapt. She proposed that the male principle can be characterized as self-assertion, separation, independence, control, competition, focused perception, rationality, analysis, clarity, discrimination, and activity. The female principle is described as interdependence, cooperation, receptivity, merging, acceptance, awareness of patterns, awareness of wholeness, and synthesizing. Although males and females can access both types of values, evidence exists that females in organizations adapt to male norms while being evaluated against female stereotypes. Marshall concludes, "The male domination of cultures goes largely unrecognized in organizational life and in mainstream organizational theory."

Patrice Buzzanell (1994) described feminist organizational communication theorizing as discussing "the moral commitment to investigate the subordinated, to focus on gendered interactions in ordinary lives, and to explore the standpoints of women who have been rendered invisible by their absence in theory and research." Buzzanell discussed how gender is socially constructed and enacted in organizations, with messages, structures, and practices becoming the contexts for gender construction and negotiation. Organizational communication is therefore the focal process for this construction and negotiation.

Buzzanell (1994) examined three traditional themes in organizational writings— competitive individualism, cause-effect/linear thinking, and separation or autonomy—and contrasts them to feminist organizational communication theory. The ethic of competitive individualism creates organizational winners and losers based on competition and a need to excel over others. This competitive ethic typically casts women in the role of the "other," whereas stereotypical expectations and behaviors cast women as "losers." Buzzanell contrasted the competitive ethic with the cooperative enactment of organizations in which opportunities exist to understand how women translate the cooperative ethic into talk and behavior. She called for understanding how people communicate in cooperative-oriented and feminist-based organizations and contrasting that talk with how people communicate in competitively driven groups. Also not as extensively explored in communication work, most of the above discussion also applies to racial and ethnic differences.

The second theme, cause-effect/linear thinking, is based on the superiority in traditional society of the rational, direct, and solution-oriented. Feminist organizational communication theory asks questions about alternatives and explores the double binds created for women who are negatively sanctioned for adopting the scientific male style and who also are devalued for choosing stereotypical feminine communication patterns. Race perspectives also challenge the superiority of tradition models which limit contributions that do not follow a traditional white-male communication model.

The third theme, separation and autonomy, is based on socialization practices that urge men to become separate and autonomous through action, work, and status; women, by contrast, are socialized for nurturing, being attractive, following authority, and being well liked. Feminist organizational communication theory offers the potential to examine the consequences of these socialized differences for both men and women. Feminist theory explores the importance of integrating emotion in communication theory while promoting discussions of developing the authentic self.

Karen Ashcraft and Brenda Allen (2003) extended the concepts of feminist theory to understanding issues of race in organizations. Ashcraft and Allen claimed that not only are organizations fundamentally gendered but also fundamentally raced. Many of the assumptions in organizations about the contributions of women apply to people of color. Additionally, notions exist which suggest that discrimination and marginalization will be eliminated when more people of color and women are in more diverse organizational positions. To date the facts simply do not support this perspective, making gender and race of ongoing concern for organizational excellence.

When discussing the Meaning-Centered approach, we discussed organizational socialization or attempts by organizations to help members learn appropriate behaviors, norms, and values. Connie Bullis (1993) used feminist theory to develop an alternative perspective. Bullis described why it is important to consider how socialization practices can construct women as marginalized others. Bullis challenged us to think about voices marked as outsiders, unsocialized, uncommitted, disloyal, absentee, unemployable, or dropouts. Her work and the work of others has raised important questions about socialization processes that function both to marginalize as well as socialize. Think for a moment about your own experiences. Have you ever considered yourself marginalized? If so, what were the communication experiences contributing to this feeling? If not, can you identify examples of times when others may have been excluded during socialization communication?

Feminist and race perspectives can assist Bill Drake in asking questions about whether all managers are being heard. Have important voices been discounted, contributing to his current problems? Has he mistakenly assumed that all good ideas and inputs were equally valued? Although we cannot know the answers without more details of the case, we can see how these questions give Bill Drake additional ways to understand Coronado's problems. We continue our discussion of important Emerging Perspectives in Chapter 3.

Institutions and Organizational Communication

Both the Functional and Meaning-Centered approaches have been criticized for focusing too intensely on single organizations without adequate regard to influences in the larger environment. A discussion of **institutions** and organizational communication has begun as a partial answer to this criticism. The definitions of institutions vary. The word *institution* is sometimes used interchangeably with the term *organization*. A particular high-prestige organization may be referred to as an institution in its field. Institution sometimes refers to what John Lammers and Joshua Barbour (2006) described as "supraorganizational entities or governing

Institutions ■ High-prestige organizations; process, practice, or groupings of similar organizations that are prominent parts of our environments; relatively stable traditions, practices, standards, customs, rules, and laws.

bodies such as the economy, the state, or a religion. A given level of aggregation has been said to be the institutional level (e.g., contrasted with the individual, group, or organizational levels). The traditional professions, such as medicine, law, and clergy, are sometimes referred to as institutions. Institution has also been used to describe specific customs and practices (e.g., the institution of marriage) as well as rules and laws (e.g., the institution of criminal justice)" (p. 358). In other words, institutions provide our environments relatively stable traditions, practices, standards, customs, rules, and laws.

If institutions are more permanent and established than individual organizations, the question becomes: how does an organization or groups of organizations, processes, or practices become institutionalized? Based on the work of Pamela Tolbert and Lynne Zucker (1996), Tim Kuhn (2005) described a process of institutionalization which involves innovation, habitualization, objectification, and sedimentation. Organizational communication is fundamental in this description of the institutionalization process. Tolbert and Zucker and later Kuhn described the process of institutionalization as beginning when an innovation or new understanding enters a field of practice, organization, or related group of organizations. In order for the innovation to be sustained, the habitualization phase must occur, whereby the innovation becomes part of patterned approaches to problem solving usually used by a limited set of individuals who have contact with each other across organizations.

The Internet provides a useful example. The needs in the scientific and military communities for the transmission, retrieval, and linkage across time and space of large volumes of information gave rise to what today we call the Internet. The communication and technological advances occurred over several decades with the initial protocols and uses of the emerging technology primarily reserved for academics, scientists, and a lesser number of military personnel. Once the introduction of the innovation was stabilized and habitualization among this somewhat limited group occurred, the objectification phase rapidly emerged.

The objectification phase is characterized by social consensus about the value of the innovation, often based on limited knowledge about the specifics of the innovation but agreement that based on convincing arguments of merit the innovation has significant potential. Once this legitimacy has been established, the sedimentation phase occurs. Sedimentation refers to the spread of the innovation and its persistence over time. Likely everyone reading this book would agree the Internet has become an institution of our time and vital to the subject of our study, organizational communication.

In further explanation of the importance of institutions, Lammers and Barbour suggested institutions bring us observable routines that go across many settings or organizations. For example, the school you currently attend is in many ways unique; yet, many routine practices in your school can be found in similar schools throughout the world. Your school is part of the institution of education. Lammers and Barbour also suggested institutions manifest beliefs, which influence decisions and choices that individuals make. You probably have beliefs defining a good school based not only on the school you attend but also on what you know about the institution of education in general.

Lammers and Barbour noted that institutions are established through associations among people and are characterized by low rates of change with fixed and enduring qualities, often formalized with specific rules for conduct and specific prescriptions for rational purpose and how to get things done. This institutional perspective suggests that understanding organizational communication in specific circumstances must be informed by understanding the broader institutional context in which specific organizations and individuals find themselves. What does an institutional perspective mean for Bill Drake? Is it possible that his personal institutional influences differ significantly from others on his management team? In some respects Bill Drake must deal with the fact that "quality" is no longer as institutionalized at Coronado as he would like. How would you advise him using an institutional perspective?

Global Cultures and Organizational Communication

Most of us are aware of a myriad of changes, usually referred to as globalization, made possible for both individuals and organizations by emerging communications technologies. Fewer of us have been exposed to the profound cultural differences influencing organizational communication in a global workforce. It is fair to say, there are no overarching global principles for effective organizational communication. In fact, many legitimately argue much of what we describe as effective communication is U.S.-centric or at best Eurocentric.

Robert House, Paul Hanges, Mansour Javidan, Peter Dorfman, and Vipin Gupta (2004) led a ten-year study of sixty-two societies to describe varying values and practices related to functioning in a world of global collaborations. This massive study included 170 social scientists and management scholars from around the world with 17,300 participants in 951 organizations. It identified nine core dimensions of **global cultures**: uncertainty avoidance, power distance, institutional collectivism, in-group collectivism, gender egalitarianism, assertiveness, future orientation, performance orientation, and humane orientation. The differences here can be profound and create differences in how individuals and groups may approach global collaborations. For example, societies with higher uncertainty avoidance will have a tendency to formalize their interactions with others, exhibiting low tolerance for breaking rules and showing stronger resistance to change. On the other hand, societies with lower uncertainty avoidance tend to be more informal in their interactions with others, exhibiting tolerance for breaking rules and supporting more change. It is relatively easy to imagine how working with these differences can challenge collaborators across cultures.

The value of assertiveness provides another excellent example. Societies valuing high assertiveness tend to favor dominant, tough behavior with an emphasis on success and progress. Societies with low assertiveness values view dominant and tough behavior as socially unacceptable and favor people and relationships over success and progress. High-assertiveness cultures tend to value direct and unambiguous communication, whereas lower-assertiveness cultures favor speaking indirectly and emphasizing "face-saving." Although the study

Global cultures ■ Regional or country-specific societal values and practices including core dimensions such as uncertainty avoidance, power distance, institutional collectivism, in-group collectivism, gender egalitarianism, assertiveness, future orientation, performance orientation, and humane orientation.

conducted by House and his colleagues provides important guidance for our thinking, it must not be considered comprehensive or inclusive of all valuable ways of knowing and communicating. Communication in global environments will require new understandings informed by many voices not traditionally part of our organizational dialogues.

There is no innate right or wrong in the ranges of cultural values and communication approaches, but the myriad of differences has the potential to influence collaborations across cultures with particular emphasis on power relationships, treatment of others, and marginalization of voices lower in dominance. It is fair to say that global cultural differences affect all of the basic assumptions we use as we work in increasingly diverse environments. In our Coronado case, Bill Drake does not have to deal with global differences. Think for a moment how much more complicated his problem might be if his customers were global and his manufacturing units were in several different countries.

Technology and Organizational Communication

Emerging communications technologies influence organizational structure, processing of information, newcomer socialization, interactions among work groups, interactions with customers, the speed of work, information security, individual privacy, networks for innovation, problem solving, decision making, and a host of other organizational experiences. Access to and control of technology are powerful communication influences changing the way work is performed, how people relate to each other, how power is exercised, and a host of organizational participation practices. We will discuss use of technology in greater detail in later chapters, but it is important to understand that the emergence of these technologies changes fundamental assumptions in all of the theoretical perspectives we discussed.

Think back to our discussion of networks in the Functional tradition. Will these new technologies challenge what we currently know about information flow? The Meaning-Centered perspective is focused on influence, power, and cultures, among other issues. The virtual nature of work and the vast geographic distances over which work is performed among people of diverse backgrounds complicate a vision of organizations as composed of relatively homogeneous individuals with backgrounds that can be easily understood by coworkers.

Postmodernism, critical theory, and feminist and race theory ask important questions about how reality is constructed in organizations. However, these perspectives also face challenges from the increasing complexity of a technologically linked global work environment. Some of their assumptions about participation and power will be called into question by global cultural differences expressing divergent value orientations. Our purpose here is not to understand fully this complexity but to recognize its emergence as part of our individual and collective competency challenges. Think again of our Coronado case. Technology likely will be an increasing part of Bill Drake's environment. If he is not getting the information he needs now, what might a more technologically sophisticated environment bring in terms of benefits and problems?

Emerging Perspectives: Summary of Essential Issues

Emerging Perspectives for organizational communication describe communication as a **constitutive process**, often described as **communication constitutes organization (CCO)**, and critique and challenge basic assumptions of message meaning and transfer, power and domination, and notions of rationality associated with hierarchical and patriarchal systems. Communication as a constitutive process brings about self and social environments. Communication literally produces organizing, decision making, and influence. **Postmodernism** rejects former (modern) notions of authority and power, stability of meanings, and concepts of effectiveness. **Deconstruction** is the method of postmodern analysis, with its emphasis on the exposure of the myths we use to explain the way things are and the uncovering of interests involved in socially constructed meanings.

Critical theory shifts our attention to power and abuses of power through communication and control in organizations. Organizations are depicted as political decision-making sites with potential for both domination and codetermination. **Feminist and race theory** focus on the marginalization and domination of women and people of color in the workplace and how the valuing of diverse voices contributes to an equality for differences rather than the equality of sameness characteristic of the Functional and Meaning-Centered approaches. Finally, Emerging Perspectives must include an understanding of the increasing influence of **institutions, global cultures, and technologies** for organizational communication.

Return to the Coronado case presented at the beginning of this chapter. Examine how the Functional, Meaning-Centered, postmodern, critical, and feminist and race perspectives help us understand Bill Drake's issues. What are the differences? Where can you find similarities?

Practical Theory and Organizational Communication

The Functional tradition, Meaning-Centered approach, and Emerging Perspectives all can be described in some respects as practical theory for organizational communication. Simply put, the Functional, Meaning-Centered, and Emerging Perspectives approaches all help us ask questions, understand, critique, and think about how to stimulate excellence in organizational communication. J. Kevin Barge and Robert Craig (2009) describe the importance of practical theory when they explain

> . . . three broad approaches to practical theory . . . (1) mapping, (2) engaged reflection, and (3) transformative practice. First, *practical theory as mapping* begins by creating a high-quality map of reality through scientific, interpretive, or critical methods that subsequently can be used to inform practice. . . . Second, *practical theory as engaged reflection* explicitly addresses the reflexive relationship between theory and practice—how each can inform the other—and, therefore, reflects an integration of practical and theoretical discourses. . . . Third, *practical theory as transformative practice* . . . from this perspective is viewed as a useful resource for theorists and practitioners to help them make sense of situations and take action that is intended to improve these situations." (p. 59)

The remainder of this text will assist you in utilizing a variety of practical theories to develop excellence in diverse communication competencies.

CHAPTER HIGHLIGHTS

The Functional tradition, the Meaning-Centered approach, and Emerging Perspectives for understanding organizational communication help us ask questions important for analyzing problems. You should now review summary sections for each perspective. Figure 2.4 identifies key questions from each perspective. These questions can be used throughout the text as we analyze a variety of organizational problems—a practical theory approach. ■

The Functional Tradition

1. How effective are organizing, relationship, and change messages?
2. What types of formal and informal communication networks exist? What network roles can you identify? Are they adequate?
3. Is channel use appropriate for effective communication?
4. Is the load on the communication system part of the problem?
5. What types of communication distortion exist?
6. Does the organization get good input communication from its environment? How effective is throughput and output communication?
7. Is the system open or closed?

The Meaning-Centered Approach

1. Do organizing activities help reduce message equivocality?
2. How effective is decision-making communication?
3. Do most organizational members identify with the organization? How do you know?
4. What attempts are made at organizational socialization? Are they appropriate and effective?
5. How does power relate to the problem?
6. Do organizational stories, rituals, and events provide important information?
7. What type of culture exists? Is it effective? How do you know?
8. How can the communication climate be characterized? Is that appropriate? What should change?

Emerging Perspectives

1. What are the hidden power relationships?
2. Are women and others marginalized?
3. Describe abuses of power.
4. Do stories, rituals, and events sustain hierarchical and patriarchal systems?
5. Is decision making characterized by domination or codetermination? How can change occur?
6. How is rationality conceptualized and presented?
7. How do institutions influence particular organizations?
8. How do global cultural differences influence organizational collaborations?
9. Describe how technology influences issues of power, marginalization, culture, and participation in decision making.

FIGURE 2.4
Analyzing Organizational Problems

WORKSHOP

1. Form groups of four to six members each. Using your school as an organization with which all class members are familiar, identify organizing, change, and relationship messages. Groups should compare lists. How much agreement exists? How much disagreement? What accounts for the differences?

2. In small groups, read either The United Concepts Advertising Agency Dilemma Case or The "Newcomers Aren't Welcome Here" Case that follows and select from Figure 2.4 the questions that best help you understand the problems in the case. Answer at least six questions and then prepare answers to the following questions.

The United Concepts Advertising Agency Dilemma Case

1. How would you advise Jane?
2. What would you tell Chris and John?
3. What would you tell Frank Donnell?

The "Newcomers Aren't Welcome Here" Case

1. What should Joe and Henry do?
2. Could Bernie have handled the announcement in a manner that would not have alienated Joe and Henry?
3. What do you think is going to happen?

Groups should report to the class as a whole and compare and contrast questions selected and answers.

THE UNITED CONCEPTS ADVERTISING AGENCY DILEMMA CASE

Jane Peters was having the best morning of her career. Since coming to United Concepts Advertising as an account executive, she had been successful in acquiring new business, but nothing as big as the Raven Furniture account. Raven was the largest chain of furniture stores in the West, and landing the account meant something not only in the West Coast offices of United Concepts but in Chicago and New York as well.

Jane knew that her creative team, John and Chris, was largely responsible. The close working relationship among the three was the best Jane had experienced in her fifteen years in the advertising industry. In fact, Jane began to think of ways to make John and Chris more visible to her boss, Frank Donnell. After all, Frank was pleased that the agency got the Raven account. Perhaps he could be persuaded to promote John and Chris to senior creative positions.

Three Weeks Later

Jane was exhausted. Getting the Raven account up and going was not only requiring long hours but was also complicated by the resistance of some of the top management at Raven. She had never imagined there would be resistance at Raven to changing agencies and considerable disagreement about the United Concepts proposal. In fact, dealing with the various people at Raven was taking too much time. Her other accounts were not getting the service they needed, and Chris had just made a major error in the Raven ad scheduled to run this weekend. Jane caught the mistake as it was about to go to the printer. Although it was costly to adjust the error at that point, she was relieved but shaken at how close they had come to a major problem. Jane considered approaching Frank Donnell for more help on the account.

One Week Later

The creative meeting wasn't working. John and Chris were angry with each other and could not agree on an approach for Raven's Christmas promotion. They complained that Jane was too busy to work with them the way she used to and blamed her for rushing the creative process. Jane was sympathetic but told John and Chris that they did not understand her current pressure. The meeting ended with the first real tension the group had experienced. Jane went to see Frank Donnell and asked for help, additional people, and promotions to recognize the real efforts of John and Chris.

Two Weeks Later

Jane was angry as she read her memo from Frank Donnell. Yes, her request for one additional staff person would be honored, but no promotions for Chris and John. Company policy prohibited the creation of additional senior creative positions in the West Coast office. Jane began to draft an angry response. Raven people were just beginning to appreciate their work. How was she going to continue to motivate Chris and John? Would they resent the new person? Was the Raven account worth all this trouble? ■

THE "NEWCOMERS AREN'T WELCOME HERE" CASE

Joe and Henry have worked for Temple Air Conditioning and Heating for over twenty years. Both men are competent workers who were hired by Temple's founder, Bernie Jones. In fact, Joe, Henry, and Bernie still have an occasional beer together on Friday nights after work. Bernie is always complaining that the good old days are over and that nobody should have so much paperwork to run a heating and air-conditioning business. Joe and Henry don't think things have really changed all that much except that the houses keep getting bigger and fancier. Joe and Henry have worked as a team for the last fifteen years without a supervisor. They are part of the reason Temple has a good reputation for quality work and fast service. Joe and Henry don't spend time with other installation teams and don't see any reason why they should.

Early Monday Morning

Bernie's announcement was a blow. He was bringing in a college-educated person to supervise the installation teams. Joe and Henry could hardly believe what they were hearing. They should have known something was up when Bernie called everyone together before the trucks went out on Monday morning.

JOE: Who does he think he is, bringing in some college guy—what do we need another guy for?

HENRY: Yeah, Bernie is losing it. He knows how this place got built—off our backs. I am not going to work for anybody, let alone somebody with a fancy degree.

JOE: I always looked up to Bernie—and I thought he felt the same way about us. Obviously we were wrong. After twenty years, to be wrong about a guy makes you feel stupid.

HENRY: What do you think we should do?

JOE: How would I know?

HENRY: Well, I'm not going to take this lying down. Are you with me?

JOE: Sure, we can make Temple fall apart. ■

3. Emerging Perspectives challenge many current notions of organizational communication. Add to the following list of myths any common assumptions you can identify about organizational life.

Myth List: Men are stronger leaders than women during organizational crises.

Women are more nurturing managers than men.

Management must exercise control for organizations to succeed.

Only a select few are capable of innovating.

For each myth on the list, discuss the following questions:

1. How do notions of power contribute to this statement?
2. Does this statement marginalize men or women? What does it mean for other important differences people exhibit?
3. Describe abuses of power related to this statement.
4. How much genuine participation occurs in decision making if this statement is true?
5. What is the basis of rationality for the statement?
6. How are these statements viewed in different parts of the world?

Listen to the discussion. Is it difficult to deconstruct or critique myths of how things happen? Why? Why not? ■

TIPS FOR EFFECTIVE COMMUNICATION

1. Identify several examples in which you believe you have been misunderstood. Take each of these examples and determine how you might have created more clarity with your message and the channels you chose for message sending. Ask for feedback about what others have understood you to mean when you send an important message.
2. Describe what is important to you in a working relationship. Ask others to describe what is important to them.
3. Learn to watch for individuals who do not participate in a discussion or project. Encourage them to participate by asking for their ideas and input.
4. Seek out individuals from cultures different from your own. Talk with them about your culture, and encourage them to share their experiences.
5. Pick out two countries about which you know very little. Use the Internet and other approaches to increase your awareness of these countries. Think about how you would communicate with a work colleague from each country. ■

REFERENCES AND SUGGESTED READINGS

Albrecht, T. L., and B. Hall. 1991. Relational and content differences between elites and outsiders in innovation networks. *Human Communication Research* 17: 535–561.

Allport, G., and L. Postman. 1947. *The psychology of rumor.* New York: Holt.

Alvesson, L. M., and S. Deetz. 1996. Critical theory and postmodern approaches to organizational studies. In

Handbook of organizational studies, eds. S. R. Clegg, C. Hardy, and W. R. Nord, 191–217. London: Sage.

Ashcraft, K., and B. Allen. 2003. The racial foundation of organizational communication. *Communication Theory* 13: 5–38.

Barge, J. K., and R. T. Craig. 2009. Practical theory in applied communication scholarship. In *Routledge handbook of applied communication research,* eds. L. R. Frey and K. N. Cissna, 55–78. New York: Routledge.

Barnett, G. 1988. Communication and organizational culture. In *Handbook of organizational communication,* eds. G. Goldhaber and G. Barnett, 101–130. Norwood, NJ: Ablex.

Brown, M. H. 1985. That reminds me of a story: Speech action in organizational socialization. *Western Journal of Speech Communication* 49: 27–42.

Browning, L., R. W. Greene, S. B. Sitkin, K. M. Sutcliffe, and D. Obstfeld. 2009. Constitutive complexity: Military entrepreneurs and the synthetic character of communication flows. In *Building theories of organization: The constitutive role of communication,* eds. L. Putnam and A. Nicotera, 89–116. New York: Routledge.

Bullis, C. 1993. Organizational socialization research: Enabling, constraining, and shifting perspectives. *Communication Monographs* 60: 10–17.

Buzzanell, P. M. 1994. Gaining a voice: Feminist organizational communication theorizing. *Management Communication Quarterly* 7(4): 339–382.

Cheney, G. 1983. On the various and changing meanings of organizational membership: A field study of organizational identification. *Communication Monographs* 50: 342–362.

Conrad, C. 1994. *Strategic organizational communication: Toward the twenty-first century.* New York: Holt, Rinehart and Winston.

Cooren, F., and G. Fairhurst. 2009. Dislocation and stabilization: How to scale up from interactions to organizations. In *Building theories of organization: The constitutive role of communication,* eds. L. Putnam and A. Nicotera, 117–152. New York: Routledge.

Corman, S. R., and M. S. Poole, eds. 2000. *Perspectives on organizational communication: Finding common ground.* New York: Guilford Press.

Craig, R. T., and K. Tracy. 1995. Grounded practical theory: The case of intellectual discussion. *Communication Theory* 5: 248–272.

Cronen, V. 2001. Practical theory, practical art, and the pragmatic-systemic account of inquiry. *Communication Theory* 11: 14–35.

Cushman, D., S. King, and T. Smith. 1988. The rules perspective on organizational communication research. In *Handbook of organizational communication,* eds. G. M. Goldhaber and G. A. Barnett, 55–94. Norwood, NJ: Ablex.

Dahle, T. L. 1954. An objective and comparative study of five methods of transmitting information to business and industrial employees. *Speech Monographs* 21: 21–28.

Davis, K. 1967. *Human behavior at work.* New York: McGraw-Hill.

Deetz, S. 1992. *Building a communication perspective in organization studies I: Foundations.* Paper presented at the Speech Communication Association, October, Chicago.

Deetz, S. 1994. *Transforming communication, transforming business: Building responsive and responsible workplaces.* Cresskill, NJ: Hampton Press.

Deetz, S. 2001. Conceptual foundations. In *The new handbook of organizational communication: Advances in theory, research, and methods,* eds. F. M. Jablin and L. L. Putnam, 3–46. Thousand Oaks, CA: Sage.

Donnellon, A., B. Gray, and M. Bougon. 1986. Communication, meaning and organized action. *Administrative Science Quarterly* 31: 43–55.

Eisenberg, E., and H. L. Goodall. 1993. *Organizational communication: Balancing creativity and constraint.* New York: St. Martin's.

Eisenberg, E., and P. Riley. 1988. Organizational symbols and sense-making. In *Handbook of organizational communication,* eds. G. Goldhaber and G. Barnett, 131–150. Norwood, NJ: Ablex.

Eisenberg, E. M., and P. Riley. 2001. Organizational culture. In *The new handbook of organizational communication: Advances in theory, research, and methods,* eds. F. M. Jablin and L. L. Putnam, 291–322. Thousand Oaks, CA: Sage.

Fairhurst, G. T., and L. Putnam. 2004. Organizations as discursive constructions. *Communication Theory* 14, 5–26.

Ferguson, K. 1984. *The feminist case against bureaucracy.* Philadelphia: Temple University Press.

Hart, Z., and V. Miller. 2005. Context and message content during organizational socialization: A research note. *Human Communication Research* 31: 295–309.

House, R., P. Hanges, M. Javidan, P. Dorfman, and V. Gupta, eds. 2004. *Culture, leadership, and organizations: The globe study of 62 societies.* Thousand Oaks, CA: Sage.

Jablin, F. 1982. Formal structural characteristics of organizations and superior-subordinate communication. *Human Communication Research* 8(4): 338–347.

Jablin, F. M. 2001. Organizational entry, assimilation, and disengagement/exit. In *The new handbook of organizational communication: Advances in theory, research, and methods,* eds. F. M. Jablin and L. L. Putnam, 732–818. Thousand Oaks, CA: Sage.

Jablin, F. M., and L. L. Putnam, eds. 2001. *The new handbook of organizational communication: Advances in theory, research, and methods.* Thousand Oaks, CA: Sage.

Katz, D., and R. Kahn. 1966. *The social psychology of organizations.* New York: Wiley.

Kuhn, T. 2005. The institutionalization of Alta in organizational communication studies. *Management Communication Quarterly* 18: 618–627.

Lammers, J., and J. Barbour. 2006. An institutional theory of organizational communication. *Communication Theory* 16: 356–377.

Level, D. A., and W. P. Galle. 1980. *Business communications: Theory and practice.* Dallas, TX: Business Publications.

Littlejohn, S.W., and K. Foss. 2008. *Theories of human communication.* Belmont, CA: Thomson Wadsworth.

Louis, M. R. 1980. Surprise and sense making: What newcomers experience in entering unfamiliar organizational settings. *Administrative Science Quarterly* 25: 226–251.

Lyon, A. 2004. Participants' use of cultural knowledge as cultural capital in a dot-com start-up organization. *Management Communication Quarterly* 18: 175–203.

Marshall, J. 1993. Viewing organizational communication from a feminist perspective: A critique and some offerings. In *Communication yearbook/16,* ed. S. Deetz, 122–143. Newbury Park, CA: Sage.

McPhee, R. D., and P. K. Tompkins, eds. 1985. *Organizational communication: Traditional themes and new directions.* Beverly Hills, CA: Sage.

McPhee, R. D., and P. Zaug. 2009. The communicative constitution of organizations: A framework for explanation. In *Building theories of organization: The constitutive role of communication,* eds. L. Putnam and A. Nicotera, 21–47. New York: Routledge. Reprinted from McPhee, R. D., and P. Zaug. 2000. The communicative constitution of organizations: A framework for explanation. *Electronic Journal of Communication* 10: 1–2.

Miller, K. 1999. *Organizational communication: Approaches and processes,* 2nd ed. Belmont, CA: Wadsworth.

Mintzberg, H. 1973. *The nature of managerial work.* New York: Harper and Row.

Monge, P. 1990. Theoretical and analytical issues in studying organizational processes. *Organization Science* 4: 406–430.

Monge, P., and E. Eisenberg. 1987. Emergent communication networks. In *Handbook of organizational communication,* eds. F. Jablin, L. Putnam, K. Roberts, and L. Porter, 304–342. Newbury Park, CA: Sage.

Morley, D. D., and P. Shockley-Zalabak. 1991. Setting the rules: An examination of the influence of organization founders' values. *Management Communication Quarterly* 4: 442–449.

Morley, D. D., P. Shockley-Zalabak, and R. Cesaria. 1997. Organizational communication and culture: A study of 10 Italian high-technology companies. *Journal of Business Communication* 34: 253–268.

Mumby, D. 1987. The political function of narratives in organizations. *Communication Monographs* 54: 113–127.

Mumby, D. K. 1993. Critical organizational communication studies: The next 10 years. *Communication Monographs* 60: 18–25.

Mumby, D. K., and L. L. Putnam. 1992. The politics of emotion: A feminist reading of bounded rationality. *Academy of Management Review* 17: 465–486.

Pacanowsky, M., and N. O'Donnell-Trujillo. 1983. Organizational communication as cultural performance. *Communication Monographs* 50: 126–147.

Pepper, G. 1995. *Communicating in organizations: A cultural approach.* New York: McGraw-Hill.

Poole, M. S. 1985. Communication and organizational climates: Review, critique, and a new perspective. In *Organizational communication: Traditional themes and new directions,* eds. R. D. McPhee and P. K. Tompkins, 79–108. Beverly Hills, CA: Sage.

Poole, M. S., and R. D. McPhee. 1983. A structural analysis of organizational climate. In *Communication and organizations: An interpretive approach,* eds. L. Putnam and M. Pacanowsky, 195–219. Beverly Hills, CA: Sage.

Poole, M. S., D. R. Seibold, and R. D. McPhee. 1985. Group decision-making as a structurational process. *Quarterly Journal of Speech* 71: 74–102.

Putnam, L. 1983. The interpretive perspective: An alternative to functionalism. In *Communication and organizations: An interpretive approach,* eds.

L. Putnam and M. Pacanowsky, 31–54. Beverly Hills, CA: Sage.

Putnam, L., A. Nicotera, and R. McPhee. 2009. Introduction: Communication constitutes organization. In *Building theories of organization: The constitutive role of communication,* eds. L. Putnam and A. Nicotera, 1–19. New York: Routledge.

Putnam, L., and M. Pacanowsky, eds. 1983. *Communication and organizations: An interpretive approach.* Beverly Hills, CA: Sage.

Redding, W. C. 1983. Stumbling toward identity: The emergence of organizational communication as a field of study. In *Organizational communication: Traditional themes and new directions,* eds. R. D. McPhee and P. K. Tompkins, 15–54. Beverly Hills, CA: Sage.

Riley, P. 1983. A structurationist account of political culture. *Administrative Science Quarterly* 28: 414–437.

Rogers, E., and R. Agarwala-Rogers. 1976. *Communication in organizations.* New York: Free Press.

Schall, M. S. 1983. A communication rules approach to organizational culture. *Administrative Science Quarterly* 28(4): 557–581.

Scott, C. R., S. R. Corman, and G. Cheney. 1998. Development of a structurational model of identification in the organization. *Communication Theory* 8(3): 298–336.

Shockley-Zalabak, P., and D. D. Morley. 1989. Adhering to organizational culture: What does it mean, why does it matter? *Group and Organization Studies* 14: 483–500.

Shockley-Zalabak, P., and D. D. Morley. 1994. Creating a culture: A longitudinal examination of the influence of management and employee values on communication rule stability and emergence. *Human Communication Research* 20(3): 334–355.

Smircich, L. 1983. Concepts of culture and organizational analysis. *Administrative Science Quarterly* 28: 339–358.

Smircich, L., and M. Calás. 1987. Organizational culture: A critical assessment. In *Handbook of organizational communication,* eds. F. Jablin, L. Putnam, K. Roberts, and L. Porter, 228–257. Newbury Park, CA: Sage.

Stohl, C. 2001. Globalizing organizational communication. In *The new handbook of organizational communication: Advances in theory, research, and methods,* eds. F. M. Jablin and L. L. Putnam, 323–375. Thousand Oaks, CA: Sage.

Tangirala, S., and R. Ramanujam. 2008. Exploring nonlinearity in employee voice: The effects of personal control and organizational identification. *Academy of Management Journal* 51: 1189–1203.

Taylor, J. R. 2009. Organizing from the bottom up? Reflections on the constitution of organization in communication. In *Building theories of organization: The constitutive role of communication,* eds. L. Putnam and A. Nicotera, 153–186. New York: Routledge.

Tolbert, P., and L. Zucker. 1996. The institutionalization of institutional theory. In *Handbook of organization studies,* eds. S. Clegg, C. Hardy, and W. Nord, 175–190. Thousand Oaks, CA: Sage.

Tompkins, P., and G. Cheney. 1982. *Toward a theory of unobtrusive control in contemporary organizations.* Paper presented at the Speech Communication Association Convention, November, Louisville, KY.

Tompkins, P., and G. Cheney. 1983a. Account analysis of organizations: Decision making and identification. In *Communication and organizations: An interpretive approach,* eds. L. Putnam and M. Pacanowsky, 123–146. Beverly Hills, CA: Sage.

Tompkins, P., and G. Cheney. 1983b. Communication and unobtrusive control in contemporary organizations. In *Organizational communication: Traditional themes and new directions,* eds. R. D. McPhee and P. K. Tompkins, 179–210. Beverly Hills, CA: Sage.

Van Maanen, J., and E. Schein. 1979. Toward a theory of organizational socialization. In *Research on organizational behavior,* eds. B. M. Straw and L. L. Cummings, 209–264. Greenwich, CT: JAI Press.

Weick, K. 1979. *The social psychology of organizing,* 2nd ed. Reading, MA: Addison-Wesley.

Ziegler, J. 2007. The story behind an organizational list: A genealogy of wildland firefighters' 10 standard fire orders. *Communication Monographs* 74: 415–442. ∎

Communication Implications of Major Organizational Theories

DEVELOPING COMPETENCIES THROUGH ...

KNOWLEDGE   Describing Scientific Management theories for organizations
Describing Human Behavior theories for organizations
Describing Integrated Perspectives theories for organizations
Describing Postmodern, Critical, and Feminist theories for organizations

SENSITIVITY   Awareness of communication implications of Scientific Management theories
Awareness of communication implications of Human Behavior theories
Awareness of communication implications of Integrated Perspectives theories
Awareness of communication implications of Postmodern, Critical, and Feminist Perspectives

SKILLS   Applying theory to familiar organizations
Practicing analysis capabilities

VALUES   Understanding Scientific Management, Human Behavior, Integrated Perspectives, and Postmodern, Critical, and Feminist Perspectives in contemporary organizations
Clarifying the importance of values in organizations

▶ THE DAVIS INSTRUMENT COMPANY'S MANUFACTURING CRISIS

Pam Martin was not surprised that the three supervisors in her section were disagreeing about how to train on the new MCF system. Joan, Henry, and Frank rarely agreed on how to solve section problems. Even though Pam had been their manager for over two years and knew each of them to be highly competent, the three seemed to view their work at Davis very differently. The problem for today's staff meeting was no exception. The new MCF system was being installed throughout all Davis Instrument Company's manufacturing areas to computer-automate and control assembly work previously done by highly skilled workers. The system would not replace any existing employees but would require training on new machines and computer controls. Over time, productivity would be expected to increase, and those employees who had early training on the system would be in positions for rapid advancement. All three of Pam's employees had supported acquiring the new system and thought that it was in the best long-term interests of Davis, but Joan, Henry, and Frank did not agree on how to select employees for training on the MCF and how to restructure work teams to implement the new process.

Joan argued Pam and the supervisors should just decide. After all, early training on the system should fit the best workers with the highest aptitudes for computers to the new jobs. Yes, of course that meant that other good workers would not have as much chance for advancement, but tough decisions are what management gets paid to make. Joan contended the supervisors were in the best position to judge how to restructure the work teams. She proposed that the supervisors draw up a list of new job assignments, announce them to the group, and develop a timetable for system implementation.

Henry strongly disagreed. He voiced concern that his work team was worried about the new assignments. Henry believed that the affected workers should have some say in the assignment decisions. He supported letting each work team give their supervisors a plan for reassignment that the supervisors would then use for final decisions. He contended individuals were more likely to be motivated and accept the changes willingly if they had a part in determining how the changes were to be implemented.

Frank thought both Joan and Henry represented extreme positions that really did not serve the best interests of Davis. He proposed the three supervisors draw up overall criteria for the new positions and the job assignments needed for each work team. They should then present the reorganization plan to their work teams and have individual meetings with each worker to determine interest and skill fit for each of the new positions. Frank agreed with Joan that some tough decisions about particular individuals would have to be made. He also agreed with Henry that better motivation would result if each individual had some input about the future assignment.

Pam knew all three wanted the project to succeed. The question was how to get Joan, Henry, and Frank to agree on an approach.

1. Joan, Henry, and Frank are all competent supervisors. What accounts for their differences?
2. Is it possible they have different types of people in their work teams?
3. Can you describe how each of the three views the role of supervisor?
4. How do you think they view their work groups?
5. Do they have different theories of how organizations work? ■

INTRODUCTION

Joan, Henry, and Frank have different views about how organizations should operate. They all agree the MCF system is a needed change but disagree about how that change should be made. Their disagreement can be traced, at least in part, to the different ways they view workers and organizations.

In Chapter 2 we established three major perspectives for studying organizational communication: the Functional tradition, the Meaning-Centered approach, and Emerging Perspectives. In this chapter we identify and describe major organizational theories developed in fields others than communication and evaluate their communication implications. We use the communication perspectives from Chapter 2 for our evaluation. We look at how researchers describe the ways in which organizations should work, what types of assumptions are made about people in organizations, and what these descriptions and assumptions mean for organizational communication.

We examine four major perspectives or schools of organizational thought: the Scientific Management, Human Behavior, Integrated Perspectives, and Postmodern, Critical, and Feminist Perspectives schools. The four can be distinguished from one another by the questions researchers representing each viewpoint ask about organizations. Theorists representing the Scientific Management school ask questions about how organizations should be designed, how workers can be trained for maximum efficiency, how the chain of command works, and how division of labor should be determined.

Human Behavior theorists are concerned about the influence of individuals in organizations, what motivates workers, and how motivation affects the organization. These theorists believe organizational design and structure reflect basic assumptions about human behavior. They describe organizational relationships and people as resources. Human Behavior approaches are frequently discussed as human relation and human resource theories.

The development of what we call the Integrated Perspectives school can be traced to criticisms of Scientific Management and Human Behavior approaches. In the Integrated Perspectives approach, researchers ask questions about how structure, technology, and people relate to their environments. They are concerned with relationships among organizational design, employee motivation, communication participation, and organizational values, because these factors relate to the organization's ability to function in its environment. In some respects, the Integrated Perspectives approach reflects a merger of much of the thinking developed by Scientific Management and Human Behavior researchers. Finally, Postmodern, Critical, and Feminist Perspectives present a critique of power and domination in organizations, and of rationality as described by the Scientific Management perspective, and seek to examine the privilege of certain organizational members and the marginalization of others.

This chapter contributes to *knowledge* competencies by describing major organizational theories representing Scientific Management, Human Behavior, Integrated, and Postmodern, Critical, and Feminist Perspectives. We foster *sensitivity* competencies by examining communication implications found in theory. We develop analysis *skills* by combining knowledge and sensitivity competencies for application to familiar organizations and case studies. Finally, knowledge, sensitivity, and skill competencies influence *values* through evaluation of Scientific Management, Human Behavior, Integrated, and Postmodern, Critical, and Feminist Perspectives theories in contemporary organizations and by examining the importance of values for successful organizations. (The contributions of numerous individuals are used to describe the various theoretical perspectives in this chapter. Birth and death years for some of these individuals are provided to help you develop a time perspective for their work. When no dates are provided, you can assume the individuals referenced are current scholars.)

THE SCIENTIFIC MANAGEMENT SCHOOL

In his classic work *Principles of Scientific Management* (1913), Frederick Taylor described the Scientific Management school when he attempted to convince readers the inefficiency in most organizations is caused by a lack of systematic management and that "the best management is a true science, resting upon clearly defined laws, rules, and principles, as a foundation." This foundation, from the Scientific Management point of view, rested on "scientifically" designed organizations characterized by carefully developed chains of command and efficient division of labor.

Three men—Frederick Taylor, Henri Fayol, and Max Weber—were largely responsible for developing the major concepts of the Scientific Management approach. All three were contemporaries living and writing during a period from the middle of the nineteenth century to World War I. The approaches of Taylor, Fayol, and Weber are used to describe the **Scientific Management Perspective**.

Scientific Management Perspective ■ Theoretical approach to organizations that emphasizes organizational design, worker training for efficiency, chains of command, and division of labor. The perspective rests on the assumption that work and organizations can be rationally or "scientifically" designed and developed.

Principles and Basic Activities for Scientific Management

Frederick Taylor (1856–1915) is often referred to as the father of Scientific Management. Taylor's work experience, ranging from common laborer to chief engineer, served as the basis for the development of the four essential elements he viewed as the foundation of scientific management: (1) careful selection of workers, (2) inducing and training workers by the scientific method, (3) equal division of work between management and workers, and (4) discovering the scientific method for tasks and jobs.

Taylor (1913) held management responsible for devising the scientific method of work. He contended allowing workers to determine how tasks should be performed fostered inefficiency. Furthermore, he believed management is responsible for identifying "one best way" to perform tasks and that management should be exacting in teaching workers this scientific method for task performance. Taylor believed close contact between management and workers would eliminate the necessity for peer communication and what he called "soldiering," the unhealthy influence of the peer group.

Time and motion ■ Technique for determining the efficiency of production through work observation and time measurements; used to develop work standards that can be measured for efficiency.

Taylor is famous for his introduction in industry of the **time and motion** study. Taylor believed if tasks were scientifically designed and workers extensively trained, the efficiency of production could be determined by timing the amount of work (motion) performed by individuals and teams. His "one best method" of task design was intended to produce the adoption of work standards that could be measured to increase efficiency and overall productivity.

Taylor believed scientific management could be accomplished only with a well-defined chain of command and very specific division of labor. He held management responsible for developing the chain of command and organizing a division of labor based on well-defined work standards and measurement of standards to increase efficiency. Taylor's concepts were extremely influential in the early 1900s and continue to influence how we design organizations, establish performance standards, and measure work efficiency today.

Principles of Management

Henri Fayol (1841–1925) is credited with the first known attempt to describe broad principles of management for the organization and conduct of business. A French mining engineer, Fayol spent his working career as an engineer and later managing director of Comambault, a floundering mining company before Fayol assumed leadership. Fayol enjoyed enormous success as director of Comambault and was widely credited with turning a financially troubled company into a stable and thriving institution. Fayol founded the Center for Administrative Studies and, as a leading industrialist, attempted to influence the French government to apply his principles of administration. His early papers on general administrative theory became the influential text *General and Industrial Management,* first published in 1916.

In *General and Industrial Management* (1949), Fayol proposed fourteen principles of administration or management that he viewed as essential for effective organization. Management was responsible for developing well-defined assignments for workers. Fayol placed responsibility for the exercise of *authority* with management. He also emphasized a difference between authority as a result of job title versus what he called "personal" authority, authority based on intelligence, experience, moral worth, ability to lead, and past service. Although he did not describe it as such, Fayol recognized the importance of what is now called credibility in leadership.

Fayol's principle of *unity of command* carried specific recommendations for communication. He contended orders should come from only one superior and that a bypass of the chain of command would be a source of problems. He generally believed messages should move from supervisors to subordinates following the formal organizational chart. Fayol described the *scalar chain* as the movement of messages both vertically and horizontally throughout the organization. In fact, his discussion of the scalar chain is the only known treatment of horizontal communication found in organizational literature until the writings of Chester Barnard in 1938. Fayol defined the scalar chain as "the chain of superiors ranging from the ultimate authority to the lowest ranks. The line of authority is the route followed— via every link in the chain—by all communications which start from or go to the ultimate authority." Fayol described the chain as carrying messages in vertical directions. As such, the chain would have an equal capacity to carry messages vertically, both downward and upward. Fayol admitted that at times the chain required too much time for messages to travel effectively through all the links. He suggested that when the necessity for rapid message exchange occurred, it would be advisable to use a "gang plank" whereby peers communicated directly without regard to the scalar chain. This "gang plank" has become known in organization and communication literature as **Fayol's bridge.**

Fayol's bridge ■ Horizontal communication between peers.

Fayol also valued what he called *equity,* or a combination of kindliness and justice toward all. He viewed equity as necessary to encourage workers to carry out duties with devotion and loyalty. Another principle of administration Fayol emphasized was *initiative,* the ability to think through and execute plans. He considered the manager who permitted the exercise of initiative within a work group to be superior to the one who could not.

Fayol's concept of *esprit de corps* was based on his belief that the strongest organization exhibited union of purpose. Fayol suggested that esprit de corps could be achieved by implementing his principle of unity of command. In advising managers about establishing esprit de corps, he warned against dividing and ruling and the abuse of written communication. Fayol suggested that when giving an order that required explanation, "usually it is simpler and quicker to do so verbally than in writing. Besides, it is well known that differences and misunderstandings which a conversation could clear up, grow more bitter in writing."

In addition to his principles of administration, Fayol identified five basic activities of management. These activities—planning, organizing, commanding, coordinating, and controlling—encompassed all his principles of administration and served as a summary of Fayol's view of the overall responsibility of management.

Planning was described by Fayol as the development of operational strategies for the organization and the forecasting of future needs. Organizing was the use of people and materials to implement the organizational plan or goals. Commanding was the management function of obtaining maximum or optimum return for the organization from human and material resources. Coordinating was the function of integrating the efforts of all organizational members. Finally, controlling required management to establish how closely to its plan the organization was operating. Although Fayol wrote early in the 1900s, his activities of management and principles of administration continue to receive extensive attention and are influential in the operation of contemporary organizations.

Principles of Bureaucracy

Max Weber (1864–1920), a German sociologist, is frequently referred to as the father of **bureaucracy**. Heavily influenced by socialist philosophy, Weber developed his theory of bureaucracy as a response to the abuses of authority he believed to be present in early patrimonial (advancement by inheritance) systems. To Weber, the bureaucratic model for organizations should be based on authority relationships that emphasize depersonalization and task competence.

Bureaucracy ■ Organizations based on formalized rules, regulations, and procedures, which make authority rational as opposed to charismatic or traditional.

Weber (1947) identified three types of authority: charismatic, traditional, and bureaucratic. Charismatic authority is based on the specific characteristics of the person exerting authority. Personal attributes of the individual inspire others to follow. This authority is nonstructural (does not go with specific jobs) and usually nontransferable from person to person. In other words, charismatic authority is individually based, and when the charismatic leader leaves the organization, the authority or ability to influence leaves with him or her. Weber believed charismatic authority contributed to unstable organizations and disorderly transition of power from one person to another.

Traditional authority, according to Weber, is associated with the customs of a group or society. Although generally more stable than charismatic authority, traditional authority passes from individual to individual based on custom or tradition rather than ability or task competence. A family-owned company, for example, traditionally remains in the family from one generation to another, regardless of the abilities of others who might want to head the organization. Outsiders are simply not members of the family.

Weber believed bureaucratic authority represented the ideal for organizations. Bureaucratic authority was to rest on formalized rules, regulations, and procedures that made authority "rational-legal," not based on personal charisma or tradition.

Bureaucratic leaders were to be selected according to rules and regulations designed to promote the most competent for the particular job. This ideal bureaucracy, with its rational-legal authority mode, was designed to counteract nepotism, favoritism, and unbalanced decision making. As did Taylor and Fayol, Weber called for division of labor and for task specialization. He supported a formal **chain of command** and hierarchical structure. Impersonality in interpersonal relations was valued, and employment selection and promotion were to be based on competence.

> **Chain of command** ■ Formal authority and reporting structure of an organization.

Weber's ideal bureaucracy can be described as having a hierarchy of authority with a scalar chain of command. This chain of command would be organized according to task specialization and should represent division of labor appropriate to the required tasks. Also, the chain of command should operate with standardized rules and procedures designed to emphasize "rational" decision making and task competence. The rules and procedures of the bureaucracy should emphasize the employment of qualified personnel, not necessarily those who have family or personal connections or whom tradition might select, but personnel with the best task competencies for a particular job. To secure qualified personnel, detailed definitions of job expectations and responsibilities would have to be developed in accordance with the rules and procedures of the organization. Communication in the bureaucratic system should be formal and follow the chain of command. According to Weber, the ideal bureaucracy should place primary emphasis on the goals of the organization and put individual interests secondary to organizational productivity.

Communication Implications of Scientific Management Theories in Contemporary Organizations

Communication, from the Scientific Management point of view, was to be a tool of management designed to facilitate task completion and as such was to operate as one of many organizational variables. Communication activities were to be specialized, as were tasks and jobs. Specifically, communication was required to train workers and give daily instructions concerning job requirements. Communication activities were to be formal, and interpersonal communication of a social or personal nature was to be discouraged, particularly among peers. Horizontal communication was to occur infrequently and only when following the chain of command was too time-consuming and cumbersome. Scientific Management theorists envisioned more messages flowing from supervisors to employees than from employees to supervisors. Status differences between managers and workers were to be encouraged and were believed essential for enforcing organizational rules and regulations.

By looking at the dates of the writings of Taylor, Fayol, and Weber, we may be tempted to believe that the Scientific Management viewpoint is outdated and provides limited usefulness in understanding today's organizations. Dates, however, can be misleading. A careful examination of most contemporary organizations reveals numerous Scientific Management principles still in operation. Think for a moment about the massive numbers of financial transactions processed and distributed by large organizations throughout the globe twenty-four hours per day seven days per week. Also think about globally distributed reservation centers, telephone service centers, and product help desks. Most are organized around very carefully defined task specialization with workers deviating from defined protocols only with supervisor permission. These massive organizations exhibit many of the characteristics of the Scientific Management Perspective.

The Davis Instrument Company from the beginning of this chapter is another example. Davis has a chain of command for its manufacturing units. Pam is a manager responsible for three supervisors, who in turn each direct a team of workers. Davis can be described as having a division of labor that is in the process of change because of the introduction of the new MCF system. This change will require extensive task instruction and the careful selection of the "best" workers for the new jobs. Davis holds management responsible for determining how the system is to be implemented. Furthermore, Joan exhibits a Scientific Management Perspective when she argues that Pam and the supervisors should decide about job assignments without worker input. She believes managers should be responsible for work design and for structuring their teams for maximum efficiency. Based on what we have learned about the principles of administration proposed by the Scientific Management theorists, Joan's proposal represents their views.

Local, state, and national governments have been organized with many of the principles from the Scientific Management school. Not only do these organizations have hierarchies and chains of command, but also the transfer of power is governed by rules and regulations similar to those proposed by Weber. Although votes for officials may be based on their personal charisma, the successful candidate assumes office only after following the prescribed election rules. Both state and federal civil services have detailed job descriptions for most positions, with promotions governed by rules and regulations designed to eliminate favoritism and emphasize overall ability. Obviously, one can argue with how well these principles work in actual practice, but their design is a distinct legacy from the Scientific Management theorists.

Think about your school from the Scientific Management viewpoint. Are scientific principles reflected in admission policies and the rules and regulations that govern the granting of degrees? How would you characterize the division of labor between students and teachers? Is there a chain of command? Do scientific principles influence communication? Attempt to characterize the effectiveness of the scientific principles you identify and extend your analysis to other organizations to which you belong. For most organizations, you will be able to identify at least some of the principles first described by Taylor, Fayol, and Weber.

THE HUMAN BEHAVIOR SCHOOL

The Human Behavior school shifts the emphasis from the structure of organizations, work design, and measurement to the interactions of individuals, their motivations, and their influence on organizational events. The **Human Behavior Perspective** assumes work is accomplished through people and emphasizes cooperation, participation, satisfaction, and interpersonal skills. Theorists representing this viewpoint

Human Behavior Perspective ■
Theories of organizations that emphasize the interactions of individuals, their motivations, and their influence on organizational events.

see organizational design and function as reflections of basic assumptions about human behavior.

Major Human Behavior Theories

Principles of Coordination   Mary Parker Follett (1868–1933) was ahead of her time in proclaiming productive organizations must be concerned with the desires and motivations of individuals and groups. An honor graduate of Radcliffe College, Parker Follett was not a businessperson in the usual sense but came to her interest in profit-making organizations from her work in political science, government, and social administration. A frequent lecturer in both Europe and the United States of America, Parker Follett is best known for her concern for the steady, ordered progress of human well-being. Years ahead of other theorists, Parker Follett characterized conflict as potentially constructive and described collective responsibility and integration as supportive of business excellence. Parker Follett is famous for her psychological foundations of the smoothly operating organization. Although less well known than Scientific Management theorists, Parker Follett, in her shift to the psychological and motivational processes of workers, made significant contributions to the emergence of behavior theories for understanding organizational life.

The Hawthorne Effect   Elton Mayo (1880–1949) did not expect to be credited with beginning the Human Behavior point of view. As an influential Harvard professor, he was interested in expanding the understanding of the work environment as described by Frederick Taylor. When the famous Hawthorne studies began, Mayo experimented with the alteration of physical working conditions to increase productivity.

The Chicago Hawthorne plant of the Western Electric Company was the site of the research. In 1927, Mayo led a research team from the Harvard Graduate School of Business Administration in a series of experimental studies designed to improve the physical working environment for increased productivity. Management at the Hawthorne plant was aware that severe dissatisfaction existed among workers, and previous efforts by efficiency experts had failed both to reduce tension and to increase productivity. Mayo and his colleagues began to experiment with altering physical conditions to determine a combination of conditions that would increase productivity. They worked with factors such as lighting, noise, incentive pay, and heating. As the studies progressed, they found little support for the expected relationship between improved working conditions and improved productivity. They became aware that other unexpected factors were interacting with physical factors to influence work output. During their study of changes in lighting intensity, Mayo and his colleagues observed that work output increased when lighting intensity increased. That was a result that could be interpreted in terms of Taylor and the Scientific Management viewpoint. Yet they also observed that work output increased when they decreased lighting intensity. That result ran counter to not only Taylor but also any previously established principles of Scientific Management. In fact, output increased no matter how the physical variables changed. Mayo and his colleagues (1945) came to understand that a powerful and previously unrecognized influence in the experimental setting was the attention the researchers were paying to the workers. The attention encouraged a group norm that emphasized increased production no matter how the researchers altered the physical environment. This effect, widely known as the **Hawthorne effect,** was the first documentation in industrial psychological research of the importance of human interaction and morale for productivity. The Hawthorne studies became the first organized attempts to understand the individual worker as key to the overall production process. As a result of the Hawthorne research, production could no longer be viewed as solely dependent on formal job and organizational design.

Hawthorne effect ■ Group norms that influence productivity apart from the physical production environment.

Theory X–Theory Y ■ McGregor's description of management assumptions about workers. Theory X characterizes assumptions underlying Scientific Management theory, and Theory Y is associated with assumptions common to Human Behavior perspectives. Theory X managers assume that workers dislike work and will avoid responsible labor. Theory Y managers believe that workers can be self-directed and self-controlled.

Theory X and Theory Y In his famous work *The Human Side of Enterprise* (1960), Douglas McGregor (1906–1964) proposed his **Theory X–Theory Y** concept as a way to distinguish between the Scientific Management and Human Behavior Perspectives. A former president of Antioch College and a Massachusetts Institute of Technology professor of management, McGregor was interested in the basic assumptions about human nature inherent in both scientific and humanistic theories of management and organization.

McGregor presented Theory X as a summation of the assumptions about human nature made by those favoring the Scientific Management ideas of Taylor, Fayol, and Weber. McGregor believed hierarchical structure, management control of influence and decision making, close supervision, and performance measurement were based on assumptions about how to motivate human behavior.

Although McGregor believed Theory X accurately characterized the assumptions underlying Scientific Management theory, he doubted these assumptions provided the best evidence of how to motivate workers, contribute to employee satisfaction, or stimulate high levels of productivity. Building on the work of Mayo and others, he proposed Theory Y as an alternative to Theory X and as a way to understand individual motivation and interaction within organizations (see Figure 3.1).

McGregor has been criticized for what some have called a polarized either/or approach to human nature. McGregor responded that Theory X and Theory Y are assumptions that may be better understood as ranges of behaviors from X to Y. Managers, as such, can draw on both sets of assumptions, depending on the situation and specific people involved.

McGregor and also Rensis Likert (discussed below) are sometimes associated with both the Human Behavior and Human Relations Perspectives. Although similar in most respects, Human Relations views extend the focus beyond the specific behaviors of workers to evaluate how the entire organization can encourage the productive and effective use of people as resources, thereby supporting organizational productivity.

Participative Management As a professor of sociology and psychology and director of the Institute of Social Research at the University of Michigan, Rensis Likert

Theory X Assumptions	Theory Y Assumptions
1. People dislike work and will avoid work when possible.	1. People view work as being as natural as play.
2. Workers are not ambitious and prefer direction.	2. Workers are ambitious and prefer self-direction.
3. Workers avoid responsibility and are not concerned with organizational needs.	3. Workers seek responsibility and feel rewarded through their achievements.
4. Workers must be directed and threatened with punishment to achieve organizational productivity.	4. Workers are self-motivated and require little direct supervision.
5. Workers are not highly intelligent or capable of organizational creativity.	5. Workers are creative and capable of organizational creativity.
6. Organizations have difficulty in using human resources.	6. Organizations have difficulty in using human resources.

FIGURE 3.1
Douglas McGregor's Theory X and Theory Y

(1903–1981) conducted extensive research to determine how management differed between successful and less successful organizations. His classic work, *New Patterns of Management* (1961), advanced his theory of **participative management** based on comparisons between productive and less productive work groups.

Likert, in *New Patterns of Management,* set forth a new theory—participative management—that rejected many of the assumptions on which Scientific Management was founded. His employee-centered management was based on effectively functioning groups linked together structurally throughout the entire organization. In other words, Likert proposed the management process should depend on participative groups formed to have overlapping individual membership among groups. Figure 3.2 illustrates how an organizational chart using the Likert concept might look.

Participative management ■ Likert's theory of employee-centered management based on effectively functioning groups linked together structurally throughout the organization.

Likert supported his participative management theory with extensive research in high- and low-production situations. He believed proper understanding of the differences or variability in human performance could help build productive organizations. Taylor had interpreted variability in performance as a need to establish specific procedures and production standards; Likert's interpretation called for an increase in participation by organizational members at all levels.

In an attempt to demonstrate the importance of participative management, Likert offered an extensive comparative analysis of management systems ranging from highly authoritative systems to the ideal of participative management. In highly authoritative systems, management closely controls and directs work with little reliance on workers for problem solving. A general atmosphere of distrust discourages free-flowing communication. In more benevolent authoritative

(The arrows indicate the linking pin function.)

FIGURE 3.2
Likert's Linking Pin Concept

R. Likert, *New Patterns of Management,* 1961, p. 113. Reproduced with permission of The McGraw-Hill Companies.

systems hierarchical management control exists, but some trust and confidence are placed in workers. Likert also described consultative systems where management actively seeks worker input but retains control of important decisions. Finally, Likert proposes the ideal of participative management, which he describes as trust between management and employees and by decisions being made throughout the organization. Accurate communication flows in all directions, and people are motivated because of their participation in organizational events and in shaping their own futures. Goal setting, as well as appraisal of how well goals are being met and the overall effectiveness of the organization, takes place at all organizational levels.

Likert's participative management system was put into practice through a structure of interlocking groups, with members having multiple group memberships. These multiple group memberships provided links among groups, or what is now known as the famous "linking pin" function. This system of organization underscored Likert's commitment to broad participation at all organizational levels. Likert (1961), in describing the benefits of linked groups, predicted "fuller and more candid communication throughout the organization—upward, downward, and between peers." In sum, Likert's concept of participative management rested on his contention that the supportive atmosphere of the effective group promoted creativity, motivated people to use the communication process as both senders and receivers, and exerted more influence on leadership than in other types of systems.

Communication Implications of Human Behavior Theories in Contemporary Organizations

Effective communication was a cornerstone of the Human Behavior Perspective. Management was to trust employees, and employees were to feel free to discuss job-related concerns with their supervisors. Peer-group interaction was not only recognized but was also viewed as a potentially positive influence for productivity. The human behavior theorists recognized both formal and informal communication networks carrying task and social support messages. Interactions at all levels were expected to be extensive and friendly, with substantial cooperation throughout the organization. From the Human Behavior viewpoint, communication was vital to the use of human resources and good organizational decision making.

Most contemporary organizations include not only Scientific Management ideas but also much of the thinking generated from the Human Behavior theorists. The Davis Instrument Company is an example. Davis is structured according to many of the principles of Scientific Management, but Davis also exhibits the influence of Parker Follett, Mayo, McGregor, and Likert. Pam Martin makes decisions about the new MCF system with participation from her employees. She uses a group process to address issues and solve problems. Earlier we identified Joan as articulating a Scientific Management approach. We can expand our analysis and describe Henry as representing the Human Behavior viewpoint when he calls for extensive involvement from the various work teams in determining their new training and job assignments. Both Henry and Frank reflect Theory Y assumptions about people when they contend workers are more motivated when involved in decisions that directly affect them. In fact, when we thoughtfully analyze the Davis case, it is possible to conclude that both Scientific Management and Human Behavior ideas are in evidence and that both will contribute to the success or failure of the new MCF system.

Most contemporary organizations are similar to Davis in their combined usage of Scientific Management and Human Behavior ideas. Committees, project teams, and work units all are examples of the use made of groups in modern organizations. Training for managers and supervisors emphasizes developing interpersonal skills for working effectively with employees. New employees attend orientations designed to help them understand and become a part of the organization. Awards honor a variety of creative contributions, and profit-sharing and merit-pay plans attest to the importance of employee involvement for organizational success. These examples and many others exist side by side in today's organizations with hierarchical structures, division of labor, chains of command, and final management responsibility in decision making.

Earlier you described your school from a Scientific Management point of view. Now think about that same organization from the Human Behavior viewpoint. What assumptions are made about the basic nature of students? Is there an honor code for academic achievement, or are exams tightly monitored and cheating vigorously punished? Is creativity expected from students? Is there a supportive atmosphere that contributes to effective communication among students and with teachers? Attempt to characterize your school in terms of Theory X and Theory Y. Does one work better than the other? If so, why? If not, how do they work in combination? Finally, describe which of the Human Behavior concepts you believe to be the most influential for effective communication.

INTEGRATED PERSPECTIVES VIEWPOINTS

Both Scientific Management and Human Behavior approaches have been criticized for their failure to integrate organizational structure, technology, and people with the larger environment in which organizations exist. The Scientific Management theorists concentrated on organizational structure and work design with little attention to people and organizational environments. The Human Behavior theorists were concerned with people but also tended to ignore influences beyond organizational

Integrated Perspectives ■ Theories that attempt to explain how people, technologies, and environments integrate to influence goal-directed behavior.

boundaries. In reaction to these criticisms, a number of organizational researchers have developed **Integrated Perspectives** viewpoints. These theorists attempt to explain how people, technologies, and environments integrate to influence all that happens in organizations.

Process and Environmental Approaches

Process and environmental approaches to organizational theory attempt to describe how complex processes such as decision making influence the internal operation of organizations and are influenced by external environments. Researchers using these perspectives seek to explain how human and technical systems interact with the broader environments in which organizations operate and in so doing seek to test basic assumptions from both Scientific Management and Human Behavior viewpoints. To describe process and environmental approaches, we discuss the decision-making approach of Herbert Simon; sociotechnical integration as described by Eric Trist and Kenneth Bamforth; contingency theory as introduced by Joan Woodward, Paul Lawrence, and Jay Lorsch; and systems theory as explained by Daniel Katz and Robert Kahn. Finally, we explore what is described as the new organization science and learning organizations using the work of Margaret Wheatley, Peter Senge, Gareth Morgan, and others.

Decision-Making Approach Herbert Simon (1916–2001) offered a description of organizations that differed from both the Scientific Management and Human Behavior viewpoints. Simon (1957) proclaimed organizational behavior is a com-

Decision-making approach ■ Simon's concept that organizational behavior is a complex network of decisions, with decision-making processes influencing the behavior of the entire organization.

plex network of decisions with decision-making processes influencing the behavior of the entire organization. According to Simon, organizations can be understood in terms of what types of decisions are made at various organizational levels and with what types of information. As such, Simon viewed the **decision-making approach** as the essential organizational process.

Bounded rationality ■ Assumption that people intend to be rational, but with limited information-processing capacity, human decision making is based on selective perception and therefore exhibits "limited" rationality.

Understanding the limitations of human decision making was important to Simon's model. Along with Richard Cyert and James March (Cyert and March, 1963), Simon introduced the concept of **bounded rationality** as a way to understand information processing and decision making. Specifically, the concept of bounded rationality assumed people intend to be rational, but with limited information-processing capacity, human decision making is based on selective perception and therefore exhibits "limited" rationality. Simon argued individuals often make organizational decisions while realizing their decisions are based on partial information. Simon called this process "satisficing," or the making of decisions with partial information in the hope the decision will be good enough, if not the best.

Sociotechnical Integration   The concept of **sociotechnical integration** rested on two assumptions first described by Eric Trist (1911–1993) and his student Kenneth Bamforth[1] (1951) as a result of their work with a British coal-mining operation: (1) organizational production is optimized through optimizing social and technical systems, and (2) a constant interchange exists between the work system and the broader environment.

Sociotechnical integration ■ Theoretical attempt to balance human social-psychological needs with organizational goals; an assumption that organizational production is optimized through optimizing social and technical systems.

The sociotechnical approach attempted to balance human social-psychological needs with organizational goals. Communication in the sociotechnical approach related to work, to the needs of the environment, and to the personal needs of workers. Trist and Bamforth tested the sociotechnical concept in a British coal-mining operation. Workers were trained to rotate as necessary through all the tasks required by new machines. This cross-training was designed to introduce variety and interest into the work environment. Also, each work team was permitted to set its own rate of production and was responsible for handling its own problems and conflicts. The output of these autonomous groups was compared with groups with more traditional and "scientifically" designed assignments. In the Trist and Bamforth experiment, the sociotechnical groups outperformed their scientific group counterparts by approximately 34 percent, or 1.8 tons of coal per shift.

These experiments led Trist and Bamforth to conclude meaning in work could be established through group assignments that permit individuals to be included in entire task cycles rather than work on isolated parts of a job. The autonomy of groups in setting their own standards and making decisions about their own problems could give individuals a sense of self-determination that closer supervision and control could not achieve. This emphasis on group-set goals and responsibilities could contribute to a solidarity of purpose that could help integrate individual and organizational goals. This integration would be productive for both individuals and organizations. This work has become an important foundation for team-based organizations discussed later in our text.

Contingency Theory   The **contingency theory** began with research by Joan Woodward (1916–1971) on one hundred British manufacturing firms in an effort to develop a list of characteristics that would indicate differences in organizational structure. Woodward's (1965) classification included organizations with little technological complexity and those with extensive reliance on complicated technologies. Her findings relating differences in technology to differences in organizational

Contingency theory ■ Approach that rejects the "one best way" to organize in favor of the view that no specific set of prescriptions is appropriate for all organizations. As such, an organization must adapt to changing circumstances and the needs of individuals and the environment in which the organization operates.

---

[1]Birth date unknown.

structure became the foundation of modern contingency theory, or the realization that differences in organizations are due to differences in goals and environments.

Contingency theory rejects the "one best way" to organize as described by Scientific Management's theorists. Contingency theory also finds the Human Behavior approach lacking an explanation of the complex relationships among units within the organization and the larger environment in which the organization operates.

Paul Lawrence and Jay Lorsch (1969) described contingency theory as the establishment of internal organizational operations contingent or dependent on external environmental needs and individual needs. Lawrence and Lorsch viewed organizations as having three primary relationships that determine how organizations operate and respond to their environment. Specifically, organizations have what Lawrence and Lorsch called "interfaces" at the organization-to-environment, group-to-group, and individual-to-organization levels. They suggested organizational design and operation should be based on these three interfaces, which differ for all organizations.

Proponents of the contingency view suggest there is no specific set of prescriptions appropriate for all organizations. Organizations must adapt to changing circumstances and the needs of individuals and the environments in which the organizations operate. In other words, contingency theory suggests considerable judgment is required to understand effective organizational operation because that operation "all depends on the situation."

Systems theory ■ Describes organizations as made up of subsystems that take in materials and human resources, process materials and resources and yield a finished product to the larger environment.

The Systems Approach Closely related to contingency theory, **systems theory** grew in direct response to criticisms of both Scientific Management and Human Behavior philosophies. The systems approach emphasizes interaction with the larger environment. In systems theory, the organization takes in materials and human resources (inputs), processes materials and resources (throughputs), and yields finished products (outputs) to the larger environment. Along with inputs, throughputs, and outputs, the ideal system should have a self-corrective mechanism whereby feedback or inputs from the environment can be processed into adaptation of throughputs and, potentially, outputs. The system's self-corrective mechanism is called the system's cybernetic, which in the ideal system is the management team. In systems theory, the law of equifinality attests to the multiple-action courses possible for the achievement of a goal. Equifinality rejects the concept of a single course of action to reach a single goal.

Daniel Katz (1903–1998) and Robert Kahn (1918–1991) and other systems theorists advanced a principle of optimization, or looking for maximum output in return for minimum input. Maximum return for minimum input is affected by feedback from the environment and management's ability to adjust. Thus, systems may be described as open or closed, mechanistic or organic. An open system exchanges information with its larger environment. A closed system limits exchange with the environment and seeks to operate as a self-contained unit. Katz and Kahn (1966) related the closed organizational system to a closed thermodynamic system, contending they both will approach a condition of maximum entropy with no further possibility of useful work. The open system, on the other hand, fights entropy and seeks a dynamic equilibrium among input, throughput, and output. The open system exhibits the law of equifinality and has a sound self-corrective mechanism. The organic system is suited to change, whereas the mechanistic system functions best in stable conditions. The organic system compares favorably with descriptions of open systems, whereas the mechanistic system may be compared with closed systems.

Systems theory as described by Katz and Kahn is undergoing an important transformation brought about by rethinking the basic nature of systems and system relationships to the environment. These newer approaches emphasize how systems (entire organizations or parts of organizations) attempt to maintain themselves during ever-constant change. The approach asks questions about external environmental influences that are more complex than previously understood—not just the immediate competitive, economic, or social environment but global and political influences ranging from known to unknown environmental changes. The newer approaches also describe how systems can influence their larger complex environment. These approaches do not replace earlier systems theory descriptions but instead expand notions about the complexity of our ever-changing environment. They borrow language from the study of biology and physics in asking us to think in a more comprehensive way about influences for organizations and organizational influences in our larger environment. These approaches become especially relevant as we address global realities and rapid technological change. Gareth Morgan (1997), in his important book *Images of Organizations*, explained, "Traditional approaches to organization theory have been dominated by the idea that change originates in the environment. . . . The organization is typically viewed as an open system in constant interaction with its context, transforming inputs into outputs as a means of creating the conditions necessary for survival. Changes in the environment are viewed as presenting challenges to which the organization must respond" (p. 253). Morgan described the work of two Chilean scientists, Humberto Maturana and Francisco Varela, who are credited with describing **autopoiesis**, a new approach to systems theory. Morgan took an example from a biological organism to explain:

> **Autopoiesis** ■ Process describing each element in a system simultaneously combining the maintenance of itself with the maintenance of the other elements of the system.

> The bee as an organism constitutes a chain of self-referring physiological processes with their own circular organization and lives within a society of bees where relations are also circular. In turn, the relationship between the society of bees and the wider ecology is also circular. Eliminate the bees and the whole ecology will change, for the bee system is linked with the botanical system, which is linked with insect, animal, agricultural, human, and social systems. All these systems are self-referential and turn back on each other. A change in any one element can transform all the others. . . . An understanding of the autopoietic nature of systems requires that we understand how each element simultaneously combines the maintenance of itself with the maintenance of the others. (p. 254)

Management theorist Margaret Wheatley (1992) described autopoietic structures as each having a unique identity and a clear boundary, yet being merged with its environment.

Supporting a transformation in systems thinking, Wheatley used insights from quantum physics, self-organizing systems, and chaos theory to present a view of systems theory with new possibilities for connections and change. Wheatley argued, as do many physicists, that the relationships in the quantum world are not just interesting but all there is to reality.

This notion of complex, fluid, ever-changing relationships answers conceptual questions about influences for organizational behavior. We no longer have to attempt to decide whether the individual or the system is more influential; relationships continually shift and change depending on individuals and the moment. This notion of pervasive relationships—a relational universe—as described in quantum theory suggests we do not create reality but we evoke potentials that are already present. Wheatley (1992) identified this notion as closely related to Karl Weick's concept of enactment in organizations: how we participate in the creation of organizational realities. She further contended information is the creative energy both for organizations and the universe. This notion places organizational communication as a primary process for all organizational systems.

Learning Organizations   In addition to the descriptions of autopoiesis and increased system complexity, systems theory has been extended to the concept of designing organizations to learn in a brainlike way (Morgan, 1997). Frequently referred to as **learning organizations**, these organizations gain knowledge from continuous processes of information exchange between the organization and its environments. Chris Argyris of Harvard and Donald Schön (1930–1997) of the Massachusetts Institute of Technology (MIT) first brought the learning to learn concept to managerial attention. Peter Senge of MIT popularized the concept of the learning organization in his now-famous work *The Fifth Discipline* (1990).

Learning organizations ■
Organizations gaining knowledge from continuous processes of information exchange between the organization and its environments.

Senge (1990) provided five new "component technologies" that he claimed are gradually converging to innovate learning organizations. Senge contended the five disciplines must develop as an ensemble.

Senge's Five Disciplines:

1. *System thinking:* the ability to think about connections and patterns and to view systems as wholes, not individual parts of the patterns.
2. *Personal mastery:* developing special levels of proficiency. Personal mastery is the discipline of continually clarifying and deepening our personal vision, of focusing our energies, of developing patience, and of seeing reality objectively. As such, it is an essential cornerstone of the learning organization, the learning organization's spiritual foundation. An organization's commitment to and capacity for learning can be no greater than that of its members. The roots of this discipline lie in both Eastern and Western spiritual traditions and in secular traditions as well.
3. *Mental models:* deeply ingrained assumptions, generalizations, or even pictures or images that influence how we understand the world and how we take action.
4. *Building shared vision:* the capacity to hold a shared picture of the future we seek to create. When there is a genuine vision, people excel and learn, not because they are told to but because they want to.
5. *Team learning:* learning that starts with dialogue, the capacity of members of a team to suspend assumptions and enter into genuine "thinking together." The discipline of dialogue also involves learning how to recognize the patterns of interaction in teams that undermine learning.

Cultural Approaches

Cultural approaches to organizational theory describe how organizational members collectively interpret the organizational world around them to define the importance of organizational happenings. In other words, cultural approaches to organizational theory explain organizational behavior in terms of the influence of cultures that exist both internally and externally to the organization. Cultural research attempts to identify how a unique sense of the place (culture) contributes to individual behavior and organizational effectiveness. Cultural research focuses on how cultures form, whether cultures are "strong" or unified, how subcultures manifest themselves, and how organizational cultures respond to fragmentation. Organizational communication is central to most culture research, making cultural perspectives important for our study.

Cultural approaches ■ Theories that describe how organizational members collectively interpret the organizational world around them to define the importance of organizational happenings. Approaches to theory that explain organizational behavior in terms of the influence of cultures that exist both internally and externally to the organization.

Organizational Culture Formation Edgar Schein (1985b) defined organizational culture as "a pattern of basic assumptions—invented, discovered, or developed by a given group as it learns to cope with its problems of external adaptation and internal integration—that has worked well enough to be considered valid and, therefore, to be taught to new members as the correct way to perceive, think, and feel in relation to those problems." In support of this definition, Schein provides a model of culture with three distinct levels: (1) artifacts and creations, (2) values, and (3) basic assumptions. Artifacts and creations are the most visible level of culture, consisting of the physical and social environment created by organizational members. Artifacts and creations can be seen by members of the culture and by observers. Artifacts and creations include architecture, technology, furniture, dress, and a variety of written documents. Behaviors such as decision making, meetings, and networks also are included. The second level, values, refers to both individual and group preferences for the way things should be in the organization. Values are harder to observe, although relationships between values and behaviors have been established by a variety of scholars. Finally, Schein described as his third level basic assumptions. Basic assumptions are the core of what individuals believe to be true about the world and how it works. Basic assumptions form around humanity's relationship to nature, the nature of reality and truth, the nature of human nature, the nature of human activity, and the nature of human relationships.

Schein (1983) also provides a model of how organizational cultures begin. According to Schein, the history of new organizations suggests they share the following initial steps: (1) the founder (or founders) has an idea for a new enterprise; (2) a founding group is created with members who have initial consensus about the idea; (3) a founding group acts to bring structure and resources to the idea; and (4) the initial functioning of the group is based on the idea; that is, the group begins to develop a history. Schein suggested, "In this process the founder will have a major impact on how the group solves its external survival and internal integration problems. Because the founder had the original idea, he or she will typically have biases on how to get the idea fulfilled—biases based on previous cultural experiences and personality traits" (p. 17).

In later work, Schein (1985a) suggested the functions of culture differ by growth stages of organizations. During the birth and early growth stages of organizations, for example, the founder or family dominates the organization and culture functions to hold the organization together, emphasize socialization, and develop commitment. Organizational midlife is characterized by the spawning of subcultures and loss of key goals, values, and assumptions. Organizational maturity brings cultural constraint on innovation with an emphasis on preservation of the past.

The Strong Culture Perspective   Early culture studies placed an emphasis on what has been described as "strong or unified" cultures developed by leadership (management) in order to guide an organization to excellence. The concept suggests effective leaders identify values important for success and then literally build cultures reflective of those values. Joanne Martin and Peter Frost (1996) described these studies as representing an integration view in which "top managers could build such a culture by articulating a set of values and then reinforcing those values, again and again, with formal policies, informal norms, stories, rituals, and jargon. In time, and with consistency, those values would become shared—with enthusiasm—by all employees. This would set up a domino effect: higher commitment, greater productivity, and ultimately, more profits" (p. 602).

Two examples of the integration perspective illustrate the strong culture approach. First, Terrence Deal and Allen Kennedy, in their book *Corporate Cultures: The Rites and Rituals of Corporate Life* (1982), identified five basic elements of organizational culture: business environment, values, heroes, rites and rituals, and the cultural network. Each contributes to managing behavior and, according to Deal and Kennedy, "helps employees do their jobs a little better." Essentially, a strong culture contributes to managing the organization by spelling out in general terms how people are to behave while helping people feel better about what they do, enabling hard work and excellent productivity.

Deal and Kennedy (1982) suggested the business environment is "the single greatest influence in shaping a corporate culture." What companies do in their competitive environments shapes the reality of how organizations manage activity and whether they are successful. Values emerge that help individuals determine where the emphasis of their efforts should be placed. In other words, organizational values help people become dedicated to a cause, which in turn guides decisions about all types of behaviors. These strong values are not, however, without their dangers. Strong organizational values may limit change and encourage obsolescence when organizational values come in conflict with changing environments requiring new decisions and approaches. Regardless of whether their impact is positive or negative, values, according to Deal and Kennedy, are the core of corporate culture.

Deal and Kennedy (1982) contended heroes are the real live human successes who become role models for the culture's values. Stories and myths about the behaviors of heroes help organizational members determine what they have to do to succeed and what is valued by the organization. Rites and rituals also serve this function. Deal and Kennedy identified management rituals such as formal meetings in which rituals develop about the number held, the setting, the table's shape, who sits where, and who is in attendance. Recognition rituals, ranging from formal events honoring outstanding service to informal traditions, also identify what the organization holds to be important and help to integrate individual and organizational goals. Finally, Deal and Kennedy suggested informal organizational communication is the cultural network and as such is the only way to understand what is really going on. From the Deal and Kennedy perspective, culture is the organizational process that most contributes to shaping organizational outcomes. The communication of culture therefore both shapes behavior and reflects the operating reality of the organization.

Our second example comes from Thomas Peters and Robert Waterman in their best-seller *In Search of Excellence* (1982), in which they reported the results of their study of sixty-two successful representatives of U.S. industry. Among the organizations studied were Hewlett-Packard, Frito-Lay, Delta Airlines, McDonald's, Boeing, and numerous others selected because of their prestige in the business world, overall financial performance, industry position, and innovativeness as measured by their ability continually to bring new products and services to changing markets. As a result of their work, Peters and Waterman (1982) identified eight cultural themes, or strongly held values characterizing these excellent, innovative companies, as follows:

1. *A bias for action.* Excellent companies made decisions. They were analytical but not paralyzed by too much information. When they had a problem, they took action.
2. *Close to the customer.* Service, reliability, innovative products, and continual concern for customer needs were fundamentals for the excellent companies. The close-to-the-customer value also resulted in new product ideas and served as the basis for innovation.
3. *Autonomy and entrepreneurship.* Excellent companies wanted leaders in all types of organizational activity. They encouraged risk taking and innovation and gave people responsibility for their own ideas. People were not so tightly controlled as to lose creativity.
4. *Productivity through people.* Workers at all organizational levels were the source of quality and the source of productivity. Excellent companies fought against a we/they management/labor attitude.
5. *Hands-on, value-driven.* The basic philosophy and values of the organization contributed more to achievement than did any specific technology or material resource. Values were seen to influence behavior and were considered the core of excellence.
6. *Stick to the knitting.* Excellent companies stayed in the businesses they knew. They did not diversify beyond what they understood in terms of either technology and service or customers. They grew by doing what they did extremely well.
7. *Simple form, lean staff.* None of the excellent companies was run with complicated organizational structures. In fact, many of the top corporate staffs were running multi-billion-dollar organizations with fewer than a hundred people.
8. *Simultaneous loose-tight properties.* These companies were both centralized and decentralized. Autonomy and entrepreneurship were encouraged at all levels within the organizations. Decision making was often decentralized, yet core values were very centralized and rigidly supported.

The Subculture Perspective At the same time the strong culture perspective was gaining momentum, numerous researchers began to question the validity of the strong/unified culture approach, believing it to be an oversimplification of organizational life with too much emphasis on management and not enough emphasis on the experiences of people throughout the organization. Multiple cultures within organizations were identified and described as subcultures often reflective of cultural groups in society as a whole. Subcultures were found in occupational groupings both within and beyond a particular organization. For example, computer programmers, accountants, lawyers, teachers, and video producers might belong to a subculture in a given organization and also identify with the culture of their profession or occupation in general. Subcultures could be identified and associated with almost any type of difference in perception or situation such as status, seniority, gender, race, ethnicity, or even geographic location. Martin and Frost (1996) described the research that focused on subcultures as differentiation work. They suggest, "These studies have in common a willingness to acknowledge inconsistencies (i.e., attitudes versus behavior, formal policies versus actual practices, etc). They see consensus as occurring only within subcultural boundaries. They acknowledge conflicts of interest, for example, between top management and other employees or within a top management group."

The Fragmentation Perspective The last perspective we discuss is developing in some respects due to the ever-increasing complexity of understanding organizations. Just as systems theory is advancing in part due to globalization and the increasing use of sophisticated technology, cultural perspectives are informed by the rapidly changing nature of work and organizations. An individual entrepreneur works from a home office with clients around the globe. Large organizations partner on a new product while competing in other product lines. Few individuals expect to work for one organization throughout their work lives. Notions of change and flux are the norm, not the exception. Understanding culture from this perspective has been called the fragmentation approach. Martin and Frost (1996) explained:

> According to the advocates of the fragmentation view, the relationships among the manifestations of a culture are neither clearly consistent nor clearly inconsistent; instead, the relationships are complex, containing elements of contradiction and confusion. Similarly, consensus is not organization-wide nor is it specific to a given subculture. Lack of consistency, lack of consensus, and ambiguity are the hallmarks of a fragmentation view of culture. . . . Change is a constant flux, rather than an intermittent interruption in an otherwise stable state. Because change is largely triggered by the environment or other forces beyond an individual's control, fragmentation studies of change offer few guidelines for those who would normatively control the change process. (p. 609)

In other words, the fragmentation view suggests the strong culture and subculture views do not adequately explain the nature of change for most organizations and individuals. The fragmentation view sees issue-specific consensus more likely than the shared consensus in either strong cultures or subcultures.

Regardless of the perspective taken, culture is identified as central to understanding all types of organizational experiences with communication as the main process for cultural manifestations. Because of the centrality of communication to culture, we close this section on integrated perspectives with a sensemaking model, which in many respects could be applied to any of the perspectives we have discussed.

Sensemaking Model   The work of Karl Weick is an excellent example of what we mean by integrated perspectives. Many familiar with Weick's work would argue that he should be characterized as writing from a systems perspective, whereas others contend he more readily advances concepts aligned with culture studies. The discussion in Chapter 2 of his views of enactment of organizations carries a distinctively "systems" flavor. Here, however, we place his sensemaking model in the cultural perspectives section because of its focus on the intersection of simultaneous interpretation and action. Weick's provocative statement, "The outcome comes before the decision," helps us understand the dynamic nature of his sensemaking model, which includes authoring as well as interpretation. Weick (1995) explained:

> The process of sensemaking is intended to include the construction and bracketing of the textlike cues that are interpreted, as well as the revision of those interpretations based on action and its consequences. Sensemaking is about authoring as well as interpretation, creation as well as discovery. . . . A crucial property of sensemaking is that human situations are progressively clarified, but this clarification often works in reverse. It is less often the case that an outcome fulfills some prior definition of the situation, and more often the case that an outcome develops that prior definition. (pp. 8–11)

Weick referred to the central role an individual's own actions play in determining what is the "sense of situations." He argued it is a mistake to think that we make decisions in organizations according to well-developed plans. He proposes that we make decisions and then render them sensible by explaining the meaning of our decisions. Weick (1995, pp. 61–62) identified sensemaking as having seven distinguishing characteristics and provides a recipe for understanding each of the characteristics:

1. *Grounded in identity construction.* The recipe is a question about who I am as indicated by discovery of how and what I think.
2. *Retrospective.* To learn what I think, I look back over what I said earlier.
3. *Enactive of sensible environments.* I create the object to be seen and inspected when I say or do something.
4. *Social.* What I say and single out and conclude are determined by who socialized me and how I was socialized, as well as by the audience I anticipate will audit the conclusions I reach.
5. *Ongoing.* My talking is spread across time, competes for attention with other ongoing projects, and is reflected on after it is finished, which means that my interests may already have changed.
6. *Focused on and by extracted cues.* The "what" that I single out and embellish as the content of the thought is only a small portion of the utterance that becomes salient because of context and personal dispositions.

7. *Driven by plausibility rather than accuracy.* I need to know enough about what I think to get on with my projects, but no more, which means sufficiency and plausibility take precedence over accuracy.

Individual and organizational sensemaking activities illustrate the intersection of interpretation and action. Sensemaking can therefore be understood as part of the cultural web of the organization as well as a highly individual process. Weick (1995) related organizations and sensemaking processes: "Both organizations and sensemaking processes are cut from the same cloth. To organize is to impose order, counteract deviations, simplify, and connect, and the same holds true when people try to make sense."

Taken as a whole, these descriptions of cultural development, transmission, and sensemaking reflect basic assumptions about the dynamic nature of culture and its propensity to change across time.

Communication Implications of Integrated Perspectives in Contemporary Organizations

The Integrated Perspectives viewpoints present a diverse set of implications for organizational communication. The systems theorists all describe organizations with changing needs and environments, even though descriptions of the relationship to environments vary. Thus, the effectiveness of communication relates not only to what happens within the organization, but also to how the organization communicates with its environment, its customers, and community. The cultural approaches, on the other hand, are more specific about the importance of communication in carrying messages about the culture and influencing behavior through cultural expectations.

With the contributions of process and environmental theorists we talked about the importance of the external environment and began to merge much of the thinking from the Scientific Management and Human Behavior approaches. Also, with the advent of the cultural approaches, communication was described as the process through which shared realities are generated and through which values, identification, and socialization occur.

There are numerous examples of the importance of organizations adjusting to their external environments. Beginning in late 2008 and continuing today, many big U.S.A. financial institutions have ceased to exist while others are losing competitive position to foreign institutions. The widespread use of wireless networks has enabled countries in Africa and China, for example, to literally bypass hard-wired technologies, creating an unprecedented competitive advantage for manufacturing and other services previously dominated by U.S.A. and European companies. The back-to-basics emphasis in education has been in response to concerns students are not developing competencies needed for global environments. The list could go on. The contribution of Integrated Perspectives theorists in describing the need to acknowledge the influence of the external environment has improved our ability to think comprehensively about organizations and how people and technology relate to larger environments.

Concern for organizational culture is readily apparent in contemporary organizations. Organizations publish vision and mission statements, conduct training programs that identify the values of the organization, and hold annual events of special cultural significance. Schools have graduation ceremonies; sales organizations have annual awards banquets; and special traditions emerge to celebrate promotions, achievements, and a variety of other organizational events. Moreover, a record number of organizational members formally study the cultures of those globally dispersed individuals and organizations with whom they can expect to do business.

The significance of the Integrated Perspectives approaches can be seen in a return to the Davis Instrument Company's manufacturing changes. The introduction of the new MCF system is in response to market pressure to remain cost-competitive. The concern for how to reassign and train workers illustrates essential sociotechnical relationships among environmental needs for change, human needs during change, and the changing requirements of new technology. What happens next at Davis will depend on some factors not readily apparent in the case. What are the general expectations of the Davis workforce regarding change? What does the "culture" suggest is going to happen? The decisions Pam Martin's supervisors make will be accepted or resisted, at least in part, based on their cultural fit with the shared realities of Davis and with the organizational values held by Davis employees. To advise Pam Martin and the supervisors effectively, we would need to know more about how things really work at Davis.

Think for a moment about organizations with which you are familiar. How have they adjusted to their environments? Is your school state-funded or dependent on private revenue? For either case, think about environmental influences that school administrators must consider when planning programs and asking for monetary support. Now describe the shared values of your school. How are they communicated? Can you identify some of the rites and rituals that influence student identification and socialization? Where is consensus present and where is it fragmented? Finally, attempt to define what you would say to a new student about what it takes "to be successful around here."

POSTMODERN, CRITICAL, AND FEMINIST PERSPECTIVES

Although all the perspectives discussed describe power relationships within organizations and although Integrated Perspectives place considerable emphasis on the subjective and interpretive dynamics in organizations, little attention is paid to power as domination or the challenging of traditional hierarchical and patriarchal systems of authority. Postmodern, Critical, and Feminist organizational theories provide that critique and examine alternatives for organizational life.

Postmodern and Critical Perspectives focus on power and domination and on challenges to hierarchy, bureaucracy, and management control.

> **Postmodern and Critical Perspectives** ■ Theories that focus on power and domination and on challenges to hierarchy, bureaucracy, and management control.

Postmodern Perspectives Stewart Clegg, in his work *Modern Organizations* (1990), built on the concepts of French philosophers such as Jean-François Lyotard (1984) and Jean Baudrillard (1983), who describe the postmodern condition as highly ordered, technologically specialized, mass-mediated, and demanding of precision, speed, flexibility, and adaptability in individual performance. These continuous and often conflicting demands promote numerous constructions of reality, foster ambiguity, raise distrust of traditional authority, and stimulate alternative sensemaking. We focus on Clegg's description of the postmodern organization to assist our understanding of the ever-evolving ways in which we come to know organizational life.

Scientific Management, and to some extent the other organizational perspectives discussed, called for task specialization, mass consumption, and specialized jobs for which workers were thoroughly and completely trained. Clegg contended postmodernism rejects these concepts. Clegg characterized postmodern organizations as flexible structures needing workers with multiple skills who are capable of continual learning. Market niches replace mass consumption, and smaller is better if organizations are doing what they do best. Bureaucracy is replaced by workplace democracy in which all employees are valuable sources of decision making. Market needs are primary, and teams replace the emphasis on the individual contributor. Top-down management is made obsolete by self-managing teams, and quality is a part of all processes, not the "inspected-for-quality" mentality of the past. Management is a responsibility fulfilled at a point in time rather than a permanent occupation, and rewards are based more on groups or teams than on individuals. Trust is fundamental among all managers and employees, with an emphasis on broad support for planning and decision making.

Critical Theory Critical theory is what the name implies: a criticism; a critique of society, organizations, and social constructions. Tracing its roots to the work of Karl Marx and others, Critical theory today takes as a central theme the issues of power and power abuse in organizations and society as a whole. Although Critical theory continues, as Marx did, to look at problems with capitalism and oppression in society, current theorists do not expect revolution but seek ways to generate more genuinely participatory and democratic organizations. Jurgen Habermas, along with theorists such as Michel Foucault (1926–1984) (see References and Suggested Readings for more information), rejects the concept of rational science as the basis of valid knowledge on which arbitrary capitalism is constructed. Habermas calls for the use of Critical theory (criticism, critique, and so forth) to reconstitute reason and rationality as processes for positive social change. According to Habermas, communicative process is the basis for change and, as discussed in Chapter 2, carries a notion of constitutive process, literally foundational to all organizing, influence, and decision making.

The concepts of Habermas and other critical theorists challenge notions that management exists as a naturally emergent, value-free set of practices and persons. Critical theorists call for a third paradigm in contrast to scientific and interpretive approaches to management and organization. Specifically, critical theorists seek understanding of organizational life nested in the broader context of society through understanding of power and political relationships. Mats Alvesson and Stanley Deetz (1996) characterized the rise of both Critical theory and Postmodernism as responses to social conditions. Our current complex society has many positive capacities but also dangerous forms of domination. These forms of domination often are hidden from ready observation. It is the role of critical inquiry to surface these abuses.

Feminist Organization Theories   Marta Calás and Linda Smircich (1992) helped expand the realm of issues discussed by critical theorists through their application of feminist approaches to the critical study of organizations. Calás and Smircich, along with others, have moved beyond treating gender as one of many variables important to organizational and management studies to critique basic assumptions in organizational research. Specifically, **Feminist Perspectives** require that organizational theory be examined for its promotion of patri- archy as a particular understanding of power and gender relationships. Theorists examine the male worldview, with particular attention to considerations of valuing the man as rational and the woman as supportive and nurturing. As such, women's experiences and voices are marginal- ized; they are of value but less than centrally important to organizational power relationships.

Feminist Perspectives ■ Theories that critique the gendered assump- tions of modern organizations and call for the recognition and valuing of multiple voices and perspectives.

Karen Ashcraft (2006) described the influence of Feminist Perspectives in inte- grating the public and private lifeworlds previously separated by traditional bu- reaucracy. Ashcraft explained:

> Scholars have long characterized bureaucracy as hostile to feminism, the institu- tional arm of male dominance. Bureaucracy took root as the boundaries between public and private lifeworlds sharpened and crystallized, along with men's and women's respective roles in the world. . . . For feminists, this was no historical coincidence; bureaucracy helped to define and divide public and private spheres of human activity by casting suspicion on private (i.e., subjective, emotional, sex- ual—in a word, feminized) subjects as irrational, chaotic forces. . . . At issue, then, is not that bureaucracy splits selves better left whole, but that it (re)pro- duces a public sphere prone to devalue feminine subjects. . . . Feminists view formalization as especially suspect, as it conceals gender bias under a cloak of impartiality. In response to such critique, feminist organization is generally conceived as the pursuit of empowerment by way of a kind of collectivism—one that seeks a harmonious integration of public and private lifeworlds. (p. 61)

Ashcraft's comparisons of common bureaucratic and feminist organization de- scriptions help us understand distinctions between the two. Bureaucracy views the primary goal of organization as a means to an end such as optimum performance, whereas the feminist organization is the end in itself (such as gender empower- ment). The power structure of bureaucracy is hierarchical with authority central- ized at the top, whereas the feminist organization is egalitarian with authority decentralized and grounded in consensual decision making. The division of labor in bureaucracy is formal and specialized; in the feminist organization it is informal, contributing to community building. Bureaucracy defines professionalism as ra- tional and impersonal, with separation of public and private lives. Feminism values emotional and personal integration, in which work is fully integrated with private selves. Control in bureaucracy rests on formal, exhaustive, standardized rules. Control in the feminist organization reflects a shared culture of informal norms and ideological commitments.

In earlier work Ashcraft (2001) proposed the concept of "organized disso- nance" as the strategic union of forms presumed hostile, such as bureaucracy and feminist forms. In her more recent contributions, Ashcraft (2006) concluded newer forms of organizations are more likely to be hybrid rather than purely bureaucratic or feminist: "Put simply, it seems likely that *most* new forms are relatively hybrid and paradoxical in character, that—for postbureaucratic organizing—dissonance may be more rule than exception. From this vantage point, feminist bureaucracy enriches the study of new forms not as a novel instance, but as an illustrative case that embodies tensions common to much postbureaucratic practice" (p. 58).

Communication Implications of Postmodern, Critical, and Feminist Perspectives in Contemporary Organizations

The Postmodern, Critical, and Feminist organizational theory approaches discussed focus on the centrality of organizational communication for understanding organizational relationships and the construction of broader social relationships. Organizing, relationship, and change messages are acknowledged in Postmodern, Critical, and Feminist Perspectives; however, message functions are examined relative to power relationships, abuses of power, and the capacity of all messages to incorporate multiple meanings and ambiguity. Postmodern, Critical, and Feminist Perspectives stress multiple meanings or interpretations and reject notions of broadly shared organizational realities. Communication is viewed as literally constituting the organization and the process by which power is understood, including dominant voices marginalizing women and others. Postmodern, Critical, and Feminist Perspectives propose a value of increased participation and democracy among workers, with an emphasis on the value of all organizational voices.

The delayering of organizations—reduced numbers of hierarchical levels and managers—is evident in numerous organizations, with self-managing and high-performance teams replacing traditional notions of supervision. Postmodern and Critical Perspectives describe these changes in terms of power shifts, interdependence, and increased needs for flexibility and adaptation as contrasted with task specialization and shared meanings. Organizations of today and tomorrow are populated with increasingly diverse workers. Customers and markets are both diverse and specialized. Adaptation, flexibility, and change are more common than unusual, and organizations regularly examine new approaches requiring increased and changing skills from the workforce. Hierarchy is challenged, and ambiguity increases. Shared practices are required among those with fewer and fewer of the same messages or interpretations. Feminist issues affecting women and minorities struggle to come to the forefront of organizational concerns. Globalization and the changing workforce all evidence Postmodern, Critical, and Feminist challenges in organizational life.

The Davis Instrument Company's problems can be viewed from Postmodern, Critical, and Feminist approaches. Davis needs to change. The old relationships are not working as effectively as in the past. The practices of Davis reflect assumptions about shared realities and how power relationships should contribute to decisions. Multiple meanings, ambiguity, and flexibility are issues facing management and the entire organization. To understand the Davis problem requires us to think about the assumptions that guide Davis decision making and whether worker voices are marginalized as contrasted to the concerns of managers and supervisors.

CHAPTER HIGHLIGHTS

In this chapter, we discussed Scientific Management, Human Behavior, Integrated Perspectives, and Postmodern, Critical, and Feminist Perspectives for studying organizations and their communication implications. We described the **Scientific Management** stance as a "scientific" approach to the design of organizations. Organizational design is based on a carefully developed chain of command and efficient division of labor. In the Scientific Management point of view, communication is viewed as management's responsibility, with task- and rule-related messages moving along formal networks in a downward direction. As such, messages are expected to be low in equivocality. Decision making and influence are management-controlled variables of the organization. Culture is not considered and may be viewed as inappropriate.

The **Human Behavior** viewpoint shifts the emphasis away from the structure of organizations, work design, and measurement to the interactions of individuals, their motivations, and influence on organizational events. Human Behavior theorists describe communication as performing organizing, relationship, and change functions, with all organizational members participating. Networks are both formal and informal, and message equivocality can be characterized as higher than the Scientific Management theorists envisioned. Decision making occurs throughout the organization, particularly if the organization demonstrates a supportive climate. The peer group is viewed as a primary source of influence.

Integrated Perspectives viewpoints grew out of criticisms of both the Scientific Management and Human Behavior viewpoints. These viewpoints, according to their critics, had failed to integrate organizational structure, technology, and people with the larger environments in which organizations exist. The Integrated Perspectives approaches attempt to explain how people, technology, and environments interact to influence goal-directed behavior. Cultural approaches attempt to explain organizational behavior in terms of the influence of culture. The communication implications resulting from the work of the Integrated Perspectives theorists are diverse, with communication viewed both as a central process for organizational effectiveness and as dependent on the needs of a particular organization.

The **Postmodern, Critical,** and **Feminist Perspectives** focus on power and domination or the challenging of traditional hierarchical and patriarchal systems of authority. Postmodern organizations are described as flexible structures needing workers with multiple skills who are capable of continual learning. Market niches replace mass consumption, and workplace democracy replaces bureaucracy. Teams replace the emphasis on the individual contributor. Critical theory is what the name implies: a criticism or critique of society, organizations, and social constructions. Finally, Feminist perspectives challenge the gendered assumptions of modern organizations and call for the recognition and valuing of multiple voices and perspectives. ■

WORKSHOP

1. Form groups of four to six members each. Identify organizations in your community with which group members have some familiarity. Discuss whether these organizations represent Scientific Management, Human Behavior, Integrated Perspectives, or Postmodern, Critical, and Feminist viewpoints. Do any of the organizations represent combined approaches? How effective is communication in the various organizations?

2. A Guide to Case Development and Analysis (see below) should be used as you begin to examine increasingly complex organizational cases and prepare cases from personal interviews and experiences.

3. Using the Guide to Case Development and Analysis, analyze the cases that follow: "What Do You Mean I'm Not Going to Graduate?" and "We Never Had to Advertise Before." Propose ways to approach the problems identified in the cases.

A Guide to Case Development and Analysis

Case studies help close the gap between reading about organizations and theory and knowing what to do in an actual organizational situation. Cases are examples or illustrations of organizational problems to which we apply the theory we study to determine how best to solve problems.

A case gives information about the organization, its people, and its problems. Information is used to analyze what contributed to the problems and determine how the problems presented in the case might be treated. When preparing an original case, your personal business experiences or interviews with organizational members can be used to identify interesting communication problems. Problems are usually presented (either orally or in writing) in story or narrative forms with enough clarification so others can generate solutions. Case development and analysis can be approached through a three-step process. The process begins by asking questions and developing answers in each of our competency areas: knowledge, sensitivity, skills, and values.

1. IDENTIFY AND DESCRIBE THE SITUATION OR PROBLEM

Knowledge

What are the major and minor problems in the case?

What communication theories apply to these problems?

What organizational theories or perspectives are apparent?

What information is missing?

What assumptions are we making about the organization, its people, and their problems?

Sensitivity

Who or what appears to be most responsible for the communication problems?

What are the shared realities in the organization?

Are the principal individuals good communicators? If not, what are their limitations?

Are the principals in the case assuming responsibility for their communication behaviors?

Skills

What skills do the case principals exhibit?

What additional skills are needed?

How could these skills be developed?

What overall organizational skills are lacking?

What are the major organizational strengths?

Values

What is important or valuable to the involved individuals?

Do they share similar values?

How would you describe the culture of the organization?

Are individual and organizational goals compatible?

2. DEVELOP ALTERNATIVES AND TEST THE "REALITY" OF POSSIBLE SOLUTIONS

What should be done?

How many alternatives can be generated?

Can alternatives be combined?

What can be done?

Are the people involved willing to change?

3. PROPOSE SOLUTIONS AND SUGGEST IMPLEMENTATION PLANS

Explain your reasoning for solution selection.

Identify who is responsible for what.

Determine a timetable for implementation.

Suggest how your solution might be evaluated.

THE "WHAT DO YOU MEAN I'M NOT GOING TO GRADUATE?" CASE

Central University is a large Midwestern school noted for its fine undergraduate liberal arts programs. All students entering the university are required to complete humanities, social science, mathematics, natural science, and foreign language requirements. The foreign language requirement has been strengthened in the last two years, and all students are required to complete four semesters of a language or pass a competency examination.

The foreign language requirement has not been received favorably by the student body. Petitions to the university's committee on academic progress are often requests for exceptions to the requirement so as to graduate in a desired semester. To minimize these complaints and better inform the student body about the nature of the requirements, the committee has asked that Admissions and Records revise Central's bulletin to place the requirements section in a more prominent position. The advising service also has been asked to name all juniors and seniors who have not completed the requirement.

Jane Jordan is one of the students who, in her second semester of her senior year, has received a notice from the advising office that she will not graduate on schedule because of a one-semester deficiency in Spanish. Jane is furious and goes to the head of the committee on academic progress with her complaint. Jane claims that she was admitted to Central before the requirement was put in place and that although she had to drop out for two semesters to work, she should be graduated under her original admission requirements. Jane admits that she was advised of the new requirement when she returned to Central but was assured by an advisor that she could get out of it because of her original admission date and generally good academic record. Jane further contends that she has a job waiting at the end of the semester and will be harmed if required to stay at Central another term. The head of the committee on academic progress ponders what to do.

Questions for Discussion

1. What are the communication problems in this case?
2. Who is responsible?
3. Is Jane approaching the problem correctly?
4. What should the head of the committee do? ■

▶ THE "WE NEVER HAD TO ADVERTISE BEFORE" CASE

John Murphy and his father, Al, are arguing again. In fact, it seems they argue most of the time now. Today's argument is over whether to begin radio advertising for their appliance repair shop.

Al Murphy founded Murphy's Appliance Repair some twenty-five years ago. John literally grew up in his father's business and had been eager to finish college and prepare to take over daily operation when his father retired. Neither man had anticipated their numerous differences of opinion.

Al believes that he knows the business better than anyone and that John's ideas are too new and costly for any successful operation. John, on the other hand, believes there is increasing competition in their part of town and that resting on past success is dangerous. John wants to add additional automated machinery and advertise, as two of their competitors are doing. John sees the changes as progressive and necessary to the long-term survival of the business.

John has never had trouble communicating with his father before. He wonders what he can say to make his point. After all, the business has to support not only his father and mother but John's family as well. He has every right to make decisions if he is to have so much responsibility. Al feels much the same way. How can this disagreement be happening? He had looked forward to John's entrance into the business. Has college ruined his understanding of business? Isn't it supposed to be just the other way around?

Questions for Discussion

1. What is happening between John and Al?
2. Is advertising the real issue?
3. Are their values different?
4. What would you suggest that John do?
5. What can Al do? ■

TIPS FOR EFFECTIVE COMMUNICATION

1. Evaluate the Scientific Management principles in operation in two organizations with which you have close contact or membership.
2. Evaluate Human Behavior concepts in two organizations with which you have close contact or membership.
3. Evaluate process and environmental and cultural approaches in two organizations with which you have close contact or membership.
4. Evaluate Postmodern, Critical, and Feminist Perspectives in two organizations with which you have close contact or membership.
5. Verbally describe your findings to a member of each of the selected organizations. Ask for their perspectives or comments. How similar or dissimilar are your observations? What accounts for the similarities and differences? ■

REFERENCES AND SUGGESTED READINGS

Alvesson, M., and S. Deetz. 1996. Critical theory and postmodernism approaches to organizational studies. In *Handbook of organization studies*, eds. S. Clegg, C. Hardy, and W. R. Nord, 191–217. Thousand Oaks, CA: Sage.

Alvesson, M., and H. Willmott, eds. 1992. *Critical management studies*. London: Sage.

Ashcraft, K. 2001. Organized dissonance: Feminist bureaucracy as hybrid organization. *Academy of Management Journal* 44: 1301–1322.

Ashcraft, K. 2006. Feminist-bureaucratic control and other adversarial allies: Extending organized disso-nance to the practice of "new" forms. *Communication Monographs* 73: 55–86.

Barnard, C. 1938. *The functions of the executive*. Cambridge, MA: Harvard University Press.

Baudrillard, J. 1983. *Simulations*. New York: Semiotext.

Baudrillard, J. 1990. *Cool memories*. London: Verso.

Bennis, W. G. 1986. *Leaders and visions: Orchestrating the corporate culture*. New York: The Conference Board.

Calás, M. B., and L. Smircich. 1992. Using the F word: Feminist theories and the social consequences of organizational research. In *Academy of management proceedings,* ed. F. Hoy, 335–339. Washington, DC: Academy of Management.

Calás, M. B., and L. Smircich. 1996. From "the woman's" point of view: Feminist approaches to organization studies. In *Handbook of organization studies,* eds. S. Clegg, C. Hardy, and W. R. Nord, 218–257. Thousand Oaks, CA: Sage.

Clegg, S. 1990. *Modern organizations.* Newbury Park, CA: Sage.

Cyert, R. M., and J. G. March. 1963. *A behavioral theory of the firm.* Englewood Cliffs, NJ: Prentice Hall.

Deal, T., and A. Kennedy. 1982. *Corporate cultures: The rites and rituals of corporate life.* Reading, MA: Addison-Wesley.

Eisenberg, E., and H. L. Goodall. 1993. *Organizational communication: Balancing creativity and constraint.* New York: St. Martin's.

Fayol, H. 1949. *General and industrial management,* trans. C. Storrs. London: Pitman.

Follett, M. P. 1924. *Creative experience.* New York: Longman Green.

Foucault, M. 1972. *The archaeology of knowledge.* London: Tavistock.

Foucault, M. 1979. *The birth of the prison.* Hammondsworth, UK: Penguin.

Katz, D., and R. Kahn. 1966. *The social psychology of organizations.* New York: Wiley.

Kilduff, M., and A. Mehra. 1997. Postmodernism and organizational research. *Academy of Management Review* 22(3): 453–481.

Lawrence, P., and J. Lorsch. 1969. *Developing organizations: Diagnosis and action.* Reading, MA: Addison-Wesley.

Likert, R. 1961. *New patterns of management.* New York: McGraw-Hill.

Lorsch, J., and P. Lawrence. 1970. *Studies in organization design.* Homewood, IL: Irwin.

Lyotard, J. 1984. *The postmodern condition: A report on knowledge,* trans. G. Bennington and B. Massumi. Minneapolis: University of Minnesota Press.

March, J. G., and H. A. Simon. 1958. *Organizations.* New York: Wiley.

Martin, J., and P. Frost. 1996. The organizational culture war games: A struggle for intellectual dominance. In *Handbook of organization studies,* eds. S. Clegg, C. Hardy, and W. R. Nord, 599–621. Thousand Oaks, CA: Sage.

Mayo, E. 1945. *The social problems of an industrial civilization.* Boston: Graduate School of Business Administration, Harvard University.

McGregor, D. 1960. *The human side of enterprise.* New York: McGraw-Hill.

Metcalf, H. C., and L. Urwick. 1940. *Dynamic administration: The collected papers of Mary Parker Follett.* New York: Harper and Row.

Morgan, G. 1997. *Images of organizations.* Thousand Oaks, CA: Sage.

Pasmore, W. A., and J. J. Sherwood. 1978. *Sociotechnical systems: A sourcebook.* San Diego, CA: University Associates.

Peters, T. J., and R. H. Waterman Jr. 1982. *In search of excellence.* New York: Harper and Row.

Roethlisberger, F. J., and W. J. Dickson. 1939. *Management and the worker.* Cambridge, MA: Harvard University Press.

Schein, E. H. 1983. The role of the founder in creating organizational culture. *Organizational Dynamics,* summer, 13–28.

Schein, E. H. 1985a. How culture forms, develops, and changes. In *Gaining control of the corporate culture,* eds. R. H. Kilmann, M. J. Saxton, and R. Serpa, 17–43. San Francisco: Jossey-Bass.

Schein, E. H. 1985b. *Organizational culture and leadership.* San Francisco: Jossey-Bass.

Senge, P. 1990. *The fifth discipline.* New York: Doubleday/Currency.

Simon, H. A. 1957. *Administrative behavior.* New York: Macmillan.

Smith, A. 1937. *The wealth of nations* (Cannon ed.). New York: Modern Library.

Taylor, F. W. 1913. *Principles of scientific management.* New York: Harper.

Trist, E. L., and K. W. Bamforth. 1951. Some social and psychological consequences of the long-wall method of coal-getting. *Human Relations* 4: 3–38.

Weber, M. 1947. *The theory of social and economic organization,* trans. A. Henderson and T. Parsons. New York: Free Press.

Weick, K. 1995. *Sensemaking in organizations.* Thousand Oaks, CA: Sage.

Weick, K., and S. Ashford. 2001. Learning in organizations. In *The new handbook of organizational communication: Advance in theory, research, and methods,* eds. F. Jablin and L. Putnam, 704–731. Thousand Oaks, CA: Sage.

Wheatley, M. 1992. *Leadership and the new science.* San Francisco: Berrett-Koehler.

Woodward, J. 1965. *Industrial organization: Theory and practice.* London: Oxford University Press. ■

Organizational Communication

Values and Ethical Communication Behaviors

DEVELOPING COMPETENCIES THROUGH ...

KNOWLEDGE   Describing individual and organizational values
             Defining ethical communication
             Identifying criteria for the evaluation of ethical communication behaviors
SENSITIVITY Awareness of our personal value systems
             Understanding the complexity of ethical dilemmas
             Distinguishing between what we would do and what we should do
SKILLS   Assessing personal value systems and behaviors
             Applying skills to case and dilemma analysis
VALUES   Relating values to individual behavior and organizational effectiveness
             Understanding ethical behavior as contributing to choice, growth, and
                development

▶ THE PRESIDENTIAL FACT-FINDING (WITCH-HUNT?) CASE

Alyne Carter was surprised to receive a call requesting her to come to the office of the president of Melton Corporation. Alyne had never had an appointment with the president, and she was concerned about what he wanted to discuss. The president was relatively new to Melton, and rumor had it that the board of directors had hired him as a "hatchet" man to terminate some long-term Melton managers who were associated with the failure of one of Melton's major land development projects. Alyne's boss, Jim Johnson, had received criticism from some board members, although he was not directly involved with the development project.

Melton had a long history of being a good place to work, with open communication and support for taking risks, even though risks sometimes resulted in failures. Management at Melton had traditionally believed their speculative land development business would be most successful if they developed properties other companies had chosen to ignore. The strategy had generally worked, with the Briarwood project a major and important exception. The failure of Briarwood and the loss of several million dollars had upset important board members and had contributed to the resignation of Melton's president.

Alyne Carter did not work on the development side of Melton's business. She reported directly to the vice president in charge of personnel and human resource development, Jim Johnson. Alyne and Jim had a good working relationship based on mutual trust and admiration. Alyne was concerned when she heard criticism of Jim as well as the general rumors that people were going to be fired. The upcoming meeting with the new president increased her fears.

When Alyne left the meeting, she knew her concerns were real. The discussion with the new president had confused her and had left her wondering what to do. Although he had been perfectly pleasant, she knew he was looking for information to use against her boss. The president had begun the meeting by asking her to describe her work at Melton. He then said he needed to ask her some hypothetical questions about her department's management, recruitment, and promotional practices. Following several general questions, the president said that the rest of their conversation must stay within his office. He then proceeded to ask her if pressure had come from certain managers to hire several key individuals thought to be responsible for bad decisions in the Briarwood project. The president specifically asked if Jim Johnson had approved her hiring recommendations and whether any of her recommendations had been reversed in the last six months. Alyne attempted to answer the questions directly, although she felt as if she were walking into some unknown trap. She wished she had called Jim to tell him she had been asked to see the president. He might have been able to give her some insight about what was going on. The president closed the meeting by again suggesting their conversation was not to leave the room. He also made a somewhat vague reference to his responsibility to make unpopular changes in the best interest of Melton. He said he hoped she would understand and realize he had to do his job in the best way he saw fit.

Alyne could not believe this type of meeting had taken place at Melton. The rumors about a hatchet man certainly seemed correct. She knew she had been told not to talk about her discussion with the president, but she thought that Jim should know. Was it unethical to break her promise to the president? Where did she owe her loyalty? Was the president engaged in fact-finding or in a witch-hunt? ■

INTRODUCTION

Alyne Carter faces a question of values and ethics. She has inadvertently become involved in a communication situation that makes her uncomfortable and violates what she believes to be basic Melton company values. Alyne has been told by the president of Melton that their conversation should be kept in confidence, yet she believes her boss, Jim Johnson, should know about the president's fact-finding and veiled threats of future action. Alyne is caught between respecting directions from the president and valuing her loyalty to her boss. She has to decide about her values in this situation and what constitutes ethical behavior. Part of her decision will be based on a determination of whether Melton's president has engaged her in unethical communication.

Although an uncomfortable situation, Alyne's dilemma unfortunately repeats hundreds of times a day in all sizes and types of organizations. Individual and organizational values clash, making determinations of ethical behavior difficult.

Organizational values appear to change, leaving employees perplexed about what communication behaviors are valued and what behaviors should no longer be exhibited. Individual organizational members try to determine whether personal ethics and business ethics can or should mix.

Corporate and government scandals intensify our questions about values and ethics. Do we have broad structural and decisional problems in the way organizations are governed and led, or are these high-profile problems based on individual defects? Regardless of the position taken, most would agree communication is at the center of the political, legal, and social processes in which the scandals take center stage. Furthermore, in a global environment do we have a tendency to view values and ethics from our specific cultural perspectives? Do we impose our values on complicated organizational issues? What types of social responsibility and social justice issues are embedded in values and ethics for both organizations and individuals? The chapters that follow all, in one way or another, describe individual, group, and organization-wide processes with important value and ethical dimensions. From notions of individual performance to the relationship of the organization to its broader environment, values and ethics are a part of all that we and others experience.

This chapter is designed to help you think about how values and ethics influence human communication within organizations. The chapter also introduces you to value and ethical dilemmas commonly encountered by communication professionals. The chapter attempts to contribute to the development of *knowledge* by defining values and ethics, identifying individual and organizational values, and establishing frameworks for evaluating ethical communication behaviors. We develop *sensitivity* for relationships among organizational cultures, values, ethics, and decision making. We practice analysis *skills* through personal assessment of values, by identifying value themes in organizational philosophy statements, and by evaluating ethical behaviors in typical organizational communication situations. We encourage *values* development through an understanding of the importance to organizations of personal and organizational value systems and through discussions of the role of ethical communication behaviors for communication competency and effectiveness. We apply all four competencies—knowledge, sensitivity, skills, and values—to a case study, practical examples of value and ethical dilemmas, a decision-making simulation, and the development of a personal values and ethics statement for organizational communication.

VALUES IN ORGANIZATIONAL COMMUNICATION

Although most of us frequently use the word *value*, we often do not stop to thoughtfully consider what the concept really means to us. If asked, could you readily identify your value system for others? How did it develop? Who or what has influenced your choices? How does your value system influence your communication behaviors?

Generally speaking, value refers to the relative worth of a quality or object. Value is what makes something desirable or undesirable. **Values** are attitude sets which are subjective assessments

Values ■ The subjective assessments made about the relative worth of a quality or object.

about the relative worth of a quality or object. Richard Johannesen, in his important book *Ethics in Human Communication* (1983), stated that "values can be viewed as conceptions of The Good or The Desirable that motivate human behavior and that function as criteria in our making of choices and judgments." Family belonging, achievement, financial security, prestige, and hard work are all values that have some degree of importance for most of us. Johannesen and others suggest that the importance of our personal values influences a wide variety of our decision-making activities and behavior choices. In other words, we are more likely to make choices that support our value systems than choices that will not. Let us say that financial security is a strong value for an individual. When faced with a choice of jobs, chances are the individual will carefully examine each organization for potential financial and job security. The job applicant who values financial security may well take a lower salary offer with a well-established company over a higher-paying offer from a new, high-risk venture. Another job seeker with different values, possibly adventure and excitement, might choose the newer company simply for the potential risk and uncertain future.

Values therefore become part of complex attitude sets that influence our behavior and the behavior of all those with whom we interact. What we value guides not only our personal choices but also our perceptions of the worth of others. We are more likely, for example, to evaluate highly someone who holds the same hard-work value we do than someone who finds work distasteful. We may even call this person lazy and worthless, a negative value label.

Before reading further in this chapter, stop for a few minutes and attempt to describe your personal value system. What are your priorities? Have you ever stopped to think about their influence on your activities and your evaluations of others? Think about how your personal values may influence your communication behavior.

Organizational Value Systems

Most organizations promote a set of values designed to guide and govern behaviors throughout the organization and between the organization and its external environment. Organizational value sets have been described by some researchers as the bedrock of an organization's culture. Although most organizations make explicit a set of organizational values, it is also true that values other than overtly stated ones guide behavior in most organizations.

Milton Rokeach (1973) defined a value system as "an enduring organization of beliefs concerning preferable modes of conduct or end-states of existence along a continuum of relative importance." Based on the Rokeach definition, Leonard Goodstein (1983) contended that "in any organization, the members generally have a set of beliefs about what is appropriate and inappropriate organizational behavior. Furthermore, these beliefs can be ordered in importance in a reliable fashion by the members of the organization." In other words, organizational value systems help organizational members to understand what the organization holds as important and how the unique sense of the place should influence their personal decision making and behavior.

Values are part of the shared realities generated through organizational communication. These shared values are reflected in organizational myths, stories, mission statements, physical surroundings, slogans, and decision making, for example. Indeed, it is fair to say that organizational values are transmitted, maintained, and changed through organizational communication processes.

Organizational values are seen in the decisions members make. Terrance Deal and Allen Kennedy (1982) suggested that "if employees know what their company stands for, if they know what standards they are to uphold, then they are much more likely to make decisions that will support those standards." Research conducted by David Palmer, John Veiga, and Jay Vora (1981) supported the important link between values and decision making. They found that "value profiles were relatively successful in predicting managers' decision preferences and in providing further evidence of the linkage between personal values and decision making." In other words, an individual's value system, when coupled with the more general value system of the organization, influences the decisions individual organizational members will make.

Organizational values not only influence the behaviors of current members but also contribute to the type of person who gets hired and the types of career experiences employees are likely to have. Some organizations value very specific types of educational backgrounds, whereas others are more likely to look for particular work experiences. Some organizations value promotion from within, whereas their counterparts never fill important vacancies from among existing employees. During times of economic difficulty, organizations valuing long-term commitment to their employees may reduce work hours or salaries for everyone rather than lay off a portion of their workforce. Other organizations with less employee-centered values may decide that layoffs are the most efficient and effective way to deal with a business downturn. Arguments can be made for either position. The values of the organizations, however, are likely to guide the alternatives even considered by their respective management teams.

It is important to note stated values are not always the values in use in practical circumstances. Patrick Lencioni (2002) provided an interesting example: "Take a look at this list of corporate values: Communication, Respect, Integrity, Excellence. They sound pretty good, don't they? Strong, concise, meaningful. Maybe they even resemble your own company's values, the ones you spent so much time writing, debating, and revising. If so, you should be nervous. These are the corporate values of Enron, as stated in the company's 2000 annual report. And as events have shown, they're not meaningful; they're meaningless" (p. 113). In other words, values in practice not just stated values govern whether behavior is ethical, effective, or abusive, flawed, or even illegal.

Organizational Values, Globalization, and Diversity

There is a danger, of course, in thinking about organizations as having singular sets of values reflecting the closely held beliefs of all organizational members. Within an organization, diverse functions, leadership, and histories all contribute to differences in what is desirable and important. Differences in values within and between organizations are only expected to increase. As discussed throughout this book, the diversity of the workforce combined with the forces of globalization not only bring new challenges for working together and new organizational forms but also contribute to value diversity within organizations.

David Strubler (1993) provided an interesting illustration of value diversity within organizations in his study of what he called hybrid companies for which large numbers of Japanese and Americans work together either in the United States of America or in Japan. Strubler suggested the cultural and value dimensions of context, face-saving, and truth can help us understand how value differences within and between organizations contribute to potential misunderstanding and difficulty. According to Strubler, the Japanese, coming from a high-context culture, have a high volume of commonly shared information that makes implicit communication more desirable than more explicit information exchanges. By contrast, the U.S.A. workers' generally low-context culture is heavily dependent on explicit information exchange, often supported by extensive written documentation. In addition, although both cultures are concerned with face-saving, the Japanese generally place a higher imperative on face-saving behaviors than do Americans. Strubler related: "Consequently, high face-saving cultures view indirect (implicit) communication as preserving one's sense of dignity. Open argumentation in Japanese culture is considered unethical. Low face-saving cultures such as found in the U.S. view indirectness as unethical and typically favor argumentation as a method of settling difficulties. . . . In low context cultures, an emphasis is placed on the explicit written or spoken word. Truth is objective and absolute. When truth is violated (someone does not keep his or her word) guilt is experienced. In high context cultures, an emphasis is placed on relational (harmonious) communication" (p. 12).

Both Japanese and American cultures recognize the subjective and objective nature of truth, but value differences frequently have been observed. Strubler (1993) described, "Japanese often accuse Americans of being brash. Americans accuse Japanese of being deceitful. Often there is a failure to understand one another's cultural imperatives." Obviously, these types of cultural and value differences extend to numerous types of work settings. Competent communicators therefore begin to appreciate their personal responsibilities to understand how value differences may influence a variety of important organizational communication settings.

Diversity in values does not occur solely in the global business environment. As the workforce includes increasingly diverse cultural groups, organizations, often attempting to have their own distinct value systems, will increasingly reflect value differences and similarities across groups. These value differences and similarities are important for both individuals and organizations. A large body of research, for example, continues to demonstrate that **value congruence** (the similarity between individual and organizational values) between employees and their organizations has a significant effect on organizational commitment, employee work satisfaction, and turnover. Taylor Cox (1993), in his work on cultural diversity in organizations, described the importance of understanding this dynamic of value congruence and how it might work in multicultural organizations. Cox stated:

Value congruence ■ The similarity between individual and organizational values.

> The message . . . of value congruence may seem somewhat ambiguous. It may seem to suggest that diversity results in lower organizational performance. However, this is only true if we make certain assumptions about organizations such as that they should seek to assimilate all entrants into a monolithic culture, which tends to produce culture clash for entering members who are different

---

Company A

As a company, we want to share timely and accurate information on policies, programs, and activities. We want the information to be consistent and available to all employees. This is a goal that all managers should help to achieve. The company believes communication about our business creates a motivated and creative workforce.

Company B

The mission of Company B is as follows: Command, control, and support the workforce. Modernize the workplace. Prepare to support other divisions of the company. Train, motivate, and maintain individual capabilities. Provide a motivated environment that will attract and retain motivated and challenged workers.

Company C

Our philosophy in managing is to plan aggressively and anticipate events rather than let them drive us. Our program for our personnel must include fair compensation, appropriate benefits and working conditions, and an opportunity for advancement based on skills and ability. Our company will endeavor to participate in and offer educational programs necessary to ensure the qualified training of personnel, with a primary emphasis on improving customer service. All of these efforts are adopted to support our goal of excellence.

FIGURE 4.1
Organizational Value Statements

from the traditional norm. Instead, my intended message is that the importance of value congruence illustrates the need for multicultural organizations, one feature of which is that the organizational culture specifies alternatives that are equally appreciated rather than the one best way. Thus it is important to bear in mind that person-organization fit, in a cultural sense, is a function of the flexibility and inclusiveness of the organization as well as the individual. (p. 22)

Think about the values of your school. Can you describe these values in any order of priority? How do they influence the policies and procedures that you as a student are asked to follow? What kinds of formal and informal messages transmit these values to students? What values do students transmit to the administration and faculty?

Figure 4.1 provides three examples of organizational value statements. Each statement is taken from the new employee handbook of the three organizations. Without knowing anything else about these organizations, think about the value systems that you believe the messages represent.

Which of the three most closely fits your personal value system? Which least fits your values? Would value statements such as these make a difference in the organizations for which you would want to work? If so, why? If not, why not?

Individual Values

Most agree that value congruence even in a broad sense is important for allowing an individual to identify positively with the organization. In other words, a closeness between "this way is the way I believe things are" and "this way is the way I believe things should be" generally means the individual is satisfied with the organization and can personally commit to organizational values and beliefs. One of the difficulties, of course, is thoughtfully understanding the real values of an organization before one becomes a member. The process of matching individual and organizational values also is complicated by the lack of individual understanding of how value systems relate to work life. (The self-analysis exercises for career planning in Chapter 12 are designed to help you think about your values as they might relate to career and job selection.)

Value Orientations Beginning in 1960, Gordon Allport, Philip Vernon, and Gardner Lindzey suggested personal values can be described in terms of six orientations: theoretical, economic, aesthetic, social, political, and religious. Theoretical values focus on the discovery of truth, knowledge, and order, whereas economic values focus on the useful and practical and on material acquisition. We express aesthetic values in our concerns for artistic experiences and in our desire for form and harmony. We express social values in our relationships with others and our love and service commitments. Political values relate to needs for power, influence, leadership, and domination, and religious values relate to needs for unity and meaningful relationships to the world.

Terminal and Instrumental Values Milton Rokeach's (1973) value survey identified terminal and instrumental values. **Terminal values** can be viewed as concern for "end states of existence," or desirable goals, and **instrumental values** are desirable behaviors or modes of conduct that relate to and influence terminal values. Figure 4.2 lists the terminal and instrumental values Rokeach identified. A possible relationship between terminal and instrumental values can be illustrated through the example of someone with a high priority on the terminal value of accomplishment and instrumental values of being ambitious, capable, imaginative, intellectual, logical, and self-controlled. That is not to suggest, of course, that these are the only instrumental values that go hand in hand with a sense of accomplishment. Obviously, there could be others. Terminal values, however, are generally accompanied by combinations of instrumental values that individuals perceive to be harmonious.

Terminal values ■ Concerns for end states of existence or desirable goals.

Instrumental values ■ Desirable behaviors or modes of conduct that are related to and influence terminal values.

Work Values The personal values discussed apply to all aspects of our lives, not just the time we spend in organizations. Few attempts have been made to explore personal values as they specifically apply to work environments. Roger Howe, Maynard Howe, and Mark Mindell (1982) identified five value dimensions that they believed affect our organizational lives: locus of control, self-esteem, tolerance of ambiguity, social judgment, and risk taking.

Locus of control ■ Value we place as organizational members on connections between our efforts and the success or failure of the organization.

Locus of control refers to the value we place as organizational members on connections between our efforts and the success or failure of the organization. In other words, do we value personal control over success or failure, or do we value an organizational environment in which circumstances beyond our control contribute to success or failure? Do we, for example, want to be personally responsible for meeting sales quotas, or do we prefer to provide support to others who have the final quota responsibility? Our locus of control value also relates to whether we value organizational advancement as a result of our own efforts (personal control) or as the result of luck, politics, or random selection (external control).

The **self-esteem** dimension relates to the value we place on recognition for work, positive feedback, and the use of our contributions. This value represents our concern for being trusted and perceived as making worthwhile contributions to the organization.

> **Self-esteem** ■ Value we place on recognition for work, positive feedback, and the use of our contributions.

Tolerance of ambiguity as a value refers to the importance we place on structured or unstructured work environments. Our preference for one right answer or our comfort with a variety of possible approaches for decision making relates to the level of ambiguity we personally value. Those with a low tolerance for ambiguity may value one right answer and structured environments, whereas those higher in tolerance for ambiguity may prefer less structure and more opportunity for creative and diverse approaches.

> **Tolerance of ambiguity** ■ Value or importance we place on structured or unstructured work environments.

The value we place on the feelings of others and our general assumptions about why people work can be described as our **social judgment.** Our concerns for sensitivity, empathy, and social insight relate to the importance we place on working relationships with others.

> **Social judgment** ■ Value we place on the feelings of others and our general assumptions about why people work.

Risk taking concerns the importance we place on quick rather than deliberative action and whether we prefer our own sense of job fulfillment as opposed to job security. Our risk-taking value influences the degree of security we require in work situations, our tolerance for ambiguity in decision making, and whether we are willing to attempt tasks we have not previously encountered or have few qualifications for accomplishing.

> **Risk taking** ■ Value that explores the importance we place on quick rather than deliberative action and whether we prefer our own sense of job fulfillment as opposed to job security.

Figure 4.2 summarizes the three value approaches that have been described. After reviewing these lists, consider which additional values you would add. Which of the three approaches best represents your personal value system? Could the three be combined?

APPRAISING YOUR INDIVIDUAL VALUE SYSTEM

Understanding what is important to us and what our values are contributes to our ability to identify the careers and organizations in which we can be most productive and satisfied. Personal value assessment also helps us identify the ways values influence behaviors and evaluations of whether communication is ethical or not. Before beginning to explore ethics in organizational communication, we provide a self-analysis of personal values to give you insight into your value system. This assessment exercise is based on the assumption that consistent behaviors reflect value systems. Our approach in Figure 4.3 is by no means the only valid measure of a value system. We present this scale as a useful way to begin to think about the relationship of values and behaviors. As you complete the appraisal, consider additional questions that might be asked and additional values not represented in the appraisal. The scoring form for your appraisal is located on pages 134–135.

Value Orientations	Work Value Dimensions
Theoretical	Locus of control
Truth	Internal
Rationale	External
Order	Self-esteem
Knowledge	Recognition
Economic	Trust
Material acquisition	Worth
Usefulness	Tolerance of ambiguity
Pragmatism	Structured work
Aesthetic	Unstructured work
Artistry	Social judgment
Harmony	Assumptions about others
Form	Interpersonal sensitivity
Social	Risk taking
Love	Action-oriented
Concern for others	Uncertainty as challenging
Service	
Political	
Power	
Influence	
Domination	
Leadership	

Rokeach Terminal and Instrumental Values

Terminal Values	Instrumental Values
A comfortable life	Ambitious
An exciting life	Broad-minded
A sense of accomplishment	Capable
A world at peace	Cheerful
A world of beauty	Clean
Equality	Courageous
Family security	Forgiving
Freedom	Helpful
Happiness	Honest
Inner harmony	Imaginative
Mature love	Independent
National security	Intellectual
Pleasure	Logical
Salvation	Loving
Self-respect	Obedient
Social recognition	Polite
True friendship	Responsible
Wisdom	Self-controlled

FIGURE 4.2
Three Approaches to Describing Personal Values

Instructions: Read the following twenty-four statements, which indicate six defined values. Circle the number for each question that is most descriptive of you. Use this scale:

    4 = definitely true
    3 = mostly true
    2 = undecided whether statement is true or false
    1 = mostly false
    0 = definitely false

1. I intend to retire by age fifty with enough money to live the good life.   4 3 2 1 0
2. I take pleasure in decision making, particularly when other individuals are involved.   4 3 2 1 0
3. I enjoy now, or have enjoyed in the past, a close relationship with one or both of my parents.   4 3 2 1 0
4. I especially enjoy and appreciate beauty and beautiful objects, events, or things.   4 3 2 1 0
5. I enjoy creating projects of my own.   4 3 2 1 0
6. I feel a rich life has many friends and much friendship in it.   4 3 2 1 0
7. I am most valuable to clubs and groups when I am an officer rather than just a member of the group.   4 3 2 1 0
8. I enjoy both giving and going to parties.   4 3 2 1 0
9. I would choose a class in art, drawing, or sculpture over a class in math.   4 3 2 1 0
10. I think holidays should be spent with family and close relatives.   4 3 2 1 0
11. I like fine things and have expensive tastes.   4 3 2 1 0
12. I think decorating one's apartment or house is a fun thing to do.   4 3 2 1 0
13. I expect to earn more money than the common person on the street.   4 3 2 1 0
14. I take pleasure in buying special gifts for members of my family.   4 3 2 1 0
15. I am often considered a take-charge type of person in small groups and organizations.   4 3 2 1 0
16. Had I the talent, I would write, draw, or create art of some kind.   4 3 2 1 0
17. I have a close friend with whom I talk about almost everything.   4 3 2 1 0
18. I enjoy owning good music, literature, and artwork.   4 3 2 1 0
19. I think it is good and fun to make something out of nothing.   4 3 2 1 0
20. I agree with the phrase that money can't buy happiness but it sure makes life much more comfortable.   4 3 2 1 0
21. I think that spending time with one's family is an activity that is both necessary and enjoyable.   4 3 2 1 0
22. I often have to aid those close to me in making choices regarding both important and unimportant things in life.   4 3 2 1 0
23. I would give up sleep in order to spend time with some good friends.   4 3 2 1 0
24. When I see a new building or house, I first think about how it looks and then how it will be used.   4 3 2 1 0

FIGURE 4.3
Values Appraisal Exercise

This scale was prepared and tested by Sherwyn P. Morreale.

ETHICS IN ORGANIZATIONAL COMMUNICATION

The Abuse of Ethics

Although we may not easily define what we mean by ethical behavior, most of us are aware that abuses are all around us. We know students who have engaged in plagiarism or cheated on exams. We may have committed these or similar behaviors ourselves. We hear the excuses as reasons: "Everyone is doing it and no one ever gets caught"; "I was desperate. I didn't understand the material and the professor wouldn't help"; "I can't let my family down"; "I have to get a good job and a B won't do." The statements are troubling and the statistics are worse. In 2004 several research sources estimated that over one-third of undergraduate college and university students were using the "cut and paste" method of Internet plagiarism each year (McCabe, 2004). But the abuses certainly do not rest with students alone. The early years of the twenty-first century have seen a rash of corporate and government scandals. Enron, Global Crossing, Synergy, Xerox, Adelphia, Tyco, and WorldCom are but a few major corporations at which significant abuses resulted in the loss of billions of dollars, unemployment for thousands, and criminal charges leveled at leadership. Deceptive messages, illegal accounting practices, taking corporate profits for individual gain, creating phantom entities to record transactions and disguise debt, and a variety of strategies to avoid taxation were used to secure questionable and illegal advantage, resulting in scandal and public outrage. The global financial crisis beginning in 2008 can be traced to multiple ethical abuses as well as outright illegal behaviors. Although some of the most visible scandals could be linked to individual behavior, increasingly organizational structures and cultures were assessed blame.

Stockholders and boards (organizational governance structures) were held accountable for permitting manipulation of performance for the interests of a powerful few. Short-term financial results as a mark of success crippled several well-known companies. The leaders of boards of directors were ousted for authorizing the acquisition of personal, private telephone records in an effort to investigate information leaks. A chief executive officer was fired for violating patent agreements with federal prosecutors. At the same time, chief executive officer (CEO) compensation in the form of bonuses made front-page news following massive infusion of funds from the U.S.A. federal bail-out and stimulus funds. Corporate social and ethical responsibility has became a topic of discussion as never before. The remainder of this chapter provides ways to evaluate these critical ethical issues.

Defining Ethics

So far, this chapter has described values as what makes something desirable, a subjective assessment of worth that motivates human behavior and serves as a yardstick against which we measure choices. Ethics, although related to values, are the standards by which behaviors are evaluated for their morality: their rightness or wrongness. When applied to human communication, **ethics** are the moral principles that guide our judgments about the good and bad, right and wrong, of communication, not just communication effectiveness or efficiency.

Ethics ■ Moral principles that guide judgments about good and bad, right and wrong, not just effectiveness or efficiency.

Johannesen (1983) helped make the distinction between values and ethics:

> Concepts such as material success, individualism, efficiency, thrift, freedom, courage, hard work, prudence, competition, patriotism, compromise, and punctuality all are value standards that have varying degrees of potency in contemporary American culture. But we probably would not view them primarily as ethical standards of right and wrong. Ethical judgments focus more precisely on degrees of rightness and wrongness in human behavior. In condemning someone for being inefficient, conformist, extravagant, lazy, or late, we probably would not also be claiming they are unethical. However, standards such as honesty, truthfulness, fairness, and humaneness usually are used in making ethical judgments of rightness and wrongness in human behavior. (p. 1)

From this perspective it is fair to say that our values influence what we will determine to be ethical. Values, however, are our measures of importance, whereas ethics represent our judgments about right and wrong. This close relationship between importance and right and wrong is thought to be a powerful influence on our behavior and how we evaluate the behavior of others.

Making Ethical Decisions

Three general decision-making frameworks can be identified for their approaches to our subject of ethics: utilitarian theory, theory of rights, and theory of justice. First, utilitarian theory evaluates behavior based on outcomes or consequences for those involved. Second, the theory of rights emphasizes individuals' entitlements or privileges as members of a society. Finally, a theory of justice emphasizes balance or equity. These three perspectives are mostly a product of Western cultural values. It is important to note, especially in light of global environments, other cultures may have different values that define differently morally acceptable actions. Thus, ethics is not a concrete science. Even in our own culture, solutions to moral dilemmas are not always clear. Indeed the three perspectives that follow are potentially contradictory with one another.

Utilitarian Theory   Utilitarian theory rests on the principle that our actions are judged by their consequences or outcomes. The statement "The ends justify the means" is often used to describe this philosophical viewpoint. Utilitarianism charges decision makers with determining the various possible outcomes in a given situation and then determining which will benefit the greatest number of individuals.

Theory of Rights   The theory of moral rights asserts that all individuals have certain inalienable rights that are defined by society and that these rights must be respected in all situations, including the workplace. The most familiar rights for Americans are those found in the U.S.A. Constitution's Bill of Rights. Cavanagh, Moberg, and Velasquez (1990) suggested the following as commonly accepted basic moral rights:

1. *The right of free consent.* Individuals have the right to be treated only as they freely consent to be treated.
2. *The right to privacy.* Individuals have a right to a private life outside the purview of the public.

3. *The right to freedom of conscience.* Individuals have the right to refuse to do anything that goes against their moral or religious beliefs.
4. *The right of free speech.* Individuals have the right to speak freely as long as what they say does not violate others' rights. (The concept of others' rights remains subject to debate and various legal interpretations.)
5. *The right to due process.* Individuals have a right to a fair and impartial hearing to avoid a violation of their rights.

This theory is fairly easy to use as a guideline if individuals agree that we all have the same entitlements. Unlike utilitarian theory, which has to weigh the effects of the decision for the majority, the theory of rights is more clear-cut. That is, if a right is being violated, the action is not ethical. For example, because the use of e-mail and the Internet has increased exponentially, there have been instances when employers have monitored employees' messages unbeknownst to employees. Court cases have upheld the monitoring of employee e-mail and Internet use, but the practice raises moral questions based partly on the theory of rights. Is it ethical to monitor employees' e-mail, texting, and Internet use according to the theory of rights? Most would answer that it is. Although individuals have a right to privacy, that right does not extend to their time on the job. Although monitoring one's correspondence without one's knowledge may lower trust levels, it is not unethical. An organization might even justify the practice using utilitarian theory by concluding that it would benefit the organization (the greatest number) to know what is being communicated by employees.

Theory of Justice The theory of justice requires that all decision makers be guided by fairness, impartiality, and equity if their actions are to be considered ethical. Thus, treatment of individuals should not be based on arbitrary characteristics, and any differential treatment should be defendable. Treatment also should be consistent and impartially enforced. For example, most organizations have experienced some form of employee reduction or downsizing. One of the ethical issues an employer faces is deciding which departments or individuals will be let go. Do you make the decision based on performance or seniority?

The theory of justice would consider that whatever direction you take, you must be fair, equitable, and impartial. If organizations decide they will base layoffs on seniority, they must first develop a strong reason for their decision. Then, that criterion must be used in all termination decisions. Finally, any subsequent decisions that affect those who are laid off must apply equally to all (e.g., severance packages). The theory of justice has gained in importance with the advent of issues of corporate social responsibility, sustainability, and a host of highly visible ethical and legal abuses.

Think about an ethical decision you have had to make. Which of these perspectives did you use? Would your decision have been the same with each of the three theories? Why? Why not?

Defining Ethical Communication

Is it ever ethical to tell a lie? Am I being ethical if I deliberately withhold information I know you need but have not asked for directly? Should I compliment a person to be pleasant, even though the compliment may be insincere? Is it ethical to withhold from my boss information about a mistake I have made? How honest should someone be in giving criticism to another? Chances are you have had to answer several of these questions in your personal determination of ethical communication behaviors. Daily we come into contact with situations requiring us to make judgments or choices about what is right, ethical, or moral. In the case of a compliment, we may spend little time debating what is ethical, whereas a decision to withhold information from the boss requires serious consideration and considerable worry.

We all face the question of trying to determine ethical communication behavior. Our answers to ethical questions are based on our communication competencies—knowledge, sensitivity, skills, and values—and are related to our overall communication effectiveness. As previously discussed, ethical communication is an important prerequisite for effectiveness for both individuals and entire organizations.

Josina M. Makau (2008) explores the relationship of communication to ethics. Makau concludes, "Communication—the use of available resources to convey information, to move, to inspire, to persuade, to enlighten, to connect—is an inherently ethical undertaking. Regardless of context, communication involves choice, reflects values, and has consequences. These three key elements of communication form the basis of its ethical makeup" (p. 435). Ronald Arnett (1985), in synthesizing the status of ethics scholarship in communication, pointed to communication behaviors that support **choice making** as a "central component in the ethics of communication." Joseph DeVito (1976), in contrasting ethical and unethical communications, suggested ethical communication supports individual choice based on accurate information about alternatives. Unethical communication prevents individuals from acquiring needed information important for choices. Examples of unethical behaviors include lying, extreme emotional appeals, and preventing communication.

Choice making ■ Selection of options based on knowledge of alternatives.

Thomas Nilsen (1966) described communication he believed to be morally right as that which provides the listener with the information needed to make a choice and the reasoning that would make a rational decision possible; it must then help the listener to make the most reasonable choice. As Arnett's (1985) status of ethics scholarship suggested, although there is disagreement about what is ethical, there is consensus about the centrality of choice making for ethical communication.

Paul Keller and Charles Brown (1968) suggested ethical communication fosters conditions for growth and development. Keller (1981) further contended it is possible to be committed to a position while at the same time remaining open to new information. This openness to new information is viewed as fundamental for growth and development. Ethical communication can also be described as based on values that support the innate worth of individuals. Communication is ethical when it values the essential dignity of human beings and supports the ability of individuals to realize their full potential. Christopher Lyle Johnstone (1993) suggested, "In communication that is ethically sound, the conversations in which we participate—our own inquiries—are always open-ended and inconclusive. None of us possess the 'truth.' It is to be found in the 'becoming' of dialogue." Whether ethical communication is described as supporting informed choice making, contributing to growth and development, or valuing the innate worth of human beings, it depends on individuals taking responsibility for personal behaviors. This personal responsibility underscores the importance of developing criteria or guidelines for ethical communication behaviors.

Influences for Ethical Organizational Communication

Individual value systems, organizational value systems and cultures, and the standards of given professions all influence the ethics of organizational communication. Employees have individual value systems and make individual judgments about the rightness or wrongness of communication behavior. Even in organizations in which openness is encouraged, an individual employee may choose not to notify a supervisor of a serious mistake. The individual judges this behavior as ethical because of his or her intent to correct the problem. The employee's supervisor, on the other hand, may consider it unethical to withhold information that could affect the productivity of the group. An absolute judgment about the rightness or wrongness of the employee's behavior is difficult. It is possible to understand, however, that individual and organizational values can differ, contributing to different interpretations of ethical behavior.

Matthew Seeger, Timothy Sellnow, Robert Ulmer, and Julie Novak (2009) describe applied ethics, which "focuses on issues of ethical decision making and problem solving in professional and organizational communities. . . . Typically, the focus of applied ethics is on identifying norms, standards, guidelines, and processes of professional and organizational practices, and methods for promoting ethical decision making. . . . For example, the role of professional codes of conduct in promoting discussion, informing decision making, and resolving practical ethical problems is central to applied ethics. . . . Professional standards not only help to ensure that ethics are addressed but also elevate the status and effectiveness of various professions" (p. 282). Seeger and his colleagues go on to suggest that "ethical principles are applied in organizational communication contexts through three general approaches, either individually or as part of an integrated ethics program: (1) ethical codes of conduct; (2) ethics training; and (3) strategies to create more accessible, open and responsive structures and procedures" (p. 291). The importance of ethical standards for the communication professional was underscored by W. Charles Redding (1979), who described the impact of consultants on the careers or earning capacities of large numbers of individuals. Specifically, Redding contended that irreparable damage can be done in these high-risk consultant–client situations. Redding (1991), in a continuation of his earlier concerns, categorized common organizational messages that he classified as unethical. Redding concluded that coercive, destructive, deceptive, intrusive, secretive, and manipulative messages all violate important ethical standards.

Formal codes of ethics such as those that guide the medical and legal professions are not as common in the communications professions. Codes of ethics for journalists do exist, but codes are yet to be developed for the more general organizational communication professions.

Evaluating Ethical Behavior

Seeger, Sellnow, Ulmer, and Novak (2009) provide guidance for evaluating ethical behavior. Specifically, the Seeger research team believe that

> communicators must be sensitive to the ethical implications of their communication choices. . . . Part of this sensitivity involves recognition of the ethical dimensions of decisions so that they may be fully considered in the decision process.

... Second, communication is viewed as the process whereby decision makers sort through various value positions and determine which should take prominence in a given context. Argument, debate, discussion, and consensual decision making, for example, all have a role to play in sorting through conflicting values. ... Standards and values that encourage participation, voice, and free exchange of information help to ensure that relevant values are represented. (p. 283)

Most of us do not continually think about evaluating our own behavior and the behaviors of others along ethical lines. We do, however, tend to make conscious ethical evaluations when in doubt about what we should do or when the behaviors of others cause us concern about the rightness or wrongness of their actions. An important part of our communication competency is therefore determining how we should approach evaluating ethical communication behaviors.

Karl Wallace (1955) developed a set of guidelines for the evaluation of behavior that he first applied to our political system and that Rebecca Rubin and Jess Yoder (1985, pp. 14–15) extended to the assessment of communication skills in an educational setting. These guidelines are appropriate for consideration in most organizational communication situations.

1. The **habit of search**. Ethical communication willingly explores the complexity of any issue or problem. This exploration requires generating valid information and evaluating new and often controversial findings.

   Habit of search ■ Ethical communication that willingly explores the complexity of any issue or problem.

2. The **habit of justice**. Ethical communication presents information as openly and fairly as possible and with concern for message distortion. Not only is information accurate, but information is also presented for maximum understanding.

   Habit of justice ■ Ethical communication that presents information as openly and fairly as possible with concern for message distortion.

   When we receive and evaluate information, the habit of justice requires that we examine our own evaluation criteria and potential biases that contribute to distortion in meaning.

3. The **habit of public versus private motivations**. Ethical communication is based on sharing sources of information, special opinions, motivations, or biases that may influence our position. Hidden agendas are discouraged for both message senders and receivers.

   Habit of public versus private motivations ■ Ethical communication based on sharing sources of information, special opinions, motivations, or biases that may influence positions.

4. The **habit of respect for dissent**. Ethical communication not only allows but also encourages opposing viewpoints and arguments. This habit of respect for dissent in an open environment supports generation of the best ideas through thoughtful examination, disagreement, and new idea presentation.

   Habit of respect for dissent ■ Ethical communication that encourages opposing viewpoints and arguments.

When applied to the organizational setting, these guidelines suggest individuals and groups engage in ethical communication behaviors when they thoughtfully analyze problems and issues, are open to diverse types and sources of information, conduct their deliberations openly without hidden agendas, and not only respect different viewpoints but also encourage disagreement and dissent to produce superior ideas and solutions. From this perspective, unethical organizational communication behavior suppresses the examination of issues, withholds relevant information to pursue personal interests or motivations, and uses dissent to press for personal rather than organizational advantage. In other words, ethical communication behaviors promote participation, transparency, and accountability and support courageous actions.

ORGANIZATIONAL CONUNDRUMS

The word *conundrum* refers to a problem or a puzzle. The organizational conundrums discussed here illustrate the problems and perplexing dilemmas that routinely raise ethical issues for all organizational members.

After reviewing the research identifying ethical concerns in organizational communication, Seeger, Sellnow, Ulmer, and Novak (2009) identified the following ethical issues: privacy and voice; free speech, diversity, persuasion and coercion, change, power and domination, authority and control, organizational democracy, discourse and dialogue, legitimacy and corporate social responsibility, recruitment and socialization, ethical climate, and public relations. Carl Anderson (1997) identified four organizational goals that are often framed as incompatible: economic performance, competence, the learning organization, and the organization as community. These incompatibilities are a foundation for ethical dilemmas. Economic performance refers to the goal of profit, with its inherent measurement and assumption that some organizations will succeed while others fail. Competence refers to the tangible or intangible assets that yield sustainable competitive advantage. To improve the competencies supporting efficiency, methods such as restructuring, reengineering, quality control, process redesign, and downsizing have been increasingly employed. The learning organization refers to an organization's capacity to change strategies, tactics, or performance. The organization as community refers to the respect for rights and fulfillment of duty. Anderson explained, "These four goals are in fact interdependent. Over the long run, competence and learning are necessary to sustain economic performance. A strong community is fundamental to all three. Dilemmas occur because decisions that improve competence, learning, and performance can easily hurt community" (p. 28).

Ann Plamondon (1997) identified organizational climates in which ethical dilemmas arise. Specifically, she described a climate of broken organizational promises, a climate in which no one takes responsibility, a climate of denying participation and dissent, a climate requiring whistle-blowing, and a climate of cultural relativism. Broken promises occur when promises do not match organizational action. Promises of increased compensation, promotions, participation in decision making, and many other forms of desired change are often made to stimulate improvement and then are either ignored or cannot be fulfilled. Bureaucracies often encourage shifting responsibility from level to level or to no particular organizational position or person. No one is responsible for delaying needed action. "I was just following orders or policy" is a common statement used to deflect responsibility for bad decisions, poor actions, and unethical behaviors. Hierarchical structures often limit participation and dissent. Not only can this limitation contribute to poor decisions, but also it often becomes a form of control requiring employees to support decisions and actions with which they have significant disagreement. Illegal behavior in a climate of control contributes to the need

for **whistle-blowing,** the exposure of illegal behavior to organizational outsiders. Finally, a climate of cultural relativism suggests
that in a global environment, ethical behavior will be different for
different cultures. Certainly cultures vary in a global environment. A belief in a climate of cultural relativism, however, has been used as defense for selling products
in other countries that are banned in the United States of America as well as for engaging in questionable workplace and environmental practices. Numerous examples can be found throughout the globe of leaders engaging in practices they know
will harm others or the environment with the defense that these practices create
jobs and profits critical for economic development. Can you think of recent examples in which any of these "climates" have gained public notoriety? What are the
ethical issues involved in product recalls, environmental abuses, or whistle-blowing cases? Have you ever been caught in one of these climates? What did you do?
What should you have done?

> **Whistle-blowing** ■ The exposure of illegal behavior to organizational outsiders.

Michael Hackman and Craig Johnson (2009) describe as courageous followership
the ethical responsibilities of those who report to leaders. They suggest assuming
personal responsibility and taking accountable action are ethical responsibilities.
Furthermore, the courage to serve refers to the ethical responsibility of supporting
leaders through hard and sometimes unglamorous work. Followers also are asked
to exhibit the ethical responsibility of challenge. As Hackman and Johnson state,
"Inappropriate behavior damages the relationship between leaders and followers
and threatens the purpose of the organization. Leaders may break the law; scream
or use demeaning language with employees; display an arrogant attitude; engage in
sexual harassment; abuse drugs and alcohol; and misuse funds. Courageous followers need to confront leaders acting in a destructive manner" (p. 360). Hackman
and Johnson discuss the courage to participate in transformation, with followers
identifying what needs to be changed, providing honest feedback, suggesting resources, creating a supportive environment, modeling openness to change and empathy, and providing positive reinforcement for positive new behaviors. Finally,
Hackman and Johnson discuss the courage to leave: "When leaders are unwilling
to change, courageous followers may take principled action by resigning from the
organization. Departure is justified when the leader's behaviors clash with the
leader's self-proclaimed values or the values of the group, or when the leader de-
grades or endangers others" (p. 362).

Many leaders and organization members are aware that the continued ability
to carry out their operations occurs within a system (our world) that has limits.
Issues such as climate change, natural resource depletion, and the energy crisis are
hitting organizations head-on, requiring attention to aspects of the business beyond quarterly financial results. In order to deal with these challenges, many organizations have adopted the principles of sustainability as a guiding framework
for operations. *Sustainability,* expressed in simple terms, suggests that every individual should "Leave the world better than you found it, take no more than you
need, try not to harm life or the environment, make amends if you do" (Hawken,
1993). For some, sustainability is a moral or ethical mandate, others see it as a
legal requirement, whereas others treat these issues as a cost of doing business.
Some even consider sustainability practices and processes to be a business opportunity or competitive advantage. Regardless of the perspective taken, this new concept

is strongly value-laden with ethical implications for leadership, decision making, employee involvement, education and training, and communication to networks of stakeholders. (For more information on sustainability, see Laura Quinn's essay and case study in the Workshop section.)

The organizational conundrums discussed all ask in one way or another the question of whether an organization can support a core of social values, act in ethical ways, and become or stay financially successful in an increasingly complex world. George Cheney (1999) used the term *organizational integrity* to describe whether organizations can keep to humane and democratic commitments while growing, enjoying financial success, and perhaps even becoming more centralized and bureaucratized. The issues are complex and critical. They are not easy. In addition, the conundrums include us all. The remaining chapters in this book help you think about and build competencies to deal with these challenges. The next section specifically discusses common ethical dilemmas frequently faced in our organizational lives.

ETHICAL DILEMMAS IN ORGANIZATIONAL COMMUNICATION

Although ethical issues can arise over virtually any type of communication, several recurring organizational communication situations have ethical implications. These situations—representing skills and abilities; communication behaviors related to money; communication behaviors related to information collection, dissemination, problem solving, and decision making; personal communication behaviors; communication behaviors related to technology; destructive communication behaviors; planned organizational communication (internal policies and decisions and external communication); and communication behaviors related to courage, responsibility, trust, and ethics—are frequently encountered by the communication professional.

Representing Skills and Abilities

We present our skills and abilities to potential employers when seeking a job. The way in which we communicate what we know reflects an ethical decision about fair representation of our abilities. Most of us have known someone who has told an interviewer about a skill that we knew the individual did not possess. Although we would say that this behavior is not strictly ethical, we know our friend is highly motivated and will attempt to do a good job if hired. Does this motivation make the behavior acceptable, however? What is the ethical standard we should apply?

Once hired, we may attempt to seek good assignments designed to help us advance. How do we represent our abilities as compared with others in our work group? Do we keep information about mistakes from our supervisor to appear more competent than our peers? Do we blame others for problems even though we legitimately bear part of the responsibility? How can we behave ethically and still risk what others might think about our competencies if they know we have made a major mistake?

When in a supervisory or managerial position, we are responsible for giving feedback to others about their performance. Are we hesitant to give negative information to a problem employee, thereby creating a false sense of security? Are we making an important ethical decision, or are we making a realistic appraisal that the person in question can't handle bad news and would be demoralized if we were more direct?

The representation of skills and abilities also influences problem identification. Consultants and human resource development specialists are frequently asked to help define organizational problems and propose training and related development activities for problem solution. These professionals face the dilemma of defining a problem they may or may not have the skills to solve. When the consultant is external to the organization, defining a problem as needing skills other than those the consultant possesses costs the consultant potential earnings. The organization must hire someone else to meet its needs. On the other hand, defining the problem or need in terms of services the consultant can provide is subject to serious questions of integrity. The concerns are much the same for the internal communication professional.

Communication Behaviors Related to Money

Communication surrounding fees for services, salaries, and personal versus organizational money is subject to ethical evaluation. The communication consultant, in pricing a training program to a potential client, must base the worth of services on personal credentials, program complexity, general market value of the program, and fees the consulting organization expects to pay. Should a consultant, for example, charge different organizations different fees for essentially the same services? How should fees and services be described? How can the consultant establish charges for diagnosing a problem that is not fully understood? The answers to these and other questions represent decisions about ethical communication.

One ethical question is whether general salary information should be available to all employees or whether salaries should remain confidential to individual employees. The communication of performance review and wage administration information also is a management communication decision with ethical consequences. Individuals communicate their ethical standards regarding organizational money when they use expense accounts, buy services or products for the organization, and establish department budgets. One way to examine our communication behaviors relating to organizational money is to determine whether we would approve of our behavior if we were the sole owner or head of the organization.

Many communication professionals face ethical dilemmas as a result of payment for services. It is not uncommon, for example, for a communication consultant to work simultaneously for competing organizations. Do both clients need to know that the consultant is employed by the other? Internal communication specialists encounter information concerning personal problems of employees such as alcoholism or drug abuse. Are these specialists ever entitled to withhold information from the organization that pays their salary? How should these decisions be examined? All these questions and more have ethical implications for the behaviors of individuals and for overall organizational policy.

Communication Behaviors Related to Information Collection, Dissemination, Problem Solving, and Decision Making

Most communication professionals are involved in collecting organizational information. They interview, conduct surveys, facilitate meetings, advise and counsel individuals, review documents, and in a variety of other ways generate data important to the conduct of their jobs. During data collection activities, professionals make ethical decisions concerning what should remain confidential, who has a need to know, how accurate the information is, and what the criteria for interpretation are. These same ethical issues relate to information dissemination. Should sensitive information be kept private, going only to affected individuals? Does a guarantee of confidentiality prohibit the use of the information, even though the organization could be improved if the information surfaced? Who has a need to know? How accurate is the information, and is it subject to varying interpretations? Most experienced professionals know that their ability to handle these sensitive questions ethically contributes to their personal credibility. Even if ethical considerations were not important in and of themselves, practicing communication professionals find that the exercise of ethical standards is essential to their overall organizational effectiveness. Research on effective leaders supports this perspective. As we discuss extensively in Chapter 7, effective leaders are known for their abilities to generate trust and behave consistently. Outstanding leaders practice their individual standards (ethics and values) in a manner that helps others accept the challenge of their organizational vision.

Information collection and dissemination are part of the problem-solving and decision-making processes of organizations. As a result, the concern for ethics extends beyond simply collecting and disseminating information. For example, what are the ethical implications of attempting to solve problems with limited alternatives? Are solution alternatives available from all affected by decisions? Is it ethical to make decisions without input from those affected? Why? Why not? Finally, will the impact of decisions support organizational values and represent ethical standards? How do we know? Most would agree these are important questions without easy answers. However, thoughtful consideration of these questions and others links communication and ethics to critical organizational processes.

Personal Communication Behaviors

Thus far, we have been talking about the ethics of organizational communication as related to specific types of organizational responsibilities. Although these areas include personal behaviors, there is yet another area of personal behavior important for consideration. This area, broadly described as our personal communication style, refers to the ethics of our individual behaviors, regardless of our job responsibilities. Do we, for example, behave autocratically, enforcing our will by refusing to consider the opinions of others and attempting to win at any cost? Is this autocratic preference ethical when it stifles the good ideas of others? Do we, as a result of high communication apprehension or a preference for conflict avoidance, refuse to participate in decision making even though we have information appropriate to the decision? When we are employed by the organization, is it ethical to withhold the best of our thinking? Does our style help others to examine issues critically, or do we use the power of our positions or the force of our personalities to get our own way? How can we examine the ethics of our approaches?

Most of us have been either victims or carriers of gossip. We find talking about others interesting and exciting. We may not be as excited when we know others are discussing our personal or professional lives. Gossip is prevalent in most organizations. Gossip, however, carries important value and ethical implications. What responsibility do we have to verify the accuracy of our communication about others? What is the difference, if any, between gossip and truth not officially released by the organization? What are the implications of engaging in gossip? What should we do when we are the subjects of gossip, whether true or otherwise? Closely related to the gossip that occurs in most organizations is the subject of organizational confidentiality. Most organizations require at least some level of confidentiality from employees. Confidentiality is designed to protect organizational information necessary for competitive advantage. Confidentiality usually extends to information about customers and other types of product or service data. Many organizations require employees to sign confidentiality agreements providing security of information about customers, products, and services. Have you ever provided what you knew to be confidential information to others? What were your reasons? What would you do if your boss asked you to keep information about a major mistake confidential from others? These questions and others can be answered through self-assessment and understanding of our personal ethical standards.

Communication Behaviors and Technology

Maintaining confidentiality and security of information for e-commerce is an increasingly complex organizational responsibility. Disclaimers on the Internet and in other publications describe organizational commitments to confidentiality. Yet leaks of confidential information are frequent, and identity theft from breaches of electronic confidentiality occur for almost one in eight individuals every year. The breaking of confidentiality is a frequent and costly organizational occurrence. Indeed, the broad use of technology for purchases and exchange of important information carries both an ethical and legal responsibility for individuals and organizations.

As more and more workers use technology on a daily basis, issues about its workplace use increase. Many people have desktop access to e-mail, the Internet, organizational databases, videoconferencing, and a host of other programs and links. Some organizations regularly monitor the e-mail and Internet use of their employees. Others limit Internet access to only selected sites known to be associated with business needs. Still others publish policies directing the type of communication behaviors expected on e-mail and when using the Internet. Many organizations, for example, prohibit individual advertising when using company electronic resources. Others, by contrast, establish Web pages for employee exchange of personal information, including the desire to sell personal property. All these issues have ethical and trust implications. Do you know anyone who uses a corporate e-mail account for personal correspondence? How much time is devoted to this activity during a workday? Is that ethical? Why? Why not? How many people use their organization's Internet provider for personal Internet access? What are the implications of these behaviors?

In addition to the various uses made of organizational technologies, ethical questions can be asked about the approach to communication we select when using telemediated channels. Research consistently supports the reality that many people will be more harsh and critical using e-mail than in face-to-face interactions. Others use e-mail to raise issues they will not raise in other forums. There are strengths and weaknesses to these approaches. The question to ask, however, is whether it is ethical to use a technology that distances us from our receivers to engage in an exchange we will not "own" in less distanced communication. How can we approach understanding this issue? What does your own personal behavior suggest?

Destructive Communication Behaviors

A number of communication behaviors such as deception, invasion of privacy, aggression, incivility, sexual harassment, and discrimination are almost universally considered unethical. Unfortunately, these behaviors occur daily within all types and sizes of organizations. In describing destructive behaviors, Craig Johnson (2007) contended, "Like the dangerous aspects of ourselves, the shadow side of organizations must be acknowledged and confronted. There is little hope of transforming organizational systems unless we first address the behaviors that undermine any change effort." Lying is the most obvious form of deception and is a deliberate attempt to either provide false information or mislead others with only marginally truthful information. But deception also occurs when individuals remain silent even though they have information that could alter understanding in particular situations. If we are honest with ourselves, most of us recognize we have engaged in deception at one time or another. We may not as readily recognize how deception lowers trust and impairs problem solving and decision making. In other words, many of us do not thoughtfully consider both the ethical and performance implications of deception.

We set boundaries around how much information we communicate in our work environment about our personal lives and private thoughts and positions. We worry about who has access to our personal information such as financial or medical records. Most of us consider it unethical when someone searches our desk, records a telephone conversation without our knowledge, forwards an e-mail without our permission, or reveals information we have shared in confidence. The rise of technology surveillance in the workplace raises new issues about personal rights and privacy. But as Johnson (2007) pointed out, "Arrayed against privacy rights is the organization's right to gather information about its members."

Aggression, incivility, sexual harassment, and discrimination are communication and physical behaviors with destructive and unethical consequences. Incivility usually refers to a broad range of behaviors that disregard and violate generally accepted norms of respect. Behaviors termed as lacking in civility range from discourteous driving to e-mails that demean or discount. According to Stephen Carter (1998), some studies indicate the majority of us experience incivility weekly. A somewhat lesser number are believed to experience incivility on a daily basis. Can you think of a time when you have been a victim of incivility? When have you engaged in a behavior others might consider lacking in civility?

Although incivility impacts performance, aggression is even more deliberate in its attempts to harm or injure. Aggressive behaviors include both physical and communication threats such as sabotage, insults, and refusing to interact or provide needed information. Johnson (2007) helped us understand the unethical and negative consequences of aggression:

> Not surprisingly, aggression can do extensive damage to both individuals and the organization as a whole. Victims may be injured, experience higher stress levels leading to poor health, become fearful or angry or depressed, lose the ability to concentrate, and feel less committed to their jobs. Observers who witness aggressive incidents may suffer some of the same negative outcomes. They, too, experience more anxiety and a lowered sense of well-being and commitment. At the organizational level, performance drops as a result of aggressive actions. Workplace aggression is correlated with lower productivity, higher absenteeism and turnover rates, lawsuits and negative publicity. (p. 218)

Sexual harassment and discrimination behaviors are both unethical and illegal. These behaviors inhibit or deny basic rights and opportunities to those victimized and often result in legal action against those engaged in harassing or discriminatory acts. Unethical and illegal behaviors harm individuals and organizations. Although most of us do not engage in the extremes of these behaviors, developing our personal communication competency requires we remain aware of our behaviors and learn to confront negative behaviors in others. Later chapters specifically address development of competencies for these difficult situations.

Planned Organizational Communication

Organizations regularly communicate a variety of policies and procedures with ethical implications. Hiring processes and decisions, promotional policies, assignment of work, and working conditions are all evaluated for their ethical consequences. Do organizations genuinely open positions and promotions to the most qualified, or are those in a close network of in-group relationships most likely to succeed? Are all employees given opportunities for development and challenging work assignments, or do entire segments of the workforce have little challenge and opportunity? Are working conditions free of hazards both physically and psychologically? Are employees able to engage in free statements of their concerns and positions? The answers to these questions and others become the ethical climate of the organization.

Organizations also communicate ethical decisions to their external publics. The quality of products and services can be evaluated for ethical dimensions. Planned organizational communication such as advertising, public relations, and government and stockholder interactions is more likely to be governed by formal codes of ethics or legal standards and requirements than other aspects of organizational communication. Advertising is subject to government regulations that include ethical standards about what constitutes truth in advertising. Full disclosure of financial information is required for stockholder and government relationships, and public relations efforts are subject to ethical standards established by the journalism profession. Despite these standards, we can all think of times when we have questioned the ethics of advertising and can remember when organizations attempted to manipulate the public with less than full disclosure about products or services. The global environment places a special challenge on understanding ethical communication when ethical standards vary greatly across cultures.

Courage, Responsibility, Trust, and Ethics

Engaging in ethical behavior is both an individual and organizational responsibility. Increasingly, organizations seek individuals with ethics training and the ability to translate that knowledge into both formal and informal communication behaviors. Communication professionals are expected to behave ethically and have the capability to advise others in the development of messages, policies, and practices that support ethical standards. Communication professionals write press releases, develop Internet and e-mail policies, develop and guide organizational assessments of climate and culture important to problem solving and decision making, manage risk and crisis communication, and deal with numerous other situations involving significant ethical implications. At times ethical behaviors are courageous and difficult behaviors. At all times ethical behaviors contribute to the trust necessary for individual and organizational excellence. Preparation for these responsibilities begins with self-awareness and clarity about personal values and ways to assess ethical communication behaviors. The following section provides specific opportunities to apply ethical standards.

DEVELOPING ETHICAL STANDARDS IN ORGANIZATIONAL COMMUNICATION

We discussed how to determine whether communication is ethical. We also identified some common ethical dilemmas faced by communication professionals. We have not, however, attempted to apply ethical standards to the behavior choices we can expect to encounter in organizational settings. Following are shortened versions of ten organizational dilemmas I encountered during my consulting experiences. For each dilemma, attempt to determine what you would actually do if faced by this situation and what you should do. If what you would do and should do are different, state why. Finally, after analyzing all ten situations, attempt to determine what criteria you used in applying ethical standards.

Ethical Dilemmas in Organizational Communication

1. You are the newly appointed personnel director for a large beverage distributor. Your new job responsibilities include screening all applicants for promotions to management positions. Your company's usual procedure is for the personnel director to screen applicants and select the top three for further interviews with management. You also know that the president of the company does not want a woman on his personal staff. Your current decision is difficult because your most recent vacancy is on the president's personal staff and your top three applicants are female. You can send the three applicants to the president and wait to see what happens. You can rethink your selection criteria and try to have a male applicant in the top three. You can reopen the position, hoping to attract additional qualified

applicants. You can confront the president about his discriminatory posture. You also have other options. What would you do? What should you do?

2. A crew member from the night shift's manufacturing group has come to you as her personnel liaison with a concern about drug use on the production line. She won't give you any specific details for fear of those involved finding out who has turned them in. She suggests that you should investigate immediately but warns against involving her in any way. She asks you not to tell the other personnel liaisons because the grapevine has it that one of them may be involved. You can go to your boss and work with her in deciding what to do next. You can try to investigate on your own. You can bring up the drug problems the plant is experiencing at a staff meeting and watch closely to see if there are any unusual reactions from your peers. You can tell your source to give you more specific information before you will do anything. You can ignore the problem because of lack of evidence. You have other options. What would you do? What should you do?

3. You have overheard a conversation between your manager and the manager of a department in which your best friend is employed. From their conversation, it is apparent that your friend is not pleasing her manager and she will definitely be passed over for the promotion she badly wants. You don't want to see her hurt, and you happen to know she has a job offer from another group within your organization. Should you tell her about the conversation and urge her to take the new offer? Should you remain silent because of the manner in which you heard the information? Should you go to your boss and tell him that you accidentally overheard the conversation and are concerned because your friend might turn down a good job offer? Should you urge your friend to confront her boss? You have other options. What would you do? What should you do?

4. You are the lead copywriter in an advertising agency handling a major chemical products account. Your copy is frequently criticized by the chemical manufacturer's marketing director. He wants a stronger sell, even if that means omitting much of the disclaimer information associated with the safe use of the products. He contends that people buying chemicals should take individual responsibility for safety and that the company should not be required to devote scarce ad and package label space to full disclosure of the potential hazards. You realize that he may even be willing to test whether government regulating agencies will restrain his actions if he refuses to comply with industry product-labeling requirements. The issue comes to a head when you receive copy proofs changed by the marketing director to omit disclosure information that you believe should remain in the new ad series. Your immediate boss is out of town on vacation and cannot be reached. You either have to let the changes go or confront the marketing director. You know he will not appreciate your interference. You can let the copy go as is. (You have documented evidence that the marketing director, not your agency, made the changes.) You can refuse to make the changes, thereby jeopardizing the account. You can ask to be removed from the account. You can go to the marketing manager's boss in the chemical company. You have other options. What would you do? What should you do?

5. You have received a job offer from one of your current employer's principal competitors. The offer was unsolicited and has come as a surprise. Although this type of offer is not uncommon in the advertising business, you are unsure how to respond. The vice president urging you to come to work for her also mentioned

that one of your current employer's largest accounts is talking with her group about changing agencies. You have reason to believe that the account is pleased with your work and wonder if her offer is not aimed at increasing the chances of taking business away from your employer. So far, the vice president has not asked you any questions about the account. You are scheduled to meet her for lunch next week. Should you tell your employer that you are considering another position? Should you refuse to discuss the account in question if the vice president mentions it? How can you learn whether the offer has a hidden business agenda? Do you have a responsibility to your current employer to tell him a major account is being solicited by another firm? What would you do? What should you do?

6. You are the member of a task force asked to recommend to the city council how the city's Park and Recreation Department can better serve low-income members of your community. Two members of your group believe the city government should reduce its budget, and they view your assignment as an ideal way to make that statement. You disagree. The task force is charged with making programming recommendations. The Park and Recreation Department is charged with incorporating those recommendations into their budget, which must be approved by the council. You support more programs for low-income areas of your community and hope some of your recommendations will be part of the final report. Several group members agree with you, two strongly disagree, and several are undecided. At the next-to-last task force meeting before the report is due to council, a reporter asks to interview a member of the task force in order to get a progress update. The two members with whom you have had the most disagreements are late to the meeting. Others in the group suggest you talk with the reporter. You agree, hoping for an opportunity to express your support for low-income programming. As the interview begins, you wonder whether your remarks should reflect the various perspectives present in the group or whether it is appropriate to represent your personal view. Should you tell the reporter that members both support and disapprove of increased park and recreation programming? Should you tell the reporter that the final report to council is very likely to contain a dissenting opinion and you are not sure which side of the issue will receive majority support? Will this type of dissent weaken the effectiveness of the report? Should you represent your position because the other two members are late and would have had an opportunity to speak to the press had they arrived on time? What would you do? What should you do?

7. You are a member of a project team charged with designing a new service support training program for your organization's 150 customer support representatives. The representatives are generally knowledgeable but resistant to a new training program. Your team members include two of your peers from the training department and two customer support representatives. The initial design meetings have been productive, but you become aware that the two customer support representatives expect you and your coworkers to do the work. They will critique what you propose. Further, you know that at least one of the customer support representatives is talking with others in his work group about your ideas. You have learned that some representatives think you don't know what the work really is and can't possibly design a good program. You want the program to be good but are concerned with the rumors and lack of work from two members of your team. Should you confront the representatives? Should you ask team members for more effort? What would you do? What should you do?

8. You are a member of a self-directed work team charged with processing travel requests for over 3,000 salespeople worldwide. Your team has been praised for quality work and cost savings. In fact, your group has reduced processing costs by 40 percent over previous groups. One longtime member of your team is not pulling her share of the load. Jane is excellent with her accounts but is not helping other team members when they are overloaded. Jane is popular with management and many of the salespeople you support. Other team members have asked you to talk with Jane. You think that the entire team should engage in this conversation. To make matters worse, you learn that Jane, but not the rest of the team, has received a coveted customer support award. Jane has not mentioned this award to the team. Should you ask Jane about the award? Should you insist the team join you in talking to Jane? What would you do? What should you do?

9. You have been asked by your boss to evaluate the e-commerce strategy the marketing department of your company proposes. You have reason to believe that your boss doesn't really understand the proposal because she has little experience with potential Internet business applications. You don't have the experience to do the evaluation but know you must make a response within the next week. You decide to review the Internet strategies of your major competitors. To your surprise, you find that your company's marketing proposal ignores several features for customer service that all your competitors are using. When you discuss this omission with the director of marketing, he laughs at you for what he considers your lack of experience and suggests that you have no right to question his judgment. You are concerned about your lack of experience but believe you have some valid concerns. You don't want to put your boss in a bad position by opposing a proposal from another department. Should you talk with your boss? Should you present your concerns despite the marketing director's opposition? What would you do? What should you do?

10. You are a senior member of a global marketing team charged with developing a major promotion for your organization's new line of consumer products. The products are intended to be introduced simultaneously in eighteen countries including the United States of America, several European countries, and large segments of Asia. The company's international marketing director prefers that your team develop a single promotional theme for, as he puts it, "the globe." You are concerned because team members from Asia contend this is dangerous and culturally inappropriate. Several team members consider the initial promotional copy brash and insulting. You and some of your European counterparts believe the copy is direct and will gain instant attention from potential consumers. You must present a proposal to the marketing director within a week. You can ask the director for more time. You can present the significant disagreement to the director even though you know he will not be pleased. You can have the team vote, knowing that the majority will support the theme some find offensive. What other options do you have to resolve this dispute? What would you do? What should you do?

After analyzing these examples, are the behaviors you would do and should do always the same? If they were different, what caused the difference? What contributed to similarities? Was it difficult to determine what was ethical in a given situation? Can you identify the standards you used as your criteria? After considering these examples, can you see the relationship between competency and ethics?

CHAPTER HIGHLIGHTS

Values are the subjective assessments we make about the relative worth of a quality or object. These assessments are thought to guide our behavior in making choices and judgments. Both individuals and organizations have value systems that are expressed through communication behaviors. **Ethics** are the standards by which behaviors are evaluated for morality, for rightness or wrongness. When applied to human communication, ethics are the moral principles that guide our judgments about the good and bad, the right and wrong of communication, not just communication effectiveness or efficiency. Values and ethics are a part of all communication and organizational experiences. ∎

WORKSHOP

1. Divide into groups of four or six members each and discuss the ten ethical dilemmas presented in this chapter. Compare your individual responses with those of other group members. As a group, what would you do? What should you do?

2. Either individually or in small groups, write a statement describing the values of your ideal organization. Describe your ideal organization's ethical communication behaviors.

3. "People, Planet, and Profit: Sustainability and the Triple Bottom Line" by Laura Quinn examines the ethical basis of the concept of sustainability. As you read her essay, prepare to discuss as a class the value and ethical implications of using sustainability as part of organizational strategy and organizational communication.

4. The "GreenBean Coffee, Inc.—Is It Our Responsibility?" Case by Laura Quinn helps us assess how the concept of sustainability might influence problem solving and decision making in the example of a company seeking to uphold high values while operating as an industry leader. Discuss as a class what the case suggests about individual and corporate social responsibility.

People, Planet, and Profit: Sustainability and the Triple Bottom Line

Laura Quinn, Ph.D.[1]

Imagine a world in which organizations participate in the global economy in ways that enhance the safety and well-being of all individuals and protect our natural habitats while creating a fair and equitable state of wealth for everyone. Wouldn't this be wonderful? Is it possible? With innovation, creativity, and a commitment to expanded values, there is a new framework, called sustainability, helping businesses make this dream a reality.

We all know our current state of global affairs isn't in the best condition. In fact, issues of global warming, ozone depletion, pollution, unemployment, and unfair labor practices, to name just a few, are daily elements of our local, national, and international news. Indeed, the future of our planet and its inhabitants (us!) is in question; some would say it is in a state of jeopardy. However, dwelling on our current state of "doom and gloom" will not help the situation. What will help is identifying a way of working and living that is financially feasible, fair and equitable to all, and, at the same time, protects our planet—this is what sustainability is all about.

All types of organizations from countries around the world are taking on what some would call a revolutionary approach to running their day-to-day operations. This new approach, referred to as sustainability, asks organizations to go beyond the traditional evaluation of success, profitability, and the bottom line to expand these measures to include the triple bottom line (TBL). The TBL Perspective asks businesses to look beyond profits as the main measure of success and also to include the impact their operations have on people and the planet. While still focusing on the economic value an organization produces, the TBL expands to measure the social and environmental value the organization creates or, unfortunately, destroys. Organizations adopting a triple-bottom-line stance consider the impact

---

[1]Laura Quinn, Ph.D., is an associate at the Center for Creative Leadership. She has responsibility for leadership development programs and sustainability research.

of their operations, strategies, and decisions on their employees, their industry, their community, their environment—the "whole system" of the organization.

Certainly, this expanded viewpoint requires organizations to pay attention to a complex, integrated network of factors. When using the TBL, it is not enough to ask, "How much does it cost?" or "What will our profit be?" Organizations implementing the TBL will employ a broader scope of questioning to include (but not limited to) the following:

To Address People

- Do we treat our employees with respect?
- Do our employees earn "livable" wages and have good working conditions?
- Are we a diverse organization, treating people of all types in a fair manner?
- Do we ensure the health and safety of our people? Our communities?
- Do our stakeholders trust us?
- Does our organization uphold ethical values and practices?

To Address Planet

- What is the impact of our product or services on the environment?
- Do our operations create pollution and harmful waste?
- Are we efficient and effective in our consumption of energy and resources?
- Do we recycle?

To Address Profit

- Can we make and sell our products or services for a profit?
- What do we need to do to maintain our profitability?
- Are we competitive in the marketplace?
- How can we ensure continued innovation and competitive advantage?

Of course, paying attention to the triple bottom line is not necessarily easy; the TBL requires integration, openness, and thoroughness within an organization's communication systems. The TBL requires strong leadership, a commitment to ethics and values, and patience. It is important to recognize that as organizations pursue the TBL, the emphasis on each factor is not always the same or equal. The TBL factors are linked and require different levels of consideration at different times and in different situations. For example, a decision on em-

ployee policies may come up that doesn't have a strong environmental impact but does have a definite impact on employees, wages, and jobs (people and profit). This decision would not have an equal emphasis on the environmental factor. Yet another decision may be needed on the new types of chemicals used in the manufacturing process of an organization; this decision would clearly involve all three factors. In this case, the organization would want to know: How much does the new chemical cost? Is it toxic? If so, what can be done with the waste? What impact does this waste have on the environment? Where will this waste be dumped? Who will this affect? Most important, do we have an alternative that isn't toxic, or is there another process that doesn't require a toxic chemical? The complexity added by the TBL factors requires organizations to rethink and reconfigure their organizational communication processes in ways that address triple-bottom-line effects. Specifically, consideration must be given to the following:

- *Leadership*—Leaders must create a new vision for the organization that expands beyond traditional values and approaches. Instead of focusing on short-term strategies, leaders must think of the legacy of their organization's impact on the world. Goals and objectives must incorporate a whole-systems perspective, with a focus on innovation, interconnections, and long-term impact.
- *Values/Ethics*—The TBL Perspective requires the adoption of a broader, more encompassing set of organizational values and ethics. Instead of being driven by the single value of creating shareholder wealth, organizations must also place value on factors such as social justice, environmental quality, fair employment and trade practices, and community involvement.
- *Decision Making/Problem Solving*—As the three factors of the TBL are incorporated, they necessitate that new criteria be developed for evaluating effective decisions and solutions to problems. Decision criteria must expand, beyond considering costs, to consider the impact of decisions on people, including vendors, employees, and community members, and on the environment, including the efficient use of natural resources, the creation of waste and pollution, and the effect on the supply chain.
- *Employee Involvement/Employment Practices*—In order to implement the TBL, it is imperative that employees at all levels of the organization be involved. Addressing the factors of the TBL is a complex process, and ensuring the participation of all employees will help provide a whole-systems

perspective for decisions, processes, and strategies. Also inherent in the triple-bottom-line perspective is the fair and inclusive treatment of employees. Employment practices must contribute to the employee's sense of safety, well-being, and respect.

- *Education/Training*—Certainly, the TBL requires a new way of thinking and behaving. To ensure that everyone has a shared understanding of the principles and perspectives of the TBL, some form of continuous training and education will be needed to teach everyone about the different factors, as well as the skills needed to deal with a new and greater level of complexity.
- *Communication Networks/Stakeholder Engagement*—As the TBL addresses complex issues within and beyond the organization's boundaries, organizations must ensure that communication networks are broad and diverse and include the entire system of the organization. Creating frequent forums for dialogue with stakeholders such as employees, vendors, customers, community members, environmental groups, nonprofit groups, and government officials is an essential part of understanding and managing the TBL.

So what do organizations get when they adopt a TBL stance? Of course, the main benefit of adopting the TBL is that of becoming a responsible global citizen. In addition, there are strategic advantages, cost savings, and the building of goodwill that develop around an organization's efforts with the TBL. Anytime an organization is more comprehensive and forward thinking in its strategies and operations, it can compete more effectively in its own market, whether it is a manufacturing organization or a community nonprofit organization. TBL organizations have been shown to experience the following advantages as a result of their efforts toward sustainability:

- Increased stakeholder satisfaction and loyalty
- Ease in hiring and maintaining talented employees
- Increased productivity
- Increased employee morale
- Reduced expenses and waste
- Increased revenue and market share
- Better risk management
- Increased capability for adapting to market/industry/customer changes
- Improved innovation
- Positive community relations

Although much technological and scientific knowledge helps organizations transition to this new way of conducting business, the organizational communication challenges of the TBL are just beginning to be addressed. The field of organizational communication can and must play a significant role in helping these organizations move forward to sustainability with the triple bottom line. The TBL organization's ultimate goal is to participate in commerce as a first-class global citizen, helping to make the world a better place for current and future generations. The field of organizational communication can play a significant role in helping organizations along on this worthwhile and necessary journey.

GreenBean Coffee, Inc.—Is It Our Responsibility?

Laura Quinn, Ph.D.

GreenBean Coffee, Inc., currently holds the number one position in the U.S. coffee market; they have surpassed their industry competition with the growth of their neighborhood coffee shops, grocery store retailing, and online marketing and sales. No one ever thought GreenBean could pull this off, but with a reputation for quality and value, employer-of-choice practices, and progressive environmental policies, many customers traded in their loyalties to other coffee retailers and committed to GreenBean's products and business practices. Indeed, GreenBean's mission and values emphasize their commitment to being "good global citizens," treating people fairly, and not harming the environment while running a profitable business. As of today, GreenBean has retail shops in all fifty states, with a handful of international locations. They are planning to grow internationally.

Recently, an international environmental organization, Groovy Planet, came to GreenBean to address the issue of beans growing in South America. Groovy Planet's studies have confirmed the use of toxic pesticides in the coffee-farming practices in South America. Residues from these pesticides are contaminating the water supply in South America; in addition, the employees of the South American coffee growers are experiencing increased asthma, respiratory, and dermatological health issues as a direct result of contact with these pesticides. Groovy Planet has not gone to the press with this information but indicates it will in order to get the U.S. coffee industry to take action. Groovy Planet has contacted GreenBean Coffee first because of its role as industry leader, as well as its company values. South American coffee farmers supply GreenBean, Inc., with 100 percent of their raw beans.

As GreenBean's senior staff gets together to address this issue, the product development team presents the following facts: GreenBean's coffee bean supplier, not GreenBean, is the purchaser/user of the toxic pesticides; GreenBean purchases the beans with the stipulation that the beans will be washed prior to shipment to the United States of America so the pesticides will not affect GreenBean's customers; the employees with health issues are not employees of GreenBean. GreenBean has found an organic pesticide with the same protective qualities of the toxic pesticide, but the coffee growers require GreenBean to pay the additional costs for the use of this product. Using the new organic product would result in a need for a reduction in profit margin or an increase in price.

(NOTE: Because of GreenBean's quality and reputation, it is already the price leader in the coffee market.)

Questions for Discussion

1. Is dealing with the toxic pesticides GreenBean's responsibility?
2. Is GreenBean violating any company values? If so, which ones?
3. How should GreenBean communicate with its coffee suppliers? With Groovy Planet? What should this communication entail?
4. Is GreenBean's reputation at stake?
5. What should GreenBean do? ■

TIPS FOR EFFECTIVE COMMUNICATION

1. Evaluate your communication for its honor and respect for all persons.
2. Listen actively and ask for clarification when you believe you may not understand.
3. Ask others for input even when you are fairly certain you will disagree.
4. Provide information openly and honestly.
5. Encourage others to participate in difficult discussions.
6. Support civil disagreement.
7. Challenge behavior that devalues others.
8. Apologize for and correct personal negative behaviors.
9. Support others to confront wrongs.
10. Provide credit and support for ethical behaviors. ■

REFERENCES AND SUGGESTED READINGS

Allport, G., P. Vernon, and G. Lindzey. 1960. *Study of values.* Boston: Houghton Mifflin.

Anderson, C. 1997. Values-based management. *Academy of Management Executive* 11(4): 25–46.

Arnett, R. C. 1985. *The status of ethics scholarship in speech communication journals from 1915 to 1985.* Paper presented at the Speech Communication Association Convention, November, Denver, CO.

Bennis, W., and B. Nanus. 1985. *Leaders: The strategies for taking charge.* New York: Harper and Row.

Carter, S. 1998. *Civility: Manners, morals, and the etiquette of democracy.* New York: HarperPerennial.

Cavanagh, G., D. Moberg, and M. Velasquez. 1990. The ethics of organizational politics. In *Foundations of organizational communication: A reader,* eds. S. Corman, S. Banks, C. Bantz, and M. Mayer, 243–254. New York: Longman.

Cheney, G. 1999. *Values at work: Employee participation meets market pressure at Mondragón.* Ithaca, NY: ILR Press/Cornell.

Cox, T. 1993. *Cultural diversity in organizations.* San Francisco: Berrett-Koehler.

Deal, T. E., and A. A. Kennedy. 1982. *Corporate cultures: The rites and rituals of corporate life.* Reading, MA: Addison-Wesley.

DeVito, J. A. 1976. *The interpersonal communication book.* New York: Harper and Row.

Goodstein, L. D. 1983. Managers, values, and organization development. *Group and Organization Studies* 8(2): 203–220.

Hackman, M., and C. Johnson. 2009. *Leadership: A communication perspective.* Prospect Heights, IL: Waveland Press.

Hawken, P. 1993. *The ecology of commerce: A declaration of sustainability.* New York: HarperBusiness.

Howe, R., M. Howe, and M. Mindell. 1982. *Management values inventory.* San Diego, CA: University Associates.

Howell, W. S., and E. G. Bormann. 1988. *The process of presentational speaking,* 2nd ed. New York: Harper and Row.

Johannesen, R. L. 1983. *Ethics in human communication,* 2nd ed. Prospect Heights, IL: Waveland Press.

Johnson, C. 2007. *Ethics in the workplace: Tools for organizational transformation.* Thousand Oaks, CA: Sage.

Johnstone, C. L. 1993. *Ontological vision as ground for communication ethics: A response to the challenge of postmodernism.* Paper presented at the Speech Communication Association Convention, November, Miami.

Keller, P. W. 1981. Interpersonal dissent and the ethics of dialogue. *Communication* 6: 287–303.

Keller, P. W., and C. T. Brown. 1968. An interpersonal ethic for communication. *Journal of Communication* 18(1): 73–81.

Lee, G. 2006. *Courage: The backbone of leadership.* San Francisco: Jossey-Bass.

Lencioni, P. M. 2002. Make your values mean something. *Harvard Business Review,* July, 113–117.

Lippitt, G., and R. Lippitt. 1978. *The consulting process in action.* La Jolla, CA: University Associates.

Makau, J. M. 2008. Ethical and unethical communication. In *21st Century Communication: A Reference Handbook,* ed. W. Eadie, 435–443. Thousand Oaks, CA.: Sage.

McCabe, D. 2004. *An executive summary of the status of academic integrity within academic communities.* Durham, NC: Center for Academic Integrity.

Nilsen, T. R. 1966. *Ethics of speech communication.* Indianapolis: Bobbs-Merrill.

Palmer, D. D., J. F. Veiga, and J. A. Vora. 1981. Personal values in managerial decision making: Value-cluster approach in two cultures. *Group and Organization Studies* 6(2): 224–234.

Plamondon, A. 1997. Ethics in the workplace: The role of organizational communication. In *Organizational communication: Theory and behavior,* ed. P. Yuhas Byers, 90–113. Boston: Allyn and Bacon.

Posner, B., J. Kouzes, and W. Schmidt. 1985. Shared values make a difference: An empirical test of corporate culture. *Human Resource Management* 24(3): 293–309.

Redding, W. C. 1979. Graduate education and the communication consultant: Playing God for a fee. *Communication Education* 28(4): 346–352.

Redding, W. C. 1984. *Professionalism in training—Guidelines for a code of ethics.* Paper presented at the Speech Communication Association Convention, November, Chicago.

Redding, W. C. 1991. *Unethical messages in the organizational context.* Paper presented at the International Communication Association Convention, May, Chicago.

Rokeach, M. 1973. *The nature of human values.* New York: Free Press.

Rubin, R., and J. Yoder. 1985. Ethical issues in the evaluation of communication behavior. *Communication Education* 34: 13–17.

Seeger, M., T. L. Sellnow, R. R. Ulmer, and J. M. Novak. 2009. Applied communication ethics: A summary and critique of the research literature. In *Routledge handbook of applied communication research,* eds. L. R. Frey and K. N. Cissna, 280–306. New York: Routledge Taylor and Francis Group.

Shockley-Zalabak, P., and D. Morley. 1989. Adhering to organizational culture: What does it mean? Why does it matter? *Group and Organization Studies* 14(4): 483–500.

Stewart, L. 1993. *Ethical issues in organizational diversity.* Paper presented at the International Communication Association Convention, May, Washington, DC.

Strubler, D. 1993. *Ethics in hybrid Japanese/American organizations: A question of whose values.* Paper presented at the Speech Communication Association Convention, November, Miami.

Wallace, K. R. 1955. An ethical basis of communication. *Speech Teacher* 4(1): 1–9. ■

Scoring the Values Appraisal Exercise (Figure 4.3, p. 111)

Instructions (Part 1). Below are the six defined values indicated by the twenty-four statements in Figure 4.3. Enter the number you circled for each statement next to the number for that statement. Then total your score for each value.

Values:	Money	Power	Family	Aesthetic	Creative	Social
	1___	2___	3___	4___	5___	6___
	11___	7___	10___	9___	12___	8___
	13___	15___	14___	18___	16___	17___
	20___	22___	21___	24___	19___	23___
Totals:	___	___	___	___	___	___

Instructions (Part 2). Now plot your own personal values profile. Use the preceding totals for each of the six values and plot them on the chart that follows.

	Money	Power	Family	Aesthetic	Creative	Social
16						
15						
14						
13						
12						
11						
10						
9						
8						
7						
6						
5						
4						
3						
2						
1						
0						

Individuals in Organizations

DEVELOPING COMPETENCIES THROUGH . . .

KNOWLEDGE   Describing diversity in the workforce
Describing intrapersonal and interpersonal experiences of individuals in
    organizations
Describing theories of motivation

SENSITIVITY   Relating motivation to communication behaviors
Being aware of communication preferences in organizational experiences
Understanding how perceptions of communication competencies affect
    work satisfaction
Describing the importance of trust for interpersonal relationships
Describing emotion in organizations
Identifying positive attitudes for valuing diversity

SKILLS   Valuing diversity
Practicing active listening
Practicing analysis capabilities

VALUES   Relating individual communication experiences to organizational identifi-
    cation, work performance, communication, and job satisfaction
Identifying personal needs in work settings
Relating valuing diversity to interpersonal effectiveness

▶ DAVE GREEN'S FIRST REAL JOB

Dave Green was excited. Today was his first day in the Human Resource Department of AMX Corporation, one of the best-known management training firms in the country. Landing a job with AMX had not been easy. On his campus alone, ten candidates had interviewed with the AMX recruiter. He had been told AMX had over 200 total applications from which to choose.

    Dave knew his degree in organizational communication was a good choice. Even so, he had been apprehensive about finding just the right job. The training position in the Human Resource Department was perfect, and working for Sally Johnson—one of the best trainers in the Midwest—was a real opportunity. Of course, he still worried about exactly what would be expected and whether he really was ready.

Dave's initial assignment was to work with a team of three experienced researchers and trainers to locate materials for a new training program Sally was developing. Although Sally had assured him the three wanted more help, Dave wondered about his reception into the group. After all, they had been with AMX for several years and had worked together for Sally for more than two years. How would they feel about his becoming a member of the team?

As Dave prepared for his first meeting with Sally and the group, he began to think about what he might say and ask. How should he describe his skills? What techniques could he use to best understand their expectations of him? What were his goals in this job?

In this chapter we follow Dave's experiences with AMX Corporation. We try to understand his experiences as they might relate to our attempts to develop communication competencies important for working with supervisors, employees, and peers. ■

INTRODUCTION

It is not unusual to be both excited and apprehensive when beginning a new semester, starting a new job, or joining a new volunteer group. We aren't completely sure what to expect. What will the people be like? Will our competencies meet the expectations of others? As individuals, we bring skills and abilities to organizations and expectations about what we hope will happen. We want to be successful, but like Dave Green, we wonder if our communication competencies are appropriate to the task.

Think for a moment about the organizations of which you are a member. How did you feel when you first enrolled in your school, were hired for your job, or joined a new church? How do you feel now? How would you describe your organizational experiences? Which give you the most satisfaction?

In previous chapters, perspectives for understanding organizational communication have been described and major organizational theories have been studied. Now we relate what we know about organizations as a whole to how individuals experience organizational life. Although we view organizations as entities in which many people work together for goal achievement, we all experience organizations as individuals. Understanding our individual experience is important for developing communication competencies that contribute to personal satisfaction as well as to overall organizational effectiveness.

This chapter is designed to contribute to *knowledge* by defining and describing concepts of motivation and identifying the primary characteristics of a diverse workforce, including supervisor, employee, and peer relationships. We develop *sensitivity* competencies through awareness of individual predispositions for organizational communication behaviors and by identifying effective and ineffective message strategies and tactics. We develop *skills* by applying knowledge and sensitivity competencies in a variety of activities and practicing active listening. Finally, we develop *values* through awareness of the relationship of communication to cultural intelligence, valuing diversity, and trust in interpersonal relationships.

INDIVIDUALS IN ORGANIZATIONS

Working in organizations is an important fact of life for almost everyone, so important, in fact, that for most people, organizational experiences influence how we evaluate our individual self-worth and achievements. Yet how do we understand these experiences? How do they relate to developing communication competencies for organizational excellence?

An individual's organizational experiences result from the attitudes, beliefs, preferences, and abilities the individual brings to the organization; how the organization seeks to influence the individual; and what types of organizational relationships the individual develops. Each person brings to an organization his or her personal needs, predispositions for behavior, communication competencies, expectations, and skills. Individuals also develop relationships with supervisors, peers, employees, customers, and vendors that become primary information sources about all aspects of organizational life. The organization in turn establishes goals, policies, procedures, and reward systems that influence individual expectations and job experiences. In other words, we all have individual identities separate from the organizations of which we are a part, we develop relationships with others based in part on our perceptions of ourselves and our experiences, and we engage in the day-to-day give-and-take of these relationships within the context of specific organizations.

Donald Campbell (2000) described the emergence of the notion of the proactive organizational member. According to Campbell, proactive individuals are interpersonally effective, exhibit task and job competence, are expected to be committed to their work, and engage in taking initiative. Proactive individuals use independent judgment, exhibit personal integrity, and are guided by high values. The description of the proactive individual closely resembles what we have been describing as organizational communication competency.

An individual's relationship with his or her supervisor is one of the most important of the primary communication experiences in organizational life. It is so important, in fact, that the quality of this relationship usually determines how the individual identifies with the organization as well as the individual's job and organization satisfaction. Peers also are an important source of information and support. Communication experiences with supervisors and peers are so influential that they contribute to the quality and quantity of an individual's work. The research of J. David Pincus (1986) has related quality and quantity of work—job performance—to perceptions of organizational communication experiences. In particular, quality of supervisory communication and information exchange within peer groups has been significantly related to revenue and workload measures of the overall organization. In other words, individuals who are satisfied with organizational communication experiences are more likely to be effective performers and to be satisfied with their jobs than those who have less positive communication relationships.

Figure 5.1 illustrates the primary communication experiences of individuals in organizations and relates these experiences to organizational outcomes such as communication and job satisfaction. The next sections of this chapter explore intrapersonal and interpersonal experiences in organizations and identify strategies and tactics for increasing individual communication effectiveness. Chapter 6 discusses individuals and small-group experiences.

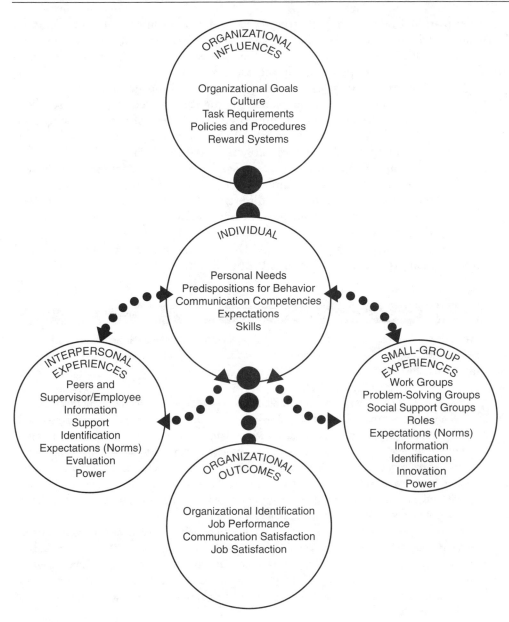

FIGURE 5.1
Individuals in Organizations: Primary Communication Experiences

THE INTRAPERSONAL EXPERIENCE

Most of us want to identify with the organizations for which we work. We want to be thought of as good performers with high work standards. Certainly, most of us want to be satisfied with organizational communication as well as other aspects of our jobs. Earlier we found people's work satisfaction is related to a variety of organizational relationships. If true for us, it becomes important to understand what contributes to these relationships. Among the primary influences on our relationships with supervisors, peers, and all employees are the individual characteristics we possess, characteristics that can be described as our **intrapersonal experience** or as some would describe our personal identity. The intrapersonal experience is based in part on self-concept, which in turn is influenced by a variety of past experiences, including various group affiliations. Our intrapersonal experience is composed of our personal needs, self-concept, predispositions for behavior, communication competencies, and expectations. We quickly recognize the intrapersonal experience is complex and differs from individual to individual. Understanding and appreciating these differences become central to building effective and satisfying organizational relationships. Before we discuss ways of understanding the intrapersonal experience, we return to Dave Green and his first real job. We look at what Dave brings to AMX as a way of understanding individual intrapersonal experiences within organizations.

Intrapersonal experience ■ Composed of our personal needs, predispositions for behavior, communication competencies, and expectations.

▸ DAVE GREEN: THE INTRAPERSONAL EXPERIENCE

Dave knows the AMX job will be a test of what he has learned. He has always been a top student. He was proud to be listed on honor rolls, and he graduated in the top 10 percent of his class. He has thought a lot about the AMX interview questions concerning his strengths and weaknesses and ultimate career goals.

Dave knows he has good verbal skills and has been able to work effectively in groups. In fact, on most group projects during his university days he volunteered to do the oral presentations, something many of his fellow students dreaded. In return, Dave has not always done his share of the research and writing. He remembers describing himself to the AMX interviewer as a leader, yet he wonders if that will be at all appropriate when he is the new member of an experienced work team. As Dave thinks about his new job, he is inclined to wait and let others take the lead until he has more experience. After all, he wants the people at AMX to think that he is competent and worthy of their decision to hire him.

As Dave begins his new job, he expects his work to be very different from his four years of college. He believes AMX is a top company with highly competent people. He is somewhat apprehensive about his ability to produce in a team of experienced researchers and trainers. Also, he believes his new boss will have high expectations of his abilities, abilities that as yet have not been thoroughly tested. As learned in Chapter 2, Dave is in the anticipatory phase of socialization. ■

Motivation

Dave Green would say that he is beginning his new job at AMX with high **motivation**. He wants to succeed and looks forward to the chance to demonstrate his abilities. He has a generally positive sense of self. Chances are the AMX interviewers offered him the job because they also believed he was motivated to achieve. What exactly is motivation, and how does motivation relate to intrapersonal experience and communication competency?

Motivation ■ Intrapersonal experiences that influence behavior.

Put simply, *motivation* is the term used to describe intrapersonal experiences that influence behavior. We don't see the motivation, but we see behavior. We infer unseen internal reactions have motivated that behavior. Dave Green, for example, tells the interviewer he is eager to work for such a well-respected management training firm. Dave's statement is observable behavior. The interviewer, however, infers Dave's statement of eagerness reflects his motivation to succeed at AMX. Taking the interview and Dave's qualifications as a whole, the interviewer decides Dave is positively motivated to behave in a way desirable to AMX. As a result, Dave gets the job.

Chances are we can all recall times when we were highly motivated to do a good job and other times when we were not motivated at all. We recognize what feeling motivated is and can understand that in some way that feeling influenced our behavior. What causes that internal experience? What happens to motivate us?

Social scientists take many different approaches to describe the somewhat ambiguous concept of motivation for behavior. Abraham Maslow, for example, contended behavior is influenced by internal needs. He thought needs such as safety and security, prestige, and self-actualization are more important in understanding an individual's behavior than influences in the external environment. Frederick Herzberg, on the other hand, described behavior as a result of both internal and external motivators, and B. F. Skinner viewed reinforcement from the external environment as the primary influence for behavior. In their criticism of need satisfaction theories, Gerald Salancik and Jeffrey Pfeffer provided an important link between motivation and communication theory when they proposed that workers' job attitudes are a function of their communication activities.

Hierarchy of Needs Theory   Abraham Maslow (1908–1970) is famous for what has been described as his **Hierarchy of Needs** theory, which proposes that human behavior seeks either to increase need satisfaction or to avoid a decrease in need satisfaction. According to Maslow (1954), individuals focus attention on needs that are not met and are motivated to seek satisfaction of those needs. Maslow described needs in an ascending hierarchy beginning with physiological needs, followed by safety and security needs, love and social belonging, esteem and prestige, and self-actualization (see Figure 5.2).

Hierarchy of Needs ■ Maslow's description of human behavior based on an ascending order of physiological, safety and security, love and social belonging, esteem and prestige, and self-actualization needs.

Physiological needs are the basic body needs of food, sleep, sex, and survival. Although these needs vary from individual to individual, Maslow contended that until these needs are reasonably well met, individuals do not focus their behavior on higher-level needs. From an organizational perspective, many physiological needs are met by the regularity of a paycheck, which provides food and basic physical survival.

Maslow believed the satisfaction of safety and security needs also varies from individual to individual. What constitutes freedom from physical harm and security to one individual may not represent that same safety to another. Individuals in organizations satisfy their safety and security needs when they believe their jobs are relatively secure and when working conditions are free of physical harm.

FIGURE 5.2
The Need Levels in Maslow's Hierarchy of Needs

Love and social belonging needs are met through family affiliations, friend-ships, and a variety of peer groups that provide social support and affection. As with all other needs, the degree to which individuals seek love and social belonging varies. Social belonging needs in organizations are generally thought of as being sat-isfied through peer and supervisory and employee relationships and through simi-larities between the organization's values and the values of individual members.

Maslow described esteem and prestige needs as the desire for self-respect and the respect of others. Esteem and prestige are both internally defined and influ-enced by perceptions of what is prestigious to others. In organizations, esteem and prestige needs are satisfied through performance evaluation, job titles, status sym-bols, and the pride individuals feel in their work contributions.

Self-actualization is at the top of Maslow's hierarchy. According to Maslow, self-actualization is the belief that one has satisfied his or her full potential and is engaged in activities for which he or she is uniquely suited. As such, self-actualization cannot be explained in terms of a specific organizational responsibility or recogni-tion but in terms of how an individual believes his or her abilities are used within the organizational setting.

Maslow's Hierarchy of Needs has several important implications for com-munication behavior. The theory implies individual communication behavior in some way reflects an assessment of need satisfaction. Observation of individual communication behavior can therefore provide important evidence about what is motivational to an individual at a given time. The individual who communicates insecurity about his or her acceptance in a work team may be focusing on low fulfillment of love and social belonging needs. A supervisor, according to Maslow, is unlikely to be able to motivate this individual by describing the prestige associated with a new job assignment that further removes the individual from peer approval.

Maslow's theory implies it is not motivational to communicate about needs that are reasonably well met. Although money and fringe benefits are important, communication designed to motivate at these lower-level needs frequently does not accurately assess the love and social belonging, esteem and prestige, and self-actualization needs of individuals. Maslow's theory also suggests if communication behavior in the organization does not meet the perceived needs of the individual, the individual will continue, in what is essentially healthy behavior, to seek need satisfaction. Thus, complaints and conflict that are often viewed as counterproductive organizational behaviors may be healthy individual behaviors in pursuit of personal need satisfaction.

As Dave Green begins his job at AMX, he is concerned about his acceptance in an experienced work team. Using Maslow's concepts we would say Dave is concerned about his love and social belonging needs. He is therefore likely to pay particular attention to communication with his peers and to behave in ways he believes appropriate for their acceptance.

Motivation–Hygiene Theory The **Motivation–Hygiene theory** of Frederick Herzberg (1923–2000) emphasizes the influence of both internal and external factors in explaining human behavior. Herzberg's (1966) theory proposed that satisfaction and dissatisfaction are not polar opposites. In other words, what produces dissatisfaction in the work environment, if corrected, will not necessarily produce satisfaction or motivation. His research suggested environmental factors (hygiene factors) such as status, interpersonal relations, supervision, policies, working conditions, and salary all influenced whether workers were dissatisfied. For example, if salaries were too low, dissatisfaction was predictable. If salary adjustments were made, however, satisfaction or motivation would not necessarily occur, although dissatisfaction might be lessened. The factors he found to be motivational were work itself, achievement, growth and responsibility, recognition, and advancement.

> **Motivation–Hygiene theory** ■
> Herzberg's description of human behavior based on the influence of both internal and external factors. The theory proposes that satisfaction and dissatisfaction are not polar opposites and that what produces dissatisfaction with work when corrected will not necessarily produce motivation.

Herzberg concluded many organizations attempt to motivate workers through hygiene factors, when hygiene factors can only be expected to relate to whether workers are dissatisfied, not whether they are truly motivated. From a communication perspective, Herzberg's Motivation–Hygiene theory suggests dissatisfaction can be relieved by satisfactory communication and action directed toward hygienic work factors. Motivation, however, will not be achieved by such communication. Motivational communication is more likely to be effective when directed to achievement, recognition, challenging work, increased responsibility, and growth and development.

Herzberg's concept of motivation, applied to Dave Green, suggests Dave will be motivated by his desire to be competent (to achieve) in his new work setting. From the Herzberg perspective, Dave's apprehension about joining an experienced work team is based on his motivation for challenging work and growth and development.

Rewards Theory   B. F. Skinner (1904–1990), in contrast to both Maslow and Herzberg, proposed that human behavior can be motivated and is influenced by **rewards** in the individual's environment. According to Skinner (1953), behavior reinforced through positive feedback or tangible rewards will be perpetuated, whereas behavior that does not receive positive reinforcement will be unlikely to continue. When applied to the organizational setting, the paycheck is a form of feedback that reinforces behavior expectations. Supervisors provide feedback on behavior to employees, and peer groups develop norms of expected behaviors that when exhibited by individuals are rewarded with continued group membership. Skinner's theory does not take into account individual needs, as Maslow's does, nor admit to complex relationships between satisfaction and dissatisfaction, as does Herzberg's Motivation–Hygiene theory. Skinner's theory does suggest that communication about rewards will be motivational only as long as rewards are linked to specific behaviors. In other words, if behavior is to be influenced, communication must be directed at specific behaviors, and linkages must be understood by people the organization seeks to influence.

Rewards ■ Positive feedback or tangible reinforcements for organizational behaviors.

Skinner's theory of what motivates behavior suggests Dave joined AMX because of what he knows about the organization and his belief that he has landed a prize job. His reward in obtaining the job will probably influence his attempts to exhibit behaviors that support the norms of his new work team. According to Skinner, these norm-conforming behaviors, if supported by positive feedback or tangible rewards from his peers and supervisor, will motivate Dave to perpetuate their use and become one of the group.

Social Information Processing Theory   Gerald Salancik (1943–1996) and Jeffrey Pfeffer in criticizing need satisfaction theories proposed that a person's needs and attitudes can be understood in terms of the **Social Information Processing theory**. This theory proposes people's needs and attitudes are determined by the information available to them at any given time. Salancik and Pfeffer (1978) suggested three basic determinants of attitudes or needs: (1) the individual's perception of the job or task characteristics, (2) information the social environment provides to the individual about what attitudes are appropriate (i.e., social information), and (3) the individual's perception of the reasons for his or her past behaviors. Thus, Salancik and Pfeffer described needs differently from the internal-drives portrayal of Maslow. Salancik and Pfeffer conceptualized needs as the results or outcomes produced by an individual's perceptions and by the social information available in the work environment.

Social Information Processing theory ■ Proposes that a person's needs and attitudes are determined by the information available at any given time.

Salancik and Pfeffer identified four ways in which social information influences attitudes: (1) overt, evaluative statements of coworkers directly shape individual worker attitudes; (2) frequent talk among coworkers about certain dimensions of the job and work environment focuses attention on what is considered to be important or salient in the work setting; (3) information from coworkers, or social information, helps an individual worker interpret and assign meaning to environmental cues and events in the work setting; and finally, (4) social information influences the way an individual interprets his or her own needs. Thus, Salancik and Pfeffer argued job attitudes are a result of social information in the work setting coupled with the consequences of past individual choices. The organization, then, can be viewed as having influence on attitudes by contributing information to the attitude formation process. The Social Information Processing theory challenges notions that individuals have stable, relatively unchanging internal needs. Salancik and Pfeffer proposed the communication activities of an organization act as a primary influence on attitude formation, which in turn is influential in understanding human behavior. In support of this perspective, later work suggests information in the organizational environment (sometimes referred to as passive information) has even a greater impact on reducing ambiguity for individuals than active attempts by individuals to seek clarifying information.

Dave Green's transition from school to AMX helps us understand the somewhat complex relationships proposed by Salancik and Pfeffer. Dave Green expresses a positive attitude about his experiences during college. The same Dave Green also expresses uncertainty about his ability to meet the expectations at AMX. Salancik and Pfeffer contend that the individual's perception of the job or task characteristics shapes attitudes or needs. Thus, it is expected Dave's perception of his competency will differ based on his understanding of the differences between college and AMX.

During college Dave made effective use of his verbal skills and ability to work in groups by volunteering to organize and make oral presentations researched and written by other classmates. Chances are Dave considered these tasks an appropriate use of his abilities (the approach met his needs), at least in part because his classmates approved of his efforts in the group and made known their dread of doing the presentations themselves. In other words, they influenced Dave with social information: (1) overt, evaluative statements about Dave's positive contributions and (2) frequent talking about certain important dimensions of the project (oral presentations).

Also, Dave told the AMX interviewer he was a leader, yet we see that he is inclined to let others take the lead until he has more experience at AMX. From the Salancik and Pfeffer perspective, Dave's attitude is probably shaped by his assignment of meaning to environmental cues, specifically the competence of the experienced team he is joining as a junior member. The Social Information Processing concept suggests Dave does not have a stable need to lead and that the difference in this need between college and AMX is based on the social information available to him about the differences in the expectations and realities of the two environments.

Relating Communication and Motivation   Regardless of their differences in perspective, the theories of Maslow, Herzberg, Skinner, and Salancik and Pfeffer relate motivation and attitudes to communication experiences and behaviors. Earlier we inferred from Dave Green's communication behavior that he was highly motivated as he began his new job at AMX. To illustrate the communication and motivation relationship further, the statements in Figure 5.3 have been taken from transcripts of conversations with workers asked to describe what motivates them in their

Maslow's Hierarchy of Needs Theory

1. Physiological needs. "I work because I have to put food on the table."
2. Safety and security needs. "I like to work here because there is a real commitment to no layoffs. The last place I worked wasn't like that."
3. Love and social belonging. "The people I work with are my best friends; we would do anything for each other."
4. Esteem and prestige. "This job has given me the visibility I need to advance."
5. Self-actualization. "My work is ideally suited for my talents. In some ways it doesn't seem right to take money for doing what I love to do."

Herzberg's Motivation–Hygiene Theory

Hygiene Factors:

1. Salary. "The pay here is good, and I give them a good return on their money."
2. Supervision. "I like my supervisor. We were really unhappy with the previous guy."
3. Status. "I like having my own office and a secretary. I've never had that before."

Motivation Factors:

1. Achievement. "I really feel a sense of accomplishment in this job."
2. Work content. "The work is challenging, and I think we are putting out a good product."
3. Responsibility. "They let us take real responsibility here. People expect the best but they don't always look over your shoulder."

Skinner's Positive Reinforcement Theory

1. Rewards. "We get a bonus if we outproduce our quota."
2. Rewards. "My supervisor was really complimentary about the design of the new system. I believe that my efforts are recognized."

Salancik and Pfeffer's Social Information Processing Theory

1. Social information. "My boss really helped me identify what was important for this job. I think that I have responded with efforts that are recognized by the organization."
2. Social information. "My coworkers really helped me learn the ropes. You can make a lot of mistakes in this job if you don't learn what your work team needs and wants."

FIGURE 5.3
Worker Examples of Personal Motivation

work. The statements have been categorized as they reflect the motivational theories of Maslow, Herzberg, Skinner, and Salancik and Pfeffer.

Predispositions for Organizational Communication Behaviors

Predispositions or preferences for organizational communication behaviors are an important part of an individual's intrapersonal organizational experience. Predispositions are personally held preferences for particular types of communication situations or behaviors. These preferences are a result of intrapersonal needs (motivation), personal self-concept, past experiences, current information, and self-perception of communication competency. Predispositions for oral communication, for example, have been found to be related to our occupation choice, job satisfaction, productivity, advancement, and job retention. Thus, we infer that communication predispositions and preferences influence behavior and are therefore important for individual organizational experiences.

Communication Apprehension   One of the most frequently researched of communication predispositions is what James McCroskey (1982) has described as **communication apprehension** (CA). Generally defined as an individual's level of fear or anxiety associated with either real or anticipated communication with others, CA has been found to be meaningfully associated with such important organizational outcomes as occupation choice, perception of competence, job satisfaction, advancement, and job retention. In other words, individuals with high communication apprehension are more likely than others to be in

Communication apprehension ■ Predisposition for behavior described as an individual's level of fear or anxiety associated with either real or anticipated communication with others.

jobs with low communication requirements, to believe themselves less competent than others, to exhibit lower job satisfaction than their counterparts, and to not advance in their organization as their technical skills might suggest they could. They will also spend less time than others with the organization. Virginia Richmond and McCroskey (2009) have related concepts such as shyness, willingness to communicate, argumentativeness and tolerance for disagreement, and aggressiveness to communication apprehension. While it is not the purpose of our text to describe all of these diverse constructs, awareness of the role of communication predispositions and preferences remains important for understanding individuals in organizations.

Dave Green does not appear to be high in communication apprehension, shy, or unwilling to communicate. His past experiences in groups suggest he will volunteer for public speaking situations and is generally comfortable with his verbal skills. He can be expected, more than a person with higher communication apprehension, to integrate with his work group and successfully use his abilities at AMX.

Leadership and Conflict Preferences

In addition to different levels of apprehension, individuals differ in their desire to lead others and in their perception of what is effective leadership. Individuals also differ in how they approach conflict. Leadership and conflict preferences have been theorized to influence choice of communication strategies and tactics in leadership and conflict situations. Numerous researchers have described both leadership and conflict predispositions and preferences in terms of an individual's combined concern for tasks or goals and people relationships. These two concerns combine with past experiences and an assessment of the present situation to influence behavior. Various predispositions for leadership and conflict behaviors are generally described as preferences for collaboration, compromise, avoidance, competition, or accommodation. For example, an individual with a strong competitive predisposition may not cooperate with the ideas of others in the same manner as an individual with a collaborative or accommodative predisposition. The individual with strong avoidance predispositions may attempt to avoid leadership responsibilities and conflict situations, as would the person with high communication apprehension. We describe these preferences in detail in later chapters, and you will be provided with an opportunity to assess your individual predispositions for leadership and conflict.

Communication Competency

Individuals' perceptions of their communication competencies—knowledge, sensitivity, skills, and values—influence their organizational experiences. When individuals believe their competencies are lower than those of others, that fact may well limit the responsibilities they will accept. On the other hand, individuals who assess their competencies as comparable to those of others may willingly accept new responsibilities as challenging and worthwhile. Perception of competency is, of course, related to communication apprehension and leadership and conflict preferences, but it is also related to past experiences, the presence or absence of particular skills, and deliberate attempts to improve competencies. As such, perception of competency can be described as a summing up of preferences and predispositions for organizational communication behavior.

INTERPERSONAL EXPERIENCES

Much of our time in organizations is spent interacting with other people. A variety of interpersonal communication relationships is important for individual job involvement, satisfaction, identification, commitment, and productivity. This variety is important in understanding yet another dimension of how individuals experience organizations. As you might expect from the discussion of the intrapersonal experience, predispositions and preferences influence the types of interpersonal relationships individuals establish. Preferences, however, are inadequate to explain fully what happens in what are called primary dyadic relationships in organizations. The relationships supervisors and employees and peers establish are governed not only by individual predispositions, but also by important task and social considerations as well as increasing diversity in the workplace. Before we explore the primary interpersonal relationships of supervisors and their employees and individual peer interactions, we return to Dave Green and observe some of his early **interpersonal experiences** at AMX.

Interpersonal experiences ■ Descriptions of important one-on-one organizational relationships such as supervisors and employees and peer to peer.

▶ DAVE GREEN: INTERPERSONAL EXPERIENCES

Dave was pleased that John, the senior writer on the team, had asked him to lunch. Dave had worried John might treat him like a kid because John did remind Dave a bit of his own father. He could learn a lot from John and certainly wanted John to think he was doing his job. Maybe John could fill him in on what his boss, Sally Johnson, really expected. The first few weeks of Dave's job at AMX had left him both elated and confused. Sally was friendly and seemed anxious for him to succeed, yet he wasn't sure what her expectations were. She had assigned him to do some research for part of the new project, but organizing and presenting the material were left up to Dave. Dave wasn't comfortable with asking her just what she wanted for the end product. He wasn't sure if Sally wanted a particular approach or didn't care as long as the material was good. John had told him yesterday that Sally would listen to a variety of approaches if the information were interesting and important. Dave was somewhat apprehensive about what Sally would find interesting. This lunch with John was timely. Maybe he could run some ideas past him and get a better feel for what he should do. ■

Dave's dilemma about his assignment is not unusual. Establishing expectations in supervisor–employee relationships can be difficult, especially in the beginning of a job. Dave is fortunate to have a peer like John who can help him define Sally's expectations and give him support as he adjusts to new challenges and ways of doing things. Dave experiences what was described in Chapter 2 as encounter socialization.

Successfully meeting Sally's expectations will influence not only how Sally feels about Dave, but also Dave's entire organizational experience. As researchers Sue DeWine and Frank Barone (1984) suggested that "perceived organizational communication relationships are considered to be the most important contributor to job satisfaction as an organizational outcome."

FORMING INTERPERSONAL RELATIONSHIPS

Most relationships in organizations begin on a relatively impersonal basis. We base our understanding of people on what we know about their membership in a specific group, culture, or role and make predictions about communication on general versus individual, specific information. Our effectiveness in interpersonal relationships relates to our awareness of differences and similarities in groups and our willingness to test the accuracy of our understanding. In addition, effectiveness relates to our ability to accept differences as legitimate and important for organizational effectiveness. Dave Green begins his relationship with Sally Johnson based on his understanding of professional women and his expectations of what managers do. As Dave becomes acquainted with Sally, the relationship becomes more interpersonal, with Dave and Sally responding to each other not just as members of groups but also as unique individuals. Relationships are key to our socialization both as we enter an organization and throughout our work life. In Chapter 2 we discussed anticipatory, encounter, and metamorphosis socialization as important processes through which we learn appropriate behaviors, norms, and values of an organization. In general, we can conclude that as relationships develop we gather information that helps us establish the general norms or rules of how our interactions will progress.

Interpersonal relationships in organizations are formed for important task and social considerations. Unlike our personal relationships, the organization actually structures for us many interpersonal encounters necessary for task accomplishment. To become effective in these diverse relationships, it is important to understand how we are attracted to others and how the impressions we form influence our communication behaviors.

We are attracted to others by physical and personality characteristics. We attribute, for example, more positive characteristics to those we identify as more physically attractive than to their less attractive counterparts. Research also indicates we are most likely to find attractive those individuals who are similar to us in attitudes and beliefs and in relatively close physical proximity. The influences of similarity and physical proximity often prove problematic when establishing interpersonal relationships in organizations. The organizational requirement to work with those very different from us and in both close and distant proximity challenges us to examine how we form impressions and how we evaluate the competencies of others. In other words, do we evaluate as more competent and worthy of trust those organizational members who are most like us and with whom we have frequent contact? What are the implications of such an evaluation?

In addition to evaluations based on similarity and physical proximity, we tend to like most of those individuals who reward or reinforce us. We prefer people who compliment rather than criticize. Again this pattern of impression formation, although certainly understandable, can limit the amount of developmental feedback we solicit or accept from diverse organizational members. Positive feedback, although comforting, does not always stimulate the growth necessary to increase our competency.

Although research does suggest we are most comfortable with those similar to us and those who reinforce us, we also form positive impressions of those who have complementary rather than similar characteristics. For example, talkative individuals may form their most satisfying relationships with less talkative peers, and some supervisors may prefer submissive to more dominant employees. In general, however, research suggests we are most likely to form positive impressions of those who we find physically attractive; have similar attitudes to ours; and are of the same race, religion, age, and general social class. We also make assessments about individuals occupying positive positions of prestige or credibility in work groups or in the organizational hierarchy. JC. Bruno Teboul and Tim Cole (2005) suggested that "in organizational settings, humans strive to develop relationships with the highest complementary and highest similar (partners) available. Consequently, they classify other employees at any given time as high and low preference partners."

We are more likely to establish satisfying interpersonal relationships based on similarity than relationships characterized by diversity. The implications for organizational effectiveness are obvious. Fully competent organizational members must not limit themselves only to the familiar but must be open to establishing satisfying and effective interpersonal relationships with both similar and dissimilar others. Dave Green will face this challenge as he joins members of a team different in age, sex, and ethnicity.

Supervisors and Employees

The supervisor–employees (subordinate) relationship can be described as the primary interpersonal relationship structured by the organization. Because it is formed to support task and job requirements, almost everyone in an organization—except perhaps at the very top of the hierarchy—is involved in such a dyad. Dave Green and Sally Johnson form the supervisor–employee dyad of our AMX case.

Both supervisors and employees bring a wide variety of personal characteristics and predispositions to their relationships. The interaction of these characteristics influences the satisfaction each person feels with the other and helps determine the overall effectiveness of the relationship. A supervisor, for example, who thinks an employee shares similar values is more likely to view that employee as competent. Employees, on the other hand, are more likely to be satisfied with both work and supervision if they perceive a high degree of communication competency in the relationship. Research suggests an employee's perception of the supervisor's ability to listen, respond quickly to employee messages, and be sensitive and understanding is the strongest predictor of satisfaction with both work and supervisor. Employees' satisfaction with their supervisors also has been found to be directly related to their perception of their own personal communication competence. Vincent Waldron and Marilyn Hunt (1992) found that individuals reporting high-quality relationships with their supervisors were more likely to engage in informal, friendly interactions with their supervisors, to conform to formal and informal requests, to attempt to clarify expectations, and to accept criticism from supervisors than were individuals reporting lower-quality relationships.

Supervisor–employee relationships frequently have been described in terms of Leader–Member Exchange (LMX) theory. LMX theory suggests leaders have limited time and resources and share both their personal and positional resources differently with their employees. Jaesub Lee (1997), in synthesizing much of this research, suggested "leaders tend to develop and maintain LMXs with their subordinates that vary in quality, ranging from high (in-group) to low (out-group). In-group exchange is a high quality relationship characterized by high levels of information exchange, mutual support, informal influence, trust, and greater negotiating latitude and input in decision influence. At the other extreme is out-group exchange, a low quality relationship in which the opposite is observed (e.g., more formal supervision, less support, and less trust and attention from the superior)" (p. 269). LMX has been linked to a variety of communication behaviors with both supervisors and peers.

Related to this notion of LMX is what has been called the "Pelz effect" or the supervisor's upward LMX with his or her own boss. As early as 1952, Donald Pelz found supportive communication from supervisors perceived to have high upward influence was more satisfying to employees than supportive communication from supervisors perceived to be low in the ability to influence their own supervisors. Relating the Pelz effect to LMX, Lee (1997) concluded employees who perceived a positive LMX with their supervisors and who perceived their supervisors to have high upward influence were more likely to engage in cooperative communication as contrasted to competitive communication within the work group.

In later work, Lee (2001) found individuals in high-quality LMX relationships were more likely than those in low-quality relationships to believe supervisors distributed resources fairly and used fair procedures and processes. Furthermore, these perceptions influenced how much employees reported sharing information, ideas, and resources with work group peers. In other words, the less favorable the relationships with the supervisor, the more likely individuals were to withhold information even from their peers.

Other studies support the importance of communication competency for the supervisor–employee relationship. Numerous studies report supervisors who are high in communication apprehension are not as well liked as those lower in apprehension, and highly apprehensive employees are not as likely as others to seek supervisory positions. In general, we can say relationships between supervisors and employees are influenced by a wide variety of communication behaviors; the predispositions, preferences, and abilities of both supervisors and employees; and overall work environments.

What is the nature of communication between supervisors and employees? For one thing, it is frequent and time-consuming. Supervisors may spend from one-third to two-thirds of their time communicating with employees. Research also suggests employees want and seek interaction with their supervisors. In fact, employees are more likely to seek both formal and informal help from their supervisors than from peers or their own employees.

Communication between supervisors and employees is diverse and complex in content and both face-to-face and mediated with a variety of technologies. Patricia Sias (2009) has described supervisor–employee relationship functions as leadership, information exchange, feedback and appraisal, mentoring, and power and influence. Supervisors initiate discussions to establish task requirements and performance expectations; act as information sources; provide feedback and appraisal; engage in formal and informal mentoring; and utilize both appropriate and inappropriate methods to influence, exercise power, and generally control the work environment. Employees also are information sources for supervisors, providing upward feedback and responding to or resisting influence attempts. The effectiveness of these message exchanges contributes to employees' job satisfaction, quality of work performed, commitment, creativity, and overall communication satisfaction.

Research on supervisor–employee communication reports a "positivity bias" in upward communication. Paul Krivonos (1982) summarized many of the findings about upward communication in the following four categories: (1) employees tend to distort upward information, saying what they think will please their supervisors; (2) employees tend to filter information and tell their supervisors what they, the employees, want them to know; (3) employees often tell supervisors what they think the supervisor wants to hear; and (4) employees tend to pass personally favorable information to supervisors while not transmitting information that reflects negatively on themselves. Janet Fulk and Sirish Mani (1986) suggested the perception of supervisors' downward communication, or the extent to which supervisors are perceived as actively withholding information, influences the accuracy of upward messages. The more the supervisor withholds, the more employees withhold and distort. In general, we can say if trust levels between supervisors and employees are low, and if employees have mobility aspirations they believe their supervisors can influence, there is likely to be a positivity bias that distorts upward communication.

The work of Kathleen Krone (1992) suggested employees who are most likely to attempt to influence their supervisors report having high control over their work and high participation in decision making. Supervisors with empowered (control over work and decisions) employees are more likely to ask employees for their opinions, and employees believe their upward influence is likely to be successful. Eric Eisenberg and H. L. Goodall (1993) referenced the work of Patricia Riley and Eric Eisenberg when they suggested: "The primary skill individuals must cultivate in managing their boss is advocacy—the process of championing ideas, proposals, actions, or people to those above you in the organization. Advocacy requires learning how to read your superior's needs and preferences, and designing persuasive arguments that are most likely to accomplish your goals. The advocacy approach differs sharply from traditional views of superior–subordinate communication, which emphasize the importance of subordinate compliance and dramaturgy, of playing the good underling, and making your boss look good" (p. 230).

We can certainly see why individuals want to be positively perceived by their supervisors, but we can also readily understand that a bias for positive upward communication may not be effective for the organization. When a positivity bias distorts upward communication, supervisors may not receive timely information about problems. Thus, needed information about innovation and change may be slow in coming, particularly if the supervisor is perceived as resistant to new ideas. Trust between supervisors and employees is the key to improving accurate communication and reversing the possible negative effects of a positivity bias. And trust is established through the communication competencies that both parties bring to relationships. In other words, the knowledge, sensitivity, skills, and values exhibited by both supervisors and employees contribute to the quality of relationships and to ultimate effectiveness.

The relationship between a supervisor and an employee is influenced not only by the amount of openness and support between the two but also by the amount of influence the supervisor has in satisfying the employee's needs. Much research supports the notion that employees base upward influence messages on their perception of how their supervisor attempts to influence them, the ability or power of the supervisor to influence others positively on behalf of his or her employees, and the perception on the part of employees about whether upward influence will indeed affect organizational decisions. Markku Jokisaari and Jari-erik Nurmi (2009) reported levels of supervisor support were directly related to employee role clarity, job satisfaction, and changes in salary levels. Employees reporting high perceived supervisor support also reported role clarity and job satisfaction that was greater than employees perceiving lower supervisor support. Additionally, employees reporting high supervisor support enjoyed rates of salary increases that were higher than employees with less supervisor support.

The quality of the supervisor–employee relationship also relates to the expectations of the supervisor. Donald Campbell (2000) identified common supervisor expectations important for employees: job and task competence, interpersonal effectiveness, organizational orientation, enterprising qualities, and personal integrity. One of the important characteristics of supervisor–employee communication is the frequent gap in information and understanding between what the supervisor perceives and what an employee believes to be true. Supervisors and employees frequently differ on such important issues as basic job duties, performance expectations, amount and quality of communication exchange, and desirability of employee participation in decision making. John Hatfield, Richard Huseman, and Edward Miles (1987) reported supervisors overestimate, according to employees, the amount of positive verbal recognition they give. In addition, supervisors report giving less negative feedback than their employees report receiving. Finally, the greater the perceived gap in verbal recognition, the lower the employee's satisfaction with supervision and overall job satisfaction.

Another type of relationship frequently developed between supervisors and employees is the mentor-to-mentee relationship. This relationship is based on mutual trust and respect and the desire of the mentor (usually a supervisor/manager or another person higher in position or senior in longevity with the organization than the mentee) to assist in career development for a specific individual. The mentor engages in coaching and advice extending beyond immediate job requirements to include information on how to be viewed as a successful contributor to the organization and how to make decisions likely to result in favorable organizational recognition. Research consistently has supported the importance of mentoring for career advancement. Unfortunately, much of this research suggests mentors are most likely to select for mentoring those individuals who are similar to the mentor. These findings present challenges for an increasingly diverse workforce.

After being exposed to some significant findings from the research on supervisor–employee (subordinate) relationships, how would you advise Sally and Dave? Describe the adequacy of the performance expectations she has established. How can she build trust with Dave? What should Dave do? Think about any supervisor–employee relationships in which you have been involved. How candid were you in upward communication? Describe what trust means to you.

Peers

Although secondary in importance to supervisor–employee relationships, peer relationships are an important part of an individual's organizational experiences. Relationships with peers are characterized by both task and social interaction: peers communicate job information, advice, evaluation of performance, and personal feedback. Peers help us "learn the ropes" and identify with the organization. Peers help us learn about the culture of the organization, share tasks, and trouble-shoot work-related problems. Peers often engage in socializing outside the work environment and share in a variety of important life events. Communication in the peer relationship frequently is more candid and of a more personal nature than communication with supervisors. As with supervisor relationships, peers are important for motivation, commitment, creativity, and overall satisfaction. It is fair to say that most of us will spend more time with our peers than with our supervisors.

Peers are members of a work group to which an individual belongs. Peers also are members of other groups at the same approximate structural level within the organization as well as individuals who are internal customers of a product or service produced by a given work group. Simply put, peers are all organizational members of approximately the same organizational structure, role, and responsibility levels.

Increasing research focuses on the one-to-one aspect of peer relationships. There is broad support for the importance of peer interactions for providing integration, or a sense of belonging, in organizational life. For example, individuals who are high in communication apprehension are less likely than others either to send or to receive integrative messages at the peer level. These same individuals also report less communication participation overall than their peers and lower overall communication satisfaction. On the other hand, individuals who have been promoted to management and those who expect vertical mobility are more likely than others to have developed a sense of belonging with their peers and organization.

Peers are central to the advice networks in which most individuals participate. Advice networks form around information transfer, communicate professional values, and contribute to both retarding and stimulating innovation. Peers can help one another solve problems and determine what approaches are best with particular supervisors. Dave Green has positive expectations about his interactions with his more experienced peer, John. Dave hopes John will be able to clarify his first assignment from Sally. Although Dave likes John, he is not certain how John evaluates Dave's abilities.

Beverly Davenport Sypher and Theodore Zorn Jr. (1987) described how peers evaluate each other in terms of liked and disliked coworkers. Liked coworkers were most frequently depicted as considerate, personable, and exhibiting integrity-related behaviors. The higher in the organization the employee and the more he or she had mobility aspirations, the more ability to influence was wanted from liked peers. Lack of integrity led the list of descriptors for disliked coworkers, followed by self-centered and insecure behaviors. The Sypher and Zorn research specifically addressed the importance in peer relationships of the sensitivity and value components for communication competency.

Patricia Sias and Daniel Cahill (1998) explored factors and communication changes associated with the development of workplace friendships among peers. Sias and Cahill explain:

> We found that peer friendships experienced three primary transitions: from coworker/acquaintance-to-friend, friend-to-close friend, and close friend-to-almost best friend. The coworker-to-friend transition was perceived to be caused primarily by working together in close proximity, sharing common ground, and extra-organizational socializing. Communication at this transition became broader, yet remained relatively superficial. The friend-to-close friend transition was associated primarily with problems in one's personal and work experiences. Communication at this transition became broader, more intimate, and less cautious. The close friend-to-almost best friend transition was associated primarily with life events, work-related problems, and the passage of time. Communication became less cautious and more intimate. (p. 273)

Generally, workplace friendships are believed to provide overall positive benefits for organizational members. Studies have associated workplace friendships with improved workplace performance, reduced stress, favorable perceptions of personal support, a positive work environment, and the ability to engage in change and innovation. In recent work, Thomas Feeley, Jennie Hwang, and George Barnett (2008) found employees who were active in their social networks and had a number of workplace friends were more likely to remain with their employer than individuals with fewer workplace connections.

One special category of workplace friendship deserves our specific attention: romantic relationships. Romantic relationships have been known to contribute to personal satisfaction and happiness and to serious workplace problems including termination. Many organizations have specific policies about romantic relationships within the work environment. Most organizations do not permit an individual in either a married or romantic relationship to have evaluative or approval authority over a romantic partner. Other organizations discourage employment of both partners in a romantic relationship. Peers often are uncomfortable with romantic relationships in peer groups, believing subtle or overt favoritism may block group effectiveness. The romantic relationship is subject to a variety of ethical implications. Organizational travel policies, opportunities for advancement, compensation, and a host of other issues are complicated by the romantic relationship. However, numerous individuals have handled this relationship with high integrity and without organizational damage.

It is important to recognize that peer relationships can be negative. Patricia Sias and Tara Perry (2004) described five primary factors contributing to poor peer relationships and actual relationship deterioration: problem personality, distracting life events, conflicting expectations, promotion, and betrayal. Peer and other relationships may deteriorate when annoying personality traits outweigh other benefits of the relationship. Relationships also deteriorate when a peer's personal problems interfere with his or her work and the overall relationship. Peers often distance themselves when conflicting expectations about appropriate behaviors cannot be resolved. The promotion of one individual to authority over the other and betrayal of trust or the withholding of important information also are contributors to deteriorating relationships. Bullying and mobbing are specific examples of the abuse of power in peer relationships. Sias (2009) has described bullying as "a dyadic phenomenon in which a bully repeatedly continually harasses and abuses a specific victim. Such abusive behaviors include verbal abuse, undermining the victim's work, and belittling the victim. . . . *Mobbing* is basically a group version of bullying that involves a group of people 'ganging up' on a victim. Employees who mob a coworker actively seek out communication with the victim with the intent to torment, hurt, and frustrate, rather than simply ignore, the victim" (p. 68). Research suggests difference from the majority population often contributes to bullying and mobbing. Specifically, homosexuals and ethnic and racial minorities often are targets of efforts to isolate and ostracize. However, women, older workers, people with physical and cognitive disabilities, those with certain religious perspectives, and many others have been the targets of the destructive behaviors known as bullying and mobbing.

In an exit interview conducted in a highly successful West Coast research and development lab, one computer engineer claimed both of his peers were aware that the line of reasoning he used for his design had been previously rejected by their manager. Neither peer shared information, permitting the engineer to pursue six months of research with a high likelihood of failure. When asked why the manager did not know of the line of inquiry the engineer was pursuing, the engineer replied his peers had advised him to be somewhat vague with his manager, a person who rarely examined the specifics of the projects under his direction. Was the engineer set up to fail? Although not clear from the interview, his peer relationships were certainly destructive and probably contributed to an organizational performance that did not reflect his abilities or the needs of the company.

Customers, Clients, and Vendors

Individuals also form important interpersonal communication relationships with internal and external customers or clients as well as vendors or suppliers of the organization. These relationships are based initially on task concerns but frequently emerge into social support relationships as well. Customers generally are considered to be those who purchase products or services from an organization while clients are those who are in a professional advice or service relationship with the organization. Vendors are individuals or entire organizations who provide products or services to organizations other than their own. Customer, client, and vendor relationships are based on exchanges of information about products, services, timing, delivery, quality, and cost. These relationships often are established through telemediated channels but remain important to the goals of all the parties involved in the relationship.

The ability to assess expectations is critical to the nature of customer, client, and vendor relationships. Customers, clients, and vendors have specific expectations about needs, services, or products, which are unrelated to the personal characteristics of the individuals expected to support these requirements. Based on previous interactions with others, customers and clients often can be aggressive and demanding. Vendors, on the other hand, want to please their customer, sometimes making truthful exchange about schedules, quality, and pricing difficult. Customer, client, and vendor relationships may be transient or long term. Effective customer, client, and vendor relationships often are based on rapidly assessing needs, connecting to identified needs, and responding with both organizational and customer, client, or vendor needs in mind. Supervisors and peers frequently provide advice about these relationships, and individuals often are evaluated based on the satisfaction and production related to communication exchanges with customers and vendors. As the marketplace becomes more diverse and international, communication with customers, clients, and vendors requires increasingly complex competencies. We describe these relationships more fully when we talk about strategic communication in Chapter 10.

Communication Networks and Interpersonal Relationships

We introduced the concept of communication networks (formal and informal patterns of communication that link organizational members together) in Chapter 2. Dave's experiences help expand on the earlier discussion and explain the various networks we can expect in most any type of organization. Cynthia Stohl (1995) suggested networks can be described at four interdependent levels: personal, group, organizational, and interorganizational. Peter Monge and Noshir Contractor (2001) explained: "Communication networks are the patterns of contact between communication partners that are created by transmitting and exchanging messages through time and space." Dave will participate in all levels as he links not only with his primary work team and supervisor but also with others throughout the organization and with other organizations. Richard Farace, Peter Monge, and Hamish Russell (1977) identified three general properties of the links found in organizational networks: symmetry, strength, and reciprocity. They described a symmetrical link as persons equally exchanging information during an interaction. In other words, the network is symmetrical when both parties have approximately the same amount of give-and-take. Symmetrical links are common among peers when interacting about work problems or social interests.

The opposite of the symmetrical link is the asymmetrical link, in which one individual gives more information than another. Common organizational examples of asymmetrical links are supervisors giving directions to employees or instructors lecturing to students. In most cases, more information is sent from supervisors to employees and from instructors to students than the other way around.

The network property of strength refers to the frequency and length of interactions among linked individuals. Strong links communicate more frequently than weak links and usually have longer periods of interaction. The strength of communication links predicts who is influential among organizational members. The stronger the communication link among people, the greater the chances of linked individuals influencing one another's behavior.

The final property, reciprocity, describes the level of agreement among organizational members about their network links. In other words, do individuals agree or disagree about the type of link they have with one another? Disagreement about whether individuals are linked frequently can be understood in terms of the different perceptions individuals bring to communication relationships. For example, an employee may perceive a symmetrical link to his or her supervisor, whereas the supervisor would describe the link as somewhat weak and certainly asymmetrical. Independent observation could help to understand the discrepancy, but the perceptions of each individual would still influence their overall relationship.

Individuals perform diverse roles in networks. Common roles such as liaisons, bridges, gatekeepers, participants, nonparticipants, and isolates all function differently in communication networks. Liaisons link or connect groups with common information without being members of either group. Bridges link groups together by having membership in two or more groups. Both liaisons and bridges engage in what is described as boundary spanning. Boundary spanning occurs when one holds a role in a particular organization and is also responsible for linking or representing that organization to the external environment and to other organizations. Boundary spanning also occurs when individuals have multiple group memberships, requiring them to represent one group or groups to others.

Gatekeepers are positioned in networks to control the flow of information through a communication chain. Gatekeepers routinely receive information and determine whether to transmit that information to the next link or links in the chain. Managers are gatekeepers in relation to their employees. Administrative assistants are gatekeepers because they filter messages and may even determine who can reach their bosses. Employees can keep problems from their managers in a gatekeeper role. Anyone in the network can function in this role.

A network isolate can be described as an individual with few or no communication links throughout the organization. Isolates often are apprehensive about communication and deliberately avoid interaction with others. Few organizational members are complete isolates, however. Individuals or groups may be isolates from other groups. Competition between groups, for example, may weaken communication links and contribute to isolation, and individuals or groups may be isolated from certain communication functions while participating in others. An individual or group may be involved in the sending and receiving of organizing and relationship messages without being connected or linked (i.e., involved) in change messages or the innovative function.

Finally, there are the network participants and nonparticipants. Participants are individuals who participate in linked communication behaviors but who are not usually in liaison or bridge roles. They are typically seen as members of the group but not influential to other groups. Nonparticipants are formal members of groups but do not affiliate with others in the group to the extent that participants do. According to Gerald Wilson, H. Lloyd Goodall, and Christopher Waagen (1986), nonparticipants differ from isolates in that nonparticipants have demonstrated more communication and relationship abilities. Nonparticipants refrain from communication out of choice, not out of inability or fear. Figure 5.4 illustrates the communication links.

Network roles influence whom organizational members use as references to manage the uncertainty of organizational environments. Priti Shah (1998) explained individuals select social referents to help them evaluate and comprehend their performance, compensation, career trajectories, and work responsibilities. These social referents are particularly important during times of uncertainty.

The final type of link discussed here is called "weak ties," or our communication links that are less developed and generally more limited in space, place, time, and strength of emotional bonding. Beginning with the work of Mark Granovetter (1973), the notion of weak ties has been seen as important in organizations because individuals with many weak ties have increased access to information primarily because of the diverse nature of those links. In other words, individuals who are closely linked have the potential to all end up with the same information. Information coming from diverse sources provides the potential for different perspectives and new ideas. Technology and global connectivity make the concept of weak ties increasingly important. The ability to bring diverse individuals, information, and perspectives to organizational innovation, creativity, problem solving, and decision making has never been greater.

In addition to the focus on individual network roles, communication networks are described in terms of their overall size (numbers of members), inclusiveness (numbers of individuals in the network as contrasted to the numbers of isolates), density (ratio of pairs of nodes that are mutually reachable to total number of pairs of nodes), centralization (comparison of the links of the most central network individual with other network members), and a host of other features. Monge and Contractor (2001) described the importance of understanding that both formal and emergent networks exist side by side in organizations, with individuals having membership in multiple networks. They suggested "the distinction between formal and informal structures in organizations has diminished significantly in recent years and may become increasingly irrelevant in the coming decade. Reasons for this center on shifts in organizational structure and management philosophy. Prominent among these are changes to more team-based forms of organizing, the adoption of matrix forms of organizational structure, and shifts to network forms of organizing. At the core of these changes has been the explosion of lateral forms of communication made possible by new information technologies that facilitate considerable point-to-point and broadcast communication without regard for traditional hierarchy" (p. 446).

Individuals in Organizations

FIGURE 5.4
Black Boxes Illustrate Gatekeeper, Liaison, Bridge, and Isolate Communication Links

A word of caution about structure of networks is important. The increase in technologically linked networks has given rise for some to describe a division between network structures and the content of messages. However, content and structure are better understood as integrated and not to be separated for either individuals or entire organizations.

Diversity and Interpersonal Relationships

Most organizations employ men and women of different ages, ethnicity, race, sexual orientations, religions, physical and cognitive abilities, and values. Most of us will form as many interpersonal relationships in organizations with people who are different from us as with those with whom we have much in common. William Johnston (1987), in the Hudson Institute's famous Workforce 2000 report, described U.S.A. **workforce diversity** by five demographic facts: (1) the population and overall workforce are growing more slowly than at any time since 1930; (2) the number of younger workers is declining as the average age of the workforce and population rises; (3) women will continue to enter the workforce in record numbers; (4) minorities will be a larger proportion of the new labor force; and (5) immigrants will increase their participation as workers at the highest level since World War I. Johnston referred to these trends as facts based on the globe's known demographic profile.

Workforce diversity ■ Description of workers that emphasizes differences in age, gender, race, ethnicity, and values.

Sandra Ketrow (1992) provided an additional perspective: "According to Worldwatch Institute (September 12, 1992), women rather than men are the family breadwinners in most of the world, where sex discrimination against them is a major cause of poverty. If such discriminatory attitudes prevail through overt or implicit interaction in organizations, attention to sex and gender as they relate to work performance and work- or task-related communication is crucial as we watch the balance of numbers shift in our workplaces" (p. 3).

Lea Stewart (1993) put global population statistics in perspective: "By 2050, half of the U.S. population will be African American, Hispanic American, Native American, and Asian American. These demographic changes are a clear motivation for embracing cultural diversity in organizations. Although organizational cultures tend to try to reproduce themselves . . ., the culture of the past can no longer be replicated. The Organization Man no longer exists to fill middle management jobs in the same way as his predecessors did. . . . Thus, accepting cultural diversity is a necessity" (p. 2).

The increasingly diverse workforce results in differences in communication styles, needs for social support, languages, and values that all stimulate our abilities to form effective interpersonal relationships. Diverse people bring different intrapersonal attitudes, experiences, expectations, and competencies to organizations. These differences can contribute to organizational effectiveness when those with different styles and values work together in interpersonal relationships characterized by mutual understanding and satisfaction. Differences, however, can produce conflict, tension, stereotyping, harassment, discrimination, abusive control, and exclusion, all of which contribute to a variety of negative organizational outcomes. Evidence exists that negative outcomes continue with sex and racial/ethnic segregation of occupations, salary differences for women and minorities not explained by performance or education differences, and different evaluations of behaviors for women, minorities, and white males. Patricia Amason, Myria Allen, and Susan Holmes (1999) underscored the importance of the communication of social support as organizations adapt to multicultural issues such as cultural stereotyping, language barriers, and employee attempts to acculturate. In a study of Hispanic employees' acculturative stress and social support, Amason, Allen, and Holmes reported that for both Hispanics and Anglos, perceptions of support from supervisors did not differ, but social support communication was more likely to occur between members of the same racial/ethnic group. Of particular importance was the finding that praise and help with personal problems from Anglo to Hispanic peers was highly valued and significant in contributing to positive acculturation. Brenda Allen (2007) helped us understand

> reports, along with the chronic statistics about race-related socioeconomic disparities, reveal that race persists as a source of social inequality. However, many white persons in the United States seem to believe that racial discrimination is basically a thing of the past. Along with some persons of color, they sometimes invoke the language of color-blindness. . . . white people often seem to deem their racial identity as a nonissue, due greatly to invisible privileges of whiteness. During everyday interactions, they usually are not conscious of their race, and they are likely to claim not to notice others' race. They frequently conceive of racism as isolated, atrocious acts committed by dysfunctional individuals. These differences in perspectives derive from how all of us learn about race through dominant discourses, across various contexts and relationships. (p. 260)

Regardless of the positive or negative nature of interactions, the importance of interpersonal experiences for organizational life is well established. Whether an individual is a newcomer to the organization, a transferred or relocated worker, or a longtime member of a work group, we can see why it is important to understand how we form relationships in a diverse workforce and in particular how supervisor and employee and peer-to-peer relationships influence our organizational experiences.

TRUST AND INTERPERSONAL RELATIONSHIPS

Most people consider trust a critical factor in all types of interpersonal relationships, including those established in organizations. Although a somewhat ambiguous term, *trust* can be viewed as positive expectations about the behavior of others based on roles, relationships, experiences, and interdependencies. In work that Kathleen Ellis, Ruggero Cesaria, and I have conducted (Shockley-Zalabak, Ellis, and Cesaria, 2000; Ellis and Shockley-Zalabak, 2008), we discuss the central role that organizational communication plays in the behavioral dimensions of trust. The work we reviewed generally supports (1) accurate information, (2) explanations for decisions, and (3) openness in communication behaviors affecting perceptions of trustworthiness and overall job satisfaction. Information flow has the strongest relationship with trust in a supervisor. Adequate explanations and timely feedback on decisions are associated with higher levels of trust, as is communication that is accurate and forthcoming. Managers and supervisors who freely exchanged thoughts and ideas with their employees enhanced overall perceptions of trust. Research generally supports a concept that describes trust in overall organizational policies, processes, and programs as predictive of trust in top management. Perceptions of trust also are related to confidence that employees express in the competence of organizational leadership. This competence refers to leadership not only at the top management level but also at the supervisory and coworker levels. Here workers judge whether their supervisors and coworkers are competent and therefore trustworthy. At a peer and group level, the perception of competence and trust among peers and their leaders predicts the completion of goals for effective group outcomes. As we form interpersonal relationships, we make evaluations about the trustworthiness of others while understanding others are forming similar perceptions of us. We know trust is fluid and can move rapidly from trust to distrust. We also know from our experiences that once trust is lost it is often a difficult process to rebuild or regain. Fully competent organizational members learn to think about their behaviors in terms of whether they contribute to or detract from building trust. Fully competent organizational members know that in one way or another all of their behaviors are about trust in relationships.

WORKPLACE EMOTION, BALANCE, AND INTERPERSONAL RELATIONSHIPS

All of us can relate to emotion and interpersonal relationships. We also know emotion is part of workplace interpersonal relationships. Understanding the various types of workplace emotion and how they relate to balance between the personal and professional contributes to our abilities to understand complex organizational environments. Katherine Miller, Jennifer Considine, and Johny Garner (2007) identified five types of emotion in the workplace: emotional labor, emotional work, emotion with work, emotion at work, and emotion toward work. They distinguished the five with the following descriptions:

> . . . *emotional labor,* involves the display of emotion that is some way defined and controlled by management and, as a result, is often perceived as inauthentic. . . . *emotional work* includes emotion that, like emotional labor, is a part of the job itself but which is a natural outgrowth of job-related communication. Both emotional labor and emotional work stem from the work itself and involve interaction with some kind of client (e.g., customer, patient, student). . . . *emotion with work,* involves emotion that emerges through relationships and interaction with other employees in the workplace. . . . *emotion at work,* considers emotion that has its genesis outside of the workplace (e.g., worries from home, grief, excitement about a sports team) but is experienced in the workplace. . . . *emotion toward work* as the emotional experience in which the work or job is the target of the emotion. (pp. 232–233)

We will discuss further emotional labor and emotional work in Chapter 9.

Relationships with supervisors and peers generate emotions. Most of us have been uncomfortable with workplace displays of anger or sadness. Fewer of us are uncomfortable when joy and happiness are the expressed emotions. We have been told to keep our personal and professional lives separate, knowing that at times it is literally impossible to do so. And most of us have experienced either loving or hating a particular job. The issue is not whether emotion at work is relevant to our interpersonal relationships but how emotion impacts work and relationships.

The virtual work environment brings additional challenges for emotional expression. E-mail exchanges routinely feature punctuation marks to assist with the lack of nonverbal cues such as smiles or frowns. Previous written messages have not featured these expressions. As Stephen Fineman, Sally Maitlis, and Niki Panteli (2007) reported:

> We see this inventiveness in other ways too, such as substituting the non-verbal signals that convey face-to-face feeling and presence with the need for prompt, even instant, virtual messaging—and the ensuing anxiety should this not occur. . . . Indeed, the meaning of silence during virtual exchanges appears to have its own experiential and cultural architecture. For example, while studies in the US and the UK have shown that silence in virtual communication leads to frustration and has negative effects on team bonding. . . . there is evidence that East Asian participants are likely to regard silence as desirable and more respectful first-response when receiving an e-mail form an organizational superior. . . . It seems that, in the increasingly global virtual environment, members will confront cultural understanding about how virtual communications should be framed and understood. (p. 557)

Most of us have experienced anger expressions in telemediated communication that might not have occurred in face-to-face exchanges. Others can report times when misunderstandings escalated because of a lack of clarity in electronic message exchanges. Regardless of whether emotion is expressed in face-to-face or through telemediated channels, we readily understand its importance for our individual experience of work and interpersonal relationships. Can you identify a time when you felt your emotional expression at school or work was appropriate? Do you have an example when you wish you had reacted differently? What makes the difference?

TECHNOLOGY AND INTERPERSONAL RELATIONSHIPS

Most of the discussion to this point has focused on interpersonal relationships with people with whom we have face-to-face interactions. Although these relationships are vitally important, we have just illustrated that the virtual work environment is creating new challenges and experiences. Technology has changed and is changing literally all types of relationships in which we engage. We no longer work only with those with whom we have face-to-face contact. We work across time zones, different languages, cultural differences, and geographic locations. We work with people without extensive information about their backgrounds, values, or experiences. We are expected to work effectively with others, using a variety of communications technologies. For organizations today and more tomorrow, basic communication competencies include abilities to use electronic mail, computers, voicemail, fax machines, the Internet and World Wide Web, group decision support systems (GDSS), a variety of management information systems, and video and computer conferencing. In thinking about the use of complex technologies and interpersonal relationships, Thomas Friedman (2002) described (based on the work of Linda Stone) the notion that we are engaged in continuous partial attention. We listen to a conversation, answer our cell phone, send an e-mail, respond to a text message, check tweets and blogs, and make a business decision almost simultaneously. We rarely engage in sustained attention, yet all of these actions are part of our communication relationships.

The selection of one communication medium over another has been linked to whether the medium has the ability to support immediate feedback, can provide verbal and nonverbal information, uses natural language, and exhibits a personal focus. Using these criteria, face-to-face communication can be described as rich in information. Rich channels are more likely to be used for ambiguous and important messages, whereas channels low in richness are better suited to deal with unambiguous tasks. Research links the use of advanced communications technologies such as video and computer conferencing, group decision support systems, or personal digital assistants to organizational members' assimilation into organizations and to the reduction of a variety of uncertainties about organizational life. Jennifer Waldeck, David Seibold, and Andrew Flanagin (2004) found that organizational members described the use of advanced communication and information technologies as effective for their organizational assimilation. Although face-to-face interaction remained the highest-rated medium for assimilation, advanced technologies were a strong preference over all other traditional media such as print publications or telephone interactions. The advanced technologies were evaluated as convenient, useful, and important tools for communicating and seeking information.

More and more of us regularly use e-mail, instant messaging, texts, blogs, and video technology to exchange messages about tasks and social information. For a growing number of **teleworkers** (individuals who work at home or in other than organizationally owned or controlled spaces), telemediated communication is their primary process for establishing relationships, working on task-related concerns, and communicating the results of their work. Research suggests that for teleworkers, e-mail carries task information but contains more messages (than for workers in organizationally controlled physical space) about social/relational issues, innovations/suggestions, and grapevine information. How teleworkers develop relationships and relate to the organization is of increasing importance. Craig Scott and C. Erik Timmerman (1999) reported teleworkers who spend approximately 50 percent of their time as virtual employees are more likely to identify with the organization and its values than those who telecommute more frequently. Nicolle Ellison (1999) reported traditional managerial paradigms are challenged by arrangements wherein employees work primarily off-site. Ellison found that telework seemed to exacerbate tensions between organizational subcultures and between managers and employees. Employee and supervisor trust remained an issue. Teleworkers, more than their less "virtual" counterparts, socialized with clients, friends, and family as contrasted to coworkers. Finally, Sherry Thatcher and Xiumei Zhu (2006) described the impact of telecommuting on identity. Specifically, they propose that telecommuting can alter identification with the work group and require greater effort to bring congruence between an individual's

> **Teleworkers** ■ Individuals who work at home or in other than organizationally owned or controlled spaces.

self-perception and the perception of important others with whom the teleworker may have little to no face-to-face interaction.

All types of interpersonal relationships are affected by technology. Teleworkers submit work mostly without daily close supervision by management. Technology use in general promotes less face-to-face interaction. Myria Allen, Stephanie Coopman, Joy Hart, and Kasey Walker (2007) helped us understand how technology contributes to complexity in managing privacy boundaries between information employees seek to keep private and information the organization requires to reduce uncertainty. Many workers, for example, report using organizational e-mail and Internet access for personal use. Often that use is a violation of organizational policies; however, it is common practice and the violation is not enforced in many organizations. In other circumstances organizations investigate employee behavior with organizationally owned technologies, including reviewing employee e-mail use. Many job applicants are surprised to learn employers routinely evaluate prospective employees based on applicants' social networking posts and other social media usage. Working across time zones and geographies also means working across cultures and languages and with those with whom we have very little personal experience. Trust becomes increasingly important to virtual environments because we must act, perform, and behave without the cues with which we are most familiar. Although the nature of these changes requires further exploration, it is fair to say that technology will continue to change the types of interpersonal relationships we form and how we evaluate these relationships for effectiveness.

INCREASING INTERPERSONAL EFFECTIVENESS

Thus far, intrapersonal and interpersonal experiences common in organizational life have been examined in an attempt to understand how motivation influences communication behavior and how dyadic relationships are formed and shaped through communication. The importance of our own personal communication competency and our perception of the competency of others as it relates to satisfaction with interpersonal relationships and overall job satisfaction has been described. Yet the specific skills that individuals can use to improve communication effectiveness have not been identified. Now comes a discussion of the importance of cultural intelligence, valuing diversity, active listening, and descriptive message strategies.

Cultural Intelligence

The term *cultural intelligence* refers to an individual's ability to understand the behaviors of other people in terms of three classifications: those that are universally human, those that are specific to an individual, and those that are rooted in culture. Although the three classifications certainly overlap, the notion of cultural intelligence helps us assess our own reactions and responses based on a more comprehensive understanding of individual behaviors. Is the behavior to which we react something that most individuals do in certain circumstances? Is the behavior universally human? Is the behavior something that this particular individual seems to choose in this situation? How unique is the behavior?

Finally, can this behavior be described in terms of the individual's culture? How do I know? The culturally intelligent individual learns to assess his or her reactions by understanding the complexity of behavior and being willing to explore alternative explanations.

Valuing Diversity

Barriers and Positive Approaches   Understanding that the workforce is diverse does not automatically give us the ability to relate effectively to that diversity. In fact, most of us have had uncomfortable interactions with people who seemed to discount us and our abilities. We in turn have probably left others with that same sense of uneasy concern.

As we consider our personal communication competency, we can increase our effectiveness by understanding barriers to **valuing diversity** and positive approaches helpful in increasing understanding.

Valuing diversity ■ Ability to understand and appreciate the contributions that differences in people can make to organizations.

Several important barriers to valuing diversity help explain problems that frequently occur among men and women of differing cultures, ages, ethnicity, race, sexual orientation, religion, and values. For each barrier there are positive approaches that can improve effectiveness. The following discussion of barriers and positive approaches helps us examine our personal behaviors and better understand others.

Barrier One: Preconceptions and Beliefs That Foster Inaccurate Information and Confusion between Perceptions of Behaviors and Actual Behaviors.   Despite research to the contrary many continue to believe both young people and older people lack the competence and wisdom to make important organizational contributions. We often discount without thinking the contributions of those we place in particular categories; that is, we do not look at their behavior but what our inaccurate information suggests would be their potential contributions. In our culture, research continues to suggest the behaviors of male professionals have a wider range of acceptance than females. This is particularly true for white males, more than their racially or ethnically diverse counterparts. In other words, white males are generally more valued when their behaviors are deemed to be intelligent, aggressive, and ambitious than when females and nonwhite males exhibit similar behaviors. When we consider global cultural differences, the opportunities for preconceptions and beliefs that foster inaccurate information and confusion are virtually endless.

Positive Approach: Personalize Knowledge and Perceptions.   We can learn to separate our preconceptions, beliefs, and attitudes from actual behaviors. We can continually open our awareness to new information and new ways of understanding others. We can understand that knowledge is individual in nature and that others may legitimately view what is factual or correct very differently from us. In our organizational relationships, we can learn to describe what is accomplished, the merit of an idea, or the quantity of work performed. We can consciously separate, or personalize, these descriptions from beliefs about people of a given culture, national origin, age, sex, race, ethnic group, religion, or sexual orientation.

Barrier Two: Stereotypes That Limit the Potential Contributions of Individuals Based on Their Membership in a Group or Class. Stereotypes simplify our ability to understand the world by making predictions about people based on the group or class to which they most obviously belong. Stereotypes emerge from basic, widely believed characteristics of a given group. Although stereotyping in a diverse environment makes the world more predictable and deceptively approachable, in and of itself stereotyping invites inaccuracy and undervalues diversity. Stereotypes emerge not only about specific groups or classes of people but also about who should be more powerful, exhibit dominance in interrelationships, and generally engage in social control. Put simply, stereotypes give us a false aura of similarity and predictability that limits individual potential. Think about the specific stereotypes which apply to the groups of which you are a member. What stereotypes do you use?

Positive Approach: Tolerance for Ambiguity. Learning to tolerate and value ambiguity is the positive counterpart to the negative effects of stereotyping. An attitude of tolerating ambiguity accepts as normal an environment that requires us to know people as individuals, not as members of a group or class. A tolerance for ambiguity is a sensitivity competency important as we enter new situations of all types. Frustration and discomfort may be normal reactions to ambiguity, but the sorting through and making sense of diverse relationships are essential characteristics for interpersonal effectiveness.

Barrier Three: Prejudices That Produce Negative Emotional Reactions to Others. Prejudice arises from beliefs that given groups of people are generally inferior or that a given group interferes with important basic values. Prejudice is associated with discomfort about the unfamiliar and associated with behaviors we personally find offensive. The chances are that we have all had prejudices at one time or another. We react emotionally and negatively to others without accurate information or even direct personal contact. Prejudiced behavior can be overt, as in refusal to work with a given group of people, or subtle, as in appearing to accept an individual as equal while carefully controlling the amount of influence he or she can exert in any given situation. Prejudice limits interpersonal relationships by arbitrarily devaluing groups of individuals based on negative emotional reactions. In addition, as previously discussed, anything that hampers effective communication limits organizational effectiveness.

Positive Approach: Nonjudgmentalness. We all want to feel valued as individuals. Prejudice, or prejudging on the basis of the group to which we obviously belong, robs us of our individuality and limits effective interpersonal relationships. Nonjudgmentalness, or the positive opposite of prejudice, is exhibited by people who give others an opportunity to explain themselves. Nonjudgmental people base their reactions—whether positive or negative—on explanations, not group membership. Nonjudgmentalness requires active listening (a skill discussed later in this chapter) and a willingness to base our evaluations on an understanding of the other's point of view. When persons believe they have been heard, they are generally more receptive to hearing both positive and negative reactions.

Barrier Four: Stylistic Differences in Personal Communication That Inhibit Interpersonal Relationships. We all have style, personal and individual expressions of attitudes about ourselves and our culture. We speak, dress, and behave nonverbally with personal style influenced by culture. We develop vocabulary, syntax, idioms, slang, and dialects reflecting both our past and our present. Our speech style develops within the context of our background. What we view as appropriate and effective is a result of our evaluation of our past and present experiences. The same is true for our dress and nonverbal behaviors. Although we may recognize how our style develops, many of us remain uncomfortable with others who have different styles. Some people appear aggressive and threatening when they engage in their own culturally acceptable behaviors. Others physically stand too close, invading our personal space. We move away, signaling a form of disrespect we do not intend. When others are enthusiastic in speech, we may consider them illogical, based on our preference for details. We become uncomfortable with one another and thereby limit our interpersonal effectiveness. Style differences frequently block the substance of what we can contribute to one another.

Positive Approach: Display of Respect. A display of respect for differences begins with the attitude that differences are desirable. Respect includes specific recognition that although stylistic differences are normal, they are a possible source of misunderstanding. A display of respect includes active listening and nonverbal behaviors that encourage interactions with others. A display of respect also includes monitoring our own behaviors to minimize misunderstanding of our intentions. A display of respect is a sensitivity competency based on a genuine valuing of diversity.

Brenda Allen (2004) recommended we increase our effectiveness with others by being mindful, being proactive, and filling our communication toolbox. Allen suggests:

> As you monitor your thoughts, attitudes, and feelings, look for evidence of dominant belief systems. Ask yourself if you are relying on stereotypes or making assumptions about social identity groups, including those you belong to. Notice when you have negative or emotional responses to phrases, words, images, and objects related to social identity groups. Track how you routinely respond to certain differences. Mark moments when you experience discomfort while interacting with members of other social identity groups. In addition, look for signs of how you are privileged. This advice applies to everyone, including persons who self-identify as disadvantaged, because most of us embody privileged and nonprivileged social identity groups. (p. 191)

Allen went on to advise proactive behaviors, which include identifying ways to help support others. She presented a mental checklist to assist individuals in being both mindful and proactive (see Figure 5.5). Finally, Allen recommends filling a communication toolkit (developing skills) in order to inform intrapersonal, interpersonal, and organizational communication about difference. The next section describes some of the communication concepts and skills important for this toolkit.

- What preconceived notions do I have about this person based on social identity characteristics (whether we seem different or similar)?
- Are those notions positive, negative, or neutral?
- What's the source of those preconceptions?
- Will my preconceptions facilitate or impede communication?
- Am I open to learning about this person and myself during this interaction? Why or why not?
- Am I willing to be changed as a result of this interaction or experience?
- What communication tools can I use to try to create genuine communication?

FIGURE 5.5
Brenda Allen's Checklist for Mindful and Proactive Interactions

Based on Brenda Allen, *Difference Matters: Communicating Social Identity,* 2004, p. 202.

Active Listening

Myths and Barriers Listening is as fundamental to effective communication as talking. It is important in organizations. Supervisors talk and incorrectly assume employees are listening; groups engage in lively debate, hearing one another but not arriving at similar meanings; organizational members argue without understanding that they support essentially the same position.

Active listening ■ Processes of hearing, assigning meaning, and verifying our interpretations. Increases the accuracy of message reception, enabling responses based on what was said, not on what might have been said.

Several important myths about listening and barriers to **active listening** help explain the ineffectiveness described in our examples. The following discussion of myths helps us understand our personal listening habits and the listening habits of others.

Myth One: Listening and Hearing Are the Same Thing. Fact: Hearing is the physiological process in which sound waves strike the eardrum, creating vibrations for transmission to the brain. Listening extends the physiological process to the assignment of meaning to sounds. Listening is therefore essential for message decoding.

Myth Two: Listening and Hearing Are Physiological Processes. Fact: Hearing is a natural physiological process, but effective listening extends the physiological process of hearing into the skill of accurate decoding and assignment of meaning. In fact, more people speak well than listen well, although what we choose to say in most situations is a result of our listening skill.

Myth Three: Everyone Listening to the Same Message Receives the Same Message. Fact: Because listening involves individual decoding and assignment of meaning, listening will be different for everyone.

In addition to myths that confuse listening and hearing, several important barriers to effective listening (the act of receiving and interpreting communication) have been identified. First described by Ralph Nichols (Nichols and Stevens, 1957), listening barriers are important for understanding individual habits that interfere with accurate message reception.

Barrier One: Labeling Communicators and Subjects as Uninteresting or Unimportant. Although at times these labels may be accurate, many of us determine early in an interaction or presentation that we don't understand the subject, don't like the person, or find little of interest or importance in the message. We then tune out the speaker and spend our time thinking about other matters. By not listening to the message, we have no way to assess accurately the value of what we might have heard.

Barrier Two: Emotionally Resisting Messages. Often we react quickly to emotionally charged words or subjects. Internally we think of ways to respond to the speaker and argue our position. In this process we often quit listening to what is being said. We make judgments and respond to those judgments as if the speaker's position were accurately known to us. Criticisms from supervisors and peers often are met with emotional listening resistance. We hear only the negatives and do not attend to offers of help or ways to improve our performance. We are overstimulated and do not accurately receive messages that could help us grow and develop.

Barrier Three: Criticizing Personal Style Rather Than Messages. We often find ourselves criticizing the way a message is presented and ignoring its content or value. We don't like the message being "read" to us, we find the speaker lacking in experience, or we don't care for the negative tone of the boss. Our listening focuses on delivery and approach. Stylistic elements rather than content capture our attention.

Barrier Four: Failing to Identify Listening Distractions. Believe it or not, listening for facts can be distracting. Trying to listen accurately for a series of facts is not only difficult but also frequently distracts from the overall meaning of the message. Taking notes can distract from meaning, as can attempts to memorize what we hear. Physical noise, interruptions, and unidentified sounds also contribute to ineffective listening.

Barrier Five: Faking Attention. Many of us get into the habit of faking attention whether the speaker is interesting or not. We have a lot on our minds and use our listening time for reflecting. We develop behaviors such as head nodding and eye contact that are designed to make the speaker believe we are listening. In reality we have tuned in to our own special world. At times we may not even be aware that we have begun to fake attention. Most of us can recall a time when we intended to listen and suddenly realized that we had not heard a word. Obviously, when we miss most of the message we reduce our chances for accurate communication.

Barrier Six: Misusing Thought Speed and Speech Speed Differential. We can think three to four times faster than we talk. Thus, we have time for our minds to wander as we attempt to listen. For most people, the thought speed and speech speed difference is not used to increase listening effectiveness but to think of other subjects while another person speaks. We sometimes think of our own response, we think of subjects unrelated to the speaker's message, and we use the time to jump from subject to subject. Listening experts tell us our time would be better spent in internally restating the speaker's message, drawing analogies and examples related to the subject, and determining what questions to ask. In other words, effective listeners use the differential time to make sure they understand the message.

Barrier Seven: Not Listening. At times we simply do not want to hear what is being said. We deliberately attempt to dismiss the information presented. We do not want to be influenced by what we hear. Emotional resistance to particular types of content fosters intentional strategies to avoid hearing. We use technology with ear devices to block sound, we consciously talk to ourselves, or we use personal digital assistants to read or send messages: often we visually signal our distaste for the message. The more positive approach is to evaluate the reasons for our distaste. Is it the message? Is it the speaker? If we determine we simply cannot listen to the content, experts suggest we determine alternative strategies, such as those described in the next section, for more directly confronting the reasons for our extreme displeasure.

Guidelines for Good Listening

Active listening includes the processes of hearing, assigning meaning, and verifying our interpretations. Skill in active listening supports effective communication by increasing the accuracy of message reception. Accurate message reception in turn enables better responses, responses based on what was said, not on what we think might have been said.

Active listening begins with an attitude about our role in the communication process. A positive active listening attitude begins with a genuine concern for understanding messages as others intend, to sense meaning from another person's point of view. This attitude includes empathy for others and a willingness to control our emotions to facilitate mutual understanding. Skillful active listeners control mental arguments, avoid jumping to assumptions and conclusions, and are careful not to stereotype others.

Active listeners stop talking long enough to hear what others have to say. When others have finished talking, active listeners frequently paraphrase or feed back what they have understood. They allow people to verify the accuracy of those perceptions or to explain what inaccuracies exist. Active listeners use questions for meaning clarification and do not interrupt attempts to explain ideas or positions.

Active listeners summarize main points and evaluate facts and evidence before responding. Thus, the skill of active listening is as important for disagreements as for agreements. This skill is practiced to foster understanding of another's position, not necessarily to generate agreement with that position. In fact, most communication scholars argue that an individual is in a better position to disagree if he or she has accurately understood the meaning of another's ideas.

Descriptive Messages

By now you are aware that none of us ever fully experiences another person's meaning. Instead, we interpret that meaning through communication. The message strategies and tactics we adopt are our attempts to make our meanings understandable to others. Thus, it is important to develop message skills that help others accurately interpret our meanings.

Descriptive messages ■ Messages characterized by ownership of perceptions and conclusions and language that presents facts, events, and circumstances all parties in communication are likely to observe or experience personally.

Descriptive messages can help us accurately exchange information with others. In organizations we frequently communicate with people with whom we have little in common and little or no personal relationship; they don't know us and we don't know them. Yet our ability to be understood is crucial to our performance and contributes to the functioning of our organization. Descriptive messages can help us accurately exchange information with supervisors, peers, and employees, as well as with those with whom we have little regular contact.

Descriptive messages are characterized by two basic tactics: **message ownership** and **descriptive language**. Message ownership refers to the ability to "own" our perceptions and conclusions without undue reference to others or attempts at blame. Descriptive language describes rather than evaluates and does so in language that presents facts, events, and circumstances all parties are likely to observe or experience personally.

Message ownership ■ Attempts to communicate verbally individual perceptions and feelings without attempting to establish blame or find unnecessary corroboration.

When I own my own messages, I verbally communicate my personal perceptions and feelings without attempting to establish blame or find unnecessary corroboration. The use of the pronoun *I* replaces the *you* message so often associated with blame. The pronoun *I* also replaces vague ownership references such as *we, some,* and *they.* Figure 5.6 illustrates effective and ineffective message ownership tactics.

Descriptive language ■ Language choice based on facts, events, and behavior as opposed to language choice describing attitudes, blame, or other subjective and vague concepts.

Descriptive language is used to describe what all parties to the communication can reasonably be expected to observe. Those using descriptive language avoid evaluation by choosing facts and observable behavior over interpretations of facts and behaviors. Descriptive language users talk about facts, events, and behavior,

Effective	Ineffective
I am angry with you.	You always make me mad.
I don't understand the technical terms you are using. They seem to me to be specific to engineering. I am not an engineer.	You're talking like an engineer.
I am responsible for doing this job as part of our contractual agreement.	You have problems with authority.
I am telling you directly and honestly what my findings are.	You are being a bit paranoid.
I need this specific information to complete this report.	How do you expect me to do my job without adequate information?
I am concerned about the level of costs on Project X.	We think costs are running wild on Project X.
I am worried about the mistakes in your last report.	Some of us think you haven't been yourself lately.

FIGURE 5.6
Message Ownership Tactics

Effective	Ineffective
I need information for cost overruns for _____ product to finish my audit report by _____ date.	You were to have provided me all the information necessary to finish this report on the costs.
Which part of the cost overrun data is not being submitted? Can you tell me why that particular information seems inappropriate to you?	Why don't you understand my request? What do you mean my request for information is not appropriate?
I do not have a response to my memo of _____ date requesting _____ data.	You are not being straightforward with the agency.
My position suggests that I need A, B, and C to prepare the report. I understand that you are willing to give me A and C but not B. Is that correct?	I know what I need to finish the report and so do you, but you are not willing to give it to me.

FIGURE 5.7
Descriptive Messages

not attitudes, blame, or other subjective and vague concepts. In other words, descriptive language use tells what is needed, what happened, or what is in question. This statement is not to say that effective communication never evaluates behavior; rather, descriptive language use is based on the assumption that it is difficult to exchange accurate information about the adequacy (good or bad) of facts and behaviors until all parties understand the specific facts or behaviors of reference. For example, when an important report is late and departments are in conflict, chances are the conflicting individuals can agree that the report must have a new due date. It is less likely that these same individuals will similarly interpret who caused the delay and who should bear the most responsibility and blame. From an organizational point of view, completion of the report is the primary goal of the communication. Of secondary consideration is agreement on blame for the failure.

Descriptive messages combine tactics of message ownership with selection of descriptive language and can be both statements and questions. They are useful for summarizing during active listening. Figure 5.7 presents effective and ineffective examples of descriptive messages.

CHAPTER HIGHLIGHTS

An individual's organizational experiences result from the attitudes, beliefs, preferences, and abilities the individual brings to the organization, how the organization seeks to influence the individual, and the types of relationships an individual develops. An individual's communication experiences relate to quality and quantity of job performance, job satisfaction, and communication satisfaction.

The **intrapersonal experience** of individuals in organizations is composed of personal needs, predispositions for behavior, communication competencies, and expectations. Personal needs have commonly been referred to as **motivation**.

Predispositions for organizational communication behaviors are personally held preferences for particular types of communication situations or behavior. **Communication apprehension**—an individual's level of fear or anxiety associated with either real or anticipated communication with others—influences a wide variety of organizational outcomes, as do preferences for leadership and conflict behaviors. Perceptions of communication competency can be described as an overall summation of preferences and predispositions for organizational communication behaviors.

Diversity characterizes the paid workforce of today and tomorrow. The diversity of the workforce refers not only to women, minorities, and immigrants, but also to the overall aging of workers and increased participation by the physically challenged. The resulting differences in communication style and values all stimulate our abilities to form effective interpersonal relationships. We form **interpersonal relationships** in organizations for important task and social considerations. Unlike our personal relationships, the organization actually structures for us many interpersonal relationships necessary for task accomplishment. The relationship an individual develops with his or her supervisor is one of the most important of the primary communication experiences in organizational life. Peers also are an important source of information and support. Communication experiences with supervisors and peers relate to how well individuals perform and their overall measures of organizational satisfaction.

Interpersonal effectiveness can be achieved through **cultural intelligence, valuing diversity, active listening, message ownership,** and **descriptive language.** These skills contribute to communication competency for interpersonal communication. ■

WORKSHOP

1. Write a letter to a hypothetical new employer describing how best to motivate you. Describe the working environment that you would find personally motivational. After your letter is completed, compare it with the various motivational theories described in this chapter. Which theory or theories can be applied to your letter?

2. You and another member of your class (preferably someone you do not know well) should take turns describing what you find important in a work environment. This exchange should take ten minutes. Each of you can ask questions of the other. At the end of ten minutes, complete the following What Do People Really Want? rankings. Rank your preferences and what you believe to be the preferences of your partner. After both rankings are complete, you and your partner should exchange ranking sheets and discuss on what basis rankings are made.

3. Write a paper about Dave Green's experiences. Using the theory and recommendations for increasing effectiveness found in the chapter, describe specific actions Dave Green can take to enhance his individual experience and relationships at AMX. Papers can be used for class discussion or as a hand-in assignment.

4. Write a paragraph about what valuing diversity means to you. In groups of four or five, read the paragraphs and then compose a paragraph combining ideas. Present the final product to the entire class.

5. To build skills and practical experience with the technique of active listening, select a controversial issue appropriate to the class. (An issue that students raise or one that relates directly to work problems is recommended.) Form groups of six students each. Two volunteers from each group should represent opposing opinions on the issue. The remaining group members should form a circle around the two volunteers. The only rule that must be followed is that before either volunteer responds to the other, the listener must state to the other's satisfaction what the speaker has just said. In other words, no replies are allowed until the speaker is satisfied that the listener can restate the original message. With the group observing, the two members should proceed to discuss the issue. Group members are to act as monitors and may intervene if the rule has been violated. After ten minutes of discussion, the class should describe how active listening influenced the issue under consideration. (Alternative exercise form: all members of the class can participate in the activity by forming pairs of participants for issue discussion.)

What Do People Really Want?

For the following ten work-related items, you will develop a ranking (1–10) of their importance to you and project how the person with whom you have been interacting will rank the items. You will then compare your self-rankings with your partner's projection of your rankings and compare your projections with his or her self-rankings. Discuss the similarities and differences in rankings.

Remember, rank what is important to you and what you believe is important to your partner in a work environment.

	My Personal Ranking	My Partner's Ranking of Me
1. Sensitivity to personal problems		
2. Interesting work		
3. Salary		
4. Job security		
5. Loyalty of company to employees		
6. Tactful and constructive criticism		
7. Appreciation for work		
8. A sense of belonging		
9. Good working conditions		
10. Opportunities for advancement		

	My Ranking of My Partner	My Partner's Self-Ranking
1. Sensitivity to personal problems		
2. Interesting work		
3. Salary		
4. Job security		
5. Loyalty of company to employees		
6. Tactful and constructive criticism		
7. Appreciation for work		
8. A sense of belonging		
9. Good working conditions		
10. Opportunities for advancement		

TIPS FOR EFFECTIVE COMMUNICATION

1. Develop a specific set of expectations you have for a work environment. When considering a job, ask questions about these expectations and honestly describe your expectations to others.

2. Ask questions about expectations for both task and communication behaviors in any work setting you consider.

3. Identify specific individuals from whom you can seek advice about your communication competencies and overall development needs. Set a time to talk with each individual and listen actively to what is said.

4. Identify by name your closest network of friends and advisors. How diverse is your network?

Identify specific ways in which you can expand your networks. Develop a plan.

5. Identify emotional responses you have to phrases, words, images, and objects related to diverse identity groups. When your responses are negative, develop alternative positive responses. (Based on Allen, 2004.)

6. Select three conflict situations you have either participated in or observed. Develop message ownership and descriptive language strategies to address these conflicts.

7. Develop five descriptions of your values, expectations, and skills designed to help others build trust in you.

8. Identify a time when your personal use of technology was ineffective and misunderstood by others. Develop personal strategies to monitor your use of technology for improved interpersonal relationships.

9. Practice improving your listening in situations that you typically find boring or irritating.

10. Select an interpersonal relationship you currently have that is in need of improvement. Attempt to use some of the information from this chapter to improve this relationship. ■

REFERENCES AND SUGGESTED READINGS

Albrecht, T. L., and B. Hall. 1991. Relational and content differences between elites and outsiders in innovation networks. *Human Communication Research* 17: 535–561.

Allen, B. 2004. *Difference matters: Communicating social identity.* Long Grove, IL: Waveland.

Allen, B. 2007. Theorizing communication and race. *Communication Monographs* 74: 259–264.

Allen, M., S. Coopman, J. Hart, and K. Walker. 2007. Workplace surveillance and managing privacy boundaries. *Management Communication Quarterly* 21: 172–200.

Amason, P., M. Allen, and S. Holmes. 1999. Social support and acculturative stress in the multicultural workplace. *Journal of Applied Communication Research* 27: 310–334.

Athanassiades, J. 1973. The distortion of upward communication in hierarchical organizations. *Academy of Management Journal* 16: 207–226.

Baird, J. E. Jr. 1977. *The dynamics of organizational communication.* New York: Harper and Row.

Booth-Butterfield, M., and S. Butterfield. 1986. Effects of evaluation, task structure, trait-CA, and reticence on state-CA and behavioral disruption in dyadic settings. *Communication Monographs* 53(2): 144–159.

Brislin, R. W. 1988. Prejudice in intercultural communication. In *Intercultural communication: A reader,* eds. L. Samovar and R. Porter, 339–344. Belmont, CA: Wadsworth.

Bruno Teboul, JC., and T. Cole. 2005. Relationship development and workplace integration: An evolutionary perspective. *Communication Theory* 15: 389–413.

Campbell, D. J. 2000. The proactive employee: Managing workplace initiative. *Academy of Management Executive* 14: 52–66.

Carmichael, C. W. 1988. Intercultural perspectives of aging. In *Intercultural communication: A reader,* eds. L. Samovar and R. Porter, 139–147. Belmont, CA: Wadsworth.

Cox, T. 1993. *Cultural diversity in organizations.* San Francisco: Berrett-Koehler.

Daly, J. A., and J. C. McCroskey. 1975. Occupational desirability and choice as a function of communication apprehension. *Journal of Counseling Psychology* 22(4): 309–313.

Dansereau, F., and S. Markham. 1987. Superior–subordinate communication: Multiple levels of analysis. In *Handbook of organizational communication,* eds. F. Jablin, L. Putnam, K. Roberts, and L. Porter, 343–388. Newbury Park, CA: Sage.

DeVito, J. A. 1988. *Human communication: The basic course,* 4th ed. New York: Harper and Row.

DeWine, S., and F. Barone. 1984. *Employee communication and role stress: Enhancement or sabotage of the organizational climate?* Paper presented to the Organizational Communication Division of the International Communication Association Convention, May, San Francisco.

Downs, C., and T. Hain. 1982. Productivity and communication. In *Communication yearbook 5,* ed. M. Burgoon, 435–453. New Brunswick, NJ: Transaction Books.

Downs, C. W., and M. D. Hazen. 1977. A factor analytic study of communication satisfaction. *Journal of Business Communication* 14: 63–73.

Earley, P., and S. Ang. 2003. *Cultural intelligence: Individual interactions across cultures.* Stanford, CA: Stanford University Press.

Eisenberg, E., and H. L. Goodall Jr. 1993. *Organizational communication: Balancing creativity and constraint.* New York: St. Martin's.

Eisenberg, E., P. Monge, and R. Farace. 1984. Coorientation of communication rules in managerial dyads. *Human Communication Research* 11: 261–271.

Ellis, K., and P. Shockley-Zalabak. 2008. The organizational trust profile: A comprehensive instrument to measure organizational trust. In *Increderea organizationala: Trust: The bedrock of individual and organizational excellence,* eds. E. Avram and P Shockley-Zalabak, 31–60. Bucuresti, Romaniei: Editura Universitara.

Ellison, N. 1999. *Dispersed work environments: A case study in communication technology and organizational culture.* Paper presented at the International Communication Association Convention, May, San Francisco.

Falcione, R., J. McCroskey, and J. Daly. 1977. Job satisfaction as a function of employees' communication apprehension, self-esteem, and perceptions of their immediate supervisor. In *Communication yearbook 1,* ed. B. D. Ruben, 363–376. New Brunswick, NJ: Transaction Books.

Farace, R. V., P. R. Monge, and H. M. Russell, 1977. *Communicating and organizing.* Reading, MA: Addison-Wesley.

Feeley, T. H., J. Hwang, and G. Barnett. 2008. Predicting employee turnover form friendship networks. *Journal of Applied Communication Research* 36: 56–73.

Fineman, S., S. Maitlis, and N. Panteli. 2007. Virtuality and emotion. *Human Relations* 60: 555–560.

Folb, E. A. 1988. Who's got the room at the top? Issues of dominance and nondominance in intracultural communication. In *Intercultural communication: A reader,* eds. L. Samovar and R. Porter, 121–130. Belmont, CA: Wadsworth.

Friedman, T. 2002. *Longitudes and attitudes.* New York: Farrar, Straus and Giroux.

Fulk, J., and S. Mani. 1986. Distortion of communication in hierarchical relationships. In *Communication yearbook 9,* ed. M. McLaughlin, 483–510. Newbury Park, CA: Sage.

Gibbons, D. 2004. Friendship and advice networks in the context of changing professional values. *Administrative Science Quarterly* 49: 238–262.

Granovetter, M. 1973. The strength of weak ties. *American Journal of Sociology* 78: 1360–1380.

Harris, P., and R. Moran. 1996. *Managing cultural differences: Leadership strategies for a new world of business.* Houston, TX: Gulf.

Hatfield, J., R. Huseman, and E. Miles. 1987. Perceptual differences in verbal recognition and relative job satisfaction. *Communication Research Reports* 4: 8–13.

Herzberg, F. 1966. *Work and the nature of man.* Cleveland, OH: World.

Jablin, F. M. 1978. Message-response and openness in superior–subordinate communication. In *Communication yearbook 2,* ed. B. D. Ruben, 293–309. New Brunswick, NJ: Transaction Books.

Johnston, W. 1987. *Workforce 2000.* Indianapolis, IN: Hudson Institute.

Jokisaari, M., and J. Nurmi. 2009. Change in newcomers' supervisor support and socialization outcomes after organizational entry. *Academy of Management Journal* 52: 527–544.

Ketrow, S. 1992. *Cultural diversity and organizational communication: The gender perspective.* Paper presented to the Applied Communication Section of the Speech Communication Association Convention, October, Chicago.

Krivonos, P. D. 1982. Distortion of subordinate to superior communication in organizational settings. *Central States Speech Journal* 33(1): 345–352.

Krone, K. 1992. *Communicative and relational consequences of centralized authority structures.* Paper presented at the Speech Communication Association Convention, October, Chicago.

Lee, J. 1997. Leader–member exchange, the "Pelz effect," and cooperative communication. *Management Communication Quarterly* 11(2): 266–287.

Lee, J. 2001. Leader–member exchange, perceived organizational justice, and cooperative communication. *Management Communication Quarterly* 14: 574–589.

Lengel, L. 2008. Computer-mediated communication. In *21st century communication: A reference handbook,* ed. W. Eadie, 543–549. Thousand Oaks, CA: Sage.

Maslow, A. 1954. *Motivation and personality.* New York: Harper and Row.

McCann, R. M., and H. Giles. 2006. Communication with people of different ages in the workplace: Thai and American data. *Human Communication Research* 32: 74–108.

McCroskey, J. C. 1982. *An introduction to rhetorical communication,* 4th ed. Englewood Cliffs, NJ: Prentice Hall.

Miller, K. I., J. Considine, and J. Garner. 2007. Let me tell you about my job: Exploring the terrain of emotion in the workplace. *Management Communication Quarterly* 20:231–260.

Miller, K. I., and P. R. Monge. 1985. Social information and employee anxiety about organizational change. *Human Communication Research* 11(3): 365–386.

Monge, P., and N. Contractor. 2001. Emergence of communication networks. In *The new handbook of organizational communication: Advances in theory, research, and methods,* eds. F. Jablin and L. Putnam, 440–502. Thousand Oaks, CA: Sage.

Nichols, R., and L. Stevens. 1957. *Are you listening?* New York: McGraw-Hill.

Pace, R. W. 1983. *Organizational communication: Foundations for human resource development.* Englewood Cliffs, NJ: Prentice Hall.

Pearson, J. C. 1988. Gender and communication: Sex is more than a three-letter word. In *Intercultural communication: A reader,* eds. L. Samovar and R. Porter, 154–162. Belmont, CA: Wadsworth.

Pelz, D. 1952. Influence: A key to effective leadership in the first line supervisor. *Personnel* 29: 209–217.

Pincus, J. D. 1986. Communication satisfaction, job satisfaction, and job performance. *Human Communication Research* 12(3): 395–419.

Ray, E. 1993. When the links become chains: Considering dysfunctions of supportive communication in the workplace. *Communication Monographs* 60(1): 106–111.

Read, W. 1962. Upward communication in industrial hierarchies. *Human Relations* 15: 3–15.

Richetto, G. M. 1969. *Source credibility and personal influence in three contexts: A study of dyadic communication in a complex aerospace organization.* Unpublished doctoral dissertation, Purdue University, Lafayette, IN.

Richetto, G. M. 1977. Organizational communication theory and research: An overview. In *Communication yearbook 1,* ed. B. D. Ruben, 331–346. New Brunswick, NJ: Transaction Books.

Richmond, V. and J. McCroskey. 2009. *Organizational communication for survival.* Boston: Pearson.

Roberts, K., and C. O'Reilly. 1974. Measuring organizational communication. *Journal of Applied Psychology* 59(3): 321–326.

Ruben, B. D. 1988. Human communication and cross-cultural effectiveness. In *Intercultural communication: A reader,* eds. L. Samovar and R. Porter, 331–339. Belmont, CA: Wadsworth.

Salancik, G., and J. Pfeffer. 1977. An examination of need-satisfaction models of job attitudes. *Administrative Science Quarterly* 22: 427–456.

Salancik, G., and J. Pfeffer. 1978. A social information processing approach to job attitudes and task design. *Administrative Science Quarterly* 23: 224–253.

Scott, C., and C. E. Timmerman. 1999. *Communication technology: Use and multiple workplace identifications among organizational teleworkers with varied degrees of virtuality.* Paper presented at the International Communication Association Convention, May, San Francisco.

Scott, M. D., J. C. McCroskey, and M. F. Sheahan. 1978. Measuring communication apprehension. *Journal of Communication* 28: 104–111.

Shah, P. 1998. Who are employees' social referents? Using a network perspective to determine referent others. *Academy of Management Journal* 41(3): 249–268.

Shockley-Zalabak, P., K. Ellis, and R. Cesaria. 2000. *Measuring organizational trust.* San Francisco: International Association of Business Communicators.

Shockley-Zalabak, P., and D. Morley. 1984. High apprehensives within the organization: How and with whom do they talk? *Communication Research Reports* 1(1): 97–103.

Sias, P. M. 2009. *Organizing relationships.* Thousand Oaks, CA: Sage.

Sias, P., and D. Cahill. 1998. From coworkers to friends: The development of peer friendships in the workplace. *Western Journal of Communication* 62(3): 273–299.

Sias, P., and T. Perry. 2004. Disengaging from workplace relationships: A research note. *Human Communication Research* 30: 589–602.

Skinner, B. F. 1953. *Science and human behavior.* New York: Macmillan.

Smith, A. F., and S. A. Hellweg. 1985. *Work and supervisor satisfaction as a function of subordinate perceptions of communication competence of self and supervisor.* Paper presented to the Organizational Communication Division of the International Communication Association Convention, May, Honolulu, HI.

Smith, P. C., L. M. Kendall, and C. L. Hulin. 1969. *The measurement of satisfaction in work and retirement.* Chicago: Rand McNally.

Snavely, W., and J. McNeill. 1985. *A path analytic study of the impact of organizational and interpersonal stressors on job tension, satisfaction, and turnover propensity.* Paper presented to the Organizational Communication Division of the International Communication Association Convention, May, Honolulu, HI.

Snyder, R. A., and J. H. Morris. 1984. Organizational communication and performance. *Journal of Applied Psychology* 69(3): 461–465.

Stewart, L. 1993. *Ethical issues in organizational diversity.* Paper presented at the International Communication Association Annual Conference, May, Washington, DC.

Stohl, C. 1995. *Organizational communication: Connectedness in action.* Thousand Oaks, CA: Sage.

Sypher, B. D., and T. E. Zorn Jr. 1987. *Individual differences and construct system content in descriptions of liked and disliked coworkers.* Paper presented to the Organizational Communication Division of the International Communication Association Convention, May, Montreal.

Thatcher, S., and X. Zhu. 2006. Changing identities in a changing workplace: Identification, identity enactment, self-verification, and telecommuting. *Academy of Management Review* 31: 1076–1088.

Tompkins, P., and G. Cheney. 1983. Account analysis of organizations: Decision making and identification. In *Communication and organizations: An interpretive approach,* eds. L. Putnam and M. Pacanowsky, 123–146. Beverly Hills, CA: Sage.

Waldeck, J. H., D. R. Seibold, and A. J. Flanagin. 2004. Organizational assimilation and communication technology use. *Communication Monographs* 71: 161–183.

Waldron, V., and M. Hunt. 1992. Hierarchical level, length, and quality of supervisory relationship as predictors of subordinates' use of maintenance tactics. *Communication Reports* 5(2): 82–89.

Wilson, G. L., H. L. Goodall Jr., and C. L. Waagen. 1986. *Organizational communication.* New York: Harper and Row. ∎

Groups in Organizations

DEVELOPING COMPETENCIES THROUGH . . .

KNOWLEDGE   Identifying types of groups in organizations
Describing working in groups
Describing group processes
Describing group communication roles
Describing the team-based organization

SENSITIVITY   Relating individual communication behaviors to effective participation
in groups
Understanding positive and negative participation behaviors
Evaluating personal skills for group participation

SKILLS   Practicing effective group participation
Practicing analysis capabilities

VALUES   Relating group effectiveness to individual participation behaviors
Identifying responsibilities for self-managing groups
Understanding the concept of workplace democracy

◤ DAVE GREEN'S SMALL-GROUP EXPERIENCES

Dave had been at AMX for over three months. He would be glad when his first presentation to Sally and the group was behind him. It wasn't that they had not been helpful. The weekly planning meetings Sally held with the team were useful, and he was beginning to get more familiar with what to expect. John was clearly the leader. He talked more than any of the others, at least when Sally was present. The staff meetings usually began with an overall progress report of the week's activities, with some attention given to any problems encountered since the last meeting. Dave had observed that few serious difficulties were aired during the meetings. He wasn't sure if the others approached Sally for individual problem solving. As for him, he had not experienced a serious problem, except not knowing what Sally expected. John had helped with clarifying expectations on more than one occasion. The staff meetings were the forums for formal presentation of researched materials. Dave had observed two such presentations in the last three months. Next week was his turn, and he expected that the group would be supportive.

In addition to the staff meetings, the research team met informally about once every two weeks. Again, John seemed to call and run the meetings. Dave was not sure how the others felt about John's leadership but assumed that both Ralph and Susan supported him. At two of these meetings, Dave had been a little uncomfortable with being assigned some work from John. He wasn't quite sure what, if anything, to do about the assignments. After all, John seemed an accepted informal leader and John had been personally supportive of Dave. ■

INTRODUCTION

Peer relationships are more frequently discussed as small-group rather than as one-on-one organizational experiences. Most individuals in organizations spend considerable time in groups. Membership in work, problem-solving, and social support groups is common and influences how we experience organizational life. Dave Green is the new member of his team. His new job gives him formal membership in the group. He hopes that he will become part of an informal social group, but AMX as an organization won't make that happen. Dave's social support network will depend on his informal relationships at AMX.

Small-group experiences ■
Individual involvement in the formal and informal groups formed within organizations for task or social support.

Most of us have memberships in multiple groups. Families, work organizations, athletic teams, friendships, and volunteer groups are only a few **small-group experiences** in which most of us are involved. We join these groups in different ways and for different reasons. In our organizational lives, our jobs often define membership in certain groups. Our skills and visibility within the organization may determine membership in other types of groups, and our interpersonal relationships determine the extent of our membership in social support networks. In this chapter we explore the types of primary-group relationships in organizations and the roles individuals play in these groups, and then we examine Dave Green's reflections on his early group experiences.

This chapter is designed to contribute to *knowledge* competencies by discussing groups common to most organizations, identifying individual experiences in groups, and describing group processes. We foster *sensitivity* competencies by relating individual participation to group effectiveness, distinguishing between positive and negative participation behaviors, and evaluating personal communication skills for participation. We develop *skills* by practicing positive participation behaviors and analyzing transcripts and group participation. Finally, we develop *values* by relating group effectiveness to individual participation behaviors and by identifying responsibilities for self-managing groups.

SMALL-GROUP EXPERIENCES

Dave Green became a member of Sally Johnson's staff by virtue of his new job assignment. His first three months on the job have helped him learn about how the group works, what the expectations are, how issues are handled, and what his role or roles will be. Dave is also a member of an informal work group unofficially led by John. This group also has informal rules and operating procedures. He is less clear about his responsibilities to John but in general finds the group supportive and helpful. Dave's AMX experiences are common to most organizations. Some of the groups to which we belong are formally structured with specific goals, rules, and procedures. Others are more informal, blending task and social roles, and still others serve a purely social support function.

Organizations have many different types of formal and informal groups. Work teams, quality teams, sales teams, problem-solving groups, management teams, and unions are only a few examples of formally structured organizational groups. Informal groups come together for social events, athletic competition, coffee breaks, gripe sessions, and a variety of other purposes. Both types of groups are important for individual task accomplishment and social support.

We talk about groups as if they are easily described and recognized, but what exactly is a group? How do we identify group members and the types of activities in which groups actually engage? John Baird (1977) has provided a definition of groups that has endured over time. Baird suggested a group can be defined as "a collection of more than two persons who perceive themselves as a group, possess a common fate, have organizational structure, and communicate over time to achieve personal and group goals." This definition places communication relationships at the core of group activity. As such, groups can be understood in terms of how they are formed and structured, how individuals understand their dependence on one another, and how members communicate.

Organizations form groups to fulfill a variety of organizational needs. Work groups are formed for maximum task efficiency and effectiveness. Problem-solving groups address ongoing organizational issues as well as emergencies. Groups meet regularly to review organizational operations and make future plans, to negotiate labor–management agreements, and to respond to financial crises or unusual pressure from competition. Groups such as quality teams are formed to systematically examine new and better ways of doing things. The underlying assumption is that the efforts of numbers of individuals exceed individual efforts requiring energy and creativity for either completing tasks or examining issues.

Groups also contribute to establishing the shared realities of the organization. Expectations about member conduct can be found in most groups. Members communicate expectations to new members and evaluate behavior as either conforming to or disregarding the group rules. Dave learns the communication rules of his work team. For example, he learns John expects to be the informal leader and apparently Ralph and Susan accept this situation. Dave attempts to determine whether the lack of problem discussion in staff meetings is a communication rule or the absence of any real problems during his tenure with AMX. He also tries to determine what the group expects to be discussed in group settings and what should be handled privately with Sally. These rules and others become the realities Dave shares with his work team.

The next several sections of this chapter help us to understand Dave's experiences by describing the types of groups commonly formed in organizations, experiences individuals have in groups, and groups processes. Finally, we discuss how we can increase effective group participation by working individually and cooperatively.

TYPES OF GROUPS

Organizations have many different types of formal and informal groups for important task and social considerations. In Chapter 5, we discussed relationships in primary work groups between supervisors and employees and among peers. Most of us will have multiple group memberships in addition to our primary work team. We are taking the perspective we will be part of multiple **bona fide groups,** that is, groups with permeable boundaries and interdependent with the broader environment. In other words, our membership in multiple groups brings relationships between and among groups. No one group has rigid boundaries. Groups are influenced by their members' experiences in other groups. The broader environment influences what issues we address and the resources with which we work. Think for a moment about your current group memberships. Can you understand how your membership in one group influences what you experience in another group? Are there ever conflicts in experiences and expectations? How are groups of which you are a member influenced by external circumstances? Next, we identify some of the specific types of groups common to organizations. Although we discuss these groups as separate types, they, in fact, meet the definition of bona fide groups. Chances are you will be a member of several of these group types simultaneously.

> **Bona fide groups** ■ Groups that have permeable boundaries and are interdependent with the environment.

Primary Work Teams

The first group assigned to us when we enter an organization is our **primary work team.** What we have been hired to do places us structurally within the organization and identifies our supervisor and related peer group. Work teams vary in size and formality. Some will work closely together, whereas others exchange infrequent information. Carl Larson and Frank LaFasto (1989) identified three common features of competent work-team members: (1) the possession of essential skills and abilities, (2) a strong desire to contribute, and (3) the capability of collaborating effectively.

> **Primary work team** ■ Group to which an individual is assigned on organizational entry.

In research on effective teams, Larson and LaFasto found effective work teams had members whose technical abilities were relevant to the team's objectives and who valued commitment and contributions to the team. Effective teams were characterized by the understanding of individual members concerning the relationship of their personal efforts to team effectiveness. Finally, Larson and LaFasto reported: "A consistent response . . . was the importance of selecting team members capable of working well with others . . . some people are capable of dealing with others in a collaborative fashion, and some are not." Larson and LaFasto concluded their data collected from effective teams strongly suggested people who could not collaborate should be removed from team efforts.

John Cragan and David Wright (1986) identified some of the different types of work teams we are likely to encounter. Their descriptions of long-standing work groups, project teams, and "prefab" work groups help us to understand the different team structures organized to meet particular work needs. **Long-standing teams,** for example, are formed when the overall responsibilities of the team change slowly with time and when team membership can be expected to remain relatively stable. Long-standing work teams have well-defined organizational responsibilities, enabling selection of new team members based on qualifications previously identified as important for the group. Dave Green joins such a group at AMX. The training function is well established and is expected to continue over time. AMX has experience with the types

> **Long-standing teams** ■ Relatively permanent groups of individuals organized for task accomplishment.

of people who are successful in training and development jobs. As such, they have developed a list of qualifications they believe new members of the department should possess. Dave Green matches their initial expectations and enters a relatively long-standing group.

University departments are examples of long-standing teams. Although advances in knowledge change the content of courses, the general responsibilities for teaching, research, and service remain. Our government is another long-standing example. Congress, state and local governments, the Supreme Court, the president and cabinet members, and numerous other entities are examples of groups established by law but supported by the customs of the society as a whole. In most organizations, personnel, financial, legal, and overall management responsibilities are carried out by long-standing teams. Long-standing teams develop ways of doing things that not only make qualifications for new members clear but also identify expected behaviors for members. Long-standing teams have the strength of team history and practical experience. They can, however, limit creativity and change when group traditions block rapid adaptation to new circumstances.

Project teams form with highly specialized individuals to accomplish a specific project in a fixed period of time. These teams have specific goals, such as the design of a new product or the integration of technologies across the organization. Project teams are commonly used in high-technology industries for the research and design of products and processes. Their formation is based on the technical expertise needed for a given line of inquiry. Project teams draw membership from other teams in the organization, and assignments may be viewed as temporary or relatively permanent, depending on the needs of the project. When members come from different functions throughout the organization (e.g., marketing, research and development, manufacturing), the team is often described as a cross-functional project team. Project teams have been part of the space program for many years and are common in telecommunications, electronic, computer, and research-based industries. Because of the nature of their formation, project teams do not have the history and traditions of long-standing work groups. They must quickly clarify goals, roles, and responsibilities in order to establish working relationships necessary to meet project guidelines and timetables. The formation of project teams permits an organization to respond rapidly to changing markets. Team members, however, may have difficulty in establishing trust and mutually satisfying working relationships when pressured by deadlines and the technical complexity of a challenging assignment. In research on project teams, Karen Brown, T. D. Klastorin, and Janet Valluzzi (1990) reported high-performing project teams more than their less successful counterparts were characterized by lower opinions of peers at the beginning of the project and were more likely to highly value technical expertise. These authors' results indicated project teams that began with harmonious interpersonal relations may not perform as well as those that experienced early disharmonies. Information exchange throughout the duration of the project, however, was linked to ultimate success. Robert Keller (1994), in his work with research and development project teams, found that the more challenging (nonroutine) the team's assignment, the more prevalent the requirement for high information processing to achieve project quality.

Project teams ■ Work groups established for the duration of a specific assignment.

Prefab group ■ Work group designed and structured for frequent replacement of members. Prefab groups have detailed individual assignments requiring limited experience to produce specified products.

Whereas project teams are associated with high-technology research and development efforts, the **prefab group** is the invention of the U.S.A. service industry. As Cragan and Wright (1986) described the prefabricated group, "the job descriptions of this type of work group have been meticulously defined and rigidly structured so that a collection of people with no previous experience of working together can quickly form a work group that will produce a predictable level of productivity." Fast-food restaurants and supermarket check-out lines are examples of the use of prefab groups. The prefab group is efficient and predictable. Behavior expectations are specifically and clearly established. The group is designed to produce an average level of production and not expected to solve problems, introduce creativity into the process, or adapt to new situations. Prefab groups are best utilized for the production of goods and services but are not appropriate to meet problem-solving needs.

Self-managing team ■ A small number of people with complementary skills who are committed to a common purpose, have a defined set of performance goals, and execute an approach for which they hold themselves accountable.

Self-managing teams are formed to give individual team members more responsibility, authority, and accountability for their work. Jon Katzenbach and Douglas Smith (1993) defined a team as "a small number of people with complementary skills who are committed to a common purpose, set of performance goals, and approach for which they hold themselves accountable." The growth of the numbers of self-managing teams in organizations is a result of the need to reduce management layers and the realization that high-performing teams potentially can outproduce work groups in more traditional hierarchical structures. Support is found throughout numerous organizations for the assertion that teams outperform individuals, particularly when multiple skills and experiences are required. Individual performance is frequently enhanced within a climate of group goals. Katzenbach and Smith contended, "Hierarchy and teams go together almost as well as teams and performance. Teams, in fact, are the best way to integrate across structural boundaries and to both design and energize core processes." Self-managing teams usually schedule their own work, cross-train team members, troubleshoot process and product problems, set evaluation criteria, conduct peer evaluation, and recommend product and process improvements. Clay Carr (1992) suggested teams are most likely to succeed when they have clear, worthwhile, and compelling goals and when team members understand they are expected to commit themselves to these goals. Carr's work also supports the notion teams must be rewarded for team, not individual, success. When John Courtright, Gail Fairhurst, and Edna Rogers (1989) compared traditional hierarchical structures with self-managing teams, they found the self-managing environments were characterized by a variety of question-and-answer combinations, conversational elaboration, and a lack of managerial orders and commands. In contrast, competitive interchanges, interruptions, and statements of nonsupport typified interaction in the more traditional hierarchies. James Barker and Phillip Tompkins (1993) reported workers in self-managed teams tend to identify more strongly with their team than with their company, particularly in terms of loyalty.

Directional Groups

Another category of important groups in organizations involves those formally charged and structured to provide overall direction for the organization.

Management teams, standing committees, and boards of directors are examples of groups empowered both structurally and legally to develop vision and policy for the organization. Generally viewed as powerful organizational groups, **directional groups** review the plans and performance of most other units within the organization. Directional groups establish policy and are generally responsible for both the oversight and the performance of the organization.

Directional groups ■ Groups formally charged and structured to provide overall direction and oversight of the organization.

Most directional groups can be described as cross-functional teams or groups. People with different functional backgrounds bring important complementary knowledge and expertise to their assignments. These different backgrounds become resources for the group to use as it addresses its primary responsibilities. For example, most leadership groups include people with diverse backgrounds such as finance, customer service, research, marketing, sales, and public relations.

Directional groups, frequently referred to as executive leadership teams, set strategic direction for the organization and often must seek approval of another directional group, the board of directors, to implement that direction. An example from a Fortune 50 company (corporation in the top fifty in dollar volume in the United States of America) illustrates the significance of the directional group. The chief executive officer and executive team of this large computer company launched an e-business initiative with the approval of the board of directors. The initiative included the purchase of another company known for technical expertise in e-business. The results were marginal, resulting in a drop in stock prices with market analysts questioning basic leadership decisions. Within five months the chief executive officer and several members of the executive team submitted their resignations, and the board of directors quickly moved to replace leadership with senior executives responsible for the product lines that had formerly been the long-standing strengths of the corporation. This type of experience is common for members of directional groups based on the significant influence they have on major organizational decisions.

Directional groups frequently are criticized for their failure to fully understand organizational issues or to make timely decisions in the best interest of the organization and its various stakeholders. Directional groups often are composed of representatives from various constituencies both within and outside the organization and come to decisions representing various and often opposing interests. Directional groups depend on effective leadership to establish processes that support decision making. Directional groups usually depend less on the personal communication competencies of individual members than on the information-seeking and communication processes that the group adopts for problem solving and decision making.

Quality Teams

Quality teams are the result of a specific application of group problem solving that has gained popularity in the United States of America. The term *quality team* applies to a group that meets regularly to identify and propose solutions to problems affecting product or process quality. Although the use of problem-solving teams began as

Quality teams ■ Groups charged with responding to quality or quantity problems and to issues raised by management.

early as the turn of the twentieth century, the emphasis on quality teams as we know it today began after World War II when Edward Deming introduced his statistical quality control methods to Japanese management. By the early 1970s, over 6 million Japanese workers participated in what were initially called quality circles, or attempts to have line workers and leaders spend voluntary time solving product quality problems. The success of quality circles in Japan and increasing concerns for product quality in the United States of America have generated intense interest in this participative process of quality control.

Typically, quality teams are groups of volunteers who work in the same general area with the same general technology. Groups are led by supervisors or elected group members and are charged with responding to quality or quantity problems and to issues raised by management. Emphasis is placed on training quality circle members in group dynamics, problem solving, communication, and quality control. Quality teams are formed around the idea that groups can more quickly and effectively identify problems and propose solutions; that workers at all levels want to participate in problem solving, not just task implementation; and that innovations proposed at all levels within organizations can improve quality and productivity. Quality teams have made documented improvements in productivity. They must, however, be supported by access to useful information for problem solving and by genuine management responsiveness to change.

Quality teams have been used frequently in manufacturing situations and are credited with many improvements in the U.S.A. electronics industry in the 1990s and 2000s. Quality teams are used regularly in health care settings and are associated with cost reductions in the financial-transactions-processing industry.

Marshall Scott Poole and his colleagues (2000) have investigated the adoption of quality improvement initiatives by intact teams (teams with the same overall goals as quality teams but formed with members of an ongoing work group). Their work in an integrated health care system indicated quality improvements are most successful when the work groups enjoy a good deal of autonomy in their work and have high task variability and task interdependence. When interaction styles support creativity and efficiency, attitudes toward quality initiatives are more positive, and implementation efforts increase.

Task Force Groups

Task force groups ■ Groups of individuals with diverse specialties and group memberships who are charged with accomplishing a specifically designed task or project.

Task force groups form to bring together individuals with technical specialties who are members of other organizational groups, to accomplish a specifically designed task or project. Like project groups, task force groups form around the technical specialties of their members. Unlike project teams, task force groups generally do not create products or implement processes but plan the initiation of projects or organizational changes. Simply put, task force groups are study groups charged with making recommendations. A task force may research and evaluate how to restructure organizational responsibilities. For example, a major high-technology firm was unable to recruit successfully approximately 60 percent of the job applicants to whom they made offers. In their concern for recruiting effectiveness, top management formed a task force to study recruiting responsibilities and make recommendations for changes. Membership of the task force was selected from all organizational groups with any recruiting responsibility. Management gave the task force specific responsibilities and a time frame in which to present conclusions. Task force groups have the advantage of focused responsibilities and potential membership from qualified individuals throughout the organization. They frequently face challenges, however, because individual members may seek to protect the position of their primary work groups. Task force groups are generally more successful when members agree change is needed and when they work cooperatively for organizational versus subgroup goals.

Steering Committees

Steering committees resemble task force groups in the composition of their memberships, but what task force groups recommend, steering committees implement. Formed with diverse organizational membership, steering committees implement organizational plans, processes, or change. Whereas the task force might recommend a new recruiting process for the high-technology firm, a steering committee might be formed to implement recommendations and monitor the progress of the new plan. Steering committees literally steer the progress of a plan, goal, issue, or program. They give organizations the advantage of broad participation in the oversight of a project. Steering committees have been criticized, however, as rubber-stamp groups in which no one takes definite responsibility, permitting the best-laid plans to miss the mark or actually fail. Research suggests authority and responsibility to bring about change are critical for successful steering committees.

> **Steering committees** ■ Groups of individuals with diverse specialties and group memberships who are charged with implementing organizational plans, processes, or change.

Focus Groups

Like quality teams, **focus groups** represent a group process gaining in organizational use. Focus groups are collections of individuals who are familiar with a problem or issue and are asked in a somewhat unstructured format to describe the issue and any recommendations they might have. Focus groups have been used by advertising and marketing organizations to understand consumer preferences, identify effective message strategies, and evaluate potential new products. The successful use of focus groups in advertising and marketing has stimulated their application to numerous other organizational issues. Focus groups are formed to discuss problems, not to take responsibility for final recommendations or implementation of change. Focus groups can be used to gather information and get reactions quickly to proposed courses of action. The groups are frequently formed to identify new types of training needs, assess employee morale, uncover poorly defined problems, and make policy recommendations. They provide excellent information when made up of individuals with adequate concern for or information about the subject under discussion. On occasion, focus group members have voiced frustration about not knowing the outcome of their efforts. Forward-thinking companies, when using employee focus groups, are careful to provide feedback mechanisms.

> **Focus groups** ■ Collections of individuals who have familiarity with a problem or issue and are asked in a somewhat nonstructured format to describe the issue and make recommendations; formed to discuss problems but not to take responsibility for final recommendations or implementation of change.

Geographically Diverse Teams

Geographically diverse teams ■ Groups of individuals who form a work team but are separated in distance and linked through technology.

Sometimes referred to as networked or virtual teams, **geographically diverse teams** emerge to link people together across time zones, distance, language, and a variety of other personal and organizational circumstances. Geographically diverse teams communicate using networked computers, video, and audio connections. Geographically diverse teams include individuals who work out of their homes (commonly called telecommuters) as well as individuals separated by miles and even continents.

Sales, transaction processing, manufacturing, and service support functions increasingly are organized as geographically diverse teams. Although many of the same issues apply as with other organizational groups, geographically diverse teams are heavily dependent on technology and the ability of group members to solve complex problems without face-to-face interaction. Many organizations, however, find that geographically diverse teams need some face-to-face meeting. For example, one large computer manufacturer using teams with membership in a variety of countries brings team members together quarterly to discuss problems and operating norms and to work on issues brought about by their geographic separation. Most of us will experience working in geographically diverse groups over the next several years. This reality underscores the importance of a combination of human and technological communication competencies.

Social Support Groups

Social support groups ■ Formed as subgroups of larger task groups or among people with similar organizational interests; function to stimulate trust and cohesiveness among group members.

Work teams, quality teams, task forces, steering committees, and focus groups can all be **social support groups.** Formed for task considerations, most continuous groups provide informal social support to group members. Social support groups form as subgroups of larger task groups among people with similar organizational interests and among friends. They have few formal task responsibilities as such but often support task accomplishment by stimulating trust and cohesiveness among group members. Social support group membership has been associated with organizational and communication satisfaction and competency. Individuals apprehensive about communication are less likely to be members of diverse social support groups and are more likely than others to work in relative isolation. Those comfortable with their communication competencies are more likely to be involved in diverse groups and are more likely than their more highly apprehensive counterparts to exhibit communication and job satisfaction.

Communities of Practice

Communities of practice ■ Groups of individuals with similar professional backgrounds who interact regularly to innovate and improve performance.

Another type of group, **communities of practice**, is emerging in mostly informal but with some structured versions, to provide professional development and stimulate innovation among groups of similar professionals. The term *communities of practice* (CoPs) refers to networks of individuals who interact regularly to work on innovating and improving with regard to their particular technical specialty or problem. Made famous by software developers, communities of practice use expertise both within an organization and across organizational boundaries. CoPs generally come together voluntarily with no specific reporting structures or accountabilities and often have membership geographically dispersed across differing organizations or different division or business units within a given organization. CoPs focus on learning and problem solving and rarely have formal leaders. The generation of new knowledge is dependent on broad participation of interested professionals. Joel Iverson and Robert McPhee (2008) described three basic processes of CoPs: mutual engagement, shared repertoire, and negotiation of a joint enterprise. Specifically, mutual engagement refers to the level of communication and interaction within a CoP. Shared repertoire identifies the knowledge and capabilities within the group of people, while negotiation of the joint enterprise describes a set of tasks which CoP members seek to influence. Organizations increasingly depend on CoPs for knowledge sharing and innovation. Some organizations are formally establishing CoPs among groups of like professionals. Without question, the use of CoPs is more readily available to both individuals and organizations with sophisticated communications technologies.

As you can readily see, groups are important for our organizational experiences. In many cases, our competencies will be evaluated through our group participation. The next section of this chapter describes a growing application of groups in organizations—the team-based structure.

THE TEAM-BASED ORGANIZATION

Based on the successful use of teams in a variety of industries, one of the fastest growing of all contemporary organizational changes is the move to team-based structures. Characterized as a "flat organization" with fewer managers and supervisors than a traditional hierarchy, the **team-based organization** is composed of a variety of teams with defined responsibilities and accountabilities for which managers provide mostly indirect supervision. Self-managing teams, discussed earlier in this chapter, are the cornerstone of the team-based structure.

Team-based organization ■ Organizational structures with fewer managers and networks of self-managing teams.

The growing number of team-based organizations is in direct response to increased global competitiveness requiring overhead reductions and increased productivity. A by-product of this need to improve competitive positioning is the potential in the team-based structure (but not necessarily the reality) of a more mature treatment of the workforce. In other words, the opportunity to work in self-managing teams and team-based organizations replaces the close supervision of hierarchies with individuals and groups who self-monitor, innovate, and produce quality work with little or no supervision.

Team-based organizations and the concept of teamwork frequently are confused. The term *team-based organization* refers to a structural change from hierarchy to flat and often networked configurations of teams. Teamwork is the ability of individuals to work collaboratively. Teamwork is required for successful team-based structures, but teamwork also is important for hierarchy. Team-based organizations alter the way in which work is organized, supervised, and rewarded, whereas teamwork is the interactional process through which work is accomplished.

Over 70 percent of major corporations today have team-based structures in parts of their operations. Many small organizations also use team organizational forms. Research indicates team-based organizations generally outperform more hierarchically organized structures in terms of product and service output, less absenteeism, fewer industrial accidents, more worker flexibility, quality improvements, and overall employee job satisfaction. Michael Hackman and Craig Johnson (2000) reported research covering fifteen years that describes team-based structures as more innovative, able to share information, involved, and task skilled than more traditional organizational structures. Examples include AT&T Credit Corporation, where teams process 800 lease applications a day as contrasted to 400 a day before the team structure was implemented; Corning, where teams are credited with decreasing defect rates from 1,800 parts per million to 9 parts per million; Federal Express, with a reduction in service errors by 13 percent in one year; and General Mills, with 40 percent more productivity in factories with team-based structures compared with traditional factories. Needless to say, the implications of this change affect most of us and challenge our ability to work effectively in groups.

A useful way to understand a team-based organization is to examine four important aspects of organizational life: goals, roles, relationships, and processes. In both team-based structures and hierarchies, overall goals guide all aspects of work. In a hierarchy, management generally is responsible for goal setting with limited input from workers. In the team-based organization, the overall business goals of the organization are established by management, but work unit goals are established by team members, who monitor their own results. Numerous examples exist of teams establishing goals that exceed the productivity of their counterparts in hierarchies. A team-based organization requires a more diverse role set from individual team members. For example, team members not only set productivity and quality goals, but they also monitor and report results, conduct team meetings, provide feedback to team members, problem-solve, evaluate performance, and provide input on needed process or product changes. In essence, team members assume many of the supervision responsibilities formerly residing with management. In a team-based structure, relationships with customers, vendors, and others in the organization are managed directly by the team, whereas in a hierarchy supervisors and managers initiate change and provide communication links throughout the organization. Finally, processes such as conflict management, problem solving, decision making, and leadership become team member responsibilities, more so than in more closely supervised models. Again, these processes require highly developed communication competencies from all team members. In a recent national employer survey, team skills were listed as a major requirement for college graduates and also a major deficiency as employers evaluated their new college hires.

Team skills usually are divided into two categories: task and maintenance roles. Task roles represent the processes in which the team engages to achieve its goals, whereas maintenance roles deal with literally maintaining the ability of the team to work together. Task roles include problem analysis, idea generation, idea evaluation, abstract ideas/vision identification, solution generation, solution implementation, goal setting, agenda making, discussion clarification, disagreement identification, and consensus identification. Maintenance roles include group participation, group climate, and conflict management. Later sections of this chapter have more discussion about task and maintenance roles and increasing participation effectiveness.

The team-based organization with its use of self-directed work teams is not without issues and concerns. First, working in a self-directed work team requires a complex mixture of competencies both technical and communicative. Many technically capable people report difficulty adapting to providing and receiving peer feedback. In addition, career advancement is less well understood in team-based organizations than in hierarchies with more established paths to increasing responsibility and associated prestige. The question of who gets credit for what is an issue as well as whether team members are adequately compensated by the organization for their contributions to increased competitiveness. Critics also charge that team-based structures have a potential for exploitation based on continual pressures to increase productivity.

Of particular importance to the subject of this text are the issues in teams surrounding participation. Paul W. Mulvey, John Veiga, and Priscilla Elsass (1996) have studied self-limiting behavior in teams when individuals either surrender their positions or withhold effort, a process they call "raising a white flag." Mulvey, Veiga, and Elsass reported the top six reasons for self-limiting behaviors are (1) the presence of someone with expertise, (2) the presentation of a compelling argument, (3) lacking confidence in one's ability, (4) an unimportant or meaningless decision, (5) pressure from others to conform to the team's decision, and (6) a dysfunctional decision-making climate. These issues and others are fundamental to the functioning of teams and to individual satisfaction with the work unit.

High-Reliability Organizations

The term **high-reliability organization** has been developed to describe organizations in high-risk industries where the success of the organization is in recovering from or mitigating failures and crises. Police and fire departments, certain security organizations, and a host of organizations dealing with medical and hazardous events can be designated high-reliability organizations. All of us are impacted by the work of groups/teams in high-reliability organizations and some of us will spend significant time in high-reliability groups. High-reliability organizations focus on what can go wrong. Often interagency or interorganizational teams are required to bring order out of chaos during huge mega fires, hurricanes, floods, earthquakes, or terrorist events. Teams in high-reliability organizations develop redundancy in communication strategies, technologies, and tactics in order to avoid oversimplification of facts and interpretations. Missed information may be as important as exchanged information. Unlike most other organizational teams, simulations often are used to practice communication strategies and tactics to guide action during crisis. Strategies and tactics continuously are reviewed for improvement, and postevent analysis is common. Communication protocols are more formal than informal although informal communication certainly exists in high-reliability teams. Again, unlike other groups, high-reliability organizations frequently record and publish transcripts of communication during

High-reliability organization ■
Organizations in high-risk industries designed to mitigate failure and intervene in crises.

crisis responses. The high-reliability organization is an important example of the significance of excellence in organizational communication for problem solving during often difficult and even extremely dangerous situations.

GROUP PROCESSES

We previously said that the organization actually structures many of the groups to which we belong. Although certainly accurate, this notion of group formation only begins to help us understand how groups evolve and develop. We can be more effective group participants when we become familiar with a variety of group processes.

Workplace Democracy

Workplace democracy ■ Principles and practices that emphasize employee goals, feelings, and participation.

George Cheney (1995) describes **workplace democracy** as a system of governance which truly values individual goals and feelings (e.g., equitable remuneration, the pursuit of enriching work, and the right to express oneself) as well as typical organizational problems (e.g., effectiveness and efficiency, reflectively conceived). Workplace democracy actively fosters the connection between those two sets of concerns by encouraging individual contributions to important organizational choices and allowing for the ongoing modification of the organization's activities and policies by the group.

Workplace democracy, as described by Cheney, may or may not be found in structured hierarchies, team-based organizations, or high-reliability organizations. In fact, few organizations incorporate practices that fully support all aspects of his definition. The rise of employee-owned organizations, worker cooperatives, and employee stock ownership plans begins to address democracy issues. Clearly, globalization, change, innovation, and increased competitive pressures are closely linked to genuinely valuing people for their contributions. It is fair to conclude organizations are challenged to increase employee input on a wide variety of issues that not only affect the work directly but also affect all aspects of organizational life. Group communication processes are at the heart of these challenges.

Group Norms and Communication Roles

Dave Green joins a work group that has been together for some time. In a very real sense his membership may influence the group to re-form to include the new member. Obviously, the others know one another well. Their sense of tension with one another is predictably less than the tension of coming to know Dave. Dave, on the other hand, must establish new relationships with Sally, John, Ralph, and Susan. His tension is probably the highest in the group as he attempts to absorb the most new information.

Dave is anxious to understand the expectations of Sally and the others in his work group. He observed that very little conflict is voiced in group meetings. He wants to know whether this is a behavior expectation of the group—a norm—or whether few potentially conflicting issues have come before his group in the short period of his membership. Dave is concerned, as we all are in new groups, about the expectations the group holds and how the members will evaluate him. Simply put, Dave is concerned about AMX norms.

Group norms are unwritten behavior rules, ways of doing things that groups develop over time, usually through tacit rather than explicit agreement. Norms reflect what the group deems desirable, and they can be said to be cultural beliefs about effectiveness or appropriateness. Groups have general norms that apply to all members and role-specific norms that apply to individual members in such roles as leader, secretary, information collector, and critic. Generally speaking, group members disapprove and sometimes punish members who violate norms. We can only imagine what might occur if Dave Green openly disagreed with John in one of Sally's staff meetings. We don't know if the absence of conflict is an AMX norm, but we suspect that based on his observations, Dave will be cautious in initiating conflict. Dave will attempt to establish his role in the group by understanding its norms or expectations.

> **Group norms** ■ Unwritten behavior rules, ways of doing things, that groups develop over time. Norms reflect what groups deem desirable and can be said to be cultural beliefs about effectiveness or appropriateness.

Previously, we described organizational communication as the construction of the multiple realities and cultures of organizations. We also can observe communication activities in groups as they contribute to shared group realities and culture. One way is by examining the roles group members enact and how these roles are encouraged or discouraged in the group.

Individuals assume different roles in groups. As a newcomer to the AMX team, Dave has a task role but also a newcomer role. At first Dave's group may expect less from his task role because he is a newcomer who does not yet know the ropes. Dave can probably get more help from the group while he is still a newcomer than when the group believes that he has had enough time to become socialized and make an equal contribution.

Dave also brings to his group predispositions for a variety of communication behaviors. His predispositions and his communication roles will interact with the predispositions and roles of other group members to create the shared realities of the group.

Kenneth Benne and Paul Sheats (1948) developed three important classifications of **group communication roles:** group task roles, group maintenance roles, and self-centered roles. **Task roles** help groups accomplish goals, whereas **maintenance roles** promote social support among group members. **Self-centered roles** support individual goals and may or may not be compatible with overall group goals and relationships.

> **Group communication roles** ■ Task, maintenance, and self-centered categories for description of behaviors that individuals exhibit in groups.
>
> **Task roles** ■ Communication roles that help groups accomplish goals.
>
> **Maintenance roles** ■ Communication roles that promote social support among group members.
>
> **Self-centered roles** ■ Communication roles that support individuals' goals and may or may not be compatible with overall group goals and relationships.

When members perform group task roles, they make suggestions, contribute new ideas, ask for facts, and provide information important for the group to make decisions. They may offer opinions or seek opinions as well as clarify information used to perform tasks or contribute to group direction. Members also perform task roles when they summarize and evaluate ideas. Group maintenance roles provide support to the group, reconcile differences or suggest areas of agreement, relieve tension, and find positions that most group members can support. Finally, self-centered roles focus more on individual desires than on group process and often are seen in someone

Task Roles	Maintenance Roles	Self-Centered Roles
Initiator	Social supporter	Negative blocker
Information requestor	Harmonizer	Dominator
Information giver	Tension reliever	Attacker
Procedure facilitator	Energizer	Clown
Opinion requestor	Leader	
Opinion giver	Follower	
Clarifier	Compromiser	
Summarizer–evaluator	Gatekeeper	

FIGURE 6.1
Group Communication Roles

blocking ideas, dominating the conversation, clowning around to avoid responsibility, or engaging in other generally negative behaviors. Figure 6.1 lists common group communication roles. The Workshop section at the end of this chapter provides additional description and practice in observing how these roles influence group processes.

Generally speaking, group task and maintenance roles are productive for group interaction, whereas self-centered roles are destructive and contribute to ineffectiveness. Chances are, however, most of us engage in all these roles at one time or another. Communication competency for group settings relates to our ability to identify the roles we are likely to use and to analyze group needs in order to use these roles for effective problem solving.

Although the roles we have just described are frequently observed in organizational groups, they by no means represent all the possible communication roles. You can probably add to the list from your group experiences. Which communication roles are you likely to fulfill? Does your answer differ depending on the group in which you find yourself? If so, why? If not, why not?

WORKING IN GROUPS

Most of us will spend the majority of our work time in some form of group effort. Norms, and group communication roles do not fully explain some of the subtle influences on our group experiences. Why are we more comfortable in some groups than in others? What makes one group more prestigious than another? Why is it that certain group memberships help our career and others hinder professional success? How can we determine the differences?

There are no definite answers to these questions. Generally speaking, we are more comfortable in groups when the group goals and our individual goals are compatible. When our personal needs are met, we are more likely to attempt to meet the needs of others and to exhibit cohesive behavior within the group. The more positive we feel about our personal communication competencies, the better able we are to work in groups successfully. Moreover, when we respect the competencies of others, we consider the time and energy invested in group experiences to be worthwhile. Next we discuss three aspects of working in groups—diversity, creativity and collaboration, and the virtual experience—as examples of the importance of communication competency for group participation effectiveness.

Diverse Work Groups

We all bring our previous experiences and backgrounds to group participation. As our workforce and markets become increasingly diverse and global, an important component of our personal communication competency is the ability to work effectively in groups with those who have backgrounds different from our own. As Taylor Cox Jr. (1993) suggested, "It is important to acknowledge that all members of organizations, not just members of minority groups, have salient group identities. To the extent that gender affects organizational experience, it affects both men and women. To the extent that racioethnic identity has effects, it affects Whites and non-Whites. If accountants are disdained in favor of engineers, both engineers and accountants are affected. Appreciation of this simple fact, that we all have group identities which affect our own behavior and how others treat us, is a vital step toward building personal competence for working in diverse groups" (p. 61).

Most of us can understand culturally diverse groups are affected by different communication roles and approaches of members. The key notion is not that differences exist but how the group engages with these differences as it works on both task and relationship issues. Research continually supports the importance of effective communication for group productivity. So what is effective communication within diverse groups? Although there is no definitive answer to this question, the competencies of members to work together to not only value differences but also use differences to enhance the group's productivity become the issue. It is fair to say that working with diverse communication approaches will literally influence the work produced by the group as well as ultimately influence the group's culture. For example, Karen Jehn, Gregory Northcraft, and Margaret Neale (1999), in their study of why differences in work groups are important, found that social category diversity (age, race, gender, etc.) had a positive affect on the morale of group members, informational diversity (using diverse types of information and perspectives) improved work products, but value diversity (group members holding significant value differences) contributed to decreased satisfaction and commitment to the group. Diverse backgrounds can contribute to different concepts of what makes groups effective. Cynthia Gibson and Mary Zellmer-Bruhn (2001) illustrate this notion of different effectiveness concepts when they talk about the importance of national perspectives in shaping how individuals view the way in which teamwork should be exhibited. For some, teamwork is viewed as similar to athletic team experiences, whereas for others teamwork is much more structured, as in a military setting.

Stephen Littlejohn and Karen Foss (2008) suggested three clusters of cultural differences are important for the functioning of diverse groups: (1) individualism-collectivism, (2) self-construal, and (3) face presentation. For example, members of individualistic cultures often view their own goals as more important than the goals of the group. Expressed views during group interactions are treated as individual statements. Members from collectivistic cultures may prefer to defer to the entire group. Some cultures support a self-construal which is independent, while others support interdependence and connections to others. Finally, the concept of face refers to image, including self-image and the image of others. Some cultures focus on making the individual look good while other cultures focus on others and creating situations where what we call face-saving for others occurs. These differences relate directly to participation in groups, consensus building in decision making, the types of conflict management approaches utilized, and whether communication is viewed as respectful or not. Although there is obviously no one answer to what constitutes effectiveness in diverse groups, it is easy to understand individuals with widely different views of what is appropriate will be challenged to find group approaches that enable all to contribute. In few other settings will our individual competencies be more challenged than when we participate in diverse groups with important work responsibilities.

Creativity and Collaboration

In addition to day-to-day task responsibilities, groups in organizations have important responsibilities for solving difficult problems, creating new products, identifying process improvements, and resolving conflict. Creativity is needed for effective performance and is not necessarily part of the capability that members bring to the group. Simply put, creativity can be understood as the development of novel and useful ideas that are important for all types of innovation. Leigh Thompson (2003) describes some of the major threats to creativity in groups: social loafing, conformity, production blocking, and downward norm setting. Social loafing occurs when group members do not work as hard as they might individually, depending on others to come up with new approaches or ideas. Conformity becomes a danger when, in order to be liked or maintain harmony, group members publicly agree with one another even when they may have some doubts about a particular solution or idea. Production blocking refers to the loss of individual ideas when others are speaking and the difficulty of listening and trying to identify where individual contributions should fit in the discussion. Finally, downward norm setting is experienced when the performance level of the group is determined by the lowest performers. Groups who work together over time often give up on ideas simply because they require too much work. Most of us have experienced these blocks to creativity in all types of group memberships. The key is to determine what types of communication behaviors can contribute to creativity and what types of behaviors act as blocks. Try to think about your membership in a group that was highly creative. What types of behaviors did group members exhibit? What happened in a group that was not as effective?

Effective collaboration processes in groups are important for enhancing creativity. Collaboration occurs through communication processes and is based, at least in part, on the "at-stakeness" members feel within the group, the transparency in the group, the high levels of mindfulness that group members achieve, and the overall synergy of the group. Avan Jassawalla and Hermant Sashittal (1999), in identifying how effectively new product development teams worked, described these processes in ways that help us understand how communication is central to collaboration. Jassawalla and Sashittal describe at-stakeness as a circumstance in which group members believe that what they do matters and that the team or group matters. Members have mostly equal stature in the group and all influence decision making. Transparency refers to the clarity that group members believe they have with one another about motivations and intentions. Hidden agendas are not present and intense information sharing occurs. Ideas are put on the table and disagreements can be handled without disturbing individual relationships. Mindfulness occurs when decisions are made that take into account various perspectives and the context of the decision. In the case of new-product-development teams, mindful decisions are ones that can be put into production and work not only for the team but also for the larger organization. Finally, synergy reflects the comfort and energy group members feel in working together and their belief in the quality of their work. Research supports the notion that groups with high synergy generally produce more creative ideas, generate better products, and are considered as a whole to be more effective than groups without this intangible but important element. Even in the most collaborative circumstances, members of a group may not agree about a creative approach. Disagreements are one of the common tensions needed for creativity. Lyn Van Swol and Emily Seinfeld (2006) reported when group members hold minority opinions they are more likely to be successful when they repeat common information rather than describing their views in totally unique ways. Van Swol and Seinfeld believe the use of commonly accepted information improves overall influence because common information can be socially validated by members of the majority in the group. Think about your own experiences. What have you done when you believed a group of which you were a member had a lot at stake? How important is it to you to understand the motivations and intentions of other group members? Can you identify a mindful decision your group made? What does synergy mean to you? Think about your communication competencies as they relate to creativity and collaboration. Where are you strong? What needs improvement?

Virtual Groups

It is a rare individual today who will not spend at least part of his or her working time in virtual groups. Loosely defined, virtual groups are teams of individuals organized either temporarily or permanently to work together linked by technology across time and space. Sales representatives become mobile workers as they transmit orders and other data to their home offices while traveling around the country. Others work an entire week at a remote location, typically visiting the office only for key meetings. Workers sometimes referred to as day extenders work in the office during traditional hours and spend additional time from a home office working with customers, with peers around the globe, or within a given organization's network. The issues of working in the virtual environment are complex. For some employees, quality of life is enhanced when workday hours can be performed from home, providing an opportunity to manage more individually work life responsibilities. Commute times are reduced, and many believe flexibility is increased. Employees are usually judged on what they do more than on what they appear to be doing. However, many virtual employees report feeling disconnected from their organizations, missing social interaction and informal relationships. Others report career damage believed to be linked to an invisibility that provides no connection to powerful organizational members. Finally, not everyone is suited to working in more isolated environments that require considerable independent action.

Organizations use virtual teams to link people with particular technical specialties across diverse geographic locations. Organizations have the potential with virtual groups to "follow the sun," with twenty-four-hour workdays and the ability to maintain close customer contact throughout the world. Additionally, virtual environments often reduce real-estate costs and overhead. However, the virtual environment does require a well-developed information technology infrastructure to support a remote workforce. Finally, managing a remote workforce requires skills many managers have never considered.

Remote workers are challenged to build trust with individuals they may never have met in face-to-face interactions. Joseph Walther and Natalya Bazarova (2007) reported geographic distribution of group members in virtual teams has an impact on how members take responsibility for individual behavior. Specifically, Walther and Bazarova found when individuals are in completely distributed groups, they take less personal responsibility and blame their partners more often than individuals working virtually but with group members who are in the same physical workplace or what is called collocated groups. Walther and Bazarova state, "When individuals work with unseen, unknown, remote partners in short-term distributed groups, those remote individuals become scapegoats for individuals' own performance decrements. In contrast, when one's group partners are less unknown, simply by virtue of being from the same geographic location or institutional affiliation—even if they have not met FtF [face to face]—individuals cannot as readily scapegoat their own misbehavior on amorphous or assumedly different partners. Rather, collocated group partners take more personal responsibility for their dysfunctional behavior" (p. 17).

Group identity is another potential issue. How do individuals develop engagement with their work and with one another? What about language and time differences? Evidence is emerging, however, that groups who work virtually over time do establish their own norms and construct an identity that assists individuals in understanding their own expectations and the expectations of others in the group.

The virtual environment is yet another challenge for communication competency. Not only is technical competency required, but also the style and tone of written messages often differ substantially from verbal exchanges. Verbal gossip is replaced by the forwarding of e-mails without the knowledge of the sender. Confidentiality takes on new meaning when messages can be transmitted broadly within a matter of seconds. Conflict in writing can be difficult to express and damaging in the permanency of the written word. Anger expressed in an e-mail has been known to disrupt relationships because the sender simply had no time to think about the appropriateness of a response. Workers use technology to connect to each other and also to increase distance. Paul Leonardi, Jeffrey Treem, and Michele Jackson (2010) report

> in distributed work arrangements the operating assumption was that distance meant disconnection in a communicative sense. In other words, people who were working away from the main office would not be as connected to office happenings as they once were. Distance was conceptualized as a communicative problem, therefore the deployment of ICTs (Information and Communication

Technologies) that afforded synchronous, data-intensive communication was thought to be a means by which to decrease the perception or experience of distance, and over-use of communication eliminated much of the desired distance of teleworkers. In person, one has little control over the extent to which their work practices are visible to others as they are available by virtue of co-presence. However, the relative invisibility of teleworkers, combined with the ability to regulate their visibility through ICT use, afforded them an opportunity to strategically create the effect of distance (through mediated communication) from their managers, coworkers, and clients. (pp. 98–99)

Cultural differences also can obscure clarity and intention. Jennifer Gibbs (2009) reported three main tensions in global virtual team interactions: autonomy–connectedness, inclusion–exclusion, and empowerment–disempowerment. Diverse cultures and time, technology, and space differences all contribute to communication challenges. Yet the opportunities for expansion of relationships and organizational excellence also exist. Part of our preparation for the future must include thinking about what it takes to work effectively in the virtual environment.

Groups and Technology Use

Increasingly organizations of all types are asking individuals and groups of employees to base change, innovation, and decision making on shared knowledge contributed to and retrieved from sophisticated internal and external databases. Some go so far as to claim successful knowledge sharing is essential to competitive advantage. Chances are as a student you use complex databases and work on group projects with others who retrieve information from similar sources. If you work on a large project you may even create your own database where group members make their contributions. For some time, research has suggested communication problems within groups or entire organizations influence members to withhold knowledge from databases, making their use less effective. Motivations stimulating or retarding knowledge sharing are complex. The challenge remains, however, to understand how individuals, groups, and organizations can generate environments and competencies to support knowledge transfer.

C. Erik Timmerman and Craig Scott (2006) reported the structural characteristics of groups such as team size, number of member locations, number of member time zones, and organizational type influence the type of technology members use for communication. However, structural characteristics are not influential in predicting group outcomes such as identification, cohesiveness, trust, and communication satisfaction. Efforts to understand argumentativeness, responsiveness, thoroughness, and engagement relate to favorable overall outcomes.

Yu Yuan, Janet Fulk, Michelle Shumate, Peter Monge, J. Bryant, and Matthew Matsaganis (2005) examined motivations to participate in organizational information sharing via collective repositories (sometimes referred to as information commons, databases, or intranets). They found social influence and technology-specific competence positively relate to individual intranet use. Specifically, individuals will be likely to contribute and retrieve information based on their perceptions of whether other team members engage in similar usage patterns. Finally, technological competence is a major contributor to individual decisions to retrieve and contribute information.

The work of Andrew Flanagin, Hee Sun Park, and David Seibold (2004) provided further insight into group performance, member satisfaction, and the use of collaborative technology. Flanagin, Park, and Seibold studied ten groups who worked together using collaborative technology over time to complete a series of seven tasks. These authors' results suggest that over time individuals become increasingly satisfied with group work using collaborative technologies. The quality of information group members provide and the equity or equality of contributions among group members is important to initial satisfaction, but the equity of contributions is more important than quality over time. In other words, when an individual contributes more than others, the individual becomes less satisfied. The more other group members contribute, the more satisfied the individual becomes. Most students have had this experience in face-to-face groups. Individuals who report they had to "carry the load" for the group often contend the experience was not a good one. Research suggests participation behaviors are key to satisfaction in technologically supported group work. Next we discuss some of the issues related to increasing our effectiveness in groups, both virtual and face-to-face.

INCREASING GROUP PARTICIPATION EFFECTIVENESS

The question now becomes how to evaluate our competencies for group participation. What types of behaviors are most productive? What should be avoided? Are there particular communication skills we should develop for group effectiveness? The next section of this chapter seeks to increase our effectiveness by identifying negative and positive group participation behaviors.

Negative Participation Behaviors

Each individual brings to group participation preferences for behavior. Research on group participation permits us to generalize about counterproductive individual behaviors.

Negative Behaviors

1. Argue stubbornly for your own ideas, positions, and conclusions. Make sure all members know exactly where you stand, and resist modifying or changing your views. Do not bother to listen actively to opposing viewpoints because of the rightness of your position.
2. Suppress differences of opinion and conflict. Use formal techniques such as agendas or majority rule to quiet opposition. Don't encourage others to express controversial opinions, and make sure the group considers only safe topics.
3. Work for quick agreement. Extended problem analysis and solution generation may contribute to dissent. Don't worry about "groupthink" because, after all, you are a group and everyone should support the same viewpoint.
4. If a stalemate occurs, pit one person against another so that there are clear winners and losers. This action will return the group to action and discourage others from blocking progress.
5. Use your power position to get others to agree with you. Don't hesitate to pull rank or threaten sanctions to preserve your ability to influence others.
6. Don't respond to e-mail requests. Send e-mails that attack others. Communicate only to selected members of the group.

Positive Participation Behaviors

The following positive participation behaviors have been adapted from the work of Cragan and Wright (1986) and others. As you review these positive behaviors, try to decide which are the most important and what additional guidelines you would suggest.

Positive Behaviors

1. Be prepared and informed when in decision-making and problem-solving groups. Review relevant materials before meetings, ask for additional needed information, formulate ideas, help with physical arrangements, and encourage other team members. Contributions to meetings should be based on knowledge about the topic, agenda, and facts that bear directly on the problem.

2. Exhibit cooperative and open-minded behaviors that encourage participation by all involved. In a group work setting, group goals have priority. Cooperation includes encouraging participation and encouraging listening and the clarification of meanings among group members. Cooperation also includes speaking with receivers in mind (concerning both content and style) to minimize message distortion. Groups tend to work best when all members accept a collective responsibility for productive outcomes.

3. Value diverse opinions and people. Promote different ideas, challenge team members to offer alternative views, support disagreement, and encourage broad participation.

4. Contribute ideas and seek information. Willingly risk ideas and opinions, ask for criticism, ask for opinions, support participation, and discourage negative evaluation.

5. Attempt to remain rational, and thoughtfully evaluate all information. Effective participation includes analyzing our own logic as well as the logic of others. Effective members exhibit enough patience for this examination to be possible. Effective members recognize good decisions are based on good information subjected to solid reasoning and evaluation.

6. Observe the participation process of the group. Members have not only a contribution responsibility but also a process responsibility for helping all members to participate thoughtfully. Those not speaking are in a position to observe when the group strays from its goals or when silent members are not given an opportunity for participation. Observation is also important for subtle cues that suggest some members may be holding important reservations that will ultimately affect their commitment.

7. Actively participate as well as observe. Active participants who seek active participation from others set a tone in the group that encourages good decision making and problem solving.

8. Stress group productivity: encourage group members, note past successes, identify group strengths, and remember group responsibilities.

9. Avoid "role ruts." Use diverse communication roles, encourage diversity among team members, and share roles with others.

10. Avoid self-centered roles. Identify disruptive behaviors, self-monitor behavior, and give feedback to those exhibiting self-centered roles.

11. Ease tensions. Facilitate positive expressions of differences, support people, evaluate ideas, and stress cooperation.

12. Support leadership. Help leaders accomplish goals, and share leadership when necessary.
13. Build group pride. Create traditions, symbols, and slogans; celebrate work, progress, and success. Celebrate interpersonal relationships.
14. Produce results. Take responsibility for group outcomes, encourage responsibility from team members, and focus on effectiveness.
15. Think about the wise use of computer-mediated communication. Respond to requests thoughtfully and understand the difference between verbal and computer-mediated interactions.

CHAPTER HIGHLIGHTS

Effective groups have essential skills and abilities, a strong desire by members to contribute, and the capability of collaborating effectively. We will work in what can be described as **bona fide** organizational groups with permeable boundaries and environmental dependence. The first group assigned to us when we enter an organization is our **primary work team.** Primary work teams have been described as long-standing teams, project teams, prefab groups, and self-managing teams. **Directional groups** are groups formally charged and structured to provide overall direction and oversight of the organization. **Quality teams** are groups of workers from the same general area or related technology who meet regularly to identify and propose solutions to problems affecting product or process quality. **Task force groups** form to bring together individuals with technical specialties who are members of other organizational groups to accomplish a specifically designed task or project. **Steering committees** resemble task forces in composition but form for the implementation of projects or to steer the progress of a plan, goal, issue, or program. **Focus groups** help organizations quickly understand issues and problems. Focus groups are not charged with final recommendations or implementation planning. **Geographically diverse teams** are work groups formed with team members separated geographically and linked through technology. Geographically diverse groups are challenged to work effectively across time zones, language barriers, and a variety of other obstacles. **Social support groups** form

across all types of formally structured groups and in less structured ways. Finally, **communities of practice** groups provide professional development and stimulate innovation among groups of similar professionals.

The **team-based organization** is a widespread organizational form used to increase overall competitiveness. Team-based organizations have fewer managers and are generally considered more productive than their hierarchical counterparts. Team-based organizations are challenged by issues of worker participation, rewards, and career issues. The **high-reliability organization** is designed for high-risk industries which need to mitigate failures and intervene in crises. Communication protocols are often formal and continually subject to analysis for improvement.

Understanding group processes is important for organizational participation. The need for increasing employee involvement and participation raises important concerns about the concept of **workplace democracy** or the valuing of individual goals and feelings about issues of primary concern to employees. **Group norms** are unwritten behavior rules, ways of doing things, which groups develop over time. Norms reflect what the group deems desirable and can be said to be cultural beliefs about effectiveness or appropriateness. Individuals assume different roles in groups. Generally speaking, three important classifications of **group communication roles** can be described: group **task roles,** group **maintenance roles,** and **self-centered roles.** Task roles help groups accomplish goals, and maintenance roles promote social support among group members. Self-centered roles support individual goals and may or may not be compatible with overall group goals and relationships. Working in groups requires communication competencies for engag-ing diversity, stimulating creativity and collabo-ration, and responding to the virtual environ-ment. Finally, our personal behaviors, both posi-tive and negative, relate to group effectiveness and satisfaction. ∎

WORKSHOP

1. Identifying effective and ineffective communica-tion roles in groups helps us to understand our own behavior and the behavior of others. Read the Group Communication Roles section that follows and attempt to identify the communication roles used by John, Henry, Tim, Mary, and Mike.
2. Read the Group Problem-Solving transcript that follows. Try to identify the communication roles exhibited by the participants. In small groups, dis-cuss answers to the questions posed at the end of the transcript.
3. Form groups of six members each and select a topic of mutual interest for discussion. One mem-ber of the group will become a nonparticipating observer. Select a topic for which a group recom-mendation for action can be made. The group will be given fifteen minutes for discussion. Although consensus is not required, each group should at-tempt to reach one or two recommendations for the issue that most members can support. During the discussion the appointed observer will fill out the Identification of Group Communication Roles form that follows. At the conclusion of the discus-sion, each participating member also should fill out the form from his or her memory of communi-cation skills exhibited by each group member. The assigned nonparticipant discusses his or her obser-vations with the group, followed by general dis-cussion of all observations.
4. Using the Identification of Group Communication Roles form for a research guide, visit a public meeting (city council, club or organization, stu-dent government, etc.). Record each participant's name across the top of the form. As the meeting progresses, identify with a small check in the ap-propriate box the various skills that individuals use during the course of the meeting. Also record any notes that will help you to determine the effec-tiveness or ineffectiveness of each participant.

Following the meeting, compare your notes with the total checks in each skill box. What type of profile was established for the most effective par-ticipants? How did the less effective members be-have? What do these observations suggest about participation skills?

Group Communication Roles

Read the following transcript of a typical group meet-ing that could occur in any organization.[1] Identify the various communication roles used by the group mem-bers. Which individuals demonstrate more effective roles? What might members do differently to improve their communication?

> The group members: John, Henry, Tim, Mary, Mike
>
> The problem: Planning the development of an im-proved employee policy manual
>
> Communication roles: Task, maintenance, self-centered

The Transcript

JOHN: I know you'll all agree that it's an honor to be chosen to be on this committee. And as you know, my background is primarily in person-nel, so I'll be glad to take primary responsi-bility for a first rewrite on the manual.

HENRY: That's good of you, John, but before moving too quickly to a rewrite, I'd like to hear some general ideas for improving the manual from all the members of our committee. Policy for the employees is a matter of importance to all of us.

TIM: Hey, you two, either of your suggestions would work well. John, if you want to do a rewrite, it might save us all plenty of time, but then again, it might also be good to base your rewrite on ideas from other committee members.

[1]Prepared by Sherwyn P. Morreale.

MARY: True, Tim, but the main point we want to keep in mind is that we, as a committee, want to write a new manual that will act as a model for other companies, something we can all be proud to have worked on.

MIKE: You're right, Mary, that's the spirit. We're all in agreement on doing the best possible job. I'd sure like to hear everybody's thoughts regarding the two possibilities we can now consider. Do you all think we should begin with a rewrite from John? Or should we begin with the manual we've got? Or are there other possible ways to go that we should consider?

JOHN: Listen, because our time is limited today, why don't I go ahead with just a simple rough draft of a rewrite. Then I'll get a copy of it to each group member before our next meeting. We can go from there.

TIM: Sounds great to me. You'll be saving all of our time and energy. When's the next meeting?

HENRY: Saving time is always a good idea. I'm with you 100 percent, Tim, but I'm a little concerned about our committee being a group that forgets to look before it leaps. Before we adjourn today, why don't we talk it through a little more.

MARY: Okay, Henry, do you think we should take more time right now and have everyone present what they think this rewrite should focus on? I'd like to hear some more ideas from everyone also. It may be our ideas will be a little different, or we may really disagree on just how the rewrite should be done.

HENRY: True, but the best final manual is going to be a product of some friendly disagreeing. So how does everybody see it? Where do we go with this rewrite job?

MARY: I think the best thing to do, at this point, is for each of us to draw up a list of the best things we see in our present manual, plus a list of its weakest points. Then together we can do a summary list of what to keep and what to improve.

JOHN: That sounds good, from a creativity point of view, but time counts here, and unless I can get on the rewrite soon, my schedule might tighten up. Then I might not have time to do a rewrite at all.

TIM: Then maybe we need to prepare these lists as quickly as possible and get them right to

John. Whichever way, though, it'll work well. We seem to know how to work together on a job like this one.

HENRY: We don't need to make a decision here on how to proceed. Let's have each person put their ideas out for, say, five minutes each. Then we can take a vote on what to do.

Group Problem-Solving Transcript

JANE (DEPARTMENT MANAGER): I think we had better get started. We have a lot to do to get ready to announce the new training plan.

SALLY (SENIOR TRAINER): Jane, I'm not sure everyone in the group really understands our plans. I think that before we decide how to introduce the program to the division we need to make sure that everyone in personnel is thoroughly familiar with what we intend to do.

JANE: That's a good point. How much information do the rest of you have?

JOHN (COMPENSATION SPECIALIST): I just know we are going to plan a training program for each employee, but I have been on vacation and don't know much more than that.

HENRY (RECRUITER): Look, I don't think each of us can be expected to know all the details. I think we should stick to our original plan and decide how a division-wide announcement should be made. The rest of us are too busy to understand all the details.

SALLY TO HENRY: I think you're very wrong. Especially in your job, you can actually attract people to this company with the type of ongoing training we are proposing.

KATHY (BENEFITS ADMINISTRATION): Sally, maybe you could describe the type of training our department will receive. That might help us understand the general concept.

JANE: Sally, I do think an overview of the program would be helpful. We do, however, have to decide on the timing of the division-wide announcement.
[Sally explains the basics of the new training program to the staff (narrative not included).]

FRANK (EMPLOYEE): I think it sounds like a very impressive program, but I wonder if we can really pull it off. Remember the time we decided to computerize all the records and start the year with a new payroll process? We were crazy. Who made that decision, anyway? Does anyone remember? Let's not have another Kent Smith [employee who left the company following the record computerization project].

SALLY TO FRANK: This one is not another Kent Smith project. I resent your implying that it is. A lot of hard work and planning have gone into identifying training opportunities that will help all our employees. I think you should keep an open mind.

JANE: Does anyone else have any questions about the program?

KATHY: Well, I think we need to move in this direction. What ideas do you need from us to make the division announcement?

SALLY: Thanks, Kathy. First of all, we need to know the timing of major communications from your individual areas to all employees. We don't want too much new information going out at once.

Try to identify the roles individuals played in the dialogue (see the list that follows). Can you determine which individuals work more cooperatively than others? Is there a leader? Are important roles missing? How would you describe this group? ◼

Identification of Group Communication Roles

Task Roles

Names of Group Members

Initiating: makes suggestions; gives ideas						
Information requestor: asks for facts, new ideas						
Information giver: submits facts, relevant data						
Procedure facilitator: takes notes; guides agenda						
Opinion requestor: seeks opinions, values, beliefs						
Opinion giver: gives opinions; expresses values, beliefs						
Clarifier: explains ideas and elaborates						
Summarizer–evaluator: restates ideas; criticizes						

Group Maintenance Roles

Names of Group Members

Social supporter: expresses togetherness; encourages others						
Harmonizer: mediates and reconciles differences						
Tension reliever: relaxes others; changes subjects						
Energizer: stimulates group activity; seeks action						
Leader: takes personal responsibility						
Follower: goes along with the group; supports decisions						
Compromiser: seeks a middle ground in disagreement						
Gatekeeper: asks opinions of nonparticipants						

Self-Centered Roles

Negative blocker: gives negative response to others						
Dominator: controls through interruptions and approach						
Attacker: acts aggressively to achieve personal status						
Clown: disrupts with jokes and diverting behavior						

TIPS FOR EFFECTIVE COMMUNICATION

1. Identify your best and worst group experience. Describe your participation behaviors in each experience. What does it suggest for future group participation?
2. Ask all members of your group to offer ideas.
3. Ask members of your group to critique your ideas.
4. When forming a group, seek diverse membership.
5. To increase balanced participation in your group, ask all members to offer a new idea. Ask that all ideas be respected and not critiqued until everyone has had an opportunity to speak.
6. Confront a group member who interrupts others. Ask the member to let others finish their thoughts.
7. Learn how to use two collaborative technologies for group decision making.
8. Learn how to determine which databases are likely to have credible information for the problems you confront. Identify less-than-credible information sources.
9. Locate a legitimate Internet-based global discussion group. Participate and observe the differing styles of the contributions.
10. Volunteer to lead a group project in which your qualifications match group needs. ■

REFERENCES AND SUGGESTED READINGS

Baird, J. E. Jr. 1977. *The dynamics of organizational communication.* New York: Harper and Row.

Bantz, C. 1993. Cultural diversity and group cross-cultural team research. *Journal of Applied Communication Research* 21(1): 1–20.

Barker, J., and P. Tompkins. 1993. *Organizations, teams, control, and identification.* Paper presented at the Speech Communication Association Convention, November, Miami, FL.

Benne, K., and P. Sheats. 1948. Functional roles of group members. *Journal of Social Issues* 4(2): 41–49.

Brilhart, J. K., and G. J. Galanes. 1989. *Effective group discussion,* 6th ed. Dubuque, IA: Brown.

Brown, K., T. D. Klastorin, and J. Valluzzi. 1990. Project performance and the liability of group harmony. *IEEE Transactions on Engineering Management* 37(2): 117–125.

Carr, C. 1992. Planning priorities for empowered teams. *Journal of Business Strategy* 13(5): 43–47.

Cartwright, D., and A. Zander. 1968. *Group dynamics research and theory,* 3rd ed. New York: Harper and Row.

Cheney, G. 1995. Democracy in the workplace: Theory and practice from the perspective of communication. *Journal of Applied Communication Research* 23: 167–200.

Courtright, J., G. Fairhurst, and E. Rogers. 1989. Interaction patterns in organic and mechanistic systems. *Academy of Management Journal* 32(4): 773–802.

Cox, T. Jr. 1993. *Cultural diversity in organizations.* San Francisco: Berrett-Koehler.

Cragan, J., and D. Wright. 1986. *Communication in small group discussions,* 2nd ed. St. Paul, MN: West.

Flanagin, A., H. Park, and David Seibold. 2004. Group performance and collaborative technology: A longitudinal and multilevel analysis of information quality, contribution equity, and members' satisfaction in computer-mediated groups. *Communication Monographs* 71(3): 352–372.

Fulk, J. 1993. Social construction of communication technology. *Academy of Management Journal* 36(5): 921–950.

Gibb, J. 2009. Dialectics in a global software team: Negotiating tensions across time, space, and culture. *Human Relations* 62: 905–935.

Gibson, C., and M. Zellmer-Bruhn. 2001. Metaphors and meaning: An intercultural analysis of the concept of teamwork. *Administrative Science Quarterly* 46(2): 274–316.

Hackman, M. Z., and C. E. Johnson. 2000. *Leadership: A communication perspective.* Prospect Heights, IL: Waveland.

Heath, R. G., and P. M. Sias. 1999. Communicating spirit in a collaborative alliance. *Journal of Applied Communication Research* 27: 356–376.

Iverson, J., and R. McPhee. 2008. Communicating knowing through communities of practice: Exploring internal communicative processes and differences among CoPs. *Journal of Applied Communication Research* 36: 176–199.

Jassawalla, A., and H. Sashittal. 1999. Building collaborative cross-functional new product teams. *Academy of Management Executive* 13(3): 50–63.

Jehn, K., G. Northcraft, and M. Neale. 1999. Why differences make a difference: A field study of diversity, conflict, and performance in workgroups. *Administrative Science Quarterly* 44(4): 741–763.

Katzenbach, J., and D. Smith. 1993. *The wisdom of teams.* Boston: Harvard Business School Press.

Keller, R. 1994. Technology-information processing fit and the performance of R&D project groups: A test of contingency theory. *Academy of Management Journal* 37(1): 167–179.

Larson, C. E., and F. M. LaFasto. 1989. *TeamWork: What must go right/What can go wrong.* Newbury Park, CA: Sage.

Leonardi, P. M., J. W. Treem, and M. H. Jackson. 2010. The connectivity paradox: Using technology to both decrease and increase perceptions of distance in distributed work arrangements. *Journal of Applied Communication Research* 38(1): 85–105.

Littlejohn, S., and K. Foss. 2008. *Theories of human communication.* Belmont, CA: Thomson/Wadsworth.

Mayer, M. 1998. Behaviors leading to more effective decisions in small groups embedded in organizations. *Communication Reports* 2(2): 123–132.

Mulvey, P. W., J. F. Veiga, and P. M. Elsass. 1996. When teammates raise a white flag. *Academy of Management Executive* 10(1): 40–49.

Napier, R. W., and M. K. Gershenfeld. 1989. *Groups: Theory and experience.* Boston: Houghton Mifflin.

Oetzel, J., T. Burtis, M. Chew Sanchez, and F. Pérez. 2001. Investigating the role of communication in culturally diverse work groups: A review and synthesis. In *Communication Yearbook 25*, ed. W. B. Gudykunst, 237–269. Mahwah, NJ: Erlbaum.

Poole, M. S., K. Real, L. Alston, B. Beal, F. Villamaria, J. Wunsch, A. Vedlitz, and T. Dacin. 2000. *Participation in quality improvement in work groups II: A longitudinal study of structural and communication process explanations in a managed care setting.* Paper presented at the International Communication Association Convention, May, Acapulco, Mexico.

Thomas, D., and R. Ely. 2001. Cultural diversity at work: The effects of diversity perspectives on work group processes and outcomes. *Administrative Science Quarterly* 46(2): 229–280.

Thompson, L. 2003. Improving the creativity of organizational work groups. *Academy of Management Executive* 17(1): 96–111.

Timmerman, C., and C. Scott. 2006. Virtually working: Communicative and structural predictors of media use and key outcomes in virtual work teams. *Communication Monographs* 73(1): 108–136.

Van Swol, L., and E. Seinfeld. 2006. Differences between minority, majority, and unanimous group members in the communication of information. *Human Communication Research* 32: 178–197.

Walther, J. B., and N. N. Bazarova. 2007. Misattribution in virtual groups: The effects of member distribution on self-serving bias and partner blame. *Human Communication Research* 33: 1–26.

Wenger, E. C., and W. M. Snyder. 2000. Communities of practice: The organizational frontier. *Harvard Business Journal* 78(1): 139–146.

Yuan, Y., J. Fulk, M. Shumate, P. Monge, J. Bryant, and M. Matsaganis. 2005. Individual participation in organizational information commons: The impact of team level social influence and technology-specific competence. *Human Communication Research* 31(2): 212–240. ∎

Leadership and Management Communication

DEVELOPING COMPETENCIES THROUGH ...

KNOWLEDGE   Describing leadership from trait, style, situational, transformational, and discursive approaches

Distinguishing between leadership and management

SENSITIVITY   Clarifying a personal theory of leadership

Understanding leadership styles, strategic objectives, and tactics

SKILLS   Assessing leadership strategies and tactics

Practicing analysis capabilities and skills using cases, transcripts of meetings, and group activities

VALUES   Relating leadership to organizational excellence

Understanding need for leadership from all organizational members

Describing principled and ethical leadership

THE CASE OF THE INVISIBLE MANAGER

John Mitchell was a superior engineer who was widely known throughout Invest Corporation for his ability to solve creatively highly complex technical problems. No one had been surprised when John was promoted approximately a year ago to laboratory manager at Invest's main research and development facility. What was surprising were the complaints from the lab that nothing was getting done. Senior lab members were particularly vocal about John's insistence on knowing every detail of their decisions before letting them move forward. They also complained about their inability to get to see him and the days on end that went by with no word from him about decisions.

Although acknowledging John's technical brilliance, several members of the lab management team openly questioned whether John would ever be a leader or even understood the difference between engineering responsibilities and those of management. John responded that his technical abilities were the type of leadership the lab needed. He believed if intelligent people were doing their jobs, they did not need close personal contact with their managers. John viewed leadership as a purely technical contribution and was amazed that some of his top engineers doubted his contributions. He could hardly believe they had labeled him their Invisible Manager. ■

INTRODUCTION

Is John right in his view of leadership? Is superior technical ability the type of leadership a management team really needs? Can both John and his managers be right? How can we define management and leadership responsibilities?

In his new position, John faces a test of his beliefs about leadership and management. He contends technical contributions are the essence of his leadership. To make complex technical decisions, he requires large amounts of detail, and the sheer volume of work has delayed his response to his managers. He believes delay is justified to improve the technical capabilities of the laboratory. He disagrees that leaders and managers need to stay in close personal contact with employees. John, however, is on a collision course with a capable group of senior lab managers. They disagree that his approach is working or that he is even exhibiting leadership. How would you help John and his managers? What does he need to understand to resolve this important problem?

Most of us have seen leadership and management situations similar to the one in which the laboratory is involved. We have been members of a group in which the leader and group members were at odds over the way a project should be accomplished. We have experienced frustration when someone like a teacher or a doctor had information or a service we needed but was not available for an appointment. We have been delayed in making plans while waiting for the decisions of others. We are influenced in all aspects of our lives by leaders or the need for leadership. Most of us act as both leaders and followers in our families, at work, and in the political and social organizations of which we are a part.

Think about the most effective leader with whom you have had direct contact. How did this person behave? What were his or her communication competencies? Now think specifically about an ineffective leader. Describe his or her behavior and communication competencies. Most of us have been influenced by leaders and have fulfilled leadership roles without giving detailed consideration to how leadership works and the competencies necessary for effectiveness. To develop communication competencies for leadership, we need to understand the importance of leadership and management communication, how leadership and management have been described, where leadership and management can differ, the determinants of leadership effectiveness, and constructive communication strategies and tactics for leadership.

This chapter is designed to contribute to *knowledge* by demonstrating the importance of leadership and management communication, distinguishing between the two, and understanding them by describing trait, style, situational, transformational, and discursive approaches. We develop *sensitivity* competencies by identifying individual preferences and styles for leadership and by becoming familiar with commonly used strategies and tactics. Sensitivity competencies, in turn, influence the use of strategic and tactical communication *skills*. We encourage *value* competencies by describing the importance of leadership for organizational excellence, identifying determinants of leadership effectiveness, and associating leadership with overall interpersonal communication competency.

Finally, all four competencies—knowledge, sensitivity, skills, and values—are applied to competency practice through self-analysis and case study.

THE IMPORTANCE OF LEADERSHIP AND MANAGEMENT COMMUNICATION

Leadership and management communication affect nearly all aspects of organizational life. Leaders help guide individuals, groups, and entire organizations in establishing goals and sustaining action to support goals. Managers fulfill specific organizationally assigned roles designed to direct and evaluate the work of others. Managers are expected to be leaders, although not all managers exhibit leadership behaviors. In fact, leadership communication can come from virtually anyone in the organization, with the effectiveness of leadership and management communication directly relating to organizational success and work satisfaction.

What exactly is meant by leadership and management communication? There are literally hundreds of definitions of what leaders do and what is considered to be leadership. Chances are our personal definition of leadership may vary from that of our friends and may even change from situation to situation. We might call an individual a leader, for example, because of the person's election to the presidency of a particular organization. At another time we might say that same individual is not a leader because he or she does not exhibit leadership behaviors expected from the president. In other words, we expected leadership from the legitimate or positional role of the presidency, but when the president does not exhibit leadership behaviors, we say the president is not a leader.

Leadership ■ Process for guiding individuals, groups, and entire organizations in establishing goals and sustaining action to support goals.

Leadership takes place through communication. Leaders communicate about needed change, translate intentions into reality, propose new strategies, and help sustain action to support decisions. Leadership communication is a process of influence whereby leaders attempt to convince followers to attain specific goals or broad organizational outcomes. The ability to influence is based on the leader's position, credibility to a follower group, analysis and technical skills, and overall communication competence. People can be assigned the position of leader, but leadership occurs not from the assignment itself but through communication behaviors in interactions with others. In other words, leadership is socially constructed in the complex interplay of communication among leaders and others within ever-changing environments. Leaders may occupy a specific role or position, while leadership is the negotiation and construction of meanings which help to support or retard a variety of actions.

Management ■ Responsibility, specifically assigned by the organization, to direct and evaluate the work of others.

Management fulfills specifically defined roles designed to facilitate work to support organizational goals. Managers are given legitimate power to influence the behavior of employees. They are charged with obtaining routine compliance with the operating procedures and expectations of the organization. It is hoped, of course, that managers can exceed routine compliance and instill in employees a desire for excellence that goes beyond merely acceptable performance. Whether resulting in routine compliance or a desire for excellence, managerial influence occurs through human communication. Based on formal supervisor–employee relationships, managerial communication directs work assignments, work evaluation, needed changes, and all other aspects of organizational action for goal achievement.

Both leadership and management communication are powerful organizational influences. Communication relationships between managers and employees influence innovation, decision making, work satisfaction, and perceptions of organizational climate. In work that Kathy Ellis and I have done (Ellis and Shockley-Zalabak, 1999), leadership and management communication were strongly related to both trust in individuals within the organization and overall organizational trust. Jaesub Lee (2001) reported the perceived quality of leader–member exchanges significantly affected perceptions of organizational rewards and fairness in a variety of processes. For example, individuals reporting low-quality leader–member exchanges (LMXs) also reported deficiencies in both formal and informal organizational rewards as well as less fairness in organizational processes than individuals with more positive communication exchanges with their leaders. Alicia Marshall and Cynthia Stohl (1993) found "two communicative activities that significantly contribute to one's level of organizational knowledge: cultivating strong relationships with managers and engaging in various leadership activities over time."

Leadership communication, whether exhibited by managers or other influential organizational members, becomes the vision of the organization that directs and redirects all organizational activity. As Warren Bennis and Burt Nanus (1985) suggested, "effective leadership can move organizations from current to future states, create visions of potential opportunities for organizations, instill within employees commitment to change, and instill new cultures and strategies in organizations that mobilize and focus energy and resources."

Leadership and management communication is part of the sensemaking activities of the organization. As we said earlier, leadership and management communication is a complex socially constructed process. It helps members develop priorities and determine what is needed by the organization. It influences decision making, transmits communication rules, and contributes to the shared realities that become the organization's culture or cultures. As such, leadership and management communication charts the course of action for the organization. The effectiveness of this communication is therefore central to organizational excellence.

THEORIES OF LEADERSHIP AND MANAGEMENT

Thousands of articles have been written about leadership and management. We talk about the need for leadership in our communities, in the organizations in which we work, and in government. Yet trying to describe how leadership and management work and how they should work remains a difficult and often controversial task. Are leaders born with leadership talents? What styles do successful leaders employ? Are some people simply in the right time and place to assume leadership responsibility? What type of leader is John Mitchell (from the beginning of this chapter)? What type of manager? Is there a difference? What can we do to increase our leadership effectiveness?

Theories of leadership and management describe leaders and managers in terms of personal traits or characteristics, preferences for leadership styles or approaches, and responsiveness to leadership requirements in specific situations. Before exploring trait, style, situational, transformational, and discursive theories of leadership, please complete the leadership experience exercise in Figure 7.1. The exercise will give you a profile of some of your attitudes and experiences with leadership that you can compare with major theories of leadership and management.

The following twenty-one statements have been used to describe leadership and leaders. Following them are four incomplete sentences that begin "My experience with leadership and leaders has taught me that ... " For each of the four incomplete sentences, select from among the twenty-one statements the five that best reflect your experiences with leadership and leaders. Statements may be used to complete more than one incomplete sentence.

Statements Describing Leaders and Leadership

1. Leaders are *born*.
2. Leadership *ability* can be *developed*.
3. Leaders are high in *intelligence*.
4. Leaders take *initiative*.
5. Leaders *deviate* from norms.
6. Leaders have *good communication* skills.
7. Leaders are in the *right place* at the right time.
8. Leaders are *democratic*.
9. Leaders are *autocratic*.
10. Leaders are *risk takers*.
11. Leaders take a *hands-off* approach.
12. Leadership is *situation-specific*.
13. Leaders *block ideas* and *punish opposition*.
14. Leaders *seek ideas* and *encourage disagreement*.
15. Leaders *ignore conflict*.
16. Leaders *solicit feedback*.
17. Leaders are *outcome-oriented*.
18. Leaders *share praise*.
19. Leaders *set goals*.
20. Leaders *blame* those who fail.
21. Leaders *control* their followers.

My experience with leadership and leaders has taught me that effective . . .

1.
2.
3.
4.
5.

FIGURE 7.1
Leadership Experiences

My experience with leadership and leaders has taught me that ineffective . . .
1.
2.
3.
4.
5.

My experience with leadership and leaders has taught me that the most important aspects of leadership are . . .
1.
2.
3.
4.
5.

My experience with leadership and leaders has taught me that the least important aspects of leadership are . . .
1.
2.
3.
4.
5.

What type of person and situation does your personal leadership theory describe? Compare your theory to the ones you will now study in Chapter 7.

FIGURE 7.1
(*continued*)

You now have before you an assessment of your personal theory of leadership. As you begin to evaluate major theories of leadership and management, think about your own personal theory and what is needed for leadership effectiveness.

Trait Approaches

Early theories of effective leadership assumed leaders had innate traits that made them effective. That is, great leaders were considered to be born with the ability for leadership. This theory of the "great man" first surfaced in the writings of the early Greeks and Romans and is prevalent today among those who believe that leadership cannot be developed, that you either have leadership qualities or you don't.

Over eighty-five years of research has attempted to define traits or personality characteristics that best predict the effective leader. Lists of desirable traits have numbered approximately eighty characteristics, but the **trait approach** has failed to define a stable set of characteristics associated with effective leadership. Even the concept of what is effective remains open to question. This approach simply does not provide a comprehensive explanation of how leaders interact with followers and meet the needs of specific circumstances.

Trait approach ■ Theory of leadership that assumed that leaders possessed innate traits that made them effective; commonly referred to as the great-man theory.

To illustrate the difficulty of establishing a trait approach for leadership, identify two leaders you would characterize as effective. Describe their personality traits and characteristics in relation to the groups they lead. Now identify two leaders whose effectiveness you question. What traits and characteristics do they exhibit? Do your effective and ineffective leaders share similar characteristics? How do they differ? What leadership traits do you exhibit? How effective are these characteristics?

Style Approaches

Style approach ■ Theories that attempt to identify a range of general approaches leaders use to achieve goals. The approaches are thought to be based on a leader's assumptions about what motivates people to accomplish goals.

The **style approach** theories for understanding leadership attempt to identify a range of general approaches leaders use to influence goal achievement. These approaches are theorized to be based on the leader's assumptions about what motivates people to accomplish goals. Particular approaches also are thought to reflect complex relationships among the personal characteristics of the leader (i.e., communication competencies, communication apprehension, and internal motivational forces), the requirements of the situation at hand, and the resources over which the leader and followers have control or influence.

Chief among the style theories is the autocratic-to-democratic continuum first proposed by Ralph White and Ronald Lippitt (1960). This continuum suggested leadership can be understood as ranging in behavior from autocratic to democratic. The three primary styles identified are autocratic, democratic, and laissez-faire.

Autocratic ■ Style of leader or manager who makes decisions with little influence from others.

The **autocratic** leader or manager makes decisions with little influence from others. This leader tells others what to do and usually enforces sanctions against those who choose not to comply. The autocratic leader views followers as essential for goal achievement but usually feels little responsibility for employee needs and relationships. Some research suggests autocratically led groups produce more in quantity than democratically led groups; however, the quality of output is better when more democracy is practiced. We have all been involved with autocratic leaders. Can you identify a successful autocratic leader and one who is not so successful? What makes the difference? Is there a best time for autocratic management? What do you lose in the process of being an autocrat?

Democratic ■ Style of leader or manager who involves followers in decision making.

Democratic leaders involve followers in decision making. They assume creativity will be greater and there will be more broad-based support for goals if participation is high. Democratic leaders assume followers are able to participate in decision making. These leaders therefore attempt to generate a climate in which problem solving can take place while preserving interpersonal relationships. Democratic leaders, as do autocrats, both succeed and fail. Now identify a successful democratic leader and one who is not so successful. As you did for the autocrats, attempt to determine the difference. What made the approach work for one and not the other? Using your personal leadership profile, attempt to place your theory on the autocratic-to-democratic continuum.

Laissez-faire ■ Style of leader or manager who behaves as a nonleader. Individuals and groups are expected to make their own decisions because of a hands-off approach from the leader.

The **laissez-faire** leader is really an example of a nonleader. This leader expects individuals and groups to make their own decisions. The laissez-faire leader takes a hands-off approach and contributes information only when asked by group members. This leader shows little direct concern for individuals or goals. Groups can succeed with

The Managerial Grid®

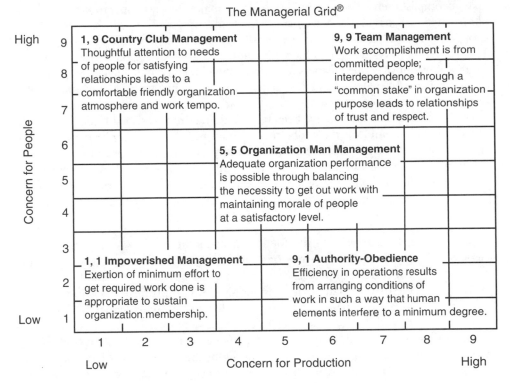

FIGURE 7.2
The Blake and Mouton Managerial Grid®

From *The Managerial Grid III: The Key to Leadership Excellence*, by Robert R. Blake and Jane Srygley Mouton. Houston, TX: Gulf Publishing Company, copyright 1985, p. 12. Reproduced by permission.

laissez-faire leaders. Their success, however, depends largely on the abilities of the group and the group's willingness to work with little or no direction. Have you ever been in a group with laissez-faire leadership? What happened? How did you feel about that type of working experience?

Perhaps the best known of the style theories for leadership and management is the one proposed in 1964 and updated through 1985 by Robert Blake and Jane Mouton. The Blake and Mouton Managerial Grid® suggested leadership styles or approaches are based on two central dimensions: concern for relationships with people and concern for task production. The balances leaders and managers make between these dimensions have become known as the leadership styles of impoverished, middle-of-the-road (organization man), country club, task (authority–obedience), and team management. Figure 7.2 illustrates the Managerial Grid® styles with the two dimensions of concern for people and concern for task.

Impoverished Management (1, 1)   **Impoverished management** is characterized by low concern for interpersonal relationships and

Impoverished management ■
Leadership style characterized by a low concern for interpersonal relationships and task accomplishment.

task accomplishment. The impoverished leader makes few attempts to influence people toward task or goal achievement. This leader frequently dislikes leadership responsibilities and lets others take responsibility that rightfully belongs to the leader. This leader often is uncomfortable with leadership and intellectually resists the need for it. Many impoverished leaders are excellent technically; they have been promoted to supervision or management because of strong technical skills. Technical skills, however, do not prepare them for managing people or letting others accomplish tasks the leaders themselves have been used to doing. Impoverished leaders may even think if people would do their jobs there would be little need for leadership. Such leaders are most often found in legitimate or formal leadership positions rather than in emergent positions as the choice of a group of peers. These leaders may be primarily responsible for the failure of a group, yet they can rarely claim much credit for a group's success. Groups with impoverished leaders often succeed despite the leader and through the emergent leadership of other group members.

Middle-of-the-Road (Organization Man) Management (5, 5)

Middle-of-the-road management ■ Style of leader who balances task and people concerns; commonly referred to as compromise management or leadership.

As Figure 7.2 suggests, **middle-of-the-road management** balances task and people concerns. Sometimes referred to as compromise leadership, the middle-of-the-road leader negotiates and compromises to achieve workable agreements and directions for action. This leader is more concerned with practical versus excellent solutions. The middle-of-the-road leader will seek the "middle" position to provide everyone with some stake in the decision. The compromise positions of middle-of-the-road leaders have been criticized as Band-Aids on the wounds of more serious problems. Critics suggest middle-of-the-road leadership promotes short-term solutions guaranteeing long-term problems. Middle-of-the-road leaders are frequently found in middle (or "organization man") management, where compromise between the needs of employees and top management seems inevitable. In fact, the difficult position of middle management has often been referred to as the sandwich position because of the pressures from below (employees) and from above (top management), pressures that often result in the need for compromise.

Country Club Management (1, 9)

Country club management ■ Style of leader or manager who emphasizes interpersonal relationships at the expense of goal achievement.

Figure 7.2 illustrates **country club management** places the emphasis on interpersonal relationships at the expense of goal achievement. The country club leader wants to be liked and to have a group of followers who feel supported by the leader. This leader provides an interpersonal relationship bond that is low on task emphasis and high in interpersonal support. Country club leaders may want the task accomplished but will not take steps to emphasize task if group members are not highly task-oriented. Country club managers are frequently observed doing the work of their employees rather than insisting their employees exhibit high standards of performance. These managers may not develop the task abilities of their employees. They may, however, lead successful groups when group members themselves have high task motivation and require only interpersonal support to maintain motivation.

Task (Authority–Obedience) Management (9, 1)

Task management ■ Style of leader or manager who is concerned with goals or task achievement while exhibiting little concern for personal relationships; commonly referred to as autocratic leadership.

Often referred to as autocratic leadership, the **task management** leader is concerned with goals or task achievement and exhibits little concern for personal relationships. This leader makes decisions and expects compliance. He or she often enforces decisions with little employee input and is willing to defend his or her position when necessary. Task leaders often exhibit win/lose conflict style preferences. The task leader values efficiency and will make quick and timely decisions. Task leadership, as do other approaches, requires having appropriate information on which to make good decisions, but by showing low concern for people, such leaders may alienate others to the point they withhold information that might improve decision making. Task leadership, however, may be appropriate when a group is hopelessly deadlocked on an issue and someone needs to take responsibility for making a decision. Furthermore, surveys of top management in leading U.S.A. companies indicate task leadership is a prevalent style preference among highly influential managers.

Team Management (9, 9)   As can be seen from Figure 7.2, **team management** is the theoretical ideal. Exhibiting high concern for both task and interpersonal relationships, team leaders emphasize goal accomplishment while supporting people. Team leadership fosters a sense of "we" with high performance standards. This leadership shares decision making and strives for problem solving designed to solve rather than postpone problems. Team leaders respect different points of view and value diversity as long as all contribute to the group effort. Team leaders, however, must have capable and willing team members for successful efforts. Although the style is highly desirable, team leaders depend on team followers for this leadership style to work. Team members who support one another but who do not have enough ability or information to work on problems will not be able to produce a high-quality decision. In other words, willingness to be a team member does not ensure a solid team, and team leadership only produces excellent results with a capable team.

> **Team management** ■ Team leadership or management is the theoretical ideal. Team leaders exhibit high concern for both task and interpersonal relationships by emphasizing goal accomplishment while supporting people.

   To better understand the styles approach to leadership, identify a series of leaders with whom you have had contact and who exhibited each of these five approaches. Try to determine how you reacted to each and how effective his or her leadership was. From your own experiences, what determines whether a particular style is effective or ineffective? What style is John Mitchell using in the lab? What style should he use?

Situational Approaches

Both the trait and style approaches failed to describe comprehensively why particular approaches work in one set of circumstances and fail in another. In response to this difficulty, **situational approaches**, or contingency approaches, were developed to understand better how leaders interact with followers and the requirements of a particular environment.

> **Situational approaches** ■ Leadership theories that explore how leaders interact with followers and the requirements of a particular environment.

   In 1967, Fred Fiedler pioneered understanding leadership styles based on the concept of contingencies. He suggested leader effectiveness could be evaluated only in relationship to how style choices related to contingencies in particular situations. Task and interpersonal relationships were important, but also to be considered were the leader's power position and how rewards and punishment were handled. Sometimes powerful leaders had good follower relationships to accomplish well-defined tasks, a favorable condition for leadership. At other times the leader's power position was in question, with an ambiguous goal to accomplish. In the latter circumstance, leader–member relationships could become strained, generating an overall unfavorable condition. According to Fiedler, the approach or style an effective leader chose depended on a combination of task, relationship, power, and situational contingencies. Along with others, Fiedler's work began to emphasize the interactional and complex nature of leadership.

Building on the work of Blake and Mouton, Paul Hersey and Kenneth Blanchard (1977) proposed a concept of leadership that suggested the appropriateness and effectiveness of leadership behaviors could not be determined by the specific behavior of the leader but by the appropriateness of the behavior in a particular situation. Hersey and Blanchard's situational leadership theory postulated that effectiveness of a particular leader was related to the leader's selection of behavior appropriate to the maturity level of the follower group. Maturity was based on achievement, motivation, ability, education, experience, and the willingness to participate responsibly in goal-oriented activities. In other words, the maturity level of the follower group was the primary factor that determined an effective leadership style. Hersey and Blanchard described situational leadership as dependent on concern for relationships, concern for task, and concern for maturity of followers. They saw four general styles of situational leadership: telling, selling, participating, and delegating. Figure 7.3 depicts the Hersey and Blanchard situational grid.

As you can tell from Figure 7.3, the telling style has high task and low relationship emphases and is best used with immature followers. The leader defines what should be done and instructs followers in how to accomplish well-established goals or tasks.

The selling style also has high task emphasis, but it has a higher relationship emphasis than the telling style. The selling style is characterized by the leader's attempt to convince followers of the importance of the goal and the leader's definition of how the goal is to be accomplished. The selling style is appropriate for a follower group mature enough to accept some responsibility for decisions and actions.

Unlike the team style of Blake and Mouton, the participating style in Figure 7.3 has high relationship and low task emphases to stimulate the creativity of a mature group of followers. The leader supports relationships and encourages participation in decision making because followers are sufficiently mature to contribute to good decisions and support decisions with appropriate action.

The final style, delegating, has low task and low relationship emphases based on high follower maturity. In other words, the leader lets followers take responsibility for decisions and actions based on a maturity level sufficient for that responsibility. The leader actually passes leadership to the group in the delegating style.

Based on the Hersey and Blanchard description of effective leadership, a mature follower group with considerable experience in a particular set of circumstances may become an immature group when faced with new challenges. An effective leader would therefore be required to delegate under the first circumstance and possibly return to the telling style when circumstances change.

As an example of how situational leadership might be applied, consider the case of an advertising account team in transition from one account to another. The creative group—artists, writers, and producers—was very familiar with the products manufactured by their former client. They knew how the products worked, what

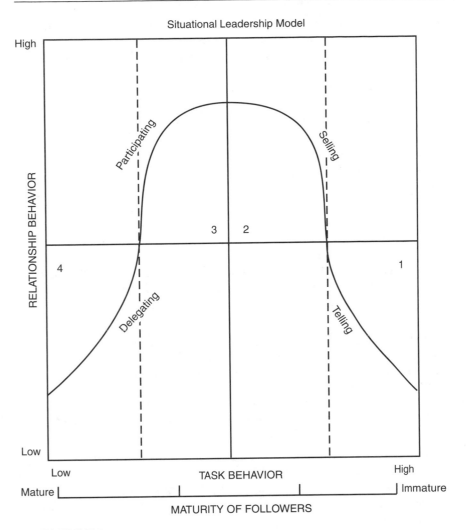

Situational Leadership Model

FIGURE 7.3
The Hersey and Blanchard Concept of Situational Leadership

P. Hersey and K. Blanchard, *Management of Organizational Behavior: Utilizing Human Resources,* 3rd ed., 1977, p. 322. Adapted by permission of Prentice Hall, Inc., Englewood Cliffs, NJ.

their advantages were over major competitors, and how to produce budget-effective commercials the client liked. When the client was sold to a major competitor, the needs of the situation changed. The entire creative team was transferred to the new owner's account with only limited responsibility to their old product line. In fact, the assignment was to integrate the old product line with the new owner's products. Quality advantages, pricing structure, client tastes, and budgets all changed. The talent of the creative staff remained the same, but the changing assignment contributed to less "maturity" in the group. The account executive supervisor could no longer use a delegating style under dramatically changed circumstances. Although not reverting to the extreme of the telling style, the group's leader used a selling style to bring about quickly needed changes without losing the account to other agencies. The account stayed with the same creative team despite a change in client ownership, attesting to the flexibility of the manager and the appropriate application of a leadership style reflecting changing needs. Leadership effectiveness, from the situational perspective, can be described as style selection appropriate to the needs of followers in a particular circumstance. Leadership flexibility is desired. With this approach, situational analysis becomes as important as task and relationship behavior.

Transformational Approaches

The trait, style, and situational approaches discussed all focus on the leader's interactions or transactions with followers. Implied in these approaches is the leader's ability to motivate followers through situational understanding and the control

Transformational approaches ■
Leadership theories that explore how leaders motivate followers by personal example, through appeals to higher-level needs, and by the establishment of vision.

of rewards and (in some cases) punishments. **Transformational approaches** to leadership suggest that inspirational leadership goes beyond the transaction between leaders and followers and literally transforms or changes situations and circumstances through personal example and the rhetorical capability for establishing vision. Michael Hackman and Craig Johnson (2009) explain:

> The transactional leader is most concerned with the satisfaction of physiological, safety, and belonging needs. To meet these needs, a transactional leader exchanges rewards or privileges for desirable outcomes—much the way a Marine drill sergeant would trade a weekend pass for a clean barracks. Transformational leaders also attempt to satisfy the basic needs of followers, but they go beyond mere exchange by engaging the total person in an attempt to satisfy the higher-level needs of self-esteem and self-actualization. Transformational leadership is empowering and inspirational; it elevates leaders and followers to higher levels of motivation and morality. (p. 103)

Hackman and Johnson, in summarizing research on transformational leaders, conclude five primary characteristics appear in one form or another. Transformational leaders are creative, interactive, visionary, empowering, and passionate. In the Workshop section of this chapter, Hackman and Johnson contribute an essay expanding these five characteristics.

J. Kevin Barge (1994) provided evidence that transformational leaders encourage extra effort from followers. Barge suggested, "Taken as a whole, the research indicates that transformational leadership is more capable than transactional leadership at empowering employees and at generating higher levels of employee commitment, satisfaction, and motivation." Transformational leaders provide a sense of vision and mission, have the capability to inspire through communication of high expectations, stimulate the use of intelligence for problem solving, and provide personal attention and coaching for followers. Barge underscores the importance of communication for transformational leadership:

> Here the combination of individualized attention and charismatic leadership emphasizes the creative function of communication. The transformational leader must assess the unique qualities of the situation and then select from a large repertoire of communication skills, rather than rely on a predetermined set of such techniques. Effective leaders model desired behavior and articulate a vision through their rhetorical and persuasive skills. The ability to compose a message that is not only

clear but also visionary and inspiring requires a sophisticated use of communicative skills. Transformational leadership cannot be scripted; its success depends to a great extent on the leader's ability to create novel communication messages, especially crafted for particular individuals, at a particular place, and at a given time. (p. 57)

As early as 1992, Warren Bennis suggested the transforming of the globe called for a new type of leader, the chief executive officer (CEO) who becomes the chief transformation officer (CTO). Bennis based the new leadership paradigm on alignment, creation, and **empowerment.** According to Bennis:

> **Empowerment** ■ Process of giving employees the maximum amount of power to do a job as they see fit; includes both responsibility and accountability for work performed.

> Today's leader needs to align the resources of the organization, particularly the human ones, creating a sense of shared objectives worthy of people's support and even dedication. . . . Today's leader must create an organizational culture where ideas come through unhampered by people who are fearful. Such leaders are committed to problem-finding, not just problem-solving. They embrace error, even failure, because they know it will teach them more than success. . . . That overused word from the '60s—empowerment—involves the sense people have that they are at the center of things rather than on the periphery. In an effectively led organization everyone feels he or she contributes to its success. Empowered individuals believe that their actions have significance and meaning. Empowered people have discretion, but also obligations. (pp. 50–51)

The concepts of transformation and empowerment begin to move us away from leadership resting only with those in positions described as leaders. A newer approach, **dispersed leadership,** is characterized by leaders attempting to develop leadership in others. Charles Manz and Henry Sims (1989) provided a view of this dispersed transformational approach which they called SuperLeadership. Simply put, **SuperLeadership** is the art of leading others to lead themselves. SuperLeaders create SuperFollowers, who become skilled self-leaders. The fundamentals of SuperLeadership include (1) establishing a vision, (2) defining goals for the leader and for the followers, (3) reinforcing individuals for good performance, (4) using constructive contingent reprimands, (5) managing and facilitating change, (6) enhancing the self-efficacy of followers, and (7) using models to teach desired and appropriate behaviors. SuperLeaders use self-management as a basis for leadership and deliberately act as models for followers. SuperLeaders encourage followers to self-set goals, create positive thought patterns, develop leadership through rewards, treat mistakes as learning opportunities, promote self-managed teams, and promote a self-leadership culture. Sims and Peter Lorenzi (1992) summarized the potential of SuperLeadership:

> **Dispersed leadership** ■ Leadership responsibilities broadly distributed throughout the organization.

> **SuperLeadership** ■ The process of leading others to lead themselves.

> "Effective organizational performance results from the interaction of the thoughts and actions of employees and managers—the practice of leadership. Empowerment of all employees is the new paradigm for organizations. Learning to work (and think) effectively requires an ongoing attention to (1) the long-term development of the manager and employee, and (2) the short-term performance of employees and managers. The achievement of a culture of self-leadership through SuperLeadership expresses our vision of the new leadership paradigm" (p. 304).

Discursive approaches ■ Examine leadership process through discourses which influence the accomplishment or lack of accomplishment of tasks and goals.

Discursive Approaches

The concepts of transformation and empowerment began a movement in leadership studies away from the positional leader as the dominant interest to a more complex understanding of communication interactions between those described as leaders and followers. Discursive leadership approaches explicitly direct our study of leadership away from specific individuals to a broad communication focus. Gail Fairhurst (2007) explained, "First, leadership is a process of influence and meaning management among actors that advances a task or goals. Second, leadership is an attribution made by followers or observers. Third, the focus is on leadership process, not leader communication alone, in contrast to heroic leadership models. . . . Finally, leadership as influence and meaning management need not be performed by only one individual appointed to a given role; it may shift and distribute itself among several organizational members" (p. 6).

Discursive leadership approaches examine discourse as influences for the accomplishment or lack of accomplishment of tasks and goals. Fairhurst characterized the term *discourse* as little "d" or big "D." The little "d" discourse refers "to the study of talk and text in social practice. Viewed as a local achievement, discourse embodies cultural meanings; it is a medium for social interaction where the details of language in use and interaction process are central concerns for analysts. . . . However, what does it mean to study talk and text? *Talk-in-interaction* represents sociality, the process of messaging and conversing. It is the 'doing' of organizational discourse, whereas *text* is the 'done' or material representation of discourse in spoken or recorded forms" (p. 6). Annual reports, e-mails, speeches, and numerous other documents all comprise texts which help us understand leadership processes in particular organizations. Fairhurst goes on to describe big "D" discourse, which "refers to general and enduring systems for the formation and articulation of ideas in a historically situated time. . . . In this view, power and knowledge relations are established in culturally standardized Discourses formed by constellations of talk patterns, ideas, logics, and assumptions that constitute objects and subjects. These Discourses not only order and naturalize the world in particular ways, but they also inform social practices by constituting 'particular forms of subjectivity in which human subjects are managed and given a certain form, viewed as self-evident and rational' (Alvesson & Kärreman, 2000b, pp. 1127–1128)" (p. 7). To understand leadership processes, discursive approaches examine talk, text, and social practices in organizations along with the enduring systems of taken-for-granted assumptions about how power and other relationships work and what is considered not only appropriate but rational. We can examine John Mitchell's situation from a discursive approach. His assumptions about needed discourse (big D) are very different from the senior engineers who report to him. They believe he is abusing power by not engaging them and providing timely information for decision making. He believes technical information is the highest form of leadership. The texts he provides (little d) are regarded by John as leadership and are not regarded by his engineers in the same manner. The engineers do not ascribe leadership to John. By examining the discourses in the lab we will understand how the differences in perceptions occur and how these differences will contribute to what happens next at Invest Corporation. Think about a group meeting in which you were involved. What types of discourses can you identify which contributed to the leadership processes in action? How can a discursive perspective help you understand leadership and how it influences a variety of organizational outcomes?

How would you describe John Mitchell's leadership from the style, situational, transformational, or discursive perspectives? Describe the assumptions John makes about his employees. Also describe the overall situation in which John is expected to provide leadership. If you were advising John, which of the theories would you use? Why?

We described trait, style, situational, transformational, and discursive approaches to understanding leadership and management communication. By now you have probably recognized these approaches are complementary, each building on the other. In other words, the approaches for studying leadership are different ways of attempting to describe leadership. We look at the traits, styles, and circumstances in which a particular leader influences his or her group. We look at talk, texts, and cultural assumptions. We use our trait, style, situational, transformational, and discursive approaches together to help explain why a particular leadership effort was successful or how the effort might have been more effective. We are not trait, style, or situational leaders but leaders who exhibit traits, styles, and reactions to specific situations. We engage in complex, varied, and ongoing discourses. The approaches just studied should help us evaluate our own efforts and better understand the efforts of others.

Throughout the discussion, leadership has been described as a responsibility of managers as well as an influence process that emerges through diverse interactions. Next we make important distinctions between leadership and management communication. These distinctions emphasize the need for managers to be leaders but recognize that leadership is a process with participation from all organizational members.

DISTINCTIONS BETWEEN LEADERSHIP AND MANAGEMENT

It is fair to say distinctions between leadership and management are really distinctions between leadership and formal authority, that is, management. Ronald Heifetz (2007) explained "when we commonly refer to the leaders of a company, a school system, a government, or a nonprofit, we generally mean the people with formal authority. And when we refer to the movers and shakers behind the scenes, or the real sources of influence in an organization or community, we generally mean the people with informal authority. We know intuitively that there is a difference between leadership and authority because we complain frequently about the lack of leadership we get form people in these formal and informal authority positions" (p. 314). Bennis and Nanus (1985) made important distinctions between leaders and managers when they suggested:

> The problem with many organizations, and especially the ones that are failing, is that they tend to be overmanaged and underled. They may excel in the ability to

handle the daily routine, yet never question whether the routine should be done at all. There is a profound difference between management and leadership, and both are important. "To manage" means "to bring about, to accomplish, to have charge of or responsibility for, to conduct." "Leading" is "influencing, guiding in direction, course, action, opinion." The distinction is crucial. Managers are people who do things right and leaders are people who do the right thing. The difference may be summarized as activities of vision and judgment—effectiveness—versus activities of mastering routines—efficiency. (p. 21)

Bennis and Nanus (1985) further contended the vision leaders provide is the clearest of all distinctions between leaders and managers. To provide vision requires marshaling the "spiritual and emotional" resources of the organization as reflected in its values, commitment, and aspirations. Management, on the other hand, is charged with directing the physical resources of the organization, its people, machines, and products. Competent managers can get work done efficiently, but excellence comes from leaders who inspire followers to emotional involvement with work and their organization. Bennis and Nanus state, "Great leaders often inspire their followers to high levels of achievement by showing them how their work contributes to worthwhile ends. It is an emotional appeal to some of the most fundamental human needs." In recent work, James Kouzes and Barry Posner (2009) identified "Being forward-looking—envisioning exciting possibilities and enlisting others in a shared view of the future—is the attribute that most distinguishes leaders from nonleaders."

The increasing complexity of a connected world places new demands on leaders and managers. The sheer volume of information available for organizational decision making complicates the development of organizational vision and the direction of organizational activities. This volume of information, when coupled with fast-paced technological changes, puts a new emphasis on the need for leadership from diverse organizational positions. In a complicated, connected world, the development of vision and the generation of emotional commitment to the work and values of an organization can no longer rest solely with leaders at the top of the organization or with the management team that directs organizational activity.

Put simply, the connected society requires leadership from diverse organizational positions. Managers will continue to fulfill specific organizational roles for the direction of work. It is hoped that those in the role of manager will also provide leadership and generate commitment to the values of the organization. The management role, however, represents the formal organizational hierarchy and, as such, is deeply involved in efficiently planning and implementing what the organization has decided to do. Managers are responsible for generating enough stability for efficient work to be accomplished. Leaders, on the other hand, are responsible for generating enough change to continually adapt to new circumstances. Thus, the competencies for effective leaders and managers are not the same. Complex organizations need leadership exhibited by those who identify emerging problems and opportunities, whether they fulfill the role of manager or not.

We can readily understand how a manager becomes a leader when inspiring employees to excellent performance. What we do not as readily see is the leadership role of the employee who identifies a needed work change, a possible new product, or an improved service opportunity and proceeds to influence others to share that vision of an improved organization. This employee's assumption of leadership responsibility is highly desirable for the fast-paced information age.

LEADERSHIP AND MANAGEMENT CHALLENGES

The new leadership and management challenges are not without internal contradictions. On the one hand, the imperative is to move to group and team self-leadership; on the other hand, if necessary, leaders are exhorted to singularly risk the future to motivate follower commitment. Leadership is described as both a lonely and a highly participative endeavor. The increasing complexity of a technologically connected global environment places new demands on leaders and managers. Ellen Van Velsor and Jean Brittain Leslie (1995), in reviewing studies of why executives derail (have negative outcomes), identified four primary themes enduring over time and across countries. According to Van Velsor and Leslie, executives derailed because they were challenged by (1) problems with interpersonal relationships, (2) failure to meet business objectives, (3) failure to build and lead a team, and (4) inability to change or adapt during a transition. Jim Collins (2009) suggests leaders and organizations who decline exhibit five general stages of decline: (1) hubris born of past success; (2) undisciplined pursuit of more in almost all categories, including profit; (3) denial of pending risks and peril; (4) grasping for solutions or, as Collins suggests, salvation; and (5) giving in to irrelevance or final endings. Think about your own leadership competencies as you read about major challenges facing leaders of today and tomorrow.

Changing Organizational Forms

Fast-paced change is the order of the day and a fundamental leadership challenge. Bennis (1992) contended "the organizations of the future will be networks, clusters, cross-functional teams, temporary systems, ad hoc task forces, lattices, modules, matrices—almost anything but pyramids." We refer to these new organizational forms as spider webs, dynamic networks, virtual organizations, and postbureaucratic organizations among others. Many describe the organizations of the twenty-first century as borderless and boundaryless.

The "middleless" organization is the new organizational design. Fewer managers with larger spans of control characterize organizational hierarchies in almost all industries. Work teams are given higher degrees of autonomy and control over immediate work situations. The goals are to increase competitiveness and improve employee morale. Traditional responsibilities of managers are replaced by passing power and control to lower levels in the organization. Managers become facilitators, coaches, teachers, and experts, whereas previously they may have been controllers, directors, planners, and rewarders. The new responsibilities are roles, not new organizational positions. Advances in communications technology give rise to the concept of networked teams and the technology form (T-form) organization. Leaders and managers must learn how to contribute to teams of people who may not be in the same geographic location and who work face-to-face only on rare occasions if at all. The T-form organization challenges leaders and managers to concentrate on using technology to design electronic work flows, production automation, technological matrixing and leveling, and virtual components.

Leaders also are faced with the fluid nature of the formal organization. Mergers with other organizations change processes, policies, markets, and leadership responsibilities. Acquisitions of other companies or product lines provide similar challenges. In 1996, Michael Hammer contended a historic chain reaction was under way, forcing deep changes in management structure, strategic planning, and financial structures precipitated by the rise of the demanding customer. This shift in focus from investors to customers was the force behind the process-centered organization. For the most part, educational background and past work experiences do not prepare leaders for the magnitude of these organizational changes.

Global and Multicultural Changes

Sims and Lorenzi (1992) provided a thoughtful discussion of several global issues affecting leadership challenges today. Sims and Lorenzi describe economic challenges that include (1) increasing competition among firms on a global basis; (2) emphasis on speed, service, and information, a mandate for flexibility and change in organizations; (3) creative and conceptual demands of a computer-based work setting, with great opportunities for value-added labor; and (4) the economic necessity of embracing previously un(der)employed workers. Sims and Lorenzi believed leaders must deal with the changing socioeconomic status and demographics of employees with a need for more training, flexibility, and lifelong learning. In the western hemisphere, employees demand greater participation in management decisions, including a shifting emphasis on teams, skill-based pay, and employee–management cooperation. Gain sharing, profit sharing, and other attempts are made to encourage and reward productivity. Finally, leaders and managers are designing flatter, more decentralized organizations, with greater employee need for self-management and concomitant accountability. Rosabeth Moss Kanter (1996), in reference to changing organizations and the world economy, called for partnering within and across organizations. According to Kanter, leaders must share and spread leadership and become learning-oriented. Leaders will come to see the community as a whole system and they will continually enlarge their network.

Alvin Toffler and Heidi Toffler (1994) suggested the world economy was undergoing its deepest restructuring since the Industrial Revolution. Today we know their prediction has come true. As Philip Harris and Robert Moran (1996) explained: "Advances in telecommunications and mass transportation, and the breaking down of national borders and cultures have led to the emergence of a global, information-oriented culture." Doug Jung and Bruce Avolio (1999) suggested leaders must understand cultural differences to stimulate high-quality individual or group performance. They discussed the differences between individualist and collectivist cultures: people in individualist cultures are expected to be more motivated to satisfy their own self-interests and personal goals, whereas in collectivist cultures the strong tendency is to support organizational values and norms. They suggested leaders must understand employee cultural orientations to make important decisions about a variety of organizational communication processes ranging from problem solving and decision making to conflict management.

High-Speed Management

The challenges described by Sims and Lorenzi, Kanter, and others are literally transforming a variety of leadership and managerial processes. In 1993, Donald Cushman and Sarah King introduced a term which has relevance today: *high-speed management*. High-speed management has as its goal the achievement and maintenance of sustainable competitive advantage through innovative, flexible, adaptive, efficient, and rapid response to environmental change. Cushman and King argued correctly that breakthroughs in information and communication technologies, increased world trade, and a volatile business characterized by rapidly changing technology all would contribute to a new perspective on leadership and management. Although the concept of high-speed management has both supporters and detractors, few challenge the notion that rapid and constant change is clearly a central issue for leaders and managers.

Inclusive-Participation Processes

Organizations of today and tomorrow must understand the concept of multiple stakeholders and how their participation in all aspects of organizational life contributes to a variety of organizational outcomes. Stanley Deetz (1993) described stakeholders (groups with organizational interests) as consumers, workers, investors, suppliers, host communities, general society, and the world ecological community. The managing process or coordination of these groups contributes to what Deetz called outcome interests: goods and services, income distribution, use of resources, environmental effects, economic stability, labor force development, lifestyles, profits, personal identities, and child-rearing practices. Regardless of the precise understanding of who is a stakeholder and the variety of potential outcome interests, a clear pattern of inclusive participation emerges for marketplace competitiveness and to meet a variety of stakeholder needs and demands. Leaders and managers are directly challenged to both address and generate these high-participation processes.

John Zenger, E. Musselwhite, K. Hurson, and C. Perrin (1993) stressed five principles of leadership important for the new inclusive-participation environments. They believed effective leaders (1) focus on the issue, not the person; (2) maintain the self-confidence of others; (3) maintain constructive relationships; (4) take the initiative to make things better; and (5) lead by example. Creating and sustaining teams requires intensive planning and persistent follow-through. The role of the leader is not to dictate solutions to problems but to help all organizational members to solve them.

Building Trust

The global financial crisis that began in 2008 produced a history-making example of distrust, a situation my colleagues and I have described as a sweeping and almost unprecedented "trust crash." Few would disagree distrust replaced trust for many if not the majority of people in the United States as unemployment rose, home foreclosures increased, and financial executives received large bonuses. One banker with whom my colleagues and I worked summed it up, "I never thought I would have to tell customers we are local, not tied in with the big guys; we are not taking any federal bailout money, and we aren't giving bonuses to our executives. Just months ago, being small and local was a disadvantage. The distrust has fractured relationships for years to come. Now people distrust us for no reason. We have to work hard to get them to trust us just because of what others have done." This bank president was stating his challenge in building trust in an environment where distrust was prevalent. In our work on trust and trust building, Sherwyn Morreale, Michael Hackman, and I (2010) describe the critical challenge for leaders of building trust. We discuss, supported by extensive research, the impact the lack of trust has in five broad categories. Distrust breeds (1) we-versus-them behaviors; (2) lower employee commitment to productivity goals; (3) fear and destructive behaviors; and (4) less favorable crises management; and (5) it is expensive in the need for monitoring and surveillance. Less certain, however, are the approaches leaders can use to build trust. Considering the magnitude of the trust deficits in many organizations, it is fair to say building trust is a primary leadership challenge and critical for a variety of important organizational outcomes.

DETERMINANTS OF LEADERSHIP EFFECTIVENESS

Thus far, we discussed whether leaders are born or can be developed, the traits associated with effective leadership, how leadership styles relate to the maturity of followers and to particular leadership situations, how leadership is understood and enacted through discourses, and how leaders contribute to establishing organizational vision. Throughout the discussion the contention has been that both leadership and management are enacted through human communication. With this perspective now comes an examination of how communication competencies, influence (power bases), and analysis abilities contribute to leadership effectiveness.

Communication Competencies as Determinants of Leadership Effectiveness

A recurring theme throughout this text has been that communication competence is necessary for organizational excellence. Knowledge, sensitivity, skills, and values must all be understood and developed for both individuals and entire organizations to be effective in our emerging information era. Nowhere is communication competency more important than when individuals attempt to lead and establish vision and direction for organizations.

Research on managerial effectiveness and perceptions of effectiveness supports the importance of communication competence. Historically leadership experts such as Chris Argyris (1962), Peter Drucker (1966), and Bennis and Nanus (1985) described communication effectiveness as a central element for overall managerial effectiveness. In recent work, Herminia Ibarra and Otilia Obodaru (2009) described men and women leaders utilizing the Global Executive Leadership Inventory (GELI). The dimensions of exemplary leadership they discuss are envisioning, empowering, energizing, designing and aligning, rewarding and feedback, team building, outside orientation, global mind-set, tenacity, and emotional intelligence. All of these important dimensions of leadership require communication competence.

Predispositions for Leadership Communication

The knowledge, sensitivity, skills, and values we bring to particular situations powerfully influence our behavior choices. Whether or not we choose to attempt leadership relates to our assessment of our own competencies, the needs of the situation, the receptivity of a follower group, and our potential ability to influence (power).

Those high in anxiety about communication, for example, are less likely to engage in leadership attempts than those lower in communication apprehension. Highly task-oriented individuals are more likely to adopt leadership styles reflecting task emphasis, whereas those preferring close interpersonal relationships are more likely to adopt styles reflecting their concern for people. Return for a moment to Figures 7.2 and 7.3. Although the grids in these figures represent behavioral approaches used for leadership and management, they also can be understood as preferences individuals bring to leadership and managerial situations. Concern for task and people relationships, when coupled with an assessment of follower maturity, influences behavior choices in specific circumstances. Yet concerns for task and people relationships, follower maturity, personal assessments of communication competence, and assessments of influence or power positions also are reflected in our predispositions for leadership communication, predispositions that subsequently influence strategic objectives and tactical choices.

Strategic Communication Objectives for Leadership

Strategic objectives for leadership communication can be described as the general game plans leaders employ for conducting communication based on personal preferences or predispositions and on assessments of the probable outcomes within particular contexts. Tactics are the specific behavior choices made by leaders to influence followers in specific situations and to support overall strategies. Strategic objectives are related to the big D discourses which relate to underlying assumptions about how the organization operates within a complex environment.

Autocratic strategies are used by leaders who seek to have followers implement decisions with little or no follower input. John Mitchell can decide the current complaints at Invest Corporation call for autocratic strategies. He can announce he will continue to determine when decisions will be made and that his technical decisions will not be subject to question. He can choose to ignore complaints that he is "invisible" and continue to view leadership as a technical contribution. These autocratic strategies are possible as long as top management supports him.

John also has choices among more participative strategies. He can encourage senior lab members to suggest ways in which he can work with them in a team atmosphere. He can compromise about the number of details he will handle personally and the amount of time he takes to make decisions. He can seek to establish more open and supportive relationships to become a more "visible" manager. Finally, John can use avoidance or laissez-faire strategies and ignore the complaints he hears. He has the avoidance option because of his legitimate power position as laboratory manager. He can ignore much of the discontent as long as he retains the support of senior management.

John's selection of strategies relates to his assessment of what is needed for leadership and his assessment of whether individuals need leadership. He also will assess how he believes power should work in this situation. As you will recall, John believes leadership is primarily a technical responsibility and intelligent people do not need close personal contact to do their jobs. These assumptions will influence what happens next at Invest.

Howard Gardner (1995), in his portraits of outstanding twentieth-century leaders, identified what he called constants of leadership with significant communication implications. Gardner suggested leaders must have a central story or message. The story must assist in creating a sense of group identity that is inclusive and encourages individuals to think of themselves as part of a broader community. He described how leaders such as Martin Luther King Jr. benefited from building on previous stories by synthesizing them in new ways. Gardner also described the relationship between the leader and what he calls the audience. This complex and dynamic interplay is based on the audience's needs and desires and the vision of the message. He used Gandhi as an example of a leader with a steadfast concentration on the same core message while exhibiting flexibility in how it was presented. Finally, the credibility of the leader is based on whether the creator of the message actually embodies or lives the story through personal example.

In an extensive study of some ninety outstanding leaders, Bennis and Nanus (1985) identified four major strategies or competencies that all ninety leaders seemed to exhibit: (1) management of attention through vision, (2) meaning through communication, (3) trust through positioning, and (4) deployment of self through positive self-regard.

The outstanding leaders of the Bennis and Nanus (1985) study commanded the attention of their followers and organizations by establishing and communicating a *vision* about where the organization should go, what it should be, and what was needed to achieve it. As Bennis and Nanus suggested, "All ninety people interviewed had an agenda, an unparalleled concern with outcome." Bennis and Nanus further suggested successful leaders not only caught the attention of others but also paid attention to others, underscoring the essential interactional relationship between leaders and followers.

The second strategy, the management of meaning through *communication*, relates to the conscious effort the leaders made to communicate so their meanings would become the meanings of every organizational level. These excellent leaders were concerned not only with what should be done but also with how to develop messages that conveyed that vision. Bennis and Nanus (1985) stated, "Getting the message across unequivocally at every level is an absolute key. Basically it is what the creative process is all about and what, once again, separates the managers from the leaders." Management of meaning rests on well-developed communication competencies and an understanding of the process of organizational communication. Without competencies and process understanding, effective leadership is problematic.

Trust as a strategy is hard to define. Bennis and Nanus (1985) described trust as the "glue that maintains organizational integrity." The leaders in the Bennis and Nanus study were trusted (although not always liked) because they were constant, predictable, and reliable. They positioned themselves as worthy of trust by exhibiting personal stability even while encouraging change and innovation. They helped their organizations develop a sense of identity (culture) and integrity (trust). Bennis and Nanus considered this sense of direction to be fundamental to these leaders' effectiveness.

Finally, the effective leaders in the study liked themselves and other people. They did not focus on failure but viewed mistakes as learning opportunities and challenges. They were like famed tightrope walker Karl Wallenda, who, until shortly before the fall that claimed his life, always focused on walking, never on falling. Bennis and Nanus (1985) contended that the Wallenda factor in leadership is the ability to focus on success, not on failure, and to frame behavior in terms of the goal, not in terms of every detail of the process.

The strategy of *positive self-regard and regard for others* closely relates to the description of developing communication competencies (knowledge, sensitivity, skills, and values) for organizational excellence. Bennis and Nanus (1985) summed up positive self-regard as three major factors: "knowledge of one's strengths, the capacity to nurture and develop those strengths, and the ability to discern the fit between one's strengths and weaknesses and the organization's needs."

Bennis (1999) concluded leaders must learn to develop a social architecture that encourages incredibly bright people to work together successfully and to engage in creativity. Leaders must constantly reinvent their organizations and learn to deploy workforces so that rather than downsizing they create new opportunities. Finally, Bennis believed leaders must learn how to create an environment that actually embraces change not as a threat but as an opportunity.

Research by Eric Eisenberg (1984) provided support to the Bennis and Nanus (1985) contention that generating vision is an important leadership responsibility. Eisenberg proposed strategic ambiguity as an organizational communication strategy that promotes unity while maintaining sufficient individual freedom to ensure flexibility, creativity, and change. Eisenberg argued that divergent organizational goals cannot always be resolved through the development of specific consensus from all organizational members. He proposed that "ambiguity is used strategically to foster agreement on abstractions without limiting specific interpretations. . . . Focusing on organizational symbolism casts leadership in a new light as well. While a primary responsibility of leaders is to make meanings for followers . . . and to infuse employees with values and purpose . . . the process of doing so is less one of consensus-making and more one of using language strategically to express values at a level of abstraction at which agreement can occur. . . . Effective leaders use ambiguity strategically to encourage creativity and guard against the acceptance of one standard way of viewing organizational reality" (p. 231).

Organizational goal and mission statements, communication rules, and organizational stories and myths all are examples of strategic ambiguity influenced by leaders. An excellent example of strategic ambiguity (vision) comes from the recurring theme to "do what's right, not what's written" of a certain large computer manufacturer. What's "right" is subject to varying interpretations across the organization. The leadership imperative, however, is to take action and act with personal responsibility, a value with high consensus even though specific interpretations often vary dramatically. In fact, conflict frequently occurs in this generally healthy organization over "what is right" and "who should decide."

So far, we have discussed autocratic, participative, and laissez-faire or avoidance strategies for leadership. We described strategies for the communication of vision, management of meaning through communication, management of trust, and management of positive self-regard and regard for others. Now we describe specific communication tactics used for each of these strategic orientations.

Communication Tactics for Leadership

Leadership tactics can be described as the communication behaviors used to support authoritarian, participative, and avoidance preferences as well as to establish vision, manage meaning, generate trust, and communicate regard and success orientations. Specific tactics are influenced by individual preferences and strategies, by communication competencies of leaders and followers, and by overall organizational values and expectations about how leadership works. Military organizations, for example, encourage authoritarian leadership, whereas organizations involved in research and development of new products usually stress more participative approaches. Still others reflect a mix of leadership processes representing the diversity of people and personalities who work together. It is important to understand that as with most tactics, the choice of specific leadership tactics illustrates the interactive nature of relationships. Both leaders and followers are involved in complex tactical interactions influenced by individual preferences and strategic objectives as well as the needs of a particular situation.

It is not possible to list or define all the communication tactics available to potential leaders. It is useful for our personal sensitivity and our skills to identify several frequently used communication tactics. Figure 7.4 presents excerpts from group problem-solving discourses in which the identified group leader illustrates a particular leadership tactic. Each example is accompanied by a description of the tactic it represents, and tactics are grouped into authoritarian, participative, avoidance, vision-setting, meaning-management, trust-generating, and positive regard and success categories.

Power Bases for Leaders

Preferences for leadership, strategic objectives, and communication tactics all contribute to how leaders influence followers. Yet behaviors alone do not adequately explain how one individual is recognized as a leader whereas another is not. We have all seen individuals who are recognized as leaders exhibit almost identical behaviors to those who never achieve leadership recognition. Frequently the difference in who is a leader and who is not is a subtle matter of credibility, a credibility that enables one person to be more influential than another. This credibility is commonly referred to as power or the **power bases** of the leader. The concept of power can best be understood as an interactive process. In other words, power does not exist in a vacuum but rather as people interact with one another within a broader system of power relationships. From this perspective, power can be understood

Power bases ■ Influence an individual has over another as a result of dependency on the powerful person. Power bases are commonly identified as legitimate, reward, coercive, referent, expert, and connection.

Organizational Narrative	Leadership Tactics

Authoritarian Tactics

"The seriousness of the problem leaves little room for continuing to think about new ideas. I believe I know what we should do and am willing to take the responsibility."

1. *Blocking ideas* by establishing responsibility

"We will first assign new sales territories; then we will put one senior salesperson in each territory; and then we will establish sales quotas."

2. *Controlling the process* of events

"I have decided we will stop development of the Henderson project. I think our direction is in Richardson Heights."

3. *Announcing goals* without consultation

"I expected you to be on my team. You can forget about my support come budget time, and you know you need that."

4. *Punishing opposition* through sanctions or withholding support

Participative Tactics

"To make the best decision we need everyone's ideas. I don't want anyone to think that he or she doesn't have a say."

1. *Seeking ideas* from all involved

"We need to make a decision on the budget, and I want everyone to have ample time to participate. Therefore, we will each spend fifteen minutes on our initial presentations."

2. *Facilitating group processes* that encourage participation

"Look, I'm glad you will disagree with me. That is the only way we will have a good solution."

3. *Encouraging disagreement* when constructive and solution-oriented

"I think opening the store at Third and Franklin is a good idea, but I need your honesty with any reservations you may have."

4. *Seeking idea evaluation*

"I believe we all agree that the new product line will work. We can easily say to stock minimum quantity of each appliance in the group."

5. *Verbalizing consensus* among group members

(continued)

FIGURE 7.4
Communication Tactics for Leadership

Avoidance Tactics

"I don't think we have any real disagreements in this group."

"Look, we have spent enough time on this problem. I don't think it is as important as you think. Let's move on."

"Whatever you want to do is fine with me. You all definitely know best."

"Look, I shouldn't have to ask you to do this. It is your job. I am not going to be a babysitter. You can take the consequences yourself."

1. *Ignoring conflict* even when obvious

2. *Changing subject* when disagreements or difficulty seem likely

3. *Agreeing with others* to avoid conflict or new ideas

4. *Refusing responsibility* for motivating others to action

Vision-Setting Tactics

"I believe we can make our bowl game the Super Bowl of college football."

"I want us to move from number five to number two during the next three months. I know with a sales force like all of you that it is only a matter of time."

"To start performing like a team we have to start acting like a team. That's why I called you here today."

1. *Visualizing abstract ideas* by symbolic association

2. *Stating desired outcomes* without undue emphasis on details

3. *Articulating reasons* for actions and goals

Meaning-Management Tactics

"I have talked about what I see ahead. I now need to know how you think that affects each group represented here today."

"Our course of action is a little like putting our own person on the moon. Awe, courage, pride, all are part of this achievement we have just experienced."

"I want everyone to hear this change at the same time. Schedule me to personally meet with each shift."

1. *Soliciting feedback* to understand message clarity and impact.

2. *Generating symbolism* to interpret events and accomplishments

3. *Managing messages* to support exchanges of meaning

Trust-Generating Tactics

"I told you the truth about the layoffs. I know it wasn't popular, but you can trust what I am now going to say. The layoffs are behind us, but we still have considerable belt-tightening to do."

1. *Communicating constancy* by linking present messages to past actions

FIGURE 7.4

"People are the most important resource this company has. For that reason I am asking all of you and all the management team to take a 10 percent pay cut so that no one will have to be without a job."

"I am asking each department head to meet with me over the next few months. I want to know what is going on and have people free to come to me."

Positive Regard and Success Tactics

"I know you consider this move a mistake. I consider that you have learned a valuable lesson."

"This is the best new product release this company has ever produced."

"Look, we are all in this together. It doesn't matter as much whose fault it was as what we need to do next."

"I know the economy is troubled, but this gives us a chance to really see what we are worth. After all, anyone can be successful when things are going well. The mark of excellence is now."

2. *Identifying values* and relating values to needed action

3. *Encouraging access* through planned communication interactions

1. *Providing support* for individual effort

2. *Offering praise* for efforts

3. *Avoiding blame* and seeking solutions

4. *Identifying challenges and opportunities* when others see problems

FIGURE 7.4
(*continued*)

as the influence an individual has over another as a result of dependency on the powerful person in a particular setting.

Power, however, is more than individual interactions. Power is fundamental to the big D discourses of organizations. The ideology of a particular organization is evidenced in its structure, in its assumptions about its specific role in a broader society, and by its overall culture. The discourses of ideology, formal structure, and culture form a sometimes hidden power structure in which all leaders and organizational members interact. Core beliefs and values along with formal structures generate what comes to be recognized as legitimate or rightful power. This legitimating of core beliefs, values, and formal structures becomes the basic authority system of the organization. Organizational culture defines through myths, stories, and ways of talking about the organization what behaviors are expected, what behaviors are to be avoided, and who importantly makes evaluative judgments. It is within these broad discourses of power that individuals exert influence and are influenced.

To understand this interaction it is helpful to think about some of the power bases available to leaders. John French and Bertram Raven (1968) gave a now classic description of five power types: legitimate, reward, coercive, referent, and expert. They also discussed connection power. Although described as individual power bases, each of these types of power is exercised within the broader discourses of organizational power.

Legitimate power ■ Power emerging from the positions, titles, or roles people occupy.

Legitimate power comes from the positions, titles, or roles people occupy. Supervisors have legitimate power over employees. As such, certain rights and responsibilities are legitimately defined and generally understood by group members. Disagreement can surround the ability of the legitimate leader, yet most agree that certain leadership responsibilities accompany the position. For example, virtually every president of the United States of America has supporters and critics; yet, despite these diverse opinions few would disagree that the individual is legitimately the president.

Reward power ■ Power based on the leader's control and distribution of tangible and intangible resources.

Reward power is based on the leader's control and distribution of tangible and intangible reward resources. A leader can influence with the promise of rewards only as long as those rewards are within the leader's control and perceived by followers as rewarding. Many people attempt to influence with rewards that others do not find important or influential. Many supervisors believe, for example, that money is the primary reward for good performance, although considerable research suggests that communication contact with supervisors is one of the most sought-after of all employee rewards. Interestingly enough, communication interaction is more often controlled by supervisors than money or other tangible benefits.

Coercive power ■ Power based on the sanctions or punishments within the control of the leader.

Coercive power can be understood as the sanctions or punishments within the control of the leader. Coercive power is the ability to punish for not complying with influence attempts. To be effective, coercive power must not be threatened beyond what the leader is willing to administer. We have all seen people lose credibility by threatening sanctions or punishments that were not within the control of the one making the threats. Although reward power can be exercised by virtually anyone, coercive power relates to the role or legitimate position an individual occupies. For example, a peer can threaten to get another peer fired, but although unpleasant, the threat is generally not considered coercive power. When a supervisor makes the same threat, though, the influence attempt takes on an entirely different meaning.

Referent power ■ Power based on others identifying with the leader.

Referent power is a result of others identifying with the leader. It is a power base only indirectly related to the leader's overt influence attempts. Referent power comes from the desire of others to use the leader as a reference or from others seeking to imitate the leader's behaviors with or without the leader's desire for them to do so. Referent power results from actions of the leader, yet the leader cannot directly exercise referent power; instead, it is assigned by others.

Expert or information power ■ Power based on information the leader knows as a result of organizational interaction or areas of technical specialty.

Expert or information power rests on what the leader knows as a result of organizational interaction or areas of technical specialty. As such, expert power does not require legitimate power for the expert to be influential. Expert power can be used without coercive power and often contributes to the development of referent power. Expert power is considered to be important for organizational excellence and is ideally the basis of effective influence attempts.

Connection power ■ Power resulting from whom the leader knows and the support he or she has from others in the organization.

Connection power is the influence leaders have as a result of whom they know and the support they have from others in the organization.

Generally conceived of as support from others in power, connection power also comes from followers. Supervisors and managers, for example, are generally in better influence positions when follower "connections" are supportive. In turn, group members are more influential when their leaders are "connected" to others in the organization. Connection power is understood by observing communication networks and how individuals are linked throughout the organization.

Situational Analysis for Leadership

Understanding the situations or circumstances requiring leadership is fundamental for effectiveness. The ability to assess thoughtfully the requirements of the problem and the group attempting its solutions contributes to the selection of effective strategies and tactics for leadership. Steven Sample (2002) suggested effective leaders often must take a counterintuitive or what he calls contrarian view. Sample wrote, "But one of the most important and contrarian points we can make about leadership is that it is highly situational and contingent; the leader who succeeds in one context at one point in time won't necessarily succeed in a different context at the same time, or in the same context at a different time."

The ability to communicate vision relates to the ability to generate vision based on sound problem analysis. Communicating outcomes relates to knowing where an organization should go and having a concept of how it can get there. In other words, good problem-solving and analysis skills are fundamental for effective leadership. Analysis skills help define problems, generate solutions, and contribute to the selection of influence strategies appropriate for leadership. Analysis skills cannot be separated from influence strategies for effectiveness. The individual who thoroughly understands a problem may not be able to influence others if communication strategies and tactics are carelessly chosen. On the other hand, we have concern for individuals who are so adept at persuasive communication that they convince groups to follow courses of action that are ill conceived or ill advised.

John Mitchell's experience at Invest is a good example. Chances are John has the technical expertise to lead the laboratory to significant technical accomplishments. No one doubts his ability to analyze technical problems. Yet John is close to failure as the manager of the laboratory. His situational analysis is only partially complete. He understands the technical direction he wants but has not communicated his vision to others and does not see any need for that type of sales pitch. John's communication behaviors do not reflect his technical excellence. His dilemma illustrates what can happen when problem analysis is not coupled with appropriate communication behaviors.

INCREASING LEADERSHIP EFFECTIVENESS

The communication competencies needed to increase leadership capabilities can be described as an expansion of those competencies necessary for interpersonal and conflict management effectiveness. The knowledge, sensitivity, skills, and values identified and developed in previous chapters all are important for effective leadership, especially if we take the position that organizations need leadership from all position levels.

As previously suggested, effective leaders understand the problems facing their group and have skill in helping diverse individuals approach common problems. Effective leaders participate in group efforts and encourage others to participate by being open-minded and exhibiting supportive behaviors. Effective leaders consult others and express sensitivity for disagreement. Effective leaders, however, will help groups make decisions when consensus is unlikely. Finally, effective leaders empower others by sharing success and credit.

Self-awareness is a key to leadership effectiveness. Understanding personal preferences, behaviors, and problem situations is fundamental to discovering why some leadership efforts succeed while others fail. Return for a moment to your personal theory of leadership. What does it tell you about your personal leadership strengths and weaknesses? What competencies need further development? When have you been most successful? Next, in an effort to help you increase your leadership effectiveness, we describe the important concept of principled leadership as well as task, procedural, and interpersonal leadership responsibilities.

Principled, Excellent, and Ethical Leadership

Principled leadership ■ Leadership that provides a consistent message, has a perspective for unleashing talent, practices ego suppression, and creates leaders.

In their extensive study of successful teams, Carl Larson and Frank LaFasto (1989) identified **principled leadership** as one of the core characteristics of why successful teams develop. According to Larson and LaFasto, principled leadership provides a consistent message, has a perspective for unleashing talent, practices ego suppression, and creates leaders.

Larson and LaFasto (1989) found that "effective team leaders begin by establishing a vision of the future. In the most common language, this need was articulated as the clear, elevating goal." In other words, principled leadership establishes and communicates a vision that creates change by unleashing the talent of team members. In later work, William Robinson (2002) described leading people from the middle rather than from the traditional hierarchy. Robinson, as did Larson and LaFasto, focused on influencing from among people, working for consensus, and using decentralization to build vision and seek opportunity. It is a view of leadership based on stimulating the talent in others and seeking to work from within as opposed to working from above.

Jim Collins (2001), in his extensive long-term study of successful organizations, described what he called Level 5 leaders as those most likely to contribute to excellence. According to Collins, Level 5 leaders "build enduring greatness through a paradoxical blend of personal humility and professional will. . . . Level 5 leaders channel their ego needs away from themselves and into the larger goal of building a great company. It's not that Level 5 leaders have no ego or self-interest. Indeed, they are incredibly ambitious—but *their ambition is first and foremost for the institution, not themselves*" (pp. 20–21). Collins went on to describe Level 5 leaders as combining humility and will, exhibiting compelling modesty, executing with unwavering resolve to get done what must be done, setting high standards, taking responsibility for problems, and giving others credit for success.

Sarah Dempsey, Patricia Parker, and Kathleen Krone (2007) challenged thinking around models of leadership in the global context which continue to favor corporate environments and include only narrow interpretations of social and cultural differences. Dempsey, Parker, and Krone suggest ways of developing global leadership competencies though engaging differences in new and more meaningful ways. Specifically, they recommended we utilize approaches for confronting difference, disrupting our fixed assumptions about difference, protecting the value of difference, and enacting a more relationship self in all aspects of leadership. In most respects building leadership effectiveness at its core is a principled process requiring a conscious ability to be aware of ourselves and others, including cultural differences.

Ethical communication behaviors are fundamental to principled leadership and excellence. As we discussed in Chapter 4, ethical communication behaviors explore the complexity of issues, present information openly and fairly with concern for message distortion, share motivations or biases that may influence positions, and encourage opposing viewpoints. Figure 7.5 summarizes the principles identified by

Team Leader Principles

1. Avoid compromising the team's objective with political issues.
2. Exhibit personal commitment to team goals.
3. Do not dilute the team's efforts with too many priorities.
4. Be fair and impartial toward all team members.
5. Be willing to confront and resolve issues associated with inadequate performance by team members.
6. Be open to new ideas and information from team members.

Team Member Principles

1. Demonstrate a realistic understanding of one's role and accountabilities.
2. Demonstrate objective and fact-based judgments.
3. Collaborate effectively with other team members.
4. Make the team goal a higher priority than any personal objective.
5. Demonstrate a willingness to devote whatever effort is necessary to achieve team success.
6. Be willing to share information, perceptions, and feedback openly.
7. Provide help to other team members when needed and appropriate.
8. Demonstrate high standards of excellence.
9. Stand behind and support team decisions.
10. Demonstrate courage of conviction by directly confronting important issues.
11. Demonstrate leadership in ways that contribute to the team's success.
12. Respond constructively to feedback from others.

Team Leader Behaviors for Decision Making

1. Trust team members with meaningful levels of responsibility.
2. Give team members the necessary autonomy to achieve results.
3. Present challenging opportunities that stretch the individual abilities of team members.
4. Recognize and reward superior performance.
5. Stand behind the team and support it.

FIGURE 7.5
Principled Leadership

Larson and LaFasto and is consistent with the work of Robinson and Collins. As you review principles for team leaders and members, identify how these principles support ethical communication behaviors.

Not only did the successful leaders described by Larson and LaFasto and Collins unleash talent through the use of guiding principles, they also suppressed individual ego displays for themselves and the team. Team members were active participants in shaping the destiny of the team, and this active participation contributed to leadership not only for the team but also within the team. Later work continues to build on the concept of principled leadership. In sum, it can be said that effective leadership promotes the development of leadership in others. Think for a moment about your own leadership attempts. Which of the identified principles did you use? Which were missing? Would you add others to the list? Next we consider how effective leaders use principled and ethical leadership for task, procedural, and interpersonal responsibilities.

Identifying Constructive Communication Behaviors for Leadership

Gail Fairhurst and Robert Sarr (1996) described the "art of framing" as managing the language of leadership. Fairhurst and Sarr contended the intricacies of communication and the difficulties of conveying even a simple message to an organization are challenges for leaders. They propose framing a message is like framing a picture. When framing is successful the message gains impact and minimizes distortions.

Framing consists of language in action, thought and reflection, and forethought. As Fairhurst and Sarr described, "Highlight the negative and a problem looks overwhelming. Accentuate the positives, and a solution seems just around the corner. . . . Our language choices are critical to the management of meaning through framing." Although framing for others is based on language choice, thought and reflection refer to how we develop internal images to describe our own mental models of the issues we wish to frame for others. Finally, forethought is both mental preparation and, for some, actually articulating various images to determine if they adequately describe the issue, position, or situation. Forethought helps prepare us for unexpected opportunities to influence others or engage in shaping meaning. Most effective leaders develop competencies for framing meaning for others. Next we consider constructive framing opportunities leaders have in the following general areas: task, procedural, and interpersonal responsibilities.

Task Responsibilities   Whether leading a major corporation or leading a group in a class project, leaders have task, procedural, and interpersonal responsibilities. In the task area, leaders are responsible for facilitating problem analysis, idea generation, idea evaluation, solution generation, and decision implementation. Leaders need to stimulate creativity and urge people to push the boundaries of their thinking. Effective leaders encourage team members to listen actively to others and expand good ideas. Leaders are responsible for promoting focused and in-depth investigation of ideas and critically evaluating all aspects of a problem. Leaders help the group address the accuracy of their information, evaluate information sources, apply information carefully to defined problems, and develop solution criteria. Review the guiding principles in Figure 7.5. Which of the principles would you apply to task responsibilities? What types of communication skills are required? Can you understand the importance of communication competency for effective leadership?

Procedural Responsibilities   Leaders also are responsible for procedures such as goal setting, agenda making, discussion clarification, and both consensus and disagreement identification. Leaders must be able to introduce ideas, give directions, and call for action. They ask for ideas and the participation of team members. Leaders remind groups of agendas and goals and generally organize group activities. Leaders actively listen as well as offer explanations for their own and others' verbalizations and behaviors. Recall the description in Chapter 6 of communication skills important for group participation. All these skills and more apply to leadership responsibilities. In effect, leaders and team members alike must develop key interaction process skills for effective group efforts. Again review the guiding principles in Figure 7.5. Which of the principles apply to procedural responsibilities? What might you add?

Interpersonal Responsibilities   Finally, leaders make significant contributions to the interpersonal dynamics of groups. Leaders contribute to participation, group climate, and conflict management. As previously suggested, effective leaders generate an environment in which team members can achieve excellence because they have the confidence to take risks. Confidence to take risks comes from the supportive climate of effective interpersonal relationships. Leaders are responsible for reflecting feelings and supporting others, empathizing, and stopping personal attacks or other counterproductive individual or group behaviors. A growing emphasis is placed on leaders as coaches for both individual contributors and teams. *Coaching* is the term applied to the process of helping others develop by providing intense and specific feedback for a range of issues related to organizational effectiveness. Coaching support includes individual behaviors and a range of team development opportunities such as goal clarity, meeting management, problem solving, and conflict resolution. What guiding principles should a leader adopt for interpersonal responsibilities? What skills are most important?

In summary, we can say that leaders affect how the task is accomplished, how people are supported within the group, and what processes and procedures the group uses to achieve its objectives. Group members also share these responsibilities, but the leader remains influential in guiding task, procedural, and interpersonal contributions.

CHAPTER HIGHLIGHTS

Leadership and **management** communication affect nearly all aspects of organizational life. **Leaders** help guide individuals, groups, and entire organizations in establishing goals and sustaining action to support goals. **Managers** fulfill organizationally assigned roles and are expected to be leaders, but leadership can come from virtually any organizational position. Theories of leadership and management emphasize **traits** such as intelligence, social maturity, initiative, and human relations abilities. **Style** theories emphasize **autocratic, democratic,** and **laissez-faire** behaviors and frequently use such categories as **impoverished, middle-of-the-road, country club, task,** and **team management. Situational** approaches build on style theories by emphasizing an interaction among leadership style, maturity of followers, and needs of a particular situation.

Transformational approaches emphasize understanding of particular situations with the establishment of vision important to motivate workers to high levels of achievement. Discursive approaches focus on talk (little "d" discourse), products of talk and interactions (texts), and underlying assumptions and power narratives (big "D" discourse) to understand how leadership is socially constructed and enacted in particular organizations or environments. Distinctions can be made between leadership and management. Managers need to be leaders, but organizations in the information society need leaders in diverse organizational positions. Strategic objectives for leadership include authoritarian, participative, and avoidance approaches. The ability to influence others relates to the **power bases** of leaders. Power bases are commonly described as **legitimate, reward, coercive, referent, expert,** or **connection power.** Situational analyses, along with strategies, tactics, and power bases, determine leadership effectiveness. Leadership effectiveness increases by understanding the guiding principles for **principled leadership** and understanding leadership responsibilities in task, procedural, and interpersonal areas. ■

WORKSHOP

1. In groups of six, identify by name examples of effective and ineffective leaders. Describe the behaviors of your effective leaders. Describe the behaviors of those you believe were ineffective. Discuss the similarities and differences in your list.
2. As you know from reading this chapter, transformational approaches to leadership are among the newest of the theories used to describe leadership. In "Leadership That Transforms," which follows, Michael Hackman and Craig Johnson help us understand this important approach to leadership. Read their comments and be prepared to discuss them and offer your own opinions.
3. Interview three leaders of your choice. Ask them about their personal theories of leadership. What do they see as the challenges facing leaders of today and tomorrow? Summarize your findings either in writing or in an oral report for class discussion.
4. The first three quotes were published in *U.S. News & World Report* on October 31, 2005. The fourth quote was published in the *Harvard Business Review* in December 2008. Read each and in small groups discuss their implications. What aspects of principled leadership do they represent?

   "I am never not aware of who I am, where I've come from—and what it took for me to give back. . . . I am here because I have walked across the backs of people who made this way for me. That's in everything that I do. I'm black and I'm female and . . . I find strength and honor in that. My responsibility is not just to myself."—Oprah Winfrey, celebrity and media company head

   "Perpetual optimism is a force multiplier."—Colin Powell, former secretary of state and chairman of the Joint Chiefs of Staff

   "You have to follow the path of doing the right thing by making decisions that are true to your mission and cause."—Howard Schultz, chairman of Starbucks

   "My job as CEO is not to make business decisions—it's to push managers to be leaders."—Sergio Marchionne, CEO, FIAT

Leadership That Transforms

Michael Z. Hackman, Ph.D. [1] *Craig Johnson, Ph.D.*

In recent years, scholars from a variety of disciplines have studied the behavior of extraordinary leaders to determine what these individuals have in common.

---

[1]Michael Z. Hackman is a professor in the Department of Communication at the University of Colorado at Colorado Springs. He received his Ph.D. in speech communication from the University of Denver. His research interests include leadership and communication, intercultural communication, and communication instruction.
Craig Johnson is a professor of leadership studies at George Fox University and director of the university's Doctor of Management program. He received his Ph.D. in speech communication from the University of Denver. His research interests include leadership and communication, and leadership/organizational ethics.

The search for common characteristics of highly effective leaders has led researchers to conclude that outstanding leaders not only move followers to action but also transform followers into leaders themselves. This model for understanding and explaining leadership has been called the Transformational Approach. Under transformational leadership, followers are motivated to work harder, to become more sensitive to moral and ethical issues, and to think and act like leaders. As a result, organizational climate and productivity often dramatically improve.

Howard Schultz is one example of a transformational leader who has had a significant impact on his organization's performance. Schultz was hired by a small Seattle company, Starbucks, in 1982. A visit to Italy convinced him that the coffee bar culture could be recreated in the United States. The company's founders and a number of outside investors were skeptical so in 1987 Schultz raised enough money to buy the firm himself. By 1992 the company began selling shares to the public and by the end of the 1990s Starbucks stock value soared more than 2200 percent, surpassing Wall Street giants such as General Electric, Microsoft, and IBM in total return. Today, as Starbucks deals with a shrinking customer base as a result of the global recession, the company has scaled back its ambitious expansion plans. Despite this setback, Starbucks continues to employ transformational principles by paying higher-than-average wages, offering stock options, providing health insurance for part-time workers, recognizing outstanding partners, and holding quarterly open forums. Other examples of transformational leaders include the late Bill Hewlett and Dave Packard of Hewlett-Packard, Herb Kelleher; the former CEO of Southwest Airlines; Jim Sinegal, founder and CEO of Costco; and Yvon Chouinard, the founder and driving force behind the Patagonia clothing and outdoor sports company.

What are the common characteristics shared by these leaders? In nearly all the classification systems of transformational leadership, five common characteristics appear. Research suggests that transformational leaders are creative, interactive, visionary, empowering, and passionate.

Creative Transformational leaders recognize that satisfaction with the status quo poses a serious threat to an organization's survival. Resting on past achievements can blind members to new opportunities and potential problems, and as organizations such as Montgomery Ward, AOL TimeWarner, and Airbus have discovered, the most successful organizations are often in the most danger. As one observer notes: "Nothing fails like success."

Transformational leaders act as problem finders who sense gaps between what is and what ought to be. They seek out new markets, products, clients, and customers which can help the organization grow and prosper.

In addition to acting as problem finders, transformational leaders foster an atmosphere that encourages experimentation and innovation. Toleration of failure is the key element of a creative climate. Transformational leaders believe failure is an important tool since those who don't fail are neither trying nor learning.

A company recognized as one of the most innovative in the world, 3M, is an example of how important it is for an organization to foster creativity. At 3M, employees are rewarded for creative success but are not punished for creative failure. Any mistake is tolerated at 3M as long as it is an original mistake. According to 3M executive Allen Jacobson, "Outsiders say we are very lenient in rewarding failure."

Actually, 3M is very insightful in realizing that nothing inhibits creativity like the fear of punishment for failure. More than 60 percent of new product ideas developed at 3M ultimately fail. However, successes like the Post-it note (those adhesive-backed note pads found in virtually every office in the world) more than compensate for 3M's product failures.

The Post-it note, like so many products at 3M, was developed using materials from a failed venture. The original compound for the adhesive on the back of the Post-it note was initially considered a failure. The adhesive compound was deemed useless because of its limited adherence to other objects—the very quality that made that adhesive a success in the Post-it note!

Interactive Extraordinary leadership is the product of extraordinary communication. Transformational leaders are masterful communicators able to articulate and define ideas and concepts that escape others. Transformational leaders spend much of their time talking with followers. They walk the shop floor or the office suite shaking hands, joking, asking questions, providing information, and, most of all, listening. Extraordinary leaders do not hole up in corporate offices.

One organization which embodies the transformational philosophy is Johnsonville Foods of Sheboygan, Wisconsin. At Johnsonville, traditional organizational structure was replaced by self-directed work teams. Middle managers adopted the leadership roles of coordinators and coaches rather than the traditional roles of supervisor and disciplinarian. These leaders were made responsible for teaching team members how to lead themselves more effectively. They coaxed, cajoled, encouraged, challenged, offered advice, and inspired team members. In short, the primary job responsibility of organizational leaders at Johnsonville Foods became one of interacting with team members.

Interaction is particularly important in times of change or crisis. In the days following the September 11 terrorist attacks, Gordon Bethune, then Continental Airlines CEO, recorded a daily voice-mail message to keep all of his 40,000 employees fully informed about the rapidly changing situation in the airline industry.

Visionary Communicating a vision to followers may well be the most important act of the transformational leader. A vision is a concise statement or description of where the organization is headed. Compelling visions provide a sense of purpose and encourage commitment. Followers achieve more and make more ethical decisions when they pursue a worthy goal.

In a study of ninety transformational leaders from government, education, music, business, and sport, Warren Bennis and Burt Nanus (1985) found that the leaders in their sample spent a good deal of time talking with employees, clients, other leaders, and consultants before developing a vision for their organization. Leaders carefully studied their organization's past, to determine the reasons for success and failures; present, to determine current strengths, weaknesses, and resources; and future, to identify possible long-term social, political, and environmental changes. The leaders then interpreted the information to construct a realistic vision that fit the norms of the group and inspired followers to put forth more effort.

To be compelling, a vision must be both desirable and attainable. According to Harvard professor John Kotter (1990), an effective vision is specific enough to provide real guidance to people, yet vague enough to encourage initiative and remain relevant under a variety of conditions. If a vision is too specific the vision may leave followers floundering when achieved.

An example of a vision statement that was too specific was President John Kennedy's vision for NASA (National Aeronautics and Space Administration). In 1962, Kennedy defined NASA's vision as "landing a man on the moon and returning him safely to earth before this decade is out." When a vision this specific is

achieved (as it was in 1969), followers may feel a sense of confusion regarding what to do next (as NASA did in the decades after the moon project).

More effective vision statements offer general guiding philosophies without detailing a specific end result. The following vision statements are examples of well-conceived organizational visions:

Ikea	To create a better everyday life for people.
Bristol-Myers Squibb	To extend and enhance human life by providing the highest-quality health and personal care products.
Disney Corporation	We create happiness by providing the finest in entertainment for people of all ages, everywhere.

These vision statements provide a general philosophy which guides the actions of members of the organization.

Empowering Transformational leaders know how to give power away and how to make others feel powerful. Transformational leaders give followers access to the funds, materials, authority, and information needed to complete tasks and to develop new ideas. These leaders allow others to make decisions rather than insisting on making all the decisions themselves. Empowered followers are energized to carry out tasks associated with their work roles. They take an active, not passive, approach toward their job responsibilities. Such intrinsic motivation is the product of four factors: *Meaning, Choice, Competence,* and *Impact*.

Meaning is the value placed on a task, goal, or purpose based on personal ideals or standards. Low levels of meaning produce apathy and detachment; higher levels focus energy and produce commitment and involvement. Leaders can foster a sense of meaning by (1) hiring those who share the group's values, (2) promoting the organization's purpose and vision, (3) clarifying work roles, (4) matching individuals with jobs they find meaningful, and (5) explaining how individual tasks support the group's mission and goals.

Choice reflects a sense of self-direction or control. Those who have choice about how to carry out their jobs (when to start, how fast to work, how to prioritize tasks) feel a greater sense of responsibility and are more flexible, creative, and resilient. Shifting decision-making authority to followers is one way to encourage a sense of self-determination. In addition, leaders empower followers by creating a participative climate which values employees and takes their ideas seriously. Years ago, a UPS (United Parcel Service) employee ordered an extra plane to make sure that packages left behind during the Christmas rush were delivered on time. Rather than punish this individual for going above the budget, company leaders praised him. His story (still told at the company) sends the message that UPS leaders will stand behind those who take initiative.

Competence is based on the individual's assessment that he or she can do the job required. It is a subset of what psychologist Albert Bandura (1977) refers to as self-efficacy or personal power. Self-efficacy is the sense that we can deal with the events, situations, and people not only at work, but in other environments as well. Followers who have a sense of self-efficacy or personal power are more likely to take initiative, to set and achieve higher goals, and to persist in the face of difficult circumstances. Constituents who believe that they have limited self-efficacy dwell on their failures instead.

Impact describes the individual's belief that he or she can influence the environment of the organization. Followers with a high sense of impact are convinced that they can make a difference in the work group's plans, goals, and procedures. Leaders can foster this perception by including workers in strategic planning and by involving them in setting collective rules and standards.

Max DePree, former CEO of the Herman Miller furniture company, goes so far as to suggest that leaders act as "servants" to their followers. As DePree explains, "The first responsibility of the leader is to define reality. The last is to say thank you. In between the two, the leader must become a servant and a debtor." The leader serves followers by providing necessary resources and encouragement to allow for the completion of assignments in the most productive manner. In the words of Jan Carlzon, the former president of Scandinavian Airline Systems (SAS), "If you're not serving the customer, you'd better be serving someone who is."

Passionate Transformational leaders are passionately committed to their work. They love their jobs and have a great deal of affection for the people with whom they work. Transformational leaders are able to encourage others because they, first and foremost, encourage themselves. This passion and personal enthusiasm motivates others to perform to their highest levels as well.

This type of passion is exemplified in a story related by Fred Smith, CEO of Federal Express. The story involves the actions of a Federal Express courier. The courier persisted in scanning and loading customers' packages even though the building was shaking and stairways were collapsing from an earthquake. The courier struggled to carry the shipment down nine flights of rubble-filled stairs to a waiting van and drove to the airport just in time for the shipment to be loaded onto a waiting plane.

Passion is a reflection of the organization and its leaders. Jim Collins (2001), who investigated companies exhibiting sustained greatness over a period of at least fifteen years, such as Nucor, Gillette, Walgreens, and Wells Fargo, found that great companies focus their energies on what they can get passionate about. For example, when Gillette executives made the choice to build sophisticated and more expensive shaving systems rather than enter the low-margin disposable market, they did so in large part because they had little enthusiasm for developing cheap, disposable razors. For executives at Gillette the technical design of shaving systems sparked the same type of excitement that might be expected from an aeronautical engineer working on the latest advancements in aviation. People who aren't passionate about Gillette are not welcome in the organization. One top business school graduate wasn't hired by the company because she simply didn't show enough passion for deodorant.

By demonstrating the characteristics of transformational leaders, individuals can begin to transform themselves and their organizations. By encouraging creativity, fostering open communication, demonstrating forward thinking, sharing responsibility, and exhibiting commitment, leaders can construct organizations prepared to meet the challenges of the future. ■

TIPS FOR EFFECTIVE COMMUNICATION

1. Volunteer to lead a group of which you are a member. Keep a journal of your experiences. Review your notes and determine where you were successful and where you have opportunities for improvement.
2. Facilitate a group in setting a vision for their work.
3. Identify a difficult concept or issue to communicate to others. Frame the issue and communicate your frame to others. Ask for feedback.
4. Write a paragraph describing your personal leadership philosophy.

5. Identify an individual you consider an effective leader. Ask for a "coaching" session with the individual. Prepare a list of specific questions focused on helping you improve your leadership potential. Listen carefully and develop a plan to put this feedback into action. ■

REFERENCES AND SUGGESTED READINGS

Alvesson, M., and Kärreman, D. 2000. Varieties of discourse: On the study of organizations through discourse analysis. *Human Relations* 53: 1125–1149.

Applbaum, R. L., E. M. Bodaken, K. K. Sereno, and K. W. Anatol. 1974. *The process of group communication.* Chicago: Science Research.

Argyris, C. 1962. *Interpersonal competence and organizational effectiveness.* Homewood, IL: Dorsey Press.

Bacon, C. C., and W. R. Ullmann. 1986. *Dimensions of interpersonal communication competence, communication accuracy, as predictors of managerial performance and job satisfaction.* Paper presented at the Speech Communication Association Convention, November, Chicago.

Bandura, A. 1977. Self-efficacy: Toward a unifying theory of behavioral change. *Psychological Review* 84: 191–215.

Barge, J. K. 1994. *Leadership: Communication skills for organizations and groups.* New York: St. Martin's.

Bennis, W. 1992. Leading change. *USC Business,* winter/spring, 47–51.

Bennis, W. 1999. Becoming a leader of leaders. In *Rethinking the future,* ed. R. Gibson, 148–162. London: Nicholas Brealey.

Bennis, W., and B. Nanus. 1985. *Leaders: The strategies for taking charge.* New York: Harper and Row.

Blake, R. R., and J. S. Mouton. 1964. *The managerial grid.* Houston, TX: Gulf.

Blake, R. R., and J. S. Mouton. 1985. *The managerial grid III: The key to leadership excellence.* Houston, TX: Gulf.

Collins, J. 2001. *Good to great.* New York: HarperCollins.

Collins, J. 2009. *How the mighty fall: And why some companies never give in.* New York: HarperCollins.

Corey, G. 1985. *Theory and practice of group counseling,* 2nd ed. Monterey, CA: Brooks/Cole.

Cushman, D., and S. King. 1993. High-speed management: A revolution in organizational communication in the 1990s. *Communication yearbook 16,* ed. S. Deetz, 209–236. Newbury Park, CA: Sage.

Davis, K. 1967. *Human relations at work.* New York: McGraw-Hill.

Deetz, S. 1993. *The negotiative organization: Building responsive and responsible workplaces.* Paper available through the Center for Negotiation and Conflict Resolution, Rutgers University, Newark.

Dempsey, S. E., P. S. Parker, and K. Krone. 2007. *Organizing tensions within transnational collective action spaces: Ana analysis of feminist transnational networks.* Paper presented at the International Communication Association meeting, San Francisco, CA.

Dobbins, G. H., and S. J. Zaccaro. 1986. The effects of group cohesion and leader behavior on subordinate satisfaction. *Group and Organization Studies* 11(3): 203–219.

Drucker, P. 1966. *The effective manager.* New York: Harper and Row.

Eisenberg, E. M. 1984. Ambiguity as strategy in organizational communication. *Communication Monographs* 51: 227–242.

Ellis, K., and P. Shockley-Zalabak. 1999. *Communicating with management: Relating trust to job satisfaction and organizational effectiveness.* Paper presented at the National Communication Association Convention, November, Seattle, WA.

Fairhurst, G. 2001. Dualisms in leadership research. In *The new handbook of organizational communication: Advances in theory, research, and methods,* eds. F. Jablin and L. Putnam, 379–439. Thousand Oaks, CA: Sage.

Fairhust, G. 2007. *Discursive leadership: In conversation with leadership psychology.* Los Angeles, CA: Sage.

Fairhurst, G. T., and R. A. Sarr. (1996). *The art of framing: Managing the language of leadership.* San Francisco: Jossey-Bass.

Fiedler, F. 1967. *A theory of leadership effectiveness.* New York: McGraw-Hill.

French, J., and B. Raven. 1968. The bases of social power. In *Group dynamics,* eds. D. Cartwright and A. Zander, 259–268. New York: Harper and Row.

Gardner, H. 1995. *Leading minds.* New York: Basic Books.

Geier, J. 1967. A trait approach to the study of leadership in small groups. *Journal of Communication* 17: 316–323.

Hackman, M., and C. Johnson. 2009. *Leadership: A communication perspective.* Long Grove, IL: Waveland.

Hammer, M. 1996. Beyond reengineering. *Executive Excellence* 13(8): 13–14.

Harris, P., and R. Moran. 1996. *Managing cultural differences: Leadership strategies for a new world of business.* Houston, TX: Gulf.

Heifetz, R. 2007. Leadership, authority, and women: A man's challenge. In *Women and Leadership*, eds. B. Kellerman and D. Rhode, 311–327. San Francisco: Wiley.

Hersey, P., and K. Blanchard. 1974. So you want to know your leadership style? *Training and Development Journal* 28(2): 22–37.

Hersey, P., and K. Blanchard. 1977. *Management of organizational behavior: Utilizing human resources*, 3rd ed. Englewood Cliffs, NJ: Prentice Hall.

Hesselbein, F., M. Goldsmith, and R. Beckhard, eds. 1996. *The leader of the future.* San Francisco: Jossey-Bass.

Ibarra, H., and O. Obodaru. 2009. Women and the vision thing. *Harvard Business Review.* January, 62–70.

Jung, D., and B. Avolio. 1999. Effects of leadership style and followers' cultural orientation on performance in group and individual task conditions. *Academy of Management Journal* 42(2): 208–218.

Kanter, R. M. 1996. World-class leaders: The power of partnering. In *The leader of the future*, eds. F. Hesselbein, M. Goldsmith, and R. Beckhard, 89–98. San Francisco: Jossey-Bass.

Kelleher, D., P. Finestone, and A. Lowy. 1986. Managerial learning: First notes from an unstudied frontier. *Group and Organization Studies* 11(3): 169–202.

Kotter, J. 1990. *A force for change: How leadership differs from management.* New York: Free Press.

Kouzes, J., and B. Posner. 2009. To lead, create a shared vision. *Harvard Business Review*, January, 20–21.

Larson, C., and F. LaFasto. 1989. *TeamWork: What must go right/What can go wrong.* Newbury Park, CA: Sage.

Lee, J. 2001. Leader-member exchange, perceived organizational justice, and cooperative communication. *Management Communication Quarterly* 14(4): 574–569.

Manz, C. 1986. Self-leadership: Toward an expanded theory of self-influence processes in organizations. *Academy of Management Review* 11: 585–600.

Manz, C., and H. Sims. 1989. *SuperLeadership: Leading others to lead themselves.* New York: Prentice Hall.

Marshall, A. A., and C. Stohl. 1993. Being "in the know" in a participative management system. *Management Communication Quarterly* 6(4): 372–404.

Peppers, L., and J. Ryan. 1986. Discrepancies between actual and aspired self: A comparison of leaders and nonleaders. *Group and Organization Studies* 11(3): 220–228.

Robinson, W. P. 2002. *Leading people from the middle.* Provo, UT: Executive Excellence.

Sample, S. B. 2002. *The contrarian's guide to leadership.* San Francisco: Jossey-Bass.

Shockley-Zalabak, P., S. Morreale, and M. Hackman. 2010. *Building the high-trust organization.* San Francisco: Jossey-Bass.

Sims, H. Jr., and P. Lorenzi. 1992. *The new leadership paradigm.* Newbury Park, CA: Sage.

Skaret, D. J., and N. S. Bruning. 1986. Attitudes about the work group: An added moderator of the relationship between leader behavior and job satisfaction. *Group and Organization Studies* 11(3): 254–279.

Snavely, W. B., and E. V. Walters. 1983. Differences in communication competence among administrator social styles. *Journal of Applied Communication Research* 11(2): 120–135.

Soares, E. J., and L. J. Chase. 1985. *Communication elements of managerial competence.* Paper presented at the International Communication Association Convention, May, Honolulu, HI.

Stogdill, R. M., and A. E. Coons. 1957. *Leader behavior: Its description and measurement.* Research monograph No. 88. Columbus: Bureau of Business Research, Ohio State University.

Tannenbaum, R., and W. Schmidt. 1958. How to choose a leadership pattern. *Harvard Business Review* 36: 95–101.

Toffler, A., and H. Toffler. 1994. *War and anti-war: Survival at the dawn of the twenty-first century.* New York: Bantam Books/Doubleday Dell.

Van Velsor, E., and J. B. Leslie. 1995. Why executives derail: Perspectives across time and cultures. *Academy of Management Executive* 9(4): 62–72.

Wheatley, M. 1992. *Leadership and the new science.* San Francisco: Berrett-Koehler.

White, R., and R. Lippitt. 1960. *Autocracy and democracy: An experimental inquiry.* New York: Harper and Row.

Zenger, J., E. Musselwhite, K. Hurson, and C. Perrin. 1993. *Leading teams: Mastering the new role.* Homewood, IL: Business One Irwin. ∎

Participating in Organizations

Developing Critical Organizational Communication Competencies

DEVELOPING COMPETENCIES THROUGH ...

KNOWLEDGE Distinguishing between decision making and problem solving
Describing problem-solving processes
Describing types of organizational interviews
Describing types of organizational presentations
Describing types of organizational communications technologies

SENSITIVITY Understanding individual and organizational influences on and barriers to decision making and problem solving
Considering the organizational and personal impact of interviews, presentations, and use of technology

SKILLS Applying analysis capabilities to group interactions and case studies
Assessing individual communication competency needs
Practicing analysis capabilities for interviews and presentations

VALUES Relating decision making and problem solving to excellence
Understanding effective communication as essential to decision making and problem solving
Understanding the importance of individual communication competencies for organizational participation
Relating effective interviews, presentations, and use of technologies to overall organizational effectiveness

THE DECISIONS, PROBLEMS, MORE DECISIONS CASE

Joan Murphy had an important and exciting dilemma. She had been offered management training positions by two of the top retailers in the country. When she had interviewed, Joan had been hoping to get an offer from one of the two, but in her wildest dreams she had not expected to hear from both. The two companies were making similar financial offers; both were in the Midwest, where she hoped to stay; and both were reported to have excellent training programs with fast promotional progress. Both alternatives were attractive. How should she decide?

Joan went to work for Dayton Retailers. The decision had been a difficult one, requiring considerable weighing of various alternatives. She felt good about Dayton and hoped they liked her work. Joan did not, however, feel comfortable with some of the behaviors exhibited by others in her management training group. Joan knew at least two of her peers in the training program were having other friends at Dayton complete their project assignments. To make matters worse, the two were getting the highest praise in the class and seemed likely to get the best assignments when the courses were over. Joan didn't think that was fair or good for Dayton. She questioned what she should do, especially when others might view her complaints as simply trying to get ahead. Joan decided to work very hard on her final presentation for the management training course to demonstrate to the trainers and the trainees as well what her capabilities were.

Joan's assignment to the Ridgefield Shopping Center was terrific. To be put in charge of junior sportswear in a thriving store was quite a plum. Her only difficulty was caused by department remodeling, which limited space to bring in new, competitive lines. Three new lines had been proposed, but space limitations permitted the stocking of only one of the three. Joan had called a meeting of the junior sportswear buyers, the top salespeople from the floor, and the floor manager to attempt to decide which of the three would be best. Joan began to think about how the group should approach the decision.

After several successful months at Ridgefield, Joan was transferred to Glencrest, a struggling store. Although she knew this position was a real learning opportunity, Joan was sorry to leave Ridgefield and the wonderful group of people with whom she was working. Joan also knew the staff of Glencrest was anything but happy to have her come. The manager Joan was replacing had been popular, and the staff was not pleased at the changes management was making. They appeared to be especially apprehensive about the new computerized inventory system due for installation. Joan knew the staff did not dislike her personally but were unhappy about management's statement the store would have to establish a better track record or suffer staff and merchandise reductions. Joan's first responsibilities were to change the sales promotions schedules for the next several months and to get the new inventory system running. She needed the cooperation of her new staff and their advice on how to develop a promotions plan that could hope to increase sales in the struggling store. After all, she did not know this market area nearly as well as Ridgefield. Joan thought about the type of group she would form for solving the Glencrest problems. She decided to interview each staff member individually to learn more about them and to understand what they might contribute to changes at Glencrest. ■

INTRODUCTION

Joan Murphy engages in communication competencies common to all types of organizational situations. Her interviewing skills resulted in two job offers. She makes an individual decision when she chooses between these alternatives. She encounters a problem when peers in her training group violate ethical standards of conduct, potentially positioning them for superior job assignments. She must prepare a final presentation for her management training course. In her first assignment, Joan must work with a group of people charged with deciding among three competitive lines. Finally, she must bring together a team capable of solving a sales problem while introducing new workplace technology.

The decisions Joan makes and the effectiveness of the problem solving in which she engages will not only affect her personal career but also influence the success of Dayton Retailers. Indeed, it is fair to say decision making, problem solving, interpersonal and small-group interactions, and presentations can be described as guiding processes for all organizational functioning. In this chapter, we define decision making and problem solving, discuss various types of organizational interviews, and describe important characteristics of organizational presentations, including training or educational presentations. In addition, the chapter describes competencies important for the use of communications technologies. We build competencies through a variety of decision-making and problem-solving cases, and we develop interviewing and presentational competencies through an understanding of basic preparation strategies coupled with practice opportunities. Finally, we ask you to examine the technologies you believe will be most important for communicating within the organizations of today and tomorrow.

This chapter is designed to develop *knowledge* by identifying critical communication competencies for participation in organizations. The competencies developed include decision making, problem solving, interviewing, presenting, and using communications technologies. We encourage *sensitivity* through awareness of individual and organizational influences for decision making and problem solving and by considering ethical and credibility issues for interviewing and presentations. We increase *skills* through decision-making and problem-solving practice, interviewing experiences, and preparation for presentations. We influence *values* by relating quality decisions and problem solving to overall organizational effectiveness and encouraging an understanding of the importance of ethical and credible individual behaviors during all types of organizational interactions including interviews and formal presentations. Finally, all four competencies—knowledge, sensitivity, skills, and values—interact during analysis and practice opportunities.

DEFINING DECISION MAKING AND PROBLEM SOLVING

Decision making and problem solving are among the most important communication processes in organizations. People working together to identify needed change contribute to innovation and creativity. Groups or individuals who cannot make a decision potentially retard progress or, even worse, contribute to negative organizational outcomes. Decision making and problem solving occur through a variety of communication processes. The effectiveness of decision making and problem solving directly influences the effectiveness of individuals as well as entire organizations.

Decision making is the process of choosing from among several alternatives, whereas **problem solving** is a multistage process for moving an issue, situation, or state from an undesirable to a more desirable condition. Although problem solving includes decision making, decision making and problem solving are not one and the same process. Decision making depends on individuals and groups choosing from among known alternatives. Problem solving is the process

Decision making ■ Process of choosing from among several alternatives.

Problem solving ■ Multistage process for moving an issue, situation, or state from an undesirable to a more desirable condition.

by which individuals and groups generate alternatives and evaluate those alternatives in light of the identified problem.

Joan Murphy engages in both individual and group decision making and problem solving. Joan and her coworkers have alternatives to consider as well as sales problems to understand and correct. The decision-making and problem-solving processes in which they engage require risks. These risks ultimately contribute to the effectiveness of Dayton Retailers.

All decision making and problem solving involve a level of risk. Decisions, whether as choices from among well-defined alternatives or the result of complex problem solving, reflect desired courses of action before the results of the action are known. Unknown results represent risk. The level of risk relates to the importance of the decision: more risk generally is associated with more important decisions. In other words, the more that can go right with a good decision is weighed against the more that can go wrong if the decision fails.

Joan Murphy faces a high-risk situation as she moves to the Glencrest store. Sales are down and the manager she replaces was popular with her employees. If Joan is successful, the store will have an increase in sales and Dayton management will view her efforts favorably. Joan has a lot to gain, and so does Dayton. If her decision-making and problem-solving efforts are ineffective, the store faces staff and merchandise reductions and Joan's own career may be damaged. A good decision-making process will not guarantee success, but a poor process will almost certainly contribute to failure. Thus, both individual and group decision-making and problem-solving capabilities influence personal and organizational effectiveness. The following sections in this chapter describe important influences and methods for decision making and problem solving and discuss a variety of problem-solving processes.

INFLUENCES FOR DECISION MAKING AND PROBLEM SOLVING

We will describe four primary factors which influence individual and group decision making and problem solving These factors—organizational culture (including power and control processes), decision/problem issues, communication competencies, and technical competencies—influence the methods used for problem solving, the quality of decisions made, and the satisfaction participants feel with decision-making and problem-solving processes.

Culture

Most scholars agree that central to the notion of organizational culture are the decision-making processes in which organizational members engage. Phillip Tompkins and George Cheney (1983) pointed out "the examination of the decision-making process provides a means of tapping the mutual influences of people and organizations." Indeed, the very activity of organizing can be described as synonymous with the decision-making process. Organizing can be seen as a conscious limitation of alternatives and therefore decision making. It is this limitation of alternatives (decisions) that becomes the shared realities of the organization or its culture.

Organizational cultures influence the methods of decision making. Some organizations expect leaders to make and announce decisions. The military, for example, does not depend on majority rule or consensus decision making for determining plans of action. The university, on the other hand, has a long tradition of consensus decision making at all organizational levels. Some organizations expect individuals to make decisions about their jobs or areas of responsibility without notifying others or seeking extensive input. Other organizations emphasize notification of others of intended plans or actions even if such actions are not expected to affect those being notified. Particular organizations may value broad participation in decision making, whereas others may emphasize limited access to decision makers. The methods and levels of participation desired for decision making and problem solving reflect organizational values and culture. Who is included in problem solving and decision making and who determines inclusion or exclusion reflect power and control processes. Power and control processes and organizational values all contribute to the culture of a given organization as it approaches problem solving and decision making.

The Decision/Problem Issue

The nature of a problem also influences decision making and problem solving. Is the problem highly complex? Does the organization have available resources to understand the problem? How important is this decision or solution to organizational effectiveness? Has the organization previously attempted to solve this type of dilemma? Timothy Kuhn and Michele Jackson (2008) helped us understand distinctions in decision/problem situations. They described determinate situations as circumstances which appear relatively routine and mundane and where alternatives and solutions are straightforward. On the other hand, they describe indeterminate situations as "interpretations of and responses to a problematic situation are less clear when there are multiple and conflicting identities, when the validation of action is uncertain, and when ambiguity marks both role requirements and action scripts. In highly indeterminate situations, information transmission will never be adequate—no matter the amount transmitted or the manner of its transmission—because what counts as being relevant or useful is not held in common" (p. 459). Complexity, resources, importance, and previous experience concerning problems all influence how individuals and organizations approach decisions. Complex problems may require more extensive involvement, a higher level of participation, more thoroughness, and greater resources than do less complex problems. The importance of the decision or problem may influence who is responsible and how much time is allocated for decision making.

Communication Competency

Throughout this text we have described the need for communication competency. Many of the competencies discussed relate to effective decision making and problem solving. What motivates us and what we believe motivates others influence the quality of our decision-making participation. Our perception of our personal competencies and our predispositions for communication help determine how and when we engage in individual and group decision making. Our interpersonal effectiveness contributes to whether we can influence others during problem solving. Our comfort or discomfort with conflict may determine whether we will contribute information if others are likely to disagree. In addition to our individual participation, the communication competencies of others influence the quality of decision making. Individuals who fail to participate even though they have needed information lower the quality of problem solving. Because decision making and problem solving occur through human communication, the ability and willingness of all involved to engage in quality participation influence the ultimate quality of decisions.

Technical Competency

The final factor to influence decision making and problem solving is technical competency. Do individuals involved in decision making have the technical background or competencies necessary to approach the problem thoughtfully? Are decision makers aware of the best available information on which to base their evaluations? Has the group been formed with a distribution of appropriate technical skills? Excellence in decision making requires a communication process that supports excellence and appropriate technical backgrounds or information. Most of us have attended meetings in which we were willing to participate and yet found that we had no relevant information for the problem at hand. We had to depend on others for our understanding. That dependence probably worked as long as other group members brought appropriate technical competencies to the decision. All too often, however, groups make important decisions without a full range of available information.

METHODS FOR DECISION MAKING AND PROBLEM SOLVING

Influenced by culture, the issue at hand, and communication and technical competencies, organizational members choose from among a variety of methods and processes for decision making and problem solving. We describe the following methods—individual approach, leader mandate, majority rule, powerful minority, and consensus—to illustrate the diversity of options available for individuals, groups, or entire organizations. It is important to note in the twenty-first century, the emphasis on decision making and problem solving is rapidly shifting from an individual to a group or team responsibility. The emphasis on group/team problem solving and decision making increasingly asks those who will actually implement a decision to make the decision. In the past, managers characteristically made decisions which were carried out at least one organizational level removed from the manager.

Individual Approaches

Individuals engage in decision making and problem solving with a variety of methods and approaches. Individuals make decisions with a range of involvement from others. At times they come to important decisions without others even knowing that a decision is being considered. An individual may decide to apply for a promotion, leave a company, or go back to school based on private evaluations of alternatives. At other times, individual decisions result from extensive interaction with others. An individual, for example, may seek feedback from peers, supervisors, or professional advisors to determine needed skill improvements. A supervisor may have discussions with other supervisors in an effort to solve a performance problem, or a supervisor may work directly with the employees in question. In any event, individual decision makers have the option to consider their alternatives alone or with others.

Leader Mandate

Groups also come to decisions with a variety of methods. When a group is hopelessly deadlocked, for example, a leader may make a decision and announce the decision to the group. The authority of the leadership position may be sufficient to enforce the decision without regard to disagreements. Some leaders prefer this method of decision making and use group members only to gather information from which the leader will arrive at the final decision. Decisions made in this fashion may or may not be of high quality. Research suggests, however, that **leader-made decisions** frequently have less group commitment than decisions in which members are more actively involved.

Leader-made decision ■ Leader of a group makes a decision and announces the decision to the group.

Majority Rule

Majority rule is a common method for decision making. When more than 50 percent of a group agree, a decision is reached. Some groups reach majority agreement informally, whereas others, such as legislative bodies, have operating rules and procedures governing majority decisions. Although faster than moving a group to true consensus, the majority-rule method may not adequately account for the views of the minority. **Majority-rule decisions** can be high in quality, but they can also ignore central issues of concern.

Majority-rule decision ■ When more than 50 percent of a group agree, a decision has been reached.

Powerful Minority

Powerful-minority decision ■ Process for decision making occurring when group membership is characterized by unequal distribution of power among members. Those members who have the most power (although in the numerical minority) are in a position to assume decision-making responsibility.

Although used less frequently than majority vote, the **powerful-minority decision** is another way groups can make decisions. When group membership is characterized by unequal distribution of power among members, those members who have the most power (although in the numerical minority) are in a position to assume decision-making responsibility. The powerful-minority method can be effective when the minority members have the best information on which to base the decision. This method fails, however, if other-than-expert power drives the decision. Examples of failure of the powerful-minority method can be found in organizational resistance to change. Longtime organizational members who control decision making through seniority and position level may retard needed changes by ignoring the expert opinions of other group members with less organizational power and influence.

Consensus

The **consensus** method results in a decision all members can agree is best and all can support. The consensus method may take more time than other methods, unless considerable agreement existed at the beginning of the process. Complete consensus is not common because it is difficult for all members of a group to believe the very best decision possible has been made. The consensus method does not rest with everyone completely agreeing but with everyone reaching a level of agreement sufficient for decision support.

Consensus ■ Method for decision making that results in all members agreeing on what is best and supporting the group decision.

BARRIERS TO EFFECTIVE DECISION MAKING AND PROBLEM SOLVING

Throughout the text we have developed a variety of knowledge, sensitivity, skill, and value competencies important for organizational effectiveness. We described individual experiences in organizations and identified positive and negative group participation behaviors. We discussed the importance of leadership and management communication. In general, it is fair to say we explored the important roles, relationships, and responsibilities that relate to organizational decision making and problem solving, the subject of this chapter.

We all have participated in groups that made bad decisions or failed to solve real problems. Think for a moment about those groups. Can you identify any particular barriers to effectiveness? What would you do differently if you were to meet again?

Barriers to effective decision making and problem solving can be described in organizational, task and procedural, and interpersonal areas. It is important for our knowledge and sensitivity competency development to understand what commonly goes wrong during problem solving even when individuals have the best of intentions.

Organizational Barriers

With virtually all types of organizations engaging in problem solving and decision making and with 80 to 90 percent of Fortune 500 companies using a variety of group decision-making processes, it is surprising to many that the American Management Association has estimated only about 50 percent of organizational decisions are ever implemented. The reasons are diverse, but two—no commitment to the decision and a lack of resources—are among the most prominent. For those decisions that get made, Paul Nutt (1999) estimated, half of the implemented decisions fail. Numerous research studies have highlighted the importance of multiple and divergent points of view for effective organizational decision making. Joseph Bonito, Mary DeCamp, and Erin Ruppel (2008) described the lack of divergent points of view in the process of information sharing in small groups. They concluded that a substantive problem was "shared information is typically discussed more frequently during discussion than unique information, and that group outcomes suffer as a result." In other words, shared information in a group was given more importance in the development and maintenance of judgments leading to decisions.

Unique information was not as valued, limiting the possibilities even considered by the group. Elizabeth Morrison and Frances Milliken (2000) argued powerful forces in many organizations cause widespread withholding of information about potential problems, contributing to poor decision making. They refer to these barriers as producing organizational silence. Morrison and Milliken suggest dynamics giving rise to organizational silence include beliefs by top management that employees are self-interested, that management knows best, and that unity is good and dissent is bad. Organizational silence can retard change and development, inhibit effective decision making, and contribute to low commitment and trust. Organizational structures and policies that become decision-making barriers include centralization of decision making and a lack of formal upward feedback mechanisms. Organizational silence is promoted when managers fear negative feedback, reject or respond negatively to dissent, and do not solicit information about negative feedback.

Organizational culture also can be a barrier to quality problem solving and decision making. Some strong cultures retard innovation by focusing on the way things have always been done. Other cultures discount or marginalize certain individuals or groups without regard to their potential contributions. Global problem-solving groups report difficulties related to the varying cultural backgrounds of group members. Organizational and globally diverse cultures help us define the expected quality of decisions within a given situation. Low or broadly divergent expectations can contribute to poor problem solving and decision making.

Finally, use of technology can be a barrier to effective decision making and problem solving. Inadequate access to technology, varying degrees of willingness to participate in telemediated communication, negative and evaluative tones in computer-mediated exchanges, and a host of other variables related to technology use can interfere with quality decision making.

Task and Procedural Barriers

Groups make poor decisions when they short-circuit problem analysis. One of the most important barriers to problem-solving effectiveness is an inadequate description of problems. Group members frequently jump to solutions that appeal to them rather than work toward solutions better suited to the complexity of the issues. In addition, both individuals and groups have been known to overestimate the positive benefits of a chosen alternative while rejecting accurate or valid information in favor of more popular but flawed data.

Groups also make poor decisions when role ambiguity contributes to confusion about responsibilities, process, or leadership. Who is responsible for what, how decisions are to be made, and what authority resides in the group are all procedural questions that when inadequately answered contribute to ineffective group decisions. The lack of agendas, too much or too little time for meetings, and a variety of other procedural issues relate to low-quality decisions.

Interpersonal Barriers

We all have observed or participated in interpersonal conflict that blocked effective decision making. We know from experience poor leadership or a variety of self-centered or ego-centered behaviors can negatively influence any group. What we may not see is group cohesion—too much to too little—can influence the quality of decisions. There are potential dangers from groupthink, or conformity behaviors that suspend critical thinking. It is important also to recognize that too little group cohesion can leave members distrustful and afraid to risk the best of their thinking. In addition, influential group members have been known to override the logic of others, leading to poor choices. Others discount the contributions of some group members and engage in disagreement behaviors without describing the substance of the disagreement.

Needless to say, so far we have only identified the major barriers to effective problem solving and decision making. What additional barriers can you identify? How can you advise a group to avoid the more serious ones?

PROBLEM-SOLVING PROCESSES

A variety of processes can be identified for both individual and group problem solving. These processes help individuals and groups move from problem identification to determination of action appropriate for problem needs. Although these processes include numerous decision-making activities, they are described as problem-solving processes because of their focus on moving situations, issues, or problems from undesirable to more desirable states. Although decision making occurs during problem solving, problem-solving processes include numerous other stages. Next, we describe three approaches to problem solving—the Standard Agenda, brainstorming, and experientially based processes. The goal of all these group-process designs and others not covered in this text is to produce creative decisions that contribute to organizational excellence. Which process is most appropriate depends on the needs of the problem, the technical and communication competencies of all involved, the culture of the organization, and a variety of other situation-specific concerns.

The Standard Agenda: A Rational Model

The **Standard Agenda** is a group application of what John Dewey (1910) identified as reflective thinking necessary for individual problem solving. It can apply to both individuals and groups. The following description of the Standard Agenda is adapted from the work of Kathryn Young, Julia Wood, Gerald Phillips, and Douglas Pedersen (2001).

Standard Agenda ■ Process for decision making based on reflective thinking, beginning with understanding the charge, and followed by understanding and phrasing the question, fact-finding, setting criteria and limitations, discovering and selecting solutions, and preparing and presenting the final report.

The Diagnostic Phase

1. *Understanding the charge.* What output is desired? Do you choose your own problem? What are your instructions? How will your work be evaluated?
2. *Understanding and phrasing the question.* Who decided it was a problem? Is the problem routine or an emergency? Has the issue been addressed before? Is everyone clear about the goal? What do the words in the question mean? Are the words specific and realistic?

3. *Fact-finding.* What are the evidences and symptoms of the problem? What is the effect of these symptoms? Has this happened before? What caused the condition? What have other interested and expert parties had to say about this issue? What might happen if the problem is not addressed? Using the answers to the previous questions, what is the problem now?

4. *Setting criteria and limitations.* What are the standards or goals by which we can judge possible solutions? What could be achieved by an effective solution? What are the legal, institutional (policy and tradition), financial, persuasive, moral, and logistical limits on decision making?

The Solution Phase

1. *Discovering and selecting solutions.* What are the alternatives? How does each meet the goals? How do they measure up against the limitations? Which provides more of what is wanted with the least new harm? Which one should be selected? Who is to do what about what, when, where, and with what projected effect, and how will it be paid for? What evaluation plan can be used to measure the effectiveness of the solution?

2. *Preparing and presenting the final report.* What must be written down and said? When, where, and to whom? How can the final report be most persuasively presented?

Brainstorming

One of the most used and popular processes for generating ideas for problem solving is **brainstorming.** In use for over forty years, the technique breaks away from linear and controlled processes and seeks creative thinking based on four basic rules: (1) criticism is not appropriate during idea generation; (2) all ideas are welcome (the more absurd, the better); (3) quantity is wanted (the more ideas, the better); and (4) combinations and alterations of ideas are sought (improve on the ideas of others and combine them). Brainstorming often is used to help understand or diagnose a problem and to elicit ideas when groups are in an alternative- or solution-generation phase. Brainstorming is used as a process in and of itself and often within the framework of the Standard Agenda. It reduces dependency on single powerful or influential individuals by encouraging broad participation without negative evaluation. Brainstorming also encourages a maximum output in a short period of time.

Brainstorming ■ Technique for generating ideas for problem solving based on methods that break away from linear and controlled processes. The process encourages maximum idea generation in a short period of time.

Experientially Based Processes

In Chapter 3 we introduced the Richard Cyert, James March, and Herbert Simon (Cyert and March, 1963; Simon, 1960) concept of bounded rationality as a way to understand information processing and decision making. Bounded rationality assumes that people intend to be rational, but with limited information-processing capacity, human decision making is based on selective perception and therefore exhibits "limited" rationality. Simon (1960) argued individuals often make organizational decisions realizing their decisions are based on partial information. Simon called this process "satisficing," or making decisions with the hope that the decisions will be good enough if not the very best. This satisficing approach frequently uses individuals' past experiences and is mindful of organizational precedents developed while handling similar problems. We all bring to our decision-making efforts masses of facts, techniques, values, knowledge, beliefs, and awareness of outcomes of previous decisions. We use intuition, feelings, fears, hopes, power relationships, and a variety of other personal and organizational concerns to select positions and courses of action. We know the fully rational or ideal solution often is simply not available or possible. We call these **experientially based processes**.

Increasingly decision making and problem solving are conducted among diverse groups of people linked through a variety of technologies. Later in this chapter we describe some of the technologies influencing participation in organizations. In addition to our discussion to this point, it is important to understand technologies influence decision-making and problem-solving methods, barriers, and effectiveness.

> **Experientially based processes** ■ Processes reflecting bounded rationality contributing to satisficing, or the generation of decisions that are good enough if not the best. Processes use a variety of past experiences, emotional reactions, and knowledge and beliefs in producing decisions often not possible with more strictly rational approaches.

INCREASING DECISION-MAKING AND PROBLEM-SOLVING EFFECTIVENESS

Effective problem solving and decision making require individuals and groups to use a broad range of communication and technical competencies. In the next section we focus on two types of skills necessary for problem solving: interaction process and fact-finding and evaluation skills. These communication competencies, coupled with competencies developed in previous chapters, form a basis for increasing our decision-making and problem-solving effectiveness.

Interaction Process Skills

Previously, we discussed individual strategies and tactics for effectiveness. Yet to be described, however, are **interaction process skills** that relate to effectiveness for decision making and problem solving. Interaction process skills are based on an understanding of the communication process; an awareness of individual predispositions, strategies, and tactics in a variety of circumstances; and knowledge and sensitivity for decision-making and problem-solving processes. Interaction process skills help individuals and groups structure problem-solving discussions, exhibit productive individual behaviors, and avoid behaviors destructive to effective decision making and problem solving.

> **Interaction process skills** ■ Skills based on an understanding of the communication process; an awareness of individual predispositions, strategies, and tactics in a variety of circumstances; and knowledge and sensitivity for decision making and problem solving.

Interaction process skills both restrict and assist in unleashing creativity during decision making and problem solving. Gay Lumsden and Donald Lumsden (1993) suggested group interactions can contribute to mind locks, or rigid assumptions about what individuals or groups should be. When interaction supports rigid mind locks, creativity shuts down. Lumsden and Lumsden gave examples of Roger von Oech's Mind Locks:

1. The right answer.
2. That's not logical.

3. Follow the rules.
4. Be practical.
5. Avoid ambiguity.
6. To err is wrong.
7. Play is frivolous.
8. That's not my area.
9. Don't be foolish.
10. I'm not creative.

Lumsden and Lumsden recommended group interactions should be characterized by encouraging playfulness, by agreeing not to judge people or ideas, by engaging in a search for different—even bizarre—idea relationships, and by consciously breaking down barriers.

As an individual, you are responsible for your skills during problem solving and decision making. Your behavior will influence not only your own satisfaction with the group but also the ability of the group to problem-solve and make an effective decision. Can you think of a time when the process skills in a group shut down good problem solving and decision making? What were the behaviors exhibited? In an effective group, what process skills did members use? Can you understand the differences?

Fact-Finding and Evaluation Skills

We make decisions based on our evaluation of the information that bears on the decision. We solve problems based on information about the problem and decisions about the adequacy of our solutions. Furthermore, we base complex decisions on the information available to us, whether or not it is the best information. It is therefore fair to say the quality of information we bring to decision-making and problem-solving processes directly influences the quality of our decisions and solutions. Our

Fact-finding and evaluation skills ■ Skills that assist in the discovery and criticism of information used in problem solving and decision making.

fact-finding and evaluation skills are central to our ability to discover and critique information used in problem solving and decision making.

To illustrate, let's assume for a moment careful planning has gone into our long-awaited vacation. We've contacted several airlines and have selected what appears to be the best fare. We have asked friends about a possible hotel and selected the one most often recommended. We arrive at our destination and are pleased with our accommodations. The newspaper in our hotel room, however, is advertising airfares to the resort area, and these fares are at least $100 less than we paid. We also find that although our hotel is very nice, there are other charming inns that give a better view of the mountains. Suddenly, our well-laid plans begin to seem inadequate; we are unsure of our choices. How did that happen with all our careful planning? The answer is relatively simple. We made decisions about our flights and hotel reservations without all the available information. We simply did not have a comprehensive awareness of our alternatives. Our initial fact-finding was inadequate.

Information Criteria

How can we evaluate the information we need? What criteria are important for our fact-finding and evaluation skills? Dennis Gouran (1979) suggested three characteristics of information should be considered in forming our decision-making rules: relevancy, sufficiency, and plausibility. *Relevancy* refers to the extent to which information bears directly on the matter up for decision. In the case of our airline reservations, the fare information acquired was relevant but did not meet the second necessary characteristic, sufficiency. *Sufficiency* refers to the amount of information necessary to establish positions or claims, or to verify what is likely to be correct. The fare schedules acquired were relevant but did not represent all of the possible fares from airlines flying our desired route. Thus, the failure to meet the sufficiency criterion cost us over $100. Finally, *plausibility*, or the extent to which information is credible, also influences our decision. Again, our rate information was credible. The airline we chose sold us the ticket for the stated price. Even though we had relevant plausible information, the lack of a comprehensive set of fare schedules (sufficiency) causes us concern about our decision. The same might be said for our hotel selection. We gathered relevant and plausible information but did not have a full set of alternatives from which to choose.

Relevancy, sufficiency, and plausibility of information affect not only individual decisions but also the quality of group efforts. The fact-finding abilities of all involved influence the effectiveness of decisions and how satisfied individuals and entire organizations are with decision making and problem solving.

Fact-finding also includes locating information in files, libraries, archives, reports, and a variety of other documents. Librarians, computer searches, the Internet, and catalog files are only a few of the resources used to identify information sources. Much to the surprise of many students, research skills previously applied to academic papers and other similar reports are valuable organizational skills when decision making and problem solving require data collection. As stated earlier, the complex information age brings more potential information to bear on problems than at any previous period in human history. This sheer volume of information complicates the fact-finding process and makes our ability to locate and evaluate data of increasing importance.

◤ THE SPENDING MORE TO SAVE MORE PRESENTATION CASE

Nancy Winslow was concerned about next week's manufacturing staff meeting. She had wanted to talk to management about her training plan and budget but not necessarily in such a potentially difficult setting. Nancy had just been notified she was to make a formal presentation justifying her request for $200,000 to train assembly workers on new equipment, including new messaging systems for work scheduling. The new equipment and communications technologies required improved reading comprehension, keyboarding, and mathematics skills. Nancy knew from her interviews with the affected workers the need for skills training was great, but she also was aware several influential managers opposed spending training time and money and favored replacing the most deficient employees. Nancy had hoped to convince the manufacturing manager of her plan before meeting with his staff. Now it was obvious she would not have that opportunity and could expect serious challenges to her proposal.

Nancy began to think about the recent interviews and needs assessment she had conducted among assembly workers. Their responses and the production data supported her training proposal, yet her findings were not designed to demonstrate whether training was a better investment than hiring new employees. Nancy wondered if she should interview someone in finance to support her point of view or leave that decision for the manufacturing management staff. The memo indicated she was to have approximately twenty minutes to present her plan, including a preliminary training design, with an additional hour for questions and answers. Nancy did not mind presenting her information but wondered exactly what her presentation goals should be. She felt uncomfortable about attempting to persuade management to train versus replace workers, although she strongly believed training was a better solution. She also was nervous about the "grilling" questions she could expect from at least two members of the staff. Nancy was apprehensive as she began to prepare her material. What information should she collect? What information should she present? Is something missing? How can she plan to respond to tough questions and challenges? ■

Nancy faces a typical organizational situation requiring data collection, interviewing, and presentation skills. She must convince management of her training plan and, in so doing, influence what happens to the employment future of several assembly workers. She wants to do a good job not only for the assembly workers but also for her reputation with the manufacturing staff. Nancy is experiencing what most of us can expect in our work lives. We will be asked to gather information and to make presentations about our work, and we will be challenged by those who may disagree with the position we represent. The decision at hand and our professional reputations will be affected by the competencies we bring to these situations.

Think about some of your experiences with interviewing, training, and presenting. What went through your mind as you began to prepare? Do you believe your current skills are adequately developed for most organizational situations?

The chances are that most of us have concerns about our interviewing, training, and presenting capabilities as well as our ability to use and understand new communications technologies. We realize that unlike the somewhat structured evaluation of our abilities during school, at work we will continually have to demonstrate our abilities by explaining and supporting our positions during both formal and informal presentations and with the use of technology.

INTERVIEWS IN ORGANIZATIONS

Interviews are a fact of life for just about everyone. We interview to get a job, we interview others who want to work with us, we receive performance feedback during interviews with the boss, we give performance feedback to others, and we gather information through interviews. Interviews are important communication activities requiring careful preparation and skilled execution. In this section, we discuss types of organizational interviews and offer suggestions for preparing for interviews. Specifically, we describe the informational interview, employment interview, performance appraisal interview, complaint interview, counseling interview, and media interview.

Informational interview ■
Interview to gather data for problem solving and decision making.

The Informational Interview

Information gathering takes place through **informational interviews.** The adequacy of our information-gathering capabilities is measured by our ability to gather relevant, sufficient, and plausible data from others and to identify sources where needed information is likely to be found. Interviews provide needed information or verify perceptions of a problem. Ideally, informational interviews take place with individuals who can plausibly be expected to have the needed facts and perceptions.

Whether they are informal or highly structured exchanges, informational interviews begin with careful planning. Planning is based on what we want to know, on who has that information, and in what form we are likely to find it. What we need to know emerges during our problem definition and our examination of the limits of our current information. We do not use interviews to gather information we already have unless there is some disagreement about its credibility.

What we need to know is influenced by our ability to define the limits of what we do not know. Although it sounds like a play on words, the concept is very important to decision making and problem solving. One of the limitations many of us exhibit during information gathering is the tendency to define what is needed in terms of what we know exists. We often do not seek enough open-ended information that may be relevant to our problem. In our vacation example, we knew we needed a nice hotel. We did not even consider our desire for a good view of the mountains in our fact-finding. We limited our fact-finding to what we knew to expect and inadvertently eliminated a highly desirable alternative.

After broadly identifying what they need to know, effective fact-finders locate sources likely to have that information. Fact-finders are faced with deciding who or what source is most accessible and who will be willing to give the needed information. Does one person have the data for our problem? Should we take a representative sample of individuals who can be expected to be affected by the problem? How precise do our sampling techniques need to be? These questions and others help fact-finders focus their efforts to find information sources appropriate for decision making and problem solving.

Once sources have been identified, the fact-finder proceeds to establish a general format for data collection. If an interview is to be conducted, the interviewer thinks about questions to ask and determines how responses will be documented for later evaluation. If written data are to be reviewed, the fact-finder decides how much will be recorded and in what format. This preparation for data collection enables the fact-finder to make better use of time spent with the interviewee or other relevant sources.

When conducting an informational interview, the interviewer must establish rapport and explain the purpose of data collection activities. During this phase of the interview, the fact-finder should establish personal credibility by introducing himself or herself, identifying the organization, and relating facts or circumstances that link the requested information to the purposes at hand. In other words, respondents are more likely to be cooperative if fact-finders introduce themselves with credentials and establish a need for the type of questions to be asked.

Once the interview begins, the fact-finder becomes concerned with framing questions that are clear and will elicit the desired information from the interviewee. Many years ago, Robert Kahn and Charles Cannell (1964) suggested what remains true today: successful interviewers adopt a receiver orientation, continually monitoring whether the interviewee understands the line of questioning and feels comfortable providing a truthful response. A communication consultant seeking information from employees about a supervisory problem, for example, may need to be careful to ensure employee anonymity in order to gather information employees think may not be safe for management to hear. The consultant must understand what employees really think, not a filtered version, to make effective recommendations. Rapport and careful selection of questions are fundamental to gathering this important but sensitive information. Interviewers must know whether interviewees want credit for their remarks or anonymity. Interviewers also must carefully monitor potential bias in the remarks of interview subjects. The ability to evaluate information continually for relevancy, sufficiency, and plausibility is necessary for fact-finders to gather information that supports effective decision making and problem solving.

Effective fact-finders frequently close informational interviews by asking for any additional information the respondent would care to offer. Interviewers also may ask subjects if there are additional issues that should be explored. These questions and others give interviewees an opportunity to add information the fact-finder may not have known existed. This step can be as important to effective solutions as information previously identified as important.

The Employment Interview

Employment interview ■ An exchange of questions between an individual seeking employment and the individuals responsible for evaluating job applicants.

When you seek a job, the **employment interview** provides an opportunity to determine if the match between you and a particular job is right. Employment interviews allow you to demonstrate you are the best person for a job, while at the same time allowing an employer to give you an accurate description of the job. When you are the interviewer, you are responsible for evaluating the responses of potential employees while accurately describing the position and your organization.

When you are the interviewee, you want to provide information about yourself that demonstrates you would be a valuable and productive member of the organization. At the same time, the employment interview provides you with an opportunity to obtain specific information about the job and the organization in which you are interested. This information will be very important to help you make an informed decision on whether to accept or reject the job if it is offered to you.

The Performance Appraisal Interview

Performance appraisal interview ■ Exchange about job performance between a supervisor/manager and an individual contributor.

Once an individual is employed in an organization or becomes responsible for the supervision of others in the organization, the **performance appraisal interview** becomes one of the most important communication events that contribute to individual development and overall organizational performance. Although formats vary extensively with specific organizational appraisal systems, the general purpose of the performance appraisal interview is to exchange between a supervisor/manager and individual contributor information about the adequacy of performance and to establish needs for development.

Although often described as an anxiety-producing experience, the effective performance appraisal interview is essential to competency development. Individual contributors can learn about others' perceptions of their performance, and managers/supervisors can learn about needs individual contributors have to perform more effectively and develop additional expertise. Both managers and individual contributors report performance issues are difficult to discuss, often leading to general statements and faint or insincere utterances of praise. When we avoid needed feedback because of our apprehension or lack of communication skills, we limit individual development and contribute to overall organizational ineffectiveness.

The Complaint Interview

The **complaint interview** is of two general types, the grievance interview and the disciplinary interview. Both types deal with organizational problems, and the effectiveness of these exchanges contributes directly to problem-solving and organizational performance. The grievance interview is designed for individuals to express specific problems to those who have legitimate organizational responsibility for dealing with the issues related to the grievance. The grievance interview can deal with issues ranging from work dissatisfaction to various forms of inappropriate behaviors such as discrimination, racism, or harassment. Grievance interviews are both informal and formal. Formal grievance interviews usually follow organizationally specific published procedures. Although difficult in nature, grievance interviews can support productive problem solving, especially when they are conducted shortly after a problem becomes troublesome.

Complaint interview ■ Question-and-answer exchange dealing with grievances or disciplinary actions.

The disciplinary interview confronts a violation of organizational rules, norms, and performance expectations. Generally, the disciplinary interview occurs between a supervisor and an individual contributor and frequently follows organizational procedures for disciplinary action. The disciplinary interview provides specific remedies for stated problems. Again, when conducted effectively, the disciplinary exchange can improve individual performance and in many cases prevent more serious action such as suspension, demotion, or termination. It is easy to understand why effective communication is crucial in both the grievance and the disciplinary interviews.

The Counseling Interview

Occurring between supervisors and individual contributors and among peers, the **counseling interview** involves an individual seeking advice and assistance from another organizational member or members. Topics of the counseling exchange include work performance, work-related interpersonal conflicts, and personal problems. People seeking counseling are asking others to provide support and assistance

Counseling interview ■ Question-and-answer exchange with individuals seeking advice from other organizational members.

with problems. Empathetic listening is important during this exchange. Depending on the nature of the problem, it may be important to remember the limitations of your individual qualifications to offer advice. Referring individuals to professional assistance should be encouraged for certain types of problems. As we discuss in Chapter 9 on organizational conflict, it is important for individuals who must make changes to generate those changes themselves without other people imposing solutions. The counseling interview always is a balance between fixing problems and helping others generate their own commitment and solution strategies.

The Media Interview

Many communication professionals represent their organizations or departments with statements to the press. The public relations professional, for example, is responsible for answering press inquiries and for assisting others in the organization to provide needed information in a manner that reflects favorably on the organization. Many other organizational members, however, are called on to talk with the press about new product developments, services, union/management issues, crises,

Media interview ■ Question-and-answer exchange between members of the press and an organizational representative.

and a host of other topics. Generally speaking, **media interviews** are most successful when you can formulate a clear objective for your statements with a limited number of key assertions. Supporting data such as anecdotes, analogies, facts, or simple statistics enhance understanding. The media interview reflects on you individually but also is a powerful contributor to the overall reputation of the organization.

INCREASING INTERVIEW EFFECTIVENESS

Preparation is the key to effectiveness for all the types of interviews described. We are responsible for developing objectives for each interview, and formulating questions and statements that will assist us in achieving those objectives. This section of the chapter provides recommendations for increasing the effectiveness of one specific type of interview, the employment interview.

Effective employment interviewing involves preparation and practice. To be prepared for an employment interview, you must acquire knowledge about yourself, about the job, and about the employer in which you are interested. You will need the following information about an organization prior to your interview:

The typical duties and salary range for the job in which you are interested.
The background of the organization. (How long has it been in operation? What is the outlook for its future?)
The products or services the organization produces.
The vision and goals of the organization.
Any specific problems or issues that might be of concern to the organization.

You also should be prepared to provide concise but descriptive answers to a variety of questions about you. For a complete listing of the twenty-six most frequently asked employment interview questions, see the Workshop section at the end of this chapter. Practice is vital to successful interviewing. Role playing is a valuable method for improving your interviewing skills. Enlist your family, friends, or coworkers to help you practice. Avoid being overly self-critical, but spend some extra practice time working on any weaknesses you identify.

Not only is what you actually say during the course of an interview very important, but so are the way you look, act, and deal with the physical environment. Nonverbal factors are significant in making a positive first impression. Your first communication with an interviewer occurs through nonverbal channels. Before you say anything, your appearance, body movements, and management of the physical environment influence the interviewer's opinion of you. There are cultural differences and organizational differences in appropriate nonverbal behaviors and management of the physical environment during an interview. Your own self-awareness and your ability to accurately perceive the environment in which the interview takes place will assist you in presenting yourself effectively.

An employment interview is a dialogue between you and the interviewer. Your verbal responses give information about you to the interviewer. These responses, plus impressions gained from nonverbal behavior, influence decisions about your potential employment.

During the employment interview, you should do more than just answer questions. You should use this time to get answers to the questions you have concerning the job you are considering. For example, any of the following questions are appropriate during an employment interview:

What are the specific duties and responsibilities of the job?
Could you describe a typical day or week in this position?
What are the training and educational opportunities?
How have those previously in this job advanced in the organization?
What are the organization's future plans and goals?
What are some examples of the best results produced by people in this job?

It is the interviewer's responsibility to close the interview. You should be prepared to summarize how your skills, interests, experiences, and goals would contribute to the job. Also you should be prepared to provide references and usually a résumé.

PRESENTATIONS IN ORGANIZATIONS

Most jobs today, and more in the future, will require employees to give presentations. We are asked to describe to management the status of a project. We train other organizational members on the use of equipment or a process. We report conclusions from our team meeting. We present ideas using technologies linking us to others throughout the world. Organizations in the twenty-first century depend more than ever on individuals providing information through **presentational speaking**. Blue-collar workers and executives alike make presentations as part of their regular job responsibilities. Presentations are used in organizations to train, inform, critique plans of action, and persuade others to support decisions. Our ability to present material effectively contributes to our organizational credibility and influences the progress of our careers.

Presentational speaking ■
Speaking in organizations that is designed to educate, inform, or persuade.

Surveys of top management in major organizations consistently suggest employees are deficient in presentation skills. Companies annually spend thousands of dollars developing oral competencies. Fully competent organizational members face the reality they will be asked to give speeches and that others will evaluate their overall effectiveness and the quality of their efforts.

Many people dread presentations. Highly apprehensive individuals will avoid job responsibilities requiring talking before groups, and when that happens, both the individual and the organization lose. Excellent organizations need contributions from all members. When fear blocks an individual from contributing, the individual loses an ability to influence decisions, and the organization loses a valuable resource.

Once we become aware of the likelihood and importance of making presentations in organizations, we start thinking about how to develop our own competencies. We ask questions about what to expect in professional settings and how to evaluate our current skills. A discussion of general characteristics of organizational presentations will answer some of these questions.

Generally, organizational presentations occur at the work location with a topic chosen to fit a particular problem or issue. Topics are specific, and speakers are expected to adhere to announced agendas. Presenters are expected to respect time constraints while effectively covering important and often complex details. Unlike many public speaking settings, the audience is usually known to the speaker and may be composed of peers, employees, and managers. In other words, the speaker will probably be involved in a continuing working relationship with members of the audience. Furthermore, most audience members will attend presentations as part of their job requirements.

Organizational presentations are characterized by a high degree of audience involvement. The presenter is frequently interrupted with questions and at times challenged on positions or technical information. Both the audience and the presenter accept responsibility for information exchange. Most effective organizational presenters are skilled at both clear and concise presentation of information and the handling of audience interaction.

The audience holds the presenter responsible for preparation and topic expertise. In fact, the overall organizational credibility of an individual can be adversely affected if he or she does not adequately prepare or presents information not credible to the audience.

Organizational presentations are usually more detailed than presentations designed for public settings. Organizational presentations frequently use computer-assisted (visual and audio) supporting materials and audience handouts. Those skilled in organizational presentations become familiar and comfortable with a variety of technologies important for enhancing understanding and retention of information. Many organizations, however, limit the advanced use of some presentation technologies, considering the time spent in presentation development wasted compared to presentations providing simple, but needed, information.

Finally, most organizational presenters must respond to questions and answers during and following presentations. The ability to respond to questions influences the credibility of the information transmitted and may contribute as much as the formal presentation to overall effectiveness. As Nancy Winslow begins to prepare for her presentation to the manufacturing staff, she considers what information they currently have about the skill level of assembly workers. She prepares visuals to detail her budget. She considers gathering data to compare training costs to the costs of hiring new, more skillful employees. In addition, she thinks about how she can answer managers who do not believe that training skill-deficient employees will meet the organization's needs.

Nancy currently works with most of the managers to whom she will make the presentation. She knows her credibility will be on the line because she is advocating a position at least two powerful members of the group oppose. How would you advise Nancy to prepare? Should she attempt to persuade the group to her position or simply make them aware of all of their options? What responsibility does she have to the assembly workers? What responsibility does she have to herself? The next several sections of this chapter describe the types of presentation options available to Nancy and make specific recommendations for increasing her effectiveness.

TYPES OF ORGANIZATIONAL PRESENTATIONS

Organizational presentations can be divided into three broad types: training/educational, informational, and persuasive. Training or educational presentations literally teach others information relevant to the organization. Informational presentations transmit knowledge from one organizational member or unit to another, and persuasive presentations are aimed at helping the organization solve problems or make decisions. Many presentations will be combinations of all three, requiring competent organizational presenters to develop skills in educating, informing, and persuading.

Training/Educational Presentations

Training/educational presentations literally teach organizational members their jobs. Groups of people are trained in new processes, interpersonal relations, communication skills, or new technologies. Presentations are designed to help others use the information the presenter has learned and is responsible for transmitting to others.

Training/educational presentations ■ Presentations that literally teach organizational members their jobs. Instructions and training are common examples.

Giving instructions is perhaps the most common form of educational presentation. In either a group or an individual setting, the presenter is responsible for organizing information clearly and concisely to enable others to meet the expectations of an assignment or task. Giving instructions may be the most frequent of all educational presentations. When presented effectively, instructions can contribute to the overall productivity of the organization. Instructions failing to convey effective information cost organizations money in mistakes, poor-quality decisions, employee frustration, and in a variety of other, less obvious ways.

Educational presentations also include technical training, basic skills training, interpersonal development and management training, and introductions of new concepts or technologies. These presentations are typically several hours in length and include diverse types of audience participation. Educational presentations train or introduce new concepts requiring competency in holding people's attention over a period of time while providing material in enough detail to generate understanding. Educational presentations are specific career responsibilities in a variety of jobs (see Chapter 12 for a more complete description) and temporary responsibilities for those with special expertise. As your educational experiences in your school will almost certainly confirm, some presenters are better than others in generating understanding. Think about a time when you were part of an effective training program. What did your instructor do well? How might you use your observations to build your skills? Now think of a time when you were not pleased with the results of your training. What made the difference? Can your observations help you understand what to avoid?

Informational Presentations

Information is the lifeblood of organizations. Problems surface through information exchanges, and problem solving occurs as individuals and organizations seek to discover information alternatives on which to base decisions. Earlier we discussed the importance of relevant, sufficient, and plausible information for problem solving and decision making. Next we provide a description of the role **informational presentations** play in generating information.

Informational presentations ■ Presentations focused on providing the most current information available. Common examples are management briefings, checkpoint meetings, and technical reports.

Informational presentations occur in a variety of organizational settings. Managers brief their employees on organizational policy. Individual contributors brief management on the status of a work project. A project team may review for management the technical problems associated with product design. Although similar to educational presentations, informational presentations are focused on providing the most current information available, as opposed to teaching the audience new information. Unlike educational presentations, which frequently assume the audience has minimal familiarity with the topic, most informational presentations assume a reasonable degree of subject familiarity by the audience. In fact, many organizational presentations that are primarily of an informational nature will begin from the point of the last information exchange rather than the beginning of the project or issue. A common example of this type of informational presentation is the checkpoint meeting, in which an individual or team will report on the status of a project based on progress from the last checkpoint. Although introductions in these presentations frequently summarize the project, little attention is paid to details previously communicated.

Management teams request informational presentations to solve problems and make decisions. Nancy Winslow is asked to bring information to the manufacturing management staff of her organization. They need to make important decisions about assembly-line workers. She considers expanding their request to attempt to persuade them to her point of view, yet her basic assignment is to inform them with relevant, sufficient, and plausible information.

Persuasive Presentations

If Nancy Winslow decides to attempt to influence the decision of the manufacturing staff, she will be engaged in persuasive communication. She will seek to influence the attitudes and beliefs of others by the arguments she makes. She will attempt to get manufacturing managers to interpret her data as she does and support her recommended training plan. Organizational members frequently are requested to make recommendations. In a very basic sense, recommending a course of action is a persuasive process.

Persuasive presentations ■ Presentations that attempt to influence the problem solving or decision making of the organization. Common examples are sales presentations, action recommendations, and resource requests.

Persuasive presentations are made to request resources, gain approval of an idea, sell a product or process, convince others to make changes, gain support for a course of action, and critique the efforts of others. Persuasive presentations focus on getting an audience to adopt the point of view of the presenter based on relevant, plausible, and sufficient arguments. These presentations guide the audience to the conclusions the presenter favors. They ask for support, for business, or for change and make a variety of other requests.

Persuasive presentations in organizations are usually task-related and contain more factual support than is common in other settings. Essentially, persuasive presentations ask for a decision from the audience that supports the intentions of the presenter. Effective presenters realize for a persuasive presentation to be successful, they must not only understand what information their audience is likely to have on the topic but also consider relevant attitudes and issues. Nancy Winslow, for example, is aware that two powerful managers generally oppose training and prefer to replace deficient workers. This awareness will drive her strategies if she decides to try to persuade the manufacturing staff. If that opposition were not present, her presentation might be organized very differently. Given her knowledge of the manufacturing managers, what advice would you give Nancy? Can she afford to ignore these two managers? Should she state her opinion but make no real effort to change their minds? What would you do if you were Nancy?

There are ethical implications in Nancy's concerns. She is concerned about the assembly workers. She can choose information for her presentation that primarily supports her training request, or she could let the managers develop their own data on replacement costs. She has a number of other options based on her evaluation of what is right and wrong in this context. Regardless of what she chooses, Nancy is engaged in making decisions that will affect her credibility with the manufacturing management staff.

INCREASING PRESENTATION EFFECTIVENESS

Thus far, we have discussed the importance of presentational speaking in organizations and described a variety of common organizational presentations. Now we identify ways in which individual competencies can be developed for presentational speaking.

Increasing Credibility

Although credibility evaluations rest with audiences, we can enhance the likelihood of a positive response if we consciously think about how to describe ourselves, our intentions, and our concerns. We can begin by considering what our initial credibility is likely to be with a particular group. What do they know about our background? How much have we interacted before? What were the results of previous exchanges? If our task competence or subject expertise is unknown to an audience, we may want to begin by briefly describing our training or experience. If our expertise is known but our position controversial, we may want to cite research and stress the competence of our sources. In addition, we can avoid needlessly calling attention to our inadequacies.

In many organizational settings, questions and challenges to presenters are common and appropriate for decision making. We can usually increase our credibility by stressing our fairness, demonstrating we have examined various alternatives, not just the ones we recommend. We can stress our concern for enduring values such as quality, creativity, or teamwork. We can stress our similarity with an audience in terms of beliefs, attitudes, values, and goals. We can point to our long-term consistency and demonstrate our concern for others through nondefensive behaviors during questioning and challenges. In general, we can increase our credibility by demonstrating we support the welfare of the group or organization, not just our own concerns. Finally, we are more likely to be perceived as credible if we present a positive orientation to the situation and are assertive and generally enthusiastic.

Audience and Context Analysis

When thinking about establishing personal credibility, we began to think specifically about our audience and the context or circumstances of our presentation. Earlier, we described effective communication as resulting from meanings being understood among people as accurately as possible. This base of interpersonal communication obviously remains true for the presentation. How can we ensure we best represent the results of our problem-solving or work accomplishments to those who have a need to know? Who are our potential audiences, and what do we want them to do? Effective presentations reflect good **audience analysis**.

Audience analysis ■ Assessment of what receivers are interested in, what they know, what their attitudes and values are, what they want to know, what the speaker's probable credibility is, and what format will be most effective.

At times, the audience will be a management team who will grant final authority or resources to implement the proposed solution. They must be convinced by our presentations of what we expect to achieve by our solutions or particular courses of action. At other times, we will announce decisions to people who are affected by them. In this case, the decision implementation and how it affects the receiver may be more important than any explanation of our decision process.

Preparation of Material

After questions about the potential audience have been satisfactorily answered, we can proceed to the selection of material for presentation. Selection of material depends on audience analysis and the assignment at hand. We select material with relevancy, sufficiency, and plausibility criteria. These criteria must be met for us individually before we can make projections about how they can be met for our expected audiences. Once material has been selected, we begin the organizing process. Material can be organized in a variety of formats.

After decisions are made about the material to be included and the organizational sequence, introductions and conclusions should be developed. Introductions attract audience attention, establish credibility for the presenter or presenters, and clarify the purpose of the presentation. As with all other presentational decisions, introductions are most effective when careful consideration is given to the needs and interests of the audience. It is difficult to capture attention if the introduction to a presentation is poorly planned.

Conclusions, particularly crucial to the success of presentations, summarize the key elements in the presentation and restate the call for needed action on the part of audience members. Effective conclusions leave the audience with a short and concrete summary of what the presenter considers most important to know. Conclusions are last impressions and influential in setting the tone for what happens next. Sometimes conclusions return to introductions to emphasize how the presentation has met the goals established then. At other times, the conclusion focuses on needed action from the audience and solicits questions to gain more direct involvement.

Preparation for Presenting

Preparation increases effectiveness and helps us manage most presentational situations. Personal preparation for presenting includes rehearsing the speech, working with visual aids, preparing notes, and timing the presentation. In addition, it is a good idea to check specific details in the room scheduled for your presentation and to arrive early to confirm arrangements. Personal preparation also includes selecting clothing appropriate for the occasion and comfortable for the presenter.

Many organizational presentations are prepared and presented by teams or groups of individuals. Many of you may have worked on a group project for which certain team members did not adhere to their allotted presentation time, making life miserable for other presenters. Groups need to rehearse and time presentations. In addition, team presentations are most effective when all team members have tightly coordinated information so no one unnecessarily repeats information.

Handling Participation

Effective presenters anticipate types of questions from their audience. They not only prepare the formal presentation but also practice answers to expected questions or challenges. Effective presenters learn to analyze questions and ask for necessary clarification before responding. If a group is relatively large, repeating a question so that all can hear increases the perception the speaker is interested in the audience and in answering the questions.

Effective presenters respond to all audience members and control domination attempts from one or two individuals. Effective presenters also ask the audience for ideas or critiques. At times, skilled presenters have questions for their audience, which increases ownership of a decision or position. Perhaps most important, effective presenters maintain supportive, nondefensive behaviors encouraging a sense of "we," or belonging with the audience. This sense of "we" is especially important for ongoing organizational relationships.

COMMUNICATIONS TECHNOLOGY IN ORGANIZATIONS

Nowhere will our communication competencies be more challenged than by the increasing use of information and communications technologies (ICTs) in all types of organizations. None of us will participate in organizations of today and tomorrow without the use of technology. Most of us are familiar with voice and text messaging, personal digital assistants, all types of phones with multimedia capabilities, fax machines, computer word processing, e-mail, and the Internet. Fewer of us are regular users of teleconferencing, high-definition conferencing, desktop publishing, spreadsheets, graphics, GDSS, and high-powered statistical and data manipulation programs. Yet, for all of us these technologies and more will be normal and required ways of participating in organizational life. Moreover, we will be required to continually learn and relearn sophisticated communications technologies to perform the basic functions of our jobs. We also will be required to determine which technologies are most appropriate for all types of content exchanges. We are in a connected age which brings both positives and negatives for organizational functioning.

Synchronous settings ■ Technology use enabling two-way communication.

Asynchronous settings ■ Technology use enabling one-way communication.

Media richness theory ■ Media richness describes a medium's capacity for feedback, the number of cues and channels available, language variety, and the focus on the recipient.

The extensive connectivity characteristic of the work world of today and tomorrow facilitates communication and coordination of work in both synchronous and asynchronous settings. **Synchronous settings** use technologies which permit simultaneous two-way communication. **Asynchronous settings** use technologies which enable one-way communication. Technologies, of course, can be both. The telephone is synchronous when we talk with another. The telephone is asynchronous when we leave a message. The same is true for a variety of computer applications ranging from e-mail (generally asynchronous) to blogs and chat applications, which often are synchronous. The media richness of various technologies also influences choice and effectiveness in communication and work settings. Richard Daft and Robert Lengel (1984, 1987) described **media richness** as the medium's capacity for feedback, the number of cues and channels available, language variety, and focus on the receiver. Generally speaking, richer mediums have more capacity for feedback, more cues and channels available, more language variety, and more focus on receivers. Less rich mediums are low or completely lacking in immediate feedback, limit the number of cues and channels available, have limited language variety, and are more sender- than receiver-focused. The original work of Daft and Lengel characterized the richest of mediums as face-to-face communication, with unaddressed documents such as bulk mail and posters as the leanest of mediums. Again, based on early work in media richness theory, it is assumed more complex and ambiguous problems are best addressed with rich media while routine information can be effectively communicated through lean media. Most of us can identify with these descriptions. When we communicate directly with others (synchronous settings), we realize how much we depend on nonverbal as well as verbal exchanges. Most of us can recall a time when an e-mail (asynchronous setting) has left us confused because we cannot assess the tone of the message.

The issues of organizational technology use are increasingly complex. Technology costs influence the selection of the combinations of technologies available to a given organization. Privacy and security issues are of increasing concern. With technologies available to employees other than in formal work settings and employees often expected to stay in contact in what were previously off-work hours, the blurring of personal and professional use of organizationally-owned technologies requires new policies and values for technology use.

Of particular concern is the effective use of technologies for decision making and problem solving. Ronald Rice and Urs Gattiker (2001) suggested ICTs have the potential to resolve problems of traditional bureaucracies by reducing organizational complexity and hierarchical structures and facilitating a better sense of member opinions through increasing participation and democratic interaction. Janet Fulk and Lori Collins-Jarvis (2001) described new and highly sophisticated electronic meeting support widely available in organizations. They identified "three generic categories of meeting technologies": teleconferencing, computer conferencing, and group support systems (GSSs). Teleconferencing supports meetings with audio and video "real-time" interaction among participants. Computer conferencing supports contributions to shared files and the text-based "real-time" interaction. Finally group support systems assist computer conferencing and teleconferencing with decision support tools, a variety of graphics, and information and meeting management tools. These technologies permit both synchronous and asynchronous work among individuals in diverse time zones and locations.

Marshall Scott Poole and Iftekhar Ahmed (2008) described the diverse range of group decision support systems:

> [GDSS] combines communication, computer, and decision technologies to support group decision making, problem solving, and subsequent activities. Communication technologies incorporated into GDSSs include electronic messaging and chat, teleconferencing, document management, calendaring, wikis, and blogs. Computer technologies include portals, service-oriented architectures, and Web-authoring tools. Decision support technologies include agenda setting, decision modeling methods (such as risk analysis or the Analytic Hierarchy Procedure), structured group methods (such as stakeholder analysis or the Nominal Group Technique), and rules for directing group discussions (such as the Parliamentary Procedure)." (p. 550)

Poole and Ahmed continued with findings from more than 50 studies comparing GDSS groups with face-to-face (FTF) groups not using GDSS:

> In terms of group outcomes, GDSS groups attain higher levels of group effectiveness than do FTF groups, when effectiveness is measured in terms of decision quality, quantity of ideas generated and considered, quality of ideas, confidence in the decision, depth of evaluation, and commitment to results. On the other hand, GDSS groups are less efficient than FTF groups in terms of time to decision and ease of decision making but more efficient on tasks that could be done in parallel (such as idea generation) or complex decision-making tasks (such as multicriteria decision analysis). Members of GDSS groups are less satisfied with their decision and decision process than are members of FTF groups. Members often reported that the GDSSs were difficult to use. Finally, GDSS groups have more trouble coming to a consensus and face more conflict than do FTF groups. (p. 554)

Keri Stephens (2007) proposed a model to facilitate the understanding of successive use of ICTs for task completion. She suggested influences for technology selection and successive use of additional technologies included the task, the traits of various media, social influences, individual differences, and organizational influences. Stephens's work underscores the reality that we will use multiple technologies for most work assignments and we continually will be making individual and organizationally directed decisions about which technologies will be most effective and how they will influence our work performance.

The potential to work in geographically diverse teams or telecommute exists in many organizations today. Communicating by e-mail, in chat rooms, on blogs, with threaded discussions, and through teleconference unites people across not only miles but also cultures and languages. The time to contemplate responses is shortened as technology collapses the time float generated when messages are sent by land or air transportation. In addition, technology permits the examination of a volume of information unknown to all previous members of the workforce.

Face-to-face communication potentially can be reduced with increased use of e-mail and other computer applications. However, the ease of electronic communication has been known to contribute to ill-conceived messages hastily developed and transmitted. Competent communicators using electronic channels will need to learn to monitor their responses, deciding wisely when more reflection or the reaction of face-to-face interaction is needed. Building trust for effective working relationships will be increasingly important. Online trust will be necessary for groups to work together and for individual and group performance to be fairly evaluated. With the new technologies we do not have to work the same hours as those with whom we interact, or even work in traditional offices. More of us will work from our homes than at any period since the Industrial Revolution. Homes routinely will be equipped with wireless modem connections, fax machines, and portable teleconferencing units. All forms of wireless communications will increase. We will engage in gathering information and making decisions with people we know less well while working with media that both distance us from others and bring us in more immediate contact across space and time.

Preparation for Communications Technology

Perhaps the most important preparation for our rapidly changing technological environments is an attitudinal preparation, the understanding that we may never completely master the technologies we use and that change will bring about the necessity for lifelong learning. The good news is research consistently demonstrates that, as we go through our careers, we are capable of new learning and increased competencies with the machines of today and those projected for the future.

In addition to accepting as normal that our learning does not stop with formal education but is an ongoing part of our organizational lives, we can prepare for communications technology by availing ourselves of opportunities to experience as many diverse applications of technologies as are readily available. Most schools and public libraries have a variety of computer as well as teleconferencing capabilities. In addition, most work organizations and more in the future will provide basic training for a variety of specific applications. It is important when we think about preparing for participation in the organizations of the future to consider how we can develop competencies in communications technology that will support the human communication competencies that we continue to develop.

CHAPTER HIGHLIGHTS

Decision making is the process for choosing from among several alternatives, and **problem solving** is a multistage process for moving an issue, situation, or state from an undesirable to a more desirable condition. Groups make decisions and solve problems through a variety of methods including **leader mandate, majority rule, powerful-minority** influence, and **consensus**. Organizational culture, the problem itself, technical competencies, and communication competencies all influence decision-making and problem-solving processes.

Problem-solving processes include the **Standard Agenda, brainstorming,** and a variety of **experientially based processes**. Decision-making and problem-solving effectiveness can be increased by developing fact-finding and evaluation skills.

Participating in organizations requires competencies in interviewing, presenting, and using a variety of communications technologies. The **informational interview, employment interview, performance appraisal interview, complaint interview, counseling interview,** and media interview are some of the major types of organizational interviews. Most jobs today, and more in the future, will require employees to give presentations. Organizational presentations can be divided into three broad types: **training/ educational**, **informational**, and **persuasive**. Nowhere will our communication competencies be more challenged than by the increasing use of information and communications technologies (ICTs) in all types of organizations. Technology will change the way we work in time, geography, culture, location, and many other ways. Communication competencies with technology will support human communication competencies. ■

WORKSHOP

1. You have been studying a variety of approaches to decision making and problem solving. You will now be asked to assume the position of training manager for Food Service Industries. As training manager you are responsible for making a series of routine business decisions. You return from your annual vacation and find a number of decision items in your e-mail. For each of the e-mail items in The Training Manager for Food Service Industries E-Mail Exercise, describe what you would do and what criteria you use for each decision. Small groups or the class as a whole will compare and discuss responses.

2. To illustrate similarities and differences in decision-making and problem-solving approaches among class members, select a current problem familiar to class members. (Cases and item 1 also are appropriate for this activity.) Divide the entire class into groups of six members each. Each group will appoint one member to be a facilitator. All groups need flip-chart paper and markers or other available technology options. Each group will have fifteen minutes to find possible solutions for the problem. (All solutions are taken, even if other group members disagree.) At the end of fifteen minutes each group will spend five minutes choosing their top three solutions (through consensus or majority vote). The top three solutions will be recorded and posted for the entire class to review. Each group facilitator reads the top three to the entire class. The class then goes "shopping" for ten minutes. Shopping is simply walking around the room and recording any solution that individual group members believe is especially productive. Groups again convene for twenty minutes. Group members begin by adding from shopping any solutions they want discussed. Within the allotted twenty minutes each group will rank their top two solutions one and two. Facilitators again record these decisions, post the findings, and report to the entire class. Discussion follows about the process and the similarities and differences in solutions.

3. The following are among the most frequently asked questions during employment interviews. Either individually or in role-playing teams, develop and practice answers to these questions. Take turns playing the role of the interviewer and interviewee.
   a. Tell me about yourself.
   b. Describe yourself.
   c. Have you done this type of work before?
   d. Why do you want to work here?
   e. Why are you interested in this job/working for this organization?
   f. What are your salary requirements?
   g. Why would you be better for this job than anyone else?
   h. What are your major strengths?
   i. What are your major weaknesses?
   j. What are your immediate employment goals?
   k. What are your long-term employment goals?
   l. What kinds of machines/technology can you use?
   m. How did you get along with your coworkers, supervisor, clients, or customers in your last job?
   n. What kind of people do you work with best?
   o. What kind of work environment do you prefer?
   p. How do you feel about pressure, deadlines, travel, relocating, overtime, or weekend work?
   q. What makes you lose your temper?
   r. What do you like to do in your spare time?
   s. What would you like to accomplish if you were hired for this job?
   t. What are the toughest problems you have faced, and how did you handle them?
   u. What kinds of decisions are most difficult for you?
   v. What have you learned from your previous experiences?

w. Describe a specific problem you have handled well. Describe an example of a work goal achieved.

x. Describe an example of how you have handled a difficult situation. Describe an example of a situation that you did not handle well. What have you learned from that experience?

y. What do you want to know about this organization?

z. Why should we hire you?

The Training Manager of Food Service Industries E-Mail Exercise

Instructions: You have been away on your annual vacation. On your return, the following items have been printed from your e-mail and marked with a priority stamp by your assistant. For each item, describe what you would do next. Can you make an immediate decision? What additional information do you need? Are you going to involve other people? Describe your criteria for each decision.

Item 1

To: YOUR NAME, Training Manager for Food Service Industries
From: Mike Barnes, Vice President of Major Accounts

I have just received two complaints about one of our newest salespersons. Topco Foods and Bestway both said Jim Johnson was rude and did not effectively represent our product line. I thought he had just been in one of your training sessions. How would you evaluate his performance? Please respond immediately.

Item 2

To: YOUR NAME, Training Manager for Food Service Industries
From: Jane Connors, Chair, Community Service Speakers Bureau, Chamber of Commerce

We know your company is an active and vital member of this community. As chair of the Speakers Bureau for our Community Outreach program, I would like to invite you to give a motivational talk on leadership at our September banquet. Mike Barnes of your company recommended you and felt you were just the person to do the job. Our program goes to press next week, so we need your response as soon as possible.

Item 3

To: All Department Heads
From: Finance

Because of a downturn in our profit projections for the next quarter, each department is being asked to reduce its fourth-quarter budget by 2 percent. Because each department's spending authority is established through finance, we need a list of those items or events you want to eliminate.

Thank you very much for your cooperation in this matter. This list should be in our office no later than Friday.

Item 4

To: YOUR NAME
From: Jerry Masters, Head of Manufacturing Services

I have a problem and know you can help. We have hired six new people for our new manufacturing process group.

We had not budgeted any training courses for the six because we did not anticipate starting the group before the first of next year. Company policy requires me to schedule them for new employee orientation, but I don't have the training funds available to reimburse your department.

Please advise how I should handle this situation.

Item 5

Dear YOUR NAME,

I was in your June 4th class on managing poor performance. I tried everything you said and now am really in a mess. In fact, the employee in question has gone to my manager and made a formal complaint.

I just want you to know that I told my manager it was all your fault and they should really look at what people are taught in those supervision classes.

Sincerely,
John Price

TIPS FOR EFFECTIVE COMMUNICATION

1. Prepare a short training presentation. Make a video of the presentation, critique yourself, and ask a knowledgeable professional to provide feedback.
2. Prepare answers to several questions frequently asked during employment interviews. Make a video of your interview responses, critique yourself, and ask a knowledgeable professional to provide feedback.
3. Learn a specific computer program for group decision making. Using the technology, work with others to solve a problem or make a decision.
4. Develop a personal description of your skills that you can use to establish your credibility for an interview or for a presentation.
5. Volunteer to lead a brainstorming group.
6. Volunteer to lead a group in using the Standard Agenda to address a specific problem.
7. Use technology to research a topic of interest with which you have limited familiarity. Evaluate the relevancy, plausibility, and sufficiency of the information you identify.
8. Identify a decision you made and then did not implement. What can you learn from this decision?
9. Identify a decision you made, implemented, and found satisfying. What can you learn from this decision?
10. Identify a decision you made, implemented, and found dissatisfying. What can you learn from this decision? ■

REFERENCES AND SUGGESTED READINGS

Baird, J. E. Jr. 1981. *Speaking for results: Communication by objectives.* New York: Harper and Row.

Baird, J. E. Jr. 1982. *Positive personnel practices, quality circles leader's manual.* Prospect Heights, IL: Waveland.

Bonito, J., M. DeCamp, and E. Ruppel. 2008. The process of information sharing in small groups: Application of a local model. *Communication Monographs* 75: 136–157.

Cyert, R. M., and J. G. March. 1963. *A behavioral theory of the firm.* Englewood Cliffs, NJ: Prentice Hall.

Daft, R. L. and R. H. Lengel. 1984. Information richness: A new approach to managerial behavior and organizational design. In *Research in organizational behavior 6*, eds. L. L. Cummings and B. M. Staw, 191–233. Homewood, IL: JAI Press.

Daft, R. L., and R. H. Lengel. 1987. Message equivocality, media selection, and manager performance: Implications for information systems. *MIS Quarterly*, September, 355–366.

Dewey, J. 1910. *How we think.* Boston: Heath.

Fisher, B. A. 1980. *Small group decision making*, 2nd ed. New York: McGraw-Hill.

Fulk, J., and L. Collins-Jarvis. 2001. Wired meetings: Technological mediation of organizational gatherings. In *The new handbook of organizational communication: Advances in theory, research, and methods*, eds. F. Jablin and L. Putnam, 624–663. Thousand Oaks, CA: Sage.

Gouran, D. S. 1979. *Making decisions in groups: Choices and consequences.* Glenview, IL: Scott, Foresman.

Hirokawa, R. 1988. Group communication and decision-making performance: A continued test of the functional perspective. *Human Communication Research* 14(4): 487–515.

Hirokawa, R., and K. Rost. 1992. Effective group decision making in organizations. *Management Communication Quarterly* 5: 267–288.

Kahn, R., and C. Cannell. 1964. *The dynamics of interviewing.* New York: Wiley.

Kuhn, T., and M. Jackson. 2008. Accomplishing knowledge: A framework for investigating knowing in organizations. *Management Communication Quarterly* 21: 454–485.

Lumsden, G., and D. Lumsden. 1993. *Communicating in groups and teams.* Belmont, CA: Wadsworth.

Morrison, E., and F. Milliken. 2000. Organizational silence: A barrier to change and development in a pluralistic world. *The Academy of Management Review* 25(4): 706–725.

Nutt, P. 1999. Surprising but true: Half the decisions in organizations fail. *Academy of Management Executive* 13(4): 75–90.

Poole, M. S., and I. Ahmed. 2008. Group decision support systems. In *21st century communication: A reference handbook*, ed. W. Eadie, 550–557. Thousand Oaks, CA: Sage.

Rice, R., and U. Gattiker. 2001. New media and organizational structuring. In *The new handbook of or-*

ganizational communication: Advances in theory, research, and methods, eds. F. Jablin and L. Putnam, 544–581. Thousand Oaks, CA: Sage.

Simon, H. 1960. The new science of management decision. New York: Harper and Row.

Stephens, K. 2007. The successive use of information and communication technologies at work. Communication Theory 17: 486–507.

Tompkins, P., and G. Cheney. 1983. Account analysis of organizations: Decision making and identifica-

tion. In Communication and organizations: An interpretive approach, eds. L. Putnam and M. Pacanowsky, 123–146. Beverly Hills, CA: Sage.

Young, K. S., J. T. Wood, G. M. Phillips, and D. J. Pedersen. 2001. Group discussion: A practical guide to participation and leadership, 3rd ed. Prospect Heights, IL: Waveland. ■

Organizational Conflict
Communicating for Effectiveness

DEVELOPING COMPETENCIES THROUGH ...

KNOWLEDGE
Defining and describing organizational conflict
Identifying conflict episodes
Describing contexts for conflict
Describing causes for conflict

SENSITIVITY
Understanding individual conflict styles and strategic objectives
Understanding group conflict approaches
Distinguishing between productive and counterproductive conflicts
Understanding how framing and sensemaking influence conflict
Identifying supportive communication climates
Understanding emotion and conflict
Understanding ethical abuses during conflict

SKILLS
Assessing communication tactics used during conflict
Developing a problem-solving process for conflict
Practicing analysis capabilities

VALUES
Developing personal awareness for conflict
Understanding individual responsibilities for productive conflict
Clarifying ethical conflict behaviors

◣ THE MIDDLESEX INSURANCE COMPANY CASE

John Fellows was excited to be named manager of the highly respected claims division for a major Midwestern insurance company. John's experience in the insurance business was varied, and at age thirty-three he had just completed extensive training on a new computer system the company hoped would eventually reduce escalating overhead costs. John was aware at least two members of his new department had applied for the job he was assuming, and he believed the company had placed him in the position partly to avoid making a choice between two competent peers.

John's initial month in the claims office of Middlesex was productive, confirming what he had been told about the competence of department personnel. Even the former applicants for his job, Joan and Tom, were cooperative and helpful. As a result of these early successes, John decided to move forward quickly with a plan to train personnel and install a new computer system.

Following his staff meeting announcement of training schedules for all employees, John was surprised and somewhat irritated when Joan complained he was moving too quickly before understanding department procedures. John decided Joan probably had not really accepted his promotion into the job she wanted. This feeling seemed to be confirmed when Tom came to John and suggested there was reason to be concerned about the morale of the department with all the upcoming changes. Tom even hinted three key people were considering asking for transfers. Although Tom did not say so, John was sure Joan was at the bottom of the trouble.

John decided to confront Joan with her lack of support for this major corporate project. Joan became defensive and denied she was resisting the change: in fact, she claimed John's misunderstanding of her concerns proved her point. To Joan, John simply was moving too fast and would create problems in systems about which he knew very little. John left the encounter wondering if maybe he had made a mistake about Joan, about Tom, or about his decision. ■

INTRODUCTION

Are John and Joan engaged in organizational conflict, or is it a personal problem? Is the new computer system the issue? Is the issue John's approach? How is Tom involved? More important, what would you do if you were John, Joan, or Tom?

As a new manager, John faces a real test of his communication competency. What John decides will affect Joan, the entire department, and possibly his future career. How would you help John decide? What does he need to understand to be an effective manager of the claims division?

Although we may not have had John and Joan's specific problem, most of us have been involved in numerous conflicts and have been faced, as John is, with important decisions. Students have conflicts with teachers over grades. Families argue about issues of responsibility or money. Coworkers have negative feelings when particular individuals carry more of the workload than others. All are examples of conflicts that test our understanding and abilities.

It is important before you read further to think specifically about some of the conflicts that have been meaningful to you. What were the issues? Who was involved? What happened? For most of us it is easier to decide what John should do in the claims division than to make decisions when we are directly involved. Yet as John and Joan discovered, conflict is an inevitable part of our daily interactions.

Certainly, if we are to be competent organizational communicators, we will be confronted with the need to solve problems effectively during conflict. To develop communication competencies for conflict, it is necessary to understand what conflict is, how it works, what role it plays in organizational functioning, and finally how individuals within organizations influence conflict outcomes.

This chapter is designed to contribute to *knowledge* by defining the concept of conflict, describing its various contexts and causes, and developing an analysis framework for understanding its process. Knowledge competencies will in turn help develop analysis skills for specific situations. We develop *sensitivity* competencies by identifying individual and group predispositions and style preferences for conflict, by understanding how framing and sensemaking influence conflict, by becoming familiar with strategies and tactics commonly used in conflicts, and by describing emotion during conflict. Sensitivity competencies influence the use of verbal and problem-solving process *skills* appropriate for each individual and the conflict at hand. We develop *value* competencies by exploring productive consequences of conflict, identifying supportive climates for conflict, and clarifying ethical conflict behaviors. As would be expected, value competencies are reflected in the use of ethical and supportive skills during conflict.

Finally, we apply all four competencies—knowledge, sensitivity, skills, and values—to the development of a problem-solving process for conflict and to competency practice through case analysis.

DEFINING AND DESCRIBING CONFLICT PROCESSES

Defining Conflict

Conflict can be described as a process that occurs when individuals, small groups, or organizations perceive or experience frustration in attaining goals and addressing concerns. At times this frustration is the result of a struggle over different values or scarce rewards, whereas other times the central issue is the status or power of involved individuals. Regardless of the reasons, for all conflict participants the process includes perceptions, emotions, behaviors, and outcomes.

> Conflict ■ Process that occurs when individuals, small groups, or organizations perceive or experience frustration in attaining goals and addressing concerns.

Conflict Contexts

Conflict can occur in any organizational setting in which there are two or more competing responses to a single event. In other words, conflict can occur in any context: intrapersonal, interpersonal, small-group, intergroup, or organization-wide or between the organization and its broader environment.

The **conflict context** influences the conflict symptoms, behaviors, and outcomes. Intrapersonal conflict, for example, is not readily observable through overt behaviors; an individual experiencing internal conflict may not discuss the problem. Yet he or she may be observed to be under pressure or generally in a bad mood. These observations are indirect symptoms of the intrapersonal conflict. When John begins to wonder about his assumptions regarding Tom and Joan and to doubt his decision about the computer system, he may begin to experience intrapersonal conflict common to us all when our perceptions differ from those around us and when our judgments are called into question. Furthermore, because John is the manager, it will be difficult for him to take a wait-and-see attitude while letting others resolve the problem.

> Conflict context ■ Any organizational setting in which there are two or more competing responses to a single event or circumstance.

The conflict between John and Joan is a good example of the interpersonal context for organizational conflict. John is excited about his job and the opportunity to put into practice his training on the new system. Although he can understand Joan wanted his job, he isn't prepared for her resistance to change. He believes she is frustrated because she was not promoted and thus discounts her concerns about his lack of understanding of the department. He also links Tom's warning about people leaving the claims area to an attempt by Joan to undermine his efforts. Joan, on the other hand, sees John as another example of a powerful manager moving too quickly without sufficient background. In addition, neither really trusts the other's motives. Chances are what happens next between John and Joan not only will affect their relationship but also will influence productivity throughout the department.

As in the interpersonal setting, conflict in the small-group context can be observed through behaviors during the conflict and by the conflict's lasting effects. The productive or destructive outcomes of conflict often are evidenced in the amount of group cohesion and productivity a team exhibits long after the actual conflict has ended. An example comes from a large West Coast electronics firm where four of ten senior research scientists left the organization within a period of fourteen months. The ten scientists had been together on a successful project for more than six years when two in the group disagreed with the direction a new product was to take. The two refused to negotiate a settlement and ordered their two principal assistants to pursue a line of research not supported by other team members. The remainder of the team approached project management with the problem and asked for resolution. Management refused to intervene, fearing alienation of the entire group if forced to take sides. Over a period of weeks, a once-productive team ceased to work together, and four key members began to look for new employment. The technical merits of the disagreement were never resolved, and in reality the team ceased to exist.

The contexts for organizational conflict are not limited, however, to interpersonal or small-group exchanges. Two separate organizational units may conflict over priorities in providing resources to each other, or an entire organization may appear to be in conflict over the fairness of pay and benefit plans. The organization-wide context, in actuality, is interpersonal, small-group, and intergroup conflict simultaneously addressing the same event or issue. Finally, the context of the organization's conflict with others—its competition, the public, the stockholders, the government—illustrates both how complex and how necessary conflict is for organizational functioning. U.S.A. automobiles and foreign competition, airline mergers and oil company mergers, concern for nuclear accidents and hazardous waste disposal, and competitive approaches to advertising and marketing are only a few examples of conflicts between organizations and their environment.

Conflict Causes

Causes of conflict ■ Causes include change, scarce resources, technology, dissent, difficult people, irrationality, incivility, diverse backgrounds and cultures, deception, emotional labor, burnout, relationships of all types, preferences, and past experiences.

Circumstances contributing to conflict and the **causes of conflict** proliferate as the pace of organizational *change* intensifies. Companies and individuals must adapt to global competition or changes in local situations with *scarce resources*, both financial and human. Competition for resources exists between units within organizations, among individuals with different agendas, and between and among organizations. Heavy workloads put conflicting time demands on employees at all organizational levels. The increasing complexity of organizational life generates conflicts, as does the use of increasingly sophisticated *technologies*. While technology use can be positive, we discussed earlier how groups working together with technology and without face-to-face contact may more readily engage in assigning blame to group members without taking personal responsibility.

You can read daily news accounts of pressures to cut costs while improving performance, whether the organization is in the private or the public sector. Changes in organizational structure, mergers, alliances, and the regulatory environment all contribute to both individual and organization-wide conflict. Some contend the increase in part-time and temporary workers generates conflict among peers because of the continuous turnover in skills. Others view management turnover during change as introducing ambiguity that in turn produces conflict.

How organizations handle and value *dissent* during decision making contributes to norms of how to handle conflict. Organizations that encourage dissent during decision making generally experience more productive conflict than those that prefer limited disagreement or participation. In addition, all organizations have as employees, customers, or vendors or are in alliances with people who exhibit difficult behaviors contributing to conflict. Some of the most frequent conflicts you will encounter in organizations occur when working with people who engage in backstabbing, demonstrations of helplessness, excuses for nonperformance, and procrastination. Dealing with *difficult people* is indeed one of the most frequent tests of our organizational conflict skills.

Most organizations experience tensions due to the many paradoxes, contradictions, and ironies in organizational life. We become aware that *irrationality* is a normal condition of organizational life and not something that, as Angela Trethewey and Karen Ashcraft (2004) suggest, should be removed or resolved. Yet paradoxes, contradictions, and ironies can contribute to conflict when handled poorly. In fact, as Sarah Tracy (2004) reported, when employees face contradictory expectations they may experience role ambiguity or role conflict leading to a variety of stressful responses.

The conditions and causes of conflict discussed so far contribute to what many describe as a rise in *incivility* in the workplace and in some cases increased aggression and violence. Workplace civility has generally been conceptualized as courteous treatment of coworkers and other contacts. It includes treating others with dignity, regarding others' feelings, and using social norms of mutual respect. Incivility, on the other hand, is characterized by intent to harm either specific individuals or the organization. Incivility manifests itself in behaviors that demean the dignity of others and violate broad social norms of mutual respect. The *diversity* of the workforce, including *diverse cultural backgrounds*, makes understanding broad social norms of mutual respect increasingly complex. As a result, intended and unintended incivilities increase. Civility and incivility take place through human communication interaction and overt behaviors. As Lynne Andersson and Christine Pearson (1999) explained:

> The need for civility becomes even greater when the interactions among people increase in complexity and frequency. . . . We face the growing challenge of relationships mediated by high-tech, asynchronous, global interaction. With history as counsel, one might assume a need for increased civility in forging and reconciling increasingly complex interactions. Yet, despite the implicit need for increasingly civil interaction, a recent poll of the American public revealed that 90 percent of the respondents think incivility is a serious problem; . . . business has started to reflect the informality of society at large. . . . As the complexity of workplace interaction increases, discourteous behavior has more nuances: there are a greater number of ways to show disregard for fellow workers. (pp. 452–453)

Also contributing to the opportunity for conflict are the various ways in which *deception* occurs within organizations. Anne Hubbell and Caryn Medved (2000) described three deception perspectives: information distortion, strategic ambiguity, and complete distortion or lying. Information distortion is a process of modifying messages to receivers. Earlier we discussed how distortion occurs as messages move throughout the organization. Whether intentional or not, distortion contributes to different perspectives and opportunities for conflict. The second perspective, strategic ambiguity, focuses on the purposeful use of vague language so that receivers can interpret a message from diverse perspectives. Again, although ambiguous messages may permit more people with different views to identify with a particular position, the lack of common understanding has the potential for conflict. An example comes from a national clothing retailer. The chief executive officer announced a major e-business initiative designed to transform the competitive position of the company. Reactions from senior managers were both enthusiastic and explosive. Some interpreted the message as a signal to move the somewhat traditional organization in new and exciting directions, but others voiced the opinion the CEO was directing focus away from their core markets and customers. Finally, lies, deceit, deception, and concealment are behaviors with obvious potential to produce conflict. They often can be characterized as serious ethical abuses.

Certain types of jobs are characterized by the conflicting and stressful situations that are a routine part of the work. For example, leaders are charged with bringing about change and often encounter serious disagreements about courses of appropriate action. Other jobs require people to respond directly to emergencies and crises, whether from customers, the public at large, or within their specific organizations. Still others must adopt a service attitude even in the face of abusive behavior. Arlie Hochschild (1983) used the term *emotional labor* to describe the work performed by those whose jobs involve a high degree of personal contact and who are expected to produce an emotional state, such as pleasure, gratitude, or self-esteem, in the people with whom they deal.

With the overall growth of the service-based economy, Geoff Anderson (1993) claimed an increasing percentage of the workforce will engage in some degree of emotional labor. Sales representatives, bill collectors, service complaint representatives, telemarketers, and flight attendants all fall within this category. These jobs and others require a separation of "true self" feelings from those that are expected to be expressed when in contact with the public. Hochschild (1983) contended these emotional labor jobs require regulated emotion because they entail voice or face contact with the public, require the workers to produce a specific emotional state or reaction in the customer, and are regulated by employer control of the emotional activities of the employee. All you need to do to understand the potential conflict in these jobs is to think back to a time when you had a disagreement with a salesclerk or someone in a customer service position. How did you react? How did that individual respond? Was it a conflict or a normal routine business interaction? What makes the difference?

All of the factors discussed relate to stress and the associated concept of burnout. Katherine Miller (1999) conceptualized workplace stress as a process in which certain aspects of the environment create strains on individuals, contributing to negative psychological, physiological, and organizational outcomes. The term *burnout* refers to the wearing out from the pressures of a situation or a job. In later work, Miller (2007) described an important distinction between emotional labor and emotional work: "Like emotional labor, emotional work is emotion that is part of the work itself. Emotional work springs from the job, not from relationships with coworkers or roles outside of the organization. Unlike emotional labor, however, emotional work usually involves emotion that is authentic, not emotion that is manufactured through surface acting or deep acting" (p. 225). In research conducted with human service workers, Miller found the compassionate communication processes of noticing, connecting, and responding to clients contributed to risks of burnout for the human service workers. In her work with financial planners Miller and Koesten (2008) further examined the role of authentic relationships development between professionals and clients as an important mediator in reduction of stress and burnout. Communication strategies associated with coping with stress and burnout include participation in decision making, receiving social support from peers and supervisors, and engaging in productive conflict. Try to identify times when you have experienced stress or burnout. Were these times or situations related to conflict? Needless to say, daily organizational life is filled with conflicts in a variety of contexts. *Relationships of all types, preferences for conflict,* and *past experiences* all contribute to organizational conflicts. The results for individuals or entire organizations rest, however, not with whether conflict occurs but with the appropriateness of conflict behaviors and the effectiveness of conflict outcomes.

Conflict Episodes

Knowing what conflict is, why it happens, and in what context it occurs contributes to our understanding of conflict as a complex interaction of both individual and group perceptions, emotions, behaviors, and outcomes. Researchers describe these complex interactions as **conflict episodes**. Scholar Louis Pondy (1967) provided a particularly useful understanding of episodes as five basic conflict stages: (1) latent conflict, (2) perceived conflict, (3) felt conflict, (4) manifest conflict, and (5) conflict aftermath. These stages are seen as influencing one another, and the total interaction determines whether the conflict is productive or counterproductive. The stages help us visualize conflict as a process and analyze specific conflicts from a process perspective.

> **Conflict episodes** ■ Descriptions of the complex interactions of both individual and group perceptions, emotions, behaviors, and outcomes during conflict.

Latent Conflict   **Latent conflict** refers to underlying conditions in organizations and individual relationships that have the potential for conflict. For example, decisions about responsibility and authority, control of resources, goals, and activities in the pursuit of goals all are necessary for organizational functioning, yet few, if any, organizations make these decisions with the total agreement of all members. In other words, the daily functioning of the organization generates disagreement and conflict.

> **Latent conflict** ■ Underlying conditions in organizations and individual relationships that have the potential for conflict.

When John became the new manager of the Middlesex claims department, his appointment over two qualified applicants—Tom and Joan—can be considered a latent conflict condition. Furthermore, the introduction of the new computer system, as with any organizational change, has the potential to generate conflict.

From the individual perspective, John, Tom, and Joan fulfill multiple roles in the department. These multiple roles may carry different and sometimes incompatible requirements, again underlying conditions for conflict. A supervisor, for example, may genuinely encourage an employee group to be open about mistakes. That same supervisor may work for a manager who is critical of mistakes and harsh in the treatment of those who make them. What the supervisor wants from the employee group is very different from what the supervisor, in the role of employee, sees as rewarded behavior. These incompatible requirements are underlying, or latent, conflict conditions.

It is important to understand latent conflict conditions always exist in one form or another, although they may or may not produce conflict. Communication competence develops from being able to recognize latent conditions without assuming conflict will automatically result.

Perceived Conflict Although latent conflict conditions always exist, individuals, work groups, or entire organizations may not see goals, individual roles, resources, or authority decisions as conflict-producing. When conditions of high agreement and mutual satisfaction exist, organizational members are unlikely to view latent conflict conditions as anything other than routine decisions necessary for smooth organizational functioning. Most organizations, however, have disagreements about even routine decisions. Who gets a promotion, which approach is best to achieve a sales goal, and how individual performance is to be evaluated are examples of decisions frequently subject to different viewpoints and misunderstandings. When individuals or groups become aware these differences exist, they are in the

Perceived conflict ■ Awareness of individuals or groups that differences exist.

perceived conflict stage of an episode.

It is important to recognize, in the perceived stage, overt conflict has not occurred, only the perception of significant frustrating differences. Also in this stage, it is possible only one person in a relationship or situation will perceive a potential conflict. Problems between supervisors and employees arise, for example, when a supervisor sees a performance problem that the employee does not. Likewise, an employee may define the lack of supervisory feedback as a problem, whereas the supervisor believes additional communication is unnecessary. These perceptual differences are characteristic of the perceived conflict stage.

The ability to analyze thoughtfully is very important in this stage. Think about your relationship with a person who is important to you and try to recall a time when you became aware that a significant difference was possible between you. What were the cues to the difference? What assumptions did you make? How did you think the difference might alter your relationship? Was the other person aware of the problem? Were his or her perceptions of the situation similar to yours? The perceptions we form as we face significant differences with others are crucial to the process of conflict because those perceptions shape and influence the next two stages, which hinge on emotions and behaviors.

Felt conflict ■ Emotional impact the perception of conflict has on potential conflict participants.

Felt Conflict Closely linked to the perceived conflict stage is **felt conflict**, the emotional impact the perception of conflict has on potential conflict participants. This stage usually precedes actual conflict behaviors and is important to behavior because it represents the merger of our perceptions and emotional reactions. It is at the felt conflict stage when we conceptualize or define probable outcomes should an actual conflict occur; in other words, it is our ego-investment stage.

Our perception of the importance of the problem, our motives and the motives of others, and the varying abilities and relative power positions of those involved all contribute to the emotional impact, or the felt conflict. For most of us, seeing a possible difference with a coworker is a different emotional experience from seeing that same possible difference with the boss; it is not that the difference with the boss is necessarily worse, only that the relationships are different. The emotional impact of the problem is linked to the value we place on the specific relationship. Put another way, the felt conflict stage is an expansion of the perceived conflict stage. Perceptions are intensified by our emotional reactions to the potential conflict. Think again about the personal situation you identified for the perceived conflict stage. How did your emotional reaction influence your behavior? What was most important to you as you considered what was going to happen? Were you aware of consciously considering your behavior choices?

Manifest Conflict   The **manifest conflict** stage has been referred to as the "action time" of conflict or the time "when the lid blows off and we really get down to business." The manifest conflict stage consists of conflicting behaviors: problem solving, open aggression, covert action, or numerous other possibilities. In this stage, communication behavior is influenced by participants' conflict preferences, perceptions of rules of interaction, power relationships, roles, and skills and abilities. All too often it is this manifest stage that we recognize as conflict, without realizing the powerful influence of previous stages.

> **Manifest conflict** ■ Actual conflict behaviors: problem solving, open aggression, covert action, and numerous other possibilities; influential for determining the productivity of the conflict and the way conflict participants will interact in the future.

Actual conflict behaviors—manifest conflict—are influential in determining the productivity of the conflict and the way conflict participants will interact in the future. Are all sides of the issue heard? Do power and influence govern what happens? How are people treated when their ideas are rejected? Group conflicts in which all members are treated with respect, for example, frequently result in decisions group members can support. On the other hand, when groups engage in personal attacks or use coercive power to enforce decisions, a very different result is predictable. Although both groups may reach reasonable decisions related to specific problems, the chances of continuing group support may be reduced if individual members feel discounted or threatened. These discounted members may contribute to future disagreements that are covert and unproductive.

Think about your personal experiences. Recall a conflict you believe was resolved productively. How did you behave? How did others behave? Was the decision a good one? How did you feel several days later? Next, recall a conflict that left you frustrated and concerned. How did this situation differ from your more productive experience? What can be learned from contrasting the two? What competencies do you think are most important for the manifest conflict stage?

Conflict Aftermath   The **conflict aftermath** (outcomes) stage is a result of the complex interactions of latent conditions, perceived conflict, felt conflict, and manifest conflict. Put simply, this stage is

> **Conflict aftermath** ■ Result of the complex interactions of latent conditions, perceived conflict, felt conflict, and manifest conflict.

what happens—in terms of both issues and relationships—as a result of the other four stages. It is the stage in which we evaluate the conflict as productive or counterproductive.

Although most of us fear conflict, most of us know conflict can be productive as well as counterproductive. Although contemporary thinking acknowledges conflict outcomes can disrupt communication, produce psychological scars, and disrupt individual relationships, groups, or even entire organizations, the view also holds that conflict permits individuals and organizations to develop new ideas and approaches and to become actively involved in necessary change. Several years ago, communication scholar Brent Ruben (1978) described what we know is true today: ". . . conflict is not only essential to the growth, change, and evolution of living systems, but it is, as well, a system's primary defense against stagnation, detachment, entropy, and eventual extinction." When applied to organizations, conflict is an essential process for continued operation. Without conflict, organizations stagnate and die.

From a practical point of view, conflict outcomes influence the quality of decisions in organizations and consume large amounts of organizational resources. Managers spend from 20 to 40 percent of their time handling conflict. Practicing managers also report managing conflict continues to become more important to organizational effectiveness. Although it is certainly obvious from this examination of conflict processes within various contexts, an often underestimated reality is the important role of individual behaviors in organizational conflict.

Many people who communicate effectively under harmonious conditions lose the ability to influence others and contribute to good decision making because they communicate poorly during conflict. Evidence suggests personal experiences with organizational conflict influence how satisfied and productive organizational members are. Additionally, relationships may actually deteriorate or end when conflict is not productive. In essence, fully effective organization members must exhibit communication competency under conflicting conditions and must contribute to productive outcomes for both themselves and the organization as a whole.

THE INDIVIDUAL IN ORGANIZATIONAL CONFLICT

Organizations bring together diverse individuals, some of whom approach conflict as you would and others with very different preferences. The various predispositions, skills, and abilities of individuals in organizations influence how organizational conflict occurs. Sensitivity to these differences is central to becoming a competent communicator within a complex environment.

Sensitivity to our own preferences and behaviors helps us develop sensitivity to differences among people. One of the best ways to develop that sensitivity is to examine our own preferences in conflicts that have been important to us. The self-report questionnaire in Figure 9.1 should be completed and scored before you study the material about conflict styles, objectives, and tactics. This questionnaire is designed to increase your awareness of your individual preferences and predispositions for conflict. Scoring forms and profile interpretations are located on page 320. Score your profile before studying the remainder of the chapter.

Before attempting to answer the following questions about your preferences and behaviors during conflict, list three conflicts that have been important to you.

1. The conflict was with _____
   about _____
   It was generally productive/counterproductive. (circle one)
2. The conflict was with _____
   about _____
   It was generally productive/counterproductive. (circle one)
3. The conflict was with _____
   about _____
   It was generally productive/counterproductive. (circle one)

Based on your memory of these conflicts and others, respond to the following questions about preferences for conflict behaviors.

Circle the number that indicates whether you strongly agree (4), are inclined to agree (3), are inclined to disagree (2), or strongly disagree (1) with each of the following statements.

1. When problems arise I prefer to let others take the responsibility for solving them.   4   3   2   1
2. I believe a middle ground can be reached in most conflicts.   4   3   2   1
3. I like everyone to be able to say what they think even if they don't agree with me.   4   3   2   1
4. I can be firm in pursuing what I think is right.   4   3   2   1
5. I try to reduce tension with others, to take people's minds off their problems.   4   3   2   1
6. Usually it is best to postpone trying to talk to someone when he or she is upset.   4   3   2   1
7. Talking about feelings and issues is important in conflict.   4   3   2   1
8. I like people to be willing to give some if I will also.   4   3   2   1
9. The goal must come first; conflict is inevitable and some people just can't take it.   4   3   2   1
10. When people are upset, I am more concerned about their feelings than any particular problem.   4   3   2   1
11. I don't like to be in unpleasant or tense situations.   4   3   2   1
12. I like to win my points.   4   3   2   1
13. Most conflicts are subject to compromise.   4   3   2   1
14. Everyone should share in the gains and bear some of the losses.   4   3   2   1
15. I will not contradict others if I believe that it will make them unhappy.   4   3   2   1

(*continued*)

FIGURE 9.1
Personal Profile of Conflict Predispositions, Strategies, and Tactics

16. I offer solutions and ask others for solutions.   4   3   2   1
17. I prefer to have everyone who is affected involved in solving a conflict.   4   3   2   1
18. Believing disagreements can destroy effectiveness, I encourage others to stay with more agreeable subjects.   4   3   2   1
19. I go after what I want, even if that makes others uncomfortable.   4   3   2   1
20. Differences usually aren't important enough to worry about.   4   3   2   1
21. I don't like to make other people feel bad by disagreeing.   4   3   2   1
22. I think the best solutions come when everyone participates and has concern for others.   4   3   2   1
23. I want others to know where I stand and will convince them of the rightness of my position.   4   3   2   1
24. Confrontation can be managed if we seek middle ground.   4   3   2   1
25. I try to help others be at ease, even if that means not pressing my point.   4   3   2   1

Again remembering the important conflicts you identified, circle a number ranging from 1 (never) to 5 (always) to describe your behaviors during conflict.

	Never		Average		Always
1. Name calling	1	2	3	4	5
2. Postponing the discussion	1	2	3	4	5
3. Proposing compromise	1	2	3	4	5
4. Expressing concern for others	1	2	3	4	5
5. Expressing concern for facts	1	2	3	4	5
6. Proposing areas of agreement	1	2	3	4	5
7. Making threats	1	2	3	4	5
8. Silence	1	2	3	4	5
9. Adding issues to the original conflict	1	2	3	4	5
10. Denying the conflict	1	2	3	4	5
11. Supporting friends even if disagreeing	1	2	3	4	5
12. Proposing solutions	1	2	3	4	5
13. Agreeing to solutions	1	2	3	4	5
14. Using formal rules to suppress conflict (voting, parliamentary procedure, etc.)	1	2	3	4	5
15. Overpowering competition	1	2	3	4	5
16. Describing gains and losses	1	2	3	4	5

FIGURE 9.1
Personal Profile of Conflict Predispositions, Strategies, and Tactics (*Continued*)

On completing the questionnaire in Figure 9.1, you will have short profiles of three conflicts you identified as important to you. These profiles are organized around conflict scholar Kenneth Thomas's (1976) basic components of individual conflict behavior: orientations/styles, strategic objectives, and tactics. You will want to refer to your profiles as we discuss each of the behavior components.

Orientations, or predispositions, for conflict are the balances individuals try to make between satisfying their personal needs and goals and satisfying the needs and goals of others in the conflict. These orientations or predispositions are commonly referred to as conflict *styles*. *Strategic objectives* are a combination of balancing the individual preferences for conflict styles with what the individual sees as feasible outcomes in a particular situation. Behavior choices, known as *tactics*, are specific communication choices that are influenced by both orientation and style and strategic objectives.

Orientations/Predispositions/Styles

Prominent conflict researchers such as Leonard Berkowitz (1962), Robert Blake and Jane Mouton (1964), Jay Hall (1969), and Kenneth Thomas (1976, 1988) all support the notion individuals have behavioral **orientations/predispositions** or styles for handling conflict. Researchers further conclude individuals have an order of preference among the styles that ultimately influence communication choices. In other words, an individual has a dominant or most preferred style, but when that style seems inappropriate in a given situation or does not work, the individual may go to his or her next preference. The self-assessment you just completed identified the preference order you used in the specific conflicts you remembered. Refer back to that preference order as we explore what these various styles mean. Think about the accuracy of your profile and whether it is an effective one for you.

Orientations/predispositions ■ Behavioral preferences for handling conflict; frequently described as avoidance, competition, compromise, accommodation, and collaboration.

Conflict styles frequently are described as five basic orientations based on the balance between satisfying individual needs and goals and satisfying the needs and goals of others in the conflict. Figure 9.2 depicts the five styles—avoidance, competition, compromise, accommodation, and collaboration—on a two-dimensional grid with individual goals/assertiveness and concern for other/cooperativeness dimensions.

Avoidance   Individuals preferring the **avoidance** style are unlikely to pursue their own goals and needs or to support relationships and the goals and needs of others during conflict. Conflict makes them very uncomfortable and often fearful. Although avoiders may have a genuine concern for goals and relationships, they do not see conflict as a positive solution. Avoiders may cope well during times of harmony but refrain—often both psychologically and physically— from participating in conflict situations.

Avoidance ■ Style of individuals who, as a result of their preferences, are unlikely to pursue their own goals and needs or to support relationships and the goals and needs of others during conflict.

Where was the avoidance style in your personal hierarchy? Can you identify friends or family who have this preference? How would you describe the impact of avoiders on decision making and on long-term relationships? The question of

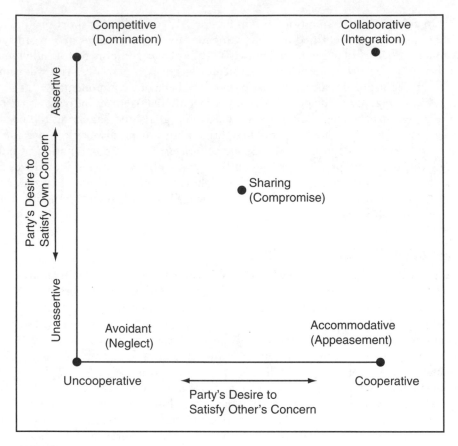

FIGURE 9.2
The Conflict Grid

K. Thomas, "Conflict and Conflict Management," in *The Handbook of Industrial and Organizational Psychology*, ed. M. Dunnette, 1976, p. 900. Copyright © 1976. Reprinted by permission of John Wiley & Sons, Inc.

impact is especially important for organizations. Although most people agree individuals within organizations have important preferences, organizations employ people to use their skills and abilities, the best of their thinking. When an individual avoids participating in decisions subject to conflict, the organization may lose important knowledge.

Competition ■ Preference for emphasizing personal goals and needs without considering the opinions or needs of others in the conflict.

Competition The individual who prefers **competition** approaches conflict by emphasizing personal goals and needs without considering the opinions or needs of others in the conflict. Competitive individuals often conceptualize conflict as win/lose and prefer to view themselves as winners. This orientation can block good problem solving, particularly if the competitive person needs input on a decision. On a more positive note, when a group is hopelessly deadlocked, competitors often believe it is their responsibility to make a decision and to take responsibility for that decision. Given ability appropriate to the problem, this approach can be organizationally effective.

How often do you use the competitive approach? How effective has it been? Can you visualize a competitor and an avoider in a conflicting situation? What would you predict will occur? Sensitivity to the impact of the competitive approach is especially important because this style can be both abusive or exactly what the organization needs. The strong competitor can be guilty of discounting other good ideas and personally attacking others in order to remain a winner. When an avoider and a competitor disagree, the competitor usually wins, with little or no resistance; but this win is good for the organization only if the competitor was right and had all the appropriate information. Can you think of a time when you really had the best information, even if others disagreed? What type of behavior was needed for an effective decision? How important was it to pursue your point of view? The competitor runs the risk of competing for the sake of competing. The competitor can, however, make a decision when others are hopelessly deadlocked. The potential positives and negatives from the competitive style illustrate the need for the sensitivity competency in communication. Competent communicators are sensitive to their preferences and the appropriateness of applying them to specific situations. In this case, competency involves knowing when competitiveness is needed and when it is counterproductive.

Compromise   Compromisers prefer to balance people concerns with task issues and often approach conflict with a give-and-take attitude that contributes to negotiation. Compromisers engage in give-and-take toward a goal or desired outcome in order to resolve the conflict situation. Most of us can identify numerous times when conflict was managed through **compromise**. Compromise works because all parties can minimize losses while establishing some gains. Indeed, organizations frequently encourage compromise, and it has become a preferred orientation in many decision-making groups.

> **Compromise** ■ Preference during conflict for balancing people concerns with task issues and exhibiting give-and-take or negotiation behaviors.

A word of caution is appropriate, however. Have you ever been involved in a compromise that didn't really work, and the problem surfaced again? Did the compromise represent good problem solving, or was it just a convenient and comfortable way out of conflict? As with the competitive approach, a preference for compromise should be matched to the needs of the situation. Individuals who are willing to compromise can help organizations make a decision from among various conflicting viewpoints. If that decision does not represent thorough problem solving and allows the issue to resurface, however, the compromise orientation should be avoided. Look again at your profile. How important is compromise to you? How effective has it been?

Accommodation   People who want to be liked, have high affiliative needs, or genuinely are concerned for the needs of others often prefer an accommodative approach to conflict. **Accommodation** is characterized by the sacrifice of personal goals to maintain relationships or in some cases to maintain peace or avoid conflict whether or not the relationship is maintained over the long term. This style can provide important support to groups engaged in making difficult decisions, but it also encourages the accommodative individual to abandon issue, goal, or task input when others appear to disagree.

> **Accommodation** ■ Preference for conflict associated with the sacrifice of personal goals to maintain relationships.

Naturally, most of us want to be liked. Again, though, the issue is organizational effectiveness. Is the accommodative individual withholding an opinion to maintain a relationship with his or her boss or coworkers? How important is that opinion to what happens in the work group? Does the accommodative style keep the individual from being a good contributor, or is his or her real contribution the support of others? These are difficult questions requiring both sensitivity and good analysis skills. Think again about the conflicts you identified in your profile. Was accommodation a preference for you or others? How did the accommodative approach work? Should it be used again?

Collaboration   When you examine Figure 9.2, the collaborative style is clearly seen as the ideal because this approach influences individuals to work for goals, to examine issues thoughtfully, and to be task-oriented while supporting others to do the same. On the other hand, **collaboration** is the most difficult of all the styles to actually use for strategic objectives and tactical behaviors. Individuals who prefer collaboration can behave collaboratively only when others assume a collaborative orientation and have enough task or goal information to solve the problem thoroughly.

Collaboration ■ Preference for ideally balancing people and task concerns during conflict.

Where was the collaborative preference in your hierarchy? Can you see why conflict researchers believe this approach has more merit than avoidance, compromise, competition, or accommodation? Now think back to the specific conflicts you used in your self-analysis. Were these problems handled collaboratively? If these problems were not handled collaboratively, describe what might have been managed differently. Also, return to John's problem at Middlesex Insurance. Try to determine what John can do to establish a collaborative approach to his problem with Joan.

Strategic Objectives

As Thomas (1976) suggested, individuals' strategic objectives in conflict are determined not only by orientations or preferences for conflict styles but also by assessments of the probable outcomes of behavior within particular contexts. Specifically, strategic objectives are determined by matching general preferences for particular conflict styles with assessments of the risks involved in a particular situation. We assess the strategies we will utilize based on our preferences and an assessment of the probable behaviors of others. Organizational role, power positions, previous experiences, and the importance of specific issues all contribute to the strategic objectives adopted by conflict participants.

A strategic choice is associated with attempting to escalate, reduce, maintain, or avoid a conflict. Strategic choices are based on what we want to happen in a particular situation. The behaviors we use—tactics—are related to our attempts to move the conflict in a desired direction. Tactics and strategies change within the conflict based on reactions from and relationships to others.

In the Middlesex Insurance case, as John reflects on his problem with Joan, he begins to establish strategic objectives. His personal preferences and decisions will affect whether the conflict escalates, reduces, stays at the present level, or is avoided. For example, if John chooses to escalate the conflict, he can announce his training schedule will be initiated as announced and those not in agreement can look for work in other departments. If John has good analysis skills, he can predict this action will probably anger Joan and possibly others. He cannot know with certainty what Joan's reaction will be, but he can assume conflict escalation is the probable outcome. John might attempt to escalate the conflict if he really wanted Joan and the others to leave, but his analysis ability probably will tell him he may be viewed with suspicion if competent people leave a department soon after he becomes manager.

On the other hand, John might attempt to reduce the conflict by asking Joan to help him understand her objections to the timetable for training. He would then be in a position to decide whether her objections were based on department operations or were primarily due to his promotion.

John could attempt to maintain the conflict at its present level by acknowledging that he and Joan have differences. He can suggest he will try his new ideas while remaining willing to listen to her objections if there are problems. John will have difficulty in choosing the strategic objective of avoidance because he and Joan have already voiced opposing views. He can, of course, back off his training schedule and not make further reference to their disagreement.

Regardless of what John decides, the result is determined by all those involved in the situation. John's strategic objective is based on his desired outcome and his best estimate of the reaction of Joan and others. His individual preferences, past experiences, and overall competency with conflict will influence his decisions and contribute to whether the outcomes are productive for the Middlesex Insurance claims department.

Communication Tactics in Conflict

Conflict tactics can be described as communication behaviors that attempt to move the conflict toward escalation, reduction, maintenance at the present level, or avoidance. The tactics adopted are influenced by individual conflict preferences and strategies and by overall organizational values about how conflict is supposed to work. For example, powerful individuals frequently use competitive and confrontational tactics, whereas individuals apprehensive about communicating use more avoidance tactics. Some organizations encourage open debate and disagreement, whereas others insist on disagreement without personal attacks or displays of anger. Still others discourage overt conflict of any type. In any case, the exchanges of communication tactics among conflict participants illustrate the interactive nature of conflict, with outcomes related to complex tactical interactions as well as orientations and strategic objectives.

Although it is impossible to list or define all the possible tactics available to conflict participants, it is important for our personal sensitivity and also for our verbal skills to identify frequently used conflict tactics. Figure 9.3 presents excerpts from actual organizational conflicts. Each example is accompanied by a description of the tactic it represents. Tactics are grouped into the following categories: tactics for conflict escalation, tactics for conflict avoidance, tactics for conflict maintenance, and tactics for conflict reduction. Strategic objectives and tactics have been summarized from the research of Joyce Hocker and William Wilmot (1991); Charles Conrad (1985); and Joseph Folger, Marshall Scott Poole, and Randall Stutman (1993).

Organizational Narrative	Conflict Tactic

Tactics for Conflict Escalation

"You have a bad attitude or you wouldn't do such sloppy and unprofessional work."

1. *Applying evaluative labels* to individuals or issues

"I know you don't want to work this out. Six months ago you weren't willing to give us the extra people for the [manufacturing] line. I can't imagine that it is any different now."

2. *Expanding the conflict* at hand to related problems or old, unsettled disputes

"It's not just me. Every member of this department thinks you are wrong. We just can't make the deadlines you keep establishing."

3. *Forming alliances* and making them known in an attempt to overpower competitors

"I don't intend to be surrounded by people who make trouble for me. You get this machine fixed this time or you can cause trouble for someone else."

4. *Making threats* with or without control of sanctions or outcomes

"I don't want to work with John on this project. You can give me Mary or Sam, but not John."

5. Deliberately *limiting the choices* of others

"I know we agreed to work this out between us, but I went to Ralph [both people's supervisor]. Your team just doesn't have the workload that mine does, and he has got to create some justice."

6. *Breaking previously agreed-upon rules* of behavior for the specific relationship

Tactics for Conflict Avoidance

(Supervisor to employee not recommended for promotion) "Being upset about Mary getting the job isn't going to help. Let's talk about it when you're feeling better. You just need to be patient and wait for another opportunity."

1. *Delaying* or procrastinating in addressing conflictive issues

(Top manager to unhappy employee) "I understand that you think your boss is unfair—and I know we have an open-door policy—but when you have a grievance you are to go to personnel and file a formal report. I will look at the issue only after you have followed proper channels."

2. *Using formal rules,* rank, seniority, majority rule, and other means of controlling processes to constrain the behavior of conflicting parties

"This issue is simply not a problem. I am not angry with you and you have no right to be mad at me. I am going to continue to believe nothing is wrong."

3. *Denying* the existence of a conflict

"I know it was important to get two more people on the night shift, and I know you really need them, but I believe that you can maintain your production level. More people would help, but your group is good and I know they can continue to do the job."

4. *Fogging the issue* by acceptance of part of the concern while ignoring other important concerns

FIGURE 9.3
Communication Tactics for Conflict

Organizational Narrative	Conflict Tactic

Tactics for Conflict Maintenance

"The only way we are going to meet this deadline is to work together. It doesn't matter right now who got us into this mess. If we don't deliver to the customer on time, we will all get blamed."

1. Describing what all parties have to *gain and lose*

(Two managers before a board of directors meeting) "No, I won't make matters worse. I have always supported you in the directors meeting. I will continue to do that even though you know I think this is not the way to go."

2. Agreeing to *honor long-term relationship* rules

"Look, I think the way you have been behaving is inconsiderate of your fellow workers, but maybe I don't have all the facts and I certainly don't know how you are feeling."

3. Combining both *escalation and reduction tactics*

"I believe we can agree that this level of budget is all we are going to have to spend between us. I will look at my travel plans if you will consider your expenditures for part-time secretarial support services."

4. *Proposing areas of agreement* and areas for compromise

Tactics for Conflict Reduction

"Now, changing the entire computer system is a major departure from our current operations. I think we need to think first of who has what type of training and how we can approach bringing people up to speed without destroying our work schedules. We then can approach purchasing and installing the new system."

1. Identifying *numerous manageable issues* and suggesting approaching "smaller" concerns

"I know we are upset that John promised we would get these shipments out over the holiday, but if we are to present our case and be listened to, we must not personally attack John or remind him that this is the second time in six months this has happened."

2. Describing *behaviors and outcomes to be avoided* during the conflict

"Obviously the report has to be corrected. I'm concerned about the amount of time that is going to take and how fatigued you must be, but I am also concerned about how we got so much inaccurate information to begin with."

3. Exhibiting concern *for both facts and feelings*

"Perhaps I was wrong to believe that we should hire another account executive before secretarial support staff. I will consider a part-time secretarial type along with the new exec."

4. Offering *compromises* from original positions

FIGURE 9.3
(Continued)

Before leaving the topic of conflict predispositions, strategies, and tactics, some words of caution are important. Although it is useful to understand our own preferences and behaviors, research reported by Hocker and Wilmot (1991) indicated most of us are prone to see ourselves as trying to solve problems while other people are using control or aggressive approaches. In other words, we are likely to view our efforts more positively than those with whom we are in conflict. In addition, emphasis on style, strategy, and tactic choices may block us from understanding that conflict is an interactional, dynamic process with others. We will be less capable of productive approaches if we, as Folger, Poole, and Stutman (1993) suggested, overemphasize a consistent, specific orientation toward conflict. Finally, most of our style, strategy, and tactics research has been conducted in the United States of America or Great Britain and has been carried out with majority groups. We know much less about preferences and orientations in cultures that are more group-oriented than individualistic. We have just begun to think through the implications of an increasingly diverse workforce and multiculturalism for organizational conflict and conflict management. As such, understanding cultural context and the limitations of any set of descriptive categories becomes an important sensitivity for productive conflict behaviors.

Emotion during Conflict

In thinking about styles, strategic objectives, and tactics for conflict, it is possible to overlook the importance of emotion and the reality that conflict stirs emotions in almost everyone. Tricia Jones (1997) described emotion as having three components: cognitive, physiological, and behavioral. The cognitive component of emotion involves the appraisal of situations that in turn evoke emotional responses. The physiological component involves the embodied experiences that literally radiate throughout the body as ongoing lived experiences. Finally, the expressive component of emotion is what we do—the behavioral response—as an expression of the cognitive and physiological experience. Jones argued conflict is emotionally defined; in other words, events that cause conflict are by definition events that elicit emotion. She related emotion to conflict strategies and tactics by suggesting that our emotional definitions of conflict affect our orientations, what we believe should occur during conflict, and our actual behavior. This view of the importance of emotional communication during conflict can help us understand our personal responses to conflict as well as approaches taken in a variety of organizational circumstances.

Anger, generally described as a very strong emotion, is a frequent experience in most organizations. Anger occurs when individuals experience humiliation, receive verbal abuse, are ignored when trying to engage in contributions or disagreements, or encounter a host of other emotion-producing interactions. Responses to anger include silence, stress, aggression, and both productive and negative conflict behaviors. Anger can stimulate creativity, but it also has been related to poor-quality work, chronic absenteeism, and even theft of company property. Although expressions of anger can be constructive and appropriate, anger displays often are associated with the types of conflict behaviors many of us fear and seek to avoid. Can you remember a time when anger contributed to how you reacted in a conflict?

Was it productive? If not, how did you respond later to your own anger? What role do you believe anger plays in organizational conflict?

Earlier we talked about jobs with high components of emotional labor or controlled emotional expressions and their potential for contributing to conflict. Unlike anger displays, which are associated rightly or wrongly with volatile conflict, the conflict experienced by those in jobs with high emotional labor components often is suppressed and surfaces in much less direct ways. Some have characterized these mostly high-visibility service jobs as contributing to workers' inability to recognize their own private feelings. Flight attendants have used the phrase "go robot" to describe their public behaviors. Vince Waldron and Kathy Krone (1991) reported personal costs associated with the suppression of emotion, which include suppressed disagreements, reduced upward information flow, and the loss of voice or the sense of being heard and responded to within the organization. Although anger and emotional suppression are somewhat different processes, we can readily see how they both become important emotional experiences for individuals and how both relate to many types of organizational conflict.

Given the pressure of today's workplace and what many consider unhealthy and unproductive approaches to conflict that focus solely on rationality, the concept of emotion in the workplace and in conflict takes on new meaning. Linda Putnam and Dennis Mumby (1993) proposed the concept of bounded emotion as a way to think about the problem of emotional control in organizations. Bounded emotionality encourages the expression of a wider range of emotions than is usually condoned in traditional organizations, while stressing the importance of maintaining interpersonally sensitive, variable boundaries between what is felt and what is expressed. In other words, many believe it is time to value emotion and the feelings, sensations, and affective responses to organizational situations that emotion brings. This valuing can benefit individuals and also a variety of organizational processes, including conflict processes.

The recognition of the importance of emotion in conflict is in direct opposition to those who believe we should discuss major points of disagreement only if we all can be "rational" and "logical." The reality of emotion is part of the fabric of organizational life. Think about times you have observed emotional displays in organizations. What happened? How did you react? Do some organizations have rules for how emotion is to be expressed? Are some emotional expressions more valued than others? For example, are anger and crying treated in the same manner? What makes the difference? Finally, think about conflicts during which you have "lived emotion" and try to remember how that experience influenced your behavior.

GROUPS IN ORGANIZATIONAL CONFLICT

In Chapter 6 we described the importance of groups for organizational functioning and discussed many of the types of groups we will probably join. Now we describe some of the specific reasons for group conflict and a variety of approaches for conflict management.

Most of us have been in groups in which tensions and conflict made us uncomfortable or blocked problem solving. It is hoped that most of us also have belonged to groups in which conflict contributed to new and better ways of doing things, actually strengthening the group's ability to work together. Think for a moment about these experiences. What made the difference? How did you feel and behave in these different circumstances?

Group Members in Conflict

Earlier we described a variety of orientations, predispositions, and styles; strategic objectives; communication tactics for conflict; and the importance of emotion. As you would expect, all these factors and more can contribute to conflict when diverse individuals participate in groups. Group members also play task, maintenance, and self-centered roles. In Chapter 6 we discussed the generally negative influence of self-centered roles and the need for balance in task and maintenance behaviors. It is easy to understand why self-centered roles and inappropriate balances of task and maintenance roles are a possible source of group conflict. In addition, although most organizations talk about the importance of teamwork, rewards usually recognize individual versus group efforts. Members of a work team, for example, will be asked to collaborate, yet each knows merit salary increases will reflect how they compare to one another, not how they produce as a group. This seeming contradiction is another source of work group conflict.

Conflict styles generally have been studied as specific to individuals. Much of the earlier discussion took that focus. Tim Kuhn and Marshall Scott Poole (2000) provided an expansion of the individual approach when they considered conflict styles at the group level "as a typical interaction pattern a group enacts when members deal with oppositions and disagreements." According to Kuhn and Poole, these group styles are "embodied in group norms about how to handle disagreements." Kuhn and Poole use the categories of avoidance, distributive, and integrative styles to access the effect of conflict styles on group decision-making effectiveness. Avoidance styles describe behavior that minimizes addressing the conflict. A distributive style, much like the competitive style, uses a confrontational approach, with one party or group essentially giving in to another. The integrative approach is characterized by cooperative and collaborative behaviors to pursue mutually positive resolutions. Building on previous work that has related decision-making quality and effectiveness to groups using competing interpretations about issues and synthesizing these interpretations into a decision the group can accept, Kuhn and Poole sought to determine if groups develop norms regarding how they will manage conflicts that carry over to affect other activities, such as decision making, even when these activities do not involve open conflict. After studying several teams over a period of time, Kuhn and Poole concluded groups that developed integrative conflict management styles made more effective decisions than groups that used confrontation and avoidance. Groups that did not develop a stable conflict style were also less effective than groups with integrative styles.

Framing and Sensemaking

How groups conceptualize or frame conflicts and how groups make sense of conflicts influence all types of organizational conflicts and the processes utilized to deal with conflicts. Boris Brummans, Linda Putnam, Barbara Gray, Ralph Hanke, Roy Lewicki, and Carolyn Wiethoff (2008) describe framing from a sensemaking perspective:

> From this perspective, framing refers to using a particular "repertoire" of categories and labels to bracket and interpret ongoing experience and inform action. In other words, it refers to the communicative process through which people foreground and background certain aspects of experience and apply a set of categories and labels to develop "coherent stor(ies) of what is going on" and make decisions about "what should be done given (those) unfolding stor(ies)." . . . Thus a framing repertoire does not refer to a set of cognitive knowledge schemas or structures of expectation (frames), existing *prior to* framing, but to a pattern of highlighting similar aspects of experience to give a coherent account of what is going on that is continuously shaped and reshaped in interactions. (p. 28)

These authors' research suggests members of groups in a dispute may or may not "rely on a similar repertoire for making sense of what is going on." In other words, people who share the same or similar experiences will focus on difference aspects of the experiences to make sense of what is happening. Brummans, Putnam, Gray, Hanke, Lewicki, and Wiethoff (2008) conclude "this study suggests that disputants develop a sense for defining a conflict situation based on their emotional investments in a conflict; their framing of risks and stakes; and their framing of the conflict's outcomes. In addition, this sense seems rooted in whether disputants are 'in it for themselves' or whether they are acting on behalf of a particular group, organization, or profession" (p. 46). It becomes important for us to understand how framing and sensemaking contribute to how conflict is conceptualized whether it is procedural, interpersonal, substantive, or a result of groupthink. The framing and sensemaking of both individuals and groups also importantly contributes to the selection of group conflict processes.

Procedural Conflict

Many types of organizational groups conflict over procedures or ways of doing things. How the group is organized, the process of decision making, who accepts responsibility, or what happens when responsibilities are not carried out all can contribute to tension and conflict within groups. Most of you have experienced this procedural conflict when preparing a project for a class. Some group members preferred majority rule, others worked for genuine consensus, and still others attempted to force their positions or opinions on the entire group.

Interpersonal Issues

One of the most common types of group conflict emerges when all members do not fairly or equally perform their responsibilities or make contributions to the group. The necessity to "carry" a member of the team raises tension and disrupts group cohesiveness. Groups also have interpersonal power clashes among members who seek influence and control. Powerful members produce conflict when attempting to force group members to take sides in essentially interpersonal disputes.

We all have observed two individuals disagreeing or disparaging each other in front of a group. We often suspect their disagreements have little or nothing to do with the issues at hand but reflect ongoing difficulties in the relationship. Unfortunately, they introduce tension and counterproductive behaviors into what might otherwise be an effective setting.

Substantive Issues

The very reason for forming groups in organizations can contribute to group conflict. Organizations should use the energy of diverse individuals to establish effective ways of doing things or to challenge existing processes in favor of new and better efforts. In effect, organizations should encourage conflicts of ideas that contribute to excellence. Individuals normally and productively can differ about positions, interests, approaches, or problems. Groups can therefore be expected to have conflicts over issues, ideas, or tasks.

Groupthink

As is true in interpersonal conflict, group conflict can range from highly productive to counterproductive. Most of us have been present at a meeting where displays of anger blocked effective problem solving. If we think carefully about our group experiences, however, we probably can remember a time when surface harmony also blocked problem-solving effectiveness.

Surface harmony, or the absence of productive conflict, can block group effectiveness when critical thinking is absent, resulting in ill-conceived courses of action. Irving Janis (1983) called the surface harmony frequently associated with highly cohesive groups **groupthink**, or the tendency of groups to suspend critical thinking and to adopt proposed solutions too quickly. Groups in danger of groupthink overestimate their own capabilities, seek information that supports their point of view, and avoid or discount contradictory ideas. Have you ever participated in groupthink? What happened? How can group members decide if they genuinely agree or are exhibiting groupthink tendencies? A discussion of a format for productive conflict provides some possible answers.

Groupthink ■ Tendency of groups to suspend critical thinking and too quickly adopt proposed solutions.

Group Conflict Management Processes

Group conflict is so important in organizations that a variety of processes for management have become commonplace. These processes are typically described as negotiation, bargaining, mediation, forcing, and arbitration. Although this chapter does not describe these processes in detail, your awareness that they are frequently used becomes part of your knowledge competency for group participation.

Negotiation is a common process in groups. Generally speaking, negotiation can be understood as a broad process involving discussions between and among individuals who are interdependent and need to come together for a decision or course of action.

Negotiation ■ Broad conflict management process involving discussions between and among individuals who are interdependent and need to come together for a decision or course of action; frequently associated with the need to compromise effectively.

Groups negotiate procedures and issues with expected give-and-take among members. The negotiation process is frequently associated with the need to compromise effectively.

Bargaining is a more structured form of negotiation. Bargaining usually involves the presentation of fairly specific proposals for the purpose of achieving a working agreement on particular issues. You are probably familiar with collective bargaining as it applies to labor and management group interactions. Yet bargaining has numerous other organizational applications. At budget time, groups may be asked to present very specific proposals for money. Representatives from each group may be asked to negotiate or bargain for fixed resources. In some cases the rules for these exchanges will be well defined, whereas in others the process is more open-ended. Regardless of the formality, bargaining is an established conflict resolution procedure in many organizations.

> **Bargaining** ■ Structured form of negotiations usually involving the presentation of fairly specific proposals for the purpose of achieving a working agreement on particular issues.

Mediation is another possible group conflict management process. In mediation a designated individual guides the negotiations or bargaining efforts of the groups in conflict. Mediation is used when negotiations are deadlocked or tensions so high that a designated leader is desirable. When mediation fails, the designated leader frequently has to rely on forcing or making a decision that the group must accept. Obviously, for mediation or forcing to be effective, the designated leader must have credibility with the opposing factions and responsibility and authority appropriate to the task. Generally speaking, mediators are members of the group or organization involved in the process.

> **Mediation** ■ Use of a designated individual for guiding the negotiations or bargaining efforts of groups in conflict.

Finally, when negotiation, bargaining, or mediation fails, organizations can manage group conflict with **third-party arbitration**. Arbitration usually involves an outside negotiator who resolves differences with formally established procedures. Labor–management disputes have been subjects of arbitration, as have a variety of legally related cases. Arbitration frequently results in ill will because of the forced nature of resolving the conflict.

> **Third-party arbitration** ■ Conflict management process involving an outside negotiator who resolves differences based on formally established procedures.

Fortunately most of us will work in groups that manage conflict through collaboration and negotiation. We know from experience that effectiveness is more likely to occur when group members voluntarily solve their own disputes than when leaders or an outside individual takes charge. (It is also important to note that in selected circumstances the group processes just described are used for individual conflict resolution.) The next section of this chapter returns to the earlier discussion of power and relates power processes to organizational conflict.

Power and Organizational Conflict

The concept of power was first discussed in Chapter 2. The discussion of conflict is an excellent time to return to this important organizational process because perceptions of power and its uses continually influence all aspects of organizational conflict. The organizational structure itself represents how formal power is intended to work. The organizational chart defines for the formal power structure who has the right to overrule whom and who makes decisions and resolves disagreements when collaboration or compromise breaks down. Formal power relationships rarely explain, however, the complexity of organizational conflict. Informal leaders, coalitions of individuals with special relationships, politics, and assumptions of superiority all influence conflict processes. We see individuals and groups with excellent ideas submitting to the ideas of more powerful organizational members and groups. This "raising the white flag" affects decision making and also structures future relationships. We observe what we call power plays in all types of organizational situations. Power plays can be described as tactics that make explicit how power should be viewed in particular circumstances in order to preserve the position of the person or persons making the "play." Technical and communicative expertises become sources of power as well as resources within the control of individuals. Information is an increasingly important organizational resource. Information resides with individuals throughout the organization, contributing to the dynamic and shifting nature of power. Our perceptions of our own power and the power of others will influence the approaches we choose during conflict. Both the wise use and the abuse of power influence how conflicts occur and what happens during conflict. Although power use during conflict can be productive, power often is associated with behaviors that marginalize others and attempt to maintain the status and position of the person or persons exercising power. Think about conflicts you have observed or in which you have been involved. How was power used? How did power influence what happened?

Conflict with Customers and Vendors

Most organizations have specific training for working with customers. Expectations about customer interactions become what we have described earlier as emotional labor. Frequently customer interactions proceed as anticipated; however, most employees have experienced times when customers become difficult as a result of personality, communication style, differing expectations, or organization-generated problems. Responding to the irate customer is a test of our abilities to critically assess the situation, exhibit effective conflict management skills, and understand the limits of our responsibility to handle the situation. Although every organization has differing expectations about customer contact, it is important to clarify those expectations and learn from particularly unpleasant situations. San Bolkan and John Daly (2009) summarize the complexity of the customer experience when they describe responses to consumer complaints:

> Managers need to know that when consumers take the time to write a complaint letter, it is beneficial to respond. In addition, it is important for people who respond to complaints to consider the content of their responses. That is, although responders might want to use excuses, justifications, and apologies to explain failure episodes to aggrieved customers, they should be aware of the potential reactions to these responses. In essence, although using excuses may be useful in reducing an organization's perceived control over a failure episode, the use of excuses might also be increasing negative perceptions of the organization. On the other hand, justifications appear to be beneficial. Providing justifications can decrease perceived negativity with the complaint situation and providing more

justifications may help decrease consumer's perceptions of negativity as well. . . . Moreover, although using apologies is likely to increase consumer' perceptions of negativity with the situation, using apologies is also likely to increase consumers' satisfaction with organizational responses and, importantly, intentions to do business with the organization in the future. . . . Finally, when responding to complaints people should try to be considerate of their customers' situations and communicate both understanding and respect for consumers. (p. 37)

Organizational vendors provide another potential challenge. Vendors provide services or products to an organization. When problems occur, the interaction with the vendor is critical to solving the problem. Identifying problem responsibility and assessing the course of corrective action are keys to effective conflict management. Working with vendor problems clearly links our problem-solving and decision-making competencies with our conflict management skills. A Workshop activity at the end of this chapter and cases in the Putting It All Together section help build our competencies for working with customers and vendors.

SPECIAL TYPES OF ORGANIZATIONAL CONFLICT: SEXUAL HARASSMENT, DISCRIMINATION, ETHICAL ABUSES

Although sexual harassment, discrimination, and numerous types of ethical abuses all have legal consequences beyond the scope of this conflict discussion, they also can be viewed as important types of organizational conflicts. Virtually all organizations have policies prohibiting sexual harassment, discrimination, and ethical abuses, yet the prevalence of these actions affects literally thousands of workers each year. The impact on individuals can be severe, but less well understood is the impact these negative conflicts have on the overall effectiveness of organizations.

Sexual harassment is an important example of power abuse that generates negative conflict. Gerald Pepper (1995) provided a useful definition of this conflict-producing abuse:

> **Sexual harassment** ■ Situation in which one person persists in behaving in a way that offends the sexual morals of another or creates employment conditions based on sexual relationships.

> Sexual harassment refers to situations in which one person persists in behaving in a way that offends the sexual morals of another or creates an expectation on the part of the harassed that his or her employment conditions are subject to change if the victim does not respond as the harasser desires. Harassment can also take the form of an overall working environment that is permeated with offensive behavior or materials. Sexual harassment may be physical or psychological, may occur between same- or different-sex individuals, may happen to both women and men, and is not a condition of hierarchical level. (p. 149)

As Debbie Dougherty (2008) describes, "Targets of the behavior have always known, and researchers have confirmed, that sexual harassment is a highly destructive workplace process. It creates stress, severe depression, and other health problems for the target and anxiety for all members of the workplace and costs millions, possibly billions to organizations in terms of increased health care costs, lost productivity, legal fees, training, and replacing targets of sexual harassment who leave the workplace to escape the predatory sexual behavior by colleagues. Sexual harassment, even less aggressive forms, is never a good thing" (p. 463). The number of individuals who experience workplace sexual harassment is difficult to determine, but research estimates range from 40 percent to as high as over 90 percent of all female workers. Estimates for abuse of men are less well documented. Sexual harassment is communicated through inappropriate verbal and nonverbal displays as well as the display of offensive objects in the workplace. Inappropriate verbal acts range from compliments with sexual overtones to terms of endearment not reflective of the workplace relationship. Nonverbal behaviors range from gestures with sexual inferences to physical acts of touching, fondling, stroking, or generally using physical presence to create a hostile environment. Displays of objects include posters or calendars with sexually explicit photos as well as use of the Internet and other communications technologies to bring sexually explicit material into the workplace. Sexual harassment includes the communication of the need to submit to sexual advances as a basis of continued employment or as a condition of advancement. Finally, harassers frequently instill fear of retaliation for reporting sexual harassment. All these behaviors occur within organizations and with customers and vendors as well.

Although sexual harassment is illegal and not supported by organizational policies, well-developed communication skills provide the most readily available assistance for women and men experiencing this abusive conflict. Harassment conflict rarely is resolved without direct intervention ranging from confronting the harasser to reporting concerns to supervisors and those charged with handling grievances. Unfortunately, many women and men have been culturally conditioned to believe many of the behaviors just described are normal and acceptable communication. Nevertheless, the impact of this type of abusive behavior limits both individual potential and satisfaction, as well as overall organizational effectiveness. Have you experienced sexual harassment? Have you participated in any of the above-described behaviors? How would you describe your current abilities to confront workplace sexual harassment?

Discrimination ■ Exclusion of individuals or groups based on personal characteristics not associated with competence or performance.

Discrimination in the workplace is both a legal and a cultural issue. Discrimination can be defined as the systematic exclusion of individuals based on characteristics such as race, ethnicity, gender, and age. Sometimes referred to as labor market discrimination, discrimination in the workplace is based on personal characteristics of workers that are not related to productivity. As with sexual harassment, discrimination is illegal, and most organizations take public stands against a variety of discriminatory practices. The experiences of women, racial and ethnic minorities, and older workers provide evidence of the continuing presence of conflicts because of discrimination. Women and racial and ethnic minorities continue to make less money than their white male counterparts in similar jobs, and the presence of the "glass ceiling" (the level above which women and minorities are not typically promoted) remains for most upper-management and leadership positions.

Bias can begin with hiring and selection processes. Job postings often require experience and backgrounds that have little or no relationship to the ability of applicants to perform the job. Often experience and/or educational requirements favor members of the majority population in an organization. Hiring decisions often favor close friends, relatives, or college connections, whereas promotions may come as a result of seniority over competence or ignoring seniority in favor of preferences for "younger" people. The potential for conflict is obvious. When competence is not the criterion for hiring and promotion, frustration and anger are understandable responses from those who are continually "outsiders."

Pepper (1995) helped us understand subtle discrimination that can reside in the culture of the organization. Pepper contends:

> Women and minorities in the workplace can profitably be understood as "marginal persons." The marginal person suffers the consequences of having no firm footing. The lack of a peer or reference group, coupled with the hostility or rejection or conditional acceptance of the desired reference group, leaves the marginal person feeling as though he or she is only a peripheral participant.
>
> Marginality offers an interesting clarification, if not a replacement, for existing theories that attempt to explain the slow progress that minorities and women have made in the workplace. Rather than relying on explanations like differences in socialization, or patriarchal organizational environments, the theory of marginality is a communication-based explanation for discrimination. It is predicated on the assumption that the marginal person, an intercultural sojourner of sorts, will continually have to wrestle with the rejection of the group left behind and the resistance of the group desired. (p. 240)

The theory of marginality focuses on the conflicts that marginalized people face with both their old and new groups. For example, research supports the difficulty of many women who are promoted from among their peers to positions of leadership. Women, more than their male counterparts, often face resistance from their former peers and hostility at worst and a lack of assistance at best from the leadership group to which they have been promoted.

The last category of special types of organizational conflict—ethical abuses—incorporates issues of sexual harassment and discrimination along with numerous other abuses in day-to-day organizational life. Dalmar Fisher (1993) identified six major areas in which ethical abuses can occur as organizations relate to their external environments: (1) products, (2) advertising, (3) finance and accounting, (4) pricing, (5) international operations, and (6) ecology. These issues and others are what Fisher describes as corporate social responsibility. He goes on to identify (1) working conditions, (2) due process and fair treatment of employees, (3) personnel policies and procedures, (4) design of work, and (5) free speech as issues with potential for ethical abuse within organizations.

Convictions of individuals for ethical abuses such as insider trading, embezzlement, sexual harassment, and discrimination are at an all-time high. In addition, research suggests that well over 50 percent of all employees have been pressured by their organizations to engage in what they consider unethical behaviors.

Employees increasingly report ethical abuses to those in positions of power. These reporting behaviors are referred to as **whistle-blowing,** or the disclosure of illegal and unethical behaviors to those who can do something about them. Reporting unethical behavior is a complicated ethical issue. Should the whistle-blower report his or her finding internally and wait for results, or should the whistle-blower go directly to the public?

Whistle-blowing ■ Reporting unethical behaviors to those who can do something about them.

The answer is not simple. The decisions individuals make about either the knowledge of or participation in ethical abuses will not only influence their own career satisfaction but also directly affect the performance of the organization.

Brian Spitzberg and William Cupach (2008) describe unwanted communication, and aggression, as a serious ethical abuse in organizations. Spitzberg and Cupach contend "when someone is neglected, ignored, insulted, criticized, yelled at, or the target of another person's communicative aggressions, the hurt can be more encompassing, more durable, and harder to ignore than a slap, push, shove, kick, or hit. People learn that bruises heal, but they have no first-aid kit for injuries to their egos. Society has never equipped people with simple treatments for being unloved, loved too much, or despised" (p. 456).

All of us will likely be faced by one or more of these negative conflict-producing situations. How we will respond relates to our knowledge, sensitivity, skills, and values. In other words, communication competency in its broadest sense will contribute to our ability to handle these special types of organizational conflict. The next section of this chapter contributes to our competencies by describing supportive climates, ethical behaviors, and principled negotiation for conflict. The section concludes with guidelines for productive conflict and a recommended format for productive problem solving during conflict.

PRODUCTIVELY ENGAGING IN CONFLICT

Thus far in this chapter, we have attempted to develop knowledge, sensitivity, and skills important for communication competence during conflict. The underlying assumption for this development has been that conflict can be productive and can make a valuable contribution to individuals and organizations. In other words, not only is conflict inevitable, but also, when productive, often it is desirable.

Before thinking specifically about possible positive outcomes of conflict, review again the conflicts you identified earlier in this chapter and in the Middlesex Insurance case. Were there positive outcomes from your personal conflicts? What do John and the entire department have to gain from productive resolution of their problem? How was conflict valuable in either your personal experiences or the Middlesex Insurance case?

In general, it can be said that a major value of conflict is its stimulus for creativity. Conflict with others forces us to evaluate and assess issues and problems. When productively managed, this evaluation can stimulate new and creative solutions that may not have emerged without competing perspectives. For example, most of us have habitual or routine ways of doing things. Frequently we do not even think about new approaches until someone challenges our effectiveness. Productive conflict can help keep us from getting in a rut. Conflict can restructure our relationships, a fact many of us fear and resist. Yet conflict can bring relationships up to date and strengthen them by addressing underlying problems and working for solutions. Both individually and organizationally, productive conflict can help us analyze goals and find effective means of achieving them.

When we adopt the perspective that conflict can be valuable, we then begin to focus our knowledge, sensitivity, and skills toward conflict as a productive process.

We think about what atmosphere is best for conflict, what contributes to ethical behaviors during conflict, and finally what types of problem-solving processes support productive conflict outcomes.

Supportive Climates, Ethical Behaviors, Principled Negotiation, and Co-Construction

Creating an environment in which individuals feel secure and encouraged to seek good solutions is a difficult yet important task. The quality of the problem-solving environment is closely linked to considerations of what constitutes ethical communication behaviors during conflict. This subtle but critical relationship between **supportive climates** and the quality of human interaction is well described by Paul Keller and Charles Brown (1968) in their interpersonal ethic for communication. Keller and Brown suggested people will be able to reach their potential only when they are psychologically free—not fearful of disagreement—and when their beliefs, opinions, and values are acceptable in their interactions with others.

Supportive climates ■ Organizational environments in which individuals feel secure and encouraged to seek good solutions; characterized by problem description, problem orientation, spontaneity, empathy, equality, and provisionalism.

Organizations annually spend millions of dollars training personnel in problem solving and conflict management with the hope this training will contribute to productive organizational outcomes. Yet the outcomes from conflict often are influenced not only by the skills and abilities of the individual conflict participants but also by the overall organizational climate, which contributes to either supportiveness or defensiveness.

Organizational climates that produce defensiveness are characterized by inaccurate perceptions of motives, values, and emotions of those in conflict. Jack Gibb (1982), in a classic study of behaviors individuals perceive as threatening, discovered that "increases in defensive behavior were correlated positively with losses in efficiency in communication. Specifically, distortions became greater when defensive states existed in the groups." Gibb concluded there are characteristic behaviors of defensive groups that are distinctly different from the characteristic behaviors in supportive groups.

Evaluation versus Problem Description   Defensive climates are described by Gibb (1982) as evaluative, whereas supportive environments are characterized by problem description. The descriptive approach attempts to fit our words as nearly as possible to our experience of reality through descriptive, nonjudgmental terms and by avoiding strong, emotion-laden words. There is a big difference between a boss who says, "You people are wasteful!" and one who says, "Our office costs are rising rapidly because of the amount of copying we do."

Control versus Problem Orientation   Defensiveness also is produced through attempts to control the behavior and responses of others. Although forcing may get short-term results, it rarely builds long-term improvement. Problem orientation is the supportive climate opposite of control. Specifically, problem orientation attempts collaboration with individuals who are being asked to make behavior changes. Think about the difference between the supervisor who says, "Get here on time or else!" and the one who says, "How can we work together to make sure you start your shift on time?" Most of us can understand the problem orientation approach in our own behavior. Try to determine when your commitment is greater: when you participate in a decision or when the decision is made for you. For most of us the answer is relatively simple: we put more time and energy into our own commitments.

Strategy versus Spontaneity   Although we all operate from strategic objectives in conflict, defensiveness is produced when we are perceived by others to be engaging in manipulative behaviors. A boss who tries to "sell" a group on an unpopular change in work requirements often produces a defensiveness based on the belief this manipulation is a fundamental form of disrespect. Spontaneity, the opposite of strategy, is reflected in behaviors that make real motives plain and generate a trust that straightforward and honest interactions are taking place. A group may not like the announcement of a schedule change, but the boss who directly provides the reasons without suggesting everyone should like the decision is more likely to generate trust. Straightforward and honest interactions (spontaneity) facilitate an individual's freedom of choice through accurate information, a requirement for ethical interpersonal communication.

Neutrality versus Empathy   Productive groups empathically support their members rather than assuming a rational neutrality based on "pure" objectivity. Productive groups also are characterized by the acceptance of others with different values and beliefs. This empathic support is closely related to the Keller and Brown (1968) notion of an interpersonal ethic for communication based on psychological freedom to express opinions and beliefs. Thinking again about our personal behavior, most of us would agree it is more comfortable to express disagreement when we know we will be thoughtfully heard than when we expect personal attack or discounting. Also, for most of us, constructively expressing disagreement is more likely to occur when we feel supported in our right to do so.

Superiority versus Equality   In general, defensive groups are more likely than supportive groups to have members intent on asserting superiority and exhibiting an unwillingness to participate equally in problem solving. In fact, defensive climates often are characterized by individuals who believe they really do not have enough in common with others to make communication possible. Although differences in individuals exist, supportive individuals and groups stress commonalities while respecting numerous and diverse contributions to solutions.

Certainty versus Provisionalism   Defensive groups, more than their supportive counterparts, are likely to have members who are certain and dogmatic about their positions. Supportive individuals are more provisional or open to experimentation in behavior, attitudes, and ideas. The provisional individual is investigative and problem-oriented rather than polarized into either-or positions. The provisional approach seeks numerous alternatives so as to find the most appropriate solution to a given problem. Again, this support for the generation of alternatives is fundamental to individual choice and ethical communication.

Ethical Communication Behaviors   The supportive conditions as described by Gibb (1982) are closely aligned to notions of ethical conflict behaviors as described by Gary Kreps and Barbara Thornton (1984). Specifically, Kreps and Thornton contended ethical conflict behaviors are exhibited when the individual stays with the issue at hand without hidden agendas; constructs reasonable, logical arguments rather than arguments designed to discount and devalue others; and keeps an open mind to new ideas while avoiding a win-at-all-costs attitude. In other words, ethical communication behaviors generate an environment in which individuals have freedom of expression and also have adequate information to make free, informed choices. Put another way, the value of productive conflict is to stimulate creativity in individuals, groups, and organizations. That creativity is most likely to emerge if we are personally safe, if we are open to many suggestions and viewpoints, and if we honestly seek the best solution from among numerous alternatives.

Principled Negotiation   Principled negotiation is based on ethical communication behaviors and supportive climates. Introduced by Roger Fisher and William Ury (Fisher, Ury, and Patton, 1991), principled negotiation is a strategy for groups of individuals in conflict to express their needs and search for alternatives that meet diverse needs. The strategy supports ethical behavior by separating people from the problem and focusing on interests, not positions. Group members are asked to develop options for mutual gain based on mutual interests. In addition, objective criteria are used to evaluate options so that all parties to the conflict can determine the fairness of decisions.

   Principled negotiation is based on the assumption that we should express disagreements and react to them with a spirit of inquiry and supportiveness rather than defensiveness. During principled negotiations, group members express concern for one another even when issue and position disagreements are obvious. Groups engaging in principled negotiation describe needs and interests in common and avoid rigid, polarized positions. Using common needs and interests as a basis, groups develop options that can be evaluated with agreed-on objective criteria. Once evaluation has been completed, groups engaging in principled negotiation can arrive at decisions with a high likelihood of broad support.

A Feminist Alternative: Co-Construction   Linda Putnam and Deborah Kolb (2000) suggested that the notion of exchange or trades is the basis of most attempts at negotiation. As such, attempts at negotiation, whether principled or not, spend more time on getting to settlements or outcomes than on understanding situations. Putnam and Kolb claimed much of negotiation and bargaining represents gendered activity because "the qualities of effective bargainers (e.g., individuality and independence, competition, objectivity, analytic rationality, instrumentality, reasoning from universal principles, and strategic thinking) are linked to masculinity. Those attributes typically labeled as feminine (e.g., community, subjectivity, intuition, emotionality, expressiveness, reasoning from particulars, and ad hoc thinking) are less valued" (p. 80). Putnam and Kolb provided what they describe as an alternative model to exchange: co-construction. Co-construction is based on all parties engaging in mutual inquiry about problems and issues. Individuals and groups blend proposals or solutions as opposed to offering different positions and then giving concessions in order to reach a solution. Individuals using co-construction attempt to talk together about the issues and question how problems may have been defined or labeled in the past. This type of communication competence focuses on individuals able to build on the ideas of others and find opportunity for joint solutions. In other words, co-construction asks individuals to work jointly to identify problems, develop understandings of the issues, and work for mutual action. Can you identify how this approach would add value to making important decisions? What makes this approach hard to do?

GUIDELINES FOR PRODUCTIVE CONFLICT

The following guidelines are presented to help you think about your personal participation in conflict. As you read, consider how each of the guidelines relates to your recent experiences during conflict and what guidelines you might add.

Monitor your personal behavior and the behavior of others for signs of destructive conflict. What are you and others doing to contribute to destructive conflict? Folger, Poole, and Stutman (1993) identified symptoms of escalation or avoidance cycles. Avoidance behaviors include marked decrease in commitment to solving the problem; quick acceptance of a suggested solution; avoidance of raising controversial aspects of any issue; people stop listening; discussion stays on safe aspects of the issue; little new information is exchanged; no plans are made to implement solutions; and evidence for claims or positions is not challenged. Escalation behaviors include dogmatically arguing for the same position; taking longer than anticipated to deal with issues; threats used to win arguments; mounting tension; nothing being solved despite hard work; hostile nonverbal communication; sarcastic behavior to relieve tension; and arguments over trivial issues. Consider these behaviors and other pertinent situations as you monitor your own experiences.

Identify common goals and interests between people or in groups. Try to think about problems in terms of common interests and goals. Avoid thinking about concrete positions and focus on common needs, desires, concerns, or fears. In organizations, legitimate and constructive disagreement often occurs about ways to implement solutions or to achieve goals. Identifying common interests and goals helps people avoid blaming and identifying other people as the problem. When people are the problem, it is important to learn to deal directly with the individual or individuals involved and not let "people conflict" contribute to poor organizational decisions.

Develop norms to work on problems. Norms or rules of behavior during a problem discussion can contribute to productive conflict by assisting individuals to identify how they will work on the problems with behaviors likely to facilitate informed decisions. Frequently adopted norms include (1) everyone in the group being responsible for assisting everyone else in presenting individual opinions; (2) avoiding win/lose statements; (3) avoiding suppression of differences by using procedures such as voting, averaging, and formal rules; (4) avoiding quick solutions; (5) making decisions only after alternative perspectives have been discussed; and (6) supporting differences of opinion and valuing diverse contributions for effectiveness.

Focus on mutual gain. Identify what everyone has to gain from productively solving the conflict. State how everyone can benefit from working on the problem.

Test proposed ideas against the criteria of mutual gain. Effective conflict resolution is more likely if opposing parties can see how their interests are protected. Avoid thinking that there is only one right answer and that if the opposing party benefits, you must therefore lose or not benefit. Develop the habit of thinking creatively in terms of mutual gain.

A Process for Productive Conflict

Individuals who observe or participate in productive conflicts frequently characterize them as good problem-solving processes. Indeed, that is exactly what productive conflict is. Earlier in the chapter, we defined conflict as frustration stimulated by competing responses or alternatives to a particular situation. When that frustration is resolved to the mutual satisfaction of involved parties and to the needs of the issue, good problem solving has occurred. The following process for productive conflict is a basic problem-solving format. Based on the concepts of supportive climates, ethical behaviors, and principled negotiation, it is designed to integrate all of our competencies—knowledge, sensitivity, skills, and values—into a productive conflict management process.

The Process

Self-Analysis of the Issues   When we experience perceived and felt conflict, the time is right to do an in-depth self-analysis about the problem. Can we describe the conflict in terms that represent observable behaviors or events to all parties? What are the limits of our understanding of the problem? What types of solutions can we propose? Who needs to change or make a decision? What can we support in resolution strategies, and what types of results are clearly not acceptable? Also, what are the power issues, roles, and relationships of the parties involved? Finally, what are our personal responsibilities for this conflict?

Setting a Meeting to Work on the Problem   Productive conflict occurs in a climate in which all participants feel supported. The setting of the meeting beforehand and the environment of the meeting itself are critical to this supportive climate. Generally speaking, all parties involved in conflict should be notified in advance about the issue for discussion. Although that will sometimes produce anticipation stress, mental preparation can occur only when everyone knows the agenda. Also, the emotional impact of conflict can be lessened and trust levels increased when people don't feel surprised by a conflict. Commitment to agreements is greater if parties have time to think about the problem and their input and limits. In addition, the meeting environment should be conducive to the free exchange of ideas, usually private and on relatively neutral ground. Individuals using the power position of their private offices may actually inhibit real problem solving. Finally, adequate time for full discussion should be allotted, with the timing of the meeting as convenient as possible for all participants.

Defining the Problem   Effective conflict outcomes occur in solving the basic problem rather than finding solutions to surface issues or discovering vastly different descriptions of the problem. Conflict participants should be encouraged to define the problem fully before any discussion of solution strategies. Problems often are poorly described because of underlying tension in the setting and a desire to get the confrontation over with as soon as possible. Clarification of the problem—through self-disclosure and active questioning—is essential to productive problem solving.

Developing Solutions   We are often relieved to be "getting through this problem" and neglect to look comprehensively at approaches and solutions. In the development of solutions it is important to think broadly about all alternatives, even those that seem to have little immediate merit. Better and longer-lasting solutions will emerge from broad rather than narrow perspectives of alternatives. All conflict participants should be encouraged to participate in solution generation. In fact, if a critically involved party to a dispute cannot offer a single solution, it may be better to adjourn the meeting temporarily to let that person consider what he or she might suggest. Forcing a decision on a nonparticipative individual may result in little commitment or sometimes actual sabotage of the solution. Ultimately, of course, action must be taken. All parties, however, must recognize the potential impact of a decision with varying ranges of agreement and commitment.

Narrowing the Choices for Action   Decisions should be discussed in light of the defined problem issues. Often decisions made with broad agreement fail because the participants have not linked their intended actions to the actual problem. If behavior change is required on the part of some but not all participants, particular care should be taken that the affected individuals participate in narrowing the choices for action. They should be encouraged to select options to which they can commit, although these options can be rejected by others if they do not meet acceptable standards. When individuals who need to change their behavior make commitments to change that they have helped generate, the long-term possibilities for successful conflict resolution have been enhanced.

Committing to Solutions   Agreeing on a solution or approach to the problem should occur only after the parties assess how that solution addresses the identified problem, whether individuals can support the decision, if those most affected have participated in the decision, and whether the solution is workable and can be implemented. Commitment to the solution comes through developing an implementation plan. Who is going to do what and in what time frame? How is the solution going to be evaluated? Is everyone clear about what we think this solution will accomplish and also what it cannot do? Finally, can we predict from this experience whether we have a solution that will work? If so, what were the keys to this outcome? If not, what were the barriers we could not surmount?

Monitoring the Process   A real key to long-term conflict resolution is effective implementation of agreed-on solutions. Effective conflict outcomes are encouraged when participants establish how they will monitor the implementation plan and when they will meet again to assess how it is working. This follow-up builds accountability into the process and also allows for celebration when solutions work and meet problem needs. This closure on the process also establishes a framework for revisiting an issue for which the solution—even if faithfully implemented—still does not satisfy the real needs of the conflict.

Although no process, set of skills, or body of knowledge will free individuals, groups, or entire organizations from the reality of conflict, the knowledge, sensitivities, skills, and values of conflict participants directly influence the productivity of conflict outcomes. Effective organizational communicators know they bear responsibilities to monitor continually their own abilities and support that process for others. In particular, productive conflicts help individuals improve their organizational relationships and are an important organizational mechanism for good decision making and adaptation to change.

CHAPTER HIGHLIGHTS

Conflict occurs when individuals, groups, or entire organizations perceive or experience frustration in the attainment of goals. Described as an **episode**, the conflict process involves the stages of (1) **latent conflict,** (2) **perceived conflict,** (3) **felt conflict,** (4) **manifest conflict,** and (5) **conflict aftermath.** Conflict episodes occur in intrapersonal, interpersonal, small-group, organization-wide, and organization-to-environment contexts. Regardless of context, participants interact in conflict with their individual preferences or styles, strategic orientations, and tactical communication behaviors. Conflict styles are described as five orientations based on the balance between satisfying individual needs and goals and satisfying the needs and goals of others involved in the conflict. These five most commonly referred-to styles are **avoidance, competition, compromise, accommodation,** and **collaboration.** Strategic objectives are determined by preferences for conflict styles and by assessment of the probable outcomes of behavior within particular contexts. Strategic objectives structure the conflict in one of four strategic directions: escalation, reduction, maintenance, or avoidance. The tactics adopted are influenced by conflict preferences and strategies

and by overall organizational values. Emotion is a critical part of conflict processes.

Group conflict is common in organizations. Framing and sensemaking contribute to how conflict processes occur. Organizations frequently manage conflict through **negotiation, bargaining, mediation,** and **third-party arbitration.** The use of a variety of power processes is prevalent during conflict. Negative and abusive workplace conflicts include **sexual harassment, discrimination,** and **ethical abuses.** Conflict outcomes are more likely to be productive if parties in conflict foster **supportive climates. Principled negotiation** and **co-construction** are approaches for conflict based on supportive climates and ethical behaviors.

A process for constructive conflict can be used to integrate all of our competencies: knowledge, sensitivity, skills, and values. The format includes self-analysis of the issues, setting a meeting to work on the problem, defining the problem, developing solutions, narrowing the choices for action, committing to solutions, and monitoring the process. In sum, productive conflict requires competent communicators who can effectively solve problems in a variety of organizational circumstances. ■

WORKSHOP

1. The following three customers are irate, and you are asked to deal with their problems.
   a. The airline for which you work has canceled Jane A.'s flight. You are asked to reschedule her on the next available flight on your airline but not to change her ticket to another airline even

though they have an earlier departure. Jane A. claims she has an important meeting and you must change to the other carrier.
   b. John B. wants to return a mechanical tool that has been removed from its package and appears to have been used. He says he does not need the

tool after all, claims he has not used it, and wants a full refund for over $500. He states he will go to the Better Business Bureau and to a television station customer hotline if you don't help him right now.

c. Joan M. is a phone complainant who is crying because the repair person from your company has not arrived within what she reports is the scheduled two-hour time window she was given earlier today. She claims her bathroom plumbing is not working and she has three small children at home. Your computer records indicate the repair is scheduled for the next day.

In groups of six, assign one person to be the customer and one to be the customer representative for each of the three situations. All six group members should engage in a role play. For each role play assign a coach for the complainant and one for the customer representative. Assign two observers who will provide feedback at the end of the role play. Role-play each situation to resolution. Following each role play have the observers provide feedback as to the effectiveness of the interaction. Ask the coaches to provide feedback. Close each role play with the participants indicating how they felt and why they chose certain approaches.

2. Interview an individual in a high-emotion labor job. Ask that person to describe his or her reactions to required emotional control. Ask the person to describe the types of conflicts he or she experiences and the methods used to manage them.

3. Attend a public meeting at which the issue for discussion is likely to produce conflict. Record the strategies and tactics used by each participant. Describe the effectiveness of the outcomes. Attempt to assess how the conflict behaviors influenced the outcomes. ■

Personal Profile of Conflict Predispositions, Strategies, and Tactics Scoring Form: Style Predispositions

1. Total your scores from questions numbered 1, 6, 11, 18, 20.   A. _____
2. Total your scores from questions numbered 2, 8, 13, 14, 24.   B. _____
3. Total your scores from questions numbered 3, 7, 16, 17, 22.   C. _____
4. Total your scores from questions numbered 4, 9, 12, 19, 23.   D. _____
5. Total your scores from questions numbered 5, 10, 15, 21, 25.   E. _____

Your scores represent a rank ordering of your preferences or predispositions for five conflict styles: (A) avoidance, (B) compromise, (C) collaboration, (D) competition, and (E) accommodation. Your highest number represents your first preference, and so on down the line. It is possible that you gave two styles the same score. This indicates that you have little difference in preference between the two. List your style preferences in order from most preferred to least preferred.

First choice _____
Second choice _____
Third choice _____
Fourth choice _____
Fifth choice _____

These styles are discussed in detail as you study Chapter 9.

Scoring Form: Strategies and Tactics

1. Total your scores from questions numbered 1, 7, 9, 15, and divide by 4.   A. _____
2. Total your scores from questions numbered 2, 8, 10, 14, and divide by 4.   B. _____
3. Total your scores from questions numbered 3, 6, 11, 16 and divide by 4.   C. _____
4. Total your scores from questions numbered 4, 5, 12, 13, and divide by 4.   D. _____

Your scores represent your average use of a variety of conflict tactics grouped into the four general conflict strategies of (A) escalation, (B) avoidance, (C) maintenance, and (D) reduction. Compare your average use figure with the scale: 1 = Never; 3 = Average; and 5 = Always.

Now return to the main text, where preferences and orientations, strategies, and tactics are discussed in detail.

TIPS FOR EFFECTIVE COMMUNICATION

1. Deal with conflict issues as soon as you can. Conflicts that go unresolved often increase in intensity.
2. When possible, work with others in face-to-face settings. Communicating through technology often escalates conflict.
3. Tell the truth if someone asks you if something is bothering you. Avoiding a conflict by denying its existence rarely works.
4. Use *I* messages and descriptive language to describe your concerns.
5. Avoid blaming others. Focus on solutions or resolution.
6. Don't agree to a solution you know you cannot honor. It will be more difficult to resolve the issue after a failed solution than to work for a resolution you and others can support.
7. Don't agree just to "keep the peace." False harmony leads to problems. Conflict is a normal part of human interaction.
8. Identify when and why you become the "difficult person."
9. Understand that a "difficult person" will stay difficult as long as you do not respond to the behavior.
10. Remember, the only behavior you fully control is your own. ■

REFERENCES AND SUGGESTED READINGS

Anderson, G. 1993. Emotions and work in a lifestyle occupation. *Journal of European Industrial Training* 17(5): 10–14.

Andersson, L., and C. Pearson. 1999. Tit for tat? The spiraling effect of incivility in the workplace. *Academy of Management Review* 24(3): 452–471.

Bennis, W., and B. Nanus. 1985. *Leaders: The strategies for taking charge.* New York: Harper and Row.

Berkowitz, L. 1962. *Aggression: A social psychological analysis.* New York: McGraw-Hill.

Blake, R., and J. Mouton. 1964. *The managerial grid.* Houston, TX: Gulf.

Bolkan, S., and J. Daly. 2009. Organizational responses to consumer complaints: An examination of effective remediation tactics. *Journal of Applied Communication Research* 37(1): 21–39.

Brummans, B., L. Putnam, B. Gray, R. Hanke, R. Lewicki, and C. Wiethoff. 2008. Making sense of intractable multiparty conflict: A study of framing in four environmental disputes. *Communication Monographs* 75(1): 25–51.

Canary, D., and B. Spitzberg. 1987. Appropriateness and effectiveness perceptions of conflict strategies. *Human Communication Research* 14(1): 93–118.

Conrad, C. 1985. *Strategic organizational communication: Cultures, situations, and adaptation.* New York: Holt, Rinehart and Winston.

Dougherty, D. 2008. Sexual harassment. In *21st century communication: A reference handbook*, ed. W. Eadie, 463–470. Thousand Oaks, CA.: Sage.

Fisher, D. 1993. *Communication in organizations*, 2nd ed. St. Paul, MN: West.

Fisher, R., W. Ury, and B. Patton. 1991. *Getting to yes.* New York: Penguin.

Folger, J., M. S. Poole, and R. Stutman. 1993. *Working through conflict.* New York: HarperCollins.

Gibb, J. 1982. Defensive communication. In *Bridges not walls*, ed. J. Stewart, 235–240. New York: Random House.

Hall, J. 1969. *Conflict management survey: A survey of one's characteristic reaction and handling of conflicts between himself and others.* Conroe, TX: Teleometrics International.

Hochschild, A. 1983. *The managed heart.* Berkeley: University of California Press.

Hocker, J., and W. Wilmot. 1991. *Interpersonal conflict.* Dubuque, IA: Brown.

Hubbell, A., and C. Medved. 2000. "*When I had to lie to my boss, I said something like this . . .*": The validation of a typology of organizational deception. Paper presented at the annual meeting of the International Communication Association, May, Acapulco, Mexico.

Janis, I. 1983. *Groupthink: Psychological studies of policy decisions and fiascoes*, 2nd ed. Boston: Houghton Mifflin.

Jones, T. S. 1997. *Emotional communication in conflict: Essence and impact.* Paper presented at the National Communication Association Convention, November, Chicago.

Keller, P. W., and C. T. Brown. 1968. An interpersonal ethic for communication. *Journal of Communication* 18(1): 73–81.

Kreps, G., and B. Thornton. 1984. *Health communication: Theory and practice.* White Plains, NY: Longman.

Kuhn, T., and M. S. Poole. 2000. Do conflict management styles affect group decision making? *Human Communication Research* 26(4): 558–590.

Martin, J., K. Knopoff, and C. Beckman. 1998. An alternative to bureaucratic impersonality and emotional labor: Bounded emotionality at the body shop. *Administrative Science Quarterly* 43(2): 429–469.

Miller, K. 1999. *Organizational communication*. Belmont, CA: Wadsworth.

Miller, K. 2007. Compassionate communication in the workplace: Exploring processes of noticing, connecting, and responding. *Journal of Applied Communication Research* 35(3): 223–243.

Miller, K., and J. Koesten. 2008. Financial feeling: An investigation of emotion and communication in the workplace. *Journal of Applied Communication Research* 36(1): 8–32.

Morris, J., and D. Feldman. 1996. The dimensions, antecedents, and consequences of emotional labor. *Academy of Management Review* 21(4): 986–1010.

Morris, J., and D. Feldman. 1997. Managing emotions in the workplace. *Journal of Management Issues* 9(3): 257–274.

Mumby, D., and L. Putnam. 1992. The politics of emotion: A feminist reading of bounded rationality. *Academy of Management Review* 17: 465–486.

Pepper, G. 1995. *Communicating in organizations: A cultural approach*. New York: McGraw-Hill.

Pondy, L. 1966. A systems theory of organizational conflict. *Academy of Management Journal* 9: 246–256.

Pondy, L. 1967. Organizational conflict: Concepts and models. *Administrative Science Quarterly* 12: 296–320.

Putnam, L., and D. Kolb. 2000. Rethinking negotiation: Feminist views of communication and exchange. In *Rethinking organizational and managerial communication from feminist perspectives*, ed. P. Buzzanell, 76–104. Thousand Oaks, CA: Sage.

Putnam, L., and D. Mumby. 1993. Organizations, emotion, and the myth of rationality. In *Emotion in organizations*, ed. S. Fineman, 36–57. London: Sage.

Putnam, L., and M. Poole. 1987. Conflict and negotiation. In *Handbook of organizational communication*, eds. F. Jablin, L. Putnam, K. Roberts, and L. Porter, 549–599. Newbury Park, CA: Sage.

Ruben, B. 1978. Communication and conflict: A system theoretic perspective. *Quarterly Journal of Speech* 64: 202–210.

Shockley-Zalabak, P. 1984. Current conflict management training: An examination of practices in ten large American organizations. *Group and Organization Studies* 9: 491–507.

Spitzberg, B., and W. Cupach. 2008. Unwanted communication, aggression, and abuse. In *21st century communication: A reference handbook*, ed. W. Eadie, 454–462. Thousand Oaks, CA.: Sage.

Thomas, K. 1976. Conflict and conflict management. In *The handbook of industrial and organizational psychology*, ed. M. Dunnette, 889–935. Chicago: Rand McNally.

Thomas, K. 1988. The conflict-handling modes: Toward more precise theory. *Management Communication Quarterly* 1(3): 430–436.

Thomas, K., and R. Kilmann. 1975. The social desirability variable in organizational research: An alternative explanation for reported findings. *Academy of Management Journal* 18: 741–752.

Thomas, K., and W. Schmidt. 1976. A survey of managerial interests with respect to conflict. *Academy of Management Journal* 19(2): 315–318.

Tracy, S. 2004. Dialectic, contradiction, or double bind? Analyzing and theorizing employee reactions to organizational tension. *Journal of Applied Communication Research* 32: 119–146.

Trethewey, A., and K. Ashcraft. 2004. Practicing disorganization: The development of applied perspectives on living with tension. *Journal of Applied Communication Research* 32: 81–88.

Waldron, V., and K. Krone 1991. The experience and expression of emotion in the workplace: A study of a corrections organization. *Management Communication Quarterly* 4: 287–309.

Walton, R., and J. Dutton. 1969. The management of interdepartmental conflict: A model and review. *Administrative Science Quarterly* 14: 73–84. ∎

Strategic Organizational Communication

Professional Applications of Organizational Communication

DEVELOPING COMPETENCIES THROUGH...

KNOWLEDGE
Describing strategic organizational communication

Describing strategic management

Defining the role of the professional communicator in strategic organizational communication

Describing the organizational environment with multiple publics and stakeholders

Describing crisis communication

SENSITIVITY
Understanding the complexity of strategic organizational communication

Developing an awareness of professional responsibilities for strategic organizational communication

SKILLS
Using analysis capabilities to select options for case problems

Assessing personal skills related to professional communication responsibilities

VALUES
Relating strategic communication to ethical and value issues faced by organizations

Understanding value dimensions of professional communication responsibilities

◣ THE PRESS AND THE STOCKHOLDERS WANT TO KNOW CASE

Linda Thomas and Brad Youngren were almost speechless. Their meeting with Jane Bevins, president of Ostern Corporation, was not what they had expected. They had known there was big trouble but nothing as complex as this problem and with so many multiple issues. Linda and Brad sat down to determine what to do next. It would be only a matter of hours before the press would be calling. They had to figure out how to approach public announcements and get more specialized information to their stockholders as well. Linda called Ostern's corporate attorneys and asked for an emergency meeting. She and Brad began to make a list of all their options.

As communication professionals in the Corporate Communications/External Relations department of Ostern Corporation, a publicly traded, midsize medical software manufacturer noted for its excellent software programs for hospital and medical practice offices, Linda and Brad are challenged to handle the public announcements of a serious earnings loss, the firing of a popular senior vice president, and the filing of a major lawsuit against Ostern. In their tenure at Ostern, a situation like this one had never happened. Until recently sales growth had averaged 200 percent a year, with the most recent year-end figures topping $1 billion. Stock prices had increased 40 percent since the first public stock offering, and confidence was high in the company's future. Linda and Brad were faced with determining how to use past credibility to help with the present situation.

Jane Bevins had laid it on the line. Mike Mitchell, the senior vice president in charge of software development, had taken shortcuts with Hospital Manager 05, a major upgrade of the Manager Programs used by over 2,000 hospital systems throughout the country. Worse yet, conversion to the upgrade, which had begun in the last quarter and was continuing, had created serious trouble in some 500 hospitals. Software flaws were creating major scheduling and inventory mistakes as well as billing errors. Interwest Hospitals, the largest chain of hospitals using the Hospital Manager programs, had notified Jane they would file a lawsuit against Ostern asking for damages due to problems with the upgrade. If that were not bad enough, Jane told Linda and Brad that her internal investigation indicated Mike had subcontracted work on the upgrade to vendors in which he had substantial personal investments. Vendors who had helped with the initial release of Hospital Manager were not even contacted for bids to work on the revisions. Jane cautioned that this information must not be used publicly, but she wanted Linda and Brad to know she had no choice but to instantly terminate Mike. The lawsuit from Interwest was to be filed on Monday, and Monday also was the day to release the most negative quarterly earnings figures in Ostern's history. Jane told Linda and Brad she believed a loss in one quarter, although not desirable, was not the major problem. What the public would learn was that Ostern had a loss, had fired a senior vice president, and was to be sued by its most important customer. Jane asked Linda and Brad to return later in the day to discuss options and approaches to handling the press, detail how to communicate with stockholders, and recommend processes for internal announcements to management and employees. ■

INTRODUCTION

Linda and Brad face a difficult situation that will challenge their professional expertise as well as influence what happens next at Ostern. The positive environment within which Ostern has operated has changed rapidly. What appears to be an internal ethical and legal problem with a senior official has resulted in significant problems with a new product release. Not only has the release created a negative earnings environment, but also a major customer with high industry visibility has been so seriously damaged they are initiating legal action to deal with their losses. Linda and Brad must develop communication messages to announce quarterly earnings to stockholders and the press, to announce the departure of Mike Mitchell, and to respond to concerns about the lawsuit. They must consider the overall reputation of Ostern, legal issues surrounding both the lawsuit and the termination of Mitchell, and a host of other issues, including internal employee reactions. Linda and Brad face a rapidly changing environment, with conflicting needs for information. Their communication efforts have ethical and value implications, and what they do will in part contribute to the future of Ostern. Linda and Brad are engaged in creating recommendations for strategic organizational communication.

In previous chapters we explored the complexities of interpersonal and group communication within organizations. We discussed ways to increase awareness of our interactions and to develop critical competencies for participating in organizations. This chapter turns to the competencies required for participating in external communications, communicating with those beyond traditional organizational boundaries. Communications, both internal and external, are considered in the context of overall strategic communication planning. We explore the ways in which communication professionals analyze situations and select and implement communication strategies—in other words, their professional and strategic application of organizational communication. We discuss a strategic planning model and explore the roles of public relations and marketing in strategic management.

We develop *knowledge* competencies through defining and describing various aspects of strategic organizational communication. We encourage *sensitivity* by exploring the multiple audiences and needs for strategic organizational communication. We practice *skills* through case and situation analysis. Finally, we influence *values* by exploring the ethical implications of strategic organizational communication.

DESCRIBING STRATEGIC ORGANIZATIONAL COMMUNICATION

In today's rapidly changing business environment, cohesive, integrated communications are gaining recognition as a means of developing competitive advantage and of allowing an organization to adapt quickly to evolving needs and demands. Professionally developed organizational communication increasingly is part of overall strategic planning and action.

What is **strategic organizational communication?** Charles Conrad (1994) stated "strategic organizational communication involves the ability to analyze a situation, select appropriate communication strategies, and enact those strategies effectively." Strategic communication is therefore goal-oriented, is based on knowledge, and is a result of considered, deliberate decisions.

Strategic organizational communication ■ Transactional processes in which organizational messages are deliberately generated; are based on environmental data, analysis, and strategy selection; and are guided by organizational objectives.

Tom Daniels, Barry Spiker, and Michael Papa (1997) described another view, one in which strategic communications are controlled by those who control organizational resources, the management. Daniels, Spiker, and Papa explained strategic communications, although generated by numerous individuals and groups within an organization, usually consist of messages selected by management and tend to reflect management objectives and biases. Although sometimes mistaken as one-way communication (originating with management), strategic communication is in fact a two-way, transactional process. Information is received by management from organizational members and the external environment, and in turn messages are sent by management to involved parties. It is a dynamic interaction.

Phillip Clampitt, Robert DeKoch, and Thomas Cashman (2000) described communication strategy as "the macro-level choices and tradeoffs executives make, based on their organizational goals and judgments about others' reactions, which serve as a basis for action." Clampitt, DeKoch, and Cashman contended organizational leadership faces continuing pressing problems such as retaining quality employees, combating organizational cynicism, and creating a dynamic, evolving workplace. They suggested: "A communication strategy can provide a hedge against employee cynicism by ensuring that dissenting opinions about decisions, practices, or policies are appropriately channeled. A well-developed communication strategy also cultivates the kind of environment more accepting of change and innovation." They went on to describe efforts at 3M to cultivate seeds of innovation by routinely recording and telling stories about breakthrough products, processes, and ideas.

Within the context of this chapter, we consider strategic communication to encompass most of the elements discussed above. Strategic organizational communication is regarded as transactional processes in which organizational messages are deliberately generated; are based on environmental data, analysis, and strategy selection; and are guided by organizational objectives.

Perspectives on Strategic Organizational Communication

Historically, many organizations have viewed various strategic communication functions—such as internal communications with employees, public relations, and marketing—as largely isolated operations. These activities often have been planned and implemented by separate departments, with limited coordination or communication among functions. In addition, a predominant view of the strategic communication process has been described as an inside-out approach in which the organization is seen as the initiator of the communication process. This orientation is a one-way communication model, beginning with an organizational objective, which is transformed into communication objectives and then culminates with action on the part of the audience, the individuals to whom the communication is directed.

There is a major shift occurring regarding the underlying assumptions and processes of strategic organizational communication. Research indicates it is more effective to view strategic communications from an outside-in perspective. This orientation recognizes the importance of an organization's environment and the need for organizations to be aware of changing environmental conditions. The orientation challenges notions of fixed organizational boundaries and permits a view that blurs distinctions between internal and external interactions. This view is supportive of the George Cheney and Lars Christensen (2001) description of internal and external communication as interrelated dimensions of organizational sensemaking.

Outside-in planning begins with an analysis of the organizational environment. By taking environmental conditions into account, communications can be designed more effectively and can be targeted more accurately to meet the needs of various organizational **stakeholders**, those individuals and groups who have an interest or

Stakeholders ■ Individuals and groups who have an interest in the organization and are able to influence the organization's ability to meet its goals.

"stake" in the organization and are able to influence the organization's ability to meet its goals. In addition, outside-in planning is concerned with more than just disseminating messages. Because this approach is based on getting to know the interests and needs of various stakeholders, it cultivates the tools required to build long-term relationships with stakeholders. Unlike the traditional inside-out model, outside-in planning lays the foundation for ongoing communication between an organization and its stakeholders.

Communication strategy differs from communication tactics. A strategic communication goal may be to foster better interdepartmental and vendor communication. Numerous tactics such as job rotations, regular meetings, or teleconferencing may be used in support of the goal. Strategy involves choice. What issues are most important? What issues can or should be ignored? Who should present what? Why should it become a major theme? When is the best timing for communication? Strategy also involves anticipating the reactions of others and planning with those reactions in mind. Strategy becomes the basis for action. Communication tactics are the actions—both planned and otherwise—that determine whether the strategic objective is realized.

A number of environmental factors contribute to the growing acceptance of a more integrated strategic approach to communication. Corporate downsizing and reengineering have flattened organizations, breaking down structural barriers and involving cross-functions and greater numbers of individuals in decision making and planning. Global competitive markets have forced corporations to become more customer-oriented, resulting in targeted communications designed to reach specific groups of people rather than a mass audience. The numbers of communication channels have increased as technologies such as digital television, e-commerce, wireless communications, and the Internet have become commonplace. We are bombarded with messages from all fronts, making integrated communications more likely to be effective in a splintered, information-overloaded world.

THE ORGANIZATION AND ITS ENVIRONMENT

Chapter 3 discussed how Integrated Perspectives theories acknowledge the importance of the interaction between an organization and its environment. An outside-in approach to strategic communication also values this dynamic relationship. As contemporary organizational environments become increasingly complex, new technologies change the ways in which organizations communicate and conduct business. Globalization occurs due to advances in communications and transportation, rapidly transitioning political climates, and the lifting of trade restrictions.

As Cheney and Christensen (2001) suggested:

In the corporate landscape of today, the issue of identity is closely tied up with the ways organizations organize their "world" in terms of communication. To begin with, the key communication elements of source, message, and receiver are all much more complicated and less easily distinguished than in prior periods. As many organizations have come to realize, the principal management problem in today's marketplace of goods and ideas is not so much to provide commodities and services or to take stands on the salient issues of the day, but to do these things with a certain distinctiveness that allows the organization to create and legitimize itself, its particular "profile," and its advantageous position. This quest for visibility has made disciplines such as public relations, issue management, marketing, and advertising chief architects of organizational identity. (pp. 241–242)

Today's rapidly changing organizational climate and its competitive customer orientation require a high degree of interaction with multiple publics.

Multiple Publics

Publics ■ A small or large group of stakeholders with interests and needs relative to a particular organization.

When studying an organization's environment, it is helpful to identify its various **publics**. As defined by Scott Cutlip, Allen Center, and Glen Broom (1985), a public is "a group of individuals tied together by some common bond of interest and sharing a sense of commonness. It may be a small or a large group; it may be a majority or a minority group." Every organization has multiple publics. Publics also may be thought of as groups of stakeholders. The changing interests, needs, and actions of publics, or stakeholders, must be considered when planning organizational strategy. Linda and Brad are aware of the multiple publics interested in Ostern's problems. Stockholders, the media, customers, employees, vendors, and others all have questions about what has happened at Ostern and what Ostern will do in the future. Yet their questions are not the same. Linda and Brad are charged with understanding the needs of these various stakeholders and creating communication exchanges to meet diverse expectations.

Edward Lawler and Jay Galbraith (1994) proposed a number of characteristics they believe put an organization at risk of becoming a corporate "dinosaur— of becoming so cumbersome and highly adapted to its historical environment that it cannot respond to today's rapidly changing climate." One of these characteristics is "lack of contact with the customer and the environment," which leads organizational members to focus on internal processes rather than on how to best satisfy customer or stakeholder needs. Another risky characteristic is the attitude "If it ain't broke, don't fix it." This cultural rule encourages employees to stick with the status quo instead of recognizing customer needs change or that there is benefit in looking to the future and considering innovation. Maintaining a high degree of stakeholder contact and a willingness and ability to adapt is critical to long-term organizational success. Increasing use of sophisticated interactive technologies provides a host of new approaches for staying in contact with a variety of publics. Employees who understand the potential of these technologies are in increasing demand.

An organization's view of its position in its environment also affects its ability to respond to environmental changes. Bill Richardson (1995) suggested organizations have a tendency "to operate from a basis of inappropriate paradigms about their strength in an environment and their 'natural' right to provide the goods and services they have traditionally provided to that environment." Organizations need to match their paradigms and planning systems to their environments.

Environmental Scanning

Because the environment is rich with useful information, many organizations routinely monitor or scan the environment for data to help shape organizational strategy. **Environmental scanning** is "the acquisition and use of information about events and trends in an organization's external environment, the knowledge of which would assist management in planning the organization's future courses of action" (Auster and Choo, 1994).

> Environmental scanning ■ The acquisition and use of information about events and trends in an organization's external environment.

Although most senior managers recognize the value of environmental scanning, many organizations do not participate in systematic scanning efforts. The frequency and intensity of scanning activities vary greatly among organizations. Some organizations passively receive external information, whereas others actively search it out. Information may be gathered informally or sporadically through members' interactions with professional organizations, attendance at off-site training sessions or conferences, or scanning newspapers and journals. Public relations and marketing specialists often compile external data through formal activities such as market research. Some organizations have even established large, complex systems or units whose sole purpose is to scan the environment.

Eric Eisenberg and H. L. Goodall (1997) pointed out that boundary spanners, or organizational members who have direct contact with the public (such as salespeople or customer service representatives), can play an important role in gathering external data. Eisenberg and Goodall point out that boundary spanners bring information into organizations from external individuals, discover trends which are important to organizations, and provide information about organizations to their external environments. Effective organizations find ways to use information gained through boundary-spanning activities.

Environmental scanning should encompass all factors likely to influence the organization, now and in the future. Such scanning usually begins with identifying internal and external stakeholders and their interests and needs. Broader scanning can point out trends and events in the competitive, economic, technological, political, social, cultural, ecological, and demographic arenas. These data may be used to forecast and strategize for the short and long term. Environmental scanning increasingly is conducted with interactive technologies. As the ability to assemble, sort, and interpret data increases, environmental scanning is predicted to play an even more important role in the development of organizational strategy.

One difficult aspect of environmental scanning, and one at which many organizations fail, is the process of distributing the information to appropriate organizational members. Computer databases and information systems are important tools for organizing, retrieving, and disseminating data.

The interpretation of information also presents challenges. Data must be evaluated, filtered, and interpreted for meaning to be constructed. Many organizations do not have methods in place for systematically interpreting data.

Although we described environmental scanning primarily as a process of monitoring the external environment, successful organizations also are aware of the events, trends, and cultural conditions that exist within the organization. Members who have responsibility for external scanning often scan internally as well. The compilation of these data can provide a rich pool of information to help guide the organization.

The Global Environment

For all types and sizes of organizations, the global environment is increasingly relevant. Globalization contributes to competition, new market opportunities, new networks of collaborations, and a host of other potentials. Customers are literally everywhere. The international/global environment, networked with sophisticated technologies, spans diverse cultures and needs, challenging the understanding of multiple publics and environmental data. New competencies are required for communicating across languages, cultural differences, political realities, and basic needs. Organizations of today and tomorrow are challenged not only to think about the diverse publics in their home countries but how messages and data that flow rapidly across the entire world will influence their opportunities and effectiveness. Knowledge of technology is necessary but insufficient to meet these challenges. An emerging area of employment for communication professionals focuses specifically on those who have cultural competence as well as an understanding of sophisticated communications technologies.

STRATEGIC MANAGEMENT

Strategic management ■ The process of formulating and implementing an organizational plan of action.

Environmental information is useful only if considered in light of its relationship to and impact on organizational activities. Through the practice of **strategic management,** external information converges with other factors to shape organizational decisions and actions. Strategic management is the process of formulating and implementing an organizational plan of action, a road map of sorts that sets direction and guides the organization among alternative courses. The purpose of strategic planning is to strengthen the organization's position in its larger environment.

Many of today's ideas about strategic management have their roots in the 1960s in the pioneering work of Harvard Business School's Kenneth Andrews and C. Roland Christensen. Andrews expanded on their work in his seminal book, *The Concept of Corporate Strategy* (1971). Andrews described strategy development as beginning with an assessment of environmental conditions and trends and the organization's internal capabilities and resources. This information could be used to determine a match between the organization's qualifications and its environment. From the area of intersection (the best match of opportunity and resources), strategy was created. Strategic management seeks to create competitive advantage by using the organization's unique qualifications to pursue opportunities existing in the environment. Although many descriptions of strategic management focus on for-profit organizations, it is important to note the processes of strategic management apply to all types of organizations attempting to meet diverse goals in complicated environments.

SWOT ■ Strengths, weaknesses, opportunities, and threats identified for strategic planning.

Andrews's model has come to be known by the acronym **SWOT:** strengths, weaknesses, opportunities, threats. In practice, the SWOT model represents these activities: the organization identifies its strengths and weaknesses as well as the opportunities and threats existing in the external environment; this information is used to design a strategy that will create competitive advantage; the strategy is implemented with consistent, coordinated, organization-wide effort. Designing the organization and implementing all aspects of activities in support of the strategy are known as strategic alignment.

Although Andrews defined strategy in rather broad terms, over the years the concept of strategy has developed to hold more precise meanings in different contexts, such as competitive or positioning strategy, business strategy, corporate strategy, and operating strategy. For the purposes of this discussion of strategic organizational communication, the focus is on the development of competitive or positioning strategy. Competitive or positioning strategy is often described as the unique quality or competence an organization has to offer, the qualities that will create competitive advantage or a distinct position among similar organizations. Eisenberg and Goodall (1997) suggested this straightforward definition: "a (competitive) strategy is a clear statement of why customers should choose a company's products or services over those of competing companies." For nonprofit organizations, a competitive or positioning strategy can be said to create a distinctiveness where donors or clients prefer the nonprofit to others offering similar services.

There are several common competitive approaches. One strategy is to be the low-cost leader in an industry, such as Wal-Mart in discount retailing. Other companies select differentiation strategies, designed to provide a unique feature within a product or service repertoire. For example, L. L. Bean offers its mail-order customers an unconditional, 100 percent satisfaction guarantee. A nonprofit may stress its low overhead, resulting in a higher amount of donor money going directly to those served by the organization. Chances are your school stresses the positive competitive position created for students with an advanced education as contrasted to those who do not continue education past high school. Other differentiation strategies may be focused on superior technical support, quality, numbers of people served, custom-order manufacture, excellent customer service, spare parts availability, or any of a long list of special features.

Over the years, many individuals have elaborated on and refined Andrews's strategic planning model. Many have specified in greater detail the various aspects of strategic planning. Most of the models are still based on the SWOT analysis and contain, in some form or another, the following phases: (1) scanning and interpreting the internal and external environments; (2) formulating a mission, or vision for the future, and transforming it into specific objectives; (3) developing strategy and implementing supporting programs; and (4) monitoring, reviewing, and revising the plan and its implementation.

Although the SWOT model remains a dominant one, it is not without its critics. Henry Mintzberg (1990, 1991, 1994) criticized the approach for its formalization of strategic planning as a detailed and detached prescriptive process. Traditional models, such as SWOT, tend to emphasize planning, or thinking, before implementation, or action. The tasks of planning managers tend to be separated from those of operating managers. Mintzberg suggested it is artificial to separate thinking and acting into separate phases. Actions influence thoughts, and thoughts influence actions; the two are intimately connected. Not only can strategies be formulated, but also they sometimes emerge from a pattern of actions: "Various people can interact and so develop a pattern that becomes a strategy. . . . Strategies can develop in all kinds of unusual ways, as people interact, mutually adjust, learn from each other, conflict, and develop consensus" (Mintzberg, 1990).

An important element of strategic management is the accurate and consistent communication of strategy to internal and external stakeholders. Although all organizational activities are involved in supporting strategy in one way or another, two functions carry a major responsibility for strategy communication and implementation: public relations and marketing.

STRATEGIC ORGANIZATIONAL COMMUNICATION

Clampitt, DeKoch, and Cashman (2000) described an effective communication strategy as having the following characteristics: (1) linking to organizational goals, (2) legitimizing certain issues and delegitimizing others, (3) shaping organizational memory, (4) making sense of the confusing and ambiguous, (5) providing a proper point of identity, and (6) continuously evolving. Further, they suggested communication strategy should be developed through a discover, create, and assess process. *Discover* refers to discerning critical issues within the context of specific circumstances. *Create* includes the process of establishing goals, developing strategy, and selecting tactics for communication, and *assess* refers to the actual implementation of strategy and its evaluation.

Public Relations

There has been little agreement over the years regarding the definition of **public relations.** In many ways, it has been a profession in search of a clear identity. Public relations, or PR, is viewed by some as one of several narrow functions, including employee communications, publicity, public affairs, media relations, or marketing support. Others see public relations as representing a broader group of activities, even encompassing all the communication activities of an organization. Glen Broom (2008) defines public relations as "'the management function that establishes and maintains mutually beneficial relationships between an organization and the publics on whom its success or failure depends' (Broom, 2009, p. 7). This definition positions the practice of public relations as a *management function* and implies that management in all organizations must attend to public relations. It also identifies building and maintaining *mutually beneficial relationships* between organizations and their publics as the moral and ethical basis of the profession" (p. 694).

Public relations ■ Strategic organizational communication involving an organization's image, internal communication, public affairs and issues management, media relations, and crisis management.

According to James Grunig (1992), his five-year study to determine the characteristics of excellent public relations programs has shown excellent programs are based on symmetrical, or two-way, communication interactions. Grunig (1990) argued that not only is a symmetrical approach more effective, but it is also "more ethical and socially responsible." Rather than focusing solely on the needs of the organization, symmetrical public relations builds mutually beneficial relationships that are more likely to be sustained over the long term.

Clarke Caywood (1997) explained how public relations, more than other functions, strengthens the outside-in perspective of an organization by building and integrating stakeholder relationships. Although public relations encompasses the full range of communication between an organization and its publics, a major PR function that receives attention is that of image building. Other specific public relations activities include the management of internal communications, public affairs and public issues, media relations, and communication during organizational crises.

Managing an Organization's Image or Reputation

To many, the term *image building* carries negative connotations of deceit and manipulation. Public relations professional Leonard Saffir (1992) explained:

> Some PR professionals deplore the word "image" because it is so often misused. They complain that too many clients think of PR people as super manipulators who can create images that bedazzle the public into buying weak stories or inferior products. Image building is a legitimate topic for a discussion of public relations. It is, to a considerable extent, what PR people do. The trouble comes when PR professionals and clients, alike, misunderstand the term. "Imaging" may involve sharpening perceptions, broadening them, or, in some cases, changing them. Imaging is not the building of illusions or the blurring of minds so the truth cannot be perceived. In thinking about images, clients and professionals should talk about skillful projection or real qualities, not the construction of something imaginary. The best approach is to take it as a given that the substance is there before anybody goes to work bringing out the image. (p. 130)

As Grunig (1992) pointed out, "Public relations practitioners use the term image to refer to many different concepts, such as reputation, perception, attitude, message, attributes, evaluation, cognition, perception, credibility, support, belief, communication, or relationship. The average person sees image as the opposite of reality. In everyday language, images are projected, manipulated, polished, and tarnished. We believe the only escape from this confusion is not to use the term. Instead, we prefer to use one of the more precise terms to which image refers— such as reputation, perception, or evaluation" (p. 33).

In light of the ambiguity of the term, our discussion of "image" focuses on the building and maintaining of an organization's reputation. For many public relations professionals, reputation management is a major responsibility and a function that is considered critical to an organization's success.

It is important to understand the factors influencing organizational reputations. Most organizations attempt to shape their reputations by drawing the attention of stakeholders to favorable qualities. Reputations, however, are dependent on much more than information communicated directly by the organization. In fact, reputation messages can be quite different from those intended. Stakeholders receive information about an organization from a variety of sources, and multiple factors come into play as stakeholders construct their views. Some form opinions of reputation based on financial performance. Others look to employment practices, quality of products or services, concern for environmental issues, community involvement, and a host of other factors to determine an organization's reputation or image. Some organizations have conflicting reputations, doing well financially but not known as good places for employees to work. And, of course, reputations for the same organization can differ from individual to individual and from group to group.

Grunig (1993), in a criticism of public relations professionals, suggested many professionals are preoccupied with image, which he views as only superficial symbolism. An emphasis on image can cause professionals to lose sight of the need to build substantive behavioral relationships between organizations and their publics. He argued for more attention to creating ongoing, interactive relationships with stakeholders.

Any discussion of image or reputation building should consider the ethical implications inherent in the process. Is the image portrayed an accurate reflection of the organization ? Does the company in fact provide quality products or services? Organizations are challenged to ensure that public relations helps people think favorably of organizations, including fostering beliefs that reputations are deserved.

Internal Communications

Internal communications ■ Planned and formalized communication prepared by communication professionals and disseminated to internal organizational members.

Internal communications, sometimes referred to as employee communications, often are developed by public relations departments. In most organizations, employees are considered an important public. Organizations increasingly are recognizing the value of building with employees long-term relationships based on mutual satisfaction.

There is an important distinction between the types of internal communication discussed here and the management of internal communications. Most of the communication discussed in earlier chapters occurs during the daily interactions of organizational members. The function of internal communications, by contrast, although often dealing with the subject matter of daily interactions, is planned and formalized communication prepared and disseminated by communication professionals to and for internal organizational members.

Internal communications specialists may be involved in a wide range of activities: seeking input from employees through surveys, interviews, meetings, or other methods; communicating the organization's mission, objectives, strategies, and programs through training activities or the preparation and dissemination of newsletters, manuals, pamphlets, and other publications; establishing formalized structures to improve the quality and flow of organizational communication; creating Web sites for internal use; determining which social media will be utilized with employees; and in general managing all communications designed to help the organization achieve its strategic objectives. Internal communications specialists increasingly use intranets, the Web, and various video interactive systems to provide information and solicit input. Internal communication portrays the values of an organization with regard to employee inclusion or exclusion in problem solving and decision making. Although most employees experience the organization through a set of peers and a manager, internal communications help employees experience the larger organization. As such, internal communications are pivotal to developing trust in the competence of the entire organization.

It is important to point out that although many organizations house the internal communications function within the public relations department that is not always the case. Internal communications may be managed by human relations, corporate communications, or other management functions.

Public Affairs and Issues Management

Public affairs and issues management involve the shaping of public opinion regarding social and political issues important to an organization. Public affairs departments inform employees about issues of importance to the organization, work with a variety of regulatory and governmental groups, are active in community-based issues, engage in political activities, and coordinate organizational public service engagement.

Public affairs and issues management ■ Shaping of public opinion regarding social and political issues important to an organization.

Issues management, a proactive function of public affairs, involves foreseeing emerging public policy issues and responding with strategies to resolve issues of importance to the organization. The strategies may be aimed at creating organizational or environmental change. An example from a city council dispute with land developers can help describe issues management. The city council of a medium-sized Midwestern community voted to permit land development of a beautiful wooded site used for many years as a recreation area by local residents. The land was not designated as a park although some efforts had been made by citizens to encourage the council to purchase the land for open space and parks. Following the council's vote for development, an active citizens' campaign attempted to block development efforts. Developers, anticipating citizen protest, mounted their own efforts, focusing not on the particular land in question but on the overall value of development to the community. Press conferences, direct mail, and advertising were all used to describe responsible growth and the need for sensitive development of beautiful land. Citizens responded with letter-writing and telephone campaigns citing examples of questionable development activities. In addition, citizens, using a somewhat obscure statute, collected signatures for a city-wide vote on development. The council was forced to call an election. The outcome—developers were permitted to build but were required to leave a significant amount of the property without houses—was a compromise. Observers believe that the developer's campaign—an example of issues management—was the primary reason they were able to continue with their plans. Citizens criticized the outcome, alleging that developers bought the issue by spending amounts of money the citizens could not hope to raise.

Raymond Ewing (1997) offered a seven-step model of the issues management process: (1) issue identification, or scanning the social and political environments for emerging issues; (2) issue analysis, or projecting how an issue will affect the organization; (3) development of a corporate policy position on an issue; (4) development of specific action plans to deal with issues; (5) implementation of action plans and communication of the organization's positions on issues; (6) review of the results, including public reactions, objections, negotiations, and organizational adjustments; and (7) continued focus on the issue "until it is resolved in a manner the company can live with during the current phase of the issue's life."

Media Relations

Media relations professionals Richard Kosmicki and Frederick Bona (1996) described the practice of **media relations**:

Media relations ■ Working with the media on behalf of an organization.

As a practitioner of media relations, you serve three masters.
One is your company, non-profit organization, or, if you work in an agency, your

client. The second is the print and electronic media. The third is the various publics who receive their information from the media. You are responsible to all three—yet you have little or no authority to influence or make final decisions. So, it takes great skill and experience to accommodate these three masters. In fact, if you're a smart communicator, you'll treat the media, print and electronic, as well as you treat your employer, client, and the audiences the media serves. (p. 59)

Effective media relations are important for strategic organizational communication. According to Thomas L. Harris (1991), the general public "continues to believe what is seen in the local and trade papers and broadcast on the evening news. Publicity has the impact of a respected third-party endorsement. . . . Media relations heightens the impact of other communications efforts."

It is important for media relations specialists to become familiar with the nature of the various media and to understand the needs of the press and their range of approaches. From newspapers to magazines, from Internet to network or cable television, each medium has its own style, scope, and audience. For example, a trade magazine is likely to target an industry audience with an in-depth article or case study; national television tends to focus on breaking news and to communicate to a broader audience (depending on the program), using visuals and sound bites. Newspapers and broadcast media alike post news on Web sites continually throughout the day and night. Media specialists have limited time to prepare responses when events are fast-moving and rapidly changing. Media outlets utilize social media such as Twitter, blogs, YouTube, and Facebook to provide public interactivity for breaking news. The length of time allowed to research and develop a story, deadline frequency, and the availability of support staff all affect the manner in which journalists function. The media relations specialist can increase the likelihood of press coverage by understanding journalists' needs and providing them with information that is timely, interesting, and newsworthy, presented in a straightforward and usable format. Knowing the various media and their methods and approaches can be invaluable in effectively establishing press contacts and managing media relations efforts.

Risk and Crisis Communication

Risk communication and crisis communication are emerging specialties for communication professionals. In recent years, we have become aware of communication processes which highlight emergent dangers and potentially shape interventions and risk management (Scott and Trethewey, 2008). We also know many organizations establish technical responses to crises without thoughtfully preparing crises communication responses. Barbara Miller and J. Suzanne Horsley (2009) clarify, "Findings suggest that although companies place great emphasis on the technical response to a crisis, the lack of crisis communication components in overall planning strategies prevents some companies from being able to adequately respond to a crisis situation." Although risk and crisis are not new organizational problems, the expanding public awareness of risk and crisis brought about by communications technologies contributes to new pressures and opportunities for organizations. Although related, risk communication and crisis communication are somewhat different processes requiring different framing and timing of messages to multiple publics. As Barbara Reynolds and Matthew Seeger (2005) suggested: "The basic goals of risk and crisis communication . . . differ. Risk messages concern the probabilities of some harm and associated methods for reducing the probability of the harm. Risk messages often are grounded in both current scientific and technical understanding of a specific risk factor as well as cultural or social beliefs regarding the risk. . . . Messages about crisis, in contrast, typically concern both what is known and what is not known about a specific event" (p. 48).

Risk communication is generally defined as the production of messages for the organization's various publics with regard to potential risks and their consequences. Risk messages often include information on how the organization is assessing or monitoring the risk, what preventive measures—if any—are in place, how the organization will respond if a perceived risk becomes a reality, and what individuals can do (self-efficacy) to reduce their personal or environmental risks. Security breaches, identity theft, health, and environmental hazards are high on many organizations' lists of issues requiring risk communication messages. As Reynolds and Seeger (2005) identified, risk communication produces messages regarding known probabilities of negative consequences and how they may be reduced. It is designed to be persuasive, is usually part of a prepared campaign including all types of mediated messages, and is controlled and structured. Safety campaigns are frequent examples of risk communication. Policies supporting technology security are communicated broadly. Disease control and health risk messages are provided by many organizations. An increasing number of organizations conduct annual risk assessments and determine issues where risk communication messages can contribute to the effectiveness and positive reputation of the organization. In most of these organizations, professional communicators are part of this assessment and message development process.

> **Risk communication** ■ Communication prepared to educate about potential risks and provide information about how to reduce potential harm.

The terrorist attacks of September 11, 2001; Hurricane Katrina; the H1N1 flu—all of these and a host of other threat experiences have challenged airlines, local government officials, the federal government, and a host of other organizations to emphasize crisis communication as never before. Virtually everyone in the United States of America and throughout the world was not only affected by these tragedies and events but also by crisis communication efforts. **Crisis communication**, simply put, is the communication response made by organizations to emergency situations. Although most U.S.A. organizations will never experience the scope of the September 11, 2001, events, most will face crises requiring major strategic communication efforts. One of the fastest-growing professional responsibilities for leaders and communication managers is the planning for what is sometimes referred to as **crisis management**.

> **Crisis communication** ■ Communication response in emergency situations designed to minimize harm to the organization and assist in understanding and responding to the emergency.
>
> **Crisis management** ■ Use of public relations to minimize harm to the organization in emergency situations that could cause damage.

Robert Ulmer (2001) identified the importance of precrisis communication in developing an effective postcrisis communication strategy. He provided a description of the crisis communication response of Malden Mills, a textile manufacturer, to a devastating fire that injured thirty-six employees and destroyed enough property to threaten to put the company out of business. Before the fire, Malden Mills' leadership had worked to establish strong relationships with employees, customers, the media, and the community. Malden Mills was the largest employer in the area at the time of the explosion. When the CEO of Malden Mills spoke to media with the fire still burning in the background, his message of constancy and commitment to rebuild was seen as consistent with his previous messages and community involvement. The postcrisis communication continued over an extended period also evidenced approaches used by Malden Mills prior to the crisis. The community, workers, and customers became advocates for the company, assisting in mitigating the financial strain brought about by the explosion. Kathleen Fearn-Banks (2008) concludes a crisis has five stages: "(1) detection, (2) prevention/preparation, (3) containment, (4) recovery, and (5) learning." The stages are not linear, with several stages potentially occurring at once. Communication professionals increasingly are involved in all stages.

Although an increasing number of organizations are developing crisis strategies and crisis communication plans, Peter Stanton (2002) provided common mistakes when in a crisis situation:

1. *Rushing to judgment.* It is essential to understand the facts before engaging in communication.
2. *Overreacting.* The most effective communicators always act judiciously.
3. *Failure to act.* Most crises do not go away by themselves and require some level of response.
4. *"Bending" the facts.* In an atmosphere of lawsuits, it is tempting to shape communication to avoid legal action. Although communication does not have to be a blunt admission of wrongdoing, it should be truthful and not invented or altered.
5. *Lack of concern/empathy/sympathy.* Concern for those affected by the crisis should be expressed before concern for shareholders or profitability. Expressions of concern for shareholders or profitability are legitimate but should be put in proper sequence.
6. *Affixing blame.* Messages about what is going to be done are more important than affixing blame.
7. *Remaining insular.* Effective messages are developed with an external as well as an internal perspective. Use of media content analysis, focus groups, and external professionals often contributes to effectiveness.
8. *Absence of teamwork.* Although the communication professional may be in charge, it is important to use the abilities and knowledge of individuals from various parts of the organization.
9. *Restricting information internally.* The focus often is on the public, with inadequate regard for the impact on the internal organization. Employees can be important ambassadors during a crisis.
10. *Failure to plan.* It is impossible to plan for a specific crisis, but it is possible to develop a plan for how the organization will respond and make decisions during a crisis.

A common mistake made during crises is an overall lack of action or communication. Although many executives feel reluctant to confront the press, it is important to use the media to communicate the organization's messages. If the organization fails to respond to media requests, the void will be filled with information from other sources. Being the first to tell the story allows the organization to define the situation and to develop a favorable public impression regarding its handling of the event.

Matthew Seeger (2006, pp. 236–242) reported the findings of a panel of crisis communication experts with regard to best practices when faced with a crisis. Seeger's findings include the following:

1. Make risk and crisis communication part of the decision process itself. Communication should not merely be involved in communicating decisions about risk and crisis after they have been made.
2. Identify risk areas and corresponding risk reduction, preset initial crisis responses so that decision making during a crisis is more efficient, and identify necessary response resources.
3. Ongoing efforts should be made to inform and educate the public using science-based risk assessments. During a crisis, the public should be told what is happening, and organizations managing crises have a responsibility to share this information.
4. Listen to the public's concerns and understand the audience. Take the public's concerns into account and respond to them accordingly.
5. Be honest and open. Honesty is necessary to build credibility and trust before and during a crisis. Openness about risks may promote an environment of risk sharing. If information about a crisis is not shared openly by the organization engaged in the crisis, the public will obtain information from other sources.
6. Collaborate and coordinate with credible sources. Developing a precrisis network is an effective way of coordinating and collaborating with other credible sources. Coordinating messages enhances the probability of consistency and may reduce public confusion.
7. Meet the needs of the media and remain accessible. The media are the primary conduit to the public. Rather than viewing the media as a liability in a crisis situation, risk and crisis communicators should engage the media through open and honest communication as a strategic resource to aid in managing the crisis.
8. Designated spokespersons should demonstrate appropriate levels of compassion, concern, and empathy.
9. Accept uncertainty and ambiguity. Risks always include some level of uncertainty. Crises and disasters are by definition abnormal, dynamic, and unpredictable.
10. Use messages of self-efficacy. Messages of self-efficacy are most effective when they recommend a range of specific harm-reducing actions to those affected by the crisis, focusing on what can be done to help others. Messages of self-efficacy need to be constructed carefully so that the reason for the action is clear, consistent, and meaningful.

Fundamental communication principles can be identified for use during a crisis. James Lukaszewski (1997) suggested establishing communication priorities: (1) those most directly affected; (2) employees; (3) those indirectly affected such as neighbors, customers, families, suppliers, government, regulators, and so on; and (4) the media and other channels of external communication. Lukaszewski suggested communicating with those most directly affected first; keeping communication local or as close to the site of the impact as possible; speaking with one voice but not necessarily with only one spokesperson; acting quickly to provide news of any adverse incident; cooperating with the media; making sound decisions; and describing how the issue involves integrity or moral or ethical dilemmas.

Many organizations prepare for potential crises by designing a crisis management plan. Plans frequently include an assessment of the types of crises to which the organization is vulnerable; the formation of a crisis team including leaders, technical responders, and communication professionals; an analysis of potential audiences who would be affected by the crisis; advance preparation of important materials needed during the crisis; and development of a crisis response center.

Employees, shareholders, and customers often are affected differently by a crisis and their needs and expectations will vary. These considerations should be taken into account when developing crisis plans. Given the high-risk nature of crisis communication and the potential for long-term, irreparable damage to the organization, crisis communication has become an important aspect of public relations.

Marketing

Marketing ■ Strategic organizational communication that is directed at bringing about an exchange between an organization and a customer.

Like the various public relations functions, **marketing** is a management process that bears major responsibility for communicating and implementing strategy. Perhaps because public relations and marketing share this responsibility, and both are involved in communicating with external publics, there is often confusion regarding their specific organizational roles. Public relations is sometimes considered part of the marketing department, or vice versa. In many organizations the two are viewed as separate but complementary functions. There is currently a trend toward integrating the two to form the most comprehensive and effective means of communicating with an organization's many publics. This trend of integrated marketing communication is discussed next.

Marketing, unlike public relations, is usually directed at bringing about an exchange between an organization and a customer. Marketing can be thought of as "a social and managerial process by which individuals and groups obtain what they need and want through creating and exchanging products and value with others" (Kotler and Armstrong, 1996). Marketing management involves analyzing markets and then planning, implementing, and monitoring programs designed to create and maintain these exchanges.

Philip Kotler and Gary Armstrong (1996) explained the relationship between marketing planning and strategic planning:

> [Marketing planning] supports company strategic planning with more detailed planning for specific marketing opportunities. . . . There is much overlap between overall company strategy and marketing strategy. Marketing looks at consumer needs and the company's ability to satisfy them; these same factors guide the company mission and objectives. Most company strategy planning deals with marketing variables—market share, market development, growth—and it is sometimes hard to separate strategic planning from marketing planning. In fact, some companies refer to their strategic planning as "strategic market planning. . . ." (p. 36)

Marketing plays a key role in the company's strategic planning in several ways. First, marketing provides a guiding philosophy—the marketing concept—which suggests company strategy should revolve around serving the needs of important consumer groups. Second, marketing provides inputs to strategic planners by helping to identify attractive market opportunities and by assessing the firm's potential to take advantage of them. Finally, within individual business units, marketing designs strategies for reaching the unit's objectives. (p. 43).

In the most effective organizations, marketing, public relations, strategic planning, and all other functions work together to develop and achieve strategic objectives and ultimately to serve the needs of customers.

Integrated Marketing Communications

During the 1990s, **integrated marketing communications** (IMC) emerged as a growing approach to the marketing process. Northwestern University's Medill School of Journalism defined integrated marketing communications as "the process of managing all sources of information about a product which behaviorally moves the customer toward a sale and maintains customer loyalty" (Harris, 1997).

> **Integrated marketing communications** ■ Process of managing all sources of information about a product that behaviorally moves the customer toward a sale and maintains customer loyalty.

IMC proponents stress the importance of building a multichannel, integrated communications strategy that communicates a single, unified message to a customer. Michael Belch and George Belch (2008) contend the movement to IMC is because "marketers recognize the value of strategically integrating the various communication functions rather than having them operate autonomously. By coordinating their marketing communication efforts, companies can avoid duplication, take advantage of synergy among various communication tools, and develop more efficient and effective marketing communication programs" (p. 816). According to Belch and Belch, the reasons for the rise are multiple, but the rapid growth of the Internet, technological advances, and changing media habits, when coupled with the rise of large retailers and the growth of database marketing, account for the need for change. Matching messages to consumer needs and integrating communications into a single message are important ways to increase the likelihood that marketing messages will be processed.

The Marketing Mix

A well-designed marketing plan coordinates multiple elements that have been designed to work together to achieve marketing goals. Numerous tools are available to the marketer; the blend of these tools is referred to as the marketing mix. The tools fall into four categories, known as the four Ps: *product* decisions (such as quality, design, packaging, services); *pricing* decisions (price, discounts, credit terms); *place* decisions (distribution channels, or the system for providing convenient access to products); and *promotion* decisions (advertising, personal selling, sales promotion, public relations).

Marketing professionals select from a range of promotional tools, including advertising, personal selling, sales promotion, and public relations strategies.

Advertising is a mass communication strategy, personal selling involves interpersonal communication, which can occur face-to-face or over the telephone (known as telemarketing), and sales promotion refers to strategies that offer added value or incentives to purchase.

For example, tools for sales promotion include contests, coupons, bonuses, and free samples. Public relations also offers unique strategies to the mix of promotional tools. Favorable publicity about a company or product tends to be more credible than advertising and may even have the effect of a third-party endorsement. A successful marketing program coordinates the various promotional tools with product, price, and place strategies to create an effective marketing mix.

Direct marketing is the fastest growing form of marketing. "Direct marketing consists of direct communications with carefully targeted consumers to obtain an immediate response" (Kotler and Armstrong, 1996). Direct marketing techniques include direct mail and catalog marketing, telemarketing, television marketing (infomercials or home shopping programs), as well as online shopping, which is the fastest-growing of all direct marketing techniques. Direct marketing provides avenues for customer feedback and is designed to encourage an immediate purchase response. As the trend toward narrowcasting advances, direct marketing strategies play an increasing role in the overall marketing mix.

Advertising

Advertising ■ Planned messages which are part of the promotional marketing mix and which utilize media to reach intended audiences to stimulate a desired impact such as product purchase or behavior change.

Advertising is the use of planned messages to target audiences through media selection to impact a purchase or behavior decision. Samuel Bradley and Timothy Laubacher (2008) describe the pervasiveness of advertising in the U.S.A. culture: "According to the trade publication *Advertising Age,* $149 billion was spent on measured media advertising in the United States in 2007. That's approximately $4500 for every woman, man, and child in the country." Donald Jugenheimer (2008) describes the advertising media process:

First , one analyzes the product, service, or idea to be promoted, along with a competitive analysis and a survey of the marketing situation. Next comes the objectives and goals, what is to be achieved with the campaign: marketing objectives, more specific advertising objectives, and even more specific media objectives. Then comes the strategies, which are plans to achieve the objectives. The strategies include the campaign targets, including geographic targets (target markets), customer targets (target groups), and media targets (target audiences). From all these analyses, it is possible to evaluate the characteristics of all the available mass media in terms of the campaign objectives and to begin to select the best media types for the campaign. Media tactics are the implementation of the plans and involve the specific media vehicles and units to be used, along with the schedules. The advertising media plan must also consider any media promotions, continuity or 'fallback' plans, the media calendar, the budget and the integration of the marketing, advertising, and media strategies and tactics. (p. 805)

Those involved in advertising are concerned not only with message development but the strategic selection of media to reach with desired frequency intended audiences. Advertising, more than public relations, is measured by sales and be-havior results.

Branding

Communication professionals in marketing, advertising, or corporate communi-cations departments are frequently responsible for branding. **Branding** is the specific process of developing product or service identification that distinguishes products or services from competi-tor organizations. Branding develops product names and state-ments (sometimes in the form of slogans) about product or service identity. Brands help create product or service identity necessary to increase sales or usage and to generate customer loyalty. Paul Mlodzik (2006) sug-gested branding "creates meaning beyond the features of the product or service . . . reduces the need to compete on price . . . builds a relationship based on meeting expectations . . . enhances the efficiency of marketing and sales efforts . . . cre-ates and enhances loyalty . . . helps mask weaknesses and aids recovery . . . builds a barrier to competition . . . extendible to products in new categories" (pp. 408–409). In sum, branding requires creativity, an understanding of customers and audiences, and the ability to make determinations of comparative advantage.

> **Branding** ■ Process of developing product- or service-naming and identity statements that distinguish products or services from competi-tor products or services.

Relationship Marketing and the Use of Marketing Databases

The practice of using communication to build long-term relationships with cus-tomers is known as relationship marketing. In relationship marketing, "there is a relationship between the buyer and the seller that normally results from inter-changes and exchanges of information and things of mutual value" (Schultz, Tannenbaum, and Lauterborn, 1992). Advances in information technologies allow companies to compile information about their customers that is necessary for maintaining ongoing relationships. As companies attempt to learn more about their customers to better serve their needs, they employ computerized databases to store, organize, and retrieve consumer data.

Most of us have experienced an Internet Web site able to identify our past pur-chases and suggest new products or services we might like based on our previous search and buying practices. At times these suggestions are helpful and at other times we wonder about the intrusion into our privacy of these powerful technolo-gies. Indeed, the proliferation of database marketing is accompanied by a growing concern about invasion of privacy.

Organizations gather customer information in numerous ways. Marketers may directly solicit responses from consumers through telemarketing, toll-free phone numbers, warranty cards, or direct mail pieces. Data from sweepstakes entries and magazine subscriptions are compiled. Companies also may track a customer's pur-chasing history by scanning the UPC (Universal Product Code) on products that are purchased, supplying data on the buying behaviors of an individual or household. This information is compiled in a computerized marketing database and can later be used to target communications to specific audiences. A marketing database is considered an important tool of integrated marketing communications.

This is an exciting and challenging time for professionals in the field of marketing. Changes in the marketing environment, advances in communications technology, and the development of new marketing tools and approaches all converge to create a dynamic and evolving profession.

Technology and Strategic Organizational Communication

The increasing presence of social media is changing strategic organizational communication in usage of media, content, frequency, reach, and timing. Essentially **social media** can be described as information created by organizations and individuals using highly accessible, mostly interactive communications technologies. Social media usage shifts individuals from more traditional ways of discovering, reading, or sharing news to the capacity to interactively turn monologue into dialogue by both consuming and generating information almost simultaneously. Although change is constant, social media have been categorized into several main groupings: social networks, blogs, message boards, podcasts, online video, RSS feeds, and wikis. Social networks are comprised of people who generally share interests and who want to explore these interests with others. Current examples include Facebook, Myspace, and Twitter. Organizations increasingly are reaching potential customers, donors, or other types of supporters using these media. Many suggest social media are changing the landscape of political campaigns, while others believe it is only a matter of time before social media replace more traditional media in advertising dollars expended. Blogs are watched daily by public relations and marketing professionals. Blogs are Web sites where individuals leave comments including both text and images. Blogs provide immediate feedback to organizations, and numerous organizations create their own public blogs. The *Huffington Post* blog is just one current example of the power of blogs. Message boards can be described as online discussion sites using technology to create the more traditional bulletin board. *Craigs List* is one of the more famous of the current message boards. Podcasts use digital media files to make diverse content available for download via Web syndication. Podcasts are in use for internal employee communication as well as for distribution to a mass audience. Podcasting usually requires subscription software. Online videos are video clips placed on the Web on sites such as YouTube. Online news clips, sporting events, music videos, and other content frequently are posted, contributing to broad reactions from diverse audiences. RSS feeds enable individuals to subscribe to Web content on any issue, trend, person, or product about which they want to stay current. RSS aggregators known as readers are necessary for subscribers to access information. Only information about individually selected topics will appear on the reader, negating the necessity to visit a variety of Web sites dealing with the selected topics. Finally wikis are a collection of Web pages designed to enable anyone with access to contribute or modify content, using a simplified markup language. The most famous broadly accessible wiki today is Wikipedia. Many organizations have in-house wikis for problem solving and publishing of important technical information. Needless to say the selection of appropriate new technologies requires expertise not common among communication professionals. Additionally, the rapid, interactive nature of social media presents new challenges for communication professionals as they engage in strategic organizational communication.

Social media ■ Information created by organizations and individuals using highly accessible, mostly interactive communications technologies.

Evaluating Strategic Organizational Communication

Strategic organizational communication is subject to a variety of measures for effectiveness. It is not the purpose of this chapter to explore all possible evaluation techniques but to raise awareness that strategic organizational communication costs organizational resources and is therefore expected to contribute to a positive return to the organization. Public relations professionals routinely report the content and frequency of all types of media coverage—both planned and unplanned. Those planning advertising campaigns report numbers of individuals reached as well as cost. Sales figures are calculated against public relations and marketing expenditures. Behaviors, such as voting, contributing money, or volunteering, are measured against the cost of efforts to stimulate these behaviors. Survey research, focus groups, competitive rankings, and a host of similar measures are used to evaluate communication effectiveness. Numbers of Web site hits, migration across Web pages, online requests, online purchases, and online donations all are calculated and contrasted with expenditures. Communication professionals are expected to understand, develop, and implement a variety of measures to determine effectiveness and direct future strategy.

ETHICAL ISSUES IN STRATEGIC ORGANIZATIONAL COMMUNICATION

As with all the forms and processes of organizational communication discussed so far, strategic organizational communication encompasses important ethical issues. In the Ostern case, Linda and Brad deal with a critical ethical abuse as well as the ethical implications of the options they recommend to Jane Bevins. Although we each have personal responsibilities for the ethics of our individual behaviors, the communication professional engaging in strategic communication efforts is combining personal responsibility with the broader concept of organizational ethical responsibilities.

Cheney and Christensen (2001) identified seven broad issues with ethical, moral, and even legal implications resulting from planned communication: (1) the posited character or integrity of the source of the message, (2) the defensibility of a particular message, (3) the legitimacy of a pattern or campaign of messages, (4) the practical impact of a message or the cumulative effect of a series of messages, (5) the openness of the structure of communication between an organization and its publics/audiences, (6) the articulation/representation of genuine public interests, and (7) the question of shared responsibility. We would add the global context and the rise of social media provide additional challenges for planned communication.

We have all questioned the truth of particular organizational messages. Advertising claims often are exaggerated, with consumer complaints frequently hidden from public scrutiny. Think of a time when you questioned the accuracy or truthfulness of an advertising message, thought that an organization was covering up product problems, or simply did not know who was believable when you were making a product or service choice. We think not only about individual integrity but also about the credibility of the organization as a whole. Strategic organizational communication is an intentional effort to shape our perceptions. Themes selected for marketing, advertising, and crisis management may focus or frame an issue away from the product or service to a more generally accepted societal good. For example, messages from tobacco, liquor, and gun manufacturers often emphasize freedom, individuality, fun, or fear over more specific product advantages or features. These ethical issues and a host of others underscore the shared responsibility between organizations and consumers for the ethical and moral evaluation of messages and their potential influence.

With the increasing complexity of organizational environments and the growing awareness of the importance of strategic communication with its ethical and legal consequences, strategic organizational communication positions in public relations and marketing represent important career options for organizational communication majors. These options and others are discussed in Chapter 12.

CHAPTER HIGHLIGHTS

Strategic organizational communication can be described as communication processes in which organizational messages are deliberately generated; are based on environmental data, analysis, and strategy selection; and are guided by organizational objectives. Strategic organizational communication messages usually are developed by communication professionals. Strategic organizational communication is based in part on environmental information and an understanding of the concepts of multiple **publics** and **stakeholders**. **Strategic management** is the process of formulating and implementing an organizational plan of action. **Public relations** and **marketing** are two types of strategic organizational communication functions that support strategic organizational direction.

Public relations functions frequently include **image management, internal communication, public affairs and issues management, media relations,** and **risk and crisis communication.** In broad terms, public relations is responsible in part for managing an organization's image or reputation. Internal communication refers to communication with employees and is frequently a responsibility of the public relations function. Public affairs and issues management involve the shaping of public opinion regarding social and political issues important to the organization. Media relations involves working with the media on behalf of an organization. Crisis communication protocols are developed to communicate during organizational crises. **Marketing** is the management communication process directed at bringing about an exchange between an organization and a customer. **Integrated marketing communications** is growing in importance, stressing strategy that communicates a single, unified message to a customer. **Advertising, branding,** and the increase in **social media usage** all contribute to the marketing mix. Emerging technologies play a significant role in public relations and marketing. Finally, ethical choices continually are required when making decisions about strategic organizational communication. ■

WORKSHOP

1. Using all the media at your disposal, including the Internet, identify a variety of marketing and public relations approaches. Bring several examples to class for discussion.

2. Locate at least two examples of crisis communication efforts. Prepare to present them to your class.

3. In groups of four, describe the image or reputation of your school. Groups should report to the class as a whole. Compare similarities. What were the differences?

4. Discuss the ethical dimensions of public relations and marketing.

5. Read the risk and crisis communication essay by Dr. Sherry Morreale. Think about her perspective. Discuss how you would approach some of the issues she raises.
6. Read the Southwest Airlines case by Adam Saffer. Discuss the use of social media. Make recommendations for social media use for your school.

Communication about Risk and Crisis in the Twenty-first Century

Sherwyn P. Morreale, Ph.D.[1]

In today's world, it seems each year brings new concerns about risks to human welfare, quality of life, and environmental protection. Most recent concerns in the United States of America relate to terrorism threats, natural disasters like hurricanes and tornadoes, and industrial-related events like the recalls of tainted products consumed by ourselves and even those we feed our pets. There are also continuing concerns about the health and safety risks people face from the degradation of our environment and the production and waste disposal methods of our manufacturing companies.

Taking these factors into account and with the increasing globalization of organizations and nations throughout the world, the need for effective risk and crisis communication policies and practices in all organizations and governments is critical. As well, the sophistication and capabilities of communication technologies now provide organizations with amazing tools and opportunities to speak to the increased public awareness of risk and crisis in today's society. Using these technologies, effective communication about risk and crisis has never been more important. All organizations, large and small, public and private, have a responsibility *and* an opportunity to dialogue openly and honestly about risk and crisis with their employees, their customers, and the general public.

To appreciate these responsibilities, let's first clarify the differences between risk and crisis communication as discussed in this chapter. Based on these differences, we can then think about the development phases or stages intrinsic in risk and crisis communication and what we as communicators can do at each stage. We can then take a look at the critical role that risk and

crisis plays in twenty-first-century society and organizations, when understood and managed effectively.

Understanding Risk and Crisis Communication   The National Research Council as early as 1983 separated the then new area of risk management into two phases: the assessment and analysis of potential risks and the management of those risks when in crisis. More exactly, the two phases are these.

Risk communication is the exchange of information and principles pertaining to the assessment and management of *risk(s)* among government agencies, industries, researchers/scholars, mass media, and the general public/interest groups. The process is one in which the communicator hopes to provide the receiver with information about the expected type (good or bad) and magnitude (weak or strong) of any outcomes from a behavior or exposure.

Crisis communication is the exchange of information and principles pertaining to the assessment and management of a *crisis* among government agencies, industries, researchers/ scholars, mass media, and the general public/interest groups. The process is one in which government agencies and organizations face a crisis, communicate about its nature, and manage the reactions of stakeholders and the public.

In sum, risk communication is *proactive*. The organization communicates about what may happen. Crisis communication is *reactive*. The organization communicates about what has happened.

The National Research Council also identified phases or stages of risk and crisis, each stage consisting of processes that if understood could help organizations address these two challenges.

Stages in Risk Communication   Risk assessment and analysis for organizations comprises seven equally important stages.

1. Identify and estimate risk.
2. Develop and analyze options.
3. Conduct overall risk analysis.
4. Make decisions from overall risk analysis.
5. Implement the decisive action.
6. Monitor and evaluate impact of the implementation.
7. Review entire process to identify strengths and weaknesses.

---

[1]Sherwyn P. Morreale, Ph.D., now a faculty member and graduate program director in the Communication Department of the University of Colorado at Colorado Springs, is the former associate director of the National Communication Association. She teaches Introductory and Advanced Organizational Communication and has researched and published extensively, including several textbooks, many research articles, and an array of edited volumes and book chapters.

Stages in Crisis Communication Crisis communication and its management comprises five stages, and as in risk assessment, effective communication is vital at every stage of the process.

1. Precrisis: Be prepared (have a crisis management plan in place), foster critical alliances with all organizational stakeholders, and test plan.
2. Initial crisis: Inform all critical organizational stakeholders and the general public, acknowledge the event with candor and empathy, and establish credibility.
3. Maintenance of the crisis: Help organizational stakeholders and the public to understand the crisis situation and the continuing risks, and provide them with timely and accurate information.
4. Resolution of the crisis: Examine the crisis situation honestly, acknowledge problems and mishaps, and explore ways to improve responses to the crisis.
5. Evaluation: Evaluate the organization's communication performance, document lessons learned, and determine specific actions to improve the crisis response plan for future scenarios.

How to Communicate in a Risk or Crisis Situation Given that communication about risk and crisis is significantly different from any other type of organizational communication, some specific guidelines will enhance the effectiveness of this type of message.

- Don't try to allay panic unrealistically and don't over reassure. Acknowledge uncertainty respectfully.
- Speak with clarity and compassion but use language sensitively, and choose your words wisely.
- Be honest, frank, and open.
- Acknowledge people's fears and address their perceptions of the risk or crisis situation.
- Listen to the public and empower people to take action.
- Be careful making comparisons to other risk situations. All crises are different.
- Coordinate and collaborate with other credible sources in the best interests of addressing the crisis expeditiously.
- Meet the needs of the media and collaborate with them to address the crisis situation.

- Finally, constantly and carefully revisit your risk and crisis management plan and re-evaluate your organization's performance in crisis.

Discussion Questions

1. What are the negative effects of risk and crisis in contemporary organizations if left unmanaged? What are the positive effects that may accrue to an organization that engages in effective risk analysis and crisis management?
2. What are the most important keys to effective risk and crisis communication for organizations doing business in the twenty-first century?
3. You are the new CEO of a large multinational organization that has not considered risk and crisis communication to be an issue. What steps will you take immediately? If a major crisis occurs during your first few weeks on the job, how will you react and handle it?
4. In small groups, list potential risk and crisis issues either at your place of work, at your university, or in your community. What should your organization or community do right now to prepare for and address each potential risk?

Southwest Airlines: Social Media in Action

Adam Saffer[2]

SITUATION ANALYSIS

Company Background

Southwest Airlines (SWA) is a Texas-based Airline company founded in 1971 by Rollin King and Herb Kelleher, who envisioned a different kind of flying experience. Their plan was simple, get passengers to their destinations on time, at the lowest possible fares, and provide them with a "good time."[3] The organization started small—servicing Dallas, Houston, and San Antonio from Dallas Love Field. Today SWA services sixty-six U.S.A. cities and carries over 100 million passengers each year.

   SWA was not an overnight success. Prior to the formation of SWA, airlines at Love Field signed an agreement to relocate at Dallas/Fort Worth International Airport to respond to anticipated growth in future air travel. SWA filed suit, stating it was not bound to the relocation as it was not a part of the original

[2]Adam Saffer is an assistant in the office of the chancellor and graduate student at the University of Colorado at Colorado Springs. His research work is in corporate social media. Data for this case were collected in Fall 2009. Verification of data was concluded in January 2010.

[3]Southwest Airlines. We weren't just airborne yesterday. Retrieved from http://www.southwest.com/about_swa/airborne.html.

negotiations. In 1979, SWA made plans to include interstate travel, which met opposition and made the company the focus of a federal regulation, the Wright Amendment. The amendment, drafted by a Fort Worth Congress member, barred interstate travel to and from Dallas Love Field, with the exception of four neighboring states (Louisiana, Arkansas, Oklahoma, and New Mexico). The exception was expanded in 1997 to include Mississippi, Alabama, and Kansas.[4] Constrained by this regulation, CEO Gary Kelley called for the repeal of the Wright Amendment, and in 2005, SWA launched the Web site, www.setlovefree.com, to educate passengers about SWA's struggle to grow. The successful campaign freeing the organization to grow marked the beginning of SWA's direct relationship with customers via Web 2.0.

Organization's Mission

Over the past thirty-eight years, the company has been able to keep a unique and effective culture of great customer service. The U.S. Department of Transportation has consistently ranked SWA with the lowest of the airline industry's ratio of complaints per passenger since it began tracking the data in 1987.[5] This distinct culture stems from SWA's mission: "The mission of Southwest Airlines is dedication to the highest quality of Customer Service delivered with a sense of warmth, friendliness, individual pride, and Company Spirit."[6] This mission directly influences the organization's use of social media.

The mission of SWA also includes what the company sees as its most important asset—its employees: "We are committed to provide our Employees a stable work environment with equal opportunity for learning and personal growth. Creativity and innovation are encouraged for improving the effectiveness of Southwest Airlines. Above all, Employees will be provided the same concern, respect, and caring attitude within the organization that they are expected to share externally with every Southwest Customer."[7]

SWA's creativity and innovativeness led them to be the first to offer ticketless travel, an airline Web site (www.southwest.com, DING!), and an airline corporate blog (Nuts about Southwest).[8] This belief in their employees is visible in the SWA use of social media. Employees are the main contributors to the blog, and it is employee comments about SWA that are retweeted.

Summary of SWA's Social Media Usage

SWA has been one of the corporate pioneers in exploring the use of social media. They were the first airline to have a Web site and corporate blog.[9] SWA also has received recognition for integrating social media: Twitter, Facebook, YouTube, and Flickr.[10] However, unlike their competition, SWA dabbles in the world of podcasts with its Red Belly Radio.[11] The seven people at SWA who make up the emerging media team sync all these media into one communication and interaction machine.[12]

Blog

As of the writing of this case, Nuts about Southwest, the company's landmark corporate blog, was the major hub for the SWA's key messages as well as social media efforts. Although the first of its kind, Kineda rated the blog as having low authority and put it on the D-list.[13] Technorati gave it an authority level of 416 on a 0–1000 scale, 1000 being the highest value.[14] The blog itself consisted of postings from members of the emerging media team, online specialists, the corporate community affairs team, the public relations team, and other employees at SWA. Postings on the blog were wide-ranging, which was expected from the variety of contributors. When SWA began service in Milwaukee, the emerging media specialist, Lindsey Reynolds, covered all aspects of the public relations event. From the volunteers at the Ronald McDonald House in Milwaukee to the actual touchdown of the plane, the

[4]Ibid.

[5]Ibid.

[6]Southwest Airlines. The mission of Southwest Airlines. Retrieved from http://www.southwest.com/about_swa/mission.html.

[7]Ibid.

[8]Southwest Airlines. We weren't just airborne, op. cit.

[9]Ibid.

[10]A. Ahles. 2009. For airlines using social media, sky no limit. *Houston Chronicle*, October 26. Retrieved from http://www.chron.com/CDA/archives/archive.mpl?id=2009_4804483.

[11]Red Belly Radio. http://www.blogsouthwest.com/podcast.

[12]H. Weber. 2009. Low-cost airlines all a-Twitter with customers. October 22. Retrieved from http://blogs.usatoday.com/sky/2009/10/lowcost-airlines-all-atwitter-with-customers-.html.

[13]Kineda. Nuts about Southwest blog rating. Retrieved from http://www.kineda.com/are-you-an-a-list-bloglebrity/?url=http://www.blogsouthwest.com/.

[14]Technorati. Nuts about Southwest blog rating. Retrieved from http://technorati.com/search?return=sites&q=nuts+about+southwest&x=3&y=10.

post covered a variety of detail in a concise manner.[15] Additionally, the corporation had their resident mommy blogger, Jessica Turner, post about the newest service location along with photos of her son in Milwaukee.[16] Yet the posts went beyond the common CSR (Corporate Social Responsibility) and major event updates by integrating corporate contests such as the "I'd rather be drinking wine . . . " campaign that linked participants to Twitter to win a free two-night stay in Napa Valley.[17] Such postings generated a high level of two-way communication between SWA and its publics. Specifically, the previously mentioned contest posting generated 167 comments even though participants were directed to Twitter. Finally, to bring home the organization's overall marketing message, SWA posted messages to incorporate the corporate campaign: "Grab your bag. It's on." The blog posted by Christi Day, emerging media specialist, titled "Why Do They Hate Your Bags?" integrated the marketing campaign with the blog. The rather short post generated a conversation, with 32 comments in a little over a month.[18]

Facebook

Facebook was a gathering space for many SWA fans to converse with other fans and also hear from the organization.[19] The wall was open for anyone to post comments but was monitored by SWA staff for foul remarks. (This monitoring was stated on the profile.) In addition to the fan comments, SWA posted promotions, comments, or contests that generated conversation among fans. The frequency of disseminating messages via this medium was inconsistent. Between November 9 and 16, 2009, there were a total of twelve messages posted on the wall from SWA and four of the total occurred on November 16 alone.

Even though there was not a regular rhythm to SWA's Facebook postings, when there was one, a conversation ensued. On October 15, 2009, there were over 125 comments posted on the SWA's Facebook fan page. SWA put two separate posting on Facebook that day: a video from Air New Zealand that generated 58 comments and 95 likes and another announcing the winner of the Red River Rivalry Plane Pull between Oklahoma

University and the University of Texas, which generated 39 comments and 64 likes. The rest of the comments for the day were fans commenting on the organization or asking questions. These types of postings were not uncommon on the page; however, the organization normally did not become active in conversations.

SWA communication with Facebook fans most often was in response to fan questions. When a question was asked, SWA often responded to the person publicly. On November 2, 2009, Lala Palelei asked about a sale that was taking place because she was planning to travel with eight children. Although the sale was over SWA commented on her post with a link to the best place to save money on tickets. Such direct contact appeared to be a common practice. On November 17, a fan posted a question as to why he had not been responded to by a representative. Within approximately fifteen minutes, SWA commented on his post stating they were researching his question. SWA posted an answer the next day. The overall two-way communication through Facebook was impossible to measure with precision, but public examples on the fan page were common.

SWA's Facebook also had a place for photos, videos, and discussions. Photos on the site were controlled and posted by the organizations. The videos were a combination of SWA-posted and user-generated. The users' postings mostly involved in-flight activities, while SWA's promoted the organization. Additionally, the page featured a "Live" tab that allowed fans to watch Web casts from the organization. Furthermore, one discussion that asked in the title "What Airport Should Southwest Fly to Next?" had received comments from 906 people and 1,023 total comments. Another feature on the page included the "Bags Fly Free" tab that incorporated the company's key messages from their advertising campaign.

Twitter

Of the social media tools used, SWA has found Twitter to be its primary means of interacting with its publics. With 870,509 followers and 3,634 total tweets, SWA averages five hours between tweets and manages to send five per day.[20] In analyzing

---

[15]L. Reynolds. 2009. It's on, Wisconsin! November 2. Retrieved from http://www.blogsouthwest.com/blog/its-on-wisconsin-0.

[16]J. Turner. 2009. Southwest flies home to Wisconsin. November 17. Retrieved from http://www.blogsouthwest.com/blog/southwest-flies-home-wisconsin.

[17]A. Rogers. 2009. I'd rather be drinking wine . . . In Napa . . . Contest. October 5. Retrieved from http://www.blogsouthwest.com/blog/i'd-rather-be-drinking-wine . . . -napa . . . contest.

[18]C. Day. 2009. Why do they hate your bags? October 6. Retrieved from http://www.blogsouthwest.com/blog/why-do-they-hate-your-bags.

[19]Facebook. Southwest Airlines fan page. http://www.facebook.com/Southwest.

[20]TweeterScore Report Card. @southwestair. Retrieved from http://sites.google.com/site/spreadsheets/spreadsheet-categories/twitsheets/tweeterscore.

the last 500 tweets as of the writing of this case, 53 percent contained links, which normally direct people to customer service or sharing a picture, and 71 percent of the 500 replied to or mentioned another account.[21]

The majority of messages sent from the Twitter account engaged with other tweeters either by replies or retweets (RTs). For example, a tweet came across that a passenger had lost a book, so SWA replied with the number to the lost and found at the airport.[22] When an inquiry or complaint was tweeted about SWA, the emerging media team responded promptly to help the tweeter. On October 2, @cupcakeproject tweeted a question about traveling with a two-month-old who does not have a birth certificate. SWA responded within five minutes asking @cupcakeproject to direct the message to @Southwestair to get the answer. Examples such as these were common, along with the occasional promotional items that linked to SWA's other social media sites. SWA's Twitter account had the highest degree of interaction with publics among all social media tools deployed by the company.

Flickr

SWA's Flickr page was similar to its competitors' in that the pictures were mostly of airplanes. This group pool had the presence of the organization. On the group pool page, the organization informed members that their photos would automatically feed into to the Nuts about Southwest blog. Moreover, SWA posted pictures to the photo stream from corporate events via SWABlogGuy, which was the only message transmitted from Flickr. The group has gathered 711 members.[23] Also resembling other Flickr accounts, SWA's had low activity in the discussion feature. Yet one discussion attacked SWA's customer service reputation with a story about a horrible experience involving the flight attendants. While the validity of the complaint made by Scooteriscrazy is unknown, seventeen different members of the group pool joined to counter the attack by sharing their enjoyable experiences when flying on SWA.[24]

YouTube

Nuts about Southwest was also the name for SWA's YouTube channel created on June 6, 2007. Since going online with

videos, SWA had collected 904 subscribers and 44,118 channel views.[25] Recently, SWA has uploaded roughly one to two videos per week. The channel has been used for a wide range of purposes; there was a combination of corporate advertisement and video press releases as well as user-generated videos. In response to being delayed on a SWA flight, Sloofus posted a video of an SWA employee entertaining passengers while they were waiting.[26] This post showed the ability to have interaction with SWA on YouTube; yet few people have posted video responses.

Of the nearly 200 videos uploaded, the most viewed was a response from SWA to claims by two passengers they had been banned for life from the airline. Other top views were the rapping flight attendant, "Day In the Life . . . " video series, and SWA commercials. According to the stats available on the videos, the most popular public on YouTube was males ranging from twenty-five to fifty-four years old.[27]

Podcasting

The final major social media tool used by SWA was podcasting. Unlike other airline organizations, SWA has incorporated podcasting into their social media strategy. The weekly podcasts, named the Red Belly Radio, were housed on the Nuts about Southwest blog site and available through RSS feeds. The audio files covered corporate events and campaigns. For example, on October 21, 2009, Red Belly Radio posted coverage of the Oklahoma University versus University of Texas plane pull. Also, the podcasts have integrated corporate contests such as the previously mentioned "I'd rather be drinking wine . . ." into the podcasts. The limitation with this social media tool is the inability for two-way communication. The only source of feedback possible is for publics to rate the podcasts on the blog site.

Taken as a whole, SWA's social media, like its culture, is an example for other organizations to examine. SWA's stronghold is the blog and Twitter, but SWA sets itself apart from other airlines with their Red Belly Radio podcasts. In sum, SWA demonstrates a dedication to reaching as many people as possible through social media. The objective of SWA, however, is not to simply make contacts but to listen, observe, and then participate with their publics. ∎

---

[21]Ibid.

[22]@southwestair. October 23, 2009. www.twitter.com/southwestair.

[23]Flickr. Southwest Airlines group pool. Retrieved from http://www.flickr.com/groups/southwestairlines/.

[24]Flickr. Southwest Airlines discussion, Southwest has the worst customer service. Retrieved from http://www.flickr.com/groups/southwestairlines/discuss/72157619412359490/.

[25]YouTube. Nuts about Southwest channel. Retrieved from http://www.youtube.com/user/NutsAboutSouthwest.

[26]YouTube. Sloofus channel. Retrieved from http://www.youtube.com/watch?v=GCkCeM8brwI.

[27]Ibid.

TIPS FOR EFFECTIVE COMMUNICATION

1. Build skills for risk and crisis communication by monitoring risk campaigns and evaluating how specific crises are approached by leadership.
2. Participate in a media training session.
3. Select a particular risk that interests you. Develop a message strategy to influence others to pay attention to the risk.
4. Seek an evaluation of your professional writing skills. Take every opportunity to seek criticism to identify areas for improvement.

5. Remember that openness, honesty, and integrity are critical for handling risk and crisis communication. The lack of these qualities can contribute both personally and organizationally to long-lasting negative outcomes. ∎

REFERENCES AND SUGGESTED READINGS

Andrews, K. R. 1971. *The concept of corporate strategy.* Homewood, IL: Irwin.

Auster, E., and C. W. Choo. 1994. How senior managers acquire and use information in environmental scanning. *Information Processing and Management* 30: 607–618.

Belch, M., and G. Belch. 2008. Integrated marketing communication. In *21st century communication: A reference handbook,* ed. W. Eadie, 689–697. Thousand Oaks, CA: Sage.

Bennis, W. 1969. *Organization development: Its nature, origins, and prospects.* Reading, MA: Addison-Wesley.

Bennis, W., K. Benne, R. Chin, and K. Corey. 1976. *The planning of change,* 3rd ed. New York: Holt, Rinehart and Winston.

Bradley, S. D., and T. C. Laubacher. 2008. Research in advertising campaign design. In *21st century communication: A reference handbook,* ed. W. Eadie, 788–796. Thousand Oaks, CA: Sage.

Broom, G. M. 2008. History and concepts of public relations. In *21st century communication: A reference handbook,* ed. W. Eadie, 689–697. Thousand Oaks, CA: Sage.

Buccholz, R. A. 1988. Adjusting corporations to the realities of public interests and policy. In *Strategic issues management,* ed. R. L. Heath, 50–72. San Francisco: Jossey-Bass.

Caywood, C. L., ed. 1997. *The handbook of strategic public relations and integrated communications.* New York: McGraw-Hill.

Cheney, G., and L. Christensen. 2001. Organizational identity: Linkages between internal and external communication. In *The new handbook of organizational communication: Advances in theory, research, and methods,* eds. F. Jablin and L. Putnam, 231–269. Thousand Oaks, CA: Sage.

Clampitt, P., R. DeKoch, and T. Cashman. 2000. A strategy for communicating about uncertainty. *Academy of Management Executive* 14(4): 41–57.

Conrad, C. 1994. *Strategic organizational communication: Toward the 21st century.* Orlando, FL: Harcourt Trade.

Cutlip, S. M., A. H. Center, and G. M. Broom. 1985. *Effective public relations,* 6th ed. Englewood Cliffs, NJ: Prentice Hall.

Daft, R. L., and K. E. Weick. 1984. Toward a model of organizations as interpretation systems. *Academy of Management Review* 9: 284–295.

Daniels, T. D., B. K. Spiker, and M. J. Papa. 1997. *Perspectives on organizational communication.* Madison, WI: Brown and Benchmark.

Dedmon, J. 1996. Thinking the unthinkable: Crisis communications. In *Dartnell's public relations handbook,* ed. R. L. Dilenschneider, 206–225. Chicago: Dartnell.

DeWine, S. 1994. *The consultant's craft.* New York: St. Martin's.

Eisenberg, E. M., and H. L. Goodall. 1997. *Organizational communication: Balancing creativity and constraint.* New York: St. Martin's.

Ewing, R. P. 1997. Issues management: Managing trends through the issues life cycle. In *Handbook of strategic public relations and integrated communications,* ed. C. L. Caywood, 173–188. New York: McGraw-Hill.

Fearn-Banks, K. 2008. Crisis communication. In *21st century communication: A reference handbook*, ed. W. Eadie, 689–697. Thousand Oaks, CA: Sage.

Fombrun, C., and M. Shanley. 1990. What's in a name? Reputation building and corporate strategy. *Academy of Management Journal* 33: 233–258.

French, W. L., and C. H. Bell. 1973. *Organization development: Behavioral science interventions for organization improvement*. Englewood Cliffs, NJ: Prentice Hall.

Goldhaber, G. M. 1986. *Organizational communication*, 4th ed. Dubuque, IA: Brown.

Grunig, J. E. 1990. Theory and practice of interactive media relations. *Public Relations Quarterly* 35(3): 18–23.

Grunig, J. E. 1992. *Excellence in public relations and communication management*. Hillsdale, NJ: Erlbaum.

Grunig, J. E. 1993. Image and substance: From symbolic to behavior relationships. *Public Relations Review* 19: 121–139.

Harris, T. L. 1991. *The marketers' guide to public relations*. New York: Wiley.

Harris, T. L. 1997. Integrated marketing public relations. In *Handbook of strategic public relations and integrated communications*, ed. C. L. Caywood, 90–105. New York: McGraw-Hill.

Henderson, B. D. 1991. The origin of strategy. In *Strategy: Seeking and securing competitive advantage*, eds. C. A. Montgomery and M. E. Porter, 3–9. Boston: Harvard Business School.

Jugenheimer, D. W. 2008. Media planning for advertising campaigns. In *21st century communication: A reference handbook*, ed. W. Eadie, 805–814. Thousand Oaks, CA: Sage.

Kosmicki, R., and F. Bona. 1996. Media relations: How to relate to the press. In *Dartnell's public relations handbook*, ed. R. L. Dilenschneider, 58–75. Chicago: Dartnell.

Kotler, P., and G. Armstrong. 1996. *Principles of marketing*. Englewood Cliffs, NJ: Prentice Hall.

Kotter, J. 1998. Cultures and coalitions. In *Rethinking the future*, ed. R. Gibson, 164–178. London: Nicholas Brealey.

Lamb, C., J. Hair, and C. McDaniel. 1992. *Principles of marketing*. Cincinnati, OH: South-Western.

Lawler, E. E., and J. R. Galbraith. 1994. Avoiding the corporate dinosaur syndrome. *Organizational Dynamics* 23: 5–17.

Lukaszewski, J. 1997. Establishing individual and corporate crisis communication standards: The principles and protocols. *Public Relations Quarterly* 42(3): 7–14.

Miller, B. M., and J. S. Horsley. 2009. Digging deeper: Crisis management in the coal industry. *Journal of Applied Communication Research* 37: 298–316.

Mintzberg, H. 1990. Strategy formation: Schools of thought. In *Perspectives on strategic management*, ed. J. W. Frederickson, 105–235. New York: HarperBusiness.

Mintzberg, H. 1991. Crafting strategy. In *Strategy: Seeking and securing competitive advantage*, eds. C. A. Montgomery and M. E. Porter, 403–420. Boston: Harvard Business School.

Mintzberg, H. 1994. *The rise and fall of strategic planning*. New York: Free Press.

Mlodzik, P. 2006. Branding and brand management: Integration and innovation. In *The IABC handbook of organizational communication*, ed. T. Gills, 400–413. San Francisco: Jossey-Bass.

Moffitt, M. A. 1994. Collapsing and integrating concepts of "public" and "image" into a new theory. *Public Relations Review* 20: 159–170.

Pace, W. 1983. *Organizational communication: Foundations for human resource development*. Englewood Cliffs, NJ: Prentice Hall.

Reynolds, B., and M. Seeger. 2005. Crisis and emergency risk communication as an integrative model. *Journal of Health Communication* 10(43): 43–55.

Richardson, B. 1995. The politically aware leader: Understanding the need to match paradigms and planning systems to powerful, "turbulent fields" environment. *Leadership and Organization Development Journal* 16(2): 27–35.

Saffir, L. 1992. *Power public relations*. Lincolnwood, IL: NTC Business Books.

Schein, E. H. 1969. *Process consultation: Its role in organization development*. Reading, MA: Addison-Wesley.

Schultz, D. E. 1995. The many views of integrated marketing communications. In *The AMA marketing encyclopedia: Issues and trends shaping the future*, ed. J. Heilbrunn, 190–194. Chicago: American Marketing Association.

Schultz, D. E., S. Tannenbaum, and R. Lauterborn. 1992. *Integrated marketing communications*. Lincolnwood, IL: NTC Business Books.

Scott, C. W., and A. Trethewey. 2008. Organizational discourse and the appraisal of occupational hazards: Interpretive repertoires, heedful interrelating, and identity at work. *Journal of Applied Communication Research* 36: 298–317.

Seeger, M. 2006. Best practices in crisis communication: An expert panel process. *Journal of Applied Communication Research* 34(3): 232–244.

Senge, P. 1998. Through the eye of the needle. In *Rethinking the future,* ed. R. Gibson, 123–146. London: Nicholas Brealey.

Stanton, P. 2002. Ten communications mistakes you can avoid when managing a crisis. *Public Relations Quarterly* 47(2): 19–22.

Stocker, K. P. 1997. A strategic approach to crisis management. In *Handbook of strategic public relations and integrated communications,* ed. C. L. Caywood, 189–203. New York: McGraw-Hill.

Ulmer, R. 2001. Effective crisis management through established stakeholder relationships: Malden Mills as a case study. *Management Communication Quarterly* 14(4): 590–615.

Wilson, G. L., H. L. Goodall Jr., and C. L. Waagen. 1986. *Organizational communication.* New York: Harper and Row. ■

Organizational Change and Communication

DEVELOPING COMPETENCIES THROUGH . . .

KNOWLEDGE   Defining organizational development and change
Identifying processes and models for development and change
Identifying approaches for planned development and change

SENSITIVITY   Developing an awareness of barriers to change
Understanding the importance of trust for productive change

SKILLS   Developing analysis capabilities through case analysis
Identifying responsibilities for change of communication professionals

VALUES   Linking effective communication to productive change
Understanding the importance of value assumptions during change

THE TECHTRON COMPUTERS "WANT TO SURVIVE, GO PUBLIC, AND THEN WHAT?" CASE

Investors (venture capitalists) knew the potential was good for Techtron Computers to challenge the dominant players in the high-speed computing market. They also knew the types of computers Techtron hoped to bring to market were a long shot for success even with their significant financial investment. The four founders of Techtron all had come from large international corporations known for their high-speed computing products designed for scientific and defense markets. To compete with their former employers was a formidable task.

The first eighteen months for Techtron had been intense. The founders had handpicked individuals from their former employers who had the potential to understand the development of new competitive products and who were willing to risk working in a start-up environment. The sixty individuals who had joined Techtron at the encouragement of the four founders all knew the risks were high, but if Techtron was successful the rewards would exceed anything they could hope for from their former employers. None of the initial employees, including the founders, had anticipated the pressure of working in a new organization or attempting to bring products to market with only a skeleton staff.

355

All of their collective experience had been in established organizations. A culture of hard work, risk taking, and living on the edge quickly emerged.

Within twenty-four months, this hard-driving Techtron culture resulted in the release of two products to market. Significant initial orders indicated the products filled a market niche and need not met by their more expensive competitors. Based on this initial success, the founders began to think about taking Techtron "public" (converting a privately owned company to a publicly traded company listed on one of the stock exchanges), returning money to their investors, and raising resources to expand the company.

The founders knew they must grow Techtron if the initial successes were to be sustained. The founders knew their initial group of employees was exceptional. They also knew this initial group was highly motivated by the potential for significant personal gain. The founders quickly realized that building products, although critical to success, was only a part of creating the changes necessary for the organization to grow and prosper. They were confronted with the need to plan for and manage change, to develop the organization, and to understand how human dynamics would influence Techtron's future. They were concerned their initial success had been their only focus. They did not know how to approach what should happen next. ■

INTRODUCTION

The Techtron founders face important decisions about organizational change—change that will determine the future of Techtron and its employees. In determining what to do, they will gather information, evaluate what they think the future holds, and involve employees, external stakeholders, and the public in decision making. All of these processes are communication-based. It is possible, therefore, to claim that organizational change takes place through communication.

Change is a somewhat ambiguous concept often simply defined as an alteration from one state to another. Others define change as differences between two sets of conditions. When referring to **organizational change,** we frequently talk about changing circumstances that place individuals and organizations in constant states of flux. Organizational change is both planned and unplanned. In the last chapter we talked about changes brought about by crisis. In this chapter we focus on changes that are more deliberate and made with a desire to improve the organization and its overall functioning.

Organizational change ■ Alterations in the organization, whether planned or unplanned.

Planned organizational change usually is the responsibility of professionals within the organization, often top leadership. However, as we focus on more participative workplaces, we see change becoming the responsibility of individuals throughout the organization. Communication about change frequently is developed and led by people with professional communication responsibilities. In this chapter we describe roles and responsibilities for planned change and how organizational development is not only an organizational process but also a professional function within the organization. Many organizations, for example, have organizational development departments similar to personnel, finance, research and development, or sales and marketing.

The founders of Techtron experienced the stress of a fast-paced and changing environment. They had to get the first products to market. They had to decide how to sell their new ideas in competition with established high-quality organizations. They now have to decide how to change the financial structure of the company. They must decide how to grow for their future. They are engaged with the pace of change. Many today describe that pace as relentless and demanding, whereas others see change as a more evolutionary process. Regardless of the perspective, organizational change develops a rate or pace based on the degree or amount of change desired, the type of change envisioned, and how much control over the change the organization can actually exert.

In this chapter we talk about the pace of change and describe examples of productive change. We explore significant barriers to change and then examine planned development and change processes. Finally, we talk about communicating change. Throughout the chapter we define professional job opportunities associated with planned development and change. We also take the position that productive change is a broadly shared organizational responsibility. Specifically, we develop *knowledge* competencies through examining models and processes for organizational change and organizational development. We develop *sensitivity* competencies through examining barriers to change and understanding characteristics of positive change. We develop *skills* by examining change responsibilities of communication professionals. Finally, we develop *values* by understanding approaches to change and the importance of productive and ethical change processes.

THE PACE OF CHANGE

For several years a best-selling book, *Who Moved My Cheese?* by Spencer Johnson (1998), dominated popular literature with its simple story of change. Johnson uses the metaphor of cheese to illustrate what people want in life, whether in an organization or any other setting. The story characters encounter unexpected change—their cheese is moved. The underlying message in the story is that change happens (someone keeps moving the cheese), and it is important to anticipate change. The message also advocates adapting to change and even enjoying the process. Figure 11.1 illustrates the concepts in *Who Moved My Cheese?* Many research-based reports also support the notion that change is all around us and what matters is not whether we encounter change, but how we respond. Think for a moment about your personal response to change. Is there a difference in your response when change is unexpected and when you plan for the change? What makes the difference?

Donald Cushman (2000), in describing his high-speed management theory of organizational communication, identified the time it takes to perform an organizational activity as key to an organization's performance or effectiveness. In talking about private sector organizations, he claimed the speed in getting a product or service to market is the "chief determinant of organizational success." Reducing product and service cycle time is necessary for competitive advantage. Cushman described the importance of continuous environmental scanning, continuous value chain analysis (comparing key outcomes to competitors' outcomes), and continuous improvement processes. Underlying this description is the assumption there is

1. Having cheese makes you happy.
2. The more important your cheese is to you, the more you want to hold onto it.
3. If you do not change, you can become extinct.
4. What would you do if you weren't afraid?
5. Smell the cheese often so you know when it is getting old.
6. Movement in a new direction helps you find new cheese.
7. When you move beyond your fear, you feel free.
8. Imagining yourself enjoying new cheese even before you find it leads you to it.
9. The quicker you let go of old cheese, the sooner you find new cheese.
10. It is safer to search in the maze than remain in a cheeseless situation.
11. Old beliefs do not lead you to new cheese.
12. When you see that you can find and enjoy new cheese, you change course.
13. Noticing small changes early helps you adapt to the bigger changes that are to come.
14. Move with the cheese and enjoy it!

FIGURE 11.1
Concepts in *Who Moved My Cheese?*

Adapted from *Who Moved My Cheese?* by Spencer Johnson (1998). New York: G. P. Putnam's Sons.

a continuous need to change and to develop proactive change strategies—in other words, leading and managing planned change.

Malcolm Gladwell, in another popular best seller, *The Tipping Point* (2002), made famous a concept previously researched in sociology, the concept of change associated with tipping points. Tipping points have been described as important thresholds or boiling points that propel the rate of change. According to Gladwell, tipping points occur when there is critical mass fostering change. As Gladwell explained:

> Sharp introduced the first low-priced fax machine in 1984, and sold about 80,000 of those machines in the United States in the first year. For the next three years, businesses slowly and steadily bought more and more faxes, until, in 1987, enough people had faxes that it made sense for everyone to get a fax. Nineteen eighty-seven was the fax machine Tipping Point. A million new machines were sold that year, and by 1989 two million new machines had gone into operation. Cellular phones have followed the same trajectory. Through the 1990s, they got smaller and cheaper, and service got better until 1998, when the technology hit a Tipping Point and suddenly everyone had a cell phone. (p. 12)

Many believe the issue of global warming and its impact on all types of organizations hit a tipping point in 2007. The economic influence of India and China is said to be a tipping point in the distribution of world power. Organizations have internal tipping points. New competition, employee discontent, ethical abuses, and crises all can contribute to rapid occurrence of tipping points, requiring response to and planning for change.

Others argue planning for continuous change is part of a "persuasive 'managerialist' bias" that positions change as necessary (whether it is or not), thereby masking the use of power vested in a few rather than in more broadly participatory processes (Zorn, Page, and Cheney, 2000). Regardless of the underlying rationale for change, most organizations support planning for continuous improvement or change. Organizational development (discussed later in this chapter), benchmarking (finding best practices in industries or specific areas of work), and reengineering (changes in work processes and structures) are but a few of the planned change practices that occur in today's organizations. How change is handled, the amount of change, who participates in deciding what to change, and a host of other issues are part of the pervasive pace of change that almost all of us experience.

DEVELOPING AND SUSTAINING ORGANIZATIONAL EXCELLENCE

Nitin Nohria, William Joyce, and Bruce Roberson (2003), in reporting a five-year study describing management practices that produced outstanding results, identified four primary practices as necessary for sustained excellence: strategy, execution, culture, and structure. Additionally, they describe the importance of talented employees, innovation, leadership, and mergers and partnerships. In the study, the organizations that excelled sharply defined strategy and clearly communicated strategy to employees, customers, partners, and investors. They developed strategy from the outside in, listening to employees, customers, partners, and investors. The execution of the high-performing companies was evidenced in delivering products and services that consistently met customers' expectations. Decision making was close to frontline employees, who were empowered to react quickly to changing market conditions. Continuous monitoring to eliminate excess and waste helped to increase productivity. The cultures of the excelling companies exhibited high expectations about performance. Although cultural values and norms differed both across and within the companies, most were characterized by empowering both managers and employees to make independent decisions to find ways to improve operations. Rewards were both performance-based and psychological. Leaders paid a great deal of attention to organizational structure (product, geography, customer, etc.), although one organizational structure was not demonstrated to be superior to another. The structures that were most effective were those that reduced bureaucracy and simplified work. Essential to effectiveness was promoting cooperation and exchange of information across the entire organization. The best people were put closest to the action, and emphasis was on systems for seamless sharing of knowledge. In sum, the high-performing companies in the study focused on planned development and change with an emphasis on excellence in people, broad participatory processes, and communication (both in listening and interacting with stakeholders) designed to produce results. These findings regarding developing and sustaining excellence are closely linked to earlier work by Warren Bennis and Patricia Biederman (1997). Bennis and Biederman reported groups who produced extraordinary results had talented people, dedicated leaders, commitment to their goals, and an ability to work together in creative collaboration. Taken together, these studies lead us to conclude that high-performing groups and organizations are examples of effective organizational development and change.

BARRIERS TO CHANGE

Although we know that change can be productive, it is a rare individual who has not experienced change that was painful. At times, people implementing change engage in self-serving destructive behaviors. In other circumstances, even well-intentioned efforts fail, creating far more problems than solutions. At other times, poor planning and execution derail efforts that might otherwise have been successful. In fact, evidence continues to mount across all types of organizations indicating that only roughly one-third of change efforts are successful. As high as 75 percent of change efforts are reported to miss their financial goals (Lewis, forthcoming). The barriers to change are diverse and often situation specific.

Complacency

Many individuals and groups simply like the way things are in the organization and do not appreciate the value change might bring. Often referred to as **complacency,** this preference for the status quo comes from a variety of sources. Leadership and management may have communicated such positive messages about the organization that no one can conceptualize why change should occur. Additionally, many are complacent in an organization that has relatively low overall performance standards with visible resources and is absent a major or visible crisis. Individuals and groups also deny the need for change when they are busy or stressed, have not had sufficient performance feedback from the environment, and/or do not have access to information about the entire organization. Have you ever experienced complacency? Can you identify what contributed to your response and what might have convinced you of the need to change your mind?

Complacency ■ The attitude of individuals or groups who prefer the status quo based on their satisfaction with current circumstances or their lack of understanding of a need for change.

Organizational Silence

One of the most important barriers to effective change is one we do not observe happening unless we engage in the behavior personally. That barrier is **organizational silence.** When individuals or groups feel compelled to remain silent in the face of issues, problems, or concerns, the organization loses vital information necessary for making change. Leaders who do not want challenges to their authority may fail in change efforts simply because they have silenced the very information they needed. Elizabeth Morrison and Frances Milliken (2000) suggested organizational silence is fostered when top leadership fears receiving negative feedback. Managers who want to avoid embarrassment, threat, or feelings of vulnerability or incompetence may, whether knowingly or not, foster conditions that employees perceive as a rationale to remain silent. Several managerial beliefs about employees also contribute to this important barrier. Three are noteworthy: (1) a belief that employees are self-interested and therefore untrustworthy; (2) a belief that leadership and management know best; and (3) a belief that unity is important and dissent is to be avoided. Have you ever been in a situation in which you remained silent even though you had information important for the problem or decision? What

Organizational silence ■ Individuals or groups refrain from offering positions or solutions during times of organizational problems and change.

contributed to your silence? Were any of the above-mentioned beliefs at work? How did others behave to influence your choice to remain silent?

Knowledge or Information Deficits

Another important barrier to productive change is the very information or knowledge used to inform the change. This barrier can be described as **knowledge or information deficits.** Often change is not informed by knowledge from individuals working most closely to the problem. At other times, change occurs without adequate information collection. And at other times, change is initiated for personal gain with little concern for available data. One of the most important aspects of this barrier is the quality of organizational participation processes. Generally speaking, broad participation throughout the organization will provide more knowledge and information important for change strategies. How can those responsible for change seek information both within and outside the organization? What types of organizational values are most likely to reduce knowledge and information deficits? What types of values contribute to increasing deficits?

Knowledge/information deficits ■ Barriers to productive change based on lack of knowledge and information from which to develop change strategy.

Risk Perception

Risk perception is a potentially powerful factor during change. When change occurs, the outcomes of the change are not immediately known. Therefore, individuals develop a **risk perception** or belief about the potential impact of the change and its overall importance and desirability. When changes are seen as unimportant, or are minor, or do not have direct impact, chances are risk perceptions will be low. For example, when a top manager leaves and employees expect that a known individual who is highly trusted will be the replacement, low risk perception is predictable. However, that same vacancy can create a much greater perception of risk if no one knows who the replacement will be and rumors begin that a change in approach to leadership is likely. Think about a time when you were worried about an upcoming change. What risks did you identify? How did you form your perceptions?

Risk perception ■ Beliefs about the potential impact of the change and its overall importance and desirability.

Uncertainty

Closely related to the concept of risk is the notion that change brings about uncertainty. Uncertainty in and of itself can be a barrier to productive change as individuals or groups try to determine how uncertainty about the future affects them. **Uncertainty,** or the ambiguity a change brings, contributes to different types of responses for different people. Some will seek to reduce uncertainty by gathering more information about the change. Others will avoid information, either because they see little direct impact or because they are so fearful of change that dealing with "facts" is troublesome. Michael Kramer, Debbie Dougherty, and Tamyra Pierce (2004) studied pilots' reactions to communication and uncertainty during the acquisition of their airline by another airline. Seeking information and communication in general did help to

Uncertainty ■ The degree of ambiguity a change brings to both individuals and groups.

reduce uncertainty but did not necessarily lead to more positive views of the change. Pilots believed their jobs were more secure once they had adequate information about the change, but they were increasingly unhappy about how their seniority was treated in the merged organization. These findings illustrate the complex process of shaping attitudes and reactions to change. Think again about your personal experiences. Can you identify a time when you were uncertain about the impact of a proposed change? What did you do to reduce the uncertainty? How did you feel once you had more information? What are the implications for those planning organizational change?

Contradictions and Misalignments

Change can fail even when those affected by change initially are in favor of the change. Paul Leonardi (2009), in studying engineers who had inadvertently stymied an organization change of which they were in favor, found contradictions and misalignments between social interactions and materiality or material features of the technology to be a barrier to change. **Contradictions and misalignments** are the confusions which result when expectations about change developed through social interactions do not match direct experiences with the change. Leonardi explains.

Contradictions and misalignments ■ Confusions which result when expectations about change developed through social interactions do not match direct experiences with the change.

> Engineers' communication with managers, coworkers, and customers led them to develop an interpretation about what the technology was supposed to do while their interactions with the material features of complementary technologies led them to develop an interpretation that the new simulation technology was not an efficient tool for that specific purpose. I show how the interpretations developed from people's material interactions moderate the effects of the interpretations developed from social interactions on willingness to use the technology in the future. I then demonstrate that, in this particular setting, engineers inadvertently stymied an organizational change of which they were very much in favor by reducing their use of the new technology. (p. 407)

Can you identify a time when you favored a change, and then, based on either interactions with others or a material aspect of the change, you determined you had been mistaken? How did you react? What might have been handled differently?

Active and Passive Resistance

Active and passive resistance to change also can be a barrier to productivity. **Active resistance** includes a variety of efforts to stop a planned change. Open disagreement, mobilizing peers to dissent, dissenting up the chain of command, voting, attempts to get others to block the change, protests, slow response to requests, overt refusal to change, and sabotage are only some of the positive and negative ways people can engage in active resistance to change. **Passive resistance** includes visible but not active disagreement with change: ignoring change messages and strategies, ambivalence, appearing to agree while not making the desired change, and a variety of other less

Active resistance ■ A variety of overt attempts to block change.

Passive resistance ■ A variety of mostly covert attempts to block change.

visible techniques. Resistance can be related to any of the above-described barriers as well as to others you can identify. Listing resistance as a barrier does not imply that at times resistance is not appropriate and necessary. There are times when resistance to ill-conceived or ill-motivated change is very appropriate and more productive for individuals and organizations than destructive change. Other times, however, resistance is based on self-interest and an unwillingness to engage in needed change. In these latter circumstances, resistance blocks progress.

Organizational Leaders

Leaders who are not effective at change implementation become change barriers. **Organizational leaders** who force change, exhibit inconsistent behaviors, show marginal support for change, set unrealistic expectations, expect others to do the work, and fail to communicate effectively contribute to failed change efforts. Whether their behaviors are intentional or not, leaders often do not understand that negative approaches to change contribute to their lack of credibility and effectiveness. Have you experienced a situation when a leader contributed to the failure? What might this leader have done differently?

> **Organizational leaders** ■ Leaders who force change, exhibit inconsistent behaviors, show marginal support for change, set unrealistic expectations, expect others to do the work, and fail to communicate effectively.

Organizational Trust

Low organizational trust generates a powerful barrier to effective change. Organizations with low trust have difficulty getting customers, employees, stockholders, investors, or the general public to believe in the possibility of productive change. The dimensions of **organizational trust** we discussed earlier in this book—concern for employees, openness and honesty, identification, reliability, and competence—often are in question when change efforts are introduced. Corporate scandals provide an excellent example. Insider trading, misuse of pension funds, criminal behavior of leaders, and a host of other factors make positive change problematic for many of the affected companies. Fear and anxiety increase when trust is low. The difficulty of regaining trust once lost should provide ample incentive for those responsible for organizational development and change to think about how to generate trust in support of long-term effectiveness.

> **Organizational trust** ■ The belief that another individual, group, or organization is competent, open and honest, concerned about employees, reliable, and identifies with common goals, norms, and values.

Organizational Decline

Finally, it is very difficult to engage in productive change when an organization is in decline. **Organizational decline** can be understood as a time when an organization is in danger of losing its abilities to meet its goals and unable to mount productive change. Jim Collins (2009) has identified five stages of decline: (1) hubris born of success, (2) undisciplined pursuit of more, (3) denial of risk and peril, (4) grasping for salvation, and (5) capitulation to irrelevance or death. And, of course, there are numerous other possibilities, including a variety of external circumstances. The issue, however, is how to assess signs of potential decline so decline can be addressed with productive change and not become an insurmountable barrier.

> **Organizational decline** ■ A time when an organization is in danger of losing its abilities to meet its goals and unable to mount productive change to increase effectiveness.

THE LEADERSHIP OF DEVELOPMENT AND CHANGE

Inherent in everything we have discussed is the responsibility of communication professionals to help organizations identify needed change and develop strategies and tactics appropriate for productive change. Because of the rapid changes associated with an information-rich society, increasing importance is attached to organizational positions responsible for guiding and directing change and development. The public relations and marketing positions discussed in Chapter 10 are directly or indirectly associated with identifying, conceptualizing, introducing, teaching, and evaluating change. Thus, helping organizations develop and change is a primary professional application of organizational communication competencies.

Organizational development ■
Educational strategies intended to change the beliefs, attitudes, values, and structure of organizations.

The leadership of development and change goes beyond public relations and marketing. Warren Bennis (1969) suggested **organizational development** is needed for dealing with continuing change and can be described as a complex educational strategy. Educational strategies are designed to promote organizational change so that adaptation to new technologies, markets, and challenges, and to the rate of change itself, can take place.

Fundamental to the Bennis notion of organizational development is the ability to identify needed change, to develop educational strategies (internal communication, training, publications, advertising, public relations) that help bring about change, and to evaluate the results of these efforts. When in Chapter 12 we discuss the responsibilities and skills required for most communication career options you will see that problem identification, design of educational strategies, and evaluation techniques are primary responsibilities for communication professionals.

Peter Senge (1998) contended the increasing interdependency of the world requires change and new learning. He described a "sense of connectedness, a sense of working together as part of a system." Senge believed the learning organization will develop capacities for change and learning not found in traditional organizations.

All types of leaders have responsibility for change. In fact, change implementers have diverse organizational positions, including direct labor jobs. Both internal and external communication specialists have professional responsibilities for a variety of organizational change processes. Whether as an employee of the organization or as an external consultant, the communication specialist collects and evaluates data, interprets data for those responsible for decision making, develops processes and plans for solutions, and evaluates the results of change and development efforts.

The manner in which change implementers, including communication professionals, provide these services can be described by a variety of processes and models: transformation; diffusion of innovation; stakeholder theory; the purchase, doctor–patient, and process models; and the appreciative inquiry process. Each process and model reflects different assumptions about change and the roles of implementers; the roles of the communication specialists; the abilities of individuals, departments, or entire organizations to define their own problems; and who has responsibility for problem solving and change.

MODELS AND PROCESSES FOR DEVELOPMENT AND CHANGE

Organizational Transformation Process

John Kotter (1998) described an eight-stage process for creating major change through successful **organizational transformation.** Kotter contended:

> It starts off with pushing the urgency rate up. What people have to do is to start focusing attention on performance data and on industry data. In other words, they've got to look objectively at how the organization is doing, and at where the industry is going, in the hope that by getting enough people looking at the real situation, those people will either become convinced that there is a crisis, or they will begin to see some major opportunities that they hadn't seen before. In either case the urgency rate goes up, and all of a sudden you've got an opportunity to get things going.
>
> The next step is to form an appropriate guiding coalition, a group that has enough power to lead the change effort. Then you've got to develop a vision, and a strategy for achieving it, and you've got to communicate that vision effectively to the whole organization. You've got to empower people to change systems and structures that stand in the way of the vision. And you've got to create some short-term wins, so that employees can begin to see visible improvements, and they can be recognized and rewarded for their part in those improvements.
>
> Next it's a question of consolidating the credibility from those short-term wins to produce even more change. And finally, you must ensure that it is all institutionalized into a new culture. (pp. 170–171)

Organizational transformation process ■ An eight-step process requiring focusing attention for change, forming guiding coalitions, developing vision and strategy, communicating to all stakeholders, empowering people to change, creating short-term wins, consolidating wins for more change, and ensuring change is institutionalized in the culture.

Diffusion of Innovation

We have described change as moving from one situation or state to another, usually intended to be positive but certainly not always productive. The processes which have been described as **diffusion of innovation** help us understand organizational innovation, diffusion, adoption, and implementation, which in turn are related to a variety of organizational outcomes, including routinization of the innovation, reinvention of the innovation, or rejection or discontinuance of the innovation. Laurie Lewis (forthcoming) describes innovation as "a creative process of generating ideas for practice. Organizational changes are sometimes generated through accidental or intentional innovation processes used by organizations to create new ways of doing or new things to do. . . . Adoption is the term we use to describe the formal selection of the idea for incorporation into an organization." Following adoption the organization determines how implementation should occur. Organizations put in practice the innovation (routinization), modify the innovation when in use (reinvention), or abandon the innovation based on failed expectations, resistance, or

Diffusion of innovation ■ Organizational process which includes innovation, diffusion, adoption, and implementation and, in turn, is related to a variety of organizational outcomes, including routinization of the innovation, reinvention of the innovation or rejection, or discontinuance of the innovation.

other factors. David Seibold, Daisy Lemus, Dawna Ballard, and Karen Myers (2009) describe diffusion of innovation from an organizational communication perspective:

> The four main elements within the process of diffusion are the innovation, communication channel, time, and social system. An *innovation* is an idea, practice, or object perceived as new by an individual, group, organization, or other entity. The *communication channel* is the medium through which messages concerning an innovation are exchanged. The relevance of *time* concerns (1) the lapse between knowledge of an innovation and an adoption or rejection decision about it—the period known as the *innovation-decision process;* (2) the time lag between early and late adopters; and (3) the adoption rate, or number of new adopters within a given time period. Finally, the *social system* is the group of interrelated units or nodes (individuals, groups, organizations, etc.) involved in the larger diffusion process.
>
> The diffusion of an innovation is facilitated by its salience within a given social system. For example, when organizational members deem an innovation to be salient, they discuss it among their social networks—extending from departmental colleagues to members of other organizations—and these discussions shape their attitudes about it. Such discussion reflects the first two stages of the innovation-decision process, which consists of (1) knowledge (which most individuals do not proceed past), (2) persuasion, (3) decision, (4) implementation, and (5) confirmation. . . . If they discuss it, . . . those conversations shape their attitudes . . ., which then shape their *decision* about whether to adopt it. If they adopt it, the next step is to *implement* the technology in the company. Finally, decision makers will seek *confirmation* that they have made the proper decision, based on outcomes associated with and reactions to the innovation. (p. 338)

Stakeholder Theory

The concept of stakeholders or multiple publics was introduced in Chapter 10. Employees, investors, customers, vendors, regulators, competitors, communities, and a host of other potential publics are stakeholders who have interactions with

Stakeholder Theory ■ Organizational theory which maps the field of potential stakeholders and guides strategic action in managing relationships with various groups of stakeholders during change.

particular organizations. Laurie Lewis (forthcoming) describes **Stakeholder Theory** as explaining "how organizations map the field of potential stakeholders and then decide strategic action in managing relationships with various groups of stakeholders." Stakeholders can play significant roles in change. Lewis describes four specific roles: opinion leaders, connectors, counselors, and journalists. According to Lewis, "Opinion leadership involves individuals or groups of stakeholders whose opinions tend to lead rather than follow other stakeholders. An innovation champion, a type of opinion leader, is said to be a leader, a sponsor, a diplomat, a salesperson, risk-taker, and a problem-solver. In the opposite vein, the *innovation assassin* . . . advises people not to use the new change." Lewis describes connectors as those who bring different types of stakeholders together across social worlds, subcultures, and niches; connectors provide social support to others during change, and journalists provide investigations during change and report findings about change not necessarily provided by the organization.

Journalists in this depiction are not without their personal positions and opinions. Journalists talk about what is good and bad about the change, raise questions and challenges, and become more important in our increasingly online stakeholder environments.

The Purchase Model

In the **purchase model,** the organization requests particular services from a communication specialist, whether an organizational employee or external consultant, to meet a need the specialist has not been involved with identifying. The communication professional may be requested to conduct a training class, write a news release, or design a publication announcing a new policy. The parties requesting the specialist's services assume they understand their own needs and have identified the specialist as capable of meeting those needs and bringing about productive change. In other words, they are purchasing the desired services. This model can be an efficient use of resources if the assignment is well defined and the specialist is capable of implementing the desired request. This model is ineffective, however, when the client does not thoroughly understand the problem or requests of the specialist services beyond the specialist's scope of responsibility or capability.

> Purchase model ■ Consulting model in which the organization relates to the specialist by requesting particular services to meet a need the specialist has not been involved with identifying.

The Doctor–Patient Model

The **doctor–patient model** is based on assumptions very different from the purchase model. In the doctor–patient model, the communication professional acts in much the same manner as a medical doctor who examines patients, identifies their symptoms, and prescribes treatment. In the organizational setting, the doctor–patient model requires the communication specialist to examine symptoms of organizational problems and prescribe appropriate solutions to meet the identified problems. As in the purchase model, the results are effective if the specialist has abilities appropriate to the task and if the organization readily accepts the diagnosis and treatment. One of the primary problems with the doctor–patient model is in the lack of organizational acceptance of proposed solutions when organizational members have little or no input into the process.

> Doctor–patient model ■ Consulting model in which the organization expects the specialist to diagnose problems and prescribe solutions.

The Process Model

The **process model** for organizational development finds members of the organization working hand in hand with the communication professional to identify problems, propose solutions, implement action, and evaluate results. In the process model, the communication specialist is responsible for guiding organizational members through inquiry and problem solving. The basic assumptions underlying the model are that organizational members are more likely to be committed to solutions they have helped generate and that the talents of the specialist are best used when working directly with those affected by the problem.

> Process model ■ Consulting model in which the organization and specialist work jointly to diagnose problems and generate solutions.

Appreciative Inquiry

Appreciative inquiry ■ An organizational change process affirming the best qualities of the organization or its employees through discovery, dream, design, and destiny.

A growing trend in planning for change is the use of a process known as **appreciative inquiry** (AI). Change planning using appreciative inquiry begins with the best qualities of the organization or its employees. The process searches for strengths to move the organization forward as opposed to focusing on weaknesses or problems. The goal of AI is to create a positive, productive environment by expanding on proven successes rather than encouraging a negative culture of fixing problems. Developed by David Cooperrider and Suresh Srivastva (1987) in the late 1980s, appreciative inquiry has four primary states: discovery, dream, design, and destiny. *Discovery* is the process for identifying the best in the situation or person. In a sense, it is appreciating the qualities that are working successfully. *Dream* is envisioning the results of a positive future. *Design* is constructing the plan to support the dream, and *destiny* is putting the plan into action. The "4-D" model is a continual cycle. Destiny naturally leads to new discoveries of strengths. Think back to our Techtron founders from the beginning of this chapter. Think about all of the change processes we discussed. Techtron founders know their employees are exceptional. What type of change process should they use to address the growth issues they face? Could they begin a change process by identifying the many strengths and positives at Techtron? Does appreciative inquiry make sense for them? Why or why not?

PLANNED DEVELOPMENT AND CHANGE

Regardless of the model or models from which change implementers work, four basic activities occur in the process of planned development and change: data collection, data evaluation, planning and implementation of solutions, and evaluation of results. The effectiveness of each of these activities contributes to the overall effectiveness of development and change. Although the activities are closely related to one another, they each require unique skills for effective performance.

Data Collection

Primary techniques for data collection include questionnaires, audits, interviews, performance data, cost analysis, and trained observation. Each technique can yield useful information, and often the techniques are combined to provide a more comprehensive understanding of potential problems and issues.

Questionnaires contain open-ended or closed questions. Entire populations may be asked to respond, or sampling techniques may be used to survey part of a population from which to generalize the results. For questionnaire data to be useful in planned change, questions must be relevant, well framed, and valid, with respondents representing a population who can be expected to understand the problem.

Organizational communication auditing is a particular type of questionnaire currently gaining in credibility and use. Such auditing is the periodic examination of important communication activities such as message-sending and message-receiving activities as they relate to important organizational outcomes. Numerous audit instruments exist and numerous others are tailored for particular organizations. Audits are used to design communication strategies, assess needs, and evaluate practices. Regardless of the procedure used, organizational communication specialists are expected to understand auditing's basic principles and to be able to use the approach as part of planned change activities.

Interviews can contribute a rich amount of data important for change and development. Whether from informal or tightly scheduled interviews, interview data can expand understanding of complex problems and identify resistance to organizational change. Interviewing requires problem knowledge, the ability to be understood by others, the ability to understand others, and skills for meaningful interpretation of interview results.

Questionnaires and interviews are techniques that gather data the organization does not already have. Other data, called performance data, exist as a result of the daily operation of the organization. These performance data come from sales reports, turnover rates, employee absenteeism, quarterly profit statements, and a host of other routine organizational measures. These data all too often are not thoughtfully used along with questionnaire and survey data to better understand needs. Communication specialists often find such performance data useful to substantiate or expand understanding of problems identified with questionnaire and interview techniques.

Gathering data about the cost of a problem also contributes to directing action toward solutions. Cost analysis may range from determining a ratio of return on an advertising campaign to assessing the dollar value of employee time spent in meetings as compared to the value derived from decisions made in meetings. Cost analysis is based on the assumption that communication behavior has both human and financial consequences. From this perspective, a seemingly inexpensive training program that fails to explain an important concept is costly.

Although cost analysis can be used to determine the cost efficiency of particular types of communication (television commercials or newspaper advertising), the primary purpose of collecting cost data is to understand the financial consequences of the event, task, or behavior within the broader context of what the organization needs. Thus, communication cost analysis frequently becomes the responsibility of the communication specialist.

Finally, trained observation is a valid technique for data collection. The communication specialist, either as a participant–observer or as an observer alone, may collect data about group processes such as decision making and problem solving. Specialists assess the effectiveness of training approaches by observing participant interactions and abilities to perform behaviors proposed during training. Skilled observation can also uncover information not previously known to the organization and therefore difficult to collect in formal questionnaires or interviews. One communication specialist's observation, for example, discovered unexpected resistance to a new policy eliminating an eating area near a production line. Although the organization provided an attractive alternative area, employees were disgruntled. Observation of the displeasure led the specialist to investigate further, finding that the production manager had increased the number of breaks per shift for each employee but had reduced the amount of time for each break. The quality assurance manager, concerned with removing food from the product assembly area, had moved the new break area further from the production line, requiring more walking time per break. The two changes, each well founded, were not compatible.

Data Evaluation

Once data are collected, evaluation and interpretation begin. In the case of questionnaires and audits, answers are tabulated and statistical analysis is used to develop a numerical description of the issues or problems under consideration. The use of appropriate statistical tests, an understanding of the limits of particular tests, and an ability to translate the numerical data into the essence of the problem are important in data evaluation. Interviews are coded to discover recurring themes or identify unique problems and creative solutions. When interview and survey data are collected for the same general problem area, data are examined for convergence, that is, whether the two forms of data yield essentially the same understanding of the problem. When they do, the specialist has added confidence in the accuracy of the findings. When findings are dissimilar, additional data may be needed to understand discrepancies.

Cost analysis data are used to evaluate communication efficiency and effectiveness and to understand the financial impact of issues and problems. These data may be used to make decisions about the amounts of organizational resources needed for change and development. Cost data also contribute to a better understanding of questionnaire and interview results. Finally, observation data are used to confirm understanding from other data, stimulate the identification of additional data needs, and bring subtle yet often crucial interpretation to data collected with more formal techniques.

Once data have been analyzed, the communication professional is responsible for interpreting data for those involved in developing solutions and making decisions about change. Data interpretation must therefore fit the needs of the proposed audience while thoughtfully and honestly reflecting the findings. This feedback stage can be especially difficult if the specialist has data that may not meet with the approval of key decision makers.

A dilemma faced by a communication consultant in a large East Coast manufacturing plant illustrates this problem. The consultant was hired to help management understand why several key supervisors had requested transfers to other divisions within the organization. Also, turnover rates for the plant exceeded the company average and absenteeism was at an all-time high. Management was perplexed because of the longtime excellent reputation of their division and the recent installation of new state-of-the-art manufacturing equipment designed to improve both quality and quantity of output. Data collected by the consultant revealed that supervisors were asking to leave because they did not trust the motives of management with regard to the new equipment. Many supervisors and a significant number of workers as well believed management was planning to use technology to eliminate jobs or at best to reduce advancement opportunities by requiring fewer and fewer lead positions on the manufacturing line. Many of the top supervisors were young and wanted to continue their career advancement, which they believed to be jeopardized by management planning. The consultant knew management would not be pleased with these findings, although the findings accurately reflected the data. The consultant was faced with the problem of presenting findings for maximum problem understanding while facilitating management to generate a solution.

A communication professional is concerned with how to facilitate understanding and generate commitment for a solution without placing blame. This component of the change process can be especially difficult for the internal communication consultant who may gain his or her primary visibility with management during the discussion of difficult problems. The ability to be effective in this type of circumstance requires careful planning and broad-based communication competency.

Data are reported in written and oral forms. Raw data and interpretations of data are identified and carefully separated. Interpretations are labeled for source and basis. Limitations of data also are specified. Frequently, reports will contain only portions of a data set. Decisions about what data to include are based on relevancy to the problem, the audience for the report, and the audience's ability to use data for problem solving. Reports identify the existence of additional data should the people involved need more detailed information.

Planning and Implementing Solutions

The planning and implementing of needed change come about in diverse ways. At times the communication professional is charged with the responsibility to develop and propose plans for change that are subject to management approval. At other times the specialist may be charged with developing and implementing plans as part of regular job responsibilities. For example, communication professionals frequently are responsible for determining organizational training needs and providing training services appropriate to those needs. In other types of problem situations, the communication professional may act as a group facilitator, with others responsible for decision making and problem solving. Finally, communication professionals may work with other organizational leaders to identify and plan for diverse types of changes.

Generally speaking, we can identify three basic approaches to organizational change: structural, technological, and behavioral. **Structural change** attempts to change an organization's basic design by altering chains of command, work functions, spans of control, and decision-making protocols. The team-based organization is an excellent example of a structural and process change made by many organizations seeking competitive advantage.

Structural change ■ Attempts to change an organization's basic design by altering chains of command, work functions, spans of control, and decision-making protocols.

Technological change attempts to introduce change designed to improve the technologies and systems used by an organization. These types of changes focus on state-of-the-art machinery, automation, and job design. In recent years, technological changes increasingly have used computerized information systems and both intranet and Internet monitoring and exchange of information.

Technological change ■ Change focusing on state-of-the-art machinery, automation, and job design.

Finally, **behavioral change** efforts focus on the use of organizational human resources. Experiences over the last many years suggest that structure, technology, and strategy changes are maximally effective only when employees are developed by and involved with organizations.

Behavioral change ■ Efforts focusing on the development and engagement of organizational employees as resources.

The communication professional is most likely to be involved with the following types of behavioral change activities: policy changes, process changes, training and development activities, and advising and counseling. Although the responsibility and level of involvement for each activity will vary from organization to organization, these primary change activities are fundamental for organizations to improve their adapting, coping, and problem-solving capabilities.

Policy refers to formally established decisions about organizational operating procedures. Organizations have personnel policies, financial policies, and customer service policies, to name just a few. For policies to be effective, they must reflect not only what the organization does but also what the organization should be doing. Effective organizations have dynamic policies that reflect changes in changing environments. Communication professionals are involved in developing personnel policies, customer relations policies, policies that govern relationships with suppliers to the organization, advertising and public relations policies, and policies that prescribe what information will be available to all organization members.

Communication professionals also involve themselves in needed *process changes*. Performance appraisal, meetings, decision making, and problem solving are only a few examples of organizational processes in which communication professionals develop plans for training organizational members in their effective use or make recommendations for process improvements.

Training and development activities are formal education strategies to help organizations perform more effectively. As already discussed, training is a primary responsibility for communication professionals. Effective training can help individuals and entire organizations develop better self-awareness, incorporate the use of new skills and processes, and adapt to the changing needs of dynamic environments. Training also is used to transmit organizational beliefs, attitudes, and values. As such, training reflects organizational culture and becomes part of the shared realities of organizational members. Training activities provide entry-level positions for many communication professionals. The development and design of effective training programs require knowledge of program or instructional design, theoretical preparation necessary to address a specific issue, and the presentation skills to facilitate active learning for adults who may or may not want to participate in the experience.

Policy, process changes, and training and development activities are generally somewhat formally structured and part of the planned operation of the organization. *Advising and counseling activities* are both formal and informal responsibilities of the communication professional. Personnel liaisons, for example, meet regularly with departments and department managers to provide advice and counsel. Counseling may examine specific behaviors, include improved ways of doing things, or focus on career development. Communication professionals, however, are frequently sought for informal advice about human relations problems and personal dilemmas organizational members face. The ability to understand and represent the interests of both the individual and the organization requires sensitivity and strong interpersonal communication skills. Effective advice and counseling help individuals reach good decisions and improve behaviors, both vital processes to organizational adaptation and change. This advising and counseling role is especially important in organizations undergoing rapid change. When individuals are asked to acquire new skills and face somewhat uncertain futures, they may need assistance in planning their personal response to the circumstances around them. The communication professional can assist the entire organization in developing flexibility for an information-rich society by individually helping members maximize their personal coping mechanisms.

Evaluating Results

Changes in policies, processes, training and developmental activities, and advising and counseling are part of the ongoing process of organizational life. Almost everyone, however, recognizes that change for the sake of change may or may not be organizationally effective. The final component of the change and development process, therefore, is the evaluation of the results.

Change can be evaluated in a number of ways and with a number of different criteria. Organizations frequently use performance measures such as profit and loss, sales quotas, manufacturing output, quality defects, and employee turnover to measure change. When a sales and profit problem has been caused by quality defects on the manufacturing line, the effectiveness of improvement efforts is measured against previous sales, profit, and defects figures.

Many organizational change efforts, however, are not directly linked to quantifiable measures of performance. Attempts to generate increased teamwork, for example, although ultimately related to profit and loss figures, cannot be immediately measured in terms of dollars and cents. Evaluation of this somewhat subjective problem can be established by looking for changes in the data that identified the problem. Data gathered by one consultant identifying a teamwork problem indicated that instead of peers and supervisors working together to solve problems, supervisors routinely went to managers for decisions they should have been making themselves. The consultant evaluated whether her team-building efforts had generated improvement by determining whether managers were still being asked as frequently for solutions. Effectiveness of teamwork efforts also was evaluated by asking the supervisors themselves how they felt about change efforts. Thus, trained observation can also be important in the evaluation of change efforts not suitable for direct performance measures.

Finally, additional data collection serves a useful role in the evaluation of change. Questionnaires, auditing, interviews, and the other techniques discussed in the data collection phase of change can be used to determine the effects of educational strategies for organizational development and change. In one very real sense, evaluation is not the end of the change process but instead is the way the process begins again. The evaluation of change gives us a new organizational point of reference from which additional change efforts can occur.

Most researchers and business practitioners agree that the rate of change in organizational life will continue to escalate. If these predictions prove true, organizational communication competencies will be increasingly desirable for those responsible for organizational decision making and problem solving. Professional positions for managing change will continue to be important, but managing change will increasingly become everyone's responsibility. Indeed, the challenges of change in an information-rich society suggest the growing importance of communication professionals for effective organizations of the future.

COMMUNICATING ABOUT CHANGE

We contend change is a communication-based process. All of the readily available evidence suggest this is true. Communicating about change, however, is a specific part of the process with specific professional communication responsibilities. Individuals throughout organizations, but certainly the leaders of marketing, public relations, advertising, sales, organizational development, human resources, and personnel positions, are responsible for seeking input from a variety of audiences and stakeholders to identify needs and opportunities for change. These same individuals also provide information about change and its expected outcomes.

Most significant planned changes are accompanied by communication strategies. At times the very effectiveness of the changes will be determined by how effectively these strategies are developed and implemented. A **communication strategy**, simply put, is the general plan for disseminating information and soliciting input during planned organizational change. A communication strategy is the explanation for organizational change, the approach for gathering input about the change, the methods of evaluating the acceptance or rejection of the change, and the methods for disseminating change outcomes.

Communication strategy ■ The general plan for disseminating information and soliciting input during planned organizational change.

Strategy involves making choices about approaches based on an understanding of the various audiences for the messages. Strategy involves goal setting and anticipating probable reactions. Communication is used to help stakeholders identify the need for change, know what is going to happen, know how it affects individuals and groups, know what is expected, and know how well the change actually works. Most change communication provides the facts of change. We are only beginning to understand that effective change messages also recognize the emotional reactions of various stakeholders and should be developed to integrate facts with consideration for underlying emotional reactions to change. Laurie Lewis (1999) concluded that more organizations disseminate information during change than gather input to guide ongoing change. Despite typical practice, evidence exists that soliciting broad input during change is a predictor of the ability to develop support for change.

In later work, Laurie Lewis, Stephanie Hamel, and Brian Richardson (2001) described models for communicating with stakeholders during change. They identified six primary models for communication: equal dissemination, equal participation, quid pro quo, need to know, marketing, and reactionary. The equal dissemination model features all stakeholders getting the same information with the same timing sequences. The equal participation model is based on disseminating information to all stakeholders and seeking input from all stakeholders. The quid pro quo approach features giving preferential communication access about change to those who provide something the organization desires, such as money, expertise, approval, power, or other resources. The need to know alternative addresses information only to those who must have information about change or those who have expressly requested information. The marketing method focuses on developing messages for specific stakeholder groups with an emphasis on the particular perspective of a given group. Finally, the reactionary method provides communication only when required by circumstances or events and is not as planned as the other approaches we have been discussing. Arguments can be made about the positives and negatives of each approach. The issue of importance, however, is to consciously think about selecting the most appropriate model or approach for a specific circumstance when communicating about planned change. In many respects, it is possible to say that framing change through communication is fundamental to leading change. Few leaders have the professional background to think about these issues. Communication professionals are expected to provide significant guidance and expertise.

Once the communication strategy has been selected, a **communication plan** deals with the implementation of strategy. The plan incorporates the goals of the strategy and crafts messages to solicit input (i.e., to actively listen) and to provide information. The plan includes an analysis of various audiences, selection of channels of communication, timing for message dissemination, timing for input and reaction to messages, and ongoing monitoring of acceptance and resistance to change. The plan must have appropriate performance indicators and be staffed with individuals with professional skills appropriate to plan implementation. The plan also includes how to communicate the outcomes of change. Although most experts agree with the conceptual elements of the plan, most also argue the plan must be fluid and evolutionary to support productive change. In most cases, these types of complicated plans are the responsibility of change leaders and those with professional organizational communication competencies.

> **Communication plan** ■ A plan to deal with the implementation of strategy. The plan incorporates the goals of the strategy and crafts messages to solicit input and to provide information. The plan includes an analysis of various audiences, selection of channels of communication, timing for message dissemination, timing for input and reaction to messages, and ongoing monitoring of acceptance and resistance to change.

CHAPTER HIGHLIGHTS

Organizational change is a somewhat ambiguous concept often simply defined as an alteration from one state to another. Organizational change is both planned and unplanned. Most organizations support planning for continuous improvement or change. How change is handled, the amount of change, who decides what to change, and a host of other issues are all responsibilities of those with professional communication competencies. Developing and sustaining organizational excellence is the rationale for change. Research supports the view that four primary practices are necessary for sustained excellence: strategy, execution, culture, and structure. Change barriers include **organizational silence, knowledge/information deficits, risk perception, uncertainty, contradictions and misalignments, active** and **passive resistance, organizational leaders, organizational trust, organizational decline,** and a host of other possibilities. The leadership of development and change often is a professional communication responsibility. **Organizational development** can be described as educational strategies intended to change the beliefs, attitudes, values, and structure of organizations. Models and processes for organizational change and development include **organizational transformation processes; diffusion of innovation; Stakeholder Theory;** the **purchase, doctor–patient,** and **process models;** and **appreciative inquiry processes.** Planned development and change include data collection, data evaluation, and planning and implementing solutions. **Structural, technological,** and **behavioral changes** all are included in change efforts. Finally, evaluating results informs the change process and prepares the organization to begin the process again. The **communication strategy** and the **communication plan** are developed in support of planned change efforts and are designed to seek input from those involved in the change and to disseminate information about the change. Strategy involves making choices about approaches based on an understanding of various audiences for messages. The communication plan is the tactical implementation of the strategy. ■

WORKSHOP

1. **The Communication Professional at Work Activity** Each of the following organizational situations will result in a request for the services of a communication professional. As you read each case, try to determine the consulting models you might use, as well as the strategy and tactics you would consider, and try to determine what information you would need to proceed. Individuals or groups should develop an overall approach to each of the six cases. (Information is missing. You will need to make some assumptions and identify them as you proceed to decide what to do.)

Jane Edwards's Problem Employee

Jane Edwards was proud of the people who worked for her in the data-processing department. They were capable and had shown a great deal of commitment and creativity during the last few difficult months of program expansion. With such a positive performance by the entire department, Jane could hardly believe the reports she was getting about George Jones. He was one of her most capable programmers. Could he really have been responsible for major errors in the new program? Did he really walk away last Friday, threatening never to come back? Should she go to him directly? Jane decides to contact her personnel liaison, Jim Hillis. She wants to know how Jim can help her understand what, if anything, is happening to George.

Questions for Discussion

1. What model is Jane putting in place to work with Jim?
2. What data does Jane have?
3. If you were Jim, what data would you need to help with Jane's problem? ■

The Case of the Poorly Written Manual

John Howard was shaking his head as he left the meeting with his boss, Joe French. Joe was right; the new technical manual was simply not up to the company's standards. Yes, he had told Joe that there were three new people in the product development and testing group, but that was no excuse. The three apparently were simply not capable writers; they might be capable product engineers, but their writing was terrible. John called the training department and asked for Susan Harris. Could Susan schedule his three new employees in her next technical writing course?

Questions for Discussion

1. What model is John putting into place to work with Susan?
2. What are his assumptions in making this decision?
3. Is this an appropriate approach to solving his problem? ■

The Transition of Stanley Manufacturing

Stanley Manufacturing has enjoyed a fine reputation in the small-home-appliance industry. Since its beginning some sixty years ago, Stanley has prided itself on maintaining a family atmosphere for its employees, who are expected to stay with Stanley for their entire working careers. Times have changed, though. Stanley's management team sees profits being eroded and more and more competitors using innovative manufacturing processes, enabling them to produce a quality product at a price lower than the Stanley line. Stanley's management team understands that Stanley Manufacturing must undergo major changes to regain a prominent position in the market. They decide to hire a consultant external to the Stanley organization to help them begin a change process.

Questions for Discussion

1. Which model is the Stanley management team putting in place?
2. If you were the consultant, what type of data would you collect?
3. How would you involve people in the Stanley organization?
4. Can an external person be useful in this situation? ■

The Crisis at Homes for the Homeless

Ardyth Gilcrease was shocked to learn from her auditors that they had identified over $500,000 of irregularities in an apartment building account that was the responsibility of her senior vice president Doug Childers. As the chief executive officer for the popular nonprofit Homes for the Homeless, Ardyth was responsible for raising funds to provide shelter for the homeless and for ensuring that the integrity of the organization was above reproach. The violations were so significant the auditors would be forced to turn the evidence over to the district attorney. Ardyth decided she must rapidly develop a team to help her understand the multiple problems ahead. She wanted part of that team to include external consultants who could assist her in navigating the major changes she knew would be coming.

Questions for Discussion

1. What type of experts should Ardyth assemble?
2. How can Homes for the Homeless prepare for the changes that a breach of integrity and negative publicity will likely bring?
3. If you were a communication consultant selected, how would you approach this problem? What specifically would you do?
4. If you were Ardyth, what would you do? How would you approach this problem? ■

Mason Financial is Working at Capacity

Jerry Reeves was not surprised to learn that his Baja team was perceived by literally everyone at Mason Financial to be working at maximum capacity. The numbers of loans processed during the past year set records for Mason and for the highly competitive loan-processing industry. Therefore, the results of Mason's annual employee satisfaction survey were disturbing. The Baja team, although receiving external praise, was reporting some of the lowest satisfaction ratings within Mason Financial. Furthermore, employees reported favoritism, unrealistic work expectations, and outright mismanagement by some supervisors. As the regional director of processing teams, Jerry was responsible for the Baja organization as well as for teams in Chicago, Atlanta, and Colorado Springs. Although teams in Chicago, Atlanta, and Colorado Springs had good records, they could not compete with the results from Baja. However, all three teams were more satisfied with Mason than their Baja counterparts. Jerry is faced with trying to understand what is happening in Baja that works for productivity but may be contributing to high employee dissatisfaction. He contacts his head of organizational development and training and asks for assistance.

Questions for Discussion

1. What are possible approaches the head of organizational development and training can use to assist Jerry?
2. What data are needed to understand these issues?
3. How should more data be collected?
4. Structure a detailed approach to assist Jerry. ■

Changes for Hewlett Designers

Hewlett Designers had a long history of successful partnerships with large corporations interested in providing customized software products for major retailers. For twenty-five years, the majority of Hewlett's customers had been large suppliers for the dominant retail chains in the United States of America. Over the past five years, Hewlett CEO, Pamela Griffith, had become aware that Hewlett should begin to look at new suppliers and a potential direct relationship with some of the major retailers. She understood, as did only some of her senior management team, that retail chain suppliers were increasingly likely to be located outside the country. Hewlett's ability to work internationally had not been tested. Additionally, they had not worked directly with retail chains. Pamela Griffith knew she must initiate a large-scale effort to evaluate how Hewlett Designers should change in order to meet future market opportunities and demands. She faced resistance from several key senior managers who thought everything was just fine.

Questions for Discussion

1. What barriers to change will Pamela Griffith face?
2. What will have to happen for productive change to take place?
3. How will organizational trust influence what happens?
4. How should the need for change be communicated? To whom? By whom? How can you decide? ■

---

2. Select one of the situations from the prior activity. Apply the appreciative inquiry 4-D step process, and think about how that would influence decisions in the case. Discuss with others how you might use the AI approach in your personal life.
3. In the case that follows, Into the Pit and Out Again: An Organizational Turnaround, Dr. Nina Polok describes a major change effort including a communication training program that contributes to a significant turnaround in a troubled organization. In small groups, discuss the case, integrating concepts of ethics, business need, planned change, and communication training. Dr. Polok has over twenty years of high-technology experience, is a trained engineer with a Ph.D. in organizational development, and currently is the director of the Bachelor of Innovation degree programs at the University of Colorado at Colorado Springs.

> ▶ **Into the Pit and Out Again: An Organizational Turnaround**

NINA POLOK, PH.D.

Surreal Day: September 11, 2001

What a tragic, surreal day this was. On the way to work this morning I heard a report on NPR about what they thought was a small airplane crashing into a tower in New York. I thought that some poor pilot had gotten disoriented or was impaired and had a horrible accident. I went on in to the plant, booted up my computer in my cubicle, did a quick check of e-mail, and headed off to the weekly staff meeting.

Our staff meetings are a little strange these days since our general manager, Kurt Wagner, is a German national who lives in Germany. The rest of the division is located in Colorado Springs. The division staff—R&D manager, marketing manager, planning manager, controller, manufacturing manager, and human resource manager (me), sit around a big table in the conference room. There's a polycom phone in the middle of the table and Kurt calls in from Germany. He's over here for a week or more at a time about one out of every four weeks.

This morning we were in our conference room, door closed, oblivious to the world outside and proceeding with our meeting. About halfway through we had just finished seeing a presentation by a financial analyst about a new process for forecasting orders that uses economic data as well as trend analysis. According to his model, business was about to turn up, and the rest of the year was looking good. This was not totally believable as we were in the midst of planning our first layoffs for later in the month. The company has never done involuntary layoffs to this extent—it's a wrenching process for all involved.

The R&D manager excused himself for a quick break. He was gone a bit longer than usual and brought back disturbing news from things he'd heard in the hallways. "That plane that crashed into the World Trade Center was an airliner. Another has crashed into the other tower and another plane went into the Pentagon. We may be under attack!" There were no TV sets on site, but we had Kurt sitting in his home office in Germany. He tuned his TV to CNN and started giving us updates about what was happening. By this time the first tower had collapsed and reporters were saying that 50,000 people worked in the World Trade Center. I turned to the R&D manager who was sitting next to me and said "The world has just changed—we just don't know how much."

We were frozen in the conference room, trying to accept the enormity of the disaster, the possibility that it wasn't over, and unwilling to leave the polycom in the center of the table, which was our only source of news. We even tried for a little while to go on with our agenda. Although it wasn't a long period of clock time, it seemed like it took forever for us to realize that any further agenda items were irrelevant, that we had better get out among the employees, get a clear source of news, and make some decisions about whether to let people go home.

We closed the plant at 3:00 P.M. so people could get home to their families. Even though it was clear by then that we were in no danger in Colorado, everyone was concerned about their children and their extended family and friends and wanted to be at home. I was worried about my two kids and whether they had heard the news yet at school and I wanted to be home to meet them. Turns out they had more access to TVs at school than I had at work. My daughter had even been watching live when the towers collapsed. We'll see what tomorrow brings. I suspect that business will suffer and a recession is likely. And I shudder to think how many thousands of people died when those towers collapsed.

A New General Manager: May 1, 2002

Today was an inflection point of sorts. Two things of note have happened. First, we have a new general manager who started today. His name is Rob Anderson, and I have high hopes that he can really help us turn around a bad business situation. Second, I completed a communications course today that I believe has the potential to also help us turn things around.

Orders have continued to decline since 9/11. We have been through two major downsizings, reducing the head count in the division by 18 percent. Thankfully, the company is paying a generous severance package that includes several months of support from an outplacement firm for each person leaving. And we have had multiple training sessions for our managers to help them deliver bad news to people being laid off, take care of the people who are staying, and take care of themselves during the entire process. I am proud of how the company and the division have handled the downsizing. We have communicated the process very clearly, and we communicate the results of decisions as soon as we can. We select the people to be laid off on the basis of a skills match with the future of the organization, and we always check to be sure we have not inadvertently created an adverse impact on women, minorities, or older employees. Still, it's been a very intense, emotional time. Some of our managers have had to lay off friends and colleagues they've known for years. People who were great contributors in the past but are lacking in skills for the future were among the first to go. The management team is somewhat traumatized, and it's hard to know if the light at the end of the tunnel is daylight or another oncoming train.

Our orders are down and our expenses are lower, but we have no visibility to anything like a profit and loss statement—we are treated as a cost center and the profit or loss is recognized higher up the hierarchy. This makes it hard to know how well we're doing and to communicate the importance of cost savings initiatives to employees. Too many things aren't visible.

The company is spending a ton of money on the implementation of a new software system while laying people off, imposing temporary pay cuts, and canceling almost all travel. The new software is known as an Enterprise Resource Planning (ERP) system and is supposed to replace hundreds of programs with one system that allows us to develop products, build them, take orders for them, and record the revenue—kind of a "soup to nuts" giant computer program. It's intended to make us more efficient and save money as well, but the implementation affects almost everyone in the company and requires hundreds of experts to help with the change.

In the midst of all of this our GM [general manager] from Germany decided to move on to another job within the company. He had been traveling to the United States at least one week a month and sometimes up to three weeks at a time. After 9/11 this became quite inconvenient, and the frequency of his trips slowed to one every five or six weeks. There are many jobs in every global company where the employees and the manager are remote from one another, but in this case all of the employees were at one site in the United States and only Kurt, the GM, was remote. The distance and the travel difficulties made it nearly impossible to be an inspiring leader in the down part of a business cycle. Kurt recognized this and took a month to seriously consider moving to the United States, which the company would have been happy to sponsor. However, in the end he decided the best thing for his family and the division was for him to move to a different GM job in the field sales organization. His is still a remote manager, living in Germany and managing a group with people located all over the world. Everyone respected Kurt's decision and the search was on for a new GM for the division.

Our new GM is from outside the company. Well, sort of. Rob worked here for many years at the start of his career, then left six years ago to work for a smaller competitor. He seems to have learned a tremendous amount from that experience, including a focus on operational excellence that we are missing and a sense of urgency about producing results that we are also missing. During the interview he showed us the metrics book he keeps on a monthly basis that includes everything you could want to know about the business, from orders and revenue to inventory levels and average discounts to new product introduction schedules. We were drooling; at the moment our systems don't allow us to easily find even half that much information. I'm looking forward to how he functions in this environment, and I'm dedicated to making sure his entry into the organization is successful.

I am also excited today about the course I just completed. It's called Communication for Results and it's unlike any other leadership training I've seen. The first session, a month ago, was two and half days long, and the second session was two days long. We each worked on a project in the interim and could take advantage of conference calls if we got stuck. The purpose of the course was intriguing, and the outcomes promised on the first day sounded very bold. The purpose was "To equip you with tools of communication and perspective that will enable you to cause consistently elevated levels of performance in yourself and others." For managers in the midst of a shrinking organization, struggling to do their work with fewer people, the idea of high performance sounded quite unrealistic given the circumstances. There were two outcomes promised. The first was "You will be able to produce increased levels of tangible business results with decreased levels of time and effort," and the second was "You will have what it takes to naturally inspire extraordinary performance in yourself and others." Frankly, these outcomes seemed impossible to achieve in any kind of classroom-based training. And yet, by the end of the course today, I felt that I had gotten these outcomes!

The content of the course is difficult to explain. It's a clever combination of experiential exercises, minilectures, and group inquiry. The fundamental assumption of the course is that if you actually look at how managers and leaders do their jobs, it's all through communicating with others—having conversations that create a possible future, or conversations that result in commitments for action, or conversations that complete a set of actions and acknowledge success. But in order to communicate effectively, it's useful to know that the message we intend is not always the message that's heard, how it gets filtered, and what we can do about it. The most powerful part of the course was the realization that my communication is often based on intentions I am not fully aware of. For example, I got insight into how critical I am of authority figures and how I use that criticism as an excuse for not taking action myself. I realized that my critical intent colors my communication and that people will hear the implicit criticism even when the content of what I say is not critical. This is deadly for a leader; people are not likely to be inspired that way! I learned ways of speaking and listening that energize people and other ways that will suck the energy right out of them. I learned some powerful ways to manage my own emotional states, crucial for leading in the face of tough circumstances. I have thirty-five pages of notes—the course is very dense—and I imagine I'll be having insights for weeks after. One thing is for sure: I feel much more optimistic, much less victimized, and more energized than I have felt in well over a year. I really want to bring this course to my organization. Maybe this plus the new GM will make the difference!

Bottoming Out: November 16, 2002

We just finished the all hands meeting for the division today, reviewing the year and talking about the plans for the coming year. To say that the numbers don't look so good would be a severe understatement. In June we went live with the new software system. Troubles in booking orders and releasing shipments cratered Q3 for the whole company, including us. Thank good-ness Rob Anderson is a trooper and can take a long-term per-spective, or he might be regretting that he took the job!

Rob and I worked together to make his entry into the organ-ization a successful one. I held meetings with the management team even before Rob arrived to debrief our experience with Kurt and talk about how we wanted to function differently with the new GM. Rob spent a lot of time talking to a wide variety of people in the division. He asked for samples of the key new products and kept them on his desk so he could explore and un-derstand their features. He talked with engineers from R&D, marketing, manufacturing, and sales about how they saw our competitive position. He made sure the entire management team took a new focus on the competition—what competitors were doing, their business results compared to ours, and their product specifications compared to ours. This information was understood at lower levels of the organization, but Rob made sure it was brought together so the entire management team could see the whole picture. We started a "war room" where we had staff meetings and posted all the relevant business informa-tion such as information on competitors, new product introduc-tions, orders and shipments, and so on, all around the room on the walls. And, we took a hard look at the management team and began to make some changes.

The first change Rob initiated was to get a new full-time controller. In an optimistic assumption about how well the new ERP system would work, the company had decided that a divi-sion could share a controller with another division. Our controller supported two divisions and worked at a site 125 miles distant from us. Although she was quite competent, the arrangement didn't work well, especially when extraordinary effort was re-quired to generate division-level data from the new systems. So we hired a new controller who devoted full-time effort initially to discovering what shape we were really in. His numbers were star-tling. We had been focused on metrics like contribution margin, but he did the work necessary to show what our profit and loss actually was. We were losing money every quarter and had been for the last year! I know it sounds crazy that we would not know this, but new organizational designs, restructuring, and the radi-cal shift to the new ERP had effectively obscured these data.

Our marketing manager was ready for a new challenge and went off to work on bringing a new product category online. So we replaced him with a new marketing manager whose experi-ence had been heavily in sales. He knew the sales organization extremely well and had great relationships there. With his help, we redesigned and refocused the marketing function. Our R&D manager retired at the end of a more than 30 year career with the company. We have just settled on a new R&D manager who will start in December.

The entire staff and almost the entire management team have now been through the Communication for Results class.

Some chose not to attend or had conflicts they couldn't re-arrange, but the people who did go came out re-energized to help us climb back to profitability. Even though we just finished another round of downsizing and may have at least one more round to go, the management team is in better shape emotion-ally than they've been in over a year. They are more able to ver-bally create a possible future for the employees that remain, are less victimized themselves, and more in touch with what's im-portant to them. Rob came out completely inspired and more in touch with what areas he should be focused on as a GM. Our goal is to achieve breakeven by Q2.

I'd call the all hands meeting we just finished a success given the circumstances. Rob spends hours getting ready for an all hands meeting. In fact, he spends more time thinking through what and how to communicate than any manager I've ever met. He is careful to provide continuity with what he showed and committed to last month and he treats all employ-ees as adults able to assess and accept business realities. He's also a whiz at PowerPoint—his visuals are compelling and re-ally make the point. People are gradually coming to trust him. There are many more questions now during the Q&A portion of the meeting, and the questions are business related. People are still justifiably worried about their jobs since we are not yet profitable, but they at least believe we are on the right track and might recover!

Breakeven at Last: May 16, 2003

Breakeven!! Even though the quarter shows a slight loss, we know we've passed through the breakeven point. Now we can start operating in the black. In our division we may also have passed the point of doing more involuntary downsizing although it is still going on all around us on this site and elsewhere in the company. The company is not out of the woods yet. But still, at least we have something worth a little celebration—though our celebrations are quite muted due to cost controls and sensitivity to people still being laid off.

We are proceeding to execute on all the tasks that are helping us achieve this business turnaround. One thing I've learned through this is that there is no one solution to a bad business situation. We make huge changes to the bottom line from making progress on lots of small fronts. We either have done or are working on changes in our pricing strategy, acceleration of new product intro-ductions, materials cost savings, reductions in corporate alloca-tions, reductions in selling costs and manufacturing overhead. Basically, we look at every line on the profit and loss statement to see where we have leverage to reduce costs or increase revenue. Every function has played a role in getting us to this point.

We are starting to build trust in the division as we continue to communicate clearly where we are and what we are doing about it. No one is happy about the state of the company—the lack of raises, the constant downsizing, the extreme cost controls.

But most employees are relieved that the division management team seems to know what they're doing.

One of the biggest challenges is to keep up the communication with our first line managers. How they view the company and the situation has a tremendous impact on the employees they supervise, so we make a concerted effort to involve them in dialogue about the division. To do this we have periodic all manager meetings to talk about the strategy of the business and to hear from them about what issues they're facing. These dialogues have helped the senior management team be aware of how certain actions are being viewed. We can then add more context so that first line managers know the "whys" as well as the "whats" of the decisions being made. We also use the information we gain from these talks in making the next set of decisions.

I have been working hard to get all our managers at all levels through the Communication for Results course. Most have attended, and I think it's helped a lot. If we are able to pull off this turnaround I intend to do some data collection at the end of the year to see whether people believe that attending the course had anything to do with our success. It's particularly difficult to measure the impact of a training program, even a very good one. But I'll be happy if I can get some thoughtful assessments of the impact by managers who attended.

A Retrospective: November 21, 2003

What a year! We can definitely call FY03 a turnaround year for this division. We were very profitable in Q4 and, thanks to that, actually made profit on the year. And in the quarter just passed, the company is profitable again, too. This is a great time for a retrospective on how we got here.

In going from a huge loss in FY02 to a profit in FY03 we did the following things.

Activity	Percent of Profit the Activity Produced
Increased orders and revenue	26.1
Lowered R&D costs	17.4
Reduced discounts on product sales	12.8
Lowered manufacturing overhead	9.1
Reduced corporate charges	7.9
Reduced cost of goods sold	7.2
Changed pricing and product options	6.5
Lowered marketing costs	6.1
Lowered selling costs	4.0
Reduced material costs	2.9

The salary savings from the layoffs are embedded in these numbers (e.g., lowered R&D costs were, in part, people). However, the total savings from all the layoffs was only 6.8 percent of the total turnaround. I believe it's impossible to turn around an organization by downsizing alone—you must find ways to generate great ideas from the people still working.

I did my anecdotal assessment of the Communication for Results course, talking exclusively to members of the plant staff. These folks took the course in the fall of 2002—two years ago! I was quite curious about what they thought the impact had been. Here's a summary of what they said:

- The course reinforced the results orientation of Rob Anderson, the new GM. It became very clear that we get paid for results and that lack of results leads to pain and suffering.
- As a result of the course we stopped blaming others, fixed our own problems first, and then continued to look for opportunities. Every line of the income statement and some on the balance sheet were fair game.
- We planned multiple ways to win on our commitments, and then added a stretch target to make the game more fun as we had learned in the course.
- We learned to look at problems as "work to do" and not add extra meaning about how bad or wrong things were.
- We gained a common language and tools that increased the speed of decisions and shortened discussion time. For example, we made clear requests, separated the conversation of what versus why, conducted more efficient meetings, and so on.
- Knowledge of the modes of communication helped us limit pretense and criticism. We gained the freedom to say what we were thinking and stop withholding. Tough issues got surfaced and addressed quickly.
- We helped each other unhook from defensive reactions.
- We considered the probable filters of our audience when we structured our communications.
- We measured ourselves and reported our progress to all employees. As we continued to meet our commitments, morale and trust improved.
- We painted the future at coffee talks and manager meetings. This had credibility once we were meeting commitments.

Even after two years, the language of the course, the tools presented, and the ways of thinking were still having a positive impact on the staff's behavior! They credited the training with having helped with the turnaround: "Communication for Results did not tell us *what* to do. Rather, it helped us be less reactive so we could figure out what to do and then it helped us do what was needed more quickly and effectively."

It's been a challenging and yet rewarding couple of years, and I'm glad I stuck it out and was able to contribute to a significant business turnaround. I have learned a tremendous amount, not the least of which is how resilient and adaptable and caring people are.

Epilogue: June 2006

The division has been profitable for thirteen quarters in a row and has reached an operating model with high operating profit and return on invested capital. In fact, they are now taking market share from competitors and growing rapidly in revenue. Increases in headcount are still tightly controlled in order to be able to weather a downturn without resorting to layoffs. The general manager who executed the turnaround has been promoted. The new GM is bringing a renewed focus on the development of people and morale is high. ■

TIPS FOR EFFECTIVE COMMUNICATION

1. Identify the questions about change that those affected by the change are likely to ask. Be prepared to answer specific questions. Select appropriate media and communication events.
2. Describe the urgency for the change and the fundamental reasons or "whys" for the change.
3. Identify key opinion leaders and ask them for their concerns, ideas, and support.
4. Form a team or group of "change leaders." Seek their input.
5. Clarify the potential positive outcomes of the change.
6. Describe clear and specific steps to accomplish the goals.
7. Provide updates during the change process.
8. Celebrate even small successes.
9. Describe the results of the change process.
10. Seek input about the results and evaluate the process for future efforts. ■

REFERENCES AND SUGGESTED READINGS

Bennis, W. 1969. *Organization development: Its nature, origins, and prospects*. Reading, MA: Addison-Wesley.

Bennis, W., K. Benne, R. Chin, and K. Corey. 1976. *The planning of change*, 3rd ed. New York: Holt, Rinehart and Winston.

Bennis, W., and P. Biederman. 1997. *Organizing genius: The secrets of creative collaboration*. Reading, MA: Addison-Wesley.

Clampitt, P., R. DeKoch, and T. Cashman. 2000. A strategy for communicating about uncertainty. *Academy of Management Executive* 14(4): 41–57.

Collins, J. 2009. *How the mighty fall: And why some companies never give in*. New York: HarperCollins.

Cooperrider, D., and S. Srivastva. 1987. Appreciative inquiry in organizational life. *Research in Organizational Change and Development* 1: 129–169.

Cushman, D. 2000. Stimulating and integrating the development of organizational communication: High-speed management theory. *Management Communication Quarterly* 13(4): 486–501.

DeWine, S. 1994. *The consultant's craft*. New York: St. Martin's.

Gladwell, M. 2002. *The tipping point*. New York: Little, Brown.

Johnson, S. 1998. *Who moved my cheese?* New York: Putnam.

Kotter, J. 1998. Cultures and coalitions. In *Rethinking the future*, ed. R. Gibson, 164–178. London: Nicholas Brealey.

Kramer, M., D. Dougherty, and T. Pierce. 2004. Managing uncertainty during a corporate acquisition. *Human Communication Research* 30(1): 71–101.

Kuhn, T., and S. Corman. 2003. The emergence of homogeneity and heterogeneity in knowledge structures during a planned organizational change. *Communication Monographs* 70(3): 198–229.

Leonardi, P.M. 2009. Why do people reject new technologies and stymie organizational changes of which they are in favor? Exploring misalignments between social interactions and materiality. *Human Communication Research* 35: 407–441.

Lewis, L. 1999. Disseminating information and soliciting input during planned organizational change: Implementers' targets, sources, and channels for communicating. *Management Communication Quarterly* 13(1): 43–75.

Lewis, L. Forthcoming. *Implementing change in organizations: A stakeholder communication perspective*. Hoboken, NJ: Wiley-Blackwell.

Lewis, L., S. Hamel, and B. Richardson. 2001. Communicating change to nonprofit stakeholders. *Management Communication Quarterly* 15(1): 5–41.

Morrison, E., and F. Milliken. 2000. Organizational silence: A barrier to change and development in a pluralistic world. *Academy of Management Review* 25(4): 706–725.

Nohria, N., W. Joyce, and B. Roberson. 2003. What really works. *Harvard Business Review* 81(7): 43–52.

Pace, W. 1983. *Organizational communication: Foundations for human resource development.* Englewood Cliffs, NJ: Prentice Hall.

Seibold, D., D. Lemus, D. Ballard, and K. Myers. 2009. Organizational communication and applied communication research. In *Routledge handbook of applied communication research*, eds. L. Frey and K. Cissna, 331–354. New York: Routledge Taylor and Francis Group.

Senge, P. 1998. Through the eye of the needle. In *Rethinking the future*, ed. R. Gibson, 123–146. London: Nicholas Brealey.

Zorn, T., D. Page, and G. Cheney. 2000. Nuts about change: Multiple perspectives on change-oriented communication in a public sector organization. *Management Communication Quarterly* 13(4): 515–566. ■

Career Options for Organizational Communication

DEVELOPING COMPETENCIES THROUGH . . .

KNOWLEDGE   Describing influences for career decisions
Identifying career option areas and educational preparation for organizational communication
Describing twenty-first-century careers

SENSITIVITY   Developing awareness of personal influences for career decisions
Understanding employment matching

SKILLS   Assessing individual career development needs
Practicing analysis capabilities for career decisions

VALUES   Relating personal and organizational values to employment matching
Understanding continuous change as important for careers

▶ THE "WHERE DO WE GO FROM HERE?" CASE

As John walked toward the student union to join his friends Jill and George, he thought about his round of upcoming interviews. Jill, George, and John were all scheduled for several of the same companies, and he knew Jill and George were concerned as well. Being almost ready to graduate had some advantages, but this job search thing was tough. Not only was John trying to determine what were good companies and how to sell himself to them, but also he was thinking about what parts of the country he would like and how it was going to feel to leave his friends. He hadn't realized it was going to be this difficult. Well, at least he wasn't alone; Jill and George were having some of the same problems, too.

As Jill waited for John and George, she began to rehearse mentally questions and answers for her upcoming interviews. Six companies scheduled in the next two days would put her skills to the test. Jill wondered if John and George were right about taking the offer with the best salary. What else should she be considering, and what about cost of living in various parts of the country? The companies she would talk with in the next two days were in four different states several hundred miles apart. What other considerations should she make?

John and George enter the union at the same time and spot Jill.

GEORGE: Sorry I'm late; I went by the library to check the annual report of Randel Corporation. John was right that their expansion has been slowing for the last two years. I will probably not consider them as seriously as I thought.

JILL: George, are you sure that is an appropriate approach? You have really liked the type of job that Randel is describing; growth certainly isn't everything. What do you think, John?

JOHN: I had been thinking that we should all take the best salary offer, but I am beginning to have second thoughts. How much consideration should we give to where we want to live and the type of products and services the company produces? I have interviews scheduled with a defense contractor, computer manufacturer, retail chain, and that government job. They all need training specialists, and I think I qualify for what they want, but they do very different things.

JILL: I was just sitting here thinking about what factors are most important to me. I expected to be so excited when this time came. I can hardly believe I am fearful of making the right choice. ■

INTRODUCTION

John, Jill, and George experience the concerns of many of us when we begin to make important decisions about the beginning of our careers. What company or organization would be best? What factors deserve the most weight in our decision? Which choice will work best in the long term? We almost need a crystal ball to help us find answers.

Our concerns really begin much earlier than during the job search process. John, Jill, and George chose organizational communication as their major. As you would expect, they are thinking about job choices that will use the skills they have developed during their years in the communication program. In a real sense, their career choices began when they selected their major and the abilities they wanted to develop with their education. The jobs they now take will reflect that overall direction and those decisions.

This chapter is designed to increase awareness of communication-related career choices. It discusses how to begin planning a career, what general career choices are available to those studying organizational communication, what skills are important, and what types of education are required. The chapter also addresses important issues influencing changing career opportunities and paradigms. Finally, the Workshop section of this chapter presents a self-analysis process helpful for career planning.

This chapter is designed to increase *knowledge* through the presentation of career options for organizational communication and through the identification of individual and organizational factors influencing careers. We develop *sensitivity* through awareness of personal experiences influential in career choices and through identification of primary responsibilities for major career options. We practice analysis *skills* with the self-analysis process and by gathering data with informational interviews. We present *values* as important in career planning, integral to the individual and organizational relationship, and central to all professional organizational activities. Finally, we apply knowledge, sensitivity, skills, and values to our interpretation of diverse career issues.

CHOOSING A COMMUNICATION CAREER

In one sense, all careers are communication careers. The majority of our organizational time is spent communicating, whether we select communication or a seemingly unrelated field as our primary area of emphasis. As proposed throughout this book, organizational communication competencies are important for us all, regardless of career choices. Although this chapter focuses specifically on communication careers, the factors important for selecting a communication career also are applicable to other choices and are basic for understanding both individual and organizational needs.

Careers are the sum total of our job experiences over time. Careers involve decisions about personal interests, aptitudes, educational preparation, and the match of our individual competencies to the needs of particular organizations. Career planning should begin while pursuing our education and continue throughout our work lives and even into retirement. We usually think of career planning as it relates to paid employment, but in reality career planning is the process by which we plan to use our competencies as they relate to all types of work environments. As such, careers are best understood as an integral part of our total lives.

How, then, should we begin to plan our careers? Put simply, an **employment match** between an individual and an employer occurs when individual competencies match organizational competencies and the individual becomes a working member of the organization. This notion of an employment match is important for understanding how individuals select jobs and how organizations select individuals for employment. Awareness of these factors is necessary for effective career planning.

Employment match ■ When individual competencies match organizational competencies and the individual becomes a working member of the organization.

Knowledge for Employment Matching

Individuals base job and career choices on what they know is available and usually with incomplete understanding of all that is possible. We gather occupational information from past experiences, the people around us, exposure during education, and the media, and in a variety of less systematic ways. Sometimes we are aware of skill and educational requirements associated with particular occupations, whereas at other times we have only a vague understanding of what competencies are required in a given profession. Individuals also have general knowledge that applies to almost all occupations. The depth and breadth of this general knowledge contribute to occupational flexibility, or the ability to fit oneself for a variety of job positions. General knowledge includes communication competencies, organizing abilities, time-management skills, critical-thinking abilities, and decision-making capabilities.

Organizations develop knowledge about the functional requirements they need in specific occupational categories. A human resource development position may carry similar responsibilities from organization to organization, but a specific human resource development position will have specific job requirements. A human resource position in one organization might require extensive training experience, whereas a similar position in another company would not include the training responsibility. In addition, organizations require the general knowledge base that we previously described for individuals. Indeed, one of the difficulties for most organizations during interviews is assessing the somewhat subjective, yet critically important, areas of general knowledge exhibited by job applicants. Research on who is promoted into top management in U.S.A. corporations suggests general knowledge in communication and decision making may be more important for long-term advancement than most technical skills.

Sensitivity for Employment Matching

Individuals bring a variety of expectations to the job search process. Salary, position responsibilities, and advancement opportunities are only a few of the expectations individuals seek to clarify in interviews. Individuals also have expectations about how employees should be treated and the type of work environment that is personally desirable. We have been oriented to work by our family experiences, by those who have acted as role models for us, and by our previous work experiences. Research indicates we are likely to be influenced in occupational choices by direct contact with individuals in specific occupations and advice from individuals personally close to us. It is therefore not unusual to find similar occupational choices—such as law, medicine, and education—made by several members of one family. These orientations, however, can be limiting. A woman, for example, who is surrounded by those who believe her best occupational choice is teaching may or may not consider other possible alternatives suitable for her abilities. That is not to say the teaching profession would be inappropriate, but to the extent it is a stereotypical expectation (a choice appropriate for women), her potential may be limited. The same is true for men. Occupational expectations of parents and influential role models can both encourage and restrict the range of possibilities considered when making educational and career choices.

Self-awareness also is an important sensitivity for career choices. What types of competencies do we bring to an employment situation? What competencies remain in need of development? What are our preferences regarding work? How do our communication, conflict, and leadership preferences influence career choices and the jobs in which we will be comfortable and productive? How well do we know ourselves and our needs?

Organizations are sensitive to finding employees who meet their expectations. Organizations develop work norms and behavior expectations they believe contribute to productivity in their particular environments. Some organizations, for example, expect workers to put in numerous hours of overtime. In an interview, the answers a prospective employee gives to questions about work and time commitments may be pivotal to the organization's assessment of the prospect's future. Organizations also develop sensitivities to changing markets and environmental needs that require new skills and abilities from their workforce. In today's labor market, most organizations expect computer and technical competencies from prospective employees; not too long ago there was only marginal concern for these skills.

Skills for Employment Matching

Individuals bring a variety of technical qualifications to their job search. The technical qualifications an individual develops should support occupational choices because technical qualifications or the lack thereof limits choice. We know that without certain skills we cannot consider certain occupations. Only the rare individual will attempt to land a computer-programming job without having technical preparation on computers. Unfortunately, far more individuals attempt to occupy communication jobs without the training or background appropriate for these responsibilities. Because we have all been "communicating" for as long as we can remember, many take for granted the technical preparation necessary for excellence in communication jobs. Yet our technical preparation is fundamental to success in the job search and in the job itself.

Our ability to translate our knowledge, sensitivity, skills, and values to a prospective employer will in large measure determine the types of jobs we are offered. Few job interviews begin with an objective test of the skills and abilities of applicants. Most organizations rely on communication exchanges—interviews, résumés, letters of application—for initial if not final screening of potential employees.

Individuals bring their technical qualifications to the job search in hopes of matching those qualifications with the organization's technical requirements. Rarely, however, is there a perfect match. Organizations generally seek the best available match between an individual's technical background and the technical requirements of a particular job. Organizations also weigh the applicant's general knowledge in communication, decision making, critical thinking, time management, and leadership. They make judgments about the current skill level of the applicant and the amount of training time necessary for the applicant to become a productive employee. Just as the individual must be able to communicate adequately his or her abilities, organizations attempt to define for the applicant the needed requirements of the job and any additional relevant information. This match between abilities and requirements is fundamental for the employment match to work successfully.

Values for Employment Matching

As in all other aspects of our life, values are a central factor in career decisions. What is important to us and what we find desirable, interesting, and stimulating all relate to our values. Our career interests are reflections of our value systems. The socioeconomic goals we hope our employment will support are a product of a complex set of values that develop throughout our life experiences. Even our achievement aspirations can be described as an extension of our personal value systems. Understanding what is important to us should guide overall career choices as well as decisions about whether specific jobs meet our needs. One of the most common employment mistakes is the acceptance of a job because it represents a good financial offer, regardless of whether the job is of interest and supports other needs. A good offer in the fullest sense is an offer that helps us support our value system.

Organizations also have value systems. Earlier the text referred to the importance of organizational culture and values. Cultures help to define what is expected and valued within particular organizations. Products, services, resource allocations, and development interests all reflect the values of organizations. As do individuals, organizations have socioeconomic goals and overall achievement aspirations. For a successful employment match, the individual's values and the organization's values need to be in harmony, if not in all respects, at least in those areas central to job performance.

An individual should begin career planning with the concept that jobs and ultimately careers are continual matches of individual knowledge, sensitivity, skills, and values with organizational knowledge, sensitivity, skills, and values. The success of these matches for both individuals and organizations begins with the ability to define and articulate competencies, a process fundamental for effective organizational communication. To assist in your planning, we provide an extensive Self-Analysis for Career Planning activity in the Workshop section of this chapter.

CAREER CHOICES IN ORGANIZATIONAL COMMUNICATION

The growth in communication career choices continues, as does the increase in numbers of students studying communication. This growth in opportunity and the diversity of potential jobs contribute to the difficulty of describing exactly what a person who studies organizational communication is qualified to do. R. Wayne Pace and Don Faules (1994) provided a useful overall description: "They apply their knowledge in public contact positions in organizations, such as sales, marketing, public relations, advertising, fund raising, and community affairs; . . . they may apply their knowledge in development positions in organizations, such as counseling, career development, organization development, internal consulting, technical training, and management development, as well as general management (both line and staff) positions" (p. 358).

Pace and Faules went on to suggest job opportunities exist for communication professionals in every major employment sector, including health care, manufacturing, retailing, banking, construction, communications, transportation, agriculture and forestry, military, education, beverages, chemicals and pharmaceuticals, computer and data processing, energy and petroleum, hospitality and recreation, insurance, justice systems, utilities, government, and the consulting and training industry.

Figure 12.1 identifies eight major career option areas and job titles within each area for those planning careers in organizational communication. As you review the descriptions of each of the eight areas, think about your self-analysis and what you will need to know to select a communication career.

OPTION AREA	JOB TITLES
Internal communication	Human resource specialist
	Training and development specialist
	Personnel liaison
	Internal publications coordinator
	Internal communication specialist
	Organizational development specialist
	Internal consultant
	Labor negotiator
	Recruiter
	Speech Writer
	Crisis communication coordinator
External communications	Advertising specialist
	Public relations coordinator
	Government relations
	Webmaster
	Industrial media producer/director
	Technical writer
	Telecommunications coordinator
	Editor
	Scriptwriter
	Video editor
	Audio editor
	Videographer
	Social media coordinator
	Community affairs coordinator
	Government affairs coordinator
	Marketing specialist
	Crisis communication coordinator
Sales	Account representative
	Retail salesperson
	Marketing specialist
	Media salesperson
	Advertising salesperson
	Real-estate, insurance, products, etc., salesperson
Human services	Fund-raiser
	Counselor
	Career development specialist
	Program specialist

FIGURE 12.1
Career Options in Organizational Communication

Education	Teacher/professor
	Administrator
	Curriculum designer
	Online education specialist
Research/information management	Associate
	Business analyst
	Content researcher
	Marketing research analyst
	Social science specialist
	Instructional design/Web specialist
Management	Trainee
	Section/branch manager
	Store manager
	Regional manager
	Corporate staff
	Sales manager
	Personnel director
	Media manager
	Advertising manager
	Human resource development manager
	Corporate communications manager
Consultant (external to employing organization)	Organizational development specialist
	Human resource development specialist
	Trainer
	Analyst

FIGURE 12.1
(*continued*)

Internal Communication

Options in **internal communication careers** are expanding. In general individuals with internal communication responsibilities engage in the following:

> **Internal communication careers** ■ Work within an organization to assist management in employee and management communication, coordinate a variety of training activities, coordinate internal communication media, facilitate team building, and develop numerous other communication activities.

1. Provide consultation, assistance, and guidance to management on matters relating to employee and management communication; coordinate employee communication programs and activities; coordinate publishing of regular employee media; advise, coordinate, and conduct attitudinal and other polls among employees; provide editorial and publishing services; and produce, edit, and distribute special publications.

2. Develop and maintain informational units to serve the needs of senior management and the communication department.

3. Develop, coordinate, and implement small-group, face-to-face communication programs to facilitate team building, problem identification, and problem solving.

Internal communication specialists must have extensive backgrounds in interpersonal and organizational communication with an emphasis on human relations. These specialists are familiar with principles of instructional design, can evaluate the designs of others, can plan and implement their own programs, and have well-developed presentational skills. In addition to speaking skills, internal communication jobs require good listening skills, an understanding of multicultural communication, and an ability to write clearly. Internal communication specialists are expected to understand appropriate uses of e-mail, various forms of conferencing, text messaging, organizational Web sites, information portals, and extranets. They also may be required to understand technical print production for internal publication responsibilities. They must be able to analyze data and must be skilled in a variety of data-gathering techniques. Most internal communication specialists are required to have a basic understanding of statistics.

External Communications

External communications careers ■ Responsibility for external public relations activities; corporate advertising; community, shareholder, financial, and government relations; and corporate literature, sales promotions, and special productions.

Those with **external communications** responsibilities engage in the following:

1. Guide and develop a full range of external public relations activities including advertising; crisis communication; community, shareholder, financial, and government relations; and the production of corporate literature, sales promotions, marketing, and special productions.
2. Direct and coordinate all activity in the development, implementation, and administration of an organizational identification system, covering all aspects of visual communication, materials, and media.
3. Evaluate, direct, and coordinate uses of new media for all types of organizational communication and e-commerce.
4. Have administrative responsibility for public relations and development departments.
5. Have responsibility for crisis communication.

External communications specialists also may be responsible for community relations, telecommunications systems, and the public relations contacts for specific individuals within or related to the corporation.

External communications specialists may be required to have a broad range of journalism and media production skills. Understanding of multicultural and global communication is a must for most external communications specialists. These specialists design and produce media in addition to supervising others (such as advertising agencies) in the design of corporate identifications ranging from logos and television commercials to e-commerce and Internet applications. They understand the fundamentals of public relations and have skills in written communication and audience analysis. Some external communications jobs require a financial background in order to direct public relations efforts in financial markets.

Sales

Those with **sales careers** represent products and services to potential customers. Sales responsibilities include preparing and making sales presentations, analyzing the market or audience, soliciting accounts, taking and handling orders, and servicing accounts. Those in sales positions are primary representatives of the organization to its external public.

Sales careers ■ Representing products and services to potential customers.

Salespeople need abilities in interpersonal and organizational communication, multicultural communication, market analysis, and the preparation and presentation of both oral and written materials. Sales positions also frequently require technical ability appropriate to specific products or services and a basic understanding of budgeting, costing, and accounting procedures.

Human Services

Human service careers generally involve nonprofit or government organizations. Job responsibilities include fund-raising through public solicitation of funds, grant writing, and other formal budget justification processes. Human service specialists may engage in individual counseling on subjects ranging from managing personal finances to job search skills. They design, administer, and evaluate a full range of programs that provide human services.

Human service careers ■ Responsibility for fund-raising, grant writing, and other formal budget justification processes. Human service professionals engage in counseling, design, administration, and evaluation of programs; they also engage in responsibilities similar to internal communication careers.

In addition to those job titles listed in Figure 12.1 for human service specialists, many of the job titles listed for the internal communication option also apply. In fact, the skills required for internal communication positions also are needed in the human service area. Human service jobs may require knowledge of direct mail, persuasive appeals in fund-raising, cost accounting, budgeting, and program evaluation.

Education

Careers in education require professional certification and advanced degrees. Those with communication backgrounds teach primarily at high school, junior college, and college and university levels. Job responsibilities include instructional design and development, presentation of educational materials, evaluation of student performance, and individual counseling and guidance. Curriculum design increasingly requires understanding of sophisticated technologies to provide quality instruction through online offerings. Educational administration opportunities exist in colleges and universities, elementary and secondary schools, preschools and day care centers, and religious education.

Careers in education ■ Teaching in high schools, junior colleges, and universities.

In addition to professional certification required for high school teachers and elementary and high school administrators, teachers need interpersonal, small-group, and organizational communication abilities. Listening is a necessary skill, as is the ability to speak and write well. Graduate degrees are required for almost everyone entering the field of education. A master's degree is necessary for elementary and secondary education positions, and a doctorate is required for most post-secondary and administrative positions. Educators are responsible for developing expertise in particular subjects, for conducting research, and for presenting material appropriate to these subjects. Educational administrators also need skills in finance, personnel management, and public relations.

Research: Information Management

Research and information management careers ■ Responsibility for the design and development of research programs to support the ongoing activities of the organization or to chart a course of change; responsibility for the acquisition and interpretation of information and the selection of technologies to support decision making and e-commerce.

Those in **research and information management careers** design and develop research programs to support the ongoing activities of the organization or to chart a course of change. Research specialists conduct interviews and surveys, evaluate data, commission data collection, and coordinate research forums. These specialists are involved in business-trend analysis, marketing and demographic research, and a broad range of social science applications to organizational life. They evaluate organizational performance with both qualitative and quantitative measures.

Depending on the focus of the position, research specialists exhibit capabilities in social-scientific research methods, marketing research, and financial analysis. Research specialists must understand data collection and evaluation procedures. They must be familiar with needs-analysis techniques and a variety of types of data interpretation. Research specialists also are responsible for interpreting their findings to the organization, which requires good skills for oral and written presentations. By far the majority of research positions require extensive knowledge of statistics and statistics software programs.

Information management is an emerging job title in all types of organizations. Information managers literally manage information the way other managers manage people. Information managers identify sources of information, recommend technologies appropriate for organizational use, subscribe to diverse databases, create databases, conduct database searches, and organize information for easy access to support decision making. Information managers may assist with instructional design for computer-based training and contribute to e-commerce development and implementation. Information management jobs require many of the same skills as those needed for more basic research. Generally speaking, information management jobs couple an understanding of basic principles of organizational communication with fairly detailed knowledge of information retrieval technologies.

Management

Management careers ■ Responsibility for planning, coordinating, supervising, and controlling many of the activities of the organization.

People in **management careers** plan, coordinate, supervise, and control many of the activities described in the other career options. Managers guide and direct employees to achieve organizational goals. Thus, managers involve themselves in a variety of personnel activities such as interviewing, hiring, performance evaluation, and employee goal setting. Managers also help to direct the activities of the organization through the use of both human and material resources. They perform communication activities to guide and direct employees, solicit employee feedback, and exchange information with other management levels and the organization's public. Managers fulfill the formal organizational role of coordinating information and activities.

Managers generally must have at least basic technical skills in the areas in which they manage. Advertising managers, for example, usually bring to their positions technical knowledge about media production. Managers need interpersonal, small-group, and organizational communication competencies. They should be able to listen, think critically, lead group decision making and problem solving, and generally speak and write well. Managers also may be required to exhibit competence in business management, finance, economics, and law.

Consulting

Those in **consulting careers** are hired by organizations to provide expertise either not in existence in the organization or more objectively supplied by someone not directly employed by the organization. Consultants help organizations identify problems, evaluate performance, find problem solutions, and implement a wide variety of change activities. Consultants design data collection activities, collect and evaluate data, and make recommendations for organizational improvements. Consultants design, conduct, and evaluate training programs. Typical topics for such programs include interpersonal communication, small-group processes, leadership, conflict management, multicultural and global communication, and problem-solving processes. Consultants also prepare a variety of written reports summarizing assignment findings.

Consulting careers ■ Work as an external advisor to organizations to identify problems, evaluate performance, find solutions, and implement a wide variety of change activities.

Consultants combine many of the skills required for internal communication and research positions. They must be able to assess quickly the quality of information they receive and establish working relationships appropriate for their assigned responsibilities. Consultants need awareness of interpersonal, group, multicultural, and organizational communication processes as well as the ability to effectively seek information both orally and in writing. Graduate degrees and extensive work experience are desirable for consulting positions.

Additional Options for Organizational Communication

Many other career options exist for those who study organizational communication. Those described here are but a few of the possibilities.

Preprofessional and Combination Options   Organizational communication backgrounds frequently are used as preprofessional preparation for training in law, social work, and business. Many of the competencies developed in an organizational communication program are favorably evaluated for entrance into a wide range of graduate programs, including, of course, graduate programs in communication. Numerous students have creatively combined organizational communication competencies with other interests such as engineering, medicine, art, and science.

Organizational Communication and Technology   Individuals who have combined organizational communication with a variety of technical specialties will find a growing number of employment opportunities. Instructional design for Internet or computer-based training, GDSS use, Web-based sales and marketing, Internet-based research, planned use of social media, and a variety of other emerging technology uses all require individuals within organizations to develop material and translate that material into a variety of technological forms. The need for content development appropriate to emerging technologies is a largely unmet need in which organizational communication students can participate. The organizational communication student who has a desire to work with digital and video media and acquires an understanding of instructional design will find a wide variety of interesting employment opportunities available.

EDUCATIONAL PREPARATION FOR ORGANIZATIONAL COMMUNICATION CAREERS

Educational preparation for organizational communication careers is most often based on a broad liberal arts background with particular emphasis on a combination of theory and practical courses. Developing competencies for the career options described here begins with an overview of the human communication process, an introduction to basic concepts and theories in organizational communication, and an understanding of how theories of organizations relate to human communication. The first part of this text was designed to introduce you to these concepts.

Preparation for a communication career also requires development of oral skills for interpersonal, small-group, and public settings. Basic research methods and statistics are essential for evaluating and collecting data, a responsibility of many communication positions.

For those selecting internal communication, human service, and research options, particular emphasis should be placed on social science courses that contribute to understanding human behavior and research techniques appropriate for behavioral science data collection and interpretation. Preparation for external communications positions is found in journalism, technical writing, public relations, and digital and other media production courses.

Courses in instructional design are important for those in education, training, and consulting. Understanding how to develop effective learning situations requires a mix of theory and practice courses and opportunities.

Those entering sales and management positions can benefit from courses in interpersonal communication, persuasion, interviewing, small-group processes, multicultural communication, and conflict management. These option areas also are supported by courses in business management, finance, and economics.

As stated earlier, most of the option areas also require a basic understanding of statistics and computers. In fact, leading organizational recruiters suggest communication professionals can best prepare themselves for good entry-level positions if they have competencies in organizational communication accompanied by special skills in video production, computers, statistics, or program design and evaluation.

For most students today, educational preparation will not stop with an undergraduate degree. Many students will continue through graduate programs, and most will participate in continuing education, whether or not in the pursuit of a formal degree. Our fast-paced information/conceptual age requires flexibility and change not only from organizations but also from us all. Part of the ability to make necessary changes comes from identifying how educational preparation strengthens our competencies and enables us to be productive members of the organizations for which we work.

CAREERS IN THE TWENTY-FIRST CENTURY

Throughout this text we have described a technologically linked global environment characterized by rapid change. Nowhere is that change more evident than in the notion of what it means to have a career and what can be expected in thinking about careers in the twenty-first century. As Thomas Friedman suggested in his best-selling book *The World Is Flat: A Brief History of the Twenty-First Century* (2006), "In the flat world (a global playing field brought about by sophisticated communications technologies), the individual worker is going to become more and more responsible for managing his or her own career, risks, and economic security, and the role of government and business is to help workers build all the muscles they need to do just that. The 'muscles' workers need most are portable benefits and opportunities for lifelong learning. Why those two? Because they are the most important assets in making a worker mobile and adaptable" (p. 369).

Although no one really can predict the future with precision, a number of current developments point to a shift from the career paradigm of the last several decades to a more person-centered versus organization-centered concept of careers. The next section contrasts old and new career paradigms, describes the protean career of the twenty-first century, introduces the boundaryless career, identifies career skills associated with new organizational forms, and raises issues for team-based careers. As you read, think about what this means for your planning. How can you create opportunities that are of special importance to you?

Old versus New Career Paradigms

Michael Arthur, Priscilla Claman, and Robert DeFillippi (1995) contrasted new versus old career paradigms in five broad categories: (1) discrete exchange versus the mutual loyalty contract, (2) occupational excellence versus the one-employer focus, (3) organizational empowerment versus the top-down firm, (4) regional advantage versus the fortress firm, and (5) project versus corporate allegiance. According to Arthur, Claman, and DeFillippi, the old career paradigm implied mutual loyalty between employees and organizations. Employee compliance was rewarded with job security. Job rewards were deferred to the future, and career opportunities were mostly standardized and prescribed by the firm. Employees often expected to stay with one organization for an entire career and relied on the organization to specify jobs and their associated occupational skill base. Employees were expected to identify with their particular firm and forgo general development in favor of firm-specific learning. In the top-down firm, management set strategic direction and defined competitiveness, and the corporate agenda generally discouraged independent enterprise. The fortress firm meant there was little identification with other regional firms, which were generally viewed as competitors. Finally, corporate allegiance meant that project goals were subordinated to corporate policy and organizational constraints. Loyalty to the work group was expected, and the organization formed a distinct boundary within which careers were expected to be pursued.

The new career paradigm is described very differently. The concept of discrete exchange means explicit exchange of specified rewards in return for task performance, basing job rewards on the current market value of the work being performed, engaging in disclosure and renegotiation on both sides as the employment relationship unfolds, and exercising flexibility as each party's interests and market circumstances change. Occupational excellence means performance of current jobs in return for developing new occupational expertise; employees identifying with and focusing on what is happening in their adopted occupation; emphasizing occupational skill and development over the local demands of any particular firm; getting training in anticipation of future job opportunities; and having training lead jobs (Arthur, Claman, and DeFillippi, 1995, p. 13).

Organizational empowerment is described as strategic positioning dispersed to separate business units with everyone responsible for adding value. Business units are encouraged to cultivate their own markets. Regional advantage means building alliances and interdependence with clusters of organizations, including competitors. Work and careers are boundaryless. Individuals move in and out of firms and work as consultants. The project becomes primary, and a successful outcome of the project is considered more important than holding the project team together. Some even suggest the new career paradigm is based on the end of jobs as we have previously known them.

The differences between these two paradigms have enormous implications for careers. The old paradigm emphasizes stability; the new paradigm emphasizes flexibility and constant change. The old was more dependent on organizational planning; the new emphasizes individual initiative. Most observers believe the twenty-first century will see a blend of both perspectives, but even with the blend, there will be increasing reliance on individual responsibility to plan for job and career transitions.

Protean Careers

Douglas Hall (1996) described the protean career: "The career of the 21st century will be protean, a career that is driven by the person, not the organization, and that will be reinvented by the person from time to time, as the person and the environment change. (This term is derived from the Greek god Proteus, who could change shape at will.)" (p. 8).

Hall described the goal of the protean career as psychological success. The individual manages the career, which is a lifelong series of changes and continuous learning. A profile of success is the ability to learn, to move from job security to employability, to think not in terms of organizational careers but of protean careers, and to consider not just the work self but the whole self. Training becomes an ongoing reality of employability, and vertical mobility—moving up—is replaced by moving across and between organizations. Hall and others contend these changes can bring more life satisfaction than the more paternalistic careers of the past. Critics express concern, however, that the lack of commitment from the organization and the overall flexibility required for the "new career" are problematic and difficult for most to conceive.

The Boundaryless Career

In many respects, careers in the twenty-first century can be described as boundaryless. More of us than in past generations will work for multiple organizations. And many more of us will work for ourselves, contracting with multiple organizations simultaneously. Some are referring to this shift away from organizational employment as *free agency,* a term previously reserved for athletes. The free agent assesses individual skills, abilities, and goals and then matches them to an ever-changing set of both short-term and long-term employment or contract opportunities. Others describe this move to self-employment as the entrepreneurial career. Entrepreneurs start their own businesses or revitalize existing but troubled organizations. Entrepreneurs develop innovative ideas and bring resources to turn these ideas into businesses or social and political organizations.

The boundaryless career also refers to the blurring of lines between work and other parts of our lives. Many of us work both in a formal office and at home. Hours of work extend with ease because technology makes communication possible twenty-four hours a day, seven days a week. It is estimated that more than half of professionals today use cellular technologies, the Internet, and e-mail most nights of the week and on weekends. Fast response is becoming a cultural norm requiring what we described earlier as continuous partial attention. The implications for family and social engagement are obvious. Our ability to consciously make choices about the integration of all aspects of our life with work becomes increasingly complex.

Working in boundaryless careers requires the development of knowledge and skills usually associated with employer responsibilities. The individual who works on contract, for example, needs expertise in negotiating and executing employment contracts that not only fairly compensate the individual for work performed but also deal with issues such as insurance, liability, and intellectual property. Retirement planning takes on new meaning even for those immediately out of undergraduate or graduate school.

For some employees, association with a profession and professional organizations replaces identification with specific employers. Professional networks and formal professional associations become primary sources of information about job opportunities. Ongoing professional development, usually identified as an employer responsibility, is frequently obtained through professional associations with or without employer reimbursement. Our professional reputations and identities are more broadly shared among a group of associates throughout the world than within the confines of our specific employers. Increasingly, we will be conscious of constructing a professional self, often articulated on our personal Web pages or blogs. The continuous challenge will be to integrate these professional identities with all aspects of our lives. The need for knowledge, sensitivity, skill, and value integration will be more important than ever. The Workshop section of this chapter attempts to provide guidance for this integration with regard to career planning.

Twenty-first-Century Organizational Forms and Career Skills

Throughout this text, we have described competencies important for organizational participation. We identified many of the specific competencies and skills needed in the twenty-first century, and you explored your own skills and thinking about development needs. We now describe career skills associated with two emerging organizational forms, networks and cellular organizations.

Networked Organization

Networked organization ■ Partners or alliances across groups and organizations to leverage the best possible resources for a given project.

The late 1970s was the beginning of the **networked organization**. Brent Allred, Charles Snow, and Raymond Miles (1996) described the rise of the networked form:

Intense international and domestic competition left many large traditional organizations slow to respond to global threats and opportunities. For example, the planning and coordinating efficiencies achieved by the global matrix organization were frequently offset by the unyielding bureaucracy it created. The extensive vertical and horizontal integration of previous decades increased the market clout of many companies, but when speed and flexibility were needed, traditional structures became burdensome. . . . To become more competitive, corporations downsized, delayered, and outsourced many functions during the 1980s. In innovative companies such as Nike, Motorola, and Novell, a new form of organization was emerging, called the network. Similar to a computer network, network organizations linked independent firms to provide the critical expertise needed for specific projects or manufacturing, and marketing a product, [and] various complementary firms were networked to provide the most efficient service at each of these stages. . . . Network firms are able to achieve maximum leverage of their core competencies by relying on their external or internal partners to perform other activities on the value chain. (pp. 19–20)

Allred, Snow, and Miles went on to describe the core competencies for the networked organization (p. 21):

■ Referral skills rely on the ability to analyze a problem and prescribe a solution within the network firm and across its partners. The traditional mentality of do it all yourself has given way to a focus on doing only what you do best. Thus, in a network, when a problem or opportunity is recognized, members are able to determine who has the best ability to address or pursue it. Referrals are made such that the best resources are brought to bear on all situations, including the use of resources outside the current network.

■ Partnering skills refer to the capacity to conceptualize, negotiate, and implement mutually beneficial outcomes. Many network organizations are multifirm, so managers within the network must know how to connect other firms' resources quickly and effectively to their own such that both parties benefit.

■ Relationship management involves giving high priority to the needs and preferences of key customers and partners. In dynamic multifirm networks, in which company participation may be periodic, relationships among past, present, and potential customers and partners must be carefully maintained.

Cellular Organization

The minimalist organizations forecast for the twenty-first century are a further evolution of what has begun with the networked form. Careers in traditional organizations involve climbing a vertical ladder, network careers move across organizations, and the **cellular organization** does not involve hierarchies at all. In the cellular organization, success does not equate to the concept of success as advancement through vertical or horizontal mobility. Allred, Snow, and Miles (1996) explained:

Cellular organization ■
Collaborative but not considered permanent association of professionals working together for a specific project or service.

> A cellular organization is made up of cells (self-managing teams, autonomous business units, etc.) that could exist on their own, but that by interacting with other cells can produce a more potent and competent organism. Common knowledge and information are shared by all the cells in a manner, akin to human DNA, that reflects heredity and guides development. . . . In the cellular firm, the organization functions not as an employer but as a facilitating mechanism to promote the application and enhancement of the knowledge-intensive skills of its membership. The firm has some of the key properties of the classical guilds and professional associations, such as sharing knowledge and accepting responsibility for member competency and performance. Within the cellular organization, members take full charge of their own careers, enjoying the learning opportunities provided by their own initiatives and those of their fellow members. An agreed set of norms promotes full self-governance as well as professional allegiance. (pp. 21–22)

The skills needed for the cellular organization include a knowledge-based technical specialty as in the past but much more attention to cross-functional and international experience. Collaborative leadership and self-management skills also are of particular importance for the cellular organization.

Regardless of the specific form of the organization of the future, the challenges are evident. For us all, becoming and staying competent will be a lifelong pursuit. The importance of understanding personal competencies and how to continually expand and develop skills for the future will remain a personal challenge throughout our careers.

Team-Based Careers

As the twenty-first century progresses, more and more of us will work in teams. A new model of career development emerges because of these experiences. Put simply, career development in teams can be described as the responsibility of the entire team. Team members serve as role models for one another, and team members usually determine both team and individual development needs and training opportunities. Individual members cross-train and move laterally within and across teams. Advancement usually is based on competency level, with more advanced team members responsible for not only task contribution but also for training and development of newer team members. Rewards are based on both team and individual results. Communication competency lies at the heart of a successful team-based career.

CHAPTER HIGHLIGHTS

Careers are the sum of our job experiences over time. Careers involve decisions about personal interests, aptitudes, educational preparation, and the match of our individual competencies to the needs of particular organizations. This **employment match** is based on the knowledge, sensitivity, skills, and values of both the individual and the employing organization. Self-analysis helps generate awareness of influences for our occupational choices and can be used to develop important criteria for career planning. Self-awareness in turn can help us evaluate the major career options in organizational communication: **internal communication, external communications, sales, human services, education, research, management,** and **consulting.** Each of these areas requires educational preparation and a diverse set of communication skills.

Individuals will assume increasing responsibility for career and job transitions in the twenty-first century. In protean careers, individuals can expect to manage their own careers, which will include a lifelong series of changes and the need for continuous learning. Boundaryless careers refer to the blurring of boundaries between traditional work and all other aspects of our lives. Boundaryless careers include contracting and the new concept of free agency and entrepreneurial activity. New organizational forms—**networked** and **cellular organizations**—will place new emphasis on participation competencies, international experience, and personal traits of flexibility and adaptability. Finally, team-based careers will emphasize the success of entire teams as well as individuals. ■

WORKSHOP
Self-Analysis for Career Planning

1. The purposes of a self-analysis are to help you understand personal influences on career choices, to identify achievements valuable to you, to define skills used in important achievements, and to make projections of the type of career and lifestyle you desire. Your self-analysis is designed to guide decisions about competency development and to identify any limitations in occupational choices you may have inadvertently created for yourself. Figure 12.2 summarizes the self-analysis activity. Your individual work sheet follows on pages 404–405.

Influences on Career Choices

Identify by name those individuals who have been most influential in helping you form expectations about work, occupations, and achievements. What have these individuals told you about what is possible?

1. Identify specific individuals who have been influential in shaping your concept of work and occupational choice.
   - What have they told you about possibilities?
   - How satisfied are they with their work?
   - How would they profile a successful person?
   - What occupations have they suggested to you?
   - What occupations do they not suggest for you?
2. Describe your ideal occupation in terms of responsibilities, skills, and measures of success.
3. Compare your "perfect occupation" with messages from those who have influenced you.
4. Define four important achievements with skills used for each achievement and values satisfied. Identify common skills used and values satisfied among the achievements. List ten skills and ten values that seem to be predictive of achievement and satisfaction for you.
5. Write a narrative describing your desired lifestyle for a five-year span following your formal education. How should this narrative influence your career choices?
6. Make ten statements about your current career planning. Identify ten questions you need answered for career planning.

FIGURE 12.2
Summary of Self-Analysis Activities for Career Planning

How satisfied are they with their work? How would they profile the successful person? What types of occupations have they suggested you should pursue? What have they told you is a waste of time?

After you have identified important "work" messages from those around you, write a one-paragraph description of your ideal occupation. Include the responsibilities the occupation entails, the skills the occupation uses, and how individuals in this occupation will know if they are successful.

Next, compare your "perfect" occupation paragraph with your answers to questions about how key people have influenced your occupational choices. Can you see their influence in your "perfect" occupation? If so, how? If not, what other influences have contributed to your selection?

Identification of Achievement Skills and Values

The next portion of your self-analysis requires careful reflection. Identify four major achievements in your life. These achievements must have one important quality: they must be very personally important. Others may have considered the achievements you identify as significant, but that is not the most important qualification. The achievements you choose should be of high personal value, regardless of external evaluation. In fact, it is common for an achievement in this category to be something of which few others are aware. These four achievements also must be achievements in which your personal efforts were primary contributions. Many people might say, for example, that they consider their family life to be an achievement, and of course it may be. For purposes of this activity, however, writing a poem, building a piece of furniture, conquering your fear of public speaking, or learning to use a computer are better examples of achievements for which you have had primary responsibility. Once the achievements have been identified, list the skills and abilities you used in these achievements and the values each achievement satisfied. (A partial skill and value list is provided in Figure 12.3.)

When you have listed important achievements, skills, and values, identify those skills and values that have contributed to more than one of your achievements.

PARTIAL SKILLS LIST

mathematical	administrative	documentation
analytical	planning	speaking
creative	organizational	financial
managerial	writing	graphic
communication	artistic	team building
persuasive	athletic	motivational
listening	research	teaching
decision making	problem solving	delegation

PARTIAL VALUES LIST

security	family happiness	power
geographic location	wisdom	expertness
justice	autonomy	love
humanitarianism	leadership	aesthetics
recognition	honesty	service
enjoyment	self-actualization	health
achievement	material wealth	knowledge
prestige	emotional well-being	religion
fame	social	creative

FIGURE 12.3
Partial Skills and Values List

You are beginning to identify through this activity those skills and values that have been most important to you over time. Which additional skills should be on your "most important" list? Which additional values? Next, list ten skills and values you believe are most likely to contribute to a sense of personal achievement. This list, if thoughtfully constructed, should be influential in career planning and occupational choice.

Describing a Desired Lifestyle

Next, write a one-page narrative describing all aspects of your most desired lifestyle for the five years immediately following completion of your education. Describe where you think you want to live, what leisure activities you envision, what family and social relationships you prefer, and how work relates to these choices.

Include in your narrative a desired level of income and any other important choices you want to consider. (We are not attempting to suggest that it is possible to define perfectly all these issues, but general themes can usually be discovered.) What do these preferences say about your choice of work? Should they be considerations in your career planning? What other influences are important?

Identifying Current Status of Career Planning

After completing all the analysis activities, list ten statements you can make about the status of your current career planning. These statements should relate to choices you have already made, skills you want to use in your future occupation, and values you want to satisfy through work. Finally, develop ten questions you want answered as a result of your self-examination. What do you need to know about occupational choices? How can you find out? Who would be good information sources? Much of what was discussed about decision making and problem solving should be used to help you examine your personal career-planning needs.

1. One way to make decisions about educational preparation for your future employment is to think about what you want to be able to present to a prospective employer on your résumé. The résumé development exercise that follows first presents basic information about résumé preparation,

followed by suggestions for you to individualize information.

2. Locate five advertisements requiring communication competencies in each of three newspapers: (1) your local paper, (2) a national paper such as the *Wall Street Journal* or the *Washington Post* national edition, and (3) a paper from a major city other than the one in which you live. Also search the Internet. Compare the advertisements. Identify the skills and experiences wanted by potential employers. What are the salary ranges? How can you prepare yourself for these opportunities?

3. Select the communication career option area (or areas) that interest you most. Identify a local professional employed in this career area. Develop a list of questions you would like answered. Make an appointment and interview this person. Report your findings to the class. (This activity can be accomplished in pairs or teams. The exercise is more meaningful if all eight option areas are reported to the class.)

4. Select a particular organization in which you are interested and to which you might want to apply in the future. Research this organization on the Internet. Report your findings during a class discussion.

5. Contact your college or university placement office. Determine what type of online job search services are available. Browse these online services to determine how they can be useful for your job search strategies. Make a list of any Web sites you visit, including a description of the types of services provided by each. Which sites will be most useful to you?

Work Sheet and Example of Self-Analysis Activities for Career Planning

NAME _____

Achievements are observable results of individual skills in action. Achievements that have lasting importance normally satisfy key values in an individual's life. This exercise is designed to help you identify both skills and values that have contributed to your personal achievements. Identification of important skills and values is a fundamental step in successful career and life planning.

Instructions. Read the instruction for each activity, reflect on it, and then write your response. Be as brief or extensive as you like.

1. Identify specific individuals who have been influential in shaping your concept of work and occupational choice.

> What have they told you about possibilities?
> How satisfied are they with their work?
> How would they profile a successful person?
> What occupations have they suggested for you?
> What occupations do they not suggest for you?

2. Describe your ideal occupation in terms of responsibilities, skills, and measurement of success.

3. Compare your perfect occupation to messages from those who have influenced you (exercises 1 and 2).

4. Identify and list four important achievements, skills used for each achievement, and values satisfied. Identify common skills used and values satisfied among the achievements. List ten skills and ten values that seem to be predictive for you of achievement.

Achievements	Skills Used	Values Satisfied
Common Skills Used		Common Values Satisfied
Ten Skills Predictive of Achievement		Ten Values Predictive of Achievement

5. Write a narrative describing your desired lifestyle for a five-year span after your education is complete. How should this narrative influence your occupational/career choices?

6. Identify ten statements you can make today about your current career planning. Identify ten questions you need answered for career planning.

Ten Statements	Ten Questions
1.	1.
2.	2.
3.	3.
4.	4.
5.	5.
6.	6.
7.	7.
8.	8.
9.	9.
10.	10.

Résumé Development Exercise

A résumé is a well-prepared description of your accomplishments, skills, and experiences written to address the needs of potential employers. Résumé formats are numerous, with the most common described as the chronological résumé (Figure 12.4) and the functional résumé (Figure 12.5).

The Chronological Résumé   A traditional chronological résumé begins with your work experiences listed in reverse chronological order, beginning with your most recent job. Dates of employment are included as well as names of employers, job titles, and duties or responsibilities. Other relevant information such as education is included. The chronological résumé tells people what your work experience is and is best used when you have consistent experience that applies to your current job applications.

The Functional Résumé   A functional résumé describes work objectives, skills, accomplishments, and education when applicable. Skills, experiences, and accomplishments are grouped according to the skills of the functions they represent. The following represent common categories for functional résumés: Administration, Bookkeeping, Communication, Computer Use, Coordination, Customer Relations/Service, Data Entry, Editing, Facilitating, Human Resource Management, Inventory Control, Management, Marketing, Negotiation, Nursing, Office Support, Problem Solving, Production, Promotion, Public Speaking, Quality Control, Record Keeping, Reporting, Sales, Supervision, Team Building, and Writing.

The functional résumé is most frequently used by new entrants to the job market, recent college graduates, and those changing career fields.

Résumé Questionnaire

1. Describe your work objectives.

2. What types of organizations are you considering?

3. Develop a list of your paid work experiences. Describe your responsibilities and accomplishments.

4. Identify your most important skills. Group them as they relate to your work objectives.

5. Assess your volunteer and college activities. How can they be used to provide additional relevant experience?

6. What should you do now to improve the résumé you will soon prepare for an employer?

7. Prepare a sample résumé.

8. Ask others to critique your efforts and make suggestions for additions. ■

Jan Waxton
5050 Warton Lane
Minneapolis, Minnesota 74329
(405) 598-8333

OBJECTIVE: Position in training department in major organization or consulting firm.

WORK EXPERIENCE:

2008 to Present   Arby's Restaurants, Minneapolis, MN
             Shift Supervisor

Supervised eight employees per shift. Delivered corporate training programs. Compiled weekly sales reports. Conducted annual performance reviews. Promoted twice in three years.

2007   IBM Corporation, Minneapolis, MN
             Human Resource Intern

Developed research summary for design of organizational change training program. Report used by design team for new training program.

RELEVANT EXPERIENCE:

2008 to Present   YMCA Volunteers, Minneapolis, MN
             Volunteer Trainer

Designed and delivered YMCA Leadership Course for over 200 volunteers. Delivered over 25 orientation presentations.

2005–2008   United Church of Christ, Minneapolis, MN
             Youth Services Volunteer

Designed and delivered Leadership Class for over 100 Youth Fellowship participants. Led over 15 other classes.

2003–2005   Memorial Hospital, Minneapolis, MN
             Volunteer Trainer

Designed and delivered Leadership Class for over 50 volunteers.

EDUCATION:

B.A.—University of Minnesota
    Major: Organizational Communication
    Minor: Human Resource Management

REFERENCES:

Available on request

FIGURE 12.4
Chronological Résumé Sample

Jan Waxton
5050 Warton Lane
Minneapolis, Minnesota 74329
(405) 598-8333

OBJECTIVE: Position in training department in major organization or consulting firm.

SKILLS:

Training:

Designed and delivered leadership programs for three nonprofit organizations. Received excellent evaluations over a two-year period.

Researched organizational change for design team in a major electronics corporation training department. Research used by design team for introduction of new training program.

Delivered training for new employees in a food-service franchise. Received excellent evaluations and two promotions over a three-year period.

Supervision:

Supervised up to eight employees per shift in a food-service franchise. Received performance appraisals exceeding expectations over a three-year period.

Writing:

Compiled weekly sales reports for management. Reports forwarded to franchise headquarters without alterations over a three-year period.

Developed research summary for design of organizational change training program. Research summary utilized by design team for training outline.

Conducted annual performance appraisal for food-service employees from compilation of weekly reports into overall written narratives for annual reviews. No review reports returned with negative comments over a three-year period.

Public Speaking:

Delivered over 50 presentations on behalf of two nonprofit organizations. Received excellent evaluations over a five-year period.

EDUCATION:

B.A.—University of Minnesota
    Major: Organizational Communication
    Minor: Human Resource Management

REFERENCES:
Available on request

FIGURE 12.5
Functional Résumé Sample

TIPS FOR EFFECTIVE COMMUNICATION

1. Think about several potential employers. Develop an answer to the question "What special skills and abilities do I have that make me the best candidate for this job?" Practice your answer with several friends or advisors.
2. Write a sample letter of application that stresses your special preparation for a job of your choice. Ask someone who will be candid with you to evaluate the persuasive nature of your letter.
3. Ask someone you admire to describe how he or she would proceed differently with career decisions if he or she had the opportunity to begin again.

4. Be honest with yourself in describing your competencies, including both strengths and development opportunities.
5. Don't worry as much about your first job offer as your ability to truthfully describe your strengths and needs in a position. (You will almost always be more successful with an employer who selected you based on a good solid assessment of what you can produce.) ■

REFERENCES AND SUGGESTED READINGS

Allred, B. B., C. C. Snow, and R. E. Miles. 1996. Characteristics of managerial careers in the twenty-first century. *Academy of Management Executive* 10(4): 17–27.

Arthur, M. B., P. H. Claman, and R. J. DeFillippi. 1995. Intelligent enterprise, intelligent careers. *Academy of Management Executive* 9(4): 7–20.

Bennis, W. 1969. *Organization development: Its nature, origins, and prospects.* Reading, MA: Addison-Wesley.

Bennis, W., K. Benne, R. Chin, and K. Corey. 1976. *The planning of change,* 3rd ed. New York: Holt, Rinehart and Winston.

DeWine, S. 1994. *The consultant's craft.* New York: St. Martin's.

French, W. L., and C. H. Bell. 1973. *Organization development: Behavioral science interventions for organization improvement.* Englewood Cliffs, NJ: Prentice Hall.

Friedman, T. 2006. *The world is flat: A brief history of the twenty-first century.* New York: Farrar, Straus and Giroux.

Goldhaber, G. M. 1986. *Organizational communication,* 4th ed. Dubuque, IA: Brown.

Hall, D. T. 1996. Protean careers of the twenty-first century. *Academy of Management Executive* 10(4): 8–16.

Miles, R. E., C. C. Snow, J. A. Mathews, G. Miles, and H. J. Coleman Jr. 1997. Organizing in the knowledge age: Anticipating the cellular form. *Academy of Management Executive* 11(4): 7–24.

Pace, R. W., and D. F. Faules. 1994. *Organizational communication,* 3rd ed. Englewood Cliffs, NJ: Prentice Hall.

Pace, W. 1983. *Organizational communication: Foundations for human resource development.* Englewood Cliffs, NJ: Prentice Hall.

Petrie, C., E. Thompson, D. Rogers, and G. Goldhaber. 1975. *Report of the ad hoc committee on manpower resources.* Report prepared for the Division IV meeting of the International Communication Association, April, Chicago.

Schein, E. H. 1969. *Process consultation: Its role in organization development.* Reading, MA: Addison-Wesley.

Wilson, G. L., H. L. Goodall Jr., and C. L. Waagen. 1986. *Organizational communication.* New York: Harper and Row. ■

Putting it All Together

The next several pages of the text contain a self-assessment instrument and cases designed to develop communication competency by applying the theory you have studied. The self-assessment instrument has been designed to help guide your choices about additional educational preparation and to identify areas for continuing competency development. The cases in the appendix are taken from real experiences of individuals with organizational communication responsibilities. These final pages have been designed to help you pull together the various competencies we sought to develop in this text. You should again complete the self-assessment of competency needs presented in Chapter 1 (Figure 1.1, repeated here as Figure A.1). Compare your answers from the beginning of the course with your answers now. What have you accomplished? What remains to be done?

After you complete your self-evaluation, compile a list of competencies you rate as highly developed. Next compile lists for those competency items rated moderately developed, somewhat limited, and needing development. What is your plan for continued growth?

CASES

The following twenty-six cases are taken from real experiences of individuals with organizational communication responsibilities. Cases address issues of emerging communications technologies and global communication and stimulate our thinking about ethics and values. Cases also raise issues about the influence of communication on decision making and vice versa. Cases explore relationships between supervisors and employees and issues of delegation, as well as male–female organizational relationships. In addition to presenting diversity and cultural concerns and identifying other problems with which a communication professional must deal, cases address individual needs in organizations, the dynamics of a team-based structure, and how people at the top of organizations view teams differently from

The following organizational communication competencies are presented for your self-evaluation. For each area, you are asked to determine whether your present competencies are highly developed, moderately developed, somewhat limited, or needing development.

As I complete this course, I would describe my KNOWLEDGE in . . .	Highly Developed	Moderately Developed	Somewhat Limited	Needing Development
1. defining and understanding organizational communication as . . .				
2. understanding major theories of how organizations work as . . .				
3. determining how an individual experiences organizational life as . . .				
4. describing what organizational conflict is and how it relates to productive organizations as . . .				
5. identifying characteristics of leadership and management communication as . . .				
6. understanding decision making and problem solving as . . .				
7. understanding strategic organizational communication as . . .				
8. locating career opportunities in organizational communication as . . .				
9. distinguishing between values and ethics in organizational communication as . . .				

As I complete this course, I would describe my SENSITIVITY to . . .	Highly Developed	Moderately Developed	Somewhat Limited	Needing Development
10. my personal responsibilities for organizational communication as . . .				
11. how "shared realities" are generated through organizational communication as . . .				
12. why and how people work together as . . .				
13. what motivates me and what is likely to motivate others as . . .				
14. the importance of interpersonal relationships with supervisors, peers, and employees as . . .				
15. personal preferences for a variety of approaches to conflict as . . .				
16. the influence of the environment of organizations as . . .				

FIGURE A.1
Self-Assessment of Personal Development Needs

	Highly Developed	Moderately Developed	Somewhat Limited	Needing Development
17. personal preferences for leadership and management communication as . . .				
18. organizational influences for decision making and problem solving as . . .				
19. past achievements, values, and skills that can guide career choices as . . .				
20. how values and ethics contribute to organizational effectiveness as . . .				

As I complete this course, I would describe my SKILLS in . . .	Highly Developed	Moderately Developed	Somewhat Limited	Needing Development
21. analyzing a variety of organizational problems as . . .				
22. developing effective organizational messages as . . .				
23. engaging in active listening as . . .				
24. contributing to supportive organizational environments as . . .				
25. participating in productive conflict management as . . .				
26. leadership communication as . . .				
27. leading and participating in effective group meetings as . . .				
28. fact-finding and evaluation as . . .				
29. gathering information for decision making and problem solving as . . .				
30. analyzing data for decision making and problem solving as . . .				
31. developing and making public presentations as . . .				
32. using a variety of communications technologies as . . .				

As I complete this course, I would describe my VALUES for . . .	Highly Developed	Moderately Developed	Somewhat Limited	Needing Development
33. accepting personal responsibility for communication as . . .				
34. relating individual communication behavior to organizational effectiveness as . . .				
35. using conflict for productive outcomes as . . .				
36. professional applications of organizational communication as . . .				

FIGURE A.1
(Continued)

As I complete this course, I would describe my VALUES for . . .	Highly Developed	Moderately Developed	Somewhat Limited	Needing Development
37. determining how leaders and managers should behave as . . .				
38. influencing my career choices as . . .				
39. understanding organizational values, ethics, and dilemmas as . . .				

After you have completed your self-evaluation, compile a complete list of items for which you rated your competencies as *Highly Developed.* Next compile lists for those competency items rated *Moderately Developed, Somewhat Limited,* and *Needing Development.* Compare your needs to when you began the course. Use your lists to continue your personal objectives for development.

FIGURE A.1
(Continued)

others. Finally, cases help us explore the difficulties of making connections when working virtually, the challenges for dual-career couples, the use of strategic organizational communication during major change, and the importance for communication planning during mistakes and crises.

I Can't Believe Our Entire World Is Wired

Ann Johnson returned to her desk perplexed. The head of information technologies (IT) for Carrier Industries had just spoken to the Carrier management team. A security breach had put some 5,000 Carrier employees at risk for identity theft. Ann believed the Carrier response to protect and provide rapid notification to employees was excellent, but she could not help but wonder about where all of these security problems would lead. As the finance manager for Carrier, Ann had seen the budget for information security grow at a larger percentage than any other budget within the company. The costs were passed on to Carrier's customers but Carrier's global market position was in danger as they needed to stay cost-competitive with products produced in India and China.

Ann wondered if Carrier should take more proactive steps to keep its employees informed of the risks and possibly consider new uses of technology to reduce expenditures on security. She felt so strongly that she put the issue on the next executive team agenda.

When Ann and her colleagues met to discuss use of information technologies and security they were amazed at the list the IT manager presented. She had known how complex technology had become, but the list made her pause and think about how everything had changed in such a short time. Carrier had long used security cameras throughout the office and manufacturing areas. What most executives did not know was that the government could under certain circumstances subpoena the recordings. E-mail, including junk e-mail, belongs to Carrier but also can be subject to outside access for a variety of legal and illegal reasons.

The cell service for managers sends ID signals to the nearest cellular towers, giving approximate locations of users. Carrier uses a Web-based notification service to determine client interests and automatically sends notices to customers who register on the company site. The site had been breached in the last year. The IT manager explained that Internet use collects digital footprints, including a host of online transactions reflecting individual preferences and a host of other interests. All Carrier customer transactions use the Internet, including billing and account records. Carrier banks entirely online. Additionally, all purchasing, payroll, and benefits tracking for Carrier are Web- and Internet-based. Finally, he confirmed that several employees using Carrier technology had been victims of phishing during the past year. (Phishing occurs when an individual responds to an e-mail designed to navigate to a fake Web site where the individual provides personal data.) His best estimate was they personally lost an average of $1,300 each.

Ann and the Carrier executive team determined they must take a more comprehensive look at technology use internally to Carrier and with their customers. They asked the IT manager to locate a consultant who could help them develop a plan.

QUESTIONS FOR DISCUSSION

1. Discuss the ethical issues for Carrier in the various technologies they use.
2. How are complex technologies changing organizational communication?
3. Discuss and list all of the considerations the leadership team will need to discuss to develop their technology plan.

How Did This Harm Occur?

As Alan Davis stares out the window of his office he considers what he should tell his attorney and how much he should attempt to protect himself if things get worse. Alan, an officer of Willis Bank, cannot believe he is going to be questioned by federal officials about his decisions in the Burning-Lewis property case. Of course, he helped Dick Johnson get over $20 million in loans from Willis, but no one could have expected the bottom to fall out of the real-estate market. Everyone was making those types of loans when he supported the Burning-Lewis deal. No other bank would have asked someone of Dick Johnson's importance to personally guarantee the loans or provide more collateral. Johnson was a multimillionaire who expected the people with whom he did business to make deals the way he wanted them. He had a record of success and the potential for Willis to win big was excellent with the new development. Alan had never even considered that Johnson would default on the second loan payment and have his company file for bankruptcy. Johnson's personal fortune was largely protected by family-member holdings untouched by bankruptcy. Furthermore, Alan never imagined the default, along with several other problem loans, would cause federal bank auditors to pay attention to Willis.

The Burning-Lewis deal had always been a gamble. The property, although near the airport, was not in the heavily developed northern section of the city. To move industry south was a challenge that Alan believed Johnson's group could influence. Alan had sold the executive loan committee of Willis on supporting the loans with his argument that if Willis did not make the deal their principal competitor would. The implications for other business in the newly developed part of the city were enormous. Several city council members had promised Alan that Johnson would be supported with tax incentives from the city. Influential council members wanted the project to move forward; Johnson had promised to build industry parks and housing developments designed over a ten-year period to bring some 100,000 new residents to the area.

Alan worries federal examiners could take exception to the "handshake" nature of the deal with Johnson. Alan had not required Johnson to provide enough hard data to justify the loan amounts based on the current market value of the property. The property itself was insufficient collateral. Alan had wanted the business and so did the Willis loan committee. They knew what was going on but now seemed ready to blame their "superstar" rather than admit other loan committee members would have done the same thing. Alan wonders if the examiners know he has purchased a condominium in one of Johnson's resort properties. He suspected at the time of the condo purchase that he had been given a "sweetheart" deal but had asked no questions. After all, that is how business is done. Alan wonders what his attorney will advise. He worries he will become the scapegoat to get the regulators off the loan committee's back.

QUESTIONS FOR DISCUSSION

1. What are the ethical issues in this case?
2. Think about the ethical implications of the following statement: Common business practice in a given industry becomes the ethical standard of practice for the industry.
3. Describe how business risk and ethical risk are similar and different.
4. Describe ethical standards for highly competitive situations.
5. How would you advise Alan Davis?

Granite City's Homeless Shelter: Doing More with Less

It was not the typical morning after a general election in the office of Lynda Ramirez, director of Granite City's homeless shelter. The results of the November elections in Granite City had been expected to bring new council members and possibly a new mayor, but no one expected an entirely new council and the tax limitation amendments. As Lynda reviewed the results in the morning paper she knew she was going to be challenged to do more with less and do it quickly.

Granite City, with a population of 500,000, had experienced rapid growth during most of the last decade. Along with rapid growth had come a threefold increase in the city's homeless population. Over the past five years the city council supported increases in the shelter's budget in order to provide needed services. As a part of city government, the shelter and Lynda both had been highly evaluated by the council.

All members of the council who had supported expanding the shelter's budget had been defeated, and the tax limitation amendments would require significant cuts in Granite City's overall budget for the upcoming fiscal year. The new council and mayor had supported the tax amendments and none had prior contact with the shelter's programs.

Lynda was not surprised when her phone rang with a message from the city manager, Rogers Davis, announcing an emergency meeting of all Granite City program heads. She knew from her assistant that the media were calling for comments, and two of her citizen board members had left worried e-mails.

The meeting with Rogers Davis and the other program heads did nothing but raise Lynda's fears. Davis estimated each of the programs would need to take a 15 percent cut by the beginning of the fiscal year. He had not met with the new council members or the mayor but indicated he must put plans in place in order to respond as quickly as possible to develop recommendations. Granite City's human resources director recommended all program heads meet with their employees and update them on the probable impact of the tax amendments. Lynda was told she should try to reassure clients of shelter programs, but she should not make promises for the future. No decision was made about media response although Davis indicated he would call the new mayor and work with Granite City's media director.

Lynda returned to her office wondering what she should tell her employees. She knew she should return the media calls and contact her citizen's board. She questioned how much she should communicate with her clients. Lynda knew she needed a comprehensive communication plan but believed more information was needed to formulate her strategy.

QUESTIONS FOR DISCUSSION

1. Describe the various communication issues in the case.
2. What should Lynda tell her employees, the board, media, and her clients? Should she contact the new council members and mayor?
3. What should Rogers Davis provide to his program heads in order to effectively deal with the situation?
4. How would you advise Lynda to proceed?
5. How would you advise Rogers Davis to proceed?

Dennison Computer Corporation—A Lesson in Organizational Culture

They were in their late thirties when they met. Four men, each successful in his own way, each dissatisfied with his job, and each a little bitten by the rock-star bug known in Silicon Valley and throughout the high-technology industry as the Steve Jobs syndrome. They wanted to make money, but more than that they wanted to be known, to be famous, to be important in an industry known for brilliance, burnout, stress, and dissatisfaction.

They met at a computer show in Washington, D.C. While most around them were outdoing each other with success stories, the four fell into serious conversation about their personal needs for something more, something beyond the big corporation with all its pressure and its inability to recognize talent.

Six months later they had begun serious plans to form their own company. They would be different; they would be successful without the baggage of their previous employers, and they would be rock stars, or at least well known enough to be respected for their computer design and business expertise.

They knew where they wanted to start. They believed that most high-capacity, high-speed computers for the scientific market were overpriced and loaded with feature sets that few used. The market in scientific computing had been sluggish, in part due to the cost of most high-quality machines. Their initial business plan described the competitive advantage they intended to bring to scientific and military markets by building a machine with the architecture and overall capacity of the industry leaders but at a fraction of the cost.

The Founders   Bob Anderson, thirty-seven, went to school and worked in Palo Alto, California. Educated at Stanford, Bob was the youngest general manager in the history of a large division of a major computer company. Prior to becoming manager, he had been the lead design engineer on a major government contract requiring sophisticated computer applications. His work on the contract was so outstanding that his company, in an unusual compensation decision, awarded him significant patent revenue rights along with a large bonus. Bob did not enjoy the position of general manager and found the company increasingly bureaucratic.

Dan Findley, thirty-nine, also from Palo Alto and Stanford, had worked with the famed Project Nemesus team, which was responsible for significant advances integrating diverse home computing systems. The project, a joint venture of three major companies, received widespread press attention and was financially successful. Dan's dissatisfaction stemmed from the amount of credit given to the lead engineer, a man known to take the ideas of others and represent them as his own. Dan decided to leave his company the day his boss was promoted to head of the corporate research and development organization. Dan believed the lead engineer and his boss had not given credit to the work of others on the team.

Chet Willis, thirty-five, graduated from the University of Oklahoma and worked for a major Dallas, Texas, instrument manufacturer. Willis had worked on design teams of four industry-leading products by the time he was thirty-two. For the last three years he had worked on a project that the company had recently canceled, believing the team was pushing an expensive technology too far ahead of the market. Chet was disillusioned because he thought his last effort was his best to date. He had invested three years of his life in a technology that might not see the market for years to come. His situation motivated him to think about joining a smaller organization. Chet believed layers of management had killed his project—not the technical merits or the market.

David Parker, thirty-eight, an MIT graduate, was a laboratory manager for a Colorado division of a major computer manufacturer. Unlike the other three, David's experience was with multiple companies; he had worked for three high-tech organizations with increasing levels of responsibility in each job. David did not like being assigned projects from others. For some time he had considered independence but lacked the initiative to begin anything on his own. Those who worked closely with David frequently described him as "in over his head but able to sell his way out of anything."

Forming Dennison   A major Texas investor was attracted to the plan prepared by Bob, Dan, Chet, and David. Bob Anderson, in particular, was amazed at how easy it had been to raise significant money. Within five months of securing start-up funding, the four had resigned their positions, moved to Dallas, and begun raiding their former employers for Dennison's workforce.

Twelve of the first fifteen employees at Dennison had worked with the founders on previous projects. All had experience with computer architecture design with specific emphasis on scientific and military applications. The other three employees, all Dallas natives, were hired to head finance, administrative, and personnel functions. The head of personnel was recruited specifically because he worked for a firm known to have a strong and generally positive culture. Bob, who had assumed the presidency of Dennison, was especially interested in building a strong culture that was different from the companies he and the others had left.

During the first six months, Bob communicated daily with all employees except for brief periods when he visited potential customers. He spent most of his time with design engineers and worked directly on certain technical issues, although Dan Findley assumed the overall responsibility for research and development. During this period, Chet Willis designed a yet-to-be-staffed manufacturing organization. David Parker traveled weekly, making contacts and asking potential customers for needed features and ideas. He also spent time with university professors interested in applications of this type of technology.

The work was exhausting; most Dennison employees averaged seventy hours per week. Excitement was intense and visitors to Dennison's makeshift headquarters noted a sense of energy. As others were hired, expectations were explicitly stated about the level of necessary commitment to be successful at Dennison. Everyone was told they would either get rich or be without work within two years. No one suggested a secure future. In fact, Dennison did not want people who needed security. One employee summed up the expectation to put Dennison above all else when he stated, "I come in on Saturday whether I have work or not. Everyone is here: you have to be seen. Last Saturday I went in my office and played cards with my son."

Friday evenings were reserved for beer and pizza parties, which featured talk of the week's events even though families were invited. As the months passed, the parties continued late into the evening with fewer and fewer family members in attendance. The tradition of working on Saturdays extended to Sunday afternoons as pressure mounted to meet deadlines.

Close to the end of the first year, the personnel manager approached Bob and the others about the pressure and stress many employees were experiencing. He noted that most employees were given deadlines without their input or an opportunity to assess the reality of the expectations. The personnel manager suggested these early experiences were pivotal to building the type of culture that would characterize Dennison in the long run. Bob laughed at the personnel manager and stated he thought he knew more about culture than the man he had hired to build one. The personnel manager asked Bob what type of culture he and the others really wanted. Although all four men could talk about the organizations they had left, they were less clear about what they wanted for Dennison.

Bob asked his personnel manager to find consultants who had worked with other organizations and knew how to build a culture. The personnel manager objected because he believed you could not buy a culture. Bob insisted outside guidance was needed. He and the other founders wanted a strong culture to help make them successful. Making that happen was the personnel manager's responsibility. If he could not accomplish this goal, they believed he should look for work elsewhere.

QUESTIONS FOR DISCUSSION

1. How would you describe the emerging culture of Dennison?
2. What assumptions about culture are exhibited by the founders? What is meant by a strong culture? What are the strengths and pitfalls of this view?
3. What should the personnel manager do? Is he responsible for building the culture as Bob suggests? What role should external consultants serve?

China, India, and Oklahoma City: Working Together, but How?

Dana Edwards loved her work. The opportunity to work for Rockwell Developers in their communications department was exactly what Dana had always wanted to do. The Oklahoma City–based company was a leader in the Southwest in developing energy-efficient office and manufacturing facilities. Dana was surprised when her boss, Al Cho, told her Rockwell had just signed a major contract for work in Beijing and New Delhi. Dana knew both China and India were in rapid growth and development, but she had never considered Rockwell would expand beyond the five-state region, which accounted for virtually all of their clients.

Al told her contacts he had developed over many years made this expansion not only desirable but significant for the growth of Rockwell. Dana would need to get as much information as possible about marketing strategies in China and India in order to develop materials for the sales force who would work in Beijing and New Delhi. The Rockwell message had to be consistent with the values of the company but still attract attention in China and India. Dana felt true alarm. She knew that Al had traveled in India and China for many years, but he was the only person at Rockwell with that background. She had never worked to design messages for countries and cultures for which she had little knowledge and no personal contacts. Dana wanted Rockwell to be successful but wondered whether the organization was making a wise decision. She began to think about how to gather information necessary for her to approach the assignment.

QUESTIONS FOR DISCUSSION

1. Dana is asked to generate messages for a global market. What are the issues she should consider?
2. What type of information does Dana need in order to approach her assignment?
3. Should Dana express her concerns about moving into a global market?
4. With whom should Dana be in contact to fulfill her assignment?

Don Augustine's Disappointed Staff

Don Augustine was concerned about his upcoming department meeting. He wanted his first group presentation to be well received but suspected the tension surrounding his arrival made that all but impossible. Don knew his appointment as marketing manager was a severe disappointment to the two internal candidates, and management's decision to transfer him to Cleveland from Los Angeles had been interpreted as a sign the Cleveland marketing function was in trouble.

At the time of his promotion, Don had worked for Axel Corporation for ten years, first as a salesperson in southern California and later as a regional sales manager for California, Nevada, Oregon, and Washington. He was well known throughout the company for establishing effective customer relationships resulting in large orders of Axel's diverse home products lines. He had no direct experience in marketing management and no previous contact with the East Coast divisions or the Cleveland marketing group.

Two of Don's new staff, Carol Simpson and Jack Riley, had applied for the marketing manager position. Carol and Jack each had more than fifteen years' experience in the marketing department. Both had been critical of their former boss for her lack of creativity and unwillingness to take the necessary risks to better establish Axel products in highly competitive East Coast markets. Carol and Jack both believed they were not considered on their own merits and were labeled as ineffective based on the history of the Cleveland office.

Shortly following his arrival in Cleveland, Don met with Carol and Jack individually. Both seemed competent yet hesitant to trust his ability to manage the function. Rumor had it that Carol was looking for a job elsewhere and that Jack was considering an early retirement. Don was not sure what losing them would mean for the staff.

Don invited all department members to his first staff meeting. He began by describing his background with the company and indicating his desire to get to know the department and all of its members. He outlined a schedule of individual meetings and made a request that department members come to these meetings with both innovative ideas and suggestions for processes and promotions that were working well and should be retained. Don was unprepared for Carol's reaction.

"Don, that all sounds good," she said. "But you have to realize everyone in this room knows that giving good ideas to the boss is the kiss of death. Either the boss gets the credit, or worse yet, nothing happens and we get blamed. Sally (the former marketing manager) got a raise even if she is now only working on a special project. My career is over with Axel. I had waited for ten years for this job to open and when it did I got labeled with her bad decisions."

Others began to support Carol's position, and although they did not blame Don personally, most indicated a strong distrust of an outsider. Several voiced displeasure that Carol had not been chosen for the job. Don noted Jack Riley sat quietly but seemed amused and watchful.

Don let the group talk without interruption, thanked them for their honesty, and restated his desire to lead an effective organization. Although his calm response seemed to be well received, he wondered how much good information he could get from a staff so angry about past problems and current changes. He decided to meet with Carol to discuss the situation.

QUESTIONS FOR DISCUSSION

1. What are the leadership issues in this case? What are the trust issues? What are the change issues?
2. How would you advise Don? Carol? What are their career options?

Dora Cartwright's Leadership Dilemma

Dr. Dora Cartwright had just been selected as the first female president of Midwestern State University, one of the largest public institutions in the country to select a woman as president. The regents had been glowing in their praise of Dr. Cartwright, and the press conference she was about to enter was sure to be a lively one. After all, Midwestern State University had been searching over a year to replace President Johnson, a highly visible and popular man in the state. And Dora Cartwright had only become a candidate within the last week.

The presidential search at Midwestern State University had been criticized by faculty, staff, students, legislators, and citizens of the state almost from the beginning. When Midwestern regents voted to hire a national search firm, many were opposed because of the firm's cost at a time when the state and the university were under financial stress. The regents had ignored the criticism and interviewed five finalists identified and researched by the search firm. None of the five received enthusiastic support from major campus constituencies. Three of the five withdrew before the end of their interviews.

Prior to being asked to apply by the president of the board of regents, Dr. Cartwright had been Midwestern's vice president of graduate programs. Her background included a variety of administrative positions at West Coast universities, and she was generally respected by the Midwestern faculty. No one, however, had urged her to actively seek the presidency. She was surprised by the regents' invitation to interview and more so when after only four hours of deliberation she was a unanimous choice. She was concerned faculty, staff, and students had not been included in the process and was relieved when search committee members from these groups told her they would support the regents' decision.

As Dora Cartwright waited for the press conference to begin she reviewed what she considered a complex and challenging leadership dilemma. First, she had not sought the position and as a result did not have a plan formulated for assuming responsibility. Second, she believed her selection was both a tribute to her past work and a compromise on which the regents could agree without reopening the search. Third, she knew she would be particularly visible as a woman assuming the top position at an institution with a hundred-year history of male leadership. Fourth, the state and university were under financial stress, making leadership difficult for anyone. She believed, for example, President Johnson's attraction to another offer was in part based on the bleak financial outlook facing the university. And finally, of immediate concern, two members of her staff had been active candidates for the position; she believed the senior staff would be less than enthusiastic about her selection. She needed their support because they possessed information critical to her success.

Dora Cartwright decided she would tell the press she was launching a ninety-day data collection process after which she would announce her strategy. Privately she began to think about how the process should evolve, who should be included, what she should ask, and how she should decide the leadership style and role that would make her an effective president for Midwestern.

QUESTIONS FOR DISCUSSION

1. How would you describe Dora Cartwright's leadership dilemma?
2. What type of communication plan can give Dr. Cartwright the information she needs?

3. Should Dr. Cartwright have taken the position? Why? Why not?

4. How would you advise Dr. Cartwright?

Kathy's Stubborn, Smart Streak

Kathy Merrell had worked for six general managers of North Electronics. Most credited her with incomparable organizational skills and a work ethic not matched by others in the company. When Pam Arnold became the new general manager of North, she knew that Kathy's organizational knowledge and history of excellent work performance would be important to her success. Pam's initial interactions with Kathy confirmed what previous managers had said. Kathy was smart, a hard worker, had excellent communication skills, and was liked and respected by the executive staff.

Pam was not prepared to hear that Kathy was going to retire in less than a year. After trying unsuccessfully to talk Kathy out of her decision, Pam began to think about next steps. So much organizational history was in Kathy's head; a plan had to be developed. When Pam proposed the plan, Kathy immediately agreed. Pam asked Kathy to take three months to develop a list of transition issues and consider when they should identify her replacement so Kathy could provide adequate training. At the end of three months, Pam was shocked when Kathy had made no progress on the issues list or even considered a timeline. Kathy said she was simply too busy to get the assignment completed. Pam knew Kathy was busy and that was exactly what worried Pam. Kathy said she would get it done when she could but did not know when that would be. Pam knew she was in trouble. The amount of information in Kathy's head was critical to the operation of the general manager's office. For whatever reason, Kathy was suddenly stubborn about protecting the information she had so carefully developed over many years. Pam wondered what she should do. She did not believe she could just wait for Kathy.

QUESTIONS FOR DISCUSSION

1. Describe the communication problems in this case.

2. How would you advise Pam?

3. What might be done to help Kathy prepare for change?

Brian James Doesn't Know What to Believe

Brian James loved his work in the financial resources department of Peterson Industries. His peers were competent and eager to help him even though he did not have the financial background common to the team. Brian had been chosen to work in financial resources because of his background in organizational communication. The manager wanted someone who could assist the team in designing communication and training to assist with Peterson's implementation of a massive new financial computer system.

After a few weeks on the job, Brian became concerned that either his peers were wrong or the management team did not understand the complexity of the system implementation. Everyone on the team talked with Brian about issues with the system, issues which if real would surely make the implementation difficult no matter how clear the communication. Brian encouraged the team to talk with management. His peers said that was impossible because management wanted only good news. Brian pushed his peers saying he could not do his work if he knew failures were almost certain to happen.

In his second month, Brian was asked to make a presentation to management about the communication plan and the timing of the initial system implementation. Brian begged the team to help him frame some of the issues but everyone refused. Brian knew he had to do something, but as the newest member of the team, he could not even begin to understand what would be a good approach. Brian made an appointment with his manager to discuss his concerns. He did not want to betray his peers but could think of no other approach.

QUESTIONS FOR DISCUSSION

1. Brian faces a difficulty in performing his responsibilities because he cannot independently assess the claims of his peers. How can he get the information he needs?
2. What should Brian tell his peers about his upcoming meeting? How should he approach his manager?
3. What communication issues does this case illustrate?

I Am Tired and Stressed

Jenny Means worked the afternoon shift in the family care unit of Coronado's largest hospice care center. Jenny was in charge of helping families with relatives in hospice to cope with daily concerns and any communication issues they might have with staff members.

Jenny knew most families with family members needing hospice care were under extreme stress. She cared about her clients and wanted to help them in any way she could. Jenny knew she had to keep a calm and positive attitude in order to be helpful. What she had not expected was the personal emotional strain of dealing with one concerned family after another. Although she worked a normal eight-hour shift, the constant needs of her clients left her stressed and tired at the end of her day. Jenny described her stress to one of the nurses who worked near her office. The nurse told Jenny some people were simply not cut out for this type of job. Jenny thought she was doing a good job with the clients and wondered how she might help herself to remain as a family advocate.

QUESTIONS FOR DISCUSSION

1. Jenny is in what can be described as a high emotional labor job. How would you advise her to use her communication skills to deal with her stress and fatigue?
2. What type of training should be developed for individuals with emotional labor jobs?

I Thought I Gave Them Everything

Henry Gonzales has been the manager of Quality Foods' Seventh Street store for four years. Henry is considered among Quality's top managers for making the once-unprofitable store the sales leader of the company. Henry works hard and expects the same of all store employees. He emphasizes financial rewards for hard work and has initiated a pay incentive plan for supervisors who are able to cut costs or increase sales in their respective departments.

Henry was angry and upset when the personnel director for Quality informed him that two of his leading supervisors had requested transfers to other Quality stores. Didn't they realize they were in the best of Quality's stores and making more money than their counterparts in less profitable operations? Did they really need more of his time, as the personnel director intimated? Why should grown people need hand-holding? Didn't they recognize that he was busy and always worked for the best interests of the store and his supervisors?

Henry wondered what he should do next. He felt inclined just to let them leave and see how they would like to work under another manager. On the other hand, they were good workers. Should he talk with them? What would he say?

Henry Gonzales is like many busy managers who lose touch with the wants and needs of those who work for them.

QUESTIONS FOR DISCUSSION

1. As you study Henry's problem, think about what you would advise Henry to do.
2. What does Henry need to know about communication competency?
3. Discuss the relationship between communication and motivation.

Ann Cartwright, Vice President of Drummond Industries

Ann Cartwright was perplexed and disturbed by the conversation taking place in hushed tones outside her office door. Apparently Tom Jackson and Jim Jurgers, both Drummond vice presidents, didn't realize Ann's door was open and that she could hear their remarks. They were saying that Ann had been promoted to vice president of marketing because she was a woman and that the president, George Miller, was unwilling to criticize her because he didn't know how to deal with a woman on his staff.

Ann had been promoted six months ago when her longtime boss, the vice president of marketing, had retired. Ann had been successful as the manager of marketing and was widely credited with developing excellent marketing plans for several new product lines and for expanding the services of the marketing department to assist the product development group in its identification of potential new lines. Her employees, both male and female, liked to work for her and believed her to be fair and direct. In fact, almost everyone seemed genuinely excited and pleased when her promotion was announced.

Ann wondered what the conversation meant and what she should do. She knew she needed both men's cooperation and certainly the trust of Drummond's president. Should she confront Tom and Jim? Should she go to the president?

Should she ignore the remarks and act as if nothing has happened? What, if anything, does this mean for her future?

Ann Cartwright's experience is similar to those reported by female professionals in all types of organizational positions. Although the number of female managers increases daily, acceptance into previously all-male management teams is mixed, often affecting the quality of working relationships. Think about what Ann should do. What communication competencies does Ann need to work with Tom and Jim?

QUESTIONS FOR DISCUSSION

1. In your view, what barriers does Ann face? What barriers exist for women in organizations?
2. If you were a corporate president or CEO, what specific measures might you take to ensure equality between the sexes in your organization?
3. What can women themselves do to accelerate more favorable attitudes toward managerial women?

The Rule Here Is to Do What Management Wants

Jim Robinson liked people on his staff to get along with one another and support group decisions. As president of Firestone Insurance, he had a history of promoting mostly white men who agreed with him. He was known for avoiding men or women who engaged in confrontation and disagreement. Jerry Douglas should have known that. He had been the sales manager for Firestone for five years and was only lately exhibiting a level of disagreement that made Robinson uncomfortable. Also, Sally Marshall, the head of finance and Firestone's only woman manager, seemed to be siding with Douglas.

Jerry contended Firestone had to hire a more diverse sales staff because additional competitors had entered several of their good sales territories, targeting Firestone customers with international affiliates. Unlike these competitors, Firestone's field sales staff were mostly white men with no international experience. Jim and others on his staff felt Jerry was being pessimistic and negative. Sally seemed to agree with Jerry, although she wasn't as outspoken as he was.

Jerry was disgusted with all his peers except Sally. The others knew he was right but were afraid to confront Jim. They told Jerry to be patient and said that Jim would eventually see his point of view. Jerry believed that being patient would cost Firestone considerable money and might cause them to lose key accounts currently being pursued by their competition.

Both Jim and Jerry were concerned. Neither liked what was happening. What would you advise Jim to do? Jerry?

QUESTIONS FOR DISCUSSION

1. Describe the culture of Firestone Insurance. How does Jim's worldview influence what is happening between Jim and Jerry?
2. What can Jerry do to influence Jim's thinking?

Two Men—Two Issues—Two Japanese Workers
Rieko McAdams[1]

Young Mr. Kobayashi   It is 5:30 P.M. and all employees are still at their desks working. They will head to a bar from work, socialize, and possibly brainstorm the next project. Mr. Kobayashi thinks about his wife and a baby girl not yet six months old. He wishes to see the baby and have a relaxed evening with his wife. Mr. Kobayashi knows that he is expected to go to the bar with his colleagues. He knows what his coworkers will say if he says he would like to go home to his wife. He knows what his superiors would think about him for not joining the group: no dedication, no drive, no loyalty, and henpecked. Kobayashi's company is an elite company in which employees dedicate their total lives by working long hours, socializing after work hours, and seeking to be recognized as company men. Kobayashi does not want to sell his body and soul to the company, but he also does not want to see others promoted before he is. He wants to be successful but would like to have time of his own.

Older Mr. Kobayashi   Mr. Kobayashi, fifty-six years old and loyal to his company, believes he is being pressured to quit his job. He has worked in the same company for over thirty years. His boss believes that Mr. Kobayashi does not exhibit the enthusiasm and drive he once did. Mr. Kobayashi's salary is twice the amount of hiring two younger employees with less experience but new and creative ideas. Mr. Kobayashi has three more years until retirement and wishes to stay with the company until then. His family includes two college students in addition to his wife. His boss offers him a choice: transfer to another branch or be demoted to a lower position. Mr. Kobayashi does not wish to move to another city. He is concerned because he believes that in Japan, a man with no work is lost. Japanese people are devoted to their work, and being fired or demoted is a terrible problem for the Japanese worker. Mr. Kobayashi's boss has no performance reason to fire him, so he pressures him to quit. This type of situation is called *kata-tataki-no-kei* in Japanese.

QUESTIONS FOR DISCUSSION
1. Discuss the problems of the two men from a cultural perspective.
2. How similar are these problems between the United States of America and Japan?
3. What are the communication issues in the cases?

---

[1]Rieko McAdams (B.A. in organizational communication, University of Colorado at Colorado Springs), originally from Japan, teaches Japanese to American students in elementary, secondary, and postsecondary schools. Prior to moving to the United States of America, McAdams worked in high-level administrative positions in Japan. Her observations are based on real circumstances, although the names have been altered.

I Thought We Were a Team

Nicki Jordan had been on a fast career track from the moment she went to work for the Federation of High School Athletes. Her drive to succeed and friendly style were exactly what the executive director, Tom Welsh, wanted. Nicki was quickly assigned to work with corporate sponsors and the Federation's board. Over the years, she became known as Tom's right hand. No one was surprised when, after Nicki had been with the organization for seven years, she was promoted to associate director and was groomed to replace Tom when he announced his pending retirement.

Nicki's first year as executive director went smoothly. She promoted her long-time colleague, Jim Masters, to her former associate director position. Jim was a highly competent accountant who had a history of working well with internal systems as well as the corporate sponsors who were the financial foundation of the Federation. In her second year as executive director, Nicki decided the growth of the Federation was such that reorganization of some of the work units was in order. She hired consultants known for their ability to understand complex organizations and develop design alternatives. She asked Jim to head the project both internally and with the consultants. Nicki was surprised when the consultants requested a private and confidential meeting. When they told her that Jim was viewed as a dictator by much of the staff, she could not believe what she was hearing. Not one person had previously raised an issue about Jim's approach. Further, Jim always told her about the positive input he received from others relative to his areas of responsibility. Were the consultants wrong? Had she missed this important information? How could she be so wrong about Jim? More important, why had no one come to her sooner?

QUESTIONS FOR DISCUSSION

1. What should Nicki do next?
2. How can she determine for herself the accuracy of the consultants' concerns?
3. If the consultants are right about Jim, what contributed to her missing this key information?

The Internal Communications Dilemma

You are new in the public relations department of Simplex Division of Newbury Corporation, a developer and manufacturer of educational products for young children. Your job is internal communications, and your boss, the head of public relations, has indicated that you have a major challenge before you.

The new head of Simplex Division is not trusted by many of the employees. Some grudgingly admit that Loren Marks came into a tough situation, but even his supporters say that he doesn't communicate well. During Marks's first six months, fifty employees were laid off; two long-term employees were demoted, resulting in grievances and lawsuits against Simplex; and significant dollars were moved from research and development to manufacturing to attempt to upgrade old systems presumed to be creating quality problems. Loren fired the research and development manager, a popular leader of eighteen years, and replaced him with a creative but emotional person from another division. Corporate organizational climate audits placed Simplex Division near the bottom among all Newbury divisions in employee satisfaction. Employees focused numerous negative comments on Loren Marks. Employees were also vocal about the lack of recognition, a fear of reprisal for speaking up, the use of organizational resources, and the uncertainties surrounding their future.

QUESTIONS FOR DISCUSSION

1. As the person responsible for internal communications, what would you do first when receiving this information?
2. How might you gather information from employees?
3. Who would you involve in planning and decision making?
4. How would you advise Loren Marks?
5. What channels would you use?
6. How would you evaluate your results?

The Reluctant Team Member

Rhonda Jenkins had worked in the credit collection department of Bass Medical Supply Corporation for over fifteen years. The announcement that credit was converting to a team-based structure came as a shock, especially amid rumors that the company would begin another round of layoffs in the fourth quarter. Rhonda liked credit and was afraid that the teams meant reductions in credit staff, especially if what she had heard about teams increasing productivity with fewer employees was true. The decision to apply for a transfer to customer support was difficult. She hated leaving her friends but didn't trust this whole team thing. After all, she had a family to support.

After only two months in customer support, Rhonda knew she had made the right move. Three people had been terminated in credit, with no plans to replace them. Rhonda was confused and upset when she learned a team-based structure was coming to customer support, based on team successes in credit. Rhonda didn't think it was a success when people lost their jobs.

Rhonda was assigned to a team of four customer support representatives. The other three were enthusiastic about the change and eager for training to develop new skills. During training each team was asked to set initial behavior expectations for the team and begin to talk about productivity goals. Rhonda explained her concerns to her new team members. The other three told her that she was making too much out of the issues and should just get on board. Rhonda ended up confronting the trainer and the entire class with her fears. The trainer was supportive and urged Rhonda to give the team a chance. Rhonda told her team members that she just could not support the effort. She would not be disruptive, but she would not participate any more than was absolutely required to stay employed.

QUESTIONS FOR DISCUSSION

1. How would you advise Rhonda?
2. What could her new team members do?
3. Describe the communication, change, and conflict issues in this case.

What Happened to the Value of Networking?

Ingress Computer Corporation was noted for excellent customer service in support of its networking products used by numerous multinational corporations with operations throughout the world. Ingress's International Customer Service team was well known for rapid response in complex situations requiring problem solving across international borders. Team members were located in six countries, communicating daily through e-mail and sophisticated GDSS and quarterly in face-to-face meetings in Rome. Other emergency meetings were conducted via video- and audioconferencing. Team leader Enrico Bardini was proud of the group he believed to be among the most knowledgeable in the industry. Bardini was surprised to receive a call from Mitchell Morgan, vice president for customer service, indicating an increase in customer complaints that suggested his team was slow to respond when systems involving more than one country were down.

Enrico decided to ask the group to discuss complaints via e-mail and to suggest potential solutions or at least explanations for recent problems. Team members responded rapidly, and their responses left Enrico even more perplexed. Yes, customer response time had slipped. The long hours of work coupled with time zone and language differences were wearing on the capabilities of individuals who worked mostly in isolation from other Ingress employees. Some members expressed the feeling that there was little appreciation for their efforts and certainly little career growth associated with their jobs. Two team members suggested more face-to-face meetings for troubleshooting, but the other four indicated that little could be done to improve the situation. All committed to trying to shorten customer response time.

Enrico reported his findings to Morgan and asked for suggestions.

QUESTIONS FOR DISCUSSION

1. Based on everything you have learned about organizational communication, describe what may be contributing to the responses Enrico received.
2. Discuss the merits and weaknesses of technologically mediated communication.
3. Describe what you would do if you were Mitchell Morgan, Enrico, or an individual team member.

The "Walking the Talk" Manager

Jeff Manson's move to the JDW Worldwide Service Center came as no surprise to those who had followed his career. Jeff had worked for the new top management of the center in two of his previous assignments at JDW. The only surprise was that he was to become a senior manager in a team-based organization reporting directly to Mary Sikes. Jeff was known for his personable style, but few who knew him would suggest that he was a true team player. Mary was just the opposite. She was known for supporting the team structure and contributing to strong overall results. Mary had been promoted to the director's role prior to the change in top management.

Mary expected all three of her direct reports to work collaboratively with the customer service teams. Jeff openly agreed with Mary about almost everything, although she was told by her new manager that Jeff had expressed concerns that the center did not have enough managerial controls. Her manager, Jeff's former boss, seemed to believe Jeff and appeared to question her assurance that Jeff would come to understand the real benefits of the team structure. When Mary asked Jeff if he had any concerns, he assured her he did not and was fully supportive of the direction of the center.

Mary's concern increased when the two teams reporting to Jeff posted quarterly results that were below their previous metrics. When she asked Jeff to help her understand, he suggested that the teams were not as mature as she had thought and that he needed to become more involved. Mary decided to speak directly with the teams. The conversations left her puzzled.

Mary learned that Jeff rarely met with the teams and had not talked with them about their current or previous results. They claimed he could not possibly know what they needed. When Mary confronted Jeff with her findings, he claimed the teams did not understand how much he had learned from observation and review of written performance results. Mary worried that Jeff was saying all the right things but was not really "walking his talk."

Mary spoke with her boss about her concerns. He assured her there was no cause for concern and that Mary was lucky to have Jeff on her staff. In fact, Mary's manager suggested that Jeff should be groomed to replace Mary when she was promoted.

QUESTIONS FOR DISCUSSION

1. How can Mary evaluate whether her concerns are valid?
2. What should Mary consider as she communicates with her boss and with Jeff?
3. What are the ethical and practical issues in this case?

Working Together at a Distance

The five members of the ComSci, Inc., product development team were located in three states with only two members of the group residing in the same city. All team members worked from their homes with a variety of networked technologies, including teleconferencing. During the first year following formation of the team, two successful products were introduced, with a third near completion. Management hailed the group as representing the future of the company. It came as a shock to almost everyone at ComSci when the development team leader, John Mercer, announced he was quitting for an opportunity to work with a competitor's development group. John claimed his team was competent and cooperative, that ComSci had rewarded him adequately, and the work they had produced was first-rate. He could not, however, continue to work with so little real connection to others. Management asked John to reconsider, but his decision was firm. The other four team members expressed dismay but concluded that they wanted to continue to work in a geographically dispersed team.

QUESTIONS FOR DISCUSSION

1. Discuss the identification and socialization issues in this case.
2. What can be done to alleviate this type of problem?
3. How can individuals and organizations assess the needs of a geographically dispersed workforce?

Career and Personal Needs Just Don't Mix

Jim and Jane Wilson rarely saw each other. Jim was a stockbroker and Jane a successful lawyer. Married since graduate school, the two were devoted to each other, to their two children, Amy and Mike, and to their careers. It was not unusual for Jim and Jane to have fewer than thirty minutes a day together, although both spent more time with Amy and Mike. Jane worried about the hurried nature of their lives, but Jim assured her they were similar to most couples they knew.

Jane had not expected to be assigned to the computer fraud case her firm had agreed to litigate on behalf of the U.S. Justice Department. The lead role was high-visibility and would engage most of her time for twelve to eighteen months. She was honored and knew this assignment would position her to become the youngest partner in the firm. Jane was not prepared for the demands of the case and found herself without a free day in the first six weeks of her assignment. Jim was supportive, but she could tell her time away from home was beginning to wear. In addition, he had major clients who wanted him to travel with them to evaluate several major investments. Jim had assumed major responsibilities for Amy and Mike. If he were to be gone for several weeks, both Jane and Jim were concerned about the children's reaction.

Jane began to feel extremely tired even in the early morning. She found herself cross with staff at work and impatient with Jim at home. She knew that stress and burnout were problems for people working on intense cases, but she believed that serious problems happened to people who were not as happy at home or as committed to work as she was. Jane was amazed when Jim sent her an urgent e-mail stating they must have an evening to talk about the pressures between their work and family life. Jane knew Jim was right but was too tired to think about how she might alter what was happening.

QUESTIONS FOR DISCUSSION

1. How would you advise Jane?
2. What would you say to Jim?
3. Can intense careers and home responsibilities mix? Discuss your answers.
4. What are the communication issues in this case?

The Competitive Leak Is More Than a Crisis

Charles Driscoll, president of Custom Industries, could hardly believe the speaker on the other end of the phone. It was 9:30 P.M. and his administrative assistant rarely called that late. Judith Anderson was at her home finishing her e-mails when she saw the unbelievable messages from Jeff Nelson, vice president of research and development for Custom Industries. The five e-mails had gone to four of Custom's major competitors as well as all of the Custom leadership team. Judith had tried to call Jeff before contacting Charles. Judith told Charles the e-mails were extremely profane in describing their competitors and contained several design secrets for two of Custom's new products. Charles quickly logged on to his system and confirmed what Judith had reported. Charles tried to contact Jeff, with no success. He quickly called his head of IT, June Stevenson, and asked her to begin looking at all e-mails originating in the last several hours from Jeff Nelson's accounts. Charles contacted Custom's attorney, Charles Bittersweet, and then called Tom Milliman, the head of public relations. Charles asked all of them to meet him at Custom's headquarters. Charles could not understand what might be happening. The language in Jeff's e-mails about Custom's competitors was totally unacceptable under any circumstances, and the release of the design secrets was both bizarre and dangerous. As Charles drove to his office, he knew that he had both a public crisis and a crisis with one of his most important leaders. Charles thought about what he should do next.

QUESTIONS FOR DISCUSSION

1. What information does Charles need to begin thinking about his next steps?
2. What will Tom Milliman need to consider from a public relations standpoint?
3. What type of crisis management approach would you recommend?

The CEO Puts Her Foot in Her Mouth

Jan Davis, communications manager for Kingfisher Retailers, was stunned. Megan Drake, president of Kingfisher, had just announced during an employee teleconference broadcast by satellite to over forty stores that she believed Kingfisher was losing its competitive edge in the electronics market and would have to engage in significant restructuring. Jan knew, of course, that revenues for the last two quarters had not met expectations and that Megan was upset. But to announce her displeasure and hint at major changes without a plan in place was dangerous for Kingfisher and for Megan herself. At the end of the conference, Megan knew she had made a mistake. She told Jan she was tired and angry at the lack of action from her senior vice presidents. She knew she should not have announced her concerns to the employees but had done so in an uncharacteristic fit of temper. Megan asked Jan what she should do next.

QUESTIONS FOR DISCUSSION

1. If you were Jan, what would you suggest?
2. What should Megan do next with regard to her senior leadership?
3. What happens when anger, fatigue, or a host of other circumstances contributes to individuals saying publicly something they immediately regret?
4. Should Megan hold another teleconference to put her concerns in context? Why? Why not?

The Only U.S.A. Communicator on the Team

Jeri Martinez had been excited when she was selected to move to Shanghai to work with the retail advertising team for Van Pelz Clothing. Her work in New York and Chicago had been recognized and she had received credit along with her team for increasing market share for Van Pelz clothing lines aimed at a teenage market. The desire of Van Pelz management to translate their U.S.A. success into the growing Asian market seemed reasonable and desirable. Jeri knew approaches in Asia would differ from U.S.A. markets, but she was not prepared for working with her new Van Pelz colleagues in Shanghai. Fong Wang and Michael Griffith were both welcoming. Both had worked for Van Pelz for over five years and told Jeri they enjoyed the company and respected their local management. Jeri was concerned about their lack of input and response to her ideas for the campaign to launch Van Pelz Asia for teens. Both Fong and Michael were pleasant in meetings but provided little in ideas for the campaign. Jeri was surprised to learn they had created a highly successful campaign for Van Pelz's adult line. She asked Fong and Michael why they were not contributing to ideas for the teenage market. Fong, appearing to reply for both of them, claimed they had not been invited to develop ideas. Jeri was perplexed. When she discussed her concerns with her Shanghai manager, Yu Zhou, he chided her for not understanding important cultural differences in her team. He told her she should be more sensitive to Fong and Michael. Jeri left Zhou's office wondering about her communication abilities. She thought she had come to Shanghai because of her abilities to work with others and to think about markets which were unusual for Van Pelz. Her conversation with Zhou and the responses of Fong and Michael raised important questions about her approaches.

1. What can Jeri do to better understand the situation she faces?
2. What are the potential cultural differences at work in this case?
3. How can Jeri determine her approach to Fong and Michael?
4. What role can Zhou play in helping Jeri?

Working across Time and Space

Lea Grimes left her office feeling frustrated and angry with her colleagues in Italy and Spain. She had told Reynolds's management team the report on potential new European clients would be on their desk by Monday. It was after 5 P.M. on Friday and still no response from Roberto Torbato (in Italy) and Santos Santana (in Spain). Lea had asked them on Monday for the information, telling them she would need data by Thursday in order to spend Friday writing a memo about the opportunities both had indicated they would try to get her what she needed. She had e-mailed three times in the last forty-eight hours without any response. Lea believed they did not get the pressure she was under. Lea, Roberto, and Santos were members of the European team for Reynolds Toys. Lea lived in Los Angeles with Roberto in Rome and Santos in Madrid. Lea coordinated European efforts from Reynolds's Los Angeles headquarters while Roberto and Santos both headed regional European sales teams. Lea reflected this was not the first time her requests had gone unheeded. She knew both men were excellent sales managers and their regions were highly profitable for Reynolds. She could not understand their delays in getting her what she needed. Management was not going to be pleased.

1. What should Lea do?
2. What could Lea have done differently in working with Roberto and Santos?
3. Based on what we know about virtual teams, what barriers are potentially in operation in this situation?

Are We a High-Reliability Team or Not?

Jason Nugent had been communication manager for the Emergency Operation Center for Western University for over five years. Each year Western's leadership team spent time with Jason in working through simulations important for response in the event Western had a natural disaster or, worse yet, a student shooting. Jason thought he had been effective and the president of Western, Janis Welton, certainly praised his work. Jason was not prepared for the new vice president for administration, Jim Jefferson. Jim had come to Western from private industry. He believed Western needed a much different emergency response operation than had previously been developed. Jim doubted the protocols Jason had developed would work in an actual emergency. He also believed the university should depend more than in Jason's plans on electronic communication with students. He wanted standard responses scripted and ready to send for approximately thirty potential emergency situations. Jason believed the potential emergency situations Western could face would be more dynamic than what Jim was envisioning. Jim ordered Jason to change the Emergency Operation Center manual and prepare to run the next scheduled simulation with the new procedures. Jason fundamentally disagreed. He believed best practices in the educational industry supported his perspective.

1. What should Jason do?
2. How can Jason determine the value in Jim's requirements?
3. Is this a conflict between two individuals who do not know each other? Is this a conflict about expertise?
4. Should Jason involve Janis Welton?

AUTHOR INDEX

A

Agarwala-Rogers, R., 68
Ahmed, Iftekhar, 277, 281
Albrecht, T.L., 65,177
Allen, Brenda, 58, 66, 162, 169, 170, 177
Allen, Myria, 162, 166, 177
Allport, Gordon, 65, 108, 133
Allred, Brent, 400, 401, 408
Alston, L., 209
Alvesson, Mats, 65, 94, 99, 224, 248
Alvin, Heidi, 228
Amason, Patricia, 162, 177
Anatol,W., 248
Anderson, Bob, 416
Anderson, Carl, 118, 133
Anderson, Geoff, 288, 321
Anderson, Mike, 8–10
Anderson, Rob, 378, 380
Andersson, Lynne, 287, 321
Andrews, K.R., 352
Applbaum, Ron, 248
Argyris, Chris, 86, 230, 248
Armstrong, Gary, 340, 342, 353
Arnett, Ronald, 115, 133
Arthur, Michael, 397, 398, 408
Ashcraft, Karen, 58, 66, 95, 99, 287, 322
Ashford, S., 100
Athanassiades, J., 177
Aug, S., 178
Auster, E., 329, 352
Avolio, Bruce, 228, 249

B

Bacon, C.C., 248
Baird, John, 177, 183, 208, 249
Ballard, Dawna, 366, 383
Bamforth, Kenneth, 82, 83, 100
Bandura, A., 248
Bantz, Charles, 133, 208
Barbour, Joshua, 58–60, 67
Barge, J. Kevin, 62, 66, 222, 248
Barker, James, 186, 208
Barnard, Chester, 4, 26, 73, 99
Barnett, George, 66, 155, 178

Barone, Frank, 149, 177
Baudrillard, Jean, 93, 99
Bazarova, Natalya, 200, 209
Beal, B., 209
Beckhard, R., 249
Beckman, C., 322
Belch, George, 341, 352
Belch, Michael, 341, 352
Bell, C.H., 353, 408
Benne, Kenneth, 195, 208, 352, 382, 408
Bennis, Warren, 99, 133, 213, 223, 225–227, 230, 232, 233, 246, 248, 321, 352 359, 364, 382, 408
Berkowitz, Leonard, 295, 321
Biederman, Patricia, 359, 382
Blake, Robert, 217, 220, 248, 295, 321
Blanchard, Kenneth, 220, 221, 249
Bodaken, E.M., 248
Bolkan, San, 308, 321
Bona, Frederick, 335, 353
Bonito, Joseph, 257, 281
Booth-Butterfield, M., 177
Bormann, E.G., 133
Bougon, M., 66
Brad, S. D., 324, 325, 328, 345
Bradley, Samuel, 342, 352
Brilhart, J.K., 208
Brislin, R.W., 177
Broom, Glen, 328, 332, 352
Brown, Charles, 115, 134, 313, 314, 321
Brown, Karen, 185, 208
Brown, M.H., 66
Browning, Larry, 53, 66
Bronowski, James, 26
Broom, G.M., 352
Brummans, Boris, 305, 321
Bruning, N.S., 249
Bruno Teboul, J. C., 150, 177
Bryant, J., 201, 209
Buccholz, R.A., 352
Bullis, Connie, 58, 66
Butterfield, S., 177
Burgoon, M., 177
Burtis, T., 209
Buzzanell, Patrice, 57, 66

C

Cahill, Daniel, 155, 179
Calás, Marta, 68, 95, 99, 100
Campbell, Donald, 138, 153, 177
Canay, D., 321
Cannell, Charles, 265, 281
Carmichael, C.W., 177
Carr, Clay, 186, 208
Carter, Stephen, 124, 133
Cartwright, D., 208
Cashman, Thomas, 326, 332, 352, 382
Cavanagh, G., 113, 133
Caywood, Clarke, 332, 352, 353, 354
Center, Allen, 328, 352
Cesaria, Ruggero, 67, 162, 179
Chase, L.J., 249
Cheney, George, 66, 68, 120, 133, 180, 194, 208, 253, 282, 326, 327, 345, 352, 359, 383
Chew Sanchez, M., 209
Chin, R., 352, 382, 408
Choo, C.W., 329, 352
Christensen, Lars, 326, 327, 330, 345, 352
Cissna, Kenneth, 66, 134, 383
Claman, Priscilla, 397, 398, 408
Clampitt, Phillip, 326, 332, 352, 382
Clegg, Stewart, 66, 68, 93, 94, 99, 100
Cole, Tim, 150, 177
Collins-Jarvis, Lori, 276, 281
Collins, Jim, 227, 240, 242, 247, 248, 363, 382
Conrad, Charles, 66, 299, 321, 325, 352
Considine, Jennifer, 163, 179
Contractor, Noshir, 157, 159, 179
Coons, A.E., 249
Cooperrider, David, 368, 382
Coopman, Stephanie, 166, 177
Cooren, François, 53, 66
Corey, G., 248
Corey, K., 352, 382, 408
Corman, Steve, 66, 133, 382
Courtright, John, 186, 208
Cox, Taylor, 106, 133, 177, 197, 208
Cragan, John, 184, 186, 203, 208

Craig, Robert, 14, 26, 29, 62, 66
Cronen, Vernon, 29, 66
Cummings, L.L., 68, 281
Cupach, William, 312, 322
Cushman, Donald, 66, 229, 248, 357, 382
Cutlip, Scott, 328, 352
Cyert, Richard, 82, 100, 260, 281

D

Daft, Richard, 276, 281, 352
Dahl, T.L., 66
Daly, John, 177, 178, 308, 321
Daniels, Tom, 325, 352
Dansereau, F., 177
Davis, K., 66, 248
Deal, Terrence, 88, 89 100, 105, 133
DeCamp, Mary, 257, 281
Dedmon, J., 352
Deetz, Stanley, 17, 26, 52, 55, 56, 65, 66, 67, 94, 99, 229, 248
DeFillippi, Robert, 397, 398, 408
DeKoch, Robert, 326, 332, 352, 382
Dempsey, Sarah, 240, 241, 248
DeVito, Joseph, 115, 133, 177
Dewey, John, 259, 281
DeWine, Sue, 149, 352, 382, 408
Dickson, W.J., 100
Dilenschneider, R.L., 352, 353
Dobbins, G.H., 248
Donnellon, A., 66
Dorfman, Peter, 60, 66
Dougherty, Debbie, 309, 321, 361, 382
Downs, Cal., 177
Drucker, Peter, 230, 248
Dutton, J., 322

E

Eadie, William, 134, 352, 353
Earley, P., 178
Edgar Schein, 87, 88
Edward, Miles, 153
Eisenberg, Eric, 66, 67, 100, 153, 178, 233, 248, 329, 331, 352
Elsass, Priscilla, 193, 209
Ely, R., 209
Ellis, Kathleen, 162, 178, 179 213, 248
Ellison, Nicolle, 165, 178
Etzioni, Amitai, 15, 26
Ewing, Raymond, 335, 352

F

Fairhurst, Gail, 53, 66, 186, 208, 224, 242, 248

Falcione, R., 178
Farace, Richard, 157, 178
Faules, Don, 389, 408
Fayol, Henri, 72–76, 78, 100
Fearn-Banks, Kathleen, 338, 353
Feeley, Thomas, 155, 178
Feldman, D., 322
Ferguson, K., 66
Fiedler, Fred, 219, 220, 248
Fineman, Stephen, 164, 178
Finestone, P., 249
Fisher, B.A., 281
Fisher, Dalmar, 311, 321
Fisher, Roger, 315, 321
Flanagin, Andrew, 165, 180, 202, 208
Folb, E.A., 178
Folger, Joseph, 299, 302, 316, 321
Follett, Mary Parker, 77, 81, 100
Fombrun, C., 353
Foss, Karen, 27, 47, 67, 197, 209
Foucault, Michel, 94, 100
Frederickson, J.W., 353
French, John, 237, 248
French, W.L., 353, 408
Frey, Larry, 66, 134, 383
Friedman, Thomas, 3, 26, 165, 178, 397, 408
Frost, Peter, 88, 90, 100
Fulk, Janet, 152, 178, 201, 208, 209, 276, 281

G

Galbraith, Jay, 328, 353
Galenes, G.J., 208
Galle, W.P., 67
Gardner, Howard, 232, 248
Garner, Johny, 163, 179
Gattiker, U., 276, 281
Geier, J., 248
Gershenfeld, M.K., 209
Gibb, J., 208
Gibb, Jack, 313, 315, 321
Gibbons, D., 178
Gibbs, Jennifer, 201
Gibson, Cynthia, 197
Gibson, R., 353, 354, 382, 383
Giles, Howard, 178
Gillis, T., 353
Gladwell, Malcolm, 358, 382
Goldhaber, Gerald, 66, 353, 408
Goldsmith, M., 249
Goodall, H.L., 66, 100, 153, 159, 178, 180, 329, 331, 352, 354, 408

Goodstein, L.D., 104, 133
Gouran, Dennis, 262, 281
Granovetter, Mark, 159, 178
Gray, Barbara, 66, 305, 321
Greene, Ronald, 53, 66
Grunig, James, 332–334, 353
Gudykunst, W.B., 209
Gupta, Vipin, 60, 66

H

Habermas, Jurgen, 94
Hackman, Michael, 5, 26, 119, 133, 192, 208, 222, 230, 244, 248, 249
Hain, T., 177
Hair, J., 353
Hall, B., 26, 177
Hall, Douglas, 398, 408
Hall, Jay, 295, 321
Hamel, Stephanie, 374, 382
Hammer, Michael, 249
Hanges, Paul, 60, 66
Hanke, Ralph, 305, 321
Hardy, C., 66, 68, 99, 100
Harris, Philip, 178, 228, 249
Harris, Thomas, L., 336, 341, 353
Hart, Joy, 166, 177
Hart, Z., 66
Hatfield, John, 153, 178
Hawken, P., 119, 133
Hazen, M.D., 177
Heath, R.G., 208, 352
Heifetz, Ronald, 225, 249
Heilbrunn, J., 353
Hellweg, Susan, 179
Henderson, B.D., 353
Hersey, Paul, 220, 221, 249
Herzberg, Frederick, 143–146, 178
Hesselbein, F., 249
Hirokawa, R., 281
Hochschild, Arlie, 288, 321
Hocker, Joyce, 299, 302, 321
Holmes, Susan, 162, 177
Horsley, J. Suzanne, 336, 353
House, Robert, 60, 61, 66
Howe, Maynard, 108, 133
Howe, Roger, 108, 133
Howell, W.S., 133
Hubbell, Anne, 287, 321
Hulin, C.L., 179
Hunt, Marilyn, 151, 180
Hurson, K., 229, 249
Huseman, Richard, 153, 178
Hwang, Jennie, 153, 178

I

Ibarra, Herminia, 230, 249
Iverson, Joel, 191, 208

J

Jablin, Fred, 6, 26, 66, 67, 68, 100,
177, 178, 179, 248, 281, 282,
322, 352
Jabusch, David, 6, 7, 26
Jackson, Michele, 200, 209, 254, 281
Janis, Irving, 306, 321
Jassawalla, Avan, 198, 208
Javidan, Mansour, 60, 66
Jehn, Karen, 197, 208
Johannesen, Richard, 104, 113, 133
Johnson, Craig, 5, 26, 119, 124,
125, 133, 134, 192, 208, 222,
244, 248
Johnson, Dick, 413
Johnson, Spencer, 357, 382
Johnston, William, 161, 178
Johnstone, Christopher Lyle, 115, 134
Jokisaari, Markku, 153, 178
Jones, Tricia, 302, 321
Joyce, William, 359, 383
Jugenheimer, Donald, 342, 353
Jung, Doug, 228, 249

K

Kahn, Robert, 67, 82, 84, 85, 100,
265, 281
Kanter, Rosabeth Moss,
228, 229, 249
Kärreman, D., 224, 248
Katz, Daniel, 67, 82, 84, 85, 100
Katzenbach, Jon, 186, 209
Keller, Paul, 115, 134, 313, 314, 321
Keller, Robert, 185, 209
Kellerher, D., 249
Kellerman, R., 249
Kendall, L.M., 179
Kennedy, Allen, 88, 89, 100,
105, 133, 246
Kennedy, G., 26
Ketrow, Sandra, 161, 781
Kilduff, M., 100
Kilmann, R.H., 100
Killmann Robert, 322
King, Sarah, 66, 229, 248
Klastorin, T.D., 185, 208
Knopoff, K., 322
Koesten, J., 289, 322
Kolb, Deborah, 315, 322
Kosmicki, Richard, 335, 353
Kotler, Philip, 340, 342, 353
Kotter, John, 246, 249, 353, 365, 382

Kouzes, James, 134, 226, 249
Kramer, Michael, 361, 382
Kreps, Gary, 315, 321
Krivonos, Paul, 152, 178
Krone, Kathleen, 152, 178, 240,
241, 248, 303, 322
Kuhn, Timothy 59, 67, 254, 281,
304, 321, 382

L

LaFasto, Frank, 184, 209, 240,
242, 249
Lamb, C., 353
Lammers, John, 58–60, 67
Larson, Carl, 184, 209, 240 249
Laubacher, Timothy, 342, 352
Lauterborn, R., 343, 353
Lawler, Edward, 328, 353
Lawrence, Paul, 82, 84, 100
Lee, Gus, 134
Lee, Jaesub, 151, 178, 213, 249
Lemus, Daisy, 366, 383
Lencioni, Patrick, 105, 134
Lengel, L., 178
Lengel, Robert, 276, 281
Leonardi, Paul, 200, 209, 362, 382
Leslie, Jean Brittain, 227, 249
Level, D.A., 67
Lewicki, Roy, 305, 321
Lewis, Laurie, 360, 365, 366,
374, 382
Likert, Rensis, 78–81, 100
Lindzey, Gardner, 108, 133
Lippitt, Gordon, 134
Lippitt, Ronald, 134, 216, 249
Littlejohn, Stephen, 6, 7, 26, 29,
47, 67, 197, 209
Lorenzi, Peter, 223, 228, 229, 249
Lorsch, Jay, 82, 84, 100
Louis, M.R., 67
Lowy, A., 249
Lukaszewski, James, 339, 353
Lumsden, Donald, 261, 262, 281
Lumsden, Gay, 261, 262, 281
Lyotard, Jean-François, 93, 100

M

Maitlis, Sally, 164, 178
Makau, Josina M., 115, 134
Mani, Sirish, 152, 178
Manz, Charles, 223, 249
March, James, 82, 100, 260, 281
Markham, S., 177
Marshall, Alicia, 213, 249
Marshall, Judi, 57, 67
Martin, Joanne, 88, 90, 100, 322

Maslow, Abraham, 141–146, 178
Mathews, J.A., 408
Matsaganis, Matthew, 201, 209
Maturana, Humberto, 85
Mayer, M., 133, 209
Mayo, Elton, 77, 78, 81, 100
McCabe, D., 112, 134
McCann, R.M., 178
McCroskey, James, 147, 177,
178, 179
McDaniel, C., 353
McGregor, Douglas, 78, 81, 100
McLaughlin, M., 178
McNeill, 179
McPhee, Robert, 47, 53, 54, 67, 68,
191, 208
Medved, Caryn, 287, 321
Mehra, A., 100
Metcalf, H.C., 100
Miles, E., 153, 178
Miles, G., 408
Miles, Raymond, 400, 401, 408
Miller, Barbara, 336, 353
Miller, Katherine, 15, 26, 67, 163,
179, 288, 289, 322
Miller, Vernon, 66
Milliken, Frances, 258, 281, 360, 283
Mindell, Mark, 108, 133
Mintzberg, Henry, 67, 331, 353
Mlodzik, Paul, 343, 353
Moberg, D., 113, 133
Moffitt, M.A., 353
Monge, Peter, 67, 157, 159, 178, 179,
201, 209
Montgomery, C.A., 353
Moran, Robert, 178, 228, 249
Morgan, Gareth, 82, 85, 86, 100
Morley, Don, 67, 68, 134, 179
Morreale, Sherwyn, 6, 26, 230,
249, 347
Morris, J.H., 180, 322
Morrison, Elizabeth, 258, 281,
360, 383
Mouton, Jane, 217, 220, 248,
295, 321
Mulvey, Paul W., 193, 209
Mumby, Dennis, 55, 56, 67, 303, 322
Musselwhite, E., 229, 249
Myers, Karen, 366, 383

N

Nanus, Burt, 133, 213, 225, 226,
230, 232, 233, 246, 248, 321
Napier, R.W., 209
Neale, Margaret, 197, 208
Nichols, Ralph, 170, 179

Nicotera, Anne, 53, 66, 67, 68
Nilsen, Thomas, 115, 134
Nohria, Nitin, 359, 383
Nord, W.R., 66, 68, 99, 100
Northcraft, Gregory, 197, 208
Novak, Julie, 116, 118, 134
Nurmi, Jari-erik, 153, 178
Nutt, Paul, 257, 281

O

Obodaru, Otilia, 230, 249
Obstfeld, David, 53, 66
Oetzel, J., 209
O'Donnell-Trujillo, Nick, 67
O'Reilly, C., 179

P

Pace, R. Wayne, 179, 353, 383,
    389, 408
Pacnowsky, Michael, 67, 68, 282
Page, D., 359, 383
Palmer, David, 105, 134
Panteli, Niki, 164, 178
Papa, Michael, 325, 352
Park, Hee Sun, 202, 208
Parker, David, 416, 417
Parker, Patricia, 240, 241, 248
Pasmore, W.A., 100
Patton, B., 315, 321
Pearson, Christine, 287, 321
Pearson, Judy, 179
Pedersen, Douglas, 259, 282
Pérez, F., 209
Pelz, Donald, 151, 179
Pepper, Gerald, 15, 26, 67, 309,
    311, 322
Peppers, L., 249
Perrin, C., 229, 249
Perry, Tara, 156, 179
Peters, Thomas, 89, 100
Petrie, C., 408
Pfeffer, Jeffrey, 141, 144–146, 179
Phillips, Gerald, 259, 282
Pierce, Tamyra, 361, 382
Pincus, J. David, 138, 179
Pink, Daniel, 3, 26
Plamondon, Ann, 118, 134
Polok, Nina, 378
Pondy, Louis, 289, 322
Poole, Marshall Scott, 47, 66, 67,
    188, 209, 277, 281, 299, 302,
    304, 316, 321, 322
Porter, L., 67, 68, 177, 178, 179, 322
Porter, M.E., 353
Porter, R., 177
Postman, I., 65

Posner, Barry, 134, 226, 249
Putnam, Linda, 53, 66, 67, 68, 100,
    177, 179, 248, 281, 282 303,
    305, 315, 321, 322, 352

Q

Quinn, Laura, 130, 132

R

Ramanujam, R., 68
Raven, Bertram, 237, 248
Ray, E., 179
Read, W., 179
Real, K., 209
Redding, W. Charles, 68, 116, 134
Reynolds, B., 337, 349, 350, 353
Rhode, D., 249
Rice, Ronald, 276, 281
Richardson, Bill, 328, 353
Richardson, Brian, 374, 382
Richetto, G.M., 179
Richmond, Virginia, 147, 179
Riley, Patricia, 66, 68, 153
Rischard, J.F., 2, 26
Roberson, Bruce, 359, 383
Roberts, K., 67, 68, 177, 179, 322
Roethlisberger, F.J., 100
Robinson, William, 240, 242, 249
Rogers, D., 408
Rogers, E., 68
Rogers, Edna, 186, 208
Rokeach, Milton, 104, 108,
    110, 134
Rost, K., 281
Ruben, Brent, 178, 179, 292, 322
Rubin, R., 134
Ruppel, Erin, 257, 281
Russell, Hamish, 157, 178
Ryan, J., 249

S

Saffer, Adam, 348
Saffir, Leonard, 333, 353
Salancik, Gerald, 141, 144–146, 179
Sample, Steven, 239, 249
Samovar, L., 177, 178, 179
Sarr, Robert, 242, 248
Sashittal, Hermant, 198, 208
Saxon, M.J., 100
Schein, Edgar, 68, 100, 353, 408
Schmidt, W., 134, 249, 322
Schön, Donald, 86
Schultz, D.E., 343, 353
Scott, Craig, 165, 201, 209
Scott, C.W., 179, 336, 353
Scott, Marshall, 179, 188

Seeger, Matthew, 116, 118, 134
    337, 339, 354
Seibold, David, 47, 67, 165, 180, 202,
    208, 366, 383
Seinfeld, Emily, 199, 208
Sellnow, Timothy, 116, 118, 134
Senge, Peter, 82, 86, 100, 354,
    364, 383
Sereno, K.K., 248
Serpa, R., 100
Shah, Priti, 159
Shanley, M., 353
Sheahan, M.F., 179
Sheats, Paul, 195, 208
Sherwood, J.J., 100
Shockley-Zalabak, P., 67, 68, 134,
    162, 178, 179, 213, 230, 248,
    249, 322
Shumate, Michelle, 201, 209
Sias, Patricia, 6, 26, 152, 155, 156,
    179, 208
Simon, Herbert, 82, 83, 100,
    260, 282
Sims, Henry, 223, 228, 229, 249
Sitkin, S.B., 53, 66
Skaret, D.J., 249
Skinner, B.F., 144–146, 179
Smircich, Linda, 68, 95, 99, 100
Smith, Adam, 100
Smith, A.F., 179
Smith, Douglas, 186, 209
Smith, P.C., 179
Smith, T., 66
Snavely, W.B., 179, 249
Snow, Charles, 400, 401, 408
Snyder, R.A., 180
Snyder, W.M., 209
Soares, E.J., 249
Spiker, Barry, 325, 352
Spitzberg, Brian, 312, 321, 322
Srivastva, Suresh, 368, 382
Stanton, Peter, 338, 354
Stephens, Keri, 277, 282
Stevens, L., 170, 179
Stewart, Lea, 134, 161, 180
Stewart, J., 321
Stocker, K.P., 354
Stogdill, R.M., 249
Stohl, Cynthia, 68, 157, 180,
    213, 249
Straw, B.M., 68
Strubler, David, 106, 134
Stutman, Randall, 299, 302, 316, 321
Sutcliffe, Kathleen, 53, 66
Swol, Lyn Van, 199
Sypher, Beverly Davenport, 155, 180

T

Tangirala, S., 68
Tannenbaum, R., 249
Tannenbaum, S., 343, 353
Taylor, Frederick, 72, 75, 79, 100
Taylor, James, 54, 68
Thatcher, Sherry, 165, 180
Thomas, D., 209
Thomas, Kenneth, 295, 298, 322
Thompson, E., 408
Thompson, Leigh, 198, 209
Thornton, Barbara, 315, 321
Timmerman, C. Erik, 165, 179, 201, 209
Toffler, Alvin, 228, 249
Toffler, H., 249
Tolbert, Pamela, 59, 68
Tompkins, Phillip, 67, 68, 180, 186, 208, 253, 282
Tracy, Karen, 29, 66
Tracy, Sarah, 287, 322
Treem, Jeffrey, 200, 209
Trethewey, Angela, 287, 322, 336, 353
Trist, Eric, 82, 83, 100

U

Ullmann, W. R., 248
Ulmer, Robert, 116, 118, 134, 337, 354

Urwick, L., 100
Ury, W., 315, 321

V

Van Maanen, J., 68
Valluzzi, Janet, 185, 208
Van Velsor, E., 227, 249
Van Swol, L., 209
Varela, Francisco, 85
Veiga, John, 105, 134, 193, 209
Velasquez, M., 113, 133
Velsor, Ellen Van, 227
Vernon, Philip, 108, 133
Villamaria, F., 209
Vora, Jay, 105, 134

W

Waagen, Christopher, 159, 180, 354, 408
Waldeck, Jennifer, 165, 180
Waldron, Vincent, 151, 180, 303, 322
Walker, Kasey, 166, 177
Wallace, Karl, 117, 134
Walters, E.V., 249
Walther, Joseph, 200, 209
Waterman, Robert, 89, 100
Weber, Max, 72, 74–76, 78, 100
Weick, Karl, 42, 43, 52–54, 68, 86, 91, 92, 100, 352

Wenger, F.C., 209
Wheatley, Margaret, 82, 85, 86, 100, 249
White, Ralph, 216, 249
Wiethoff, Carolyn, 305, 321
Wilmot, William, 299, 302, 321
Wilmott, H., 99
Wilson, Gerald, 159, 180, 354, 408
Wilson, Jane, 430
Wood, Julia, 259, 282
Woodward, Joan, 82, 83, 100
Wright, David, 184, 186, 203, 208

Y

Yoder, J., 134
Young, Kathryn, 259, 282
Yuan, Yu, 201, 209
Yuhas Byers, P., 134

Z

Zaccaro, S.J., 248
Zander, A., 208
Zaug, Pamela, 53, 54, 67
Zellmer-Bruhn, Mary, 197
Zenger, John, 229, 249
Ziegler, J., 68
Zhu, Xiumei, 165, 180
Ziegler, Jennifer, 47
Zorn, T.E., Jr., 155, 180, 359, 383
Zucker, Lynne, 59, 68

SUBJECT INDEX

A

Activities. *See* Workshops.
Active listening, 170–172
Active resistance, 362–363
Advertising, 342
Appreciative inquiry (AI), 368
Apprehension, communication, 147
Arbitration, 307
Autocratic leader, 216
Autocratic strategy(ies), 231
Autopoeisis, 85

B

Bargaining, 307
Barriers for change in organization
  active and passive resistance, 362–363
  complacency, 360
  contradictions and misalignments, 362
  knowledge/information deficits, 361
  leaders, 363
  organizational decline
    stages, 363
  organizational silence,
    360–361
  risk perception, 361
  trust and, 363
  uncertainty, 361–362
Blake and Mouton Managerial
    Grid®, 217
Bona fide groups, 184, 190–191
Brainstorming defined, 260
Branding, 343
Bullying, 156
Burnout
  concept of, 288
  emotional labor and work, 289
  for human service workers, 289

C

CCO, 52–54
Careers
  choices in organizational
      communication
    consulting careers, 395
    education, 393–394
    educational preparation for,
      396–397
    entrepreneurs, 399

external communications
    careers, 392
  human service careers, 393
  internal communication careers,
    391, 392
  management, 394–395
  options in, 390–391
  preprofessional and combination
    options, 395
  research and information
    management, 394
  sales careers, 393
  and technology, 395–396
employment matching
    knowledge, 386–387
    sensitivity, 387–388
    skills, 388
    values, 388
in education
    curriculum design, 393
    educational administrators,
      393–394
    job responsibilities, 393
    professional certification, 393–394
in twenty-first century
    boundaryless career, 399
    cellular organization, 400–401
    forms and career skills, 399–400
    networked organization, 400
    old and new career paradigms,
      397–398
    protean careers, 398
    team-based careers, 401
Climates, supportive, 313–315
Change, organizational
  barriers
    active and passive resistance, 362
    complacency, 360
    contradictions and
      misalignments, 362
    knowledge or information
      deficits, 361
    leaders, 363
    organizational silence, 360
    risk perceptions, 361
    trust, 363
    uncertainty, 361
  defined, 356

decline, 363
excellence, 359–360
leadership of, 364
models of, 365–368
pace of, 357–359
Choice making, 115
Clients, 157
Coaching, 243
Coercive power defined, 238
Communication(s)
  competency, 5, 7–8
    communication skills, 7
    definition of, 6
    and ecological model, 6
    ethical responsibility, 7
    interpersonal sensitivity, 7
    process understanding, 7
    constitutive process, 52
  contribution to organizational
      knowledge, 213
  era, 2
    characteristics of, 3
    conceptual age, 3
    convergence, 4
    information society, 3
    workers in, 4
  flows, 53
    flows should be back spaced to be
      even with era and organizational
      excellence
  organizational excellence, 4–5
  relationships
    between managers and
      employees, 213
Communication strategy, 374–375
Communications technology
  asynchronous, 276
  GDSS, 277
  organization, in, 275–278
  preparation for, 278
  synchronous, 276
    synchronous should be back
      spaced to be even with
      organization and GDSS
Communities of practice (CoPs)
  description, 190–191
  processes of, 191
  professionals., 191

Competency(ies)
defined, 360
development through
knowledge competency,
181–182, 211
sensitivity, 181–182
skills, 181–182, 211
values, 181–182, 211
Complaint interview, 267
Concepts of organizations, 15–16
Conceptual age, 3
Conflict
causes of
change, 286
dealing with difficult people, 287
deception within organizations, 288
decision making, 287
diversity of workforce, 287
incivility in workplace, 287
irrationality, 287
scarce resources, 286
technologies, 286
communication tactics in, 299–302
contexts, 285–286
customers and vendors, 308–309
defined, 285
emotion during, 302–303
episodes, 289–291
grid, 296
management processes
arbitration, 307
bargaining, 307
negotiation, 306, 315
mediation, 307
outcomes, 292
power, 307
productive/destructive outcomes, 286
productive guidelines, 316–319
stages
aftermath, 289
felt, 289
latent, 289–290
manifest, 289
perceived, 289
Congruence in organizations,
118–120
Connection power defined, 238–239
Consensus decision, organization
in, 257
Contingency theory, 83–84, 219–222
Convergence, 4
Counseling interview, 267
Country club management, 218
Crisis communication, 336–337
plans, 338
principles, 339–340

Seeger's findings, 339
stages
containment, 338
detection, 338
prevention/preparation, 338
recovery and learning, 338
Critical theory, 94
communication implications in
organizations, 96
Cultural intelligence, 166
Customers, 157, 308–309

D

Deception within organizations, 288
Decision making
barriers to effective
interpersonal barriers, 258–259
organizational barriers, 257–258
task and procedural barriers, 258
definition of, 252–253
increasing effectiveness in
criteria for providing information,
262–263
fact-finding and evaluation
skills, 262
interaction process skills,
261–262
influences of
communication competency,
254–255
culture in organization,
253–254
decision and problem issue, 254
technical competency, 255
methods for
consensus among members, 257
individual approaches, 255–256
majority rule, 256
mandate of leader, 256
powerful minority, 256
Decision-making approaches, 82
Democratic leader, 216
Development and change
communicating
about change, 374
plan, 375
data collection
auditing, 368–369
cost analysis, 369
interviews, 369
performance data, 369
questionnaires, 368–369
data evaluation
cost analysis, 370–371
evaluating results, 373
leadership of, 364

models for
organizational transformation
processes, 365
diffusion of innovation, 365
stakeholder theory, 366
purchase, 367
doctor-patient, 367
process, 367
planning and implementing
advising and counseling activities,
372–373
behavioral change, 371
policy, 372
process changes, 372
structural change, 371
technological change, 371
training and development
activities, 372
Diffusion of innovation, 367
Directional groups, 186–187
cross-functional teams, 187
executive leadership
teams, 187
failure, 187
Direct marketing, 342
Discrimination
and job postings, 310
marginalized people, 311
subtle, 311
Discourses, 224–225
Discursive approach of leaders,
224–225
Dispersed leadership, 223
Diversity of workforce, 287
and interpersonal relationships, 161
valuing, 167
barriers and positive approaches to,
167–170
groups, 197
Doctor–patient model, 367

E

Emerging perspectives for
organizational communication
CCO, 52–54
critical theory, 55–56
essential issues, 62
feminist and race perspectives,
56–58
feminist and race theory, 52
global cultures, 60–61
institutions, 58–60
postmodernism, 54–55
technologies, 61
Emotional labor, 288
Employment interview, 266

Employment matching
  knowledge for
    general knowledge, 387
    human resource development,
      386–387
  sensitivity for, 388
    self-awareness, 387
  skills for
    technical qualifications, 388
  values for
    cultures, 389
    organizations, 389
    socioeconomic goals, 388
Environments for strategic
    communication
  globalization, 327
  publics, multiple, 328
  scanning
    global environment, 330
Ethical abuses, 311
Ethical leadership defined, 240
Ethical responsibility, 7
Ethics in organizational communication
  abuse, 112
  behavior evaluating, 116–117, 315
  conundrums, 118–120
  defining, 112–113, 114–115
  ethical dilemmas and
    behaviors and technology, 122–124
    behaviors related to money, 121
    courage, responsibility and
      trust, 126
    destructive behaviors, 124–125
    developing standards, 126–130
    personal behaviors, 122–123
    planned organizational, 125–126
    skills and abilities representing,
      120–121
  influences for, 116
  making decisions, 113–114
  making ethical decisions, 113–114
Exosystem, 6
External communications careers
  responsibilities, 392
  specialists, 392

F

Fear conflict, 292
Felt conflict, 290–291
Feminist organization theories, 95–96
  communication implications of, 96
Focus groups, 189
  advertising and marketing
    organizations, 189
  description, 189
  members, 189

Formal organization, 183
Framing, 304–305
Functional tradition
  change functions, 35
  characteristics, 41
  communication
    channels, 37–38
    inputs, 31
    load, 39–40
    networks, 36–37
    output, 32
    throughput, 32
  component parts, 31
  message
    direction, 38–39
    distortion, 40
    functions, 33–34
    structure, 35–36
  open and closed systems, 32–33
  organizing functions, 34
  relationship functions, 34–35

G

Geographically diverse teams, 190
  communication, 190
  face-to-face meeting, 190
  issues, 190
Global financial crisis, 208, 229
Group communication, 14
Group conflict, 303-309
Group(s)
  contribution of, 183
  definition of, 183
  influence by members, 184
  knowledge competencies, 182
  norms and communication roles,
    195–196
    description, 195
    maintenance, 195
    predispositions, 195
    self-centered, 195–196
    task, 195
  participation effectiveness
    negative behaviors, 202
    positive behaviors, 203
  peer relationships, 182
  processes
    democracy in workplace, 194
    group norms and communication
      roles, 194–196
    norms and communication roles,
      194–196
    workplace democracy, 194
  regular meeting of, 183
  sensitivity competencies, 182
  skills and values, 182

small-group experiences
  definitions, 183
  formally structured, 183
  informal, 183
  shared realities, 183
team-based
  competitive positioning, 191
  corporations, 192
  goals, roles, relationships, and
    processes, 192
  high-reliability, 193–194
  self-directed work team, 193
  self-limiting behavior, 193
  skills, 192–193
  teamwork, 191
types, 183
  bona fide, 184
  communities of practice (CoPs),
    190–191
  directional groups, 186–187
  focus groups, 189
  geographically diverse teams, 190
  pre-fab group, 186
  primary work teams, 184–186
  project teams, 185
  quality teams, 187–188
  self-managing teams, 186
  social support groups, 190
  steering committees, 189
  task force, 188–189
working in, 196
  creativity and collaboration,
    198–199
  diverse, 197–198
  and technology use, 201–202
  virtual groups, 199–201
Groupthink, 306
Group support systems (GSSs), 276

H

Hawthorne effect, 77–78
Hersey and Blanchard concept of
    situational leadership, 221
High-reliability organizations,
    193–194
  groups/teams, 193
  missed information, 193
  success, 193
High-speed management theory, 229,
    357
Human behavior perspective, 76
  communication implications in
    organizations, 81–82
  Hawthorne effect, 77–78
  Likert's linking pin concept, 80
  in organizations, 81–82

Human behavior
    perspective, (*continued*)
  participative management, 78–80
  Theory X and Theory Y, 78–79
Human communication process, 9
  channel, 11–12
  competence, 10, 12
  construction of shared realities, 14
  context, 13
  defined, 10
  effect, 13–14
  encoding/decoding, 11
  experiences, 10
  field of experience, 12–13
  messages, 11
  noise, 12
  source/receiver, 10–11
Human service careers, 393

I

Identification, 42, 44–45
Identity, 42, 44–45
IMC. *See* Integrated marketing
    communications (IMC)
Implications for communication of
    organizational theories
  critical theory, 94
  feminist organization theories,
    95–96
Impoverished management, 217–218
Incivility in workplace, 287
Individual in organizational conflict
  orientations/predispositions/styles
    accommodation, 297–298
    avoidance style, 295–296
    collaboration, 298
    communication tactics in, 299–302
    competition, 296–297
    compromise, 297
    emotion during, 302–303
    strategic objectives, 298–299
    tactics, 299–302
Individuals in organizations, 138
  challenges for, 2
  primary communication
    experiences, 139
Individual value system, 107–108
  approaches, 110
Informal group(s), 183
Informal organization, 183
Informational interview, 264–266
Informational presentations, 272
Information power defined, 238
Information society, 3
Innovation-decision process, 366
Instrumental values, 108

Integrated marketing communications
    (IMC), 341
Integrated perspectives viewpoints
  communication implications in
    organizations, 92–93
  cultural approaches
    culture formation, 87
    fragmentation perspective, 90–91
    sensemaking model, 91–92
    strong culture perspective, 88–89
    subculture perspective, 90
  in organizations, 92–93
  process and environmental
    approaches
    bounded rationality, 82–83
    contingency theory, 83–84
    decision-making, 82–83
    learning organizations, 86
    sociotechnical integration, 83
    systems approach, 84–86
  Senge's five disciplines, 86
Internal communication careers
  responsibilities, 391
  specialists, 392
Interpersonal relationships, 148
  active listening
    myths and barriers, 170–172
  communication, 14
    links, 160
  and communication networks, 157
  cultural intelligence, 166
  customers, clients, and vendors, 157
  descriptive messages, 172–174
  and diversity, 161–162
  guidelines for good listening, 172
  message ownership tactics, 173
  peer relationships, 154–156
  supervisors and employees,
    150–151
  technology and, 164–166
  trust and, 162–163
  valuing diversity, 167
    barriers and positive approaches,
      167–169
    mindful and proactive
      interactions, 170
Interpersonal sensitivity, 7
Interviews
  increasing effectiveness, 268–269
    complaint, 267
    counseling, 267
    employment, 266
    informational, 264–266
    media, 268
    performance appraisal, 266–267
Intrapersonal experiences, 139

communication and motivation
    relating
  worker examples, 146
communication apprehension
    (CA), 147
competency, 148
hierarchy of needs theory, 141
  Maslow's, need levels in,
    142–143
leadership and conflict
  preferences, 147
motivation, 140–141
motivation–hygiene theory,
  143–144
organizational communication
  behaviors predisposition, 146
  apprehension, 147
  personal motivation, 146
  relating communication and
    motivation, 145–146
  rewards theory, 144
  social information processing
    theory, 144–145
Irrationality, 287
Issues management, seven-step
    model, 335

K

Knowledge competencies, 7–8,
    181–182, 211

L

Laissez-faire leader, 216–217
Latent conflict, 289–290
Leader-made decision, organization
    in, 256
Leader–Member Exchange (LMX)
    theory, 151
Leader(s)
  challenges before, 230
  and leadership of development and
    change
    interdependency of world, 364
    public relations and
      marketing, 364
Leadership communication in
    organization, 212–213
  approaches in
    discursive, 224–225
    situational, 219–222
    style, 216–219
    trait, 215–216
    transformational, 222–223
  challenges
    change in organization forms,
      227–228

global and multicultural
changes, 228
Leadership communication in
organization (*continued*)
excellence in leadership
defined, 240
high-speed management, 229
inclusive-participation
processes, 229
trust building, 229–230
communication tactics for, 235–237
definition of, 212
distinctions between leadership and
management, 225–227
effectiveness determinants
communication tactics, 234–237
competency in communication,
230–231
power bases for leaders, 234–239
predispositions for leadership
communication, 231
situational analysis for
leadership, 239
strategic communication
objectives, 231–234
experience of, 215
importance of, 212–213
increasing effectiveness, 239
constructive communication
behaviors, 242–243
ethical leadership, 240
excellent leadership, 240
principled leadership, 240
and management communication in
organization, 225–227
principles of, 229
tactics
definition of, 234
theories of, 213–215
trust in individuals, 213
Legitimate power defined, 238
Locus of control defined, 108–109
Low-quality leader–member
exchanges, 213

M

Macrosystem, 6
Majority rule decision, organization
in, 256
Management communication in
organization
importance of, 212–213
and leadership communication, in
organization, 225–227
strategic communication, 320–332
trust in individuals, 213

Manifest conflict, 291
Marketing mix
four Ps
place, 341
pricing, 341
product, 341
promotion, 341–342
Meaning-centered approach
characteristics, 51
communication, 46
as culture, 49–50
as influence, 44
structurational theory, 47–48
tactical rules, 47
thematic rules, 47
and decision making, 41, 44
communication cycles, 43
organizational environments,
creation/enactment, 42
organizational rules, 42–43
supervisors, 43
identification, 44–45
as influence, 44
key assumptions, 42
power, 48
socialization, 45–46
Media interview, 268
Media relations, 335–336
Media richness theory, 276
Mediation, 307
Mesosystem, 6
Messages
descriptive 172–173
encoding/decoding, 11
sources and receivers, 10
Microsystem, 6
Middle-of-the-road management, 218
Mobbing, 156
Motivation–hygiene theory,
143–144

N

Negotiation, 306–307
Networks
and interpersonal relationships,
36–37,157
boundary spanning, 158, 160
bridges, 158, 160
gatekeepers, 158, 160
isolates, 158, 160
liaisons, 158, 160
non-participants, 159
participants, 159
reciprocity, 158
roles, 159
strength, 158

symmetrical links, 158
weak ties, 159

O

Organizational change, 356–357
Organizational communication, 14
defined, 16
as meaning, 17
as messages, 17
as people, 16–17
as process, 16
as purpose, 17–18
Organizational communication,
career choices, 389
consulting careers, 395
in education, 393–394
educational preparation for,
396–397
external communications careers
responsibilities, 392
human service careers, 393
internal communication careers, 392
responsibilities, 391
management, 394–395
options in, 390–391
preprofessional and combination
options, 395
research and information
management, 394
sales careers, 393
and technology, 395–396
Organizational communication,
perspectives
emerging perspectives for, 51
communication constitutes
organizations (CCO), 52–54
critical theory, 55–56
essential issues, 62
feminist and race perspectives,
56–58
feminist and race theory, 52
global cultures, 60–61
institutions, 58–60
postmodernism, 54–55
technologies, 61
functional tradition, 30
change functions, 35
channels, 37–38
characteristics, 41
component parts, 31
inputs, 31
load, 39–40
message direction, 38–39
message distortion, 40
message functions, 33–34
message structure, 35–36

Organizational communication,
  perspectives (*continued*)
  networks, 36–37
  open and closed systems, 32–33
  organizing functions, 34
  output, 32
  relationship functions, 34–35
  throughput, 32
 meaning-centered approach
  characteristics, 51
  communication as culture, 49–50
  communication rules, 46–48
  and decision making, 41–44
  identification, 44–45
  as influence, 44
  key assumptions of, 42
  power, 48
  socialization, 45–46
 problems, analyzing, 63
Organizational conflict
 certainty and provisionalism, 314
 control and problem orientation,
   313–314
 ethical communication behaviors, 315
 evaluation and problem
   description, 313
 feminist alternative, 315–316
 groups in, 303
  with customers and vendors,
    308–309
  framing and sensemaking,
    304–305
  groupthink, 306
  interpersonal issues, 305–306
  management processes, 306–307
  members, 304
  power and, 307–308
  procedural conflict, 305
  substantive issues, 306
 neutrality and empathy, 314
 principled negotiation, 315
 productively engaging in, 312
  problem-solving environment, 313
  supportive climates, 313
 strategy and spontaneity, 314
 superiority and equality, 314
Organizational development, 364
Organizational excellence, 4–5
 developing and sustaining, 359
Organizational silence, 360–361
Organization(s)
 communications technology in,
   275–278
 formation of groups, 183
 high-reliability, 193–194
 individuals in, 182

interviews in, 266–267
leadership communication, 214
life in, 182
management communication,
  225–227
participating in, 250
presentation in, 269–271
team-based, 191–193
types of
 formal organization, 183
 informal organization, 183
and work, 1–2

P

Passive resistance, 362–363
Peer relationships, 154–156, 182
"Pelz effect," 151
Perceived conflict, 290
Performance appraisal interview,
  266–267
Persuasive presentations, 272–273
Postmodern perspectives, 93–94
 communication implications in
   organizations, 96
Powerful minority decision
 organization, in, 256
Practical theory, 29, 63
Presentations in organizations,
  269–271
 increasing effectiveness
  audience and context analysis, 274
  handling participation, 275
  increasing credibility, 273–274
  material preparation, 274
  preparation for presenting, 275
 types of
  informational presentations, 272
  persuasive presentations, 272–273
  training/educational
    presentations, 271
Primary work teams, 184–186
 effective, 184
 long-standing
  government, 185
  organizational responsibilities,
    184–185
  university departments, 185
 members features, 184
 project
  cross-functional, 185
  high-technology industries, 185
  members, 185
  prefab group, 186
 self-managing
  characterization, 186
  defined, 186

individual performance, 186
size and formality, 184
Principled leadership defined, 240
Problem-solving approach
 barriers to effective
  interpersonal barriers, 258–259
  organizational barriers, 257–258
  task and procedural barriers, 258
 definition of, 252–253
 effectiveness, 306
 groups, 183
 influences of
  communication competency,
    254–255
  culture in organization, 253–254
  decision and problem issue, 254
  technical competency, 255
 methods for
  consensus among members, 257
  individual approaches, 255–256
  majority rule, 256
  mandate of leader, 256
  powerful minority, 256
 process of
  brainstorming, 260
  experientially based, 260–261
  standard agenda, 259–260
Process model, 367
Process understanding, 7
Productive conflict guidelines, 316
 process for, 317
  choices for action, 318
  committing to solutions, 318
  defining, 317–318
  monitoring, 318–319
  self-analysis of the issues, 317
  solutions developing, 318
  work on problem, 317
Public affairs, 335
Public/mass media communication, 14
Public relations (PR)
 defined, 332
 practitioners, 333
 superficial symbolism, 334
Publics defined, 328
Purchase model, 367

Q

Quality teams, 187–188
 description, 187–188, 188
 use, 188

R

Referent power
 definition of, 238
Relationship marketing, 343–344

Reward power defined, 238
Rewards theory, 144
Risk communication, 336
  defined, 337
  plans, 338

S

Sales careers, 393
Scientific management school
  bureaucracy principles
    authority, 74
    depersonalization and task
      competence, 74
    Weber's ideal bureaucracy, 75
  communication implications in
    organizations, 75–76
  management principles
    authority with, 73
    equity, 73
    Fayol's bridge, 73
    Fayol's principle of unity of
      command, 73
    scalar chain, 73
  principles and basic activities, 72
  scientific management
    theories in contemporary
      organizations, 75–76
  time and motion, 72
Self-actualization, 141–142
Self-assessments
  career planning self-analysis,
    402–407
  individual values appraisal,
    109–111
  personal profile of conflict
    predispositions, strategies, and
    tactics, 293–294
  self-assessment of personal
    development
    needs, 18–23, 410–412
Sensemaking model, 91–92
Sensitivity competency, 8,
    181–182, 211
Sexual harassment
  conflict-producing abuse, 309
  destructive workplace process, 309
  documented, 310
  impacts, 309–310
  nonverbal behaviors, 310
  workplace relationship and, 310
Shared realities, 14
Situational approach
  Blanchard concept of, 221
  Hersey concept of, 221
  leadership, for, 219–222
Skills competency, 8, 181–182, 211

Small-group experiences
  definition of, 182
Social information processing theory,
    144–145
Social judgment, 109
Social media, 344
Social support groups, 190
  membership, 190
  responsibilities, 190
Staff meetings, 181
Stakeholders
  defined, 326–327
  theory, 366–367
Standard agenda
  meaning of, 259
  phases in
    diagnostic, 259–260
    solution, 260
Steering committees, 189
Strategic management
  communication, 332
  competitive/positioning
    strategy, 331
  defined, 330
  SWOT model, 330
    phases, 331
Strategic organizational communication
  advertising, 342–343
  branding, 343
  characteristics, 332
  databases, 343–344
  defined, 325
  employee inclusion/exclusion, 334
  ethical issues in, 345–346
  evaluating, 345
  image/reputation managing,
    333–334
  IMC, 341
  internal communications, 334
  management, strategic, 320–332
  marketing mix
    four Ps, 341–342
  marketing planning, 340–341
  media relations, 335–336
  perspectives on
    corporate downsizing and
      reengineering, 327
    environmental factors, 327
    environmental scanning, 329
    global factors, 330
    interdepartmental
      communication, 327
    outside-in planning, 326–327
    publics, multiple, 328
    stakeholders role, 326–327
    vendor communication, 327

public affairs and issues
  management, 335
public relations, 332
relationship marketing, 343–344
risk and crisis communication,
  336–339
social media, 334
technology and
  social media, 344
Strengths, weaknesses, opportunities,
  and threats (SWOT) model
  for strategic planning, 330–331
Style approach theory
  leadership, for, 216–219
Super leadership
  definition of, 223
  fundamentals of, 223
Supervisor–employee relationships,
  150–151
  categories, 152
  developed between, 154
  openness and support, 153
  quality of, 153
Surveys of top management
  organizations, in, 269
Sustainability, 119
SWOT model. *See* Strengths, weaknesses, opportunities, and threats
  (SWOT) model

T

Task force groups, 188–189
  advantage, 189
  description, 188–189
  membership and management, 189
Task management, 218–219
Team-based organization,
  191–193
Team management, 219
Technology and interpersonal
  relationships, 164–166
Teleworkers, 165
Terminal values, 108
Theory of justice, 114
Theory of moral rights
  right
    to due process, 114
    of free consent, 113
    to freedom of conscience, 114
    of free speech, 114
    to privacy, 113
Theory X and theory Y, 78–79. *See
  also* Human behavior school
Third-party arbitration, 307
Tolerance of ambiguity, 109
Training/educational presentations, 271

Trait approach of leaders
  definition of, 215–216
Transformational approach of leaders,
  223–223
Transformation process in organization
  appreciative inquiry (AI), 368
  diffusion of innovation, 365
    elements within, 366
  doctor–patient model, 367
  guiding coalition, 365
  process model, 367
  purchase model, 367
  stakeholder theory, 366–367
Trust, 162–163

U

Utilitarian theory, 113

V

Values competency, 8, 181–182, 211
Value system in organizations
  defined, 104
  values in organizations, 103
    congruence, 106
    globalization and diversity,
      105–107
    individual orientations, 107–108
    statements, 107
    systems, 104–105
    terminal and instrumental, 108
    work, 108–109
Vendors, 157, 308–309
Virtual groups, 199–201

W

Whistleblowing, 118–119, 311–312
Working in groups
  aspects of, 196
  creativity and collaboration
    communication processes,
      198–199
    disagreements, 199
    members, 199
    personal communication
      competency, 197
    participation behaviors, 202–204
  virtual groups
    communication competency,
      200–201
    cultural differences, 201
    definition, 199
    employees, 199–200
    identity, 200
    in organizations, 200
    workers, 199, 200
    working issues, 199
Workplace
  democracy description, 194
  diversity of, 287
  emotion and balance
    and interpersonal relationships,
      163–164
  incivility in, 287
Workshops, 24–25, 64–65, 97–99,
  130–133, 175–176, 205–207,
  244–247, 279–280, 319–320,
  346–351, 376–382, 402–407,
  410–412
Work values, 108